THE SPREAD OF MODERN INDUSTRY TO THE PERIPHERY SINCE 1871

The Spread of Modern Industry to the Periphery since 1871

Edited by
KEVIN HJORTSHØJ O'ROURKE
and
JEFFREY GALE WILLIAMSON

OXFORD
UNIVERSITY PRESS

OXFORD
UNIVERSITY PRESS

Great Clarendon Street, Oxford, OX2 6DP,
United Kingdom

Oxford University Press is a department of the University of Oxford.
It furthers the University's objective of excellence in research, scholarship,
and education by publishing worldwide. Oxford is a registered trade mark of
Oxford University Press in the UK and in certain other countries

© Oxford University Press 2017

The moral rights of the authors have been asserted

First Edition published in 2017

Published in the United States of America by Oxford University Press
198 Madison Avenue, New York, NY 10016, United States of America

British Library Cataloguing in Publication Data
Data available

Library of Congress Control Number: 2016952209
ISBN 978-0-19-875364-3

Links to third party websites are provided by Oxford in good faith and for
information only. Oxford disclaims any responsibility for the materials
contained in any third party website referenced in this work.

This book is dedicated to the future, our children. In O'Rourke's case, Ciara, Joseph, Gabriel, and Sophie; and in Williamson's case, Megan, Hilary, Kirk, and Amy.

Acknowledgements

We are grateful to the European Research Council, the John Fell OUP Research Fund, All Souls College, and the Oxford History Faculty's Global History Centre for their generous financial and logistical support. We are particularly grateful to Simon Mee, Aileen Mooney, Claire Phillips, Jane Smith, Rosemary Strawson, Simon Unger, Alexis Wegerich, and the staff at All Souls College for all their help in organising the conference out of which this book arose.

Contents

PART III. LATIN AMERICA

PART IV. SUB-SAHARAN AFRICA

List of Figures

List of Tables

List of Contributors

Gareth Austin, University of Cambridge

Jean-Pascal Bassino, Ecole Normale Supérieure de Lyon

Agustín S. Bénétrix, Trinity College Dublin

Loren Brandt, University of Toronto

Gerardo della Paolera, Universidad de San Andrés and CEU

Xavier Duran, Universidad de los Andes

Ewout Frankema, Wageningen University

Matteo Gomellini, Banca d'Italia

Aurora Gómez-Galvarriato, El Colegio de México

Bishnupriya Gupta, University of Warwick

Martin Ivanov, Sofia University

Morten Jerven, Norwegian University of Life Sciences

Ulaş Karakoç, Humboldt-Universität zu Berlin

Alexander Klein, University of Kent

Michael Kopsidis, Leibniz Institute of Agricultural Development in Transition Economies

Debin Ma, London School of Economics

Andrei Markevich, New Economic School (Moscow, Russia)

Graciela Márquez Colín, El Colegio de México

Aldo Musacchio, Brandeis University

Steven Nafziger, Williams College

Kevin Hjortshøj O'Rourke, All Souls College, Oxford

Şevket Pamuk, Boğaziçi University, Istanbul

Laura Panza, University of Melbourne

Dwight H. Perkins, Harvard University

Thomas G. Rawski, University of Pittsburgh

Tirthankar Roy, London School of Economics

Max-Stephan Schulze, London School of Economics

John P. Tang, Australian National University

Gianni Toniolo, Libera Università delle Scienze Sociali, Roma

Tamás Vonyó, Bocconi University

Jeffrey Gale Williamson, emeritus, Harvard University

1

Introduction

Kevin Hjortshøj O'Rourke and Jeffrey Gale Williamson

1.1 INTRODUCTION

Ever since the British Industrial Revolution, the transition to modern economic growth has been associated with industrialization. New labour-saving and energy-using technologies first originated in Britain, and then spread with a lag to countries such as Belgium and France in continental Europe and North America (Allen, 2009). The initial impact was a 'Great Divergence' in living standards between Northwestern Europe and its New World offshoots, on the one hand, and the rest of the world on the other. This divergence is now being eroded as developing economies rapidly industrialize.

But when did modern manufacturing first begin to spread to the developing world? Was it only during the 'second globalization' which began in earnest in the 1980s? Or are the roots of industrial catch-up to be found in the long period of world deglobalization which began in 1914, and saw two world wars, the Great Depression, the breakdown of formal and informal empires, and import-substituting industrialization (ISI)? Or might the spread of modern manufacturing have started even earlier, during the 'first globalization' of the late nineteenth century (O'Rourke and Williamson, 1999)?

In both globalization periods, international economic integration may have helped developing countries import new technologies, exploit their lower labour costs, and import those raw materials with which they were poorly endowed (Wright, 1990). Alternatively, trade may have made it difficult for developing countries to compete with established industries in richer countries (Williamson, 2011). In that case, the breakdown of the nineteenth-century international division of labour—which saw the industrial core economies export manufactures and import food and raw materials (Robertson, 1938; Lewis, 1978)—may have favoured industrial growth in the developing world. So what were the impacts of globalization and deglobalization on the spread of modern industry to the developing world? Were the impacts uniform, or did they depend on the characteristics of the individual countries concerned?

This volume has three goals. The first is to document the origins of modern industrial growth around the global periphery: those regions in Southern and Eastern Europe, the Middle East, Asia, Latin America, and Sub-Saharan Africa that fell behind the industrial core in Northwest Europe and North America during the Great Divergence. When did modern manufacturing first emerge in these regions, what industries did it initially involve, and how did it subsequently develop? The second is to explain these patterns of industrial development. What determined the timing of early industrialization? Did it happen spontaneously, as a result of market forces, or was government intervention required? What sorts of factor endowments encouraged early industrial development, and what sorts hindered it? How important was access to foreign markets, or alternatively, protection for the home market? What was the impact of major shocks to the international economy: world wars, the Great Depression, the spread of Communism, decolonization, the shift to market liberalism in the 1980s and 1990s? How was technology transferred to these regions? The third aim of the volume is to trace the history of modern manufacturing in the global periphery through to the present day, and to understand what determined these long-run trajectories.

We have chosen to address these questions by commissioning a series of country and regional studies, written by leading experts in the economic histories of these countries or regions. We believe that the traditional economic history approach used here has many advantages as compared with more standard cross-country regressions used by economists, for at least two reasons. First, a strong message emerging from these chapters is that the impact of factor endowments, country size, government policies, the international environment, and other factors, all tended to depend on each other. The impact of protection, for example, depended on the nature of the economy being protected, and on what other countries were doing. These interactions were so numerous and important that they would be difficult or even impossible to incorporate adequately into a standard panel regression. Second, modern manufacturing consisted of three quite distinct activities: the processing of commodities (especially for export); the production of import-competing or export-competing tradables; and the production of consumer goods for domestic markets which are quasi-non-tradable, because of high transport costs or distinctive local tastes. The same policies or international shocks could (and did) affect these three sub-categories in opposite directions, in ways that a regression explaining aggregate manufacturing output would not capture.

Chapter 2 will deal extensively with the first of these themes, and so this introduction will focus more on the second. After a brief summary of when and where modern manufacturing first emerged, we will explore the roles played by factor endowments, policy, and the international context.

Two additional introductory comments are necessary before we press on. First, there has been a flood of works dealing with industrialization in the Third World since Simon Kuznets, W. Arthur Lewis, and other giants were writing in the 1950s, 1960s, and 1970s. Why another? The answer is that this volume is about the spread of modern manufacturing, not industrialization; it deals with the origins and development of a particular sector of the economy, rather than with patterns of structural change involving all sectors. Structural change is obviously essential in explaining the transition to modern economic growth. However, studying industrialization requires an understanding, not just of the manufacturing sector, but of an additional 75 per cent of the economy—agriculture and services—as well. The development of a modern manufacturing sector is essential for industrialization, but the reverse is not true: a poor country could see its modern manufacturing sector grow rapidly without this leading to structural change. Such was the case, for example, in Southeast Europe before 1939 (Chapter 5). Indeed, the manufacturing sector could grow more rapidly than in rich industrial economies, without the country concerned converging on them in per capita GDP terms. And yet the modern manufacturing sector is crucial for long-run economic development, suggesting that there are intellectual benefits to focusing on it alone.

Second, we need to say something about our definition of the 'periphery'. As Marc Flandreau and Clemens Jobst (2005) have reminded us, the definitions of core and periphery are *ex ante* unclear, and tend to depend in practice on the purpose at hand. In our case, we are interested in the gradual spread of modern manufacturing from its original heartlands in Northwest Europe and the United States. We therefore include not only regions such as Sub-Saharan Africa and Asia, which were clearly 'peripheral' in the context of the late-nineteenth-century world economy, but also 'middle-class' or 'second-tier' countries in Southern and Eastern Europe. Modern manufacturing gained a foothold there rather later than it had done in countries like Britain and Belgium, and its experience was often less successful. We have chosen Italy to serve as representative of Southern Europe, fully mindful of the fact that it was only marginally peripheral: the judgment of Chapter 6 is that it was still a peripheral industrial nation at the time of unification, but that it had joined the industrial core by the 1930s at the latest. We feel that there are lessons to be learned from the experience of a relatively early 'peripheral' industrializer such as Italy, and what is true of that country is even truer of a country like Japan (Chapter 8).

Our five peripheral regions are thus: Southern and Eastern Europe; the Middle East and North Africa; Sub-Saharan Africa; Asia; and Latin America. These five regions were certainly poor. In 1913, their per capita incomes expressed as percentages of incomes in the three leading economies (Britain, Germany, and the United States) were: Eastern Europe 34.4 per cent; Southern Europe 42.3 per cent; Middle East 22.5 per cent; Sub-Saharan Africa 13.8 per cent; Asia 16.3 per cent; and Latin America 32.3 per cent (Maddison, 2010).

1.2 THE BEGINNING OF MODERN MANUFACTURING

Chapter 2 provides a broad quantitative overview of the spread of modern manufacturing to the global periphery, bringing together evidence on industrial (where possible, manufacturing) growth rates from 1870 to the onset of the global financial crisis in 2007. It shows that developing countries experienced rapid manufacturing growth surprisingly early, in many cases well before the First World War, although this fast growth occurred from very low initial levels of modern manufacturing output. Between 1870 and 1896, industrial output grew at 5 per cent per annum or more in Austria, Hungary, Russia, China, Chile, Brazil, Argentina, and Mexico (where annual growth was as high as 9.8 per cent). Growth slowed after 1896 in peripheral Europe and Latin America, but it accelerated in Asia, where Japan, China, and the Philippines all experienced average industrial growth rates of 5 per cent per annum or more between 1896 and the First World War. Modern factory output also expanded rapidly in Bulgaria and Romania during this period. By contrast, in the Middle East and Sub-Saharan Africa rapid industrial growth only started in the inter-war period and, especially, after 1950. The 'golden age' of 1950–73 was the high point of industrial growth not just in these regions, but across the global periphery.

The industries involved in the initial spread of modern manufacturing varied. The classic industries of the British Industrial Revolution were textiles and metallurgy, and these featured prominently during the spread of modern manufacturing to several peripheral countries as well. Textiles were particularly important in China, India, and Mexico, and they were also prominent in Austria-Hungary and Turkey. On the other hand, despite the importance of silk, they only accounted for 10 per cent of Italian manufacturing in 1870, with the engineering sector nearly twice as large. Iron was important in Mexico from the turn of the century; more generally, heavy industry was important in Austria-Hungary, Italy, and Russia. Early industrialization in Argentina involved a broader range of consumer goods (not just textiles), protected by tariffs and serving a rapidly expanding local market. In Southeast Asia and Egypt, modern industry initially focused on commodity export processing, moving into consumer goods somewhat later.

1.3 FACTOR ENDOWMENTS

Factor endowments had a profound impact on industrial policy. Labour-abundant and resource-scarce countries could enter at the bottom of the ladder, producing and exporting labour-intensive products (e.g. East Asia). Labour-scarce and high-wage peripheral countries could not exploit that strategy, and thus relied on a tariff-protected domestic market (e.g. Latin America). Where the labour-scarce economy had only a small domestic market (e.g. Southeast Asia), industrial growth was difficult.

Modern industry first emerged in high-wage economies: Britain, Northwest Europe, and North America. According to Allen (2009), this is not a coincidence: high wages, cheap capital, and abundant energy gave entrepreneurs the incentive to search for and adopt modern, labour-saving, and capital and energy-using technologies.[1] Initially, these new technologies were only economical in regions whose factor endowments corresponded with what the technologies had been designed for. But over time, the technologies improved to such an extent that it made sense to adopt them even where factor endowments were quite different. In addition, key sectors like textiles became labour-intensive relative to other industrial sectors, such as capital-intensive heavy industry. Over time, therefore, cheap labour became an

---

[1] Of course, relative factor prices are what matter. Thus it might have been abundant and cheap energy (coal) and capital, rather than scarce labour, that favoured Britain's industrial lead.

advantage in developing modern manufacturing, at least in those economies where other required inputs (financial capital, machinery, energy, skilled labour, and entrepreneurship) were in sufficient supply.

The developing economies covered in this volume were characterized by widely varying factor endowments. Sub-Saharan Africa, Latin America, and Southeast Asia were resource abundant and labour scarce, and consequently had wages that were high by developing economy standards. Our authors document these high wages (that is, high relative to other periphery countries), and show how they made it difficult to develop modern, labour-intensive manufacturing. That is, nominal unskilled wages were higher in Southeast Asia than in Japan until the 1920s, and were higher than in India and China for even longer (Chapter 11). In 1911, daily earnings in similar textile mills were 18 US cents in Japan, but 46 cents in Mexico (Chapter 12). Unskilled wages were much higher in West Africa than in India until 1945 (Chapter 14). Commodity export processing, and later import-substituting industrialization (ISI), were the typical routes to industrialization for such economies. Another response to high wages was labour coercion, which kept wage costs low in, for example, South African mining (Chapter 14) and even Soviet manufacturing (Chapter 3). Over time, however, factor endowments evolved in ways that made it easier to sustain a competitive, modern manufacturing sector. Populations grew fast, leading to falling relative wages, and bigger domestic markets; this was the case in Africa, for example, but even so that continent's recent rapid growth has in many cases been based more on commodity exports than on manufacturing.

The supply of educated labour seems to have been just as important as the supply of overall labour, and perhaps even more so, in augmenting the ability of countries to develop modern manufacturing. Lars Sandberg (1979) pointed out long ago that while physical capital can be imported from abroad, it takes much longer to accumulate human capital. Poor education may thus place an effective constraint on development—especially since human capital endowments can influence a country's ability to adapt foreign technology to local circumstances. From Abramovitz (1986) on, a vast empirical literature has documented that GDP convergence is conditional on a host of factors, including schooling, and this literature suggests that education matters because it allows countries to adopt best-practice manufacturing techniques. This volume provides ample evidence that education facilitated the spread of modern manufacturing.

From this perspective, European colonialism damaged many countries: it was not until they achieved independence that major progress was made towards providing universal primary (and later secondary) education. Racist educational policies in colonial Africa hindered development there (Chapter 14). India's British rulers viewed the sub-continent as a source of primary products, thus investing in railroads but not in schools (Chapter 10). Primary school enrolment rates were low in Southeast Asia in the 1920s, whether the colonizer was Dutch, French or British (Chapter 11). After independence, a literacy revolution took place almost everywhere around the periphery. In contrast, Japan strongly promoted education from the 1870s onwards, and this appears to have benefited its Korean and Taiwanese colonies (Chapter 8). American colonial rule benefited the Philippines in a similar fashion (Chapter 11).

When modern manufacturing began its spread to the periphery, a lack of skills was therefore often an important constraint. It follows that loosening that constraint was crucial in spurring industrial growth. Sometimes this could be achieved by importing human capital. Technical workers tended to be foreign in early-twentieth-century Mexico and Peru; they were imported from Western Europe into Southeast Europe up until the Second World War; they were also imported from Japan, China, and India into late-nineteenth and early-twentieth-century Southeast Asia (Chapters 5, 11, 12); and British mechanics and managers were important in developing early modern manufacturing in India's port cities (Chapter 10).

But importing skilled foreign labour was a costly option. A much better (long-run) solution was to increase the domestic supply of educated workers. All poor periphery countries, when independent, have tried to change their endowments and thus their comparative advantage by investing heavily in schooling. Those which underwent successful manufacturing catching-up also underwent schooling catching-up, even though it took a few decades for youth enrolment to create a literate and well-schooled adult labour force. Economists have shown econometrically how schooling has raised economy-wide productivity and GDP per capita growth. The chapters in this volume suggest that schooling's impact on manufacturing productivity has been even bigger.

Education was already improving in Southeast Europe before 1939, but Communist governments in Russia, and later Eastern Europe, invested even more heavily in human capital (Chapters 3, 5). In Southeast Asia, school enrolment rates rose sharply from the inter-war decades to the 1970s, contributing to the late-twentieth-century economic miracles of Indonesia, Malaysia, Singapore, and Thailand (Chapter 11). Newly independent countries in Sub-Saharan Africa also improved their educational systems, but not nearly as impressively, and skilled labour remained scarcer for longer (Chapter 14). India is an interesting case, in that it has been services, rather than industry, which have tended to employ better-educated Indian workers in recent decades (Chapter 10).

It is easier to overcome a shortage of financial and physical capital than human capital. Poor economies tend to have limited supplies of capital, but in periods when international capital markets are working smoothly, financial capital can be borrowed from abroad. This was certainly the case in the first global century up to the First World War for Imperial Russia, for colonial India, and for Latin America. The diaspora was also a source of financial capital for China, except during the planned economy period (Chapters 9, 13). But borrowing from abroad was only possible when international capital markets were functioning properly, which was not the case from the 1920s to the 1970s. Regions such as Latin America undoubtedly suffered as a result (Chapters 12, 13; Taylor, 1998).

Even more important than imports of financial capital were imports of equipment and machinery, which also embody up-to-date technology. These imports were crucial for countries seeking to build a modern manufacturing sector. They also had to be paid for with export earnings when international borrowing was difficult. Otherwise, these constraints would begin to bind, with potentially serious consequences for domestic manufacturing. A classic case is offered by the Soviet Union, where between 10 and 30 per cent of equipment investment was accounted for by imports in the late 1970s and early 1980s. In the inter-war period, these imports had been financed largely by grain exports, while in the post-war period they were increasingly financed by oil exports (since the USSR had by this stage become a net food importer). When first grain and then oil prices were weak, manufacturing growth inevitably slowed down (Chapter 3).

Governments attempted to relax these constraints in various ways. The USSR, India, Yugoslavia, and Romania all built up their capital goods industries, thus supplying more of their equipment needs (Domar, 1957). The USSR famously encouraged high savings rates, attempting to dramatically shift the country's factor endowment in a capital-intensive direction. Such policies worked well initially, at least in terms of boosting industrial output. Eventually, however, the strategy of prioritizing capital accumulation ran into severely diminishing returns (Chapters 3, 5, and 10).

1.4 INTERNATIONAL CONTEXT AND LUCK

By the mid-nineteenth century, the global periphery had become the commodity exporter to the industrial leaders, so world commodity price trends and their volatility were central to local manufacturing profitability and performance. That is, commodity price booms generated what we now call 'Dutch Disease': labour and capital rushed to commodity export sectors and fled domestic manufacturing. These Dutch Disease forces were powerful as the relative price of commodities soared up to the 1890s (Williamson, 2011). However, that secular boom turned into a secular bust from the 1890s to the Second World War. That is, as commodity prices fell, the relative price of manufactures rose in the global periphery. If a commodity price boom penalized manufacturing in the global periphery up to the 1890s, then the bust must surely have stimulated the growth of domestic manufactures in Asia, Africa, the Middle East, and Latin America. On these grounds alone, we would expect to find more rapid manufacturing growth in the global periphery from the 1890s to the First World War, and during the inter-war decades. And so we do: the numbers in the catching-up club increased during that half-century, and the average rates of growth of the members rose. But the catching-up did not occur everywhere, nor was it as dramatic as one might have expected. The anti-Dutch Disease pro-manufacturing forces were weaker, because these economies had developed offsets by the 1890s. Sub-Saharan Africa, Southeast Asia, and North Africa were colonies of the industrial imperialists, and imperial colonial policies, as the chapters here will show, served to suppress domestic production of tradable manufactures. In addition, export processing dominated local manufacturing by the 1890s, so that a commodity bust damaged manufacturing on those grounds. Finally, domestic demand for quasi-non-tradable consumer goods fell when export revenues and incomes fell, further damaging local manufacturing.

Latin America had gained independence early in the nineteenth century, so local manufacturing did not have to contend with anti-manufacturing colonial policy, but rather enjoyed supportive pro-manufacturing tariffs. Still, quasi-non-tradable consumer goods industries in Latin America obeyed the same laws of motion as elsewhere in the periphery. Indeed, the chapters that follow characterize these sectors as a source of endogenous manufacturing growth—positive during the commodity booms of the late nineteenth century (and the early twenty-first century) and negative from the 1890s to the Second World War.

The chapters that follow also stress the role of world markets for manufactured exports. Geography mattered: Mexico's manufacturing growth has always been favoured by its big and fast-growing northern US neighbour; Southeast Asia, Taiwan, and Korea were favoured by Japan's post-Second World War economic miracle; the same countries were favoured again by China's economic miracle after the 1980s. And Central and Eastern Europe were favoured by the fast growth of Northwest Europe up to 1913; disfavoured by European disintegration after the First World War and their membership of the Soviet bloc after 1945; and then favoured again by their reconnection to the European Union from the 1990s onwards. These contiguous relationships fostered not only trade, but foreign direct investment (FDI) and technological transfer as well.

Luck also mattered, both good and bad. Latin America dropped its trade barriers in the late 1970s, only to have China flood world markets with manufactures beginning in the 1980s. This was very bad luck. Southeast Asia started its miracle in the 1970s when Japan shifted from labour-intensive to capital-intensive technologies and used FDI to move its older technologies to Malaysia, Thailand, and other Southeast Asian countries. With a well-established competitive industry, the region was again favoured when China offered a booming market starting in the 1980s. Thus, the region was twice blessed with good luck.

1.5 POLICY

Policy has always mattered, but the policies necessary to promote modern manufacturing varied across regions and over time. We have already discussed policies designed to shift factor endowments and prices in a direction more favourable to manufacturing growth, ranging from the unambiguously beneficial (education) to the ambiguous (policies designed to spur capital accumulation) to the morally unacceptable (labour coercion). In this section we will focus primarily on trade and industrial policy.

A major point to emerge from this volume is that the relationship between openness and manufacturing growth is inherently ambiguous. This should not come as a surprise, given the extensive empirical literature on the relationship between protectionism and economic growth more generally. While the correlation between protectionism and growth is negative for the late twentieth century, it was positive during the late nineteenth century (at least for a sample of relatively rich countries) and during the inter-war period (Sachs and Warner, 1995;

Clemens and Williamson, 2004; O'Rourke, 2000). More relevant for the subject of this volume, *industrial* tariffs were positively correlated with *industrial* growth, as well as with aggregate economic growth, for the same small sample of predominantly rich late-nineteenth-century economies (Lehmann and O'Rourke, 2011).

Not only has the correlation between tariffs and aggregate growth changed over time; it has also differed across countries. Alexander Hamilton and Friedrich List believed that countries should only resort to protection once they had become sufficiently advanced that manufacturing was a feasible option. But 'sufficiently advanced' is a bit ambiguous, as the case studies in this book reveal. Certainly the relationship between tariffs and manufacturing growth has been ambiguous. By definition, one would expect tariffs to spur the growth of import-competing manufacturing industry. But, by the same token, you would also expect it to hamper the growth of export-oriented commodity processing, and early on this was the most important modern industrial activity in resource-abundant and labour-scarce regions such as Southeast Asia and Latin America.

More fundamentally, the need for protection when developing a manufacturing sector depended on underlying patterns of comparative advantage. In labour-abundant countries, labour-intensive manufacturing had at least a chance of getting off the ground without the artificial stimulus of tariffs: in labour-abundant China and India, for example, modern manufacturing first emerged during the late nineteenth century under conditions close to free trade (Chapters 9, 10). When post-colonial governments in such countries decided to actively promote industrial growth, they were fostering the development of sectors with genuine growth potential. In labour-scarce countries, on the other hand, protection was probably going to be required if labour-intensive manufacturing were to get off the ground at all: industrialization in peripheral Europe, Southeast Asia, and Latin America typically originated behind tariff barriers, which makes sense given their resource-abundant and labour-scarce factor endowments (Chapters 5, 12, 13). The long-run problem, however, was that such protection was explicitly working against the forces of comparative advantage. When these countries eventually liberalized in the 1980s or 1990s, many lost a good deal of the industry that had been built up under protection—Eastern and Southeast Europe offer good examples (Chapters 3–5).

The impact of policy was particularly dramatic in those economies which turned to Communism: Russia after the First World War, and its satellites in Eastern Europe as well as China after the Second World War. Russia, and especially Bulgaria and Romania, did not have a natural comparative advantage in manufacturing; China probably did, at least when it came to labour-intensive activities. All promoted capital-intensive heavy industry for ideological reasons, which clearly went against their initial comparative advantage. To this end, foreign trade was monopolized by the state, while it promoted rapid capital accumulation via forced savings. All of these countries eventually suffered massively due to diminished efficiency. The experience following liberalization in the 1980s or 1990s has differed greatly across these countries. While the Chinese central planners helped lay the basis for the subsequent growth miracle, by changing factor endowments, importing technology, and providing a manufacturing base that would become much more efficient, Eastern European countries like Bulgaria and Romania have deindustrialized since 1989, while even Russia has reverted to being far more of a resource-exporter (Chapters 3, 5, 9). India, which also pursued capital-intensive industrialization strategies, saw its services sector—rather than manufacturing or the primary sector—expand dramatically after liberalization. These examples suggest once again that comparative advantage determined the impact of liberalization.

Protectionism and, more generally, openness had different effects in different countries. Where technologies were imported from abroad, this was typically done by importing both machines and skilled foreign workers to operate and maintain them. This required foreign exchange, so trade openness of some sort was essential. But whereas Chinese and Indian textiles could be produced under conditions of free trade, based on cheap labour, and then sold in large local markets, peripheral European textile industries were protected, and probably had to be in order to survive import competition from industrial neighbours close by. Consumer goods industries in Latin America, which relied on the protection afforded by distance and/or trade policies, and fast-growing local markets, did well when commodity exports boomed, since this increased local demand. Export processing in labour-scarce and resource-abundant African and Southeast Asian regions—with small local markets poorly integrated by transport—relied especially heavily on international trade. Such conditions made it difficult and in some cases impossible to begin much local consumer goods production, until the Second World War and the post-war ISI years offered protection from foreign imports.

During the post-war period, labour-abundant and resource-scarce East Asia exploited its comparative advantage by subsidizing export-oriented industries. The 'gang of four' (South Korea, Taiwan, Hong Kong, and Singapore) led that charge in the 1960s. Meanwhile, labour-scarce and resource-abundant Sub-Saharan Africa, Latin America, and Southeast Asia had to fight against their comparative advantage if they wanted to develop manufacturing, by protecting their local market. They led the post-Second World War ISI protectionist charge.

Finally, several of the chapters in this volume document regional industrialization patterns which suggest the importance of location, irrespective of the country's trade policies. Modern industry in Austria-Hungary first emerged in the northwest, close to West European neighbours, in what is today Austria and the Czech Republic (Chapter 5). It also appeared in the Italian northwest, also contiguous with a big West European neighbour (Chapter 6). Factory production in China was initially located in the southeast, especially in the Lower Yangzi coastal area around Shanghai, with a smaller cluster in Manchuria (Chapter 9). Modern Indian industry first appeared in port cities such as Calcutta and Bombay (Chapter 10). In Turkey, modern factories initially clustered in Constantinople and Izmir in the west and Adana in the south, both coastal regions (Chapter 7). These regional agglomerations were typically linked to trade connections with the rest of the world: port cities offered access to foreign capital, cheap raw material imports, entrepreneurship and modern technology (as in the cases of India and China), or access to foreign export markets (as in the cases of Austria-Hungary and Italy). Symmetrically, factory production was more regionally dispersed where geography inhibited national market integration, as in Mexico, Columbia, and Chile (Chapters 12 and 13).

1.6 THE ROAD MAP

Chapter 2 (Agustín Bénétrix, Kevin O'Rourke, and Jeffrey Williamson) offers a quantitative assessment of manufacturing growth in the periphery from the 1870s to today. It shows that, on average, the periphery has experienced 'industrial catching-up' on countries with higher levels of industrial output per capita since at least the inter-war period. The remaining chapters build their narrative interpretations around this empirical summary. The chapters in Part I deal with the European periphery and the Middle East: Russia (Chapter 3, Andrei Markevich and Steven Nafziger); East and Central Europe (Chapter 4, Alexander Klein, Max-Stephan Schulze, and Tamás Vonyó); Southeast Europe (Chapter 5, Michael Kopsidis and Martin Ivanov); Italy (Chapter 6, Mateo Gomellini and Gianni Toniolo); and the Middle East (Chapter 7, Ulaş Karakoç, Şevket Pamuk, and Laura Panza). Part II of the book deals with the biggest part of the periphery, Asia: Northeast Asia (Chapter 8, Dwight Perkins and John Tang); China (Chapter 9, Loren Brandt, Debin Ma, and Thomas Rawski); South Asia (Chapter 10, Bishnupriya Gupta and Tirthankar Roy); and Southeast Asia (Chapter 11, Jean-Pascal Bassino and Jeffrey Williamson). Two chapters on Latin America follow in Part III: Mexico and Peru (Chapter 12, Aurora Gómez Galvarriato and Graciela Márquez Colín) and South America (Chapter 13, Xavier Duran, Aldo Musacchio and Gerardo della Paolera). The volume concludes in Part IV with a chapter on Sub-Saharan Africa (Chapter 14, Gareth Austin, Ewout Frankema, and Morten Jerven).

REFERENCES

Abramovitz, M. (1986). Catching up, forging ahead, and falling behind. *Journal of Economic History* 46, 385–406.

Allen, R. C. (2009). *The British Industrial Revolution in Global Perspective*. Cambridge and New York: Cambridge University Press.

Clemens, M. and Williamson, J. (2004). Why did the tariff–growth correlation change after 1950? *Journal of Economic Growth* 9, 5–46.

Domar, E. (1957). A Soviet model of growth. In *Essays in the Theory of Economic Growth*. New York: Oxford University Press, 223–61.

Flandreau, M. and Jobst, C. (2005). The ties that divide: a network analysis of the international monetary system, 1890–1910. *Journal of Economic History* 65, 977–1007.

Lehmann, S. H. and O'Rourke, K. H. (2011). The structure of protection and growth in the late nineteenth century. *Review of Economics and Statistics* 93, 606–16.

Lewis, W. A. (1978). *Growth and Fluctuations 1870–1913*. London: George Allen and Unwin.

Maddison, A. (2010). www.ggdc.net/maddison/Historical_Statistics/horizontal-file_02-2010.xls.

O'Rourke, K. H. (2000). Tariffs and growth in the late 19th century. *Economic Journal* 110, 456–83.

O'Rourke, K. H. and Williamson, J. G. (1999). *Globalization and History: The Evolution of a 19th Century Atlantic Economy*. Cambridge, MA: MIT Press.

Robertson, D. H. (1938). The future of international trade. *Economic Journal* 48, 1–14.

Sachs, J. D. and Warner, A. (1995). Economic reform and the process of global integration. *Brookings Papers on Economic Activity* 1995, 1–118.

Sandberg, L. G. (1979). The case of the impoverished sophisticate: human capital and Swedish economic growth before World War I. *Journal of Economic History* 39, 225–41.

Taylor, A. M. (1998). Argentina and the world capital market: saving, investment, and international capital mobility in the twentieth century. *Journal of Development Economics* 57, 147–84.

Williamson, J. G. (2011). *Trade and Poverty: When the Third World Fell Behind*. Cambridge, MA: MIT Press.

Wright, G. (1990). The origins of American industrial success, 1879–1940. *American Economic Review* 80, 651–68.

2

Measuring the Spread of Modern Manufacturing to the Poor Periphery

Agustín S. Bénétrix, Kevin Hjortshøj O'Rourke,
and Jeffrey Gale Williamson

2.1 OVERVIEW

This chapter documents the historical origins of industrial growth in the developing world, drawing on a vast amount of data constructed by economic historians in recent decades.[1] These origins stretch surprisingly far back into the past, in some countries even before 1890. By the inter-war period, rapid industrial growth can be found in all major regions of the developing world, and this continued into the post-war ISI (import-substituting industrialization) years. Indeed, industrial growth between 1920 and 1990 was faster in developing countries than in the leading industrial economies.

This chapter also documents per capita manufacturing growth rates in order to see when 'industrial catching-up' on the leaders first began. These per capita growth rates reflect both manufacturing productivity growth and changes in the share of the labour force employed in manufacturing.[2] The industrial catching-up which we document here is thus not comparable with the manufacturing productivity convergence which is the focus of Dani Rodrik's (2013, 2015) work, or with the GDP per capita convergence which has been explored by so many economists starting in the 1980s and 1990s (Abramovitz, 1986; Barro, 1997). When developing countries experienced industrial catching-up as we define it here, shifting resources into manufacturing (extensive development) and increasing manufacturing productivity (intensive development), both extensive and intensive development played central roles, as they have done ever since the British Industrial Revolution (Crafts, 1985).

---

[1] This chapter is a much shortened and extensively revised version of Bénétrix et al. (2015), using revised country-specific data available at <http://cepr.org/content/trade-depression>. (See also Williamson, 2010 and 2011.) The research has received generous help from many scholars listed in the 2015 paper, and also from the authors of the chapters following, whose data is used in this version.

[2] They also reflect changes in the labour participation rate.

2.2 MEASURING INDUSTRIAL GROWTH

Before we press on with the empirical analysis, we need to discuss problems of measurement. We have already pointed out in Chapter 1 that this volume speaks to output (and labour productivity) growth, not to industrialization per se. That is, in contrast with most of the previous literature, we do not measure and analyse the determinants of manufacturing output or employment *shares*. This makes our measurement problems less challenging, since we do not have to worry about the relative prices of manufacturing and non-manufacturing output. But we face other problems, especially in measuring manufacturing growth in earlier periods.

Our interest is in the spread of *modern* manufacturing embedded in large factories driven by steam, water, and electrical power. Many of the time series in the chapters that follow and in this one include small-scale, household cottage industries using traditional labour-intensive technologies. Where that is true, *modern* manufacturing output growth is understated, since the rise of factories is partially offset by the fall of cottage industries. Where we have the evidence for both sorts of industrial activities, we see that the problem is only manifested in the very early phases of growth. The inclusion of cottage industry does not seriously damage any of the conclusions reached here.[3]

This bias towards understating modern manufacturing growth early on may be offset by another bias working in the opposite direction. There is a tendency for output to be better documented in rapidly growing sectors, so that if the documented sectors are assumed to be representative of all industry, the overall industrial growth rate will be exaggerated. Crafts and Harley (1992) have shown this to have been true of the British industrial growth rate during the Industrial Revolution, thus revising the growth rate downwards. Recent work on Japan by the Hitotsubashi team similarly revises downwards the industrial growth rate during the early Meiji period. The new data in this book were constructed with an eye to this problem. While we can hardly claim that it has been purged, we believe it has been minimized.[4]

2.3 THE INDUSTRIAL OUTPUT DATA

We have collected manufacturing and industrial output data for as many countries between 1870 and 2007 as the historical records permit. Since Paul Bairoch's (1982) pioneering work more than three decades ago, scholars across the world have been building pre-1950 historical national accounts that have pushed back our quantitative knowledge of periphery GDP and its components into the inter-war or

---

[3] It should be emphasized that many cottage industries in the poor periphery were destroyed in the nineteenth century as Western European factories flooded world markets with cheap goods made by modern technologies. Thus this measurement problem is more serious in the early stages of the leaders' history, especially Western Europe, than in the poor periphery which is our focus.

[4] The previous footnote applies here as well.

even the pre-1914 period. This chapter starts with the manufacturing value-added data provided by the World Bank's World Development Indicators, supplemented by the United Nation's Industrial Statistics Database. Other frequently used sources include Smits, Woltjer, and Ma (2009), the Montevideo–Oxford Latin American Economic History Database, and the United Nations historical trade statistics database. As we went further back in time, we relied increasingly on individual country sources, including those reported in the chapters that follow in this volume.

We focus on eight periods, each with distinctive characteristics. The years before the First World War are divided into two sub-periods, before and after 1896, both of which comprised the crescendo of the first global century characterized by the gold standard, a world trade boom, liberal peripheral commercial policy (with the exception of Latin America and parts of Eastern Europe), and falling transport costs. The year 1896 is chosen as the dividing line since it marks the end of a period of falling prices (especially commodity prices, the exports in which the periphery specialized), which was followed by rising prices in the decades immediately prior to the First World War. The years from 1913 to 1920 saw the First World War, blockades, submarine warfare, the withdrawal of European manufacturers from peripheral markets, and economic chaos in the immediate aftermath of the fighting. The inter-war period from 1920 to 1938 contained the Great Depression, the collapse of world trade and commodity prices, and the rise of anti-global restrictions. The years between 1938 and 1950 saw another world war, leading again to a complete disruption of normal trade patterns. From 1950 to 1973, there was post-war reconstruction of former belligerents, and decolonization and ISI policies in the periphery. Following the oil crises and the breakdown of the Bretton Woods agreement, the years from 1973 to 1990 were ones of a pro-global and pro-market policy transition in the poor periphery, which continued up to 2007.

There are 177 countries in the 1990–2007 sample. Naturally, the further back into the past we go, the fewer are the countries whose manufacturing growth can be documented, and the smaller are the samples. Thus, our sample falls to 147 countries in 1973–90, 105 in 1950–73, 62 in 1938–50, 58 in 1920–38, 48 in 1913–20, 43 in 1896–1913, and 36 in 1870–90. The empirical analysis that follows will make an effort to deal with this issue by using both constant and variable samples.

Many of our developing country observations before 1896 come from the European periphery, but for this period we also have data for Japan, China, British India, Dutch Indonesia, Siam (Thailand), Argentina, Brazil, Chile, Mexico, Uruguay, and Ottoman Turkey. After 1896, we add Korea, Burma, the Philippines, Taiwan, Colombia, and Peru to this list. And by the inter-war period, we have information for six additional Latin American countries, as well as for Egypt, what was then known as the Belgian Congo, and South Africa. To the extent that other countries were experiencing modern industrialization before they started to collect industrial statistics, what we are documenting here probably understates the early spread of modern manufacturing.

Although the econometric analysis in section 2.7 uses country/time observations, the tables and figures below typically report the evidence by six regions. The first includes the three traditional industrial leaders: the United Kingdom (UK), Germany and the United States (US). The second includes those in the poor European periphery to the south and east. The remaining four poor periphery groups are the Middle East and North Africa (MENA), Asia, Sub-Saharan Africa, and Latin America and the Caribbean (hereafter simply Latin America). We will occasionally refer to these last four regions and the European periphery as 'the poor periphery', or as the 'followers', and to the industrial leaders as 'the core', or as the 'leaders'.

2.4 WHEN AND WHERE DID INDUSTRIAL GROWTH IN THE PERIPHERY BEGIN?

When did the poor periphery start recording rapid manufacturing output growth? The growth rates reported in Table 2.1 are computed by regressing the log of real manufacturing output on a time trend. The regional growth rates are simple unweighted averages of individual country growth rates.

Table 2.1 uses two definitions of the country groupings. The first uses the same industrial leaders throughout—the UK, Germany, and the US. The second recognizes that the UK was no longer an industrial leader in the post-Second World War era, while Japan was. The three industrial leaders from 1950 onwards are thus the US, Germany, and Japan. Of course, Japan is then removed from the poor Asian group after 1939.

What do these data tell us? Growth among the leaders was fairly steady between 1870 and 1913, averaging 3.2–3.3 per cent per annum, followed by a decline to

Table 2.1. Average industrial growth rates (per cent, per annum)

Groups	1870–96	1896–1913	1913–20	1920–38	1938–50	1950–73	1973–90	1990–2007
Leaders	3.2	3.3	1.4	1.9	0.9	5.2	1.1	2.1
Leaders*					−1.0	7.9	2.4	2.2
European Periphery	4.6	4.4	−6.3	4.7	3.1	8.8	3.1	2.8
Asia	3.0	4.4	4.3	4.3	−1.1	8.5	5.8	4.2
Asia*					−0.7	8.3	5.9	4.3
Latam and Caribbean	4.1	4.1	2.5	2.7	5.3	5.7	2.7	2.3
Middle East and North Africa	1.0	1.5	−5.4	4.7	5.0	6.3	5.9	4.4
Sub-Saharan Africa			13.4	4.6	8.6	5.5	3.5	3.9

Note: The table reports unweighted average industrial growth rates by region. Individual country growth rates are computed as the β coefficient of the following regression: $Y = \alpha + \beta t$ where Y is the natural logarithm of industrial production and t is a linear time trend. Leaders are the US, Germany, and the UK while Leaders* are the US and Germany, plus the UK before 1939, Japan after. Asia* is Asia excluding Japan after 1939.

1.4 per cent per annum during the First World War and 1.9 per cent during the inter-war period when the Great Depression did so much damage to their manufacturing sectors. Table 2.1 confirms the impressive industry-led 'growth miracle' during 1950–73. Still including the UK among the leaders into the post-war era, the leader growth rate was 5.2 per cent per annum; if instead the UK is replaced by Japan, the leader growth rate was 7.9 per cent per annum. These were, of course, the years of the German *Wirtschaftswunder* and the Japanese post-war growth miracle. After 1973, however, growth in the three post-war leaders averaged a little more than 2 per cent per annum, and it was only 1.1 per cent during 1973–90 if the UK is included among the leaders. This leader slowdown must in part have been due to the fact that war reconstruction forces were exhausted, and to the poor macroeconomic conditions following the oil crises. But long-term deindustrialization forces were probably playing the bigger role, as suggested by the continued slow industrial growth of the leaders between 1990 and 2007.

Our main interest, however, is in the performance of the periphery. The most striking finding in Table 2.1 is perhaps the strong performance of Latin America since 1870. Latin America was one of the earliest regions to experience rapid manufacturing growth, 4.1 per cent per annum from 1870 to the First World War. Indeed, Latin American manufacturing grew faster than that of the three original leaders in all periods before 2007. Growth was very rapid during the Second World War and 1950–73, in excess of 5 per cent per annum. However, after 1973 its growth rate slowed to less than 3 per cent, and it slowed again after 1990. After 1990, Latin American manufacturing growth of 2.3 per cent resembled that of a rich country that had completed its industrialization phase. In contrast, Asia, MENA, and Sub-Saharan Africa all saw much higher growth rates after 1990—around 4 per cent per annum—a performance consistent with their late-comer status.

The European periphery was an equally rapid early industrializer, with per annum growth rates of 4.4–4.6 per cent before the First World War, 4.7 per cent during the inter-war period, and 8.8 per cent during the European Golden Age. Indeed, the European periphery growth rate exceeded that of the leaders during every period after 1870, with the exception of the First World War.

While Latin America and the European periphery were both recording rapid industrial growth from 1870 onwards, other regions joined them after 1896. There was very rapid industrial growth in Asia, which exceeded that of the leaders in all subsequent periods except for 1938–50. The years between 1896 and 1913 were ones of impressive industrialization in the poor periphery: with the exception of MENA (represented here by Turkey alone), and Sub-Saharan Africa (for which we have no data), average growth rates were in excess of 4 per cent per annum in all periphery regions, greater than the industrial core.

Table 2.2 gives some country detail, showing the growth experiences of the first countries in each peripheral region achieving a ten-year average per annum growth rate of 5 per cent or higher. Latin America was led by Brazil, Chile, Argentina, Uruguay, and Mexico, while the European periphery was led by Finland, Russia, Austria, and Hungary. With the exception of Mexico, these countries first achieved ten years of 5 per cent average growth as early as the 1880s, implying that rapid

Table 2.2. Industrial growth in early members of the 'modern growth club'

Group	Country	In	1870–96	1896–1913	1913–20	1920–38	1938–50	1950–73	1973–90	1990–2007
European Periphery	Finland	1880	4.4	4.2	−5.8	6.7	4.4	6.0	3.5	6.4
European Periphery	Russia	1880	5.5	3.9	−24.4	15.7	−0.7	5.9	1.2	−1.0
European Periphery	Austria	1883	5.0	3.8	−9.6	2.3	1.3	5.8	2.6	2.8
European Periphery	Hungary	1883	5.0	3.8	−10.0	4.0	0.4	7.3	1.9	5.9
Asia	Japan	1896	3.3	5.0	6.5	6.7	−3.7	12.4	4.1	1.0
Asia	China	1900	7.8	7.8	9.4	5.3	−2.2	9.2	8.3	9.8
Asia	Philippines	1913		6.3	10.1	3.4	9.4	7.0	1.8	3.3
Asia	Taiwan	1914		5.1	9.8	4.4	−10.4	11.6	8.7	4.9
Asia	Korea	1922		8.0	3.2	7.2	−1.2	12.8	11.7	7.4
Latam and Caribbean	Brazil	1880	7.9	3.6	6.7	3.2	7.0	8.0	2.6	2.1
Latam and Caribbean	Chile	1881	6.4	3.9	1.2	2.6	6.5	5.1	2.2	3.5
Latam and Caribbean	Argentina	1886	7.6	7.6	2.0	4.2	4.2	4.9	−1.0	1.7
Latam and Caribbean	Uruguay	1886	4.1	4.0	2.7	3.2	4.8	1.3	1.5	0.1
Latam and Caribbean	Mexico	1899	2.0	3.6	−0.3	3.4	6.9	7.5	3.1	3.2
Middle East and North Africa	Turkey	1927	1.0	1.5	−10.7	8.5	−0.2	9.5	5.1	4.1
Middle East and North Africa	Egypt	1942			−0.2	0.9	6.0	5.7	5.8	5.0
Middle East and North Africa	Tunisia	1948					1.8	4.0	7.0	4.6
Middle East and North Africa	Morocco	1949					12.5	4.8	4.2	2.9
Middle East and North Africa	Algeria	1959						9.8	7.4	0.1
Sub-Saharan Africa	South Africa	1924			13.4	6.7	7.1	7.0	2.7	2.6
Sub-Saharan Africa	Congo, Dem. Rep. of	1941				2.4	13.5	3.3	−0.6	−3.9
Sub-Saharan Africa	Zimbabwe	1950					5.2	6.7	2.9	−3.7
Sub-Saharan Africa	Kenya	1964						8.8	5.4	1.7
Sub-Saharan Africa	Zambia	1966						8.3	2.4	2.8

Note: 'In' indicates the first year that a country experienced a ten-year average backward-looking growth rate greater than 5 per cent.

growth began during the 1870s. Asia was led by Japan and China, with the Philippines, Taiwan, and Korea following close behind: all but Korea had joined the 'modern industrial growth club' by the First World War.

Industrial production suffered in Turkey and peripheral Europe during the First World War, but elsewhere it continued growing rapidly. Rapid industrial growth became universal during the inter-war period: all peripheral regions, with the exception of Latin America, posted average manufacturing growth rates greater than 4 per cent during this period (Table 2.1): 4.3 per cent per annum in Asia, 4.6 per cent in Sub-Saharan Africa (the data refer only to South Africa and the Belgian Congo), and 4.7 per cent in the European periphery and MENA. Indeed, growth rates in MENA and the European periphery bucked the inter-war downward trend in that they were even higher between the wars than before 1914. Only in Latin America did industrial growth rates decline significantly between the wars, to 2.7 per cent per annum.

The Second World War led to substantial declines in manufacturing output in China, Japan, and other countries affected by the fighting, but elsewhere in the periphery output grew rapidly. Manufacturing growth was even higher in the periphery between 1950 and 1973: it reached 8.8 per cent per annum in the European periphery, 8.3 per cent in Asia, 6.3 per cent in MENA, 5.7 per cent in Latin America, and 5.5 per cent in Sub-Saharan Africa. These impressive performances were generally not sufficient to match post-war 'miraculous' growth in the US, Germany, and Japan (7.9 per cent), but were higher than the average growth rate in the US, the UK, and Germany (5.2 per cent), and *much* higher than the leaders' collective performance between 1870 and 1913 (3.2–3.3 per cent per annum).

Manufacturing growth declined in the periphery as a whole after 1973, and again after 1990, although it still remained high in Asia, MENA, and Sub-Saharan Africa, and was considerably higher than in the leaders.

In summary, rapid industrial growth began in Latin America and the European periphery in the 1870s. It spread to Asia after the 1890s, and to MENA and Sub-Saharan Africa in the inter-war years. The high point was 1950–73, and since then industrial growth has been declining.

2.5 WHEN DID RAPID INDUSTRIAL GROWTH BECOME WIDESPREAD?

We are interested not only in when modern industrial growth began in each region, but also in when it began to be widespread. Fig. 2.1 addresses this issue. We first calculate for each country the first year in which it posted a cumulative ten-year growth rate superior to 5 per cent per annum. That is, we calculate the first year for which we can document when each country joined the 'modern industrial growth club' thus defined.

The share of the countries in each region that had joined the modern industrial growth club is plotted in Fig. 2.1. The shares are monotonically increasing, since we are not concerned with the industrially mature as they permanently exit from the club (like most of the European core in the 1960s and 1970s). After all, deindustrialization and a shift to high-tech services is a natural transition for successful economies to make.

Fig. 2.1 shows the successive waves of diffusion of rapid manufacturing growth: first the European periphery, then Latin America, then Asia, then MENA, and finally Sub-Saharan Africa. By 1913, 28 per cent of the European periphery, 10 per cent of Asia, and 18 per cent of Latin America had joined the modern industrial growth club. Since club membership is based on a retrospective criterion, this implies that these countries had been growing rapidly since well before the First World War. By 1938, club membership had been attained by half of the European periphery, 18 per cent of Asia, and 26 per cent of Latin America, but still only 6 per cent of MENA and 2 per cent of Sub-Saharan Africa. By 1973 and the end of the ISI period, the threshold had been attained by 63 per cent of the European periphery, 31 per cent of Asia, 56 per cent of Latin America, 44 per cent of MENA, and 16 per cent of Sub-Saharan Africa.

Fig. 2.2 provides an alternative perspective: it measures the proportion of a region's 2007 population that was living in countries which had attained the 5 per cent growth threshold by any given year. By giving more weight to Brazil than to Saint Lucia, or to China than to Bhutan, the measured diffusion rates are increased dramatically. This suggests that population and domestic market size were an important determinant of industrial performance between 1913 and 1973, a long anti-global episode. By the First World War, the 5 per cent threshold had been attained in countries accounting for 49 per cent of the European periphery's (2007) population, 48 per cent of Asia's population, and 68 per cent of Latin

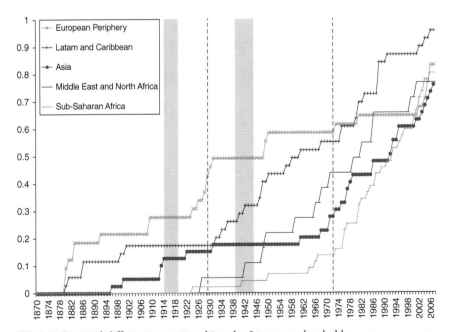

Fig. 2.1. Regional diffusion curves: reaching the 5 per cent threshold

Note: The figure shows the proportion of countries for which the ten-year backward-looking average industrial growth rate exceeded a 5 per cent threshold.

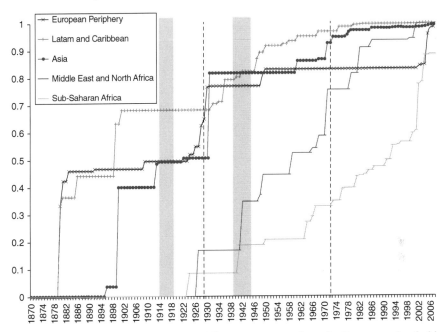

Fig. 2.2. Regional population-weighted diffusion curves: reaching the 5 per cent threshold

Note: The figure shows the proportion of the region's population in 2007 living in countries for which the ten-year backward-looking average industrial growth rate exceeded a 5 per cent threshold. Countries for which data are missing are assumed not to have exceeded this threshold.

America's population—already very large numbers. By 1938, the modern industrial growth club had been attained by countries accounting for three-quarters of the population in these three poor periphery regions. By 1973, the club had been attained in countries accounting for 83 per cent of the 2007 population of the European periphery, 94 per cent of the Asian population, 96 per cent of the Latin American population, 75 per cent of the MENA population, and even 35 per cent of the population of Sub-Saharan Africa. Industrial diffusion was virtually complete, according to this population-weighted criterion. In Asia, Latin America, and the European periphery, the years 1870–1938 were the ones that saw the greatest diffusion; in MENA, diffusion occurred largely between the Second World War and the first oil crisis; in Sub-Saharan Africa it proceeded steadily between the interwar years and the 1990s, when it dramatically accelerated. Overall, the decades between 1896 and 1938 saw the most rapid diffusion of industry to the periphery, at least as measured by output growth.

2.6 WAS THERE HISTORICAL PERSISTENCE?

To what extent were high-growth countries in one period also high-growth countries in the following period? Table 2.3 provides a list of the top ten performers for each

Table 2.3. The top ten performers by region and period

European Periphery

1870–96	1896–1913	1913–20	1920–38
Bosnia and Herzegovina	Bosnia and Herzegovina	Greece	Russia
Serbia and Montenegro	Russia	Yugoslavia	Latvia
Bulgaria	Austria	Spain	Finland
Romania	Hungary	Romania	Romania
Finland	Finland	Italy	Greece
Italy	Romania	Portugal	Bulgaria
Russia	Bulgaria	Czechoslovakia	Ireland
Austria	Spain	Finland	Estonia
Hungary	Portugal	Bulgaria	Hungary
Portugal	Italy	Austria	Poland

Asia

1870–96	1896–1913	1913–20	1920–38
Korea	China	Philippines	Korea
China	Japan	Taiwan	Japan
Philippines	Indonesia	China	China
Taiwan	Thailand	Japan	Taiwan
Japan	India	Burma	Philippines
India		Korea	India
Indonesia		Thailand	Indonesia
Thailand		Indonesia	Burma
Burma		India	Thailand

Latam and Caribbean

1870–96	1896–1913	1913–20	1920–38
Argentina	Brazil	Brazil	Colombia
Peru	Argentina	Peru	Argentina
Uruguay	Chile	Uruguay	Costa Rica
Chile	Uruguay	Argentina	Peru
Brazil	Mexico	Colombia	Mexico
Mexico	Peru	Chile	Guatemala
Colombia		Mexico	Brazil
			Uruguay
			Chile
			Cuba

Middle East and North Africa

1870–96	1896–1913	1913–20	1920–38
Turkey	Turkey	Egypt	Turkey
		Turkey	Egypt

Sub-Saharan Africa

1870–96	1896–1913	1913–20	1920–38
		South Africa	South Africa
			Congo, Dem. Rep. of

European Periphery

1938–50	1950–73	1973–90	1990–2007
Albania	Albania	Cyprus	Ireland
Bulgaria	Malta	Ireland	Lithuania
Ireland	Bulgaria	Malta	Slovak Republic
Poland	Romania	Portugal	Poland
Yugoslavia	Yugoslavia	Bulgaria	Finland
Finland	Cyprus	Latvia	Hungary
Portugal	Poland	Yugoslavia	
Spain	Spain	Italy	Czech Republic
Austria	Italy	Finland	Belarus
Czechoslovakia	Greece	Austria	Estonia

Asia

1938–50	1950–73	1973–90	1990–2007
Philippines	Singapore	Bhutan	Cambodia
Thailand	Korea	Indonesia	Myanmar
India	Malaysia	Korea	Afghanistan
Korea	Japan	Maldives	Vietnam
China	Taiwan	Taiwan	China
Japan	Thailand	Malaysia	Kazakhstan
Indonesia	Pakistan	Lao People's Democratic Republic	Bhutan
Taiwan	Mongolia	Tonga	Korea
	China	China	Malaysia
	Vietnam	Thailand	Lao People's Democratic Republic

Latam and Caribbean

1938–50	1950–73	1973–90	1990–2007
Colombia	Belize	Grenada	Trinidad and Tobago
Venezuela	Puerto Rico	St. Lucia	Costa Rica
El Salvador	Panama	Dominica	Dominican Republic
Brazil	Barbados	Paraguay	Peru
Mexico	Nicaragua	Belize	Honduras
Ecuador	Brazil	Antigua and Barbuda	Belize
Nicaragua	Costa Rica	St Vincent and the Grenadines	Nicaragua
Chile	Mexico	Puerto Rico	El Salvador
Honduras	Venezuela	Cuba	St. Kitts and Nevis
Uruguay	Peru	Ecuador	Suriname

Middle East and North Africa

1938–50	1950–73	1973–90	1990–2007
Morocco	Iran, Islamic Republic of	United Arab Emirates	United Arab Emirates
Egypt	Israel	Algeria	Oman

(*continued*)

Table 2.3. Continued

| European Periphery | | | |
1870–96	1896–1913	1913–20	1920–38
Tunisia	Algeria	Saudi Arabia	Jordan
Turkey	Turkey	Tunisia	Iran, Islamic Republic of
	Saudi Arabia	Syrian Arab Republic	Syrian Arab Republic
	Egypt	Sudan	Yemen, Republic of
	Morocco	Egypt	Saudi Arabia
	Tunisia	Turkey	Sudan
	Syrian Arab Republic	Jordan	Egypt
	Sudan	Morocco	Tunisia

| Sub-Saharan Africa | | | |
1938–50	1950–73	1973–90	1990–2007
Congo, Dem. Rep. of	Malawi	Swaziland	Equatorial Guinea
South Africa	Central African Republic	Cameroon	Mozambique
Zimbabwe	Mozambique	Cape Verde	Namibia
	Kenya	Lesotho	Uganda
	Botswana	Botswana	Lesotho
	Zambia	Mauritius	Sierra Leone
	Cameroon	Mali	Angola
	South Africa	Central African Republic	São Tomé and Príncipe
	Zimbabwe	Gambia, The	Burkina Faso
	Burkina Faso	Congo, Rep. of	Benin

region and time period, ranked by their average growth performance over the period as a whole. Certain countries appear consistently in the table: Russia, Bulgaria, China, Japan, India, and Brazil being among the most prominent. It appears that the current BRICs' rapid industrial growth is a phenomenon with deep historical roots. However, Table 2.3 shows that there also has been a good deal of churning over time, with many countries entering and exiting the leader board within a brief space of time (and, occasionally, re-entering at a later date).

Fig. 2.3 confirms that there has been relatively little persistence over time in long-run industrial growth rates. It computes the correlation coefficient between average growth rates in adjacent periods. It does so both using a consistent thirty-country sample, and using the largest sample of countries for which data exist for both periods. These correlation coefficients were quite high for the nineteenth century (0.5 in the fixed sample to 0.62 in the changing sample), and much lower in the mid-twentieth century (0.16 to 0.19) and since 1990 (0.15 to 0.49), suggesting that achieving rapid growth in one period was only a weak predictor of rapid growth in the subsequent period. While there are important exceptions, rapid long-run industrial growth was not very persistent in the twentieth century.

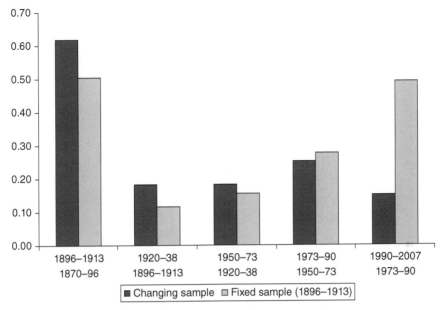

Fig. 2.3. Cross-country correlations: growth in subsequent periods

2.7 UNCONDITIONAL INDUSTRIAL CATCHING-UP

There is a vast empirical literature that asks whether poorer countries grow more rapidly than richer ones, and thus converge on the richer countries—and it has found that they do not (Abramovitz, 1986; Barro, 1997; Bourguignon and Morrisson, 2002). Instead, that literature has only found *conditional* convergence (Durlauf, Johnson, and Temple, 2005). More recently, however, Rodrik (2013) has found evidence of *unconditional* convergence in labour productivity for individual manufacturing sectors. Since we do not have comparable data for manufacturing employment, we cannot speak to the productivity issue. Instead, we ask a different question: did countries with low manufacturing output per capita systematically experience more rapid per capita growth in manufacturing output than countries with high manufacturing output per capita?

We begin by comparing rates of per capita manufacturing growth in our five peripheral regions to those in the core (in previous sections we explored aggregate rather than per capita manufacturing growth). Table 2.4 gives the difference between peripheral and leader per capita growth rates, for both definitions of the leading group. As can be seen, per capita growth rates in the European periphery exceeded those in the core throughout, except during the First World War, and Asian per capita growth rates exceeded core rates until 1990, except

Table 2.4. Catching-up: industrial growth rate relative to leaders

Panel A: Leaders are always the US, Germany, and the UK

Groups	1870–96	1896–1913	1913–20	1920–38	1938–50	1950–73	1973–90	1990–2007
European Periphery	0.9	0.6	−6.8	2.7	1.1	4.0	1.7	0.3
Asia	1.0	2.2	1.4	2.5	−2.8	2.7	2.9	0.0
Latam and Caribbean	0.2	0.2	−0.6	−0.04	1.6	−0.6	0.3	−1.3
Middle East and North Africa	−1.4	−1.0	−7.5	2.4	2.1	−0.6	2.3	−0.4
Sub-Saharan Africa			9.0	3.5	3.9	−0.002	−0.3	−0.4

Panel B: The US, Germany, and the UK before 1939, Japan after

Groups	1870–96	1896–1913	1913–20	1920–38	1938–50	1950–73	1973–90	1990–2007
European Periphery	0.9	0.6	−6.8	2.7	1.9	2.5	1.0	0.5
Asia	1.0	2.2	1.4	2.5	−2.1	1.2	2.1	0.2
Latam and Caribbean	0.2	0.2	−0.6	−0.01	2.4	−2.1	−0.5	−1.1
Middle East and North Africa	−1.4	−1.0	−7.5	2.4	2.9	−2.0	1.5	−0.2
Sub-Saharan Africa			9.0	3.5	4.7	−1.4	−1.0	−0.2

Note: Average industrial growth rates by region relative to the leaders are computed in two steps. First, we compute the average per capita growth rates for each region. Second, we subtract the GDP-weighted average of the leaders.

during the Second World War. Latin American per capita growth rates were uneven, higher than core rates in only three or four of the eight periods. The same was true of MENA and Sub-Saharan per capita growth rates: they were only occasionally higher than core growth rates. The period which saw the most uniform peripheral 'catching-up' on the core was the inter-war period.

When did it become true that per capita manufacturing growth rates were systematically higher in less industrialized countries, and when was this tendency most pronounced? In order to answer this question, we need to compare levels of manufacturing output across countries. We use two approaches. First, the World Bank's World Development Indicators report comparable manufacturing output levels for 2001, expressed in US dollars. We extrapolate these comparable 2001 output levels back in time to 1870 using our manufacturing output indices, and then divide these output figures by population taken from the World Development Indicators and Maddison (2010).

There are dangers in extrapolating manufacturing output levels backwards over such long periods, involving as they do compositional shifts, relative price changes, and the like. Therefore, we also adopted a second approach, which was to take Bairoch's (1982) data on cross-country industrial output per capita for two benchmark years (1913, 1928), and then use our annual output indices and population data to generate comparable absolute levels of per capita manufacturing output for 1870, 1896, and 1920. Similarly, we used UN data for 1967 to generate comparable absolute levels of per capita output for 1950, and World Bank data to generate comparable absolute levels for 1973 and 1990.

Armed with these time series, we can now ask: when was per capita manufacturing growth faster in less industrialized countries, where the level of industrialization is measured by manufacturing output per capita? Any industrial catching-up must have been due either to convergence in economic structure (that is, less industrialized countries seeing a faster shift of labour out of agriculture and into manufacturing), or to faster growth in manufacturing labour productivity, or both.

Table 2.5 provides the slope coefficients from regressions of the per annum, per capita manufacturing output growth rates against initial levels of per capita manufacturing output. The first column presents our preferred estimates, using the Bairoch data for 1913 and 1928, and the UN data for 1967. However, the number of observations is not constant across time periods in the first column, making the

Table 2.5. Unconditional industrial catching-up

Period	Using period-specific	Country sample					
		1870–96	1896–1913	1920–38	1950–73	1973–90	1990–2007
1870–96	−0.469	−0.169					
	(0.391)	(0.173)					
1896–1913	−0.525	−0.024	−0.259				
	(0.353)	(0.115)	(0.188)				
1920–38	−0.491**	−0.349**	−0.398***	−0.537**			
	(0.206)	(0.159)	(0.136)	(0.232)			
1950–73	−3.766***	−0.699*	−0.688**	−0.698***	−0.777***		
	(0.541)	(0.391)	(0.304)	(0.251)	(0.260)		
1973–90	−0.421***	−0.916*	−0.992**	−0.749*	−0.723**	−0.375***	
	(0.156)	(0.469)	(0.385)	(0.393)	(0.285)	(0.138)	
1990–2007	−0.348	−0.399*	−0.704**	−0.452*	−0.067	0.233	0.063
	(0.222)	(0.216)	(0.299)	(0.252)	(0.248)	(0.199)	(0.156)
Number of countries		27	32	45	57	92	146

Note: Coefficients are obtained by regressing regression-based growth rates of per capita manufacturing output on the log level of per capita manufacturing output at the beginning of the period. The first column reports coefficients using period-specific benchmarks; subsequent columns use backward extrapolation from a 2001 benchmark. See text for details. *, **, and *** indicate statistical significance at the 10 per cent, 5 per cent, and 1 per cent levels respectively. Robust standard errors in parentheses.

coefficients difficult to compare.[5] The other columns address this issue, using the data on levels constructed by extrapolating backward from the 2001 World Bank data. In each column, the sample size is kept constant over time. For example, the estimated coefficient for the inter-war period, using the sample of countries for which we have data between 1870 and 1896, is -0.349, which is significant at the 5 per cent level. That inter-war β coefficient can be compared with other periods which use the same sample, up and down the column.

We find robust evidence—a negative and statistically significant β coefficient—of industrial catching-up after the First World War. The highpoint of industrial catching-up in the periphery was the ISI period between 1950 and 1973: while strong unconditional convergence persisted after the first oil shock and up to 1990, it was slightly less pronounced than before (both in our preferred specification and in the larger country samples), and it fizzled out after 1990.

2.8 IMPLICATIONS

Rapid peripheral industrialization is not a phenomenon unique to post-Second World War 'miracles'. It took place at least as far back as the 1870s in Latin America and the European periphery, and was well under way in Asia by the end of the nineteenth century. It had become widespread in all three regions by the inter-war period. The highpoint of peripheral industrialization was not 1990–2007, as modern analysts seem to think, but 1950–73, which was also the highpoint of the periphery's industrial catching-up on the core.

As advertised in Chapter 1, the rest of this volume seeks to identify the fundamentals explaining the performance documented here.

REFERENCES

Abramovitz, M. (1986). Catching up, forging ahead, and falling behind. *Journal of Economic History* 46, 385–406.

Bairoch, P. (1982). International industrialization levels from 1750 to 1980. *Journal of European Economic History* 11, 269–333.

Barro, R. J. (1997). *Determinants of Economic Growth: A Cross-Country Empirical Study.* Cambridge, MA: MIT Press.

Bénétrix, A., O'Rourke, K. H., and Williamson, J. G. (2015). The spread of manufacturing to the poor periphery 1870–2007. *Open Economies Review* 26, 1–37.

Bourguignon, F. and Morrisson, C. (2002). Inequality among world citizens: 1820–1992. *American Economic Review* 92, 727–44.

Crafts, N. F. R. (1985). *British Economic Growth during the Industrial Revolution.* Oxford: Oxford University Press.

[5] For our six periods, the coefficients are estimated using data for 27, 32, 45, 57, 92, and 146 countries respectively. For the final two periods, this column uses benchmark data from the World Development Indicators.

Crafts, N. F. R. and Harley, C. K. (1992). Output growth and the British industrial revolution: a restatement of the Crafts–Harley view. *Economic History Review* 45, 703–30.

Durlauf, S., Johnson, P., and Temple, J. (2005). Growth econometrics. In *Handbook of Economic Growth* (Eds, Aghion, P. and Durlauf, S.). Amsterdam: North-Holland, 555–677.

Maddison, A. (2010). *Statistics on World Population, GDP and Per Capita GDP, 1–2008 AD.* http://www.ggdc.net/MADDISON/oriindex.htm.

Rodrik, D. (2013). Unconditional convergence in manufacturing. *Quarterly Journal of Economics* 128, 165–204.

Rodrik, D. (2015). Premature deindustrialization. *NBER Working Paper* No. 20935, National Bureau of Economic Research, Cambridge, MA.

Smits, J.-P., Woltjer, P., and Ma, D. (2009). A dataset on comparative historical national accounts, ca. 1870–1950: a time-series perspective. *Groningen Growth and Development Centre Research Memorandum* No. GD-107.

Williamson, J. G. (2010). When, where, and why? Early industrialization in the poor periphery 1870–1940. *National Bureau of Economic Research Working Paper* No. 16344.

Williamson, J. G. (2011). Industrial catching up in the Third World 1870–1975. *National Bureau of Economic Research Working Paper* No. 16809.

PART I

EUROPE AND THE MIDDLE EAST

3

State and Market in Russian Industrialization, 1870–2010

Andrei Markevich and Steven Nafziger

3.1 INTRODUCTION

From a low-income, agrarian base, Russia and the Soviet Union experienced an often-dramatic process of industrial growth from the late nineteenth century into the second half of the twentieth century.[1] While growth emerged from the 1880s, the economy remained primarily agricultural as late as 1913, with heavy and light industry contributing 20 per cent of national income, compared to over 40 per cent in more developed European economies (Gregory, 1982; Mitchell, 1998). After economic collapse from 1914 to 1922, the New Economic Policies of the 1920s generated significant recovery but failed to spark the industrial acceleration demanded by the Bolsheviks. Such a surge did occur following Stalin's consolidation of power in the late 1920s. In creating the emblematic 'command economy', Stalin initiated a number of policies that accelerated industrialization, which was accompanied by massive changes in all aspects of Soviet society. Stalin's industrialization drive entailed enormous human losses and welfare costs. But by the middle of the twentieth century, the Soviet economy possessed a large modern industrial sector centred on immense capital-intensive factories utilizing relatively advanced production technologies, skilled labour, and abundant resources. This impressive building of industrial capacity allowed for the military expansions of the Second World War and the Cold War, fuelled resource exploitation in Siberia and the Far East, and provided the Soviet population with meaningful increases in living standards.

However, fundamental problems within the Soviet command economy led to a decline in industrial growth rates from the 1960s onwards. The mobility of cheap labour from the countryside declined, returns to capital investment fell as misallocations increased, and incentives for innovation and worker effort in an increasingly complex economy worsened. Although autarkic policies shielded the economy from

[1] Andrei Markevich would like to thank the Hoover Institution, Stanford (Stanford, US) and the Laboratory of Russian Economic History, Higher School of Economics (Moscow, Russia), with which he was affiliated when working on this chapter.

global shocks such as the Great Depression, the limited trade and technological flows with advanced nations constrained industrial productivity growth, leading relatively inefficient firms to struggle once the economy opened at the end of the Soviet period. In contrast, a growing reliance on oil and natural resources emerged in the post-war period and carried over into the post-Soviet era. By the twenty-first century, Russia under Vladimir Putin was a post-industrial economy largely reliant on resource rents.

Our account of the long-run industrial development of Russia and the Soviet Union centres on the critical role that the state has played. From Alexander Gerschenkron's (1965) famous emphasis on substituting for the missing prerequisites of modern growth, to Stalin's formulation of the command system, to the autocratic policies of the Putin regime, the state's guiding (and often dictating) role in the industrial sector has been a constant theme of Russian and Soviet economic history. At the same time, we emphasize that even in the Soviet period, markets and market-like transactions were critical for allocating capital, labour, resource inputs, and final goods.[2] Factor and product markets were sometimes banned or otherwise inhibited by the state, but even then, informal transactions were of critical importance. With some exceptions, labour was generally free to shift towards higher returns throughout the period. Underlying the Soviet veneer of planning was a system of negotiated horizontal transactions between firms and vertical bargaining between firms and their industry superiors (Markevich, 2003; Gregory, 2004). Foreign capital, trade, and technological flows were vital for the early stages of Tsarist industrialization and continued to impact Soviet industrial development, even under conditions of professed autarky. The recent industrial experience of post-Soviet Russia has been characterized by a renewed openness to foreign capital and trade, a reversal of the emphasis on heavy manufacturing that characterized the Soviet period, and a growing dependence on resource-based sectors under tightening state control.

Before proceeding, two definitional issues must be addressed. The first is what we mean by 'industry'. In general, we refer to non-agricultural, non-service production that utilizes capital, motive power, labour, and intermediate inputs to produce a concrete final product. This encompasses heavy and light industry, mining, and the processing of agricultural products and natural resources. We rely on a newly constructed (and consistently defined) time series of per capita industrial production from 1860 to 2010, which we consider in conjunction with other qualitative and quantitative evidence of industrial activity over the period.

A second issue is what do we mean by 'Russia'? Although our core evidence on industrial output is measured in per capita terms, boundary changes require us to focus on slightly different geographies over time. By 1870, the Russian Empire included the Russian, Ukrainian, Byelorussian, and Baltic provinces of 'European Russia' as well as the Caucuses, parts of central Asia, Siberia, Bessarabia (modern

---

[2] Our emphasis on state–market interactions echoes a long literature. For example, Crisp (1991, p. 260) argues that Imperial industrialization arose out of an 'interaction between autonomous, i.e. market driven, and "induced", that is state initiated or assisted, development'.

Moldova), Finland, and the Polish provinces. Following standard practices, we exclude Finland from our account.[3] With some exceptions (that is, the Baltics), the boundaries of the Soviet Union were similar to the Tsarist ones after 1922. The largest discrepancies emerge in the last twenty-five years. The break-up of the Soviet Union in 1991 meant the disintegration of a unified statistical record. As a result, our focus in this last period is on the Russian Federation, which corresponds to the Russian Soviet Federative Socialist Republic within the old USSR.

3.2 INDUSTRIAL DEVELOPMENT UNDER THE TSARS

Historians typically date the birth of Russian industry to initiatives of Peter the Great and his successors in the eighteenth century, which fostered some large metallurgical and textile operations, based on backward production technologies and coerced (that is, serf) labour. However, it is really only in the second quarter of the nineteenth century that substantive signs of modern industrial development can be observed, and it is only after the emancipation of the serfs in 1861 that this sector's growth can be even partially documented.[4] Although tariff policies and state demand certainly helped initiate industrial growth, particularly in Poland, the Baltics, St Petersburg and the region around Moscow, serfdom and the weak legal environment for business probably did much to hinder industry prior to 1861.[5] Defeat in the Crimean War revealed Russia's economic backwardness, leading to a slow but accelerating process of economic change that lasted to the Bolshevik Revolution.

The empirical record is clearer after 1861. The research of scholars like Goldsmith (1961), Gregory (1982), and others gives us the Imperial component

---

[3] It is impossible to separate out Poland in the Imperial data. According to one estimate, Poland produced about 8 per cent of Imperial output in 1897, and per capita income was about 5 roubles more than the mean of roughly 74 roubles (Markevich, 2015a). Our industrial output series includes Poland for the Imperial period, which was more industrialized than Russia (23 against 14 roubles per capita in 1897), but we are confident that our interpretations would hold if we were able to exclude that region.

[4] Mechanization only took hold slowly in cotton spinning after Britain began to allow machinery exports (1830s), while other textile sectors remained backward and largely reliant on peasant home production. In the Moscow region, peasant households allocated much of their labour to proto-industrial activities in putting-out systems for weaving cloth, along with artisanal production of crafts and small-scale artisanal goods. Limited quantitative evidence suggests that the number of factories and the factory labour force increased steadily over the first sixty years of the nineteenth century, albeit from extremely low levels. On Russian industrial growth before 1861, see Blackwell (1968) and Kahan (1967; 1985).

[5] Although many peasants were able to move into non-agricultural employment in this period (Dennison, 2011; Fedorov, 1974), low agricultural productivity, constraints on labour mobility, and other institutional aspects of serfdom certainly limited domestic demand for industrial output (Markevich and Zhuravskaya, 2015). The installation of relatively high revenue tariffs on manufacturing goods from 1811 created some protection for domestic production, which persisted throughout the Tsarist era (Blackwell, 1968, Chapter 5). Overall, the legal environment for large-scale industrial firms remained relatively weak in the Tsarist period (Owen, 2002). Incorporation was expensive and politicized, although firms that did receive a formal charter were able to tap domestic and foreign capital markets and expand as a result (Gregg, 2014).

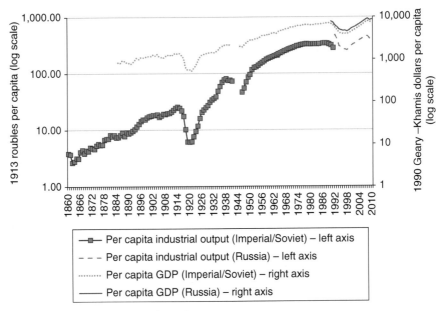

Fig. 3.1. Russian GDP and industrial output per capita

Note: The left-hand axis refers to 1913 roubles. The right-hand axis refers to 1990 Geary–Khamis dollars. One 1913 rouble was worth approximately 12.4 1990 Geary–Khamis dollars. The Imperial/Soviet series refer to GDP and industrial output per capita in either the Russian Empire (without Poland for GDP and without Finland for both series) or the Soviet Union (excluding the Baltics between the wars). The Russia series refer to the Russian Federation only. The breaks during the Second World War refer to missing data. The underlying industrial output data come from Goldsmith (1961), Gregory (1982), Markevich and Harrison (2011), Suhara (2006), Suhara (1999), and Smirnov (2013a; 2013b). Smirnov provides the data from 1991 to 2010 for the Russian Federation in the form of yearly industrial output growth rates. We apply these rates year by year, beginning with the total output number provided by Suhara (1999) for 1990 for the Soviet Union, dividing by the Russian Federation's population in each year. The sources of the GDP data are Gregory (1982) for 1885–1913, Markevich and Harrison (2011) for 1913–28, and Bolt and Van Zanden (2013) for 1928–2010. We index the pre-1928 data to 1913 and then scale it by Maddison's corresponding entry for that year to compare it to the post-1928 data.

of a Russian/Soviet industrial per capita output series for 1870–2010. This series—depicted in Fig. 3.1 and summarized in Table 3.1—includes manufacturing, mining, and fuel production, but excludes utilities and transportation.[6] While the Imperial part of the data cover the vast majority of 'modern' industrial activities, they probably miss some less formal, smaller-scale, and more traditional modes of manufacturing and mining intended for local and household consumption.[7] Such hidden production was more important earlier in the nineteenth century, which suggests that the observed growth acceleration (2.7 to 4.3 per cent between

---

[6] Although a purer manufacturing series would perhaps be preferable, decomposing available industrial data into constituent sectors is not possible for our entire period. We do not think that excluding mining or fuels would significantly change the overall patterns.

[7] Imperial statistical sources undercounted such production, as it was generally untaxed and occurred outside of the legal structure surrounding more modern industrial establishments.

Table 3.1. Russian industrial and GDP growth rates by period, 1860–2010

Period	Sub-period	Growth rate of per capita industrial output	Growth rate of GDP per capita
1860–85		2.7	NA
	1860–70	0.9	NA
	1870–80	5.3	NA
1885–1913		4.3	1.9
	1880–90	2.2	NA
	1890–1900	7.2	3.3
	1900–13	2.6	1.5
	1885–1906	4.1	1.4
	1906–13	4.7	3.3
1913–28		0.2	−0.2
	1913–21	−15.6	−11.6
	1921–8	21.9	14.7
1928–40		9.8	3.8
1940–6		−7.9 (implied)	−1.9 (implied)
1946–70		7.7	4.6
	1946–50	19.5	10.4
	1950–60	5.1	3.5
	1960–70	3.8	3.5
1970–91		0.7	1.1
	1970–80	1.8	1.4
	1980–91	−1.4	0.0
1991–2010		−0.4*	1.0
	1991–2000	−5.3*	−4.0
	2000–10	3.7	5.7

Note: See Fig. 3.1 for the underlying sources. Each period's growth rate is the compound rate implied by the end-point values for each series. For example, we take the values in the years 1940 and 1946 to establish implied growth rates during the Second World War. The 1990–2010 data refer to the Russian Federation. For the observations marked with *, we use 1992 and not 1991 as the initial points.

1860–85 and 1885–1913, Table 3.1) might overstate the pace of late-Tsarist industrialization.

Nevertheless, our aggregate data still reflect the widely accepted time pattern of Imperial Russian industrial development: slowly accelerating growth punctuated by several periods of slowdown. If the record is considered decade by decade, the 1870s, 1890s, and post-1905 periods were high growth, with the 1880s and early 1900s showing slower rates of change. Some scholars have dated the initial onset of Russia's modern industrialization to the 1840s or the Stalinist surge of the 1930s; however, we view the beginning of the transition as perhaps best situated in the early 1890s. This is consistent with Gregory (1972), who notes that the sectoral composition of the Russian economy evolved roughly in parallel with more advanced nations after 1900, although traditional production methods continued to characterize many industrial branches, and the economy remained relatively agricultural through the Revolution (Table 3.2).

Table 3.2. Value added by sector in the Imperial Russian economy, 1885 and 1913

	1885		1913	
	Total (millions of 1913 roubles)	Per cent	Total (millions of 1913 roubles)	Per cent
Agriculture	5,044	58.7	10,294	50.7
Heavy industry	175	2.0	1,632	8.0
Light industry	400	4.6	1,391	6.9
Handicrafts	565	6.5	1,311	6.5
Transportation/ communications	199	2.3	1,173	5.8
Construction	445	5.1	1,035	5.1
All other	1,765	20.5	3,456	17.0
Total	8,594		20,292	

Note: Source of these data is Allen (2003, Table 2.1), which draws on Gregory (1982), Kafengauz (1994), and others. Allen appears to draw on Kafengauz's definition in defining heavy industry as mining, metallurgy (including oil), machine building, wood products, chemicals, and motive power (i.e. engines). We aggregate several sectors to derive 'all other'.

What explains Imperial Russia's initially slow pace and subsequent acceleration of industrial growth? Famously, Gerschenkron (1947; 1965) described a sequencing that emphasized the relative stagnation of the industrial sector through the 1880s, the state's role in fostering something like a take-off in the 1890s, and a final period of high growth following the Stolypin land reforms in the mid-1900s. In Gerschenkron's account, the emancipation reforms of the 1860s reinforced the communal organization of rural society and installed collective redemption payments in return for communal land rights. These features undermined agricultural incentives, reduced labour mobility, and kept rural demand low. Only when the state stepped in during the 1890s to substitute for missing aggregate demand and to provide tariff and credit support did these 'conditions of backwardness' begin to disappear, and industrial growth took off.[8] Von Laue (1963) and others have interpreted these interventions as constituting a coherent set of industrial policies, as formulated by Sergei Witte, the Minister of Finance from 1892 to 1903.

This framework focuses on the Tsarist state's role in fostering the onset of modern industrial growth, although this interpretation has come under criticism from several directions. One important concern is empirical. Returning to the data of Fig. 3.1 and Table 3.1, the steady increase in industrial growth rates (which is echoed in the GDP per capita numbers of Table 3.1 as well) from 1861 to 1913 suggests that the discontinuities emphasized by Gerschenkron were perhaps less relevant than the secular trend. Moreover, Gregory's (1980) research on rural consumption implies that domestic demand for light industrial production was relatively robust well before the 1890s.[9] It is incorrect to state that the state played

[8] State support was particularly directed towards the railway sector. Another component of state intervention in this period was a conservative macroeconomic policy environment geared towards establishing convertibility with gold—an achievement reached in 1897.
[9] Gregory's (1980) findings on rural consumption levels contradict the argument that the rural population faced growing poverty over the late-Tsarist era. While not empirically explicit in

no role in furthering industrial growth (via railroad subsidies, trade policies, etc.) over the period, but we emphasize the continuity in policies and the role played by private sector factors.

Gerschenkron's interpretation also assumes that the post-1861 communal structure of rural Russia limited the flow of labour out of the agricultural sector, thereby raising the costs of industry. In contrast, the findings of Borodkin et al. (2008), Nafziger (2010), and other researchers imply a substantial level of short- and long-term labour migration from farms to industrial employment in cities and rural areas. This suggests that costs of industrial labour remained relatively low throughout the period, particularly given the high growth rate of the rural population.[10] Unfortunately, evidence on industrial wages across space and over time is spotty. The best information is from the work by Strumilin (1926; 1930) on St Petersburg construction workers (daily wages) and on factory workers in larger establishments across the empire (yearly salaries). We present these data in Fig. 3.2 to show that the period 1870–1913 saw relatively slow real unskilled wage growth (0.8 per cent per year) in St Petersburg, and that factory salaries were also relatively flat over the period.[11] Furthermore, although literacy was slowly rising (Mironov, 2010), the gap between illiterate and all factory workers' salaries stayed constant.[12] With the skilled labour premium remaining high, and the cost of unskilled labour low, incentives to adopt labour-saving technologies were probably limited. Although inconsistent with Gerschenkron's assertions about the commune, such factor prices perhaps led the Tsarist government to play a more active role in subsidizing, and generating demand for, more advanced industrial sectors such as armaments and railroads (Gatrell, 1994).

Late Imperial Russia's industrial producers not only employed relatively cheap unskilled labour, but also faced low energy costs due to vast charcoal and wood resources and emerging coal and oil extraction (Tomoff, 1995; McCaffray, 1996). Evidence is mixed when it comes to the cost and availability of capital. According to the calculations of Kahan (1978; 1989) and Gregory (1982), the industrial capital stock grew as fast as (8–9 per cent per year), if not faster than, other nations undergoing industrialization between the 1880s and 1913. According to Kahan, the value of industrial capital per worker increased by 55 per cent over this period.[13] Limited evidence on Russian interest rates suggests that they were slightly higher

[10] This is probably true compared to the rest of Europe as well, although evidence along these lines is limited (Khaustova, 2013).

[11] The brief spike upward in real wages in the emancipation period was probably due to disruption and unrest, rather than the end to compulsory labour.

[12] There are many possible explanations for this persistent gap, including de-skilling technological change. Preliminary evidence from Khaustova (2013) suggests that the skilled labour 'welfare ratio' was comparatively high in the Russian case.

[13] To some degree, this was enabled by financial development over the period, which was at least partially subsidized by the state. At the same time, securities markets were often quite thin, and many firms probably faced credit constraints (Gregg, 2014).

Fig. 3.2. Russian day wages and yearly salaries, 1853–1913

Note: All data are taken from Strumilin (1926; 1930). The broad dashed line is the nominal St Petersburg construction worker daily wage; the line below that marked with squares is that wage deflated by a St Petersburg price index (the price index in 1913 = 100). The shorter top line marked with triangles is the real average yearly pay for a factory worker employed by an inspected factory that was fined for some sort of violation. The even shorter solid line at the bottom is the equivalent for *illiterate* workers. Real values are all in 1913 roubles.

than in most Western European economies between 1880 and 1913, but that might have reflected greater expected returns as much as a shortfall in domestic savings.[14] Indeed, such returns, along with state investment guarantees and relative exchange rate stability, drew in huge amounts of foreign capital during the last decades of the Imperial regime. Russia became the world's largest foreign debtor during this period, with both portfolio and direct investment pouring in from France, Germany, the UK, and elsewhere (Crisp, 1976; McKay, 1970).

Despite the availability of foreign capital (and technology) and slowly improving capital markets and financial institutions, Gatrell (1986) notes that the construction costs of a modern textile factory in Russia were 75–100 per cent greater than in England in the early twentieth century. This is more consistent with Crisp's (1991) conclusion that Russian industrial firms were not overly capital intensive, than it is with Gerschenkron's (1947) assertion that enterprises maintained high investment rates (and were relatively capital intensive) to overcome labour market

[14] See the short-term rates and bond yields in Flandreau and Zumer (2004). Russian rates were comparable to those in land-rich and capital-scarce Argentina and Brazil in this period.

constraints.[15] Aside from relatively scarce managerial skills (Crisp, 1976), a key reason for the high cost of setting up a modern factory in Russia was the system of protectionism. Not only was the general tariff level rising, but considerable duties were also placed on metal products, machinery, and capital goods. These selectively imposed tariffs were generally a response to lobbying by relatively inefficient domestic producers (McCaffray, 1996). Kahan (1967) argues that this sharply raised the costs of accessing more modern technologies, thereby reducing productivity growth in industrial sectors from textiles, to chemicals, to railroads.[16] Such state policies did allow domestic producers to gain market share and increase output (Allen, 2003), but the longer-run result was a lack of competitiveness, despite access to cheap unskilled labour and energy. High prices meant that the Russian industrial sector was forced to rely on domestic demand, which, while perhaps not as limited as often asserted, was still bound by the agrarian structure of the economy and the low level of income.

In Gerschenkron's (1965) account, state efforts to overcome 'backwardness' were insufficient, and it took Prime Minister Petr Stolypin's reforms of communal property institutions in the wake of the 1905 Revolution to spark market-driven industrial development, which was cut short by the war and subsequent revolution.[17] In contrast, Allen (2003) argues that railroads and market development led to booms in agricultural output and exports (that is, extensive growth), but persistent institutional constraints, technological backwardness, and worsening terms of trade limited industrial growth through 1917. Allen's conclusions are relatively pessimistic regarding the trajectory of a hypothetical Tsarist economy after 1913—Russia did not and could not match the rapid transformation experienced by Japan before the First World War. But in our view, a combination of state policies (tariffs, credit, macroeconomic, and institutional) and market forces (relatively free factor and goods markets) did foster industrial growth from the mid-nineteenth century onwards. Change was less episodic and steadier than Gerschenkron asserted, while convergence in industrial output was more evident than Allen perceived. However, and as Table 3.2 implies, growth from a very low base did not dramatically change the structure of the Russian economy by 1913. Low levels of human capital and relative technological backwardness impeded productivity growth, while low rural incomes (perhaps linked to incentive structures in the peasant commune) limited domestic demand for industrial output.

---

[15] It might still be the case that Imperial Russian industrial firms were relatively large (in terms of labour force) and possessed more market power than similar firms in more developed economies. Although they provide little evidence on this, Cheremukhin et al. (2014) argue that concentration led to slower industrial growth than a more competitive economy would have generated.

[16] Crisp (1976, Chapters 6–8) and McKay (1970) suggest that a number of multinationals were granted special allowances for capital goods imports as part of their Russian registration or incorporation approval. The extent of such arrangements remains unknown, and the literature asserts that tariffs were typically applied quite indiscriminately and that foreign capital inflows were increasingly in the form of portfolio investment over the period.

[17] Gatrell (1994) argues that industrial growth in 1908–14 was not driven by unleashed market demand, but was the result of state spending, subsidies, and policies that attracted foreign capital to armaments and related sectors.

3.3 INDUSTRIAL GROWTH IN THE SOVIET
COMMAND ECONOMY

Following the Bolshevik Revolution, civil war, and economic collapse, substantial industrial recovery occurred under the New Economic Policy, or NEP, between 1921 and 1928 (Table 3.1). NEP entailed a mixed economy where both state policies and market relations contributed to reconstruction. Market transactions dominated in agriculture, cottage industry, and internal trade, while the government directly controlled large-scale industry, transportation, foreign trade, and credit. The dual nature of the NEP economy eventually produced crises in the relations between the Bolshevik state and self-interested private producers and consumers. These finally led to the replacement of the NEP by Stalin's command economy in the late 1920s.

Despite relatively high rates of accumulation prior to 1913, a key bottleneck for industrial development in the 1920s was the limited level of capital per worker. Almost a decade of war and revolution destroyed much of the capital stock, sparked capital flight, and roughly halved national income (almost to subsistence), which limited domestic savings. Soviet Russia lost access to international financial markets after defaulting on Imperial debts. Despite avowed Soviet interest in raising industrial output, the sector was too small to rapidly (self-)finance recovery.

The pressure to increase investment, in combination with professed Bolshevik goals regarding state control and the need to surpass capitalist countries, led to dramatic debates among the Bolsheviks regarding the policies necessary for industrial and economic growth in the 1920s (Erlich, 1960). Bukharin and his followers (the 'right') came to advocate balanced development with considerable freedom for markets. Preobrazhensky and the 'left' argued for rapid industrialization based on the redistribution of agricultural surplus towards investment in producer goods via mark-ups for manufactures and fixed grain procurement prices (the industrial-to-agricultural goods price 'scissors'). This policy, however, was difficult to realize without using open coercion toward peasants. Initial Bolshevik attempts to regulate rural–urban trade and fix relative prices for industrial and agricultural goods decreased the quantity of agricultural goods supplied and produced crises in urban procurement (the 'price scissor crises' of 1923 and 1926 and the 'grain procurement crises' of 1927 and 1928—Johnson and Temin, 1993; Gregory, 2004).

Eventually, Stalin emerged victorious over both sides and brutally realized the left's agenda by launching the collectivization of agriculture in 1929. This entailed harsh state control over grain production and distribution, and allowed for the redirection of surplus to finance industrial investment. Rapid industrialization was based on massive investment in producer goods, along with centralized planning, tight control over foreign trade with selective technological borrowing from abroad, political repression, and economic coercion. Thus, Stalin built a command economy—a state-led hierarchical system that attempted to replace markets with plan and coercion, where principals told agents what and how much to produce, where output should go, and at what 'price' transactions should occur. This system generated impressive rates of industrial growth from 1928 into the post-war period, leading to rapid (but never complete) convergence of the Soviet economy on the developed West. However, it is debatable whether this command system produced a real acceleration in the rate of industrial growth, rather than simply securing the return of the economy to its long-run development path (Fig. 3.1).[18] Moreover, this economic system ultimately generated an incentive structure that slowed industrial output growth and led to the demise of the Soviet Union.

3.3.1 The Stalinist Industrial Revolution, 1928–40

GDP growth under Stalin's industrialization reached almost 4 per cent per year, and the industrial sector grew even faster at 10 per cent (Table 3.1). Changes in composition of national income both by final use and by sector clearly demonstrate the scale of Stalin's 'great leap forward' (Table 3.3, Panels A and B). Gross investment per year doubled during the first five-year plan (1928–32) from 10 to 20 billion roubles (in 1937 prices) and increased to about 33 billion roubles by the end of the decade (Moorsteen and Powell, 1966, p. 387). The net investment share increased from 10.2 per cent in 1928 to 22.6 per cent in 1937, despite the lack of access to foreign capital markets. Most investment went into the producer goods and heavy industry sectors, which the Bolsheviks viewed as the engines of industrialization and necessary for military security. The rapid growth of military output during the first three five-year plans—from 1.3 per cent of GDP in 1928 to 18.2 in 1940—has led some authors to speculate that military power was one of the key components of the utility function of Stalin and his successors (Kontorovich and Wein, 2009), although the transition to the command economy also resulted in an increase of non-defence government consumption. These changes happened at the cost of household consumption, which fell to only half of national income by the Second World War (although per capita consumption rose a bit).

The industrial sector produced one third of value added by the end of the 1930s, in comparison to 20 per cent in 1928. The Soviet Union managed to launch a number of new sub-industries that were virtually non-existent in the Russian Empire, such as automobiles and aircraft production. Enormous growth in electricity production (from 5 billion kWh in 1928 to 48.3 billion in 1940, an increase of 866 per cent—Davies et al., 1994, p. 296) accompanied and shaped sectoral changes, with new facilities characterized by high rates of energy and natural resource usage. The growth in construction and transportation were other visible signs of a broader economic transformation.

We generally agree with the argument (Gregory, 2004) that collectivization redirected surpluses towards industrial investment and fostered cheap food for the burgeoning industrial labour force. State grain procurements rose from about

---

[18] The recent work of Cheremukhin et al. (2014) downplays the 'big push' story of Stalinist industrialization and argues that Soviet policies from 1928 to 1940 reduced factor market distortions, particularly by eliminating market power in industrial sectors.

Table 3.3. Russian/Soviet national income by final use and sector, 1913–40

Panel A	1913	1928	1937	1940
Consumption				
By households	80.5	81.6	54.9	52.2
By government:				
Defence	4.9	1.3	8.2	18.2
Non-defence	6.0	6.9	14.3	14.9
Net investment				
Domestic	11.4	10.2	22.6	14.7
Foreign	−2.9	0	0	0
Total	100	100	100	100
Panel B	**1913**	**1928**	**1937**	**1940**
Agriculture	50.7	48.3	31	29.5
Industry (including mining and fuels)	21.4	20.4	32.2	32.8
Construction	5.1	3.2	5.2	4.5
Transport	5.8	3.9	8.3	8.2
Trade	8.1	7.9	5.1	4.7
Services	8.9	16.3	18.1	20.3
Total	100	100	100	100

Note: These data are taken from Davies, Harrison, and Wheatcroft (1994, p. 272). 'Industry' in the bottom half of the table roughly corresponds to the sum of mining, light, heavy, and handicraft industries from Table 3.2. Allen (2003) slightly adjusts the 1913 numbers in calculating sectoral value-added shares.

10 million tons in 1928 to 30 million by the end of the 1930s (Davies et al., 1994, p. 290).[19] On top of that, collectivization reduced peasant incomes, which contributed to the reallocation of rural labour to the growing modern and more productive industrial sector (Allen, 2003).[20] The overall effect of this massive inflow of labour from the countryside on the productivity of the industrial labour force was most likely negative or neutral, despite considerable state investments in education during the 1920s and 1930s. Value added per worker dropped more than 25 per cent during the first five-year plan, recovering by the end of the 1930s (Harrison, 1998). The supply of cheap unskilled labour kept wages fairly low and redistributed final output in favour of capital owners—that is, the state.[21]

[19] By reducing the 'price' paid to agricultural producers in the collective farms (below that faced by the urban consumers), the state generated a form of forced savings.

[20] With a persistent gap between rural and urban real incomes, approximately 23 million people migrated from the countryside to the cities in the late 1920s–1930s (Kessler, 2002). Soviet policies also encouraged females to actively enter the labour force. More than 40 per cent of employees in large industry establishments were women by 1939 (Davies et al., 1994, p. 284).

[21] Real wages were only 60 per cent of the 1928 level by 1937 (Chapman, 1954). Despite the decrease in industrial wages, average living standards exceeded pre-1913 levels by the late 1930s, because of the reallocation of labour between sectors and an increase in employment (Allen, 2003).

Simultaneously, because of scarcity of qualified labour, the state kept the skill premium relatively high during the 1930s (Shwartz, 1952).

The resulting Stalinist 'Industrial Revolution' dramatically transformed the structure of the Soviet economy, but the overall success of such big push policies is less clear. There was a substantial gap in marginal labour productivity between industry and agriculture before Stalin (a factor of six in 1913); however, there is no evidence of idle labour (zero marginal labour productivity) in the agricultural sector. Using mass mobilization into the Russian army during the First World War, Castañeda Dower and Markevich (2014) find that a withdrawal of agricultural labour substantially less than what happened during collectivization caused a significant decrease in grain production. The scale of these economic costs (let alone the social and demographic ones) relative to gains from greater labour inputs in industry is an empirical issue that remains unexplored.

It is also debatable whether agricultural surpluses were really the main source of industrial capital accumulation. According to Millar (1974), who reconstructed the 1928–32 rural–urban trade balance, the amount of resources shifted from agriculture comprised no more than a third of accumulated capital by the end of first five-year plan. The rest came from non-rural accumulation. Millar points to two mechanisms that hindered the extraction of resources from agriculture, and their employment in industry. First, the state had to compensate for the losses in draught power caused by collectivization by providing tractors and other agricultural machines to the countryside.[22] Second, urban industrial workers relied heavily on informal markets to obtain food, and so they were affected by the rise in non-procurement prices. The consequent drop in real industrial wages meant that peasants *and* workers paid for Stalinist industrialization.[23]

Despite apparent success, especially compared to Western economies harmed by the Great Depression, the Stalinist command economy suffered from a number of fundamental flaws that undermined its efficiency and industrial development in the long run. Non-price mechanisms of resource allocation (often following political objectives) and the absence of prices reflecting true scarcity led to mistakes and path dependencies in the setting of targets under central planning, distorted investment decisions, slowed down innovation and technology adoption, and interfered with optimal factor allocations. Estimates of the resulting effects vary, but what is clear is that the scale of efficiency losses was substantial and probably worsening over time (Gregory and Harrison, 2005).[24] For a telling indicator of the long-run effects, the

---

[22] Facing confiscation, peasants preferred to slaughter and consume their livestock; the number of horses fell from 32.6 million in 1929 to 15.4 million in 1935, and the cattle population declined from 58.2 to 33.5 million (Davies et al., 1994, p. 289).

[23] Sah and Stiglitz (1984) show how a movement of the terms of trade against agriculture can undermine urban worker wellbeing. That collectivization only generated part of industrial capital accumulation roughly corresponds to Allen's (2003) view.

[24] TFP growth in the 1930s was about 1.7 per cent per annum and fell over later decades (Table 3.4). Spatial data are also suggestive. Using modern Canada and Imperial Russia as benchmarks, Mikhailova (2004) estimates that the population in Siberia and the Far East would have been 35 per cent less in 1989 if development had been entirely market driven.

industrial structure of the Soviet economy in 1989 was very similar to 1928 (Gregory, 2004).

State ownership meant that a firm could not go bankrupt, since the government would cover the costs. This inconsistency is often referred to as the soft budget constraint (Kornai, 1980). Given this, industrial enterprises tended to overinvest in risky and/or excessively large projects, since they faced fewer downside risks. Such practices also worsened factor misallocations and led to a general overuse of resources across the economy. Soviet plants used more electricity and raw inputs in comparison to similar Western enterprises (Ericson, 2013). Soviet economic thinking strengthened this effect. In professing a labour theory of value, prioritized state plants got inputs 'cheaply' and received capital assets from the state without paying market rental prices. Excessive capital intensity—coupled with misperceptions about economies of scale throughout the industrial sector, and the absence of variety as a policy objective—was associated with extremely high levels of industrial concentration.

Despite planning and state control of the means of production, quasi-'market' transactions were important in the command economy because they eased the most painful misallocations. First, rather than simply fulfilling plan mandates, producers participated in the planning process by negotiating and bargaining over output targets with industrial ministries and the state planning commission (Gosplan). Such practices led Zalesky (1980) to define the Soviet system as a 'managed' economy rather than a planned one. Second, there were extensive secondary markets for producer goods and raw materials, where enterprises exchanged resources obtained through the plan. This practice was illegal but allowed in order to correct for planning mistakes, information asymmetries with the command hierarchy, and incentive-related bottlenecks (Berliner, 1968). Third, labour market decisions remained relatively unconstrained during most of Soviet history, subject to the illegality of unemployment and residency restrictions (Sokolov, 2003).

Moreover, the USSR remained open to some market pressures from the global economy. Although capital markets and much scientific exchange remained closed, industrial modernization required foreign technologies that Russia did not have. Foreign trade—industrial machines in exchange for agricultural products and commodities—was proposed as an important engine of development in the first five-year plan (Davies and Wheatcroft, 2004). However, deteriorating terms of trade and rising trade barriers during the Great Depression put these plans under pressure.[25] Soviet imports reached 80 per cent of the 1913 level in 1931 but fell back to 20 per cent by the end of the decade (Davies et al., 1994, Table 44). Some historians argue that adverse conditions in the world economy helped foster the Soviet choice of economic autarky that persisted after the war (Dohan, 1976; Sanchez-Sibony, 2014).

---

[25] On the other hand, the Depression may have worsened the bargaining positions of international firms in negotiations with the Soviet government, thereby easing technological transfers (Shpotov, 2003). The Cold War sharply curtailed technological imports.

Where market-like incentives did not help, the state used coercion and repression to ease shortages of the command system. Stalin heavily relied on punishment and terror to maintain his regime and to realize his policies, but he also used them to provide additional incentives to economic agents (Markevich, 2015b). Because of limited scope of monetary rewards in the command system, threats of punishment and criminalization were powerful motivating tools.[26] In addition, forced labour and the Gulag system reduced effective labour costs in some industrial sectors, especially in remote parts of the country. It seems that the Gulag did lower the price of producing certain industrial products (especially in mining), but employing such labour was generally inefficient. Eventually this became clear even to the system's senior operators, which led to the dismantling of the forced labour camps after Stalin's death (Gregory and Lazarev, 2003).

3.3.2 Post-war Soviet Industrial Development: Convergence and Slowdown

The Second World War generated enormous costs for the Soviet economy, which lost about of 25 per cent of the pre-war capital stock (Moorsteen and Powell, 1966, p. 75). After the war ended, Stalin returned to massive investments in heavy industry and producer goods to enable recovery. His successors continued to employ this extensive development strategy with only a slow shift towards more consumer-oriented industrial output. The share of investment in Soviet national product continued to rise and reached almost a third by the 1980s (Ofer, 1987). The growth rate of industrial output was higher than the growth rate of GDP until the 1980s (Fig. 3.1), thereby increasing the share of industry in the economy, even as the rest of the developed world was transitioning towards post-industrial economies.[27]

Investment-led recovery gave way to the 'golden years' of Soviet economic development in the 1950s and early 1960s, when the economy experienced catch-up on Western economies in terms of industrial output and GDP per capita. This golden era did not last long, however. Growth rates of industrial production were steadily decreasing during the whole post-war epoch, becoming negative in the 1980s (Table 3.1). What lay behind this slowdown? Why did the policies that secured the impressive growth rates of the Stalinist industrial revolution stop working?

One answer is that there were diminishing returns to capital accumulation in the face of a tightening labour market, especially in industry. Cheap labour resources were largely exhausted by the early 1960s, with fewer people in agriculture or home production left to be potentially shifted into industrial employment.[28] Moreover,

---

[26] Examples include penalties for managers because of poor-quality output and prison terms because of poor labour discipline.

[27] This rising industrial share occurred alongside a decline of the agricultural sector, which led to growing food imports by the 1970s (Gaidar, 2006).

[28] The urban population exceeded the 50 per cent benchmark around 1960, and female labour participation reached almost 100 per cent by 1970 (Markevich, 2005).

Table 3.4. The growth of Soviet GDP, total factor productivity, and factor inputs, 1928–85

	1928–40	1940–50	1950–60	1960–70	1970–5	1975–80	1980–5
GDP	5.8	2.2	5.7	5.2	3.7	2.6	2.0
Labour	3.3	0.7	1.2	1.7	1.7	1.2	0.7
Capital	9.0	0.4	9.5	8.0	7.9	6.8	6.3
Land	1.6	−1.3	3.3	0.2	1.0	−0.1	−0.1
TFP	1.7	1.6	1.6	1.5	0	−0.4	−0.5
Population	2.1	−0.8	1.8	1.3	0.9	0.8	0.9
GDP per capita	3.7	3	3.9	3.9	2.8	1.6	1.1

Note: The source is Ofer (1987). Our GDP per capita growth rates in Table 3.1 are slightly different due to improvements in the underlying data since 1987. All numbers are average percentage growth rates over the period in question.

the Soviet Union had achieved full literacy and universal basic schooling by the post-war decades. Facing a slowdown in labour supply growth, an extensive growth strategy required even more rapid capital accumulation, which was either not possible or incredibly inefficient. Although it is probably part of the explanation for industrial stagnation, one problem with this interpretation is that Soviet labour productivity in industry was only about 20 per cent of the US level in 1950, reaching only 30 per cent by 1980. This suggests considerable room for capital intensification over the period (Kouwenhoven, 1996).

Another possible reason for slowing growth was the declining efficiency of the Soviet economy. Easterly and Fisher (1995) famously find that controlling for the initial level of GDP and factor inputs, the Soviet Union grew 2.28 per cent more slowly than the rest of the world in the period 1960–89. Table 3.4 demonstrates that if one applies a Cobb–Douglas production function to disaggregate growth components, Soviet total factor productivity (TFP) growth was declining during the whole post-war epoch and even turned negative around 1970.[29]

The reasons for the slowdown in Soviet TFP growth were widely discussed and debated. If one attributes the evolution of TFP purely to changes in *technology*, then sustained negative TFP growth would be a rather unique phenomenon. This is unlikely given that there was some Soviet innovation until the end of the regime. To explain this anomaly, Weitzman (1970) posited an aggregate production function with an elasticity of substitution between capital and labour of less than 1. Weitzman's approach is elegant (and supports a declining labour surplus interpretation), but it is not immediately evident why the elasticity of substitution in the Soviet Union would be so radically different from that in other countries (Allen, 2003). Given this model, it is also difficult to understand how there could have been such a break in TFP growth around 1970 (Harrison, 1998).

A likely explanation of the slowdown and eventually negative rate of measured Soviet TFP growth was a broad decline in the efficiency of resource allocation.

---

[29] Data constraints prevent us from repeating this exercise for just the industrial sector, although we would expect to find very similar results.

Secular changes in the economic environment confronted the poor incentive structure of the command system, giving rise to an institutional rather than technological interpretation of slower TFP growth. The shortcomings of the command economy already evident in the 1930s deepened during the late Soviet period. Both 'market' factors and state policies contributed to this dynamic.

First, the growing technological and organizational complexity of the economy made planning, and quasi-market bargaining between (and among) the centre and economic agents, more difficult. Complexity meant rising information asymmetries, which increased the probability of unbalanced plans, mistakes in the allocation of investment funds and scarce inputs, and 'market failures' in the distribution of final output. Due to the incentive problems they faced, economic agents were not able or willing to fully correct for these factors via secondary transactions and were unresponsive to changing consumer and producer demands. The rising share of investment spent on the modernization of old plants instead of the construction of new ones illustrates the growing misallocations. The former was more costly than the latter (roughly 55 per cent more: see Rumer, 1984); but one of the leading principles of Soviet industrial policy always was to keep all factories in operation. The government continued to follow this principle despite growing numbers of 'old' enterprises requiring reconstruction (Allen, 2003; Popov, 2007).[30]

Changes in politics and the political economy of the Soviet economy worked in the same direction. The government relinquished many of the worst aspects of economic and political coercion with the death of Stalin. Fitful attempts at economic reform and political opening from the 1960s onward strengthened the bargaining positions of economic agents—especially industrial managers—in their relations with Moscow. This further softened budget constraints because it became more difficult for the central authorities to credibly commit to not launch risky projects or to punish managers for plan failures. Moreover, the military lobby was especially strong because of the Cold War. This led to the allocation of more and better capital goods, inputs, and innovation resources towards national defence projects that had low economic payoffs. The share of Soviet military expenditures was 8–15 per cent of GDP in the 1980s, in contrast to 6 per cent in the US (Harrison, 2008). Acknowledging that the USSR could not afford the arms race was one of the factors that induced Gorbachev to initiate reforms (Ellman and Kontorovich, 1998).

Institutionally driven incentive problems and imbalanced factor allocations were especially vivid in the consumer goods and agricultural sectors, which lagged well behind the prioritized heavy industry and military production. As a result, the late Soviet period saw increasing shortages and worsening consumer goods quality. Kim (1999) found that the increase in household saving rates (from 5 to 15 per cent) between the early 1960s and late 1980s was 'forcibly' driven by unsatisfied demand in the face of fixed plan prices. The siphoning of resources from households led

---

[30] The planning process, emphasis on scale, and the geography of Soviet industrial organization generated a considerable number of one-company towns, which fostered pressures to keep plants going.

to 'hidden' inflation and rising implicit price subsidies, which grew increasingly costly for state finances (Kim, 2002).[31] But these forced savings did not fuel efficiency gains in industry, and slowing growth made attempts to satisfy growing consumption expectations of Soviet citizens even more difficult. This undermined the political loyalty of the Soviet population and reduced the stability of the whole system when coercive threats finally became non-credible by the 1980s (Harrison, 2002).

International economic policy is another example of the failure of late Soviet economic governance. While the post-war economy was relatively autarkic and never open to capital inflows, the founding of the Council of Mutual Economic Assistance (CMEA) in 1949 created a trade bloc that saw Soviet manufactured goods exported in exchange for agricultural commodities, intermediate goods, and some imports of capital goods from other Communist countries. This trade did not entail any real foreign competition for domestic producers, and it occurred in the absence of market exchange rates and prices, which eventually led to the Soviet Union effectively subsidizing exports to other CMEA members.[32] Following the OPEC crisis, Soviet leaders took advantage of newly opened fields in Western Siberia and high international prices to rapidly increase the export of oil and natural gas ($5 to $25 billion for oil alone during the 1970s—Gaidar, 2006, 2000 dollars). This financed imports that mitigated growing inefficiencies in the production of food, consumer goods, and advanced capital goods, although fixed export prices within the CMEA generated considerable opportunity costs. Overall, importing technologies from abroad provided between 10 and 30 per cent of Soviet equipment investments, and food imports accounted for between 10 and 20 per cent of the caloric intake of the Soviet population in the late 1970s and early 1980s (Hanson, 2003, p.159). However, the growing dependence on commodity export revenues made the Soviet economy vulnerable to the fall in oil prices in the early 1980s, constraining increasingly necessary imports and weakening the state's budget.[33]

The Soviet command economy initially saw high rates of industrial growth, as state-directed allocations and various market and market-like transactions channelled resources into the sector. Following the conflicting objectives of the NEP period, Stalinist policies of collectivization, encouraging human capital investment and relative labour mobility, selective technological adoptions from abroad, and an investment strategy focused on capital goods generated significant structural change, although the exact contributions of these and other factors remain unclear. The resulting industrial growth was particularly impressive in the context of the Depression, with many Western observers taken by the perceived success of the Soviet 'Industrial Revolution'. However, and following pre-Soviet trends, this

---

[31] Obviously, the causality runs both ways—the enforcement of low prices generated excess demand, which was expressed as shortages.

[32] CMEA trade comprised more than a half of all Soviet foreign trade in 1960, rising to 62 per cent by 1988 (Goodrich, 1989; Hanson, 2003).

[33] Adjustment to this adverse commodity price shock was constrained in the absence of true market prices or exchange rates.

transformation was extensive in nature, with productivity growth occurring more through factor accumulation and the transfer of resources between sectors than through innovation. Constraints on trade and technological flows from abroad limited competitive pressures on domestic firms, while the growing importance of resource exports introduced additional volatility and did little to encourage diversification. The long-run prospects of such accumulation-based growth were limited due to the incentive and information problems that lay at the heart of the command system.

3.4 THE END OF THE SOVIET UNION, INDUSTRIAL DECLINE, AND THE RISE OF THE PUTIN PETRO-STATE

In the mid-1980s, growing fiscal pressure and weaknesses in consumer and producer goods sectors led Gorbachev and a small cadre of reform-minded officials to slowly move towards ending planning, enabling the decentralization of decision making to the firm level, and hardening budget constraints.[34] However, this increase in firm autonomy in the face of still-rigid prices generated significant hoarding of inputs and final goods by firms, which caused cascading market failures across the economy. In sharp contrast to the contemporary Chinese approach, Soviet reformers paid more attention to political rather than economic reforms. Indeed, the political opening of *glasnost* meant that the failures of economic policies (and the shortages they generated) were increasingly evident to the wider public. Mounting social and political pressures culminated in the failed coup of August 1991 and the disintegration of the Soviet Union by the end of the year.

The demise of the Soviet Union generated pressure for further economic reforms in the new Russian Federation.[35] Policy-makers took a 'shock therapy' approach to market liberalization by quickly freeing prices and opening up to the global economy in the winter and spring of 1992. With price liberalization, the release of forced savings generated a spike upwards in the rate of inflation in 1991–3 (up to 800 to 1,500 per cent, depending on the price index—Table 3.5). Rather than shortages, markets came to be flooded with goods, even though collapsing incomes made it increasingly hard for households or domestic firms to buy them.

The collapse of output in the early 1990s is depicted in Fig. 3.1 and Table 3.1.[36] As noted by many observers (for example, Gaidar, 2012), the scale of Russia's aggregate and industrial decline may be overstated in the available statistics due to the rise in non-market transactions and the difficulties of valuing output in a high-inflation environment. Regardless, the early to mid-1990s did see a significant

---

[34] Managerial autonomy and several forms of quasi-ownership (cooperatives, etc.) were allowed under the Law on State Enterprises (1987) and the Law on Cooperatives (1988) (Aslund, 2013b).

[35] We focus on the Russian Federation after 1991. The experience of industry in other former Soviet Republics was roughly similar (Aslund, 2013a).

[36] In comparison to other former socialist countries, Russia's aggregate growth was better than Ukraine's or Georgia's but worse than Poland's or Kazakhstan's between 1990 and 2008 (Bolt and Van Zanden, 2013).

Table 3.5. Russian macroeconomic indicators, select years

	1990	1992	1995	2000	2005	2010
Household final consumption expenditure, etc. (% of GDP)	48.87	37.46	52.09	46.19	49.36	50.58
Gross capital formation (% of GDP)	30.13	34.61	25.44	18.69	20.08	22.62
Research and development expenditure (% of GDP)				1.05	1.07	1.13
Government final consumption expenditure (% of GDP)	20.79	13.86	19.08	15.09	16.87	18.73
Military expenditure (% of GDP)	19.09	4.73	4.07	3.56	3.58	3.85
Net exports of goods and services (% of GDP)	0.22	14.07	3.40	20.03	13.69	8.08
Energy use (kg of oil equivalent) per $1,000 GDP (constant 2011 PPP)	306.41	341.69	357.19	320.68	250.63	226.94
Inflation, GDP deflator (annual %)	15.90	1,490.42	144.00	37.70	19.31	14.19

Note: These data are taken from WDI (2014). Household, gross capital, government, and net export expenditures as shares of GDP sum to 100. R & D is part of gross capital formation, while military expenditures are mostly contained within government expenditures. Finally, note that a large part of gross capital formation was undertaken by the state.

decline in per capita industrial output of approximately 40 per cent between 1992 and 1998 (Fig. 3.1), while the share of total value added generated by the industrial sector steadily eroded from 50 to 37 per cent (Fig. 3.3). Some of this reflected the sharp end of the Soviet emphasis on industry over other sectors.[37] Within 'industry', many manufacturing sub-sectors stagnated, with the clear exception of 'other manufacturing' (Fig. 3.3), which included petroleum and metals processing.[38]

A number of factors help to explain this collapse of Russia's industrial sector. Inflation, stagnant nominal wages, and growing uncertainty sharply reduced demand for consumer goods, especially durables. The collapse of state subsidies (and falling military expenditures) meant that enterprises found their balance sheets eroding, even as they struggled to deal with the legacy of obsolete capital stocks and production technologies.[39] Rather than fire workers, firms reduced hours and wages, a reverse of standard labour market phenomena and the opposite of what transpired in much of Eastern Europe (Gimpelson and Kapeliushnikov, 2013). The decline in the real purchasing power of wages, coupled with worsening

[37] As Mau and Drobyshevskaya (2013, p. 42) state, the Soviet Union had 'an ideological commitment to industrialization' that fell apart in the late 1980s.

[38] Manufacturing as a share of GDP appears to have stayed roughly constant over the last decade— see the note to Fig. 3.3. However, the rising importance of oil and natural gas rents is also evident in Fig. 3.3. While the quantity of Russian natural gas exports rose over the period, other sources were coming online, and Russian production costs remained quite high, thereby reducing rents.

[39] Firms continued to hoard inputs and output, and engaged in barter transactions (50 per cent of inter-firm transactions by 1997—Aslund, 2013b, p. 94). Obsolete technologies and capital vintages, coupled with deteriorating labour market conditions, generated extremely low factor utilization rates and industrial productivity that persisted well after 1990 (McKinsey Global Institute, 2009). Moreover, the legacies of the geographic misallocation of Soviet industrial activity further raised the costs of inputs, labour, and transportation (Hill and Gaddy, 2003).

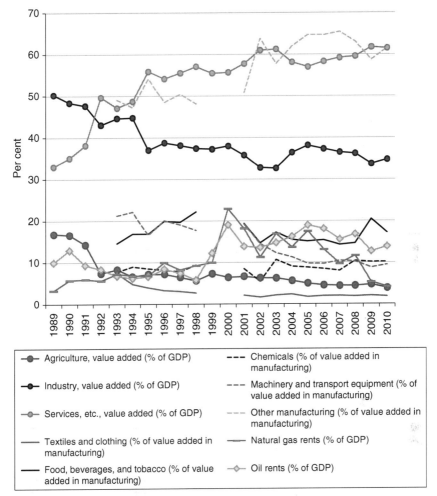

Fig. 3.3. Sectoral value-added shares and resource rents, 1990–2010

Note: These data are taken from the WDI (2014). The top three series sum to 100 per cent of GDP. The next five series sum to 100 per cent of manufacturing, which is equivalent to the industrial sector net of mining, construction, and utilities. Although earlier comparable data are unavailable, the manufacturing sub-sector of industry varied from 17 per cent of GDP in 2002 to 14.8 in 2010 (a global recession year). The two resource rent series are both equal to (output valued at world prices—costs of production)/GDP—that is, they are akin to value added.

demographic and health conditions and the obsolescence of many skills, reduced the effective supply of labour in many manufacturing sectors.

In the autumn of 1991, only 2.5 per cent of industrial output was produced by non-state owned enterprises (Ericson, 2013, p. 60). Reformers quickly moved to begin the privatization of small enterprises via auctions in early 1992. In June 1992, efforts moved on to larger firms (roughly 16,500 with more than 1,000 workers) via a voucher programme. Relatively few firms were transferred in the infamous 'loans for shares' programme, but the notoriety of these transactions, coupled with the quick rise of oligarchic control of large firms, led to a significant backlash against privatization by the late 1990s. This occurred despite evidence suggesting that oligarchic control and some forms of privatization enhanced productivity within most industries.[40] Overall, privatization did transfer the majority of productive assets into private hands by the end of the decade, and it helped lay the foundation for significant subsequent firm entry and exit in the industrial sector.[41]

Despite privatization, persistent uncertainty over ownership and control rights within firms increased borrowing costs and reduced investment in the post-Soviet period. The weaknesses of the embryonic financial system made financing new investment or upgrading outdated capital expensive. The Russian banking system was born out of the chaos of the late 1980s, when large parts of the Soviet banking system were carved up into local and firm-affiliated entities. From the beginning, the market for bank loans was relatively inefficient and highly segmented, with personal (and often political) connections of firm owners playing a central role (Schoors and Yudaeva, 2013). Moreover, unable to entice domestic depositors, many banks turned to foreign borrowing, which helped translate a foreign debt crisis into a full-blown financial crisis in 1998. Double-digit lending rates persisted into the 2000s, and the state has increasingly come to play a role in subsidizing credit.

The sharp end of Soviet trade and most capital flow restrictions in 1991 meant an increase in competition from abroad.[42] Rising imports of manufactures compounded problems for relatively inefficient domestic firms. This was particularly true for light industry, but sectors such as automobiles, computing, and aeroplanes also suffered. Relatively few firms—especially in the early years—were able to quickly adopt foreign technologies or take advantage of international capital markets, and Russian manufacturers saw little export growth.[43] Fundamentally, growing trade openness reinforced Russia's comparative advantage not in manufactures, but in commodities.

According to recent growth accounting exercises, the fall in aggregate and industrial (including mining) output in the 1990s stemmed from declining capital

---

[40] See Brown et al. (2013), who argue that privatization to domestic owners generally led to lower multi-factor productivity in manufacturing, although this correlation essentially disappears by the early 2000s. For the largest owners, Guriev and Rachinsky (2005) marshal evidence that these owners were better at accessing new sources of finance, managed their firms more efficiently, and rarely engaged in debilitating 'tunnelling' of assets.

[41] See Estrin et al. (2009). On the other hand, the poor institutional environment for businesses has constrained firm entry and reinforced concentration, especially in connection to a rebound in state ownership and control in resource-related sectors.

[42] Apart from some retrenchment in the late 1990s, Russia experienced growing integration with the global economy, culminating in accession to the World Trade Organization in 2012. Imports and exports rose sharply, with the net trade balance positive and constituting between 8 and 20 per cent of GDP from 1998 onwards (Table 3.5; WDI, 2014).

[43] However, studies of the productivity effects of Russian privatization show that enterprises acquired by foreign owners performed significantly better than state or domestically owned firms into the 2000s (Brown et al., 2013).

services, labour inputs, and TFP (Entov and Lugovoy, 2013).[44] Fig. 3.1 and Table 3.5 indicate that the rate of capital formation stabilized and industrial output rebounded in the wake of the 1998 crisis and subsequent devaluation of the rouble. Since 1998, industrial output growth has averaged roughly 5 per cent per year, driven half by capital accumulation and half by TFP growth (*ibid.*). After considerable organizational chaos and capital stock rebuilding in the 1990s, the contribution of oil and natural gas to industrial output began to rise (Timmer and Voskoboynikov, 2014). Ongoing growth in oil prices aided economic recovery (directly in terms of output, and indirectly via rising incomes and linkages to non-mining sectors), even as the installation of Vladimir Putin as President in 2000 appeared to stabilize the political system.

These two phenomena—rising oil prices and Putin's growing hold on power—reinforced each other over the 2000s, with growing state involvement in the burgeoning oil and gas sectors signalling Russia's increased dependence on natural resource-related sectors. By the 2000s, Russia was effectively a 'petro-state', as comparative advantage, high oil prices, and relative inefficiencies in other sectors served to reinforce the regime's growing focus on resource rents (Fig. 3.3) and probably undermined broader manufacturing competitiveness due to 'Dutch Disease' effects.[45] The sharp downturn in the demand for Russian oil and natural gas due to the global crisis of 2008–9 and the advent of North American shale production constituted an enormous negative shock to all parts of the Russian economy. Consequently, 2009 and 2010 saw another significant decline in Russian manufacturing and industrial output (Fig. 3.1), as direct state support shrivelled, domestic demand fell, and foreign debt and balance of payments problems raised the costs of inputs and investment.[46]

Despite improvements in economic policies in the early twenty-first century, this recent turmoil has been compounded by burgeoning state interference in the economy. In the strongest form, this reinforcement of state control has entailed the partial or complete renationalization of firms, as in the Yukos case. Although hard evidence is lacking (and observed TFP growth has been relatively robust since 1998), state interventions may have reduced the efficiency of resource allocation within and across industrial firms, limited diversification in the industrial sector, and increased the perceived risk of investment in state-connected firms, especially for foreign investors.[47] As such, it appears that the impact of Putin's policies on the

---

[44] Industry is defined here as mining, manufacturing, and utilities, and these estimates include oil and natural gas production under 'mining'. Negative TFP growth explains one-third of the aggregate output slowdown, but less than 10 per cent of industrial output's decline. Thus, the story of industrial decline—in manufacturing as well as mining—in the 1990s is much more about the decline in capital and labour services than about technological factors.

[45] There was a rise in the 'fuels' share of merchandise exports from 43 per cent in 1995 to 65 per cent in 2010 (Table 3.5; WDI, 2014). There is considerable evidence for at least some 'Dutch Disease' effects in the Russian case in the 2000s—see EBRD (2009).

[46] Despite such adverse shocks, inflation has remained high over the last five years (WDI, 2014), thus impeding nominal adjustments. However, recent political constraints on trade have possibly fostered conditions for some growth in domestic manufacturing (Connolly, 2015).

[47] R & D expenditures have fallen well behind developed economies and even China as a share of GDP (Table 3.5).

industrial sector remains rather mixed (or at least subject to the trajectory of oil prices), although manufacturing has declined in relative terms (Fig. 3.3).[48]

Despite Russia's shift towards a market economy, many institutional and statist legacies of the previous regime survived. Indeed, a large literature has emerged that credits the particularly poor performance of the 1990s, and the return to command-like controls of the Putin era, to the lack of enforceable property rights, ineffective court systems, and anti-market beliefs left over from the Soviet Union (Aslund, 2013a; Gaidar, 2012). Specialization in resource-intensive activities has probably reinforced institutional weaknesses in the industrial sector, especially through a political form of the resource curse (EBRD, 2009). While labour, capital, and goods markets have been largely liberalized, and privately owned firms are in the majority, the state's influence in all aspects of the economy has hindered and perhaps even reversed the transition process. Other than in resource-related sectors, industrial firms have found it hard to improve productivity through innovation or capital upgrading, and Russian manufacturers generally remain uncompetitive on global markets.

3.5 CONCLUSION

This history of Russian industrial development considers three distinct periods: Imperial, Soviet, and post-Soviet. Each of these entailed a very different economic system, with a distinct set of institutions, level of openness to the global economy, and industrial policy environment. Beginning with the early phase of growth in the 1880s and 1890s, accelerating during the Stalinist industrial drive, and then collapsing and only partially recovering during the last three decades, these very different eras would suggest that a unified account of Russian industrialization might be a misplaced effort.

We would disagree for at least three reasons. First, Russian industrialization provides an important contrast to the histories of industrial development in other land-rich, labour- and capital-scarce economies, including the United States, Canada, and Australia. Unlike these societies (and perhaps more like Brazil and China), Russia began the process of industrial growth with an economy that was agrarian, technologically backward, financially underdeveloped, and politically authoritarian. Russian industrialization required addressing such limitations (*à la* Gerschenkron), but it also meant a constant conflict between following comparative advantage and engaging in active policies to support underdeveloped sectors with higher growth potential—a theme explored in a number of chapters in this volume. Thus, understanding the Russia and the Soviet experiences also contributes to the debate over the roots and policy implications of 'late industrialization' and 'de-industrialization'.

---

[48] On the growing role of the Russian state, see the discussion in EBRD (2010, pp. 138–9). In general, recent Putin policies may be mimicking import-substitution industrialization policies often associated with Latin American stagnation (Tarr and Volchkova, 2013).

Second, the three different regimes offer variation to evaluate the role of 'institutions' in the development of the industrial sector. We have endeavoured to highlight a number of different channels in each period, but perhaps looking across the three regimes offers an even more useful point of systemic comparison. Indeed, the contrast between authoritarian but market-oriented institutions grounded in some form of private property rights (Imperial and post-Soviet Russia) and the authoritarian but non-market and anti-private property rights Soviet system speaks to the extractive/inclusive distinction recently employed by Acemoglu and Robinson (2012).

Finally, these three periods all provide a useful depiction of markets and state authority as joint mechanisms for the allocation of resources, information, and decision-making power within an economic system. Throughout, the Russian/Soviet state employed a wide variety of interventionist tools—subsidies, planning, coercion, trade policy, etc.—to drive the industrial development of the economy in a particular direction; one that markets acting on their own would not necessarily have produced. This means that the interaction between political objectives and economic efficiency are necessary concerns, much as scholars of other economies with high levels of state intervention (China, pre-reform India, etc.—see Chapters 9 and 10) have emphasized. At the same time, supply and demand came together very differently across the three periods, depending on how or whether the state dictated plans, targets, rules, institutions, and political objectives to influence the underlying benefits and costs for 'market' participants. Even in the Soviet economy, market-like transactions formed fundamental allocation mechanisms. The sharp swings in the relative roles and characteristics of markets and state authority drove the dynamics of industrial sector development over the last 150 years of Russian history.

REFERENCES

Acemoglu, D. and Robinson, J. (2012). *Why Nations Fail*. New York City: Crown Publishers.

Allen, R. (2003). *Farm to Factory: A Reinterpretation of the Soviet Industrial Revolution*. Princeton, NJ: Princeton University Press.

Aslund, A. (2013a). *How Capitalism Was Built: The Transformation of Central and Eastern Europe, Russia, the Caucasus, and Central Asia*. 2nd ed. Cambridge: Cambridge University Press.

Aslund, A. (2013b). Russia's economic transformation. In *The Oxford Handbook of the Russian Economy* (Eds, Alekseev, M. and Weber, S.). Oxford: Oxford University Press, 86–101.

Berliner, J. (1968). *Factory and Manager in the USSR*. Cambridge, MA: Harvard University Press.

Blackwell, W. (1968). *The Beginnings of Russian Industrialization, 1800–1860*. Princeton, NJ: Princeton University Press.

Bolt, J. and Van Zanden, J.-L. (2013). The first update of the Maddison Project: re-estimating growth before 1820. *Maddison Project Working Paper* No. 4.

Borodkin, L., Granville, B., and Leonard, C. (2008). The rural/urban wage gap in the industrialisation of Russia, 1884–1910. *European Review of Economic History* 12, 67–95.

Brown, J., Earle, J., and Gehlbach, S. (2013). Privatization. In *The Oxford Handbook of the Russian Economy* (Eds, Alekseev, M. and Weber, S.). Oxford: Oxford University Press, 161–85.

Castañeda Dower, P. and Markevich, A. (2014). Labor misallocation and mass mobilization: Russian agriculture during the Great War. *Working Paper.*

Chapman, J. (1954). Real wages in the Soviet Union, 1928–52. *Review of Economics and Statistics* 36, 134–56.

Cheremukhin, A., Golosov, M., Guriev, S., and Tsyvinski, A. (2014). The industrialization and economic development of Russia through the lens of a neoclassical growth model. *Working Paper.*

Connolly, R. (2015). Troubled times: stagnation, sanctions, and the prospects for economic reform in Russia. *Chatham House, Russia and Eurasia Program Research Paper.*

Crisp, O. (1976). *Studies in the Russian Economy before 1914.* London: Macmillan.

Crisp, O. (1991). Russia. In *Patterns of European Industrialization: The Nineteenth Century* (Eds, Sylla, R. and Toniolo, G.). London: Routledge, 248–68.

Davies, R. W., Harrison, M., and Wheatcroft, S. (eds). (1994). *The Economic Transformation of the Soviet Union, 1913–1945.* Cambridge: Cambridge University Press.

Davies, R. W. and Wheatcroft, S. (eds). (2004). *Materials for a Balance of the Soviet National Economy, 1928–1930.* Cambridge: Cambridge University Press.

Dennison, T. (2011). *The Institutional Framework of Russian Serfdom.* Cambridge: Cambridge University Press.

Dennison, T. and Nafziger, S. (2013). Living standards in nineteenth-century Russia. *Journal of Interdisciplinary History* XLIII, 397–441.

Dohan, M. (1976). The economic origins of Soviet autarky 1927/28–1934. *Slavic Review* 35, 603–35.

Easterly, W. and Fischer, S. (1995). The Soviet economic decline. *World Bank Economic Review* 9, 341–71.

Ellman, M. and Kontorovich, V. (eds). (1998). *The Disintegration of the Soviet Economic System.* New York: Routledge.

Entov, R. and Lugovoy, O. (2013). Growth trends in Russia after 1998. In *The Oxford Handbook of the Russian Economy* (Eds, Alekseev, M. and Weber, S.). Oxford: Oxford University Press, 132–60.

Ericson, R. (2013). Command economy and its legacy. In *The Oxford Handbook of the Russian Economy* (Eds, Alekseev, M. and Weber, S.). Oxford: Oxford University Press, 51–85.

Erlich, A. (1960). *The Soviet Industrialization Debate, 1924–1928.* Cambridge, MA: Harvard University Press.

Estrin, S., Hanousek, J., Kocenda, E., and Svenjar, J. (2009). The effects of privatization and ownership in transition economies. *Journal of Economic Literature* 47, 699–728.

European Bank for Reconstruction and Development [EBRD]. (2009). *Transition Report 2009: Transition in Crisis.* London: EBRD.

European Bank for Reconstruction and Development [EBRD]. (2010). *Transition Report 2010: Recovery and Reform.* London: EBRD.

Fedorov, V. (1974). *Pomeshchich'i krest'iane tsentral'no-promyshlennogo raiona Rossii.* Moscow: Moscow University Press.

Flandreau, M. and Zumer, F. (2004). *The Making of Global Finance*. Paris: OECD Development Center.

Gaidar, Y. (2006). *Gibel' imperii*. Moscow: Rosspen.

Gaidar, Y. (2012). *Russia: A Long View*. Cambridge, MA: MIT Press.

Gatrell, P. (1986). *The Tsarist Economy: 1850–1917*. London: B. T. Batsford Ltd.

Gatrell, P. (1994). *Government, Industry and Rearmament in Russia, 1900–1914*. Cambridge: Cambridge University Press.

Gerschenkron, A. (1947). The rate of growth in Russia: the rate of industrial growth in Russia, since 1885. *Journal of Economic History* 7, 144–74.

Gerschenkron, A. (1965). Agrarian policies and industrialization, Russia 1861–1917. In *The Cambridge Economic History of Europe (VI). The Industrial Revolutions and After: Incomes, Population and Technological Changes (2)*, (Eds, Habakkuk, H. and Postan, M.). Cambridge: Cambridge University Press, 706–800.

Gimpelson, V. and Kapeliushnikov, R. (2013). Labor market adjustment: is Russia different? In *The Oxford Handbook of the Russian Economy* (Eds, Alekseev, M. and Weber, S.). Oxford: Oxford University Press, 693–724.

Goldsmith, R. (1961). The economic growth of Tsarist Russia, 1860–1913. *Economic Development and Cultural Change* 9, 441–75.

Goodrich, M. (1989). Foreign trade. In *Soviet Union: A Country Study* (Ed., Zickel, R.). Washington, DC: Federal Research Division, Library of Congress.

Gregg, A. (2014). Factory productivity and the concession system of incorporation in late Imperial Russia. *Working Paper*.

Gregory, P. (1972). Economic growth and structural change in Tsarist Russia: a case of modern economic growth? *Soviet Studies* 23, 418–34.

Gregory, P. (1980). Grain marketings and peasant consumption, Russia, 1885–1913. *Explorations in Economic History* 17, 135–64.

Gregory, P. (1982). *Russian National Income, 1885–1913*. Cambridge: Cambridge University Press.

Gregory, P. (2004). *The Political Economy of Stalinism*. Cambridge: Cambridge University Press.

Gregory, P. and Harrison, M. (2005). Allocation under dictatorship: research in Stalin's archives. *Journal of Economic Literature* 43, 721–61.

Gregory, P. and Lazarev, V. (2003). *The Economics of Forced Labor: The Soviet Gulag*. Palo Alto, CA: Hoover Institution Press.

Guriev, S. and Rachinsky, A. (2005). The role of oligarchs in Russian capitalism. *Journal of Economic Perspectives* 19, 131–50.

Hanson, P. (2003). *The Rise and Fall of the Soviet Economy: An Economic History of the USSR from 1945*. London: Longman/Pearson.

Harrison, M. (1998). Trends in Soviet labor productivity, 1928–1985: war, postwar recovery, and slowdown. *European Review of Economic History* 2, 171–200.

Harrison, M. (2002). Coercion, compliance, and the collapse of the Soviet command economy. *Economic History Review* 55, 393–433.

Harrison, M. (2008). Secrets, lies, and half truths: the decision to disclose Soviet defense outlays. *PERSA Working Paper* No. 55.

Hill, F. and Gaddy, C. (2003). *The Siberian Curse: How Communist Planners Left Russia Out in the Cold*. Washington, DC: The Brookings Institution.

Johnson, S. and Temin, P. (1993). The macroeconomics of NEP. *Economic History Review* 46, 750–67.

Kafengauz, L. (1994). *Evolutsiia promyshlennogo proizvodstva Rossii*. Moscow: Russian Academy of Sciences.

Kahan, A. (1967). Government policies and the industrialization of Russia. *Journal of Economic History* 27, 460–77.

Kahan, A. (1978). Capital formation during the early period of industrialization in Russia, 1890–1913. In *The Cambridge Economic History of Europe (VII). The Industrial Economies, Capital, Labour, and Enterprise, Part 2: The United States, Japan, and Russia* (Eds, Mathias, P. and Postan, M.). Cambridge: Cambridge University Press, 265–307.

Kahan, A. (1989). *Russian Economic History: The Nineteenth Century*. Chicago, IL: University of Chicago Press.

Kessler, G. (2002). The peasant and the town: rural–urban migration in the Soviet Union, 1929–40. PhD thesis, European University Institute, Florence, Italy.

Khaustova, E. (2013). Pre-revolution living standards: Russia, 1888–1917. *Working Paper*.

Kim, B. (1999). The income, savings, and monetary overhang of Soviet households. *Journal of Comparative Economics* 27, 644–68.

Kim, B. (2002). Causes of repressed inflation in the Soviet consumer market, 1965–1989: retail price subsidies, the siphoning effect, and the budget deficit. *Economic History Review* 55, 105–27.

Kontorovich, V. and Wein, A. (2009). What did Soviet rulers maximize? *Europe–Asia Studies* 61, 1579–1601.

Kornai, J. (1980). *Economics of Shortage*. Amsterdam: North-Holland.

Kouwenhoven, R. (1996). A comparison of Soviet and US industrial performance: 1928–90. *Groningen Growth and Development Centre, Research Memorandum* GD-29.

McCaffray, S. (1996). *The Politics of Industrialization in Tsarist Russia*. DeKalb, IL: Northern Illinois University Press.

McKay, J. (1970). *Pioneers for Profit: Foreign Entrepreneurship and Russian Industrialization: 1885–1913*. Chicago, IL: University of Chicago Press.

McKinsey Global Institute. (2009). *Lean Russia: Sustaining Economic Growth through Improved Productivity*. Available at: <http://www.mckinsey.com/insights/winning_in_emerging_markets/lean_russia_sustaining_economic_growth>.

Markevich, A. (2003). Byla li sovetskaia ekonomika planovoi? Planirovanie v narkomatakh v 1930-e gg. In *Ekonomicheskaia istoriia. Ezhegodnik 2002*. Moscow: Rosspen, n.p.

Markevich, A. (2005). Soviet urban households and the road to universal employment, from the end of the 1930s to the end of the 1960s. *Continuity and Change* 20, 443–73.

Markevich, A. (2015a). Economic development of the late Russian Empire in regional perspective. *Working Paper*.

Markevich, A. (2015b). Repression and punishment under Stalin: evidence from the Soviet archives. *Working Paper*.

Markevich, A. and Harrison, M. (2011). Great War, civil war, and recovery: Russia's national income, 1913–1928. *Journal of Economic History* 71, 672–703.

Markevich, A. and Zhuravskaya, E. (2015). Economic effects of the abolition of serfdom: evidence from the Russian Empire. *Working Paper*.

Mau, V. and Drobyshevskaya, T. (2013). Modernization and the Russian economy: three hundred years of catching up. In *The Oxford Handbook of the Russian Economy* (Eds, Alekseev, M. and Weber, S.). Oxford: Oxford University Press, 29–50.

Mikhailova, T. (2004). Essays on Russian economic geography: measuring spatial inefficiency. Ph.D. dissertation, Pennsylvania State University.

Millar, J. (1974). Mass collectivization and the contribution of Soviet agriculture to the first five year plan: a review article. *Slavic Review* 33, 750–66.

Mironov, B. (2010). *Blagosostoianie naselenia i revoliutsii v imperskoi Rossii.* Moscow: Novyi khronograf.

Mitchell, B. (1998). *International Historical Statistics: Europe, 1750–1993.* 4th ed. London: Macmillan Reference.

Moorsteen, R. and Powell, R. (1966). *The Soviet Capital Stock, 1928–1962.* Homewood, IL: Richard D. Irwin, Inc.

Nafziger, S. (2010). Peasant communes and factor markets in late nineteenth-century Russia. *Explorations in Economic History* 47, 381–402.

Ofer, G. (1987). Soviet economic growth: 1928–1985. *Journal of Economic Literature* 25, 1767–833.

Owen, T. (2002). *The Corporation under Russian Law, 1800–1917: A Study in Tsarist Economic Policy.* Cambridge: Cambridge University Press.

Popov, V. (2007). Life cycle of the centrally planned economy: why Soviet growth rates peaked in the 1950s. In *Transition and Beyond* (Eds, Estrin, S., Kolodko, G. W., and Uvalic, M.). Basingstoke: Palgrave Macmillan, 35–57.

Rumer, B. (1984). *Investment and Reindustrialization in the Soviet Economy.* Boulder, CO: Westview Press.

Sah, R. and Stiglitz, J. (1984). The economics of price scissors. *American Economic Review* 74, 125–38.

Sanchez-Sibony, O. (2014). Depression Stalinism: the Great Break reconsidered. *Kritika. Explorations in Russian History* 15, 23–49.

Schoors, K. and Yudaeva, K. (2013). Russian banking as an active volcano. In *The Oxford Handbook of the Russian Economy* (Eds, Alekseev, M. and Weber, S.). Oxford: Oxford University Press, 544–73.

Shpotov, B. (2003). Bisnesmeni i buricrati: amerikanskaia tekhnicheskaia pomochsh' v stroitelstve Nizhegorodskogo avtozavoda, 1929–1931 gg. In *Ekonomicheskaia istoriia. Ezhegodnik 2002.* Moscow: Rosspen, 191–232.

Shwartz, S. (1952). *Labor in the Soviet Union.* New York: Frederick A. Praeger.

Smirnov, S. (2013a). Dinamika promyshlennogo proizvodstva v SSSR i Rossii: Chast' I. Opyt rekonstruktsii, 1861–2012 gody. *Voprosy ekonomiki* 6, 59–83.

Smirnov, S. (2013b). Dinamika promyshlennogo proizvodstva v SSSR i Rossii: Chast' II. Krizisy i tsikly, 1861–2012 gody. *Voprosy ekonomiki* 7, 138–53.

Sokolov, A. (2003). Perspektivi izucheniia rabochei istorii v sovremennoi Rossii. *Otechestvennaia istoriia* 4–5, 130–9.

Strumilin, S. (1926). Dinamika oplaty promyshlennogo truda v Rossii za 1900–1914 gg. *Planovoe khoziaistvo* 9, 239–52.

Strumilin, S. (1930). Oplata truda v Rossii. *Planovoe khoziaistvo* 7–8, 135–61.

Suhara, M. (1999). An estimation of Russian industrial production: 1960–1990. *Hitotsubashi University, Institute for Economics Research Discussion Paper* No. 373.

Suhara, M. (2006). Russian industrial growth: an estimation of a production index, 1860–1913. *Working Paper.*

Tarr, D. and Volchkova, N. (2013). Russian trade and foreign direct investment policy at the crossroads. In *The Oxford Handbook of the Russian Economy* (Eds, Alekseev, M. and Weber, S.). Oxford: Oxford University Press, 593–614.

Timmer, M. and Voskoboynikov, I. (2014). Is mining fueling long-run growth in Russia? Industry productivity growth trends since 1995. *Review of Income and Wealth* 60, S398–S422.

Tomoff, K. (1995). The role of forests in Witte's industrialization drive. *Russian History* 22, 249–83.

Von Laue, T. (1963). *Sergei Witte and the Industrialization of Russia*. New York: Columbia University Press.

Weitzman, M. (1970). Soviet postwar growth and capital-labor substitutability. *American Economic Review* 60, 676–92.

World Development Indicators 2014 (Online). [WDI]. (2014). Washington, DC: World Bank.

Zalesky, E. (1980). *Stalinist Planning for Economic Growth, 1933–1952*. Chapel Hill, NC: University of North Carolina Press.

4

How Peripheral was the Periphery?
Industrialization in East Central Europe since 1870

Alexander Klein, Max-Stephan Schulze, and Tamás Vonyó

4.1 INTRODUCTION

The origins of industrialization in Central and East Central Europe reach back into the eighteenth century (Good, 1984; Komlos 1983, 1989). Much of this part of Europe was under Habsburg rule until the demise of the Austro-Hungarian Empire at the end of the First World War.[1] The Habsburg realm's geographical location at the crossroads of Europe's west and east meant that the timing and spatial diffusion of industrialization mirrored the broader European experience. It was in the regions adjacent to western Europe, Alpine Austria and the Czech lands that 'the growth impulses from England and of the continental northwest found fertile ground first' (Good, 1984, p. 15), and where the shift from proto-industrial to modern forms of manufacturing began in the late eighteenth and early nineteenth centuries.

By the early 1870s, Austrian industrialization was well beyond the transitional phase that according to Komlos (1983) lasted to the mid-1820s, and was thus well into the 'machine-industrial phase' proper. However, as elsewhere in Europe, industrialization in the Habsburg lands, its timing and pace, was a process characterized by pronounced regional differences (Pollard, 1986). These gaps initially widened over the course of the nineteenth century, as industrial activity in Alpine Austria and the Czech lands gathered momentum. The western parts of Hungary followed significantly later with a first wave of industrial expansion in the late 1860s and early 1870s. Industrialization, though by 1913 well advanced in the western and northwestern regions of the empire, diffused only slowly to its most eastern and southeastern regions. This had profound implications for the structure and growth of the East Central European economies throughout the late nineteenth and

---

[1] We use the labels *Imperial* Austria (or Cisleithania) and *Imperial* Hungary (or Transleithania) to distinguish the two main constituent parts of the Habsburg state after the 1867 constitutional compromise from the far smaller, post-1918 successor states of Austria and Hungary in their new borders. Following Good (1984, pp. 15–17), the labels *Alpine Austria* (including the regions of Lower Austria, Upper Austria, Styria, Salzburg, Carinthia, Tyrol, and Vorarlberg) and *Czech lands* (Bohemia, Moravia, Silesia) are frequently used to identify the western and northwestern parts of the Habsburg Empire that were the most industrialized. Despite post-1918 border changes, these latter groupings correspond broadly with modern-day Austria and the Czech Republic.

twentieth centuries. It is the stark unevenness in the extent of industrial activity across the regions of East Central Europe that prompts the question of how peripheral this periphery was. We suggest that, at least in a European context, the imaginary line between the 'core' and 'the periphery' ran through the Habsburg economy—from the west/northwest to the east/southeast, reflecting the pattern of diffusion of modern economic growth emphasized in the historiography (Good, 1984; Pollard, 1986). The empire's unique position—being both close to and at the same time far away from the European industrial core—is, on the one hand, demonstrated by its prominent rank among the world's leading machinery producers: by 1913, Austria-Hungary's mechanical engineering industry, located mainly around Vienna and in the Czech lands, was in terms of output surpassed only by the United States, Britain, and Germany (Schulze, 1996). Yet, on the other hand, the Habsburg economy included large, populous regions in the east where industrialization had made little, if any, headway by the time of the First World War. Galicia, for example, accounted for about 28 per cent of Imperial Austria's population in 1910, but contributed less than 6 per cent of manufacturing output.

In the early nineteenth century, the western half of the Habsburg Empire was economically in as promising a position as the territories of Germany proper (Freudenberger, 2003). Around 1820, per capita GDP was about 7 per cent higher than in Germany; the comparative income lead was even larger for the regions that form present-day Austria.[2] That lead, though, was to disappear fast over the following decades. In this sense, then, the evidence lends some support to Alexander Gerschenkron's pessimistic assessment of nineteenth-century Austria as a case of 'failure' (Gerschenkron, 1977, p. 54). Table 4.1 reports GDP per capita for Central Europe, expressed in percentages of the German level. Four initial, general observations stand out. First, in the late nineteenth century, the Habsburg Empire, especially its Austrian half, became considerably poorer in terms of per capita income than its newly unified German neighbour. To a large extent, this falling-behind was an outcome of lower output and productivity growth in Cisleithanian *industry* which, in turn, was linked to significantly lower *levels* of human capital than in Germany (Schulze, 2007a). Second, for the late nineteenth century, there is a large development gap between Imperial Austria and Imperial Hungary (in pre-1918 borders) on the one hand, and the empire's economically most advanced regions located in what today constitute Austria and the Czech Republic, on the other. This is a reflection of the comparatively late onset of industrialization in Hungary and the eastern regions of the empire. Third, there is some evidence of modest intra-empire catching-up before 1914: the income gap between Cisleithania and Transleithania declined and so did the differentials between the territories of modern Austria, Czechoslovakia, and Hungary. Fourth, over the long run there is a remarkable absence of significant changes in the relative levels of economic

[2] Building on the estimates in Schulze (2000), Imperial Austria's GDP was extrapolated backward from its 1870 level, drawing on rates of change in agriculture and services from Kausel (1979) and in industry from Komlos (1983). Likewise for *modern* Austria, with the exception of industry, which is projected backward using Kausel's rates of change.

Table 4.1. GDP per capita in Central Europe (Germany = 100)

	1870	1890	1913	1929	1937	1950	1973	1989	2008
Imperial Austria	77	66	60						
Imperial Hungary	52	51	46						
Austria	111	95	86	91	67	95	94	99	108
Czechoslovakia	81	73	67	75	62	90	59	53	64
Hungary	59	58	54	61	54	64	47	42	52
Poland	51	53	48	52	41	63	45	34	49

Sources: (a) Imperial Austria, Imperial Hungary: Schulze (2000), with some revisions; (b) Austria, Czechoslovakia, Hungary for 1870–1913: preliminary new estimates based on revisions of regional GDPs from Schulze (2007b) and border adjustments; (c) all other: Maddison Project (http://www.ggdc.net/maddison/maddison-project/home.htm). The percentages are calculated from figures expressed in 1990 GK dollars and, except for Imperial Austria and Imperial Hungary, refer to 1990 borders.

development within the broader region that we study, including Poland for comparison. Though her initial income lead turned into a lag between 1870 and 1913, Austria was broadly on a par in level terms with the German economy (in its 1990 borders) throughout most of the modern era, with the notable exception of the disastrous episode of the 1930s. The East Central European economies, on the other hand, lagged behind both Germany and Austria and, although the size of this developmental gap did not remain constant over time, it is today astonishingly similar to what it was more than a hundred years ago.

If there is one message to take away from studying the economic history of East Central Europe in the era of modern economic growth, then it is this absence of cross-country convergence in levels of economic development over the long run. East Central Europe had begun to industrialize before the rest of the global periphery, and thus it is better described as 'half-periphery'. However, it has remained a half-periphery and has failed to catch up to, or even significantly narrow the gap vis-à-vis, the European core of advanced economies. East Central Europe thus failed to take advantage of its relative economic backwardness (Gerschenkron, 1962) and to exploit its catch-up potential (Abramovitz, 1986). After the collapse of the Soviet bloc and the following sharp depression that lasted into the mid-1990s, the income gap began to decline gradually, but so far this convergence has only just sufficed to make up for the ground lost during the socialist era.

While some of the general patterns we describe prevailed in the wider region of East Central Europe, the geographical focus is limited to the Austro-Hungarian Monarchy and its three main successor states, whose post-1918 territory remained entirely within the borders of the Habsburg Empire. The aim here is to quantify the level, structure, and trajectory of industrial development between 1870 and 2005 within, as far as possible, the borders of current-day Austria, Hungary, and the Czech and Slovak Republics. The latter two will be referred to, for the most part, as Czechoslovakia. Throughout the chapter, *industry* is defined as the sum of mining, manufacturing, and public utilities, except when otherwise stated. For the inter-war period, in particular, currently available data do not allow us to separate manufacturing from the rest of the industrial sector. For the years between 1950 and 1989, substantial differences in industry classification between the three countries make such distinction similarly difficult. However, it is not just classification issues that pose a problem when it comes to setting out long-term patterns of industrial development: state borders changed after the First World War and with the formation of the three main successor states. In most cases, the new state-level borders were not drawn along pre-war region boundaries that typically identify the contemporary statistical units of observation.

Quantitatively, we have three specific aims. First, we present near-complete time series on industrial production and compare them to the growth of gross domestic product (GDP). Second, we account for the level of industrialization by establishing the share of industry and other major sectors of economic activity in the labour force. Third, we gather evidence on the changing composition of industrial output to show how the role of modern manufacturing industries evolved over time. In this third task, we have to rely on data not entirely consistent between the pre-1914, inter-war, and post-1950 periods. This limitation is determined by post-1918 border changes, inter-temporal changes in industry classifications, and, in general, by the extent to which disaggregated data on industrial production are available. Our discussion of the evidence is, therefore, structured chronologically focusing on three main periods: 1870–1914, 1920–38, and 1950–89. In the final section we briefly consider the years following the fall of Communism and draw general conclusions about the achievements of industrialization in East Central Europe.

4.2 INDUSTRIALIZATION IN THE HABSBURG EMPIRE: DIFFUSION AND CONCENTRATION IN THE LATE NINETEENTH CENTURY

The process of industrialization in the Habsburg lands after 1870 evolved within the context of an empire-wide customs and monetary union and against the background of the 1867 constitutional settlement that established the Dual Monarchy. An increasingly dense railway network connected the regional centres of economic activity, stretching from the empire's western border with Switzerland to its eastern border with Russia, and from its northern border with Germany to the Mediterranean. The sheer geographical expanse of the empire brought with it a large degree of regional difference in broadly conceived resource endowments and in access to both domestic and foreign markets. These differences had a major impact on the location of industry and manufacturing in the empire and, by extension, its successor states. The broader outlines of the spatial pattern of industrial activity that came to characterize the second half of the nineteenth century emerged over the previous hundred years or so. Four factors, in particular, shaped this regional pattern and its concomitant differentials in manufacturing activity. First, the western and northwestern regions of the empire, i.e. those broadly corresponding with the territories of modern Austria and the Czech Republic, experienced the weakening of feudal institutions earlier than the more eastern regions, creating room for the rise of non-agricultural activity. It was here that domestic industry took hold first, that an entrepreneurial class emerged comparatively early, that foreign capital and expertise was attracted to, and where, eventually, modern forms of manufacturing began to develop (Good, 1984, pp. 14–24).[3] In 1790, 280 manufacturing firms were counted in the empire (excluding Galicia, Vorarlberg, and Tyrol). Of these, 50 per cent were located in Lower Austria and 30 per cent in Bohemia (*ibid.*)—foreshadowing the two regions' pre-eminence in Austro-Hungarian manufacturing through to 1914, notwithstanding the changing composition of regional output over time. Second, at the time of initial industrialization the western and northwestern regions of the empire were already significantly more urbanized than the rest of the country (*ibid.*), entailing agglomeration economies that were to intensify over the course of the nineteenth century.[4] Third, by 1870 the Alpine and Czech lands had a huge lead in the stock of human capital, built up over the preceding decades: new estimates suggest that the difference in average years of schooling compared to the least advanced regions in the empire was equivalent to about two and a half years, or 60 (75) per cent of the average years of schooling for Imperial Austria (Hungary) as a whole.[5] Finally, access to domestic and foreign purchasing power was crucial for the development of manufacturing, and in this respect, too, industry in Alpine Austria and the Czech lands held an advantage over the more remote regions in the empire's east.

Manufacturing in both halves of the empire expanded at significantly higher rates than the aggregate economy. Table 4.2 shows that by 1913, almost one-quarter of Imperial Austria's GDP was generated in manufacturing, while in Imperial Hungary the proportion more than doubled from less than 7 per cent in 1870 to 14 per cent in 1913. This rise in manufacturing's relative importance was the outcome of an uneven process of accelerations and decelerations in industrial activity and investment as well as changes in the output composition broadly in favour of 'modern' sectors such as metal-making, engineering, and (petro-) chemicals. Between 1870 and 1913, manufacturing output in Austria grew by about

---

[3] By the eighteenth century, Bohemia and Moravia had become centres of the textiles (linen, woollen) and glass industries, while an internationally significant mining and metallurgy sector was located in Styria, Upper Austria, and Carinthia. In the 1760s, for instance, Styria alone produced as much pig iron as England (Good, 1984, pp. 20–1). The production of textiles in the Alpine lands was in the main located in and around Vienna, Upper Austria, and Vorarlberg.

[4] By 1880 (1910), the proportion of the population resident in towns with more than 10,000 inhabitants had reached 47 (61) per cent in Lower Austria (including Vienna) and 10 (19) per cent in Bohemia (including Prague) compared to an average of 8 (14) per cent for the rest of Cisleithania; for the broader regions of Alpine Austria and the Czech lands, the figures are 23 (34) and (10) 18 per cent, respectively. From the 1860s, Budapest became the major centre of Hungarian manufacturing. Here, too, a high initial degree of urbanization is observable: in 1870, the capital city alone accounted for 14 per cent of the Danube–Tisza Basin region's population; by 1910, this proportion had increased to 29 per cent (Bolognese-Leuchtenmüller, 1978, Table 14, pp. 40–1; MSE, 1895, 1913).

[5] New approximations of regional average years of schooling were derived using regional enrolment data and the coefficients from a regression of aggregate average years of schooling in Imperial Austria and Imperial Hungary on aggregate lagged enrolment; see Schulze and Fernandes (2009) for underlying data, methods, and sources.

Table 4.2. Share of manufacturing in industrial, sectoral, and aggregate gross value added (per cent)

	Imperial Austria			Imperial Hungary		
	Industry	Secondary sector	GDP	Industry	Secondary sector	GDP
1870	96.0	63.9	19.2	89.0	58.6	6.5
1890	93.1	65.5	21.0	90.8	59.5	9.7
1913	91.9	66.6	24.8	89.2	62.3	14.1

Note: Gross value added in constant 1913 prices. Industry: manufacturing, mining, utilities. Secondary sector: industry, construction, crafts.

Source: Schulze (2000), with some revisions.

Table 4.3. Annual growth, gross valued added (per cent)

	Imperial Austria				Imperial Hungary			
	Manufacturing	Industry	Secondary sector	GDP	Manufacturing	Industry	Secondary sector	GDP
1871–1912	2.34	2.44	2.21	1.81	4.05	4.00	3.77	2.14
1871–95	1.71	1.84	1.55	1.37	4.42	4.30	4.21	2.21
1895–1912	3.23	3.29	3.16	2.43	3.48	3.53	3.08	2.02

Note: Gross value added in constant 1913 prices. Peak-to-peak measurement. Since peaks in the individual series do not necessarily correspond exactly with one another, the periods of measurement are not always identical.

Source: Appendix, Table A4.1.

2.3 per cent per annum compared with 4.0 per cent for the much less industrialized Hungary. Yet the growth rates of manufacturing (or, more broadly, industrial) output in Austria and Hungary were out of phase with one another over the period (Table 4.3): this had to do with the effects of the 1873 Vienna stock market crash. The crash led to an outflow of Austrian capital to Hungary and was a key factor in prolonging sluggish growth in Austria whilst stimulating the first major wave of industrialization in the Hungarian lands (Komlos, 1983). The repatriation of capital to Austria in the early 1890s sustained the resumption of manufacturing and aggregate growth there and was associated with a slowdown in the Hungarian half of the empire. This pattern of deceleration and acceleration was closely associated with changes in investment demand for plant and equipment, which are apparent in the temporal evolution of domestic machinery output and changes in the gross stock of machinery (Schulze, 1997, 2007a).

The pre-1873 upswing in Habsburg manufacturing was fuelled by an expansion in the money supply to finance the wars with Prussia and Italy and a record Hungarian harvest in 1867/8 coming at a time of poor harvests elsewhere in Europe (Matis, 1972, pp. 153–61). Buoyant cereal and flour exports initiated a dramatic expansion in the empire's railway network, providing a major stimulus to the domestic producer and capital goods industries that had developed in the western and northwestern regions since the late eighteenth century. These industries—engineering and iron and steel, in particular—were located primarily in Alpine Austria and the Czech lands. As rural incomes rose in response to increasing grain and land prices, demand for consumer goods expanded and led to the installation of new productive capacity in manufacturing. The associated growth in empire-wide demand for machinery provided a fillip not just to Austrian producers but also to Budapest's nascent engineering industry.[6]

Austrian manufacturing output peaked in 1871.[7] Yet what started out as the downswing following the expansionary phase of a regular business cycle was transformed into a major recession in industry by the impact of the 1873 crash, which changed longer-term expectations and investment decisions. From the late 1870s Austrian investors, seeking safe assets, engaged in large-scale purchases of new Hungarian debt. The Hungarian government was thus able to finance its regular expenditure and investment in infrastructure without crowding out private domestic investors (as much of the new debt was held in Austria). Further, the growth in Hungarian disposable incomes and in consumer demand was not constrained as the government was able to meet its fiscal targets without recourse to excessive taxation. This provided a major stimulus to both consumer and capital goods producers in a still largely agricultural economy. Hence, in Hungary the signs of depression were almost absent (despite a modest dip in activity in the 1870s). In Austria, though, the effects were rather different: 'the diminished stock of venture capital had a negative impact on industrial production until the 1890s. By attracting large amounts of Austrian capital, the Hungarian economy was therefore influential in prolonging the depression in Austria' (Komlos, 1983, p. 218). The overall outcome was a painfully sluggish recovery in Austrian manufacturing from the 1873 trough through to the mid-1880s and rapid expansion in Hungarian manufacturing into the late 1880s and early 1890s (Schulze, 2000).

As domestic demand began to pick up again in the second half of the 1880s, Austrian industrialists started installing new capacity again, going beyond mere replacement investment which had been characteristic of the preceding decade and a half. The beginning of this upturn in the late 1880s and early 1890s coincided with the reversal of intra-empire capital flows. Austrian investors turned to domestic industrial equity again (Somary, 1902, Table II, p. 39) and investment in industrial machinery was aided by a fall in Austrian long-term interest rates (Schulze, 1997). While the repatriation of Austrian capital was associated with a significant increase in Austrian manufacturing (GDP) growth of about 1.5 (1.1) percentage points over 1871–95, Hungary 'suffered less' than 'Austria gained': growth in manufacturing declined by less than 1 percentage point and the observed decrease in GDP growth is probably within the margin of error (0.2 percentage

---

[6] See Schulze (1996) on the development of Hungary's machine-building industry.

[7] According to Komlos' (1983, Table E.4) index, Austrian manufacturing grew by 8.7 per cent per annum during 1867–71 and 1.8 per cent during 1871–84. Whilst also showing a peak in 1871, the more comprehensive index documented in Table A.4.1 in the appendix increases by less than 1 per cent over the period.

points). We hypothesize that this had to do with, first, a much deeper and more sophisticated Hungarian domestic capital market than there had been in the early 1870s, as a result of significantly higher per capita incomes after more than twenty years of relatively fast economic growth; second, a shift into higher value-added manufacturing branches; and, third, comparatively high productivity growth in agriculture that sustained disposable income growth and demand for manufactured goods in a still largely agricultural economy. Throughout the late nineteenth century, agriculture in Hungary had a substantial revealed comparative advantage in crop production. The sector benefited from ready access to the higher-income markets in Austria that were largely uncontested by foreign importers due to the Habsburg customs union's external tariff (Katus, 1970; Komlos, 1983).[8] In addition, not only did crop production lend itself more readily to mechanization and machinery investment in Hungary than in most parts of the overall more mountainous and rugged Austria, but Hungary ran a trade surplus in *both* crops and livestock products with her customs union partner (Eddie, 1989).

While textiles and iron were at the centre of early industrialization in the Alpine and Czech lands, the process of industrialization in Hungary was driven initially by the agricultural processing industries, especially flour milling (Good, 1984, pp. 125–48), which drew on a productive domestic rural sector as the main source of its inputs. Yet the structure of manufacturing changed significantly in the later decades of the century in both parts of the empire and became more diversified. This raises the question of to what extent shifts to 'modern' industries were associated with changes in overall manufacturing growth. Here we consider iron and steel production, engineering (including mechanical and electrical engineering as well as transport equipment) and chemicals as representative of the 'modern sector'.[9] Of course, this is a simplification—technical change, product and process innovations occurred in other sectors, too. Table 4.4 sets out the comparative growth rates and the relative contributions to manufacturing growth made by the 'modern sector' compared to other manufacturing branches. Three observations can be made. First, the 'modern sector' grew significantly faster than the rest of manufacturing in both Austria and Hungary. Second, this held over both periods under review. Third, the evidence for Austria-Hungary conforms broadly with the general finding that industrialization typically involved a growing share not only of manufacturing in aggregate output, but also of a rising weight of the 'modern sectors' in manufacturing as a whole. In Austria, the proportion of manufacturing growth attributable to the rise of the 'modern sectors' went up from less than 23 per cent (1871–95) to almost 40 per cent at a time of overall accelerating manufacturing growth. For Hungary, the corresponding figures are 17 per cent and 25 per cent, reflecting the overall less advanced state and structure of manufacturing in Transleithania.

---

[8] Cf. Schulze (2007a) on comparative sectoral productivity growth.
[9] The category of non-engineering 'metal-working' industries, ranging from the production of nails and screws to metal furniture, has been excluded.

Table 4.4. Modern manufacturing: relative contributions to manufacturing growth (per cent, per annum)

	Modern manufacturing	Other manufacturing	Modern growth contribution	Other growth contribution	Total manufacturing
Imperial Austria					
1871–95	2.73	1.51	0.39	1.32	1.72
1895–1912	6.51	2.46	1.26	1.97	3.23
Imperial Hungary					
1871–95	7.57	4.08	0.77	3.65	4.42
1895–1912	5.35	3.13	0.86	2.63	3.48

Note: Measurement from peak to peak in total manufacturing output. For each period, relative contributions to manufacturing growth are computed as each sector's growth rate weighted by that sector's share in manufacturing at the start of the period.
Sources: See Table 4.2.

Table 4.5. Sectoral composition of labour force (per cent)

	1869/70		1890		1910	
	Imperial Austria	Imperial Hungary	Imperial Austria	Imperial Hungary	Imperial Austria	Imperial Hungary
Agriculture	62.7	78.3	61.5	79.5	54.0	73.4
Industry	18.1	7.1	19.9	8.0	22.6	11.8
Manufacturing	*17.4*	*6.6*	*18.9*	*7.4*	*21.3*	*11.0*
Mining	*0.8*	*0.6*	*1.1*	*0.6*	*1.2*	*0.8*
Utilities					*0.1*	
Construction	2.2		2.4	0.9	3.3	1.5
Services	17.0	14.6	16.1	11.6	20.1	13.3
Labour force (000s)	10,848.28	8,248.48	12,203.67	9,121.60	14,051.33	10,732.56

Source: Schulze (2007a) with some revisions.

Table 4.5 reveals some key structural characteristics of the Habsburg economy. First, throughout the period under review the empire as a whole remained a largely agricultural economy, especially so in its eastern, Hungarian half. In comparison, less than half of the labour force in Germany was employed in agriculture in 1871 and by 1910 this proportion had fallen to less than 36 per cent, while manufacturing's share had risen to more than 29 per cent (Hoffmann, 1965).[10] Note, however, that Imperial Austria had a significantly higher share of manufacturing (or, more broadly, industrial) employment in 1870 than its southern neighbour Italy and

[10] Note that Hoffmann's (1965) figures refer to Germany in its pre-First World War rather than its post-1990 boundaries. In 1910, manufacturing (including crafts as for the Habsburg Empire) accounted for 29.1 per cent, mining for 2.8 per cent, utilities for 0.3 per cent, and construction for 5.2 per cent of the total labour force.

maintained a slight lead until the First World War (cf. Chapter 6, Table 6.2). Second, the picture looks distinctly different if the focus is on those territories that after the First World War became parts of either the Austrian Republic or Czechoslovakia. Here the shares of industry and manufacturing in total employment were far higher than on average across the empire, on a par with those prevalent in Germany and well above the corresponding figures for Italy.[11] These data, then, confirm the notion of the Alpine and Czech regions as the industrial heartlands of the empire and as regions of industrial activity close to the European core.

The level differences in manufacturing and industrial employment shares within Austria-Hungary reflect the regional differentials in the timing and sectoral basis of industrialization across the empire.[12] Hungary—whether in its imperial or modern guise—came late to the game. Here, industrialization in earnest had started only during the 1860s and 1870s, aided by the inflow of Austrian funds after the 1873 stock market crash. Budapest (in the central Danube–Tisza Basin), in particular, but also the Hungarian regions on the Danube Left and Right Banks as well as the Tisza Right Bank became progressively more engaged in manufacturing over time. However, compared to Austria or Czechoslovakia, and even Imperial Austria as a whole, manufacturing played a markedly less prominent role in the Hungarian economy right up to the First World War. This is borne out by the evidence on both regional shares in manufacturing output and regional manufacturing output per head (Table 4.6).

Clearly, the spatial distribution of manufacturing across the Habsburg Empire changed over time, broadly in line with the gradual intra-empire catching-up of the Hungarian on the Austrian economy. By 1910, Budapest was firmly on the map as a major manufacturing location. Yet just as striking as this is persistence: in terms of manufacturing output per capita, the most industrialized regions in 1910 were still, by a large margin, Lower Austria and the Czech lands—just as they had been forty years earlier. In absolute terms, the per capita output lead of the established manufacturing regions over the others increased, even if it had marginally declined in percentage terms. Following New Economic Geography reasoning, regions' access to domestic and foreign markets (here: transport and tariff-cost weighted GDPs of main trading partners) is a central candidate factor accounting for a good deal of inter-regional differences in manufacturing activity. Habsburg regions' manufacturing output per head over 1870 to 1910 is indeed strongly associated with access to the home and European markets.[13] Further, regional differences in

[11] This assessment is grounded in new estimates for the successor states. They are based on the *regional* data underlying the reconstructed labour force estimates for Imperial Austria and Imperial Hungary and border adjustments; for sources and methods, see Appendix A in Schulze (2007a). For modern Austria and Czechoslovakia, the share of the labour force in manufacturing moves from *c.*22 per cent in 1870 to about 28 per cent in 1910; for Hungary, it moves from less than 9 to almost 15 per cent. Note that the 1910 figures deviate slightly from those presented in Table 4.7; this is mainly due to corrections in the estimated agricultural labour force for 1870–1910.

[12] See Table A.4.3 in the appendix for a more detailed breakdown by manufacturing branches.

[13] On the underlying Harris-type market potential measures for the Habsburg regions, see Schulze (2007b).

Table 4.6. Manufacturing gross value added by region (1990 Geary–Khamis dollars)

	Output (m.)		Regional share		Output per capita	
	1870	1910	1870	1910	1870	1910
Lower Austria	1,295	3,634	0.20	0.18	644.3	1,028.9
Upper Austria	209	471	0.03	0.02	280.7	552.5
Salzburg	41	111	0.01	0.01	266.6	516.6
Styria	243	822	0.04	0.04	211.3	569.3
Carinthia	52	154	0.01	0.01	152.9	389.9
Carniola	47	154	0.01	0.01	98.8	293.0
Littoral	101	423	0.02	0.02	166.2	473.2
Tyrol/Vorarlberg	172	500	0.03	0.03	191.8	458.0
Bohemia	2,266	5,499	0.34	0.28	436.7	812.3
Moravia	710	1,844	0.11	0.09	348.7	703.1
Silesia	180	496	0.03	0.03	347.7	655.7
Galicia	264	852	0.04	0.04	48.0	106.2
Bukovina	24	79	0.00	0.00	47.2	99.1
Dalmatia	7	60	0.00	0.00	15.1	92.4
Danube Left Bank	138	542	0.02	0.03	79.8	249.2
Danube Right Bank	178	585	0.03	0.03	73.3	189.8
Danube–Tisza Basin	198	1,379	0.03	0.07	91.5	365.9
Tisza Right Bank	105	408	0.02	0.02	69.9	230.4
Tisza Left Bank	85	372	0.01	0.02	44.7	143.3
Tisza–Maros Bank	93	394	0.01	0.02	52.9	184.0
Transylvaina	105	482	0.02	0.02	48.5	180.1
Croatia–Slavonia	62	418	0.01	0.02	33.1	156.6
Imperial Austria	5,610	15,101	0.85	0.77	272.5	540.7
Imperial Hungary	964	4,581	0.15	0.23	62.1	219.3

Source: Revised estimates based on sources and methods documented in Schulze (2007b).

human capital endowments (average years of schooling) are strongly associated with regional differences in manufacturing output per head.[14] The critical issue here is the interaction between the two. The evidence suggests that those regions that were comparatively well endowed with human capital were in a significantly better position to exploit their market potential, i.e. to realize benefits of economies of scale and specialization related to market size. The regions in the landlocked and remote east of the empire (e.g. Galicia, the Bukovina or Transylvania) were not only disadvantaged in terms of their limited access to Habsburg or foreign markets, but also constrained by previous generations' lack of investment in schooling. The southern coastal regions had a large market potential because of their cost advantages of sea transportation to growing foreign markets but, in the case of Dalmatia or Croatia–Slavonia, suffered from a poorly educated labour force. There was, then, little incentive for manufacturers to locate in these regions despite their favourable position in terms of market access. Where the human capital stock was higher, the response to the opportunities afforded by better market access was stronger, as

[14] See n. 5 above on the construction of regional average years of schooling measures.

demonstrated by the region around Trieste (Littoral). Although enrolment rates rose faster in the least developed parts of the empire than in the more advanced regions (where levels were, by Habsburg standards, already relatively high), it took considerable time before this fed into increases in average years of schooling. Those parts of the Habsburg Empire that were characterized by initially high levels of schooling, Alpine Austria and the Czech lands, were still well in the lead by 1910. Stark inter-regional differences in education investment prior to the 1870s had a lasting impact on regions' relative performance in manufacturing up to the First World War.

4.3 INDUSTRIALIZATION ON HOLD: CENTRAL EUROPE BETWEEN THE WARS

If John Maynard Keynes was correct in arguing that the economic consequences of the peace after the First World War were detrimental for Germany, then their impact beyond Germany's eastern borders can be branded catastrophic. Unlike the territory of post-war Poland, Austria, Czechoslovakia and Hungary witnessed little, if any, destruction due to war activity. The only exception is the brief conflict between the short-lived Bolshevik regime in Hungary and the *Petite Entente* formed by Czechoslovakia, Yugoslavia, and Romania, that ended with the Romanian occupation of most of Hungary in 1920. Still, the post-war settlement dislocated the economies of Central Europe. The dissolution of the Habsburg Empire severely limited access to markets and resources for industrial firms both within and beyond the pre-1914 borders (Teichova, 1985, pp. 223–7).

Different regions of the empire differed not only in their level of industrialization, but also in what branches of manufacturing they had specialized in. Thus the new borders, coupled with the animosity of the new nation states towards their neighbours, implied much-reduced market potential for many industries and the breakdown of crucial input–output linkages between firms. The milling industry of Budapest, the textile and clothing industry in Austria, or machine-tool producers in Bohemia and Moravia not only faced difficulties in accessing their once most important markets, but also in securing necessary intermediate inputs. While recent research has revealed that the negative impact of economic nationalism on market integration was already felt before the First World War, it became devastating after 1918 (Schulze and Wolf, 2011, pp. 652–73). As shown in Table A.4.2 in the appendix, the decline in industrial output across the war was comparable to, and in the case of Austria was even greater than, that of GDP—in a period when the rate of industrialization was on the rise in rest of the global periphery.

Between the wars, industrial expansion was very moderate in Central Europe, following a path quite similar to that of Germany and most of the advanced Western economies. Following a relatively successful stabilization that brought an end to hyperinflation in Austria and Hungary and restored state finances by 1924, all three countries recovered quickly up until 1929. Industrial production grew by 4.5 per cent annually in Austria, and by 8 per cent in Czechoslovakia and Hungary.

However, approximately half of this growth was lost during the Great Depression, which in both Austria and Czechoslovakia affected the manufacturing sector more strongly than the rest of the economy. In both countries, political forces prolonged the slump. While extreme political fractionalization leading to civil war tormented Austria, the government in Prague tried policies of import substitution while maintaining the gold standard, which continued to have a deflationary effect until the mid-1930s. Furthermore, the export-oriented nature of Czech industry, and its relative success during the 1920s in replacing exports to the former empire with exports to other markets, made it more susceptible to international trade shocks (Drabek, 1985, pp. 408, 429–30). Czech industry was hit hard by the rising tariffs and administrative trade barriers that emerged across Europe during and after the Great Depression (Pryor et al., 1971, pp. 35–59; Drabek, 1985, pp. 432–33). As a result, industrial output remained well below 1929 levels until 1937.

Between 1938 and 1943, the expansion of the Nazi war economy gave a large impetus to industrial growth in Central Europe, particularly in the territories annexed by Hitler in 1938. In the first two years after the Anschluss, the Austrian economy grew by more than 30 per cent, and industry by more than a half, reflecting the priority given to war preparations (Butschek, 1978, p. 65). After the announcement of rearmament in 1938, Hungary also experienced a growth spurt driven by industrial expansion. While total employment in the economy remained constant until 1943, it climbed from 330,000 to 451,000 in manufacturing, leading to a 37 per cent increase in industrial production (Ránki, 1964, p. 225; Berend and Ránki, 1960, p. 140). Recent research has revealed the staggering growth of German imports from the region after 1939, with particularly large increases from Austria and the annexed Czech lands (Scherner, 2011, pp. 79–113). Consequently, wartime industrial expansion focused primarily on mining and the primary metal industries as well as machinery and armaments.

In terms of structural development, the region did not witness much action during the inter-war period. Industrialization was put on hold; the occupational distribution of the labour force remained almost unchanged in all three countries, as reported in Table 4.7. The most important factor holding back structural modernization was the fact that agricultural productivity remained very modest, due to the lack of technological innovation, the slow spread of chemical fertilizers, and low mechanization. Thus, the farming sector had only a limited potential to release labour, which was further aggravated by the pro-agrarian political radicalization of the 1930s.

The literature, however, has pointed to several other constraints on industrial expansion. Teichova emphasized the shortage of skilled labour, which was a crucial factor limiting manufacturing growth in a period when European industry still relied heavily on craft production methods (Teichova, 1988, pp. 21–2). Eckstein stressed the decline in capital investment from the pre-1914 period, and more so after 1929, which increased the technological lag vis-à-vis advanced Western nations (Eckstein, 1955, p. 220). As shown in Figs 4.1 and 4.2 respectively, without sufficient investment in new equipment the main drivers of technological modernization in the inter-war period, electrification and motorization, made very

Table 4.7. Economically active population by sector (per cent)

	1910	1920	1930	1940	1950	1960	1970	1980	1990	2000	2008
Hungary											
Agriculture	55.8	58.2	54.2	50.0	51.8	38.1	25.0	18.4	15.3	8.4	4.9
Industry	19.4	18.1	21.7	23.2	23.6	34.8	44.7	43.9	39.7	36.8	35.5
Services	24.8	23.7	24.1	26.8	24.6	27.1	30.3	37.7	45.0	54.8	59.6
Austria*											
Agriculture	39.5	39.9	37.5	39.0	34.3	23.7	14.8	9.9	8.0	6.2	5.7
Industry	31.0	33.3	34.5	32.4	36.1	46.4	43.0	42.2	38.4	31.7	27.0
Services	29.5	26.8	28.0	28.6	29.7	29.9	42.2	47.9	53.6	62.1	67.3
Czechoslovakia											
Agriculture	42.0	39.6	37.5		37.8	25.7	16.9	13.3	12.8	6.3	3.4
Industry	34.1	33.8	35.7		37.5	46.1	48.3	49.3	45.6	45.0	39.1
Services	23.9	26.6	26.8		24.7	28.3	34.8	37.4	41.6	48.8	57.5

* The entry for 1920 reflects 1923 data; that for 1930 is an estimate based on 1934 figures and sectoral growth rates.
Sources: Austria–Butschek (2011, p. 163); Czechoslovakia–Teichova (1988, p. 9); Hungary–Eckstein (1955); for all countries after 1950: ILO (1986) and FAOSTAT Classic (http://faostatclassic.fao.org/site/550/DesktopDefault.aspx?PageID=550#ancor).

little progress in Central Europe. This relative backwardness was noticeable in comparison not only with the United States, but also with Germany, and it became more pronounced during the 1930s.

In an environment increasingly characterized by resource scarcity and trade protectionism, industrialization had several common features across Central Europe: industrial concentration to achieve economies of scale, cartelization to secure preferential access to markets and foreign technology, and product specialization to exploit market potential in niche areas. Both in Czechoslovakia and Hungary, the growth of industrial production was driven by the expansion of large-scale enterprise in primary metals, chemicals, and engineering. The three largest metallurgical companies in Czechoslovakia increased their share in steel production from 65 per cent in 1921 to 90 per cent by 1936, and owned all the export quotas allocated to the country in the International Steel Cartel (Teichova, 1988, pp. 40–1). In Hungary, the leading firms in the electro-technical industry and railway engineering managed to increase their global market share despite shrinking domestic demand. They achieved this by integrating into German-led international cartels and by concentrating on very specialized products, such as lamp and radio parts, or diesel multiple units used on small railways in remote regions around the world (Hidvégi and Vonyó, 2012, pp. 61–2). By contrast, the more traditional branches of manufacturing, such as the milling industry in Hungary, or the sugar industry in Bohemia, faced relative decline. Between 1924 and 1937, the share of metals, chemicals, and engineering products in total industrial output in Czechoslovakia increased from 22.6 per cent to 31.7 per cent (Teichova, 1988, p. 34). The same level of disaggregation is not possible for Hungary, but the statistical evidence shows that while the contribution of mining, smelting, handicraft production, and construction to national product did not change between 1924 and 1938, the share of manufacturing (which did not

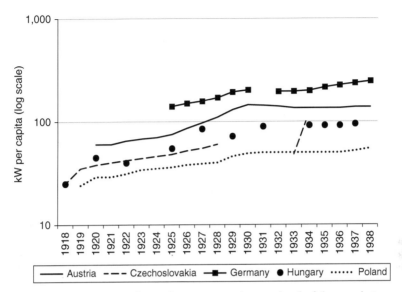

Fig. 4.1. Installed capacity in electrical power generation per head of the population
Source: Hidvégi and Vonyó (2012).

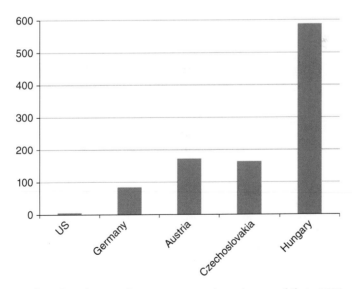

Fig. 4.2. Number of residents in the country per registered automobile in 1935
Source: Data from Hidvégi and Vonyó (2012).

include metallurgy or construction materials) increased from 15.5 per cent to 21.4 per cent (Eckstein, 1955, p. 171).

Despite the overall sluggish industrialization of East Central Europe, the region recorded some examples of the implementation of modern productivity-enhancing technologies, though these were exceptions rather than the general rule. The best-known case is the Baťa works in Zlín, the leading concern in the Czechoslovak shoe-making industry. The introduction of advanced American mass production techniques between 1924 and 1927 achieved a dramatic productivity increase that lasted into the early 1930s. Shoe production jumped from 8.9 million pairs in 1926 to 15.2 million pairs in 1927, while employment expanded by 'only' 35 per cent in the same year. Between 1930 and 1933, average weekly output per worker increased from 37 to 48 pairs and Czechoslovakia became one of the world's leading exporters of footwear (Teichova, 1985, pp. 275–6).

4.4 PLANNED INDUSTRIALIZATION IN A STATE-MANAGED ECONOMY

If the consequences of the First World War were catastrophic for Central Europe, the impact of the Second World War was apocalyptic. Hostilities on the eastern front brought unprecedented destruction. The temporary demise of the German economy and the East–West tensions emerging from the post-war settlement untied the input–output linkages between the region's industries. These were still partially the legacy of industrial development in the Habsburg Empire before 1914, but even more so the product of Nazi economic imperialism. From the mid-1930s, German foreign policy considered the region as its natural backwater and increasingly tied its economies to the Third Reich via bilateral trade agreements. The economic dependence on Germany increased further during the war, especially for the territories temporarily annexed by the Third Reich.[15] By late 1945, in Austria and Hungary, industrial production plummeted to levels that had already been surpassed by 1900 (see Tables A4.1 and A4.2 in the appendix). However, the most detrimental economic outcome of the war was the immense loss it caused in human resources. Besides the innumerable military and civilian casualties, more than a million Jews who had resided in the three countries before 1939 perished in the Holocaust. Lastly, one needs to account for the expulsion of minority Germans from East and Central Europe after 1945, in accordance with the Potsdam Agreement. Of the 16 million who voluntarily fled or were uprooted between 1944 and 1950, 3 million were expelled from Czechoslovakia and 210,000 from Hungary. Most of the expellees were deported to post-war Germany, many dying in the process, and 370,000 settled in Austria (Reichling, 1989, p. 26).

While these deportations have featured prominently in the literature on the post-war West German economy, their impact has been largely ignored in the economic

---

[15] See Hirschman (1945), Ránki (1983), and Grenzebach (1900) among others.

history of Eastern Europe. The combined effect of wartime casualties, including the permanently wounded and the mentally debilitated, and the post-war settlement, was enormous. Austria and Hungary witnessed practically no population growth between 1939 and 1950. During the same period the population of Czechoslovakia within its post-1945 borders declined from 14.7 million to 12.4 million (Maddison, 2006, pp. 416, 474–5). The *Sudetenland* was largely depopulated, and important industrial districts thus lost a vast share of their pre-war labour force.[16] Across Central Europe, the war had left behind an ill-balanced demographic structure with a notable shortage of able-bodied young and middle-aged men, who tradition-ally constituted the backbone of the industrial workforce. The Holocaust and the expulsion of minority Germans, in particular, together with substantial emigration among the bourgeois middle class, bequeathed to the tormented nations of Central Europe a plethora of industrial and commercial assets without owners, and without the necessary skills and entrepreneurial know-how to operate them.

To rebuild and re-organize the war-shattered and dislocated economies required state management, which already materialized under the national-unity govern-ments during the late 1940s, and under Allied military occupation in Austria. Popular land reforms were followed by large-scale nationalization in industry. By 1948, all large enterprises and most middle-size firms were brought under state control; private property only continued to prevail in handicraft production. The state-managed economy operated with fixed prices and wages, and the centralized allocation of resources, including both material inputs and investment. Even in Austria, most assets in heavy industry, public transport, and utilities were publicly owned, and the rest of the economy was subjected to tremendous red tape. From the immediate post-war years, governments in all three countries pursued autarkic industrialization policies with extensive planning. While central planning was never introduced in Austria, she served as the canonical example of a managed mixed economy (Berend, 1997, pp. 72–82; Seidel, 2005).

In many ways, during the early post-war period Central Europe followed a similar path to that of Latin American countries during their flirtation with import-substituting industrialization. In Austria, multiple exchange rates and tar-geted industrial subsidies were used to improve the competitiveness of domestic manufacturing. Although forced industrialization in socialist command economies applied other tools to steer economic development that often reflected military-strategic motives, it also aimed at creating industrial self-sufficiency and accelerating the process of structural change. However, from the late 1950s, industrialization in Central Europe owed much less to the East–West arms race than was the case in the Soviet Union. According to data published by the Stockholm International Peace Research Institute (SIPRI), military spending in Czechoslovakia and Hungary rarely surpassed 3 per cent of GDP between 1957 and 1989.[17]

---

[16] The border region with Germany produced about 55 per cent of Czechoslovak hard coal, 93 per cent of brown coal, 61 per cent of textiles, 38 per cent of chemicals, 45 per cent of stone and clay products, and 30 per cent of engineering products. See Shute (1948, pp. 35–44).

[17] SIPRI, *Yearbook*, diff. vols.

In establishing the quantitative record of socialist industrialization we need to treat official output data with more than a modicum of suspicion. Government statistics were distorted to a large but non-quantifiable extent. Physical output indicators are considered comparatively trustworthy, but aggregates expressed in value terms reflect unrealistic producer prices, incorrect weighting inasmuch as industry was always attributed a higher than actual share in net material product, and inappropriate methods employed in the computation of index numbers.[18] Thankfully, independent Western research revised official figures using data on physical output indicators exclusively, and applying Western accounting standards. The most substantial work was carried out by the *Research Project on National Income in East Central Europe* under the leadership of Thad P. Alton. A long series of publications report index numbers on GNP by sector of origin of product, and industrial value added, for six countries including Czechoslovakia and Hungary. We use these data to determine the composition of gross value added and of industrial production using the same industry classifications and compare these results with statistics for Austria and Germany.

Economic growth in Central Europe after 1945 was industry-driven. From its post-war nadir, industrial production recovered to pre-1939 levels by 1950 and grew rapidly for another two decades, significantly faster than the rest of the economy. In all three countries, industrial value added measured in constant prices doubled during the 1950s and tripled between 1950 and 1970 (see Table A4.2 in the appendix). In fact, industrialization reached its peak only in the 1960s and 1970s when industry and construction employed well over 40 per cent of the labour force. By contrast, the share of agricultural employment declined to less than half of its initial level during the post-war golden age. In Czechoslovakia and Hungary, industry remained the largest sector of the economy until the late 1980s.

Table 4.8 demonstrates the impact of forced industrialization in the 1950s and early 1960s in a comparative perspective. The share of industrial value added in GDP increased significantly faster in Czechoslovakia and Hungary than in Austria and Germany (GDR and Federal Republic combined). After 1968, when moderate economic reforms relaxed authoritarian controls and introduced greater flexibility for enterprise management, industrial growth slowed down considerably. However, while the rate of industrialization was declining in Germany after the oil shocks, it continued to increase until the mid-1980s in Central Europe. East of the Iron Curtain, this was largely the consequence of the slow development of the service sector. In Austria, it reflected more the overheating of industrial growth by ever-increasing state subsidies that began to rock the federal budget by the 1980s and forced the government to begin privatizing state assets.

Post-war data give us a deeper insight into the structural development of the economy and the nature of industrialization than what we have been able to establish for earlier periods. Table 4.9 shows that the share of heavy industry and

---

[18] Net Material Product was the national accounting concept used by CMEA countries. It is conceptually similar to GDP, but excludes services deemed unproductive, especially housing and the government.

Table 4.8. Share of industry* in gross value added in 1975 prices (per cent)

	1955	1965	1975	1985	1995	2005
Austria	27.3	28.7	29.2	30.0	28.7	31.5
Czechoslovakia	26.4	35.9	38,6	40.7	34.6	37.1
Hungary	24.8	32.4	32.4	33.8	35.0	39.6
Germany	32.5	34.9	35.2	33.4	27.5	27.1

* Mining, manufacturing and utilities.

Source: Own calculations based on data from G. Lazarcik (1969), Czirják (1973), Alton et al. (1982), Alton et al. (1991), DIW (Germany), WIFO (Austria), and EU KLEMS (www.euklems.net).

Table 4.9. The composition of gross industrial value added* in current prices (per cent)

	1955	1965	1975	1985	1995	2005
Heavy industry						
Austria	27.3	28.7	29.2	30.0	28.7	31.5
Czechoslovakia	26.4	35.9	38.6	40.7	34.6	37.1
Hungary	24.8	32.4	32.4	33.8	35.0	39.6
Germany	32.5	34.9	35.2	33.4	27.5	27.1
Modern manufacturing						
Austria			48.3	52.6	54.5	61.2
Czechoslovakia	56.3	58.4	57.4	63.8	53.4	62.4
Hungary	47.5	53.8	52.4	57.5	55.0	72.2
Germany	52.8	59.3	64.3	68.8	68.4	75.4

* Mining and manufacturing

Note: Heavy industry includes mining, construction materials, chemicals, primary metals, and engineering products. Modern manufacturing includes only chemicals, primary metals, and engineering products.

Source: Own calculations based on data from Staller (1975), Czirják (1968), Alton et al. (1991), DIW (Germany), WIFO (Austria), and EU KLEMS (www.euklems.net).

of modern manufacturing in gross industrial value added was similar across the region, but mining and the production of basic materials remained more important in Czechoslovakia and Hungary than in Austria and Germany. Whereas the share of modern manufacturing increased throughout the period in Austria and Germany, it stagnated in the two socialist countries from the late 1960s onward. This accords with the existing evidence pointing towards a growing technological lag between Western nations and centrally planned economies after the golden age.[19] This pattern is commonly attributed to inefficient resource allocation and the ideologically driven preference for material production over services.[20] Additionally, the austerity policies introduced to combat the budgetary effects of rising oil prices and the debt crises that emerged in the 1980s (as a consequence of lavish borrowing during the 1970s and the worsening terms of trade after 1980) also led to a reduction in investment levels, particularly investment in new machinery.

[19] See among others Kalecki (1993), and Broadberry and Klein (2011).
[20] The perhaps most elegant exposition of this view is by Kalecki (1993).

In terms of growth, Central European economies performed similarly to other peripheral regions in Europe, with some notable exceptions. As in Southern Europe and as in other countries within the Soviet bloc, the growth of industrial production slowed considerably from the 1970s and was disrupted by a temporary slump in the early 1980s. From the 1960s onwards, Central Europe was lagging behind Southern Europe in terms of average growth rates, and from the mid-1970s Austria was also pulling away from Hungary and Czechoslovakia. During the golden age, average rates of industrial expansion were also lower than in Southeast Europe, which provides evidence for convergence within the Soviet bloc. After 1980, however, this process of convergence broke down: typically the most advanced socialist economies performed best, in terms of both aggregate growth and industrial development.

In Russia (not the whole Soviet Union), the increased price of hydrocarbons created new opportunities for growth in heavy industry, not least thanks to investment in natural gas exploration and in new transcontinental pipelines.[21] In Czechoslovakia and Hungary, growth could be maintained because the relatively more advanced economic structure of both countries made them more resistant to (although by no means unaffected by) the exogenous shocks of the early 1980s. Given that modern branches of manufacturing, such as electrical engineering, and services accounted for a relatively larger share of their GDP, they were hit less severely by the oil shocks than the less developed socialist economies. Czechoslovakia and Hungary were also much less affected by the debt crises of the 1980s than Poland or Southeast Europe. Since, unlike virtually every other socialist country, Czechoslovakia did not borrow extensively during the 1970s, it did not need to tighten the belt after borrowing costs rocketed following the second oil shock. Hungary would have had to, but joined the IMF in 1982 (in a secret operation without the prior knowledge of the Soviet leadership), which improved her position as a debtor.[22] By contrast, Poland and Romania suffered prolonged depressions under severe austerity imposed by the repressive governments of General Jaruzelski and Nicolae Ceauşescu respectively; and, even if to a lesser extent, austerity also had harsh economic consequences in Bulgaria and Yugoslavia.

4.5 THE LEGACY OF INDUSTRIALIZATION: CENTRAL EUROPE AFTER 1990

The collapse of the Soviet bloc and the socialist economic system caused a major depression in Eastern Europe, affecting both Czechoslovakia and Hungary. Between 1987 and 1992, industrial production declined by 37 per cent and 28 per cent in the two countries respectively. In Czechoslovakia, the reduction in value added was more than twice as large in mining and manufacturing as in the entire economy.

[21] Hence the faster growth in total GDP in Russia (see Ponomarenko, 2002, p. 151) than in the USSR as a whole (see Maddison, 2006) after 1980.
[22] For a more detailed narrative, see Berend (1997, pp. 195 ff.).

Austrian industry initially received a boost from the opening of Eastern markets and German reunification, in particular, but this boom was short lived and turned into recession in 1991. From the mid-1990s, Central Europe enjoyed strong growth that, not unlike in earlier periods, was propelled by industrial expansion (see Table A4.2 in the appendix).

Transition to a market economy delivered first a killer blow to and then a blessing on Central European industry. The liberalization of markets, the removal of import restrictions, and the introduction of hard budget constraints finally exposed the inefficiency of state industries, leading to a sharp fall in output and employment. In subsequent years, however, privatization and a massive inflow of foreign direct investment (FDI) led to technological modernization and the rationalization of production. Industry-level data reported by the EU KLEMS project shows that productivity growth since 1995 has stemmed largely from modern manufacturing, the strongly export-oriented engineering industries in particular, where most FDI has been concentrated. Since the launching of the euro, comparative advantage in manufacturing has shifted from Southern to Central Europe. The growth impact of FDI was most noticeable in the automobile industry and electrical engineering, in which the Czech and Slovak Republics as well as Hungary emerged as major exporters within just a few years.

The quantitative evidence on structural change also reveals the relative importance of manufacturing in the growth of Central European economies. Albeit declining since the late 1980s, the share of industry in the labour force has remained considerably higher in the former Czechoslovakia and Hungary than in Austria (see Table 4.7). As shown in Table 4.8, industry's share in gross value added even increased in Hungary, where privatization and the liberalization of capital markets was completed much faster than in the Czech and Slovak Republics. The latter pursued more gradual reform programmes, and thus did not attract as much manufacturing FDI before the late 1990s. In recent years, Central Europe has experienced a period of re-industrialization and, in fact, has become proportionally more industrialized than Germany. Table 4.9 also reveals the impact of shifting comparative advantages on the structure of industrial production. The share of heavy industry and, to a lesser extent, of modern manufacturing in gross industrial value added declined sharply following the fall of Communism. By 2005, these shares had recovered, or even surpassed, their highest previous levels; nevertheless the share of modern manufacturing in Central Europe has continued to lag behind Germany.

Although transition to a market economy radically improved the development prospects of manufacturing in both Hungary and the former Czechoslovakia, the countries are still tormented by various legacies of socialism. The weakness of domestic small and medium-sized enterprises remains the main problem for industrial policy. Whereas FDI helped modernize, restructure, and often reposition large firms, small companies have had limited access to credit to finance investment in new equipment, and lack both the technical and industry-specific entrepreneurial know-how necessary to face up to the challenges of a newly globalized market environment. The legacy of state management has also been manifest in the typical responses of governments to this key problem. Tax concessions and direct subsidies to small enterprises, alongside strategic agreements with foreign multinationals offering indirect subsidies in exchange for self-imposed limitations on the share of imported inputs, did not reduce the technological backwardness and lack of know-how that still limit the growth potential of domestic firms.

Nevertheless, Central European economies weathered the storms of the transition shock more successfully than most other post-socialist countries, particularly the former Soviet and Yugoslav Republics. This can be explained by the confluence of several factors. Both their geographical vicinity to core European markets, particularly Germany, and their relatively rich endowments of skilled labour, but also their strong commitments to market reforms from the early 1990s, made Central European countries initially more attractive to Western investors than East and Southeast Europe. Czechoslovakia and Hungary, together with Poland, had already been way ahead of most other socialist countries in terms of economic reforms during the 1970s and 1980s. However, the comparatively much larger negative impact that the disintegration of the Soviet Union and the violent break-up of the former Yugoslavia had on Eastern and Southeast Europe during the early 1990s cannot be overlooked.

The quantitative evidence presented in this chapter allows us to derive several conclusions about the history of industrialization in Central Europe. First, the region stepped into the industrial age before most of the global periphery, but has not been able to narrow the developmental gap vis-à-vis the West European core. Second, economic growth in the region has been and still is industry-driven: periods of strong growth were marked by even faster industrial expansion, whereas the major calamities of the twentieth century, the world wars and the collapse of state socialism, dislocated industry more than other sectors of economic activity. Economic development in Central European countries during the last one hundred years has been shaped by these major calamities, and their response was always strongly linked to industrialization and industrial modernization. Third, growth in the contribution of industry to gross value added was strongly correlated with a rising share of heavy industry, and especially modern manufacturing, in industrial production. Finally, industrialization has always been characterized by more direct state involvement in Central Europe than in the most advanced Western economies. In this respect, Gerschenkron was right: under relative backwardness the state had to substitute for the lacking prerequisites. However, interventionist policies did not help Central European nations exploit the advantages of their relative backwardness. Falling behind the European core, not catching-up, was the experience during periods of strong state management.

APPENDIX

Table A.4.1. Indices of gross value added (constant 1913 prices, 1913 = 100)

	Imperial Austria				Imperial Hungary			
	Manufacturing	Industry	Secondary sector	GDP	Manufacturing	Industry	Secondary sector	GDP
1870	35.4	33.9	36.9	45.8	19.0	19.1	20.3	41.4
1871	41.1	39.2	42.8	48.7	20.6	20.8	23.1	40.5
1872	40.4	38.6	41.9	48.4	19.4	19.8	22.4	40.1
1873	36.4	35.0	37.5	46.4	19.6	19.9	21.3	39.7
1874	36.9	35.6	37.5	48.2	20.1	20.1	20.2	39.3
1875	37.5	36.2	39.0	48.7	18.3	18.5	17.9	39.7
1876	37.4	36.0	38.6	48.8	17.5	18.0	17.4	38.4
1877	38.2	36.9	39.4	50.2	19.5	19.8	19.2	42.5
1878	38.4	37.1	38.6	51.3	24.7	24.5	23.3	43.3
1879	38.8	37.6	39.4	49.7	22.9	22.8	21.9	43.5
1880	37.8	36.8	38.6	49.9	22.3	22.6	23.2	45.8
1881	42.2	41.0	42.8	52.4	26.9	26.7	28.0	49.8
1882	44.0	42.7	44.6	53.0	33.0	32.3	34.7	55.8
1883	45.7	44.5	46.2	54.1	37.2	36.3	41.1	54.9
1884	46.7	45.4	48.7	56.0	37.3	36.5	41.5	56.6
1885	43.2	42.3	44.0	54.7	37.7	36.8	41.2	56.9
1886	43.3	42.4	44.6	55.3	36.2	35.4	40.8	55.5
1887	47.5	46.4	49.0	58.0	37.0	36.2	39.9	58.1
1888	46.6	45.9	48.9	58.0	41.8	40.7	44.9	60.1
1889	48.2	47.5	49.7	58.0	39.1	38.5	43.5	56.8
1890	51.0	50.3	51.8	60.3	41.2	40.4	43.1	59.9
1891	53.1	52.3	54.2	61.4	47.1	45.9	48.5	62.6
1892	54.1	53.1	54.3	62.9	47.6	46.5	47.2	61.6
1893	56.9	56.0	57.7	63.3	56.4	54.6	57.6	66.4
1894	59.6	58.6	60.2	66.6	56.9	55.4	59.2	64.7
1895	61.8	60.7	61.9	67.5	59.8	58.3	63.6	71.6
1896	62.1	61.1	63.1	68.2	60.9	59.7	64.6	71.1
1897	64.6	63.7	66.1	69.4	57.2	56.6	62.3	65.9
1898	68.3	67.3	70.1	73.4	57.5	57.2	60.8	70.8
1899	69.3	68.4	70.9	75.0	62.0	61.4	65.2	73.9
1900	69.4	68.5	70.8	74.6	61.8	61.5	65.0	75.0
1901	70.4	69.7	71.7	76.4	56.4	56.6	58.2	72.7
1902	74.0	73.0	75.1	78.4	60.8	60.4	62.0	77.1
1903	74.6	73.7	75.7	78.8	64.2	63.6	64.8	80.7
1904	76.7	76.0	77.6	80.1	62.8	62.6	64.2	70.8
1905	79.3	78.5	79.9	84.4	67.1	67.0	68.7	80.2
1906	85.4	84.5	86.6	88.5	76.7	76.0	77.3	89.1
1907	92.0	91.4	91.7	91.7	78.6	77.9	80.2	84.7
1908	94.5	94.3	94.7	93.9	79.7	79.4	82.0	86.2
1909	95.4	95.4	96.2	95.1	84.6	84.3	86.6	89.4
1910	94.4	94.3	95.2	94.8	89.3	89.0	90.3	95.3
1911	99.5	98.9	98.8	96.6	95.9	95.4	94.8	94.2
1912	106.1	105.3	105.1	101.5	105.3	104.0	105.0	100.7
1913	100.0	100.0	100.0	100.0	100.0	100.0	100.0	100.0

Source: Schulze (2000), with minor corrections.

Table A.4.2. Indices of gross value added (constant prices, 1950 = 100)

	Hungary		Austria		Czechoslovakia	
	Industry	GDP	Industry	GDP	Industry	GDP
1913	37.1	71.0	84.3	91.2	48.7	64.0
1920	30.0	58.7	49.4	60.6	42.5	57.9
1921	30.0		54.4	67.1	45.5	62.5
1922			60.0	73.1	43.1	60.9
1923			59.9	72.4	47.5	65.9
1924	35.2	68.0	68.6	80.7	60.3	72.8
1925	38.5	73.1	75.3	86.2	69.3	81.3
1926	42.2	78.3	77.0	87.7	68.6	81.0
1927	47.2	81.7	78.6	90.3	76.5	87.1
1928	51.2	88.9	83.8	94.5	84.8	94.8
1929	51.2	91.8	85.6	95.9	90.3	97.4
1930	48.3	89.8	79.9	93.2	86.2	94.2
1931	44.5	85.4	71.9	85.8	80.1	91.0
1932	41.2	83.2	63.8	76.9	67.7	87.4
1933	43.5	90.7	60.7	74.4	64.0	83.6
1934	49.5	91.3	62.5	75.0	64.9	80.4
1935	56.8	95.9	64.7	76.5	66.9	79.7
1936	64.6	102.3	65.7	78.7	73.6	86.2
1937	67.0	100.0	70.2	82.9	84.3	95.9
1938	70.5	105.2	82.8	93.5		
1939	80.3	113.1	107.6	106.0		
1946	32.3	67.2	47.2	53.3		
1947	49.3	69.5	54.3	58.8		
1948	66.3	87.0	72.4	74.8	88.3	87.9
1949	78.1	94.0	86.6	89.0	91.9	92.7
1950	100.0	100.0	100.0	100.0	100.0	100.0
1951	113.1	109.7	114.5	106.8	102.8	101.8
1952	129.9	113.4	115.2	106.9	104.3	105.2
1953	136.9	115.4	117.2	111.6	105.2	104.8
1954	141.8	119.5	133.8	123.0	109.3	109.1
1955	152.4	130.3	161.4	136.6	122.7	118.4
1956	139.3	124.4	174.7	146.0	133.3	125.4
1957	154.6	134.7	183.7	154.9	146.8	133.1
1958	170.3	143.7	187.0	160.6	162.9	143.2
1959	183.2	149.5	195.8	165.1	175.7	149.5
1960	198.9	157.3	216.8	178.7	191.6	160.8
1961	216.8	165.3	227.3	188.2	203.9	167.2
1962	232.0	172.2	232.8	192.8	213.3	169.5
1963	243.1	181.6	241.7	200.6	212.3	166.3
1964	261.1	191.8	260.5	212.7	217.3	174.1
1965	275.9	193.3	271.2	218.8	230.7	180.5
1966	295.6	204.3	284.3	231.1	234.1	188.3
1967	305.3	216.1	287.5	238.1	249.1	196.4
1968	311.3	218.7	305.7	248.7	253.3	205.5
1969	314.5	225.2	342.1	264.4	257.7	209.3
1970	327.7	224.4	371.7	283.2	283.0	213.5
1971	333.0	234.4	394.7	297.7	290.4	220.8
1972	337.2	239.5	420.6	316.1	303.3	228.6

1973	351.0	251.9	443.5	331.6	315.1	236.2
1974	359.2	258.5	462.2	344.7	326.6	244.8
1975	372.9	264.0	436.1	343.4	342.2	252.0
1976	385.2	264.8	460.2	359.1	356.6	256.1
1977	403.1	281.4	481.0	375.9	369.3	267.6
1978	417.6	288.2	484.0	374.6	378.2	270.9
1979	421.7	288.8	511.4	395.0	384.0	273.2
1980	416.1	291.7	528.0	404.1	393.6	280.8
1981	422.4	293.8	509.5	403.7	401.1	279.4
1982	427.7	304.3	510.7	411.4	406.2	284.8
1983	431.8	301.2	530.3	423.0	413.8	289.1
1984	444.1	309.1	533.4	424.4	419.6	295.9
1985	444.4	301.5	560.6	433.9	427.5	298.2
1986	454.5	307.5	579.5	444.1	432.9	303.7
1987	460.9	312.3	575.2	451.5	439.8	305.2
1988	457.5	317.0	595.4	465.8	445.2	312.0
1989	442.6	309.9	619.3	485.5	445.2	314.6
1990	424.4	289.3	655.4	507.6	429.9	305.7
1991	377.7	254.9	668.3	524.6	362.6	267.3
1992	344.9	247.0	665.9	534.5	343.8	261.3
1993	356.2	245.6	654.5	536.5	306.4	262.8
1994	380.2	252.9	668.3	548.4	314.7	271.7
1995	410.2	256.6	694.7	563.7	350.1	287.7
1996	424.2	257.0	708.7	577.6	380.4	302.9
1997	466.4	265.1	734.7	590.9	365.7	305.2
1998	496.6	275.9	765.0	613.3	346.7	308.9
1999	516.6	284.7	806.2	635.0	369.3	312.4
2000	556.2	296.7	855.5	658.3	386.1	322.7
2001	557.9	307.7	882.6	664.0	391.1	333.1
2002	570.7	321.6	893.7	675.2	405.0	342.8
2003	607.9	334.0	900.6	681.1	419.8	356.8
2004	629.7	350.0	926.0	698.7	474.2	374.1
2005	657.2	363.9	949.6	715.5	520.6	399.2

Sources: GDP from Maddison (2006), industrial value added from: WIFO [Austria]; Eckstein (1955), p. 171, Czirják (1973), and Alton et al. (1982) [Hungary]; Pryor et al. (1971), Lazarcik (1969), and Alton et al. (1982) [Czechoslovakia]; after 1975, from Alton et al. (1991) and EU KLEMS (www.euklems.net).

Table A.4.3. Branch shares in total manufacturing gross value added (per cent)

	Food and beverages	Textiles and clothes	Iron and steel	Metal-working	Engineering	Brick, clay, glass	Petrochemicals
1870							
Imperial Austria	29.2	31.6	2.0	2.8	2.9	14.2	
Imperial Hungary	56.8	0.6	2.9	1.7	2.6	10.7	
1890							
Imperial Austria	31.1	30.4	3.0	3.4	4.4	9.9	0.5
Imperial Hungary	46.8	3.6	5.9	3.2	5.3	10.5	
1913							
Imperial Austria	25.0	22.0	5.5	8.6	11.1	7.4	3.0
Imperial Hungary	34.4	7.5	8.0	7.0	11.1	6.8	1.4

Note: Gross value added in constant 1913 prices.

Source: Schulze (2000), with minor corrections.

REFERENCES

Abramovitz, M. (1986). Catching up, forging ahead and falling behind. *Journal of Economic History* 46, 385–406.

Alton, T. P., Badach, K., Bakondi, K., Bass, E. M., Brumaru, A., Bombelles, J. T., Lazarcik, G. and Staller, G. J. (1991). Economic growth in Eastern Europe, 1975–1990. *Occasional Papers of the Research Project on National Income in East Central Europe* No. 115. New York: L. W. International Financial Research, Inc.

Alton, T. P., Bass, E. M., Lazarcik, G. and Staller, G. J. (1982). Economic growth in Eastern Europe, 1965, 1970, and 1975–1981. *Occasional Papers of the Research Project on National Income in East Central Europe* No. 70. New York: L. W. International Financial Research, Inc.

Berend, I. T. (1997). *Central and Eastern Europe 1944–1993: Detour from the Periphery to the Periphery*. Cambridge: Cambridge University Press.

Berend, I. T. and Ránki, G. (1960). *The Development of the Manufacturing Industry in Hungary, 1900–1944*. Budapest: Akadémiai Kiadó.

Bolognese-Leuchtenmüller, B. (1978). *Bevölkerungsentwicklung und Berufsstruktur, Gesundheits- und Fürsorgewesen in Österreich, 1750–1918*. Munich: Oldenburg.

Broadberry, S. N. and Klein, A. (2011). When and why did eastern European economies begin to fail: lessons from a Czechoslovak/UK productivity comparison, 1921–1991. *Explorations in Economic History* 48, 37–52.

Butschek, F. (1978). *The Österreichische Wirtschaft 1938 bis 1945*. Stuttgart: Gustav Fischer.

Butschek, F. (2011). *Österreichische Wirtschaftsgeschichte: von der Antike bis zur Gegenwart*. 2nd Rev. Ed. Vienna: Böhlau.

Czirják, L. (1968). Indexes of Hungarian industrial production, 1938 and 1945–65. *Occasional Papers of the Research Project on National Income in East Central Europe* No. 16. New York: Columbia University.

Czirják, L. (1973). Hungarian GNP by sectors of origin of product and end uses, 1938 and 1946–1967. *Occasional Papers of the Research Project on National Income in East Central Europe* No. 43. New York: Riverside Research Institute.

Drabek, Z. (1985). Foreign trade performance and policy. In *The Economic History of Eastern Europe 1919–1975*, Vol. I (Eds, Kaser, M. C. and Radice, E. A.). Oxford: Oxford University Press.

Eckstein, A. (1955). National income and capital formation in Hungary, 1900–1950. In *Income and Wealth*, Series V. (Ed., Kuznets, S.). London: Bowes & Bowes.

Eddie, S. (1989). Economic policy and economic development in Austria-Hungary, 1867–1913. In *The Cambridge Economic History of Europe*, Vol. 8 (Eds, Mathias, P. and Pollard, S.). Cambridge: Cambridge University Press.

Freudenberger, H. (2003). *Lost Momentum: Austrian Economic Development 1750s–1830s.* Vienna: Böhlau.

Gerschenkron, A. (1962). *Economic Backwardness in Historical Perspective: A Book of Essays.* Boston, MA: Harvard University Press.

Gerschenkron, A. (1977). *An Economic Spurt that Failed: Four Lectures in Austrian History.* Princeton, NJ: Princeton University Press.

Good, D. F. (1984). *The Economic Rise of the Habsburg Empire, 1750–1914.* Berkeley, CA: University of California Press.

Grenzebach, W. S. (1988). *Germany's Informal Empire in East Central Europe: German Economic Policy toward Yugoslavia and Rumania, 1933–1939.* Stuttgart: Steiner.

Hidvégi, M. and Vonyó, T. (2012). Nationalism and falling behind: the failure of national industrialization. *Korunk* 23, 56–65 [in Hungarian].

Hirschman, A. O. (1945). *National Power and the Structure of Foreign Trade.* Berkeley, CA: California University Press.

Hoffmann, W. G. (1965). *Das Wachstum der deutschen Wirtschaft seit Mitte des 19. Jahrhunderts.* Berlin: Springer Verlag.

International Labour Office (1986). *Economically Active Population Estimates and Projections 1950–2025*, diff. vols. Geneva: ILO.

Kalecki, M. (1993). *Socialism: Economic Growth and Efficiency of Investment.* Oxford: Oxford University Press.

Katus, L. (1970). Economic growth in Hungary during the age of dualism (1867–1913): a quantitative analysis. In *Sozial-ökonomische Forschungen zur Geschichte von Ost-Mitteleuropa* (Ed., E. Pamlényi). Budapest: Akadémiai Kiadó.

Kausel, A. (1979). Österreichs Volkseinkommen 1830 bis 1913. In *Geschichte und Ergebnisse der zentralen amtlichen Statistik in Österreich, 1829–1979* (Ed., Österreichisches Statistisches Zentralamt). Vienna: Österreichisches Statistisches Zentralamt, 689–720.

Komlos, J. (1983). *The Habsburg Monarchy as a Customs Union: Economic Development in Austria-Hungary in the Nineteenth Century.* Princeton, NJ: Princeton University Press.

Komlos, J. (1989). *Stature, Nutrition, and Economic Development in the Eighteenth Century Habsburg Monarchy: The 'Austrian' Model of the Industrial Revolution.* Princeton, NJ: Princeton University Press.

Lazarcik, G. (1969). Czechoslovak gross national product by sector of origin and by final use, 1937 and 1948–1965. *Occasional Papers of the Research Project on National Income in East Central Europe* No. 26. New York: Columbia University.

Maddison, A. (2006). *The World Economy*, Vol. II: *Historical Statistics.* Paris: OECD.

MSE: Magyar Kir. Központi Statisztikai Hivatal, *Magyar Statisztikai Évkönyv, 1872–1915.* Budapest.

Pollard, S. (1986). *Peaceful Conquest.* Reprint. Oxford: Oxford University Press.

Ponomarenko, A. N. (2002). *Retrospective Russian National Accounts: 1961–1990*. Moscow: Finansy i statistika [in Russian].

Pryor, F., Pryor, Z., Stadnik, M., and Staller, G. (1971). Czechoslovak aggregate production in the inter-war period. *Review of Income and Wealth* 17, 35–59.

Ránki, G. (1964). Problems of the development of Hungarian industry, 1900–1944. *Journal of Economic History* 24, 204–28.

Ránki, G. (1983). *Economy and Foreign Policy: The Struggle of the Great Powers for Hegemony in the Danube Valley, 1919–1939*. New York: Columbia University Press.

Reichling, G. (1989). *Die deutschen Vertriebenen in Zahlen*, Vol. I: *Umsiedler, Verschleppte, Vertriebene, Aussiedler 1940–1985*. Bonn: Kulturstiftung der deutschen Vertriebenen.

Scherner, J. (2011). Der deutsche Importboom während des Zweiten Weltkriegs: Neue Ergebnisse zur Struktur der Ausbeutung des besetzten Europas auf der Grundlage einer Neuschätzung der deutschen Handelsbilanz. *Historische Zeitschrift* 294, 79–113.

Schulze, M. S. (1996). *Engineering and Economic Growth: The Development of Austria-Hungary's Machine-Building Industry in the Late Nineteenth Century*. Frankfurt and New York: Peter Lang.

Schulze, M. S. (1997). The machine-building industry and Austria's Great Depression after 1873. *Economic History Review* 50, 282–304.

Schulze, M. S. (2000). Patterns of growth and stagnation in the late nineteenth century Habsburg economy. *European Review of Economic History* 4, 311–40.

Schulze, M. S. (2007a). Origins of catch-up failure: comparative productivity growth in the Habsburg Empire, 1870–1910. *European Review of Economic History* 11, 189–218.

Schulze, M. S. (2007b). Regional income dispersion and market potential in the late nineteenth century Habsburg Empire. *LSE Working Papers in Economic History* No. 106.

Schulze, M. S. and Fernandes, F. T. (2009). Human capital formation in Austria-Hungary and Germany: time series estimates of educational attainment, 1860–1910. In *A felhalmozás Míve. Történeti Tanulmányok Kövér György Tiszteletére* (Eds, Halmos, K., et al.). Századvég Kiadó: Budapest, 275–89.

Schulze, M. S. and Wolf, N. (2011). Economic nationalism and economic integration: the Austro-Hungarian Empire in the late nineteenth century. *Economic History Review* 65, 652–73.

Seidel, H. (2005). *Österreichs Wirtschaft und Wirtschaftspolitik nach dem Zweiten Weltkrieg*. Vienna: Manz'sche Verlags- und Universitätsbuchhandlung.

Shute, J. (1948). Czechoslovakia's territorial and population changes. *Economic Geography* 24, 35–44.

Somary, F. (1902). *Die Aktiengesellschaften in Österreich*. Vienna: Manz.

Staller, G. J. (1975). Czechoslovak industrial production, 1948–1972. *Occasional Papers of the Research Project on National Income in East Central Europe* No. 45. New York: L. W. International Financial Research.

Stockholm International Peace Research Institute (SIPRI). *Yearbook of World Armaments, Disarmament and International Security*. Diff. volumes, 1968/69 onwards. London: Taylor & Francis.

Teichova, A. (1985). Industry. In *The Economic History of Eastern Europe 1919–1975*, Vol. I (Eds, Kaser, M. C. and Radice, E. A.). Oxford: Oxford University Press.

Teichova, A. (1988). *The Czechoslovak Economy 1918–1980*. London: Routledge.

5

Industrialization and De-industrialization in Southeast Europe, 1870–2010

Michael Kopsidis and Martin Ivanov

5.1 INTRODUCTION

This chapter analyses the development of modern manufacturing in Southeast Europe (SEE), defined here as Bulgaria, Greece, Romania, and Serbia/Yugoslavia.[1] Modern manufacturing in the region started at the very end of the nineteenth century. However, industrialization only really took off after the Second World War. We thus emphasize two major sub-periods: a long preparation for take-off with two 'mini-spurts' on the eve of the First and Second World Wars; and rapid industrialization from the late 1940s, accompanied by profound structural transformation.

Southeast Europe's 'century of industrialization' occurred between two waves of de-industrialization. The first one, labelled 'Ottoman de-industrialization', occurred during the so-called 'first globalization' and was at its strongest from *c.*1815 to 1860; the second, more serious one took place during the second globalization, notably the 1990s. The connections between de-globalization and de-industrialization were different in both cases, as will be seen below.

Since large parts of Southeast Europe were in the Ottoman Empire through the end of the 1870s, we will briefly touch upon the Ottoman de-industrialization. Much has been written on this, but the literature is still far from reaching a consensus.[2] Suffice to say that the first wave of de-industrialization did not affect the few more industrial Southeast European regions in a uniform fashion. Large areas of Asia Minor, the Salonika hinterland, and Thessaly, which had good connections to supra-regional markets, were affected early in the nineteenth century, followed a few decades later by the landlocked Central Balkans. In general, the Ottoman de-industrialization was mild compared to the nineteenth-century de-industrialization of other parts of the global periphery.

---

[1] Due to a lack of data or to historical inconsistency, states like Albania and the breakaway republics of the former Yugoslavia will not be covered.

[2] The literature is vast: major contributions include Keyder (1991); Palairet (1983a; 1983b; 1997); Pamuk (1986); Pamuk and Williamson (2011); and Quataert (1994).

5.2 INDUSTRIAL GROWTH WITH PARTIAL DEVELOPMENT, 1870–1945

In his path-breaking overview of Bulgarian economic development, Gerschenkron (1962) laid the foundations of a broad consensus which still dominates the literature on industrialization in SEE. It remains widely accepted that high manufacturing growth rates in the region, confirmed in Table 5.1, 'did not reveal the specific qualities that are usually associated with a great spurt of industrial development' (Gerschenkron, 1962, p. 213). In more recent years, historians have written of 'growth without development' (Palairet, 1997; Lampe, 1986).

These respectable growth rates, however, mask the lack of fundamental structural transformation, even if modern industry grew much faster than traditional industry. Almost all scholars agree that the main indicators of structural change (e.g. the structure of GDP, occupational structure, energy consumption, productivity, factory size, capital intensity or the share of industrial exports) fail to indicate any significant transformation of the economy (Lampe and Jackson, 1982; Teichova, 1985).

Less productive, labour-intensive, low-technology consumer goods industries like food processing and textile production took the lion's share of industrial output in all Southeast European countries over the entire period. Only in Romania did these shares stay below 50 per cent, but they were high even there. During the inter-war period, low wages implied a tremendous rise of large-scale mechanized textile production throughout the region (Teichova, 1985, p. 247). No significant heavy industry emerged in Southeast Europe (Table 5.2). This was true even for resource- and especially oil-rich Romania, which according to contemporary international experts attained full-scale industrialization around 1920. Romania enjoyed the largest industrial sector and deepest domestic market in the region, as well as superior domestic industrial entrepreneurship and financing, mainly thanks to economically active Jewish and German minorities (Turnock, 1977, p. 347; Lampe and Jackson, 1982, pp. 237–77). However, oil-based industrial development in Romania mainly meant primary processing of raw materials for export, rather than highly profitable oil refining (Teichova, 1985, pp. 255–7; Berend and Ránki, 1982, p. 127).

Industrial labour productivity in Southeast Europe was perhaps only a quarter or a fifth of the levels in the most developed European countries, although the available data only permit a very rough approximation (Teichova, 1985, pp. 278–9). Bulgarian labour productivity and real wages stagnated between 1904 and 1949 (Teichova, 1985, p. 277; Ivanov and Tooze, 2007). A total factor productivity (TFP)-enhancing shift of labour from low-productivity agriculture to high-productivity industry only took place to a very limited extent, and labour productivity in modern manufacturing remained four to five times higher than in agriculture throughout the inter-war period (Vinski, 1967, pp. 268–9).

Following Gerschenkron (1962), a broad consensus on the reasons for lethargic industrialization in SEE was established and remained almost unchallenged for over fifty years: stagnant and inefficient agriculture; ill-functioning capital markets,

Table 5.1. Real growth rates of Southeast European industry, 1870–1938

Panel A, 1870–1913

		Bulgaria	Greece	Romania	Serbia/ Yugoslavia
Total industry (secondary production: total manufacturing including handicrafts output, mining, and construction)					
1870–89	(1)			3.3% (1870–89)	
1890–1913	(2)	−0.6% (1887–1911)			
	(1)			3.3% (1890–1913)	
Modern industry (factory output)					
1890–1913	(2)	18.0% (1887–1911)			
	(1)			6.6% (1890–1913)	
	(3)	14.3% (1904–11)		7.0% (1901–15)	12.5% (1901–11)
	(4)	14.6% (1904–11)		7.9% (1901–15)	
	(5)				7.1% (1898–1911)
	(6)	10.5% (1894–1911)			

Sources: (1) Axiencuc (2012, vol. 2, pp. 277–8) (1913 prices, exponential trends); (2) Ivanov (2012, pp. 374–7, 458–61, 490–3, 512–23) (1939 prices, exponential trends); (3) Lampe (1975, p. 60); (4) Jackson and Lampe (1983, pp. 392, 401); (5) Lampe and Jackson (1982, p. 250); (6) Berov and Dimitrov (1990, p. 45).

Panel B, 1920–38[*]

		Bulgaria	Greece	Romania	Yugoslavia
1920–1938	(1)		3.9%	7.3%	1.3%
	(2)	6.0% (1921–38)			
	(3)			4.3%	
	(4)	6.5% (1921–37)		9.4%	3.5% (1923–38)
	(5)	7.8% (1921–38)			
	(6)		4.5% (1921–38)		
	(7)		5.4% (1921–38)		
	(8)				2.4% (1923–38)

* Except for Greece (6) and (7) all data roughly refer to modern manufacturing excluding handicraft production. However, the transition between factory and handicraft production was gradual in Southeast Europe.

Sources: (1) Bénétrix et al. (2015); (2) Ivanov (2012); (3) Axiencuc (2012, pp. 129–30) (1913 prices, exponential trends); (4) Teichova (1985, pp. 280–2), Teichova's growth rates for Bulgaria are based on data from Chakalov (1946) for 1924–38 (Rangelova, 2000, p. 231); (5) Berov and Dimitrov (1990, pp. 130, 138, 141); (6) Christodoulaki (2001, p. 72); (7) Mazower (1991, p. 311); (8) Stajic (1959).

Table 5.2. Sectoral shares in manufacturing output, 1912–38

	Bulgaria		Romania		Yugoslavia	Greece
	1912	1938	1928	1937	1938	1938
Metallurgy and engineering	5.9	6.4	15.0	16.4	16.5	6.7
Chemicals	3.0	5.6	9.1	18.6	8.5	24.6
Woodworking	1.1	2.4	8.6	5.5	6.2	5.2
Building materials	3.6	3.9	3.9	3.6	9.1	5.1
Food processing	55.0	47.0	30.5	20.1	29.3	7.2
Textiles and clothing	19.8	28.9	14.3	22.2	22.1	36.5
Leather and fur working	5.4	2.9	5.0	4.3	4.6	10.3
Paper making and printing	0.6	2.8	4.1	4.9	3.6	4.4

Sources: Teichova (1985, p. 248); for Greece 1938: Kostelenos (1995, p. 182); for Bulgaria 1912: Berov and Dimitrov (1990, p. 51).

banks which shied away from investments in manufacturing; insufficient demand; and, most importantly, states' failure to develop programmes of rapid industrialization. Two more recent interpretations offer alternative frameworks. Palairet (1983a; 1983b; 1997) proposes an explanation centred on the alleged cultural, social, and economic 'peasantization' of the newly emerging Balkan nations. Seeing peasants in somewhat outdated fashion as the antithesis to markets, capitalism, and growth, Palairet postulates that with the rise of peasant farming following the end of Ottoman rule, the subsistence sector expanded rapidly in Serbia and Bulgaria. This caused economic retardation in all sectors, resulting in falling living standards and decreasing productivity: agrarian 'immiserizing growth' occurred, rather than industrialization (Palairet, 1997, esp. pp. 111, 177–80, 201, 310, 340, 363).

Pamuk and Williamson (2011) suggest another alternative to the iconic Gerschenkronian model of sluggish industrialization. As world export prices of agricultural commodities rose and prices of imported industrial goods fell, labour and capital were diverted from industry into the primary sector: factor endowments, including poorly developed human capital, gave Southeast Europe a clear comparative advantage in agriculture rather than manufacturing. In other words, it was not inefficient institutions that prevented Southeast European industrialization, so much as international price shocks, magnified by increased integration with world commodity markets.

Indeed, developments in labour and factor markets were hostile to industrialization. Land was abundant all over SEE, and the new Southeast European states removed existing obstacles to peasant occupation and settlement of land. Increased opportunities in agriculture put upward pressure on industrial wages. Rising labour costs led to a decline in previously flourishing textile proto-industries and a 're-agrarization' of Southeast Europe (Palairet, 1997, pp. 81, 177–81, 189–96; Petmezas, 2011, p. 37; Lampe and Jackson, 1982, p. 595). In addition, skilled and educated industrial labour was almost non-existent in Southeast Europe, except in a very few regions, and had to be 'imported' from Western Europe at a high cost (Lampe and Jackson, 1982, p. 241).

Despite these obstacles to industrialization, and the Great Depression, there is a growing consensus that on the eve of the Second World War SEE economies were undergoing a deep-seated modernization processes which facilitated rapid industrialization after 1945 (Lampe and Jackson, 1982, pp. 576–7; Teichova, 1985, p. 239). To acknowledge this is not to deny the lack of industrialization in Southeast Europe between 1870 and 1940 observed by Gerschenkron (1962), but helps to explain why sweeping industrialization could occur so quickly after 1945.

During the 1930s, states all over SEE intervened to accelerate industrialization, in reaction to the Great Depression. The import substitution required to fight dangerous external imbalances induced industrial growth in SEE above the European average.[3] Governments also supported industrialization via compulsory cartels, strict price controls, and the replacement of dwindling private investment by public industrial finance. Outside Greece a broad consensus emerged among the region's elites that only extensive state planning, combined with self-reliance as the guiding principle of development, would enable successful industrialization. A first industrialization plan was introduced in Yugoslavia. After the war, the Communists skilfully exploited this positive view of state control to implement their version of central planning (Lampe and Jackson, 1982, pp. 461–519; Teichova, 1985, p. 236; Ránki and Tomaszewski, 1986, pp. 5, 21–48).

During the inter-war years, Balkan societies underwent three fundamental changes that made rapid industrialization possible after the Second World War. First, as a consequence of rapidly advancing commercialization, peasant agriculture began to move decisively towards market-oriented intensification. Second, rural Southeast Europe experienced the most rapid demographic transition in Europe. Third, between 1900 and 1945 literacy rates dramatically increased in the entire region, and higher technical education advanced. For these reasons we prefer to speak of 'growth with partial development' instead of 'growth without development' for the period before the Second World War (Lampe and Jackson, 1982, pp. 502–3; Ivanov and Tooze, 2007, p. 698).

5.3 FROM TAKE-OFF TO DE-INDUSTRIALIZATION: MANUFACTURING IN SOUTHEAST EUROPE, 1945–2010

During the Cold War, SEE industrialization occurred no matter what the economic system: centrally planned (Bulgaria and Romania), 'market socialism' (Yugoslavia), and capitalism (Greece). The degree of pro-industrial state interventionism varied greatly among Southeast European countries. It is this ideological and institutional diversity which makes a comparison of industrialization among Southeast European

---

[3] Bulgaria's modern manufacturing, corresponding to 'large industry' in the official statistics, increased at annual rates of 8.9 per cent during 1924–9, 6.1 per cent during 1929–34, and 16.0 per cent during 1934–9 (Ivanov, 2012).

countries after 1950 especially interesting. Despite fundamental differences in their economic systems, all Southeast European countries (SEEs) followed more or less similar industrial trajectories after 1950 (Tables 5.3 and 5.4).[4] Manufacturing boomed all over SEE until the mid-1970s, but industry only became the largest economic sector in the socialist states. Around 1975 industrial growth slowed substantially, and deceleration became contraction in all socialist SEEs at the end of the 1980s: the huge 'gains' of enforced Soviet-style industrialization largely vanished within a few years. Industrial production fell back to early/mid-1970s levels during the 1990s.[5] Manufacturing growth started accelerating again in all Southeast European transition economies after 2000.

5.3.1 Stalin's Long Shadow: Enforced Industrialization in Romania and Bulgaria

In Romania and Bulgaria the transition to a socialist economy took almost a decade. The first important steps were taken in 1947–8 when all existing industrial and mining undertakings, 7,000 in Bulgaria and 35,500 in Romania, were nationalized. Many were soon consolidated into larger industrial complexes. Simultaneous forced collectivization caused a drain of labour out of agriculture unprecedented even by Soviet standards. Planners focused on boosting capital accumulation and channelling as much capital as possible into industry. Already very low living standards were reduced further in order to accelerate industrialization. By the mid-1960s structural transformation had been completed, with 'striking rapidity' in Bulgaria and Romania (Feiwel, 1982, p. 216; Montias, 1967, pp. 1–86; Tsantis and Pepper, 1979, pp. 562–67; Lampe, 1986, pp. 139–55). Manufacturing and GDP growth rates strongly exceeded those of other CMEA members, especially during the late 1940s and 1950s.[6] However, in comparison with non-Communist countries at the same low stage of development, their growth performance during 1950–73 was unexceptional, and realized at much higher human cost (Table 5.3; Crafts and Toniolo, 2010).

[4] As far as possible we used comparable data on manufacturing based on Western estimates for all socialist SEEs due to the fact that output and productivity was notoriously overestimated in official statistics, not least because of confusing Marxist concepts of social product (Alton, 1989; Ehrlich, 1992; Marer, 1993). However, even if the old Western estimates are the best available data on industrial output in socialist SEEs, they need improvement. Reconstructing manufacturing output 1950–90 according to current international standards is a task which still waits to be done.

[5] Own calculation based on data from Mitchell (2003, pp. 425–6). Due to the use of unrevised official data, the drop after 1990 is partly caused by changes in the official statistics. However, the fact remains that industrial output shrank by between one-third and one-half in former socialist SEEs during the 1990s.

[6] Around 1950, the low-productive peasant labour surplus of the European periphery was largest in the Southeast (Moore, 1945). Thus, extensive industrialization based on the forced redirection of labour from agriculture to industry probably delivered the highest productivity gains in this region, although further research is necessary to substantiate this hypothesis. The Council of Mutual Economic Assistance (COMECON or CMEA) was founded in 1949 on the initiative of the Soviet Union. Its task was to organize economic cooperation between member states.

Table 5.3. Manufacturing growth in Southeast Europe, 1950–2007 (annual rates)

Country	Official indexes, 1953–71	Western estimates, 1950-71[a]	1973–90	1990–2007
Bulgaria	12.6 (11.9)	8.3	2.8[c] (4.4)	0.1
Romania	12.1 (10.1)	7.8	3.5[c] (1.0)	0.9
Yugoslavia	10.5 (9.8)	9.2	3.2[d] (3.7)	–
Greece	–	8.2[b]	1.9	1.4

[a] For Bulgaria and Romania, Moore (1980) calculated growth rates based on revised data from Alton. Moore himself revised official Yugoslav data on manufacturing output; [b] 1950–73; [c] 1973–87, [d] 1978–88.

Sources: 1950–71: except for Greece and data in brackets, data are from Moore (1980, p. 55); for Greece and data in brackets, see Bénétrix et al. (2015). 1973–90: for Greece and data in brackets, see Bénétrix et al. (2015); for remaining data, see Alton et al. (1985), Alton (1989), and SZS/Eurostat (1990). 1990–2007: all data from Bénétrix et al. (2015, p. 30).

Table 5.4. Share of industry[a] in GDP, 1950–2010

	Romania	Bulgaria	Yugoslavia	Greece[b]
1950			21.5	21.4
1955			26.5	21.6
1960			29.0	21.8
1965	26.4	29.0	33.6	19.4
1970	35.5	34.1	36.1	22.9
1975	39.8	35.9		22.9
1980				22.6
1985				22.9
1990				20.7
1995				18.7
2000	29.0	21.3	23.4/29.0	13.9
2005				
2010	29.7	23.2	19.0/24.3	13.8

[a] Industry comprises manufacturing (including handicraft) and the energy sector (including mining) but not construction. Due to the low shares of energy, mining, and handicraft, 'industry' approximates closely to manufacturing;
[b] 1994 instead of 1995.

Sources: for Greece 1950–95: Louri and Pepelasis-Minoglou (2002, p. 334); for Yugoslavia 1950–70: Moore (1980, p. 23); for Romania and Bulgaria 1965–75: Alton (1981, pp. 41–3); for Romania, Greece, ex-Yugoslavia (Croatia/Slovenia), and Bulgaria 2000–10: Eurostat.

Faced with steadily declining manufacturing growth rates from the mid-1970s, the Communist regimes in Bulgaria and Romania were preoccupied with managing the transition from extensive to intensive growth.[7] However, industrial development

[7] According to Western estimates, annual growth rates of Bulgarian manufacturing declined from 12.2 per cent (1948–65), to 6.3 per cent (1965–76), and finally to 2.0 per cent (1977–87) (own calculation, data from Lazarcik and Wynnyczuk (1968, pp. 7, 9); Alton et al. (1985); Alton (1989)).

rested to a much larger extent than in the West on rising factor intensity (Lazarcik and Wynnyczuk, 1968; Montias, 1988, p. 542). Only after Stalin's death was it possible to cultivate national development strategies. Whereas Hungary and Poland implemented far-reaching 'liberal' economic reforms, Bulgaria and Romania strengthened central control and enlarged the scale of production (Berend, 1996; Ivanov, 2008).

Romanian Communists developed their own 'national Stalinism', connecting extreme nationalism and reckless industrialization. They advocated the expansion of heavy industries with strong linkage effects, rather than what they disdainfully called 'calico-industrialization' based on traditional consumer goods industries. The explicit target was to build up new high-technology capital goods industries which were supposed to have the highest growth impact (Montias, 1967, p. 6; Tsantis and Pepper, 1979, p. 201). Engineering and heavy chemicals were seen as the most important industries because of their diversity and strong linkage effects to all other manufacturing branches. From the mid-1950s to the late 1980s, both sub-sectors remained at the core of Romania's industrialization strategy (Tsantis and Pepper, 1979, pp. 1–7, 25–33). The strategy implied a harsh clash with the USSR and the more developed COMECON states, namely Czechoslovakia and the GDR, beginning in 1958. Until this time every country in the Eastern bloc followed a policy of 'processing-self-sufficiency', producing as many manufactured goods as possible domestically (Berend, 1996, p. 163). Driven by political and economic considerations, Khrushchev wanted to establish a productivity-enhancing international division of labour between all COMECON members. The Soviets proposed a Common Socialist Market for chemical and engineering products: no CMEA country should produce the whole range of these industrial products any longer. What this effectively meant was that Romania should concentrate on a few industrial products and curb its ambitious industrialization targets, especially concerning engineering. Romania refused to accept these plans and rejected any foreign intrusion into its industrialization policies. In retaliation the Soviet Union put the country under severe pressure by cutting or suspending economic aid. Bucharest started to look for Western partners to further develop its engineering and metal-processing industries (Montias, 1967, pp. 203–30; Berend, 1996, pp. 130–5).

Rising imports of Western high technology required higher Romanian exports. Initially machine imports were paid for with foodstuffs and raw materials, but eventually a peculiar triangular trade developed. Romania continued to export raw materials and basic industrial products to Western Europe in exchange for high technology. Trade deficits with Western Europe were financed mainly via trade surpluses with developing countries, and partly via credits. Rising oil imports were paid for with industrial exports, mainly to the Middle East. Romanian industrial equipment, including turnkey plants, found customers across the developing world. Drilling technology and farm machinery enjoyed an especially good reputation. The cheapness and robustness of Romanian products made them attractive for developing countries, but not for producers demanding high technology. Second-class machinery and other industrial products which could not be sold on world markets were delivered to COMECON partners, mainly the USSR. As a result, Romanian foreign trade with Western partners resembled that of a developing country, whereas trade with COMECON and developing economies resembled that of an industrialized nation (Tsantis and Pepper, 1979, pp. 109–39, 201–25).

The 1973 oil shock cracked this triangular trade system and aggravated the deficiencies of socialist planning. By 1975 it was clear that Romania's dependency on oil imports was endangering the competitiveness of its energy-intensive industry. Another problem was the planners' preference for large industrial enterprises, solving operational problems via strengthened central control. With 1,480 workers per industrial enterprise, compared with 712 in the USSR and 149 in West Germany, Romania probably had the world's largest number of employees per unit of production (Tsantis and Pepper, 1979, p. 200). Although Romania imported labour-saving Western technology, its industry remained highly labour intensive, reducing the productivity-enhancing rationalization effects of modern technology. Industrial firms were often forced to combine high technology with outdated machinery. Inefficient use of capital and labour caused enormous losses in productivity. Due to the inflexibility of oversized enterprises, Romanian planners preferred 'production with limited variation of specification, reduced number of types, and large serial volumes' (Tsantis and Pepper, 1979, p. 209).

Modern engineering demanded flexible adjustment to customer-specific requirements. The transition to post-Fordist production implied abandoning mass production which was well suited to the hyper-centralized Romanian system. Romania could not adapt its industry to these new conditions, and maintained its outdated industrial structure. Engineering and heavy chemical industries remained the leading sectors of the economy (Tsantis and Pepper, 1979, pp. 225, 336). The focus on energy-intensive branches implied copying Western technology of the 1950s and 1960s, which depended on low energy costs. This imitation strategy failed after the 1973 oil crisis. Building up a less energy-intensive, post-industrial, more service-based economy and creating a competitive ICT industry was beyond the capacity of centrally planned economies. Romania continued to follow an orthodox industrialization policy, neglecting the service sector and communications (Berend, 1996, pp. 191–232; Crafts and Toniolo, 2010).

After 1973, manufacturing slipped into structural crisis and long-term decline across the European 'periphery'. What aggravated the situation in centrally planned economies was the fact that their heavy-industry-based industrialization strategies were still being promoted for ideological reasons. This had fatal consequences, especially for Romania which adhered to its obsolete manufacturing structure more than any other peripheral European country (Ban, 2012). Despite rising energy prices, Bucharest continued promoting energy-intensive industry, notably oil-consuming chemicals; their expansion, labelled the second wave of socialist industrialization, tripled Romania's demand for oil between 1975 and 1980 (Ban, 2012, pp. 757–8). Consequently, Romania could not withstand the second oil price shock of 1979. Between 1976 and 1981 Romania's external debts increased from $0.5 billion (3 per cent of GDP) to $10.4 billion (28 per cent) (Ban, 2012, p. 758). By 1981 Romania was close to insolvency, but Ceaușescu wanted at any costs to prevent an IMF 'intrusion' into its neo-Stalinist industrialization programme.

He decided to pay back all debts, without reducing industrial investment. Imports were cut drastically and exports increased. As a consequence, living standards collapsed to 'near war-time levels' (Ban, 2012, pp. 756–60). These drastic measures were effective and Romania repaid its debts by May 1989, well ahead of time. However, by the end of the 1980s Romania's industrial capital stock was hopelessly outdated since technology imports had slowed for a decade. Consequently, industrial growth also slowed (Table 5.3). The decade of 'Stalinist austerity' (Ban, 2012, p. 743) severely aggravated the systemic defects of a centrally planned economy which became clear across Central and Eastern Europe after 1973.[8]

Bulgaria shared Romania's vision of a strong national manufacturing sector but Sofia chose a different route to achieve it. Bulgaria also wished to develop its own neo-Stalinist heavy industry based on engineering and heavy chemistry, and was also unhappy with COMECON's 1958 and 1970 'specialization recommendations'. These envisaged that Sofia could produce only 374 of the 3,000 types of machinery and equipment manufactured in CMEA (Montias, 1988, pp. 524–5). Bulgarian party leader Todor Zhivkov attempted to seduce rather than to confront the Kremlin. Drawing on widespread Bulgarian *Russophilia*, he proposed in 1963 that Bulgaria should join the USSR as its sixteenth republic. Only Khrushchev's removal from power prevented the plan's implementation. Nevertheless, the 'sixteenth republic' proposal had serious economic and political implications. After 1963 Bulgaria became the Soviet Union's closest and most obedient ally, and Moscow was therefore prepared to grant various concessions to Sofia. Bulgaria obtained a monopoly in the production of hauling and lifting machinery, and could specialize in food-processing, agricultural and later electronic equipment. These industries attracted most investment, and dominated Bulgarian exports after 1970. Thus, throughout the 1970s and early 1980s Bulgaria was able to adopt an export-oriented industrial policy (Montias, 1988, p. 533; Lampe, 1986, p. 156). Between 1955–7 and 1981–3 the share of machinery in major exports increased from 8.2 to 53.8 per cent (Lampe, 1986, p. 180).

Expanding Bulgarian engineering, petrochemical, and pharmaceutical industries required increasing amounts of raw materials, fuels, and semi-manufactures. Most, if not all, of the raw materials and fuels came from the USSR. To pay for them Sofia increased its exports of machinery, processed foodstuffs, and manufactured consumer goods, but rising exports between 1970 and 1983 failed to keep pace with imports, and the two oil shocks made it almost impossible to reduce the trade deficit with the USSR. By 1980 the purchasing power of Bulgarian manufacturing exports vis-à-vis Soviet oil had fallen six to seven times relative to 1970 (Stoilov, 1986, p. 18). Feeling the mounting pressure, Zhivkov played the 'sixteenth republic' card again. In 1973 a new plan for unification received a warm welcome from Brezhnev. Five years later Zhivkov appealed to Brezhnev that he should not treat Bulgaria differently from any Soviet Republic. Sofia received considerable concessions, most importantly an unspecified amount of Soviet oil far exceeding

---

[8] The prevailing consensus is that TFP growth in COMECON states slowed or was even negative after 1973, but TFP data are still lacking for all of socialist Southeast Europe.

its needs. During the early 1980s re-exported Soviet oil accounted for roughly 50 per cent of the country's total exports to the West (Montias, 1988, p. 548).

Soviet oil helped significantly in resolving Bulgaria's foreign currency debt problem. From the early 1970s, bank loans helped Sofia finance its growing trade deficit with the West. In order to service these debts, Bulgaria resorted to a triangular trade similar to that practised by Romania. Between 1970 and 1983 the share of developing countries in Bulgarian exports more than doubled from 6.5 to 13 per cent. Most of this increase was based on exports of machinery and armaments (Montias, 1988, p. 547). However, it soon became apparent that trade with developing countries was insufficient to overcome the foreign currency shortage: Bulgarian engineering exports were just enough to pay for oil imports from Arab countries, leaving a substantial deficit caused by machinery imports from Western economies. The foreign exchange imbalance was finally closed with large re-exports of Soviet oil and bridging loans from Moscow in 1977 and 1978.

The programme for industrial modernization after the 1970s oil shocks merits special attention. In reaction to the deteriorating terms of trade, the Politburo decided to promote electronics and computing: developing a high-tech sector, it was felt, would save foreign currency and fuel due to its low energy and capital intensity. Zhivkov and his team successfully gambled on the CoCom[9] embargo, which hit the Soviet Union very hard but was enforced less restrictively on insignificant CMEA members like Bulgaria. During the 1980s Sofia embarked on several projects which envisaged acquiring new technologies, adapting them to Eastern conditions, and exporting the output to the USSR (Montias, 1988, p. 556).

At first things went well, electronics and computing output tripling in a decade, and their share in exports more than doubling, reaching a peak of 19 per cent in 1987. Between 1980 and 1989 Moscow absorbed 78 per cent of Bulgarian electronics exports. But this success was a mixed blessing. The Bulgarian strategy rested on science-intensive commodities like electronic calculators, micro-computers, and CDs, but their production relied heavily on semiconductors, memory chips, and other basic elements imported from Western hard-currency countries, while the output was sold to the Soviet Union and yielded roubles. In a daring 1988 analysis, Bulgarian economists accused electronics and other high-tech branches of bringing larger expenses but not higher efficiency. Even as late as the 1980s many of the quality and incentive problems of the Bulgarian electronics industry remained. In 1986 Zhivkov himself confessed that 'the reliability and the quality of the devices are still the Achilles heel of our electronics' (Ivanov, 2008, pp. 253–4).

In summary, Soviet support was essential for Bulgaria's industrialization. The USSR provided cheap loans, acted as a guarantor for Western loans, granted explicit and implicit price subsidies, permitted specialization in several strategic industries, and offered a vast market for Bulgarian manufacturing exports. Last but not least, it supplied cheap oil that Sofia could re-export, thus financing, at least

---

[9] Coordinating Committee for Multilateral Export Controls.

partially, its machinery imports from the West. However, in less than one year Gorbachev ended this industrialization strategy. Soviet oil and trade subsidies flows dried up. After a decade of significant trade deficits, all interim commercial loans were swiftly called back and Sofia had to transfer $1.2 billion to the ailing USSR during the last two years of the Communist regime.

Taking Net Material Product (NMP), the conceptual equivalent of Western GDP, Romania and Bulgaria posted the highest growth rates of all East European centrally planned economies during 1950–89, 8.2 and 6.9 per cent respectively (Kolodko, 2000, p. 9).[10] Although they were initially 'peasant nations', by 1989 the share of industry in total employment was as high in Romania and Bulgaria as in long-established industrial countries like Czechoslovakia (Table 5.5). After 1989 both states experienced the strongest contraction of industry of all European transition economies, apart from the former USSR (Table 5.5). While in Central European transition economies de-industrialization during 1989–2000 was associated with expanding service sectors, agricultural employment shares started to grow significantly in Bulgaria and Romania. During the 1990s de-industrialization in SEE did not represent a successful structural change towards a highly productive modern service economy, but simply economic decline.

In 1990, Bulgaria and Romania displayed by far the highest degree of over-industrialization in a sample of 28 Eurasian transition economies, matched only by three other states (de Melo et al., 2001, p. 5). The main reason for the subsequent severe contraction of industry in socialist Southeast Europe was that these resource-poor economies had pursued an outdated Marxist-Stalinist industrialization model, based on energy and raw material consuming heavy industries, more than any other European COMECON state. The Soviet model was tailored for large, resource-rich, more or less autarkic economies—quite the opposite of SEE. The adjustment to new market conditions was thus extremely painful for the Bulgarian and Romanian manufacturing sectors, and this was exacerbated by delayed reforms to establish the institutional framework of a market economy. It was not until the end of the 1990s that industry finally started to recover.

5.3.2 Yugoslavia's Enforced Industrialization: A 'Third Way' to Industrialization and De-industrialization

Around 1975, economists spoke of a 'Yugoslav miracle' (Sapir, 1980; Moore, 1980), but recent accounts describe Yugoslav industrialization as failed modernization (Lydall, 1989; Dyker, 1990; Bićanić and Škreb, 1994; Allcock, 2000). Even if Yugoslav annual manufacturing growth rates came close to 10 per cent during 1950–73, 'the Yugoslav record appears to be unexceptional by standards of the noncommunist countries in the postwar period', considering the low initial level of development (Moore, 1980, p. 53). In a global perspective Yugoslavia experienced the 'standard postwar growth miracle' of an emerging economy. In contrast,

---

[10] The Maddison data on GDP per capita fully support these findings.

Table 5.5. Employment share of industry in former European COMECON states

	Employment share		Reduction
	1989	2000	
Bulgaria	45.2	28.3	−16.9
Romania	43.4	26.2	−17.2
Poland	36.9	30.8	−6.1
Slovakia	44.9	37.3	−7.6
Czech Republic	44.7	39.5	−5.2
Hungary	35.0	33.7	−1.3

Source: Raiser et al. (2003, pp. 43–5).

Yugoslav manufacturing slowed down after 1973 and even became negative just before the state's break-up in 1991 (Table 5.6). In the early 1990s manufacturing collapsed, during a transition crisis aggravated by civil wars. Manufacturing output started to increase again in Former Yugoslavia from the mid-1990s.

After 1945 Yugoslav Communists implemented the Soviet model as fast as their sister parties in other socialist SEEs. Rapid industrialization at any cost was the main economic priority in a heavily war-damaged country. Industrial production reached pre-war levels as early as 1947, when the first five-year plan (FYP) was implemented. Extremely high industrial investment, mainly in the capital goods sector, character-ized the first FYP. As in other socialist countries, this industrialization strategy required massive reductions in already low consumption levels, creating the same perilous economic imbalances as in Bulgaria and Romania (Allcock, 2000, pp. 70–6).

The break with the USSR in 1948 did not endanger industrialization. Yugoslavia immediately received substantial Western aid, and cooperation with the West was seen as the best strategy to build up a diversified modern industry. Whereas an earlier 1930s attempt to industrialize rapidly was restricted by an inability to export or borrow, easy external credit and improved access to Western markets now made rapid industrial-ization without abnormally low living standards possible (Allcock, 2000, pp. 72–3).

The introduction of workers' self-management (WSM) in 1950 ended the strict centrally planned economy and was greeted enthusiastically by non-orthodox Marxist theorists as 'third way' between capitalism and Soviet-style state socialism. Nonetheless, industrialization in Yugoslavia remained under government control, and channelling as many resources as possible into industry remained the top priority of economic policy (Moore, 1980, pp. 15–28, 151–64).[11] Before the economic reforms of the 1960s, central government held real wages low and retained control of nearly all investment funds via the taxation of corporate profits, while comprehensive price controls accelerated the growth of manufacturing.

[11] State enterprises became formally independent but were not privatized. Especially in industry, Yugoslav 'market socialism' prevented free market access of private entrepreneurs, and business bankruptcies did not occur.

Table 5.6. Industrial and manufacturing growth in Yugoslavia according to different sources using official and revised data, 1950–88

	Industrial output	Manufacturing output		Revised manufacturing output	
	Mitchell	Bénétrix et al.	OECD	Moore	Moore and SZS/ Eurostat
1950–73	8.5%	9.8%		1952–65	11.1%
1952–73			10.1%	8.8%	1965–75	6.0%
1973–90	2.0%	3.7%		1978–85	3.2%
1973–88			4.4%	1985–88	0.7%

Sources: Bénétrix et al. (2015); Mitchell (2003, pp. 425–6); OECD, Yugoslavia 1962, 1970, 1974, 1976, 1984/ 85, 1989/90, Table: Industrial Output (Appendix); 1952–75: Moore (1980, p. 42); 1978–88: SZS/Eurostat (1990).

Interestingly, the first Communist FYP (1947–52) continued the Stojadinović government's industrialization plan of 1935–9, which had promoted the development of energy production and heavy industry, based on the exploitation of domestic natural resources. This inward-oriented dual strategy, whose core element was import substitution, broke with Yugoslavia's traditional role as an exporter of raw materials. Following rapid electrification, coal, metallurgy, and metal-using industries were all developed. The next wave of industrialization comprised chemical branches, more sophisticated metal industries like automotive manufacturing as well as electrical industries. The emphasis gradually shifted from industrial raw materials and semi-manufactures to more highly fabricated products. The Marxist preference for capital goods industries remained, and contributed to extraordinarily high Yugoslav investment rates (Moore, 1980, pp. 18–20, 40–56, 93–106; Bićanić and Škreb, 1994, p. 151). Overall, Yugoslavian post-war industrialization resembled that in Bulgaria and Romania.

Until the mid-1960s Yugoslav manufacturing growth was based on a combination of extraordinary factor intensification—mainly capital deepening—and substantial technical change.[12] After 1965 a growing number of internal (political) and external (economic) factors mutually reinforced each other to slow industrial growth. Far-reaching reforms of the WSM system, aiming to decentralize economic decision making, did not create integrated domestic labour and capital markets but reinforced 'economic parochialism' (Allcock, 2000, p. 77) and economic disintegration. Even if the 'liberal' reforms of the 1960s abolished the central General

[12] The industrial capital stock increased by about 10 per cent per annum until the mid-1960s and was still growing at around 8 per cent per annum up to the end of the 1970s (Moore, 1980, p. 104; Lydall, 1989, p. 41). The contribution of technical change to manufacturing growth *c.*1955–65 was around 40 per cent (Sapir, 1980, p. 301; Moore, 1980, pp. 125–32), significantly more than in the contemporary USSR. Further research is necessary to see whether this was due to better access to modern Western technology, or whether the system of workers' self-management despite all its deficiencies was superior to central planning in allocating investment funds.

Investment Fund, they established special public investment banks controlled by large enterprises, the biggest debtors, and (local) party and municipal authorities. Inefficient capital-biased factor allocation got worse since post-reform investment financing was not governed by economic criteria, and soft budget constraints persisted. This, combined with low factor substitution elasticities, explains part of the slowdown in manufacturing growth after 1966 (Sapir, 1980, p. 294).

However, slowing TFP growth after 1970 seems more important in explaining the Yugoslav growth slowdown (Nishimizu and Page, 1982). With the 'digital revolution' Yugoslavia's manufacturing sector increasingly lost the ability to implement 'best practices'. Moreover, deteriorating terms of trade after the 1973 oil crisis demanded a swift structural adjustment away from energy-intensive manufacturing focused too much on outdated heavy industries.

However, excessive politicization of economic decision making at all levels of society, combined with rising ethnic tensions, prevented economic reforms until it was too late (Allcock, 2000, pp. 89–90).[13] The new constitution of 1974 and the 1976 Law of Associated Labour aggravated the defects of WSM and blocked true market reforms. According to Allcock (2000, p. 93), 'the entire tendency of these legislative changes was to promote rigidity and stasis by bringing into being a set of organizational forms of truly bewildering complexity', the opposite of what was required by a manufacturing sector facing increasing international competition.

Yugoslav industrialization policy aimed to develop the poor South via the creation of an industrial base. Huge public investment in manufacturing was supposed to lead to income convergence, but the opposite happened: there was divergence during 1950–90 (Vojnić, 1996). One reason was that less profitable heavy industries and mining were promoted in the poor South, in line with Marxist beliefs, whereas more profitable new industries developed in the North. Moreover, the lack of an integrated domestic labour market combined with significantly higher population growth in the South exacerbated regional divergence (Allcock, 2000, pp. 83–6).

The decline of Yugoslav manufacturing showed striking similarities to developments in Bulgaria and Romania. Yugoslavia's reaction to the first oil shock in 1973 was not to adjust by improving energy efficiency or raising exports, but to borrow abroad to bridge allegedly 'short-term' liquidity shortages. The continuing expansion of energy-consuming if 'modern' heavy industries like aluminium smelting contributed to a rising external deficit (Allcock, 2000, pp. 93–4). Yugoslavia was thus particularly hard hit by the 1979 debt crisis. During the 1980s the downward trend in TFP was for the first time accompanied by reduced gross fixed investment (Lydall, 1989, p. 41), and manufacturing declined. Industry only returned to growth after the civil wars of the 1990s; only Slovenia and Croatia had by 2007 surpassed pre-war levels of industrial output.

---

[13] Interestingly, WSM was the unspoken blueprint for many economic reforms aiming at making centrally planned economies in the Soviet sphere more efficient without introducing market reforms. The results of these 'liberal' reforms during the 1960s and 1970s were as unsatisfactory as in Yugoslavia.

5.3.3 From Europe's Most Dynamic Economy to
De-industrialization: The Case of Greece

No European economy enjoyed more rapid growth than Greece between 1950 and 1973 (Crafts and Toniolo, 2010, pp. 301–2, 306–7).[14] In contrast to the other, non-capitalist SEEs, enforced industrialization was not the cause of this exceptional growth experience. The share of secondary production and manufacturing in GDP changed only marginally *c.*1950–85 (Figure 5.1). Continuing a nineteenth-century trend, structural transformation in post-war Greece meant the transition from an agrarian to a service, rather than an industrial economy (Frangiadis, 2007; Louri and Pepelasis-Minoglou, 2002). An industrial 'take-off' only took place *c.*1963–75. From the mid-1980s the Greek economy de-industrialized, and by 2010 it was the only one in the region whose share of industry in GDP was substantially lower than six decades earlier (Table 5.4). Most experts have inter-preted Greek de-industrialization as effective structural change, helping Greece to avoid costly 'overindustrialization' and to exploit 'the opportunities of the ICT era' (Crafts and Toniolo, 2010, p. 308). However, the ongoing Greek economic crisis has given rise to doubts regarding this optimistic interpretation: was the rise of the Greek service sector really a good substitute for modern manufacturing?[15]

No other Southeast European economy managed the transition from a low-productivity agrarian economy to modern growth more smoothly than Greece. There was no forced reduction of living standards to build up a modern capital stock, because a costly 'industrialization first' strategy was rejected. Extensive American aid was all-important, especially during the critical first years after war, occupation, and civil war (Stathakis, 1993; 1995). American experts thought that Greece only had a limited economic potential that did not justify channelling resources into industry. Macroeconomic stabilization, agricultural development, the reconstruction of destroyed infrastructure, and the achievement of energy security based on domestic resources formed the top priorities. At the time this prudent 'neglect of industrial development' was heavily criticized in Greece by left and right alike. However, growth was achieved without industrialization. Due to the fact that savings and exports increased, and import substitution took place to a limited degree, Greece's dependence on external sources to offset balance of payments deficits was reduced substantially (Adelman and Chenery, 1966, pp. 2, 16–19; Ellis, 1964, pp. 238–41; Stathakis, 1995). Thus, Greece's economic development in the 1950s represented a successful Western antithesis to Stalinist heavy-industry-based industrialization at any costs. However, industrialization returned to the agenda at the start of the 1960s, as an export-led growth strategy

[14] We would like to express our deep gratitude to Leda Papastefanaki, who guided us perfectly through the rich Greek literature on Greek industrialization.
[15] The share of total services in Greek GDP increased more or less continuously between 1951–3 and 2010–12, from 43 to 82 per cent. Secondary production's share roughly stayed constant, decreasing from 23 to 14 per cent between 1984–6 and 2010–12. Primary production's share dropped continuously from 36 to 3 per cent (own calculation based on data from Louri and Pepelasis-Minoglou (2002, p. 334) and World Bank: World Development Indicators).

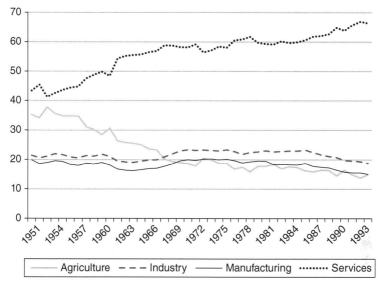

Fig. 5.1. Sectoral composition of Greek GDP, 1951–94 (per cent)
Source: Louri and Pepelasis-Minoglou (2002, p. 334).

based on manufacturing seemed to be the most promising way to fight the notoriously high trade deficit (Papandreou, 1962, pp. 101–6; Ellis, 1964, pp. 240–52).

At the time Greek manufacturing produced low-quality consumer goods almost exclusively destined for the highly protected domestic market (Ellis, 1964, pp. 243–5). Making a competitive Greek industry the principal protagonist of an export-led growth strategy was an ambitious aim. Manufacturing largely involved pre-modern, family-based, small-scale artisanal production, even though a few joint-stock companies had emerged. Many business relationships were family-centred and personalized to a degree that undermined the efficient functioning of markets (Ellis, 1964; Coutsoumaris, 1963). A system of output, credit, and factor markets had developed in manufacturing which often created local family-based monopolies (Ellis, 1964, p. 121). The Greek state protected this system. 'Greek mercantilism' entailed a restrictively managed licence system—the so-called 'expediency licences'. The state could control prices of manufactured goods. Established entrepreneurs with good relationships with the administration cooperated with banks' representatives in local markets to their advantage, restricting market access (Ellis, 1964; Coutsoumaris, 1963): 'economic parochialism' wasn't only a problem in socialist Yugoslavia. Furthermore, an underdeveloped capital market hostile to industrial finance implied that necessary investments, including foreign direct investment, failed to be realized (Ellis, 1964).

In the early 1960s the opportunity arose to remove these growth-impeding rigidities and build up modern export-oriented manufacturing. Most important was the Agreement of Association between Greece and the European Economic Community (EEC) which came into force on 1 November 1962. The following years saw a substantial reduction of Greece's extreme protectionism; the agreement and simultaneous deregulations induced a little Greek 'take-off' between *c.*1964–5 and 1973/5 (Franghiadis, 2007, pp. 185–6; Louri and Pepelasis-Minoglou, 2002, p. 333; Ellis, 1964). Greek capital formation accelerated substantially during the 1960s.[16] However, the share of industry in total investment was still very low compared to socialist SEEs, increasing only from 22.0 to 29.2 per cent between 1962–4 and 1972–4. Over the entire period 1961–88, the bulk of investment—63.4 per cent—went to the service sector.[17]

In the early 1960s the combination of legislation that was very friendly toward foreign direct investment (FDI), low wages, and steadily improving access to a large market attracted substantial FDI in manufacturing.[18] In 1962–4 about 62 per cent of manufacturing investment was of foreign origin (Germidis and Negroponti-Delivanis, 1975, p. 193; Louri and Pepelasis-Minoglou, 2002, pp. 332–7). Foreign ownership in Greek industry increased substantially during the 1960s. FDI diversified and modernized Greek industry (Tsaliki, 1991, pp. 123–4). However, foreign investment was concentrated in a few 'modern' branches like chemicals (including petroleum), basic metals, and transport equipment, but avoided traditional light industries, which nevertheless remained important (Germidis and Negroponti-Delivanis, 1975, p. 59).[19] Thus, small-scale structures and 'family bias' persisted in most Greek industries (Germidis and Negroponti-Delivanis, 1975, p. 192).

The Greek industrial take-off from *c.*1964–5 to 1973–5 led to export-led growth with manufacturing featuring prominently.[20] However, as in other SEEs, exports never matched strongly rising imports of consumer and investment goods (Tsaliki, 1991, p. 10; Germidis and Negroponti-Delivanis, 1975, p. 192). The hope that export-oriented industrialization could end the chronic payments deficit was not fulfilled.

---

[16] According to Tsaliki (1991, pp. 109–10), the annual growth rate of the real domestic non-residential net capital stock jumped from 2.4 per cent in 1951–61 to 10.0 per cent in 1961–71.

[17] Own calculation based on data from OECD, Greece 1969. In Romania the share of industry in total gross investment rose from 42.8 per cent in 1960 to 53.0 per cent in 1973 (own calculation; data for Romania from Tsantis and Pepper, 1979, pp. 562–7).

[18] The Greek state confined itself to the creation of good basic conditions for foreign industrial investment and refrained from any target-oriented industrialization policy (Ellis, 1964, pp. 272–301; Germidis and Negropontis-Delivanis, 1975, pp. 38–43).

[19] Traditionally important consumer industries (food and tobacco; textiles; clothing and footwear) still produced 45 per cent of manufacturing output in 1975 and their share remained stable during the subsequent phase of de-industrialization. Industries attracting the bulk of foreign investment (chemicals; metallurgy; machinery) slightly increased their share in manufacturing during the 'take-off' from 24 per cent (1960) to 31 per cent (1970). This percentage remained fairly stable afterwards (Louri and Pepelasis-Minoglou, 2002, p. 336).

[20] Within only ten years the share of manufacturing products in all commodity exports jumped from 10 per cent (1960) to 41 per cent (1970), increasing further to 51 per cent in 1980. The share of exports and imports in GDP increased continuously from 21.8 to 47.8 per cent between 1950 and 1985 (Tsaliki, 1991, p. 10).

Greek TFP developed favourably during the period 1950–73, stagnated during the subsequent fifteen years, and rose again after 1990 (Tsaliki, 1991, pp. 151–84; Crafts and Toniolo 2010, pp. 306–7). Productivity increased in all industrial sectors during 1958–80, most spectacularly in new branches like metallurgy, chemicals, rubber-plastics, and electric machinery (Panethimitakis, 1993). During *c*.1950–75 technical progress in Greek manufacturing depended almost entirely on capital imports connected with capital-using, non-neutral technical change (Lianos, 1976).

By the mid-1970s a decade of rapid industrialization and expanding manufactured exports to new markets in the EEC and the Middle East made experts optimistic that full-scale industrialization—built on 'modern' heavy industries—was possible and desirable for Greece. The optimism was virtually boundless (Zolotas, 1976; 1978, p. 49; Germidis and Negroponti-Delivanis, 1975, pp. 196–9). However, Greece deindustrialized. After 1974 FDI became less important in manufacturing, which negatively affected technical progress, productivity, and capital formation (Tsaliki, 1991, pp. 9, 124–5, 168–9, 180–1). The rise of Asian manufacturing had a strong adverse impact on FDI flows across the European periphery, but post-1974 democratic Greek governments did not encourage FDI, or facilitate the emergence of domestic high-tech industries.

Further research is needed to analyse the ways in which external developments (e.g. globalization) and internal developments interacted to produce the long decline of Greek manufacturing. In this context, one has to ask to what extent 'industrial inertia' caused by social and political blockages within Greek society prevented necessary structural change, resulting in radical de-industrialization. Today even the necessary structural changes in manufacturing could not substantially contribute to short-run economic recovery, simply because of the small size of the manufacturing sector. But in the long run, a competitive manufacturing sector could help to achieve self-sustained growth in a diversified Greek economy.

5.4 CONCLUSIONS

By the mid-1970s the rapidly industrializing economies of Southeast Europe seemed to be catching up successfully to the leading economies of the continent. In the opinion of contemporary experts it was only a matter of time before they would develop into mature, diversified industrial economies similar to West Germany, which in fact served as the role model for successful development in the region. Internationally competitive manufacturing sectors creating high domestic value added would end once and for all the 'eternal menace' of vulnerable Southeast European economies: notoriously high trade deficits.

However, the end of the long post-war boom disclosed fundamental weaknesses in the manufacturing sectors of all Southeast European economies which had never been redressed. Exports rose more strongly than imports during the industrializing 1960s, but the trade deficits never disappeared and rose to threatening levels following the oil crises. Industrialization never increased manufactured exports sufficiently. On the contrary, as Southeast Europe's industries lost their competitive advantage during the 1970s and 1980s, manufacturing became a burden, seriously aggravating balance of payment difficulties to the point of generating fully fledged balance of payments crises. All emerging industrial economies faced intensified international competition as a result of globalization, but no Southeast European country was able to carry out the structural changes required for its manufacturing to remain internationally competitive.

Of all SEEs, only Bulgaria made serious efforts to manage the transition to less energy-intensive and more knowledge-based modern industries, but it failed. Socialist economies were incapable of coping with changing factor prices after the first oil crisis in 1973, unable to improve their low energy efficiency. To make things worse, they did not even change their industrialization strategy, further relying on energy-wasting heavy industries. Under these circumstances, the continuing adherence to an outdated concept of rapid industrialization was a major reason leading to trade deficits and international borrowing during the second half of the 1970s. The debt crisis of 1979 hit all socialist SEEs hard, and initiated a decade of manufacturing stagnation which later became contraction.

The negative impact of industrialization on foreign trade imbalances, especially in socialist SEEs, was due to the inflexibility of centrally planned economies which prevented their adjusting hopelessly outdated industrialization strategies in a radically changing global context. However, the Greek and Yugoslav examples suggest that de-industrialization was not simply caused by a 'system failure' that could be easily addressed by 'setting institutions right'. A deep-rooted cause was 'economic parochialism', a tendency to maintain loss-making industries at any cost and to create 'closed shops' of all varieties; social inertia which obstructed necessary structural change in manufacturing. Under these circumstances the Greek solution of radical de-industrialization was the most efficient. The former socialist economies were forced to follow the Greek path during the transition crisis of the 1990s.

Despite a strongly improving human capital endowment, manufacturing in SEE never managed the transition from low- to high(er)-quality production. As a result Southeast European manufacturing lost important markets in the booming Middle East after 1973. This was especially true for engineering, which was seen as the leading sector and which despite many efforts never was able to gain a foothold in Western markets. In contrast, Asian producers conquered the low and medium price segments of Western markets offering reasonable quality. The inability to adjust manufacturing to rising quality demands on global markets not only in socialist economies but in Greece as well suggests historical deficiencies in the region independent of any economic system.

Since the end of the 1990s, manufacturing in SEE has started to recover. TFP increases have become the main source of growth all over the region, and restructured industries have adjusted to world markets (Alam et al., 2008). However, the great period of Southeast European industrialization is over. Industry is no longer the most important sector, and the number of persons employed in Southeast European industry has contracted by approximately one-third since the mid-1990s.[21] Sufficient alternative employment to compensate for severe industrial job losses has not yet emerged.

REFERENCES

Adelman, I. and Chenery, H. B. (1966). Foreign aid and economic development: the case of Greece. *Review of Economics and Statistics* 48, 1–19.

Alam, A., Casero, P. A., Khan, F. and Udomsaph, C. (2008). *Unleashing Prosperity: Productivity Growth in Eastern Europe and the Former Soviet Union*. Washington, DC: World Bank.

Allcock, J. B. (2000). *Explaining Yugoslavia*. London: Hurst & Co.

Alton, T. P. (1981). Production and resource allocation in Eastern Europe: performance, problems, and prospects. In *East European Economic Assessment: A Compendium of Papers* (Ed., Joint Economic Committee Congress of the United States). Washington, DC: US Government Printing Office, 348–408.

Alton, T. P. (1989). Comparison of overall economic performance in the East European countries. In *The Economies of Eastern Europe under Gorbachev's influence* (Ed., R. Weichhardt). Brussels: NATO.

Alton, T. P., Bass, E. M., Badach, K., and Lazarcik, G. (1985). East European GDP by origin and domestic final use of gross product 1965–1984, *Research Project on National Income in East Central Europe, Occasional Paper* No. 89.

Axienciuc, V. (2012). *Produsul Intern Brut al României 1862–2000*. Serii Statistice Seculare şi Argumente Metodologice, vol. 1–2. Bucureşti: Editura Economică.

Ban, C. (2012). Sovereign debt, austerity, and regime change: the case of Nicolae Ceauşescu's Romania. *East European Politics and Societies and Cultures* 26, 743–76.

Bénétrix, A. S., O'Rourke, K. H., and Williamson, J. G. (2015). The spread of manufacturing to the poor periphery 1870–2007. *Open Economies Review* 26, 1–37.

Berend, I. T. (1996). *Central and Eastern Europe, 1944–1993: Detour from the Periphery to the Periphery*. Cambridge: Cambridge University Press.

Berend, I. and Ránki, G. (1982). *The European Periphery and Industrialization 1780–1914*. Cambridge: Cambridge University Press.

Berov, L. and Dimitrov, D. (1990). *Development of Bulgarian Industry*. Sofia: Science and Culture Publishing [in Bulgarian].

Bićanić, I. and Škreb, M. (1994). The Yugoslav economy from amalgamation to disintegration: failed efforts at molding a new economic space 1991–91. In *Economic Transformations in East and Central Europe* (Ed., Good, D. F.). London and New York: Routledge, 147–62.

Chakalov, A. (1946). *National Income and Outlay of Bulgaria 1924–1945*. Sofia: Knipegraph.

Christodoulaki, O. (2001). Industrial growth in Greece between the wars: a new perspective. *European Review of Economic History* 5, 61–89.

Coutsoumaris, G. (1963). *The Morphology of Greek Industry*. Athens: Centre of Economic Research.

---

[21] In Bulgaria, Greece, and Romania the number of persons employed in industry decreased by 24.4, 22.0, and 37.4 per cent between 1995 and 2013; own calculation based on data from Eurostat.

Crafts, N. and Toniolo, G. (2010). Aggregate growth, 1950–2005. In *The Cambridge Economic History of Modern Europe*, Vol. 2: *1870 to the Present* (Eds, Broadberry, S. and O'Rourke, K. H.). Cambridge: Cambridge University Press, 296–332.

De Melo, M., Denizer, C., Gelb, A., and Tenev, S. (2001). Circumstance and choice: the role of initial conditions and policies in transition economies, *World Bank Economic Review* 15, 1–31.

Dyker, D. A. (1990). *Yugoslavia: Socialism, Development and Debt*. London and New York: Routledge.

Ehrlich, E. (1992). Economic growth in Eastern Central Europe after World War II. *Working Papers of the Institute for World Economics, Hungarian Academy of Sciences* No. 7.

Ellis, H. (1964). *Industrial Capital in Greek Development*. Athens: Contos Press.

Feiwel, G. R. (1982). Economic development and planning in Bulgaria in the 1970s. In *The East European Economies in the 1970s* (Eds, Nove, A., Höhmann, H.-H., and Seiden-stecher, G.). London: Butterworth, 215–52.

Franghiadis, A. (2007). *Elliniki oikonomia, 19os–20os aionas: Apo ton agona tis anexartisias stin oikonomiki kai knomismatiki enosi tis* [Greek Economy, 19th–20th Century: From the Struggle for Independence to European Economic and Monetary Union]. Athens: Ekdosis Nefeli [in Greek].

Germidis, D. A. and Negroponti-Delivanis, M. (1975). *Industrialization, Employment and Income Distribution in Greece: A Case Study*. Paris: OECD.

Gerschenkron, A. (1962). Some aspects of industrialization in Bulgaria, 1878–1939. In Gerschenkron, A., *Economic Backwardness in Historical Perspective: A Book of Essays*. Cambridge MA: Belknap Press, 198–234.

Ivanov, M. (2008). *Reformism without Reforms: The Political Economy of Bulgarian Communism, 1963–1989*. Sofia: Ciela [in Bulgarian].

Ivanov, M. (2012). *The Gross Domestic Product of Bulgaria 1870–1945*. Sofia: Ciela.

Ivanov, M. and Tooze, A. (2007). Convergence or decline on Europe's Southeastern periphery? Agriculture, population, and GDP in Bulgaria, 1892–1945. *Journal of Economic History* 67, 672–704.

Jackson, M. R. and Lampe, J. R. (1983). The evidence of industrial growth in Southeastern Europe before the Second World War. *East European Quarterly* 16, 385–415.

Keyder, C. (1991). Creation and destruction of forms of manufacturing: the Ottoman example. In *Between Development and Underdevelopment: The Precocious Attempts at Industrialization at the Periphery 1800–1870* (Ed, Batou J.). Geneva: Librarie Droz, 157–79.

Kolodko, G. W. (2000). Globalization and catching-up: from recession to growth in transition economies. *IMF Working Paper*/00/100.

Kostelenos, G. (1995). *Money and Output in Modern Greece: 1858–1938*. Athens: KEPE.

Lampe, J. R. (1975). Varieties of unsuccessful industrialization: the Balkan states before 1914. *Journal of Economic History* 35, 56–85.

Lampe, J. R. (1986). *The Bulgarian Economy in the Twentieth Century*. London: Croom Helm.

Lampe, J. R. and Jackson, M. (1982). *Balkan Economic History, 1550–1950: From Imperial Borderlands to Developing Nations*. Bloomington, IN: Indiana University Press.

Lazarcik, G. and Wynnyczuk, A. (1968). Bulgaria: growth of industrial output, 1939 and 1948–1965. *Occasional Papers of the Research Project on National Income in East Central Europe* No. 27.

Lianos, T. P. (1976). Factor augmentation in Greek manufacturing, 1958–1969. *European Economic Review* 8, 15–31.

Louri, H. and Pepelasis-Minoglou, I. (2002). A hesitant evolution: industrialization and de-industrialization in Greece over the long run. *Journal of European Economic History* 31, 321–48.

Lydall, H. (1989). *Yugoslavia in Crisis*. Oxford: Clarendon Press.

Marer, P. (1993). *Historically Planned Economics: A Guide to the Data*. Washington, DC: World Bank.

Mazower, M. (1991). *Greece and the Interwar Economic Crisis*. Oxford: Clarendon Press.

Mitchell, B. R. (2003). *International Historical Statistics: Europe 1750–2000*. New York: Palgrave Macmillan.

Montias, J. M. (1967). *Economic Development in Communist Romania*. Cambridge: MIT Press.

Montias, J. M. (1988). Industrial policy and foreign trade in Bulgaria. *East European Politics and Societies* 2, 522–57.

Moore, J. H. (1980). *Growth with Self-Management: Yugoslav Industrialization 1952–1975*. Stanford, CA: Hoover Institution Press.

Moore, W. E. (1945). *Economic Demography of Eastern and Southern Europe*. Geneva: League of Nations.

Nishimizu, M. and Page, J. M. (1982). Total factor productivity, technological progress and technical efficiency: dimensions of productivity change in Yugoslavia, 1965–78. *Economic Journal* 92, 920–36.

OECD (multiple years). *Greece: Economic Surveys by the OECD*. Paris: OECD, 1962 and years following.

OECD (multiple years). *Yugoslavia: Economic Surveys by the OECD*. Paris: OECD, 1962 and years following.

Palairet, M. (1983a). The decline of the old Balkan woollen industries 1870–1914. *Vierteljahrschrift für Sozial- und Wirtschaftsgeschichte* 70, 331–62.

Palairet, M. (1983b). Land, labour, and industrial progress in Bulgaria and Serbia before 1914. *Journal of European Economic History* 12, 163–85.

Palairet, M. (1997). *The Balkan Economies c.1800–1914: Evolution without Development*. Cambridge: Cambridge University Press.

Pamuk, Ş. (1986). The decline and resistance of Ottoman cotton textiles, 1820–1913. *Explorations in Economic History* 23, 205–25.

Pamuk, Ş. and Williamson, J. G. (2011). Ottoman de-industrialization, 1800–1913: assessing the magnitude, impact, and response. *Economic History Review* 64, 159–84.

Panethimitakis, A. J. (1993). Direct 'versus' total labour productivity in Greek manufacturing: 1958–1980. *Economic Systems Research* 5, 79–93.

Papandreou, A. G. (1962). *A Strategy for Greek Economic Development*. Athens: Contos Press.

Petmezas, S. (2011). Introduction. In *The Economic Development of Southeast Europe in the 19th Century* (Eds, Eldem, E. and Petmezas, S.). Athens: Alpha Bank, Historical Archives, 19–46.

Quataert, D. (1994). Manufacturing. In *An Economic and Social History of the Ottoman Empire, 1300–1914* (Eds, Inalcik, H. and Quataert, D.). Cambridge: Cambridge University Press, 888–933.

Raiser, M., Schaffer, M. E. and Schuchardt J. (2003). Benchmarking structural change in transition. *CEPR Discussion Paper* No. 3820.

Rangelova, R. (2000). Bulgaria's national income and economic growth 1913–45. *Review of Income and Wealth* 46, 231–48.

Ránki, G. and Tomaszewski, J. (1986). The role of the state in industry, banking and trade. In *The Economic History of Eastern Europe 1919–1975*, Vol. 2 (Eds, Kaser, M. C. and Radice, E. A.). Oxford: Clarendon Press, 3–48.

Sapir, A. (1980). Economic growth and factor substitution: what happened to the Yugoslav miracle? *Economic Journal* 90, 294–313.

Stajić, S. (1959). *Nacionalni Dohodak Jugoslavije 1923–1939 u Stalnim i Tekućim Cenama* [National Product of Yugoslavia 1923–1939]. Belgrade: Ekonomski Institut NR Srbije.

Stathakis, G. (1993). The Marshall Plan in Greece. In *Le Plan Marshall* (Ed., Ministère de l'Économie). Paris: Comité pour l' Histoire Économique et Financière, 577–589.

Stathakis, G. (1995). US economic policies in post civil-war Greece, 1949–1953: stabilization and monetary reform. *Journal of European Economic History* 3, 375–404.

Stoilov, S. (1986). *Scientific-Technical Revolution and the Strategy for Social-Economic Development of Peoples Republic of Bulgaria*. Sofia: Bulgarian Academy of Sciences Publishing [in Bulgarian].

SZS (Savezni Zavod ZA Statistiku)/Eurostat (1990). *The Comparative Study between the EEC/SFRY in the Field of Industry in 1978–1988*. Workshop at Beograd, 11 and 12 October 1990.

Teichova, A. (1985). Industry. In *The Economic History of Eastern Europe 1919–1975*, Vol. 1 (Eds, Kaser, M. C. and Radice, E. A.). Oxford: Clarendon Press, 222–322 (reprinted 2006).

Tsaliki, P. V. (1991). *The Greek Economy: Sources of Growth in the Postwar Era*. New York: Praeger.

Tsantis, A. C. and Pepper, R. (1979). *Romania: The Industrialization of an Agrarian Economy under Socialist Planning*. Washington, DC: World Bank.

Turnock, D. (1977). The industrial development of Romania from the unification of the principalities to the Second World War. In *An Historical Geography of the Balkans* (Ed., Carter, F. W.). London: Academic Press, 319–78.

Vinski, I. (1967). The distribution of Yugoslavia's national income by social classes in 1938. *Review of Income and Wealth* 3, 259–81.

Vojnić, D. (1996). Disparity and disintegration: the economic dimension of Yugoslav demise. *Ekonomski Pregled* 47, 528–63.

Zolotas, X. (1976). Guidelines for industrial development in Greece. *Bank of Greece: Papers and Lectures* No. 31, Athens: Bank of Greece.

Zolotas, X. (1978). The positive contribution of Greece to the European Community. *Bank of Greece: Papers and Lectures* No. 40, Athens: Bank of Greece.

6

The Industrialization of Italy, 1861–1971

Matteo Gomellini and Gianni Toniolo

6.1 INTRODUCTION

Between 2007 and 2012, as a result of its longest (and possibly deepest) depression since the country's unification (in 1861), Italy's manufacturing output decreased by more than 21 per cent (stats.oecd.org).[1] Even so, according to UNCTAD, in 2012 Italy was still the world's sixth largest manufacturer, slightly ahead of the United Kingdom and France, each of the three countries accounting for about 3 per cent of total world manufacturing production. This is hardly surprising given Italy's size and its natural endowments. Poor in raw materials and (outside the Po Valley) in agricultural land suitable for modern capitalist agriculture, Italy was bound to rely on manufacturing for its 'modern economic growth'. In 2011, value added by industry still accounted for 18.6 per cent of GDP in Italy as against 16.2 in the USA, 14.9 in Great Britain, and 12.5 in France (OECD, 2013). In order to prosper, as Carlo Cipolla famously said, 'Italy must manufacture goods that please the world.'

For three centuries (from around 1300 to 1600) Italy was at the core of Europe's economic activity, particularly in manufacturing. Over the following centuries the country gradually slipped to the 'periphery'. At the time of its political unification in 1861–70, its GDP per person was about 50 per cent of that of Great Britain. In the next century, Italy's convergence with the most prosperous European countries was broadly as fast as might have been expected given its initial backwardness (Toniolo, 2013). By the 1980s GDP per person was roughly similar to that of Great Britain. The history of the Italian economy moving from periphery back to core is the subject of various works (e.g. Zamagni, 1993; Castronovo, 1995; Toniolo, 2013): this chapter focuses on the role played by industrial production, particularly manufacturing, in Italy's catch-up growth.

The quantitative history of Italy's industrialization, while not matching that of Britain and the United States, is as rich as, or richer than, that of most of today's OECD countries, thanks to a nineteenth- and early-twentieth-century tradition of descriptive statistics and to the post-war work of the Statistical Office (ISTAT) and

[1] Corresponding author: matteo.gomellini@bancaditalia.it. The views expressed herein are those of the authors and do not reflect the views of the institutions represented.

individual scholars such as Gerschenkron, Fenoaltea, Ercolani, Vitali, and Carreras, to name only those most active in the field of industrial historical statistics. Industrial censuses were taken in 1911, 1921, and 1936–8. After the Second World War industrial statistics were routinely produced by ISTAT. Recently, estimates of industrial productivity growth have been extended back to the 1860s (Broadberry, Giordano, and Zollino, 2013). In this chapter, aggregate industrial value added is taken from the most recent reconstruction of national accounts (Baffigi, 2013);[2] sectoral estimates are those by Ciccarelli and Fenoaltea (2009) for the period 1861–1913; by Carreras and Felice (2012) for the inter-war period; and by ISTAT and Golinelli and Monterastelli (1990) for the second post-war period.

The chapter is organized as follows. Section 6.2 traces aggregate trends in Italian manufacturing output and productivity growth from 1861 to the early 1970s, a time when Italy's industrial system was no longer 'peripheral' by any definition. Section 6.3 focuses on 'modern' vs 'traditional' manufacturing sectors and on utilities. Section 6.4 discusses the impact on industrial output of foreign trade, tariffs, and industrial policy. Sections 6.5 and 6.6 develop a quantitative analysis of regional industrial growth. The final section pulls the main threads together to provide an overall assessment of Italy's industrial growth from the 1860s to the 1960s.

6.2 THE AGGREGATE PICTURE

According to Bairoch (1982), at the time of political unification (1861) Italy's industrial output per person was less than one-sixth (16 per cent) of the UK's, a level roughly similar to that of other peripheral West European countries (Spain, Denmark, Finland, and Norway) and higher than that of both Eastern Europe (Russia, Bulgaria, and Romania) and most non-European countries (including Japan, China, Mexico, South Africa, Australia, and New Zealand). On average Italy was less industrialized than Bairoch's 'developed countries' and more so than his 'third world'. At the same time, Italy's industrial backwardness relative to the leading manufacturing power of the day reflected more than proportionally the country's overall economic backwardness since, according to Maddison (2010), in 1870 Italy's GDP per person was about 50 per cent of the UK's level.

Italy's economic history in the 150 years following unification has been told as 'a tale of convergence and two tails' (Toniolo, 2013). As expected, during this period, GDP and productivity of this 'moderately backward country' *à la* Gerschenkron converged to those of the initially most advanced countries. Convergence in GDP per person, however, took place over the years 1896–1995 while the early post-unification decades and the post-1995 years were characterized by divergence rather than convergence. This section describes Italy's aggregate industrialization against the backdrop of its overall economic development.

---

[2] Industry is here defined as including mining and utilities, but excluding construction. It includes cottage industry and the industrial output of small workshops.

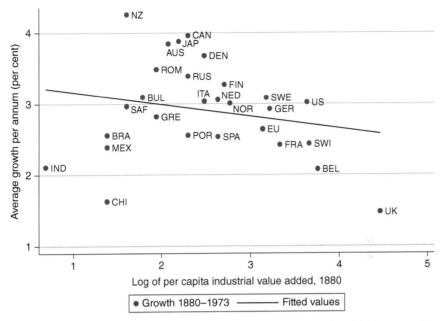

Fig. 6.1. Unconditional convergence of industrial value added (all available countries)

A feature of Italy's industrialization is that its share of world industrial output remained roughly constant over more than two centuries: it was 2.5 per cent in 1750, remained at that level until the First World War, rose to 2.7 per cent in 1938, and reached about 3 per cent in 1973 (Bairoch, 1982). In contrast, the UK's share of world industrial production was 1.9 per cent in 1750, peaked at 22.9 per cent in 1880, and declined thereafter to 4.9 per cent in 1973. A similar inverted U-shape curve characterizes Germany's share of world industry and, to a lesser extent, France's. In other words, Italy followed a pattern roughly similar to that of the overall international industrialization process.

Fig. 6.1 describes the weak unconditional convergence in industrial value added per capita realized in a sample of 30 countries during 1880–1973 (data from Bairoch, 1982).[3] Italy performs roughly as expected given its initial level of backwardness, while initially less industrially developed European countries (e.g. Bulgaria and Russia) seem to converge to the 'core' more rapidly than Italy (and Spain and Portugal).

It is worth noting that, while industrial value added grew faster in Bulgaria and the former Soviet Union than in Italy, these three countries did not significantly catch up with Italy in terms of GDP per person, indicating that Italy's 'modern economic growth' involved more than just industrialization.

---

[3] For a similar exercise, see Chapter 2 in this volume, and Bénétrix, O'Rourke, and Williamson (2015).

Table 6.1. Average annual growth rates of GDP and manufacturing

	GDP	Manufacturing value added	Manufacturing value added per full-time equivalent worker
1861–96	1.7	2.0	2.0
1896–1913	2.2	3.6	2.1
1922–9	4.0	6.3	4.2
1929–39	1.5	2.1	−0.1
1951–70	5.9	8.8	6.0

Sources: Baffigi (2013); Broadberry, Giordano, and Zollino (2013).

Italy's manufacturing history between 1861 and 1973 can be divided into five sub-periods (Table 6.1): (i) relatively slow output growth (1861–96), (ii) growth acceleration (1896–1913), (iii) rapid output and labour productivity growth (1922–9), (iv) slow growth, protection, currency revaluation, great depression, sanctions, and autarky (1929–39), (v) a long wave of catch-up growth (1951–73). The two world wars can both be characterized as 'lost decades', albeit involving very different stories and impacts on long-term manufacturing growth.

6.2.1 Before the First World War

According to Malanima (2007), Italy's industrial output and labour productivity gently declined from the beginning of the fourteenth century to the early nineteenth century when they began to pick up. At the time of unification a moderate upward trend was already detectible. Between 1861 and 1896 manufacturing value added grew on average by about 2.0 per cent per annum. Employment in the sector remained roughly constant, however, while the economy as a whole created 1.5 million new jobs. In 1896–1913 the growth rate of manufacturing accelerated to 3.6 per cent per annum. The sector's workforce increased by about 1 million (growing by 1.5 per cent per annum as against 1.0 per cent for the economy as whole). Between unification and the First World War, output per full-time equivalent worker in manufacturing increased every year by 2.0 per cent (Broadberry, Giordano, and Zollino, 2013): a respectable rate by nineteenth-century international standards.

The pattern of Italy's industrialization prior to 1914, characterized by slow growth up to the 1880s and growth acceleration thereafter, was the subject of a heated debate sparked in the late 1950s by Alexander Gerschenkron's (1962) attempt to fit the Italian case into his paradigm of European industrialization in conditions of moderate backwardness, in which 'agents', such as universal banks (created in Italy in the mid-1890s), are 'needed' to overcome the 'stumbling blocks' that obstruct the path to modern industrial growth. Rosario Romeo (1959) argued instead that the sluggish growth in the first decades after unification was due to the 'need' for social overhead capital to be created before rapid industrialization could take place. The two scholars had a lively debate in Rome, later published by Gerschenkron (1962): Romeo spotted an industrial acceleration in the 1880s, upon completion of the main rail network, while Gerschenkron dated Italy's 'big spurt' a decade later, coinciding with the appearance of German-type universal banks. Bonelli (1978) and Cafagna (1972), on the other hand, saw Italy's early industrialization as characterized by slow trend acceleration in industrial output, beginning before unification, rather than discontinuity at the end of the century.

In the late 1960s, Stefano Fenoaltea began to produce a new set of industrial value added statistics, which he continuously refined over the following decades. During the course of this exemplary work, Fenoaltea produced a new interpretation of Italy's industrialization pattern, which he saw as driven by the flow of international investments and therefore following the international business cycle (Fenoaltea, 2006). Recently, the creation of new data on the engineering sector led Fenoaltea (2014) to doubt his previous assessment of Italy's industrialization path, arguing, however, that additional work is needed to produce a new explanation.

6.2.2 The Great War and Inter-war Period

If we accept the most recent estimates (Baffigi, 2013), wartime manufacturing output grew during 1914–16 by 5 per cent per annum. (Italy entered the war in May 1915). Thereafter the war-related acceleration was not sustained, and manufacturing value added fell during the second part of the conflict and the subsequent recession. In 1922, manufacturing value added was not significantly different from 1914. The war, however, marked a qualitative turning point in Italy's industrialization, accelerating technical progress.

A period of exceptionally rapid manufacturing growth followed the post-war depression and industrial restructuring. During 1922–5, the sector grew at an average annual rate close to 8 per cent. In spite of the subsequent slowdown, the 1920s saw a remarkable performance of Italy's manufacturing, with high rates of output, productivity, and employment growth.

The 1930s can be divided into two periods: the Great Depression and the autarkic recovery. New estimates (Giugliano, 2011; Giordano and Giugliano, 2012; Carreras and Felice, 2012; Baffigi, 2013) indicate that the fall in industrial value added and employment during 1929–32 was deeper than previously believed: in three years, manufacturing output fell by 22 per cent. Recovery was slow in 1933–4 and rapid thereafter, partly driven by war-related (Abyssinian and Spanish) expenditure. In 1939 (Italy entered the conflict in June 1940), manufacturing value added was 45 per cent higher than in 1934. On the whole, Italian manufacturing was highly volatile during the inter-war years, with spurts of high growth followed by sharp slowdowns and a slump during the Great Depression. As we shall see, economic policy played an important role alongside the international business cycle.

Unlike the First, the Second World War had a strong negative impact on Italy's manufacturing production, which shrank to a quarter of the pre-war level. The decline started immediately after the beginning of the hostilities, remained relatively contained in 1941–2, and accelerated during 1943–5 when war was waged on Italian soil, and the country was divided into two separate states at war with each other.

Matteo Gomellini and Gianni Toniolo

Table 6.2. Industrial[a] employment as a percentage of total employment

Year[b]	Italy	UK	Germany	US	India	Japan
1871	15.8	42.4	29.1	24.8	12.1	10.5
1911	23.5	44.1	37.9	31.8	10.3	
1921	22.5			33.2		19.0
1931	24.5	43.7	37.4	30.2	9.1	
1936	25.6	44.5	38.2			
1951	31.1	46.5	42.1	32.9	10.2	22.9
1973	38.4	41.8	47.3	28.9	11.1	36.6

[a] Including construction [b] Italy; for some other countries, the closest available year.
Source: Broadberry et al. (2013).

6.2.3 1945–73

As in other defeated countries, the reconstruction of Italian industry was remarkably swift. In 1946, despite shortages of raw materials and the disruption of transport infrastructure, industrial value added grew by 242 per cent. The pre-war peak (1940) in manufacturing was reached in mid-1950.

In the twenty-odd years following reconstruction, cyclical stability stood in sharp contrast to inter-war volatility. The overall picture can be summarized by saying that in 1970 Italy's manufacturing sector was almost five times bigger than it had been in 1950, having grown on average by 8.3 per cent over the two decades. Between 1950 and 1958 manufacturing value added grew on average by 7.6 per cent per annum, accelerating to 10.7 per cent between 1958 and 1963. After a brief slowdown to just 2.4 per cent in 1964, growth resumed at the annual pace of 8.6 per cent until the end of the decade.

To conclude this section with a comparative perspective, Table 6.2 reports the shares of industrial employment in Italy and five other countries between 1871 and 1973. The comparison with Japan is particularly striking.

6.3 'MODERN' AND 'TRADITIONAL' SECTORS

In the beginning was silk. So the story goes, as told by a leading Italian economic historian (Cafagna, 1972). Raw silk manufacturing had a number of advantages for a relatively backward agricultural country. The cultivation of mulberry trees, for the production of cocoons, and silk spinning were useful labour-intensive complementary activities for under-employed agricultural workers, particularly in hilly areas where land productivity was not as high as at the bottom of the Po Valley. Furthermore, Federico (2005) finds strong evidence of a beneficial influence of raw silk production on engineering: already at the time of unification, Italy was the world leader in the production of silk-reeling machinery, a leadership it kept until the 1920s (Federico, 1997, 2005). In the decade before unification, a silkworm disease had considerably reduced the production of cocoons (Federico, 1997), sending the raw material price to levels only affordable by firms equipped with steam-powered machinery (Federico and Tena, 1998). Initially, boilers were produced by non-specialized engineering firms but, as technology became more sophisticated, a handful of new specialized producers emerged as the result of growing demand and weak foreign competition. A similar pattern of demand-driven production of investment goods would become common after the Second World War in the so-called industrial districts, which often developed the technology for the machinery used in the production of consumer goods. In the years immediately following unification, large-scale investment in steam-reeling resulted in the silk sector's total factor productivity growth being 3.5 times faster than the economy's average.

If silk figures prominently in the narrative of Italy's early industrialization, one should not exaggerate its importance: in 1870, the total production of textiles accounted for only 10 per cent of manufacturing value added, while engineering made up 17 per cent (Fenoaltea, 2006). If industrialization is to be the main factor in the process of 'modern economic growth', as described by Simon Kuznets, then it should rely upon industries that generate more innovation, investment, R & D, and productivity growth—in a word 'modernization'—than silk. For our purposes, considering that comparable time series for only thirteen industrial sectors are available for the entire period under review,[4] we take metallurgy, engineering, and chemical products (including rubber) to make up the bulk of the 'modern sector' (Table 6.3). This is admittedly a very rough approximation for at least two reasons: first, each sector's innovation, technical progress and R&D varied over time;[5] second, seeds of modernity, new products and new production processes abounded in other sectors (a typical example is the rapid development of viscose rayon (so-called 'artificial silk') within the 'traditional' textile sector during the 1920s).

The overall pattern of sectoral growth that emerges from Table 6.3[6] is pretty standard in any industrialization process: an increasing share of 'modern sectors' within manufacturing accompanied a growing share of manufacturing in GDP. More specific to Italy is perhaps the very rapid expansion of hydroelectric power production, which grew from almost nothing (8 million Kw) in 1890 to 2.2 billion Kw in 1913, more than doubled during the Great War (1913–20), and grew thereafter at a slower pace, close to that of the overall utilities sector.

More interesting than Italy's 'normal' industrial growth pattern over the very long run is perhaps what emerges from the observation of individual sub-periods. Before the First World War, 'modern sectors' made a relatively modest contribution to manufacturing growth. In half a century, the 'modern' share in manufacturing increased from only a fifth to less than a third of the total. On the other hand, as mentioned above, from the end of the nineteenth century to the early post-war

[4] For 1861–1913, Fenoaltea has provided a much more detailed breakdown of industrial value added, which cannot be extended to the rest of our period (Ciccarelli and Fenoaltea, 2009).

[5] For instance, in the nineteenth century and beyond blacksmiths were included in engineering value added, and small blast furnaces in that of metallurgy (Fenoaltea, 2014).

[6] Table 6.1 is from Baffigi (2013), the most recent and reliable available source. It does not, however, provide sectoral breakdowns which, in Table 6.3, are drawn from different sources (hence the discrepancies between the aggregate growth rates in the two tables).

Table 6.3. Shares and annual average growth rates of the 'modern' sector,[a] 1870–1973

	'Modern' sector's share in manufacturing		Average growth in 'modern' sectors	Average growth in manufacturing	Average growth in utilities	Average growth in electric power production
1870	0.21					
1890	0.27	1870–90	3.3	2.1	5.1	n.a.
1913	0.29	1890–1913	3.8	3.0	8.3	27.7
1920	0.28	1913–20				11.4
1925	0.35	1920–5	12.4	8.0	9.6	9.1
1929	0.37	1925–9	8.5	1.6	8.6	9.3
1939	0.47	1929–39	10.3	1.5	6.4	5.7
1951	0.45					
1973	0.56	1951–73	8.6	7.3	7.8[b]	7.6

[a] Metal making, engineering, and chemicals (incl. rubber).
[b] Energy only.

Sources: 1870–1913, Ciccarelli and Fenoaltea (2009); 1920–39, Carreras and Felice (2012); 1951–73, Golinelli and Monterastelli (1990).

period, electrification proceeded rapidly, liberally licensed by the state and financed by equity issues and long-term loans from universal banks, in response to both industrial and civil demand.

The inter-war period stands in striking contrast to the pre-war years. In 1920–5, both modern and traditional industry grew at a rapid pace, while after 1925, non-modern manufacturing almost stagnated. As discussed in the next section, tariff protection and possibly the overvaluation of the currency were instrumental in shifting resources from the labour-intensive, export-oriented sectors to the more capital-intensive ones so that, in 1939, the 'modern sector' share in manufacturing was close to 50 per cent. From this viewpoint, a case can be made that, by that time, the structure of Italian industry was more similar to that of 'core' than 'peripheral' countries. The industrialization pattern during the post-Second World War golden age looks similar to that of other countries (including 'core' ones such as Germany, France, and Japan). Average yearly growth for our 'modern' sectors outperforms the average for total manufacturing by about 1.5 percentage points, indicating that value added (and probably productivity) growth was by no means limited to the capital-intensive 'modern' industries. In fact, our definition of 'modern' itself might no longer apply to the latter part of the period.

6.4 TRADE, TARIFFS, AND INDUSTRIAL POLICY

Among the factors affecting a latecomer country's manufacturing performance and catch-up, the most frequently highlighted in the literature are comparative advantages and terms of trade, tariff and industrial policies, and the quantity and direction of foreign capital inflows (Blattman, Hwang, and Williamson, 2007;

Williamson, 2008, 2011). In what follows we briefly discuss the impact of these factors on Italy's industrialization.

Since unification in 1861–70, Italy has always been a medium-sized economy, one of the eight to ten largest in the world. Not nearly as large as those of the United States, China, or the German and British Empires, Italy's domestic market was nevertheless large enough to provide potential economies of scale for 'modern' industrial sectors. Italy's openness ratios (trade/GDP) rose from 0.2 to close to 0.3 in the second half of the nineteenth century, declined to 0.1 in the 1930s, and rose to about 0.4 in the 1970s. Throughout our period Italy's openness was lower than Germany's, higher than Spain's, and close to that of France (Federico and Wolf, 2013). Given the medium size of the economy, the choices between free trade versus protectionism, or fixed versus floating exchange rates, were less straightforward than in smaller countries. Industrial policy, which mainly took the form of the state directly or indirectly allocating resources to specific manufacturing sectors, could count on relatively large state budgets and domestic capital markets. In a word: size mattered in shaping policy options.

Touring Italy soon after unification, Richard Cobden advised the new Italian rulers to capitalize on Italy's comparative advantages (climate and art), leaving manufacturing to countries north of the Alps (possibly north of the Channel). At the time, Cobden's recommendation might not have been far off the mark. When measured by the Lafay (1992) index, a commodity-specific net exports measure of comparative advantage, until the turn of the twentieth century Italy did not enjoy a comparative advantage in manufacturing when raw silk production is excluded (Federico and Wolf, 2013, pp. 239–40). However, Lafay's index moves from −10 to 0 between the 1880s and the late 1890s, indicating that Italy was 'building' a manufacturing comparative advantage. Poor in coal, iron ore, and oil, Italy did not suffer from the 'curse of raw materials': sulphur, tomatoes, olive oil, and citrus fruits were not sufficient to develop a serious curse.

Throughout the twentieth century, by Lafay's measure, Italy had a clear comparative advantage in manufacturing production. The share of manufacturing in Italian exports rose from only 20 per cent in the 1870s and 1880s to almost 40 per cent in 1914, 50 per cent in the late 1930s (including colonial trade), and about 80 per cent in the mid-1970s. Following a standard pattern in most industrialization processes, Italy's exports, initially concentrated in a few products, became progressively diversified.

After the Second World War, Italy's share of world exports increased considerably. The composition of manufacturing exports changed, without however fully converging on that of the more advanced countries (Gomellini, 2004; Gomellini and Pianta, 2007). In particular, the country's export success was to a large extent based on goods of mid-innovative content, produced mainly by medium-sized firms. At the end of the 1960s, Italy's manufacturing still lagged behind in science-based and scale-intensive production, while exhibiting a leadership in more traditional manufacturing industrial products. The specialization in mid-tech productions that emerged in the 1960s persisted in the following decades.

Italian economic historians have largely neglected the terms of trade, possibly reflecting the belief that they did not matter much one way or the other for GDP and manufacturing growth. A recent quantitative analysis covering the period from unification to the eve of the Second World War concludes that trade diversification 'improved the Italian terms of trade but did not reduce volatility' (Federico and Vasta, 2010, p. 236). Scarcely endowed with basic industrial raw materials, Italy was exposed to the vagaries of international prices for basic commodities, for which the country was an international price taker. There are no estimates available of the impact of terms of trade volatility on the rate of growth of manufacturing; a likely guess is that it had a very moderate negative effect.

Italy's tariff history follows the European continental pattern. Born a free trader in the political and intellectual climate of the Cobden–Chevalier treaty, the Italian state leaned towards a more protectionist mood from the late 1870s onward, in tune with the main continental countries. In an effective protection framework, Gerschenkron (1955) argued that the 1887 tariff was detrimental to industrial growth because of its protection for wheat growers and the high duty on iron and steel—inputs to the promising engineering sector. Toniolo (1977) concurred but argued that the impact of the steel duty on the rate of growth of engineering was empirically modest. Other scholars (Romeo, 1959, 1988; Zamagni, 1993) were more sanguine about the tariff of 1887, invoking infant industry arguments and approving of the active involvement of the government in the promotion of industry. More recently, Fenoaltea—the leading scholar of pre-1914 industrialization—showed that the 1887 tariff and the subsequent periodic increases in the duty on wheat had a non-negligible negative impact on the growth rate of Italy's manufacturing (Fenoaltea, 2006, Chapter 4). Federico and Tena (1998) estimate that the tariff of 1887 brought the average rate of Italian protection to 50 per cent above the European average. However, while manufactured goods accounted for about 32 per cent of all imports, they accounted for only 20 per cent of the tariff revenue increase. The nineteenth-century debate on tariffs and growth went on to the present day: the prevailing view is that protection—of both agricultural and industrial goods—slowed Italy's manufacturing growth before the First World War, but the size of the damage done by the tariff is still being debated.

The 1887 tariff was introduced when a slowdown in GDP and manufacturing growth was beginning to take place. From the end of the nineteenth century to the outbreak of the Great War, industrial protection was consistently eroded by the signing of commercial treaties (Toniolo, 1990) and by a decline in the undervaluation of the real exchange rate (Di Nino, Eichengreen, and Sbracia, 2013). The period coincides, as we have seen, with an acceleration of industrial growth. By 1914 Italy's average manufacturing tariff (estimated at 18 per cent) stood at a level close to Germany's and France's, lower than Spain's and Sweden's, but much higher than that of small open economies such as Belgium, the Netherlands, and Switzerland (James and O'Rourke, 2013, p. 41).

A new protectionist turning point took place in 1925: high import duties on wheat and sugar were re-introduced, and metallurgy and a number of heavy engineering activities regained the customs' favour. A discussion of the underlying political economy of the protectionist U-turn of 1925 is beyond the scope of this chapter,[7] but it is enough to recall that 1925 was the year when Mussolini's dictatorial powers were sanctioned by law.

Italy's protectionist turn antedates by a few years the international triumph of tariffs, quotas, and exchange controls in which the country fully participated, first proclaiming a national 'battle for (domestic) wheat' and later embarking on an official programme of autarky. The latter relied on an array of allocative tools, among which import duties were just one of many.

Post-1945 tariff history closely followed the European pattern, first in the General Agreement on Tariffs and Trade (GATT), and then in the European Coal and Steel Community (ECSC) and European Economic Community (EEC) frameworks. The swift reconstruction of the Italian industrial base took place under a heavy protective shield, which included import duties, quotas, restrictions on capital movements, cumbersome authorization procedures, and managed exchange rates. The panoply of protective devices began to unwind in the late 1940s, following the Annecy conference, when Italy joined the GATT. In 1950, a *tarif de combat* was introduced, in the time-honoured tradition of entering into negotiations from a high ground. Progressive liberalization followed and, by 1957, Italy was ready to join the European Common Market and to make its currency convertible. From then onward, Italy's import duties were set in Brussels as trade liberalization in manufacturing, both among the six original members of the EEC and with the outside world, proceeded faster than was originally agreed upon in the Rome treaty.

To sum up: Italy's tariff history followed the ebbs and flows of European trade policy. Both the 1887 and 1925 duties on manufacturing were aimed at shielding so-called heavy industry from foreign competition. The former also protected cotton textiles, which were neglected in 1925. The prevailing consensus among scholars is that in both cases tariffs had a negative impact on manufacturing growth which, on the other hand, was enhanced by post-1945 trade liberalization.

When not raised mainly for fiscal purposes, which was never the case in Italy, tariffs serve two political economy purposes: consensus building (as with the notorious *pactum sceleris* between agrarian and industrial constituencies in Germany, but also in Italy) and 'industrial policy'. The latter is a broad and often ill-defined concept: for our purposes we define 'industrial policy' as the use of the state's power to influence resource allocation in order to promote industrialization (wartime policies being the extreme case in point). For better or worse, industrial policy looms large in Italy's industrialization drive. The tariff hikes of the 1880s, and 1920s and 1930s, were both part of broader policy drives aimed at promoting 'strategic' industries.

The (liberal) left that came to power in 1878 had a more hands-on attitude to industrialization than the 'Historical Right', which had been in government since

---

[7] Among recent contributions see Salsano and Toniolo (2010).

the Risorgimento.[8] Besides the tariff, a number of industrial policy tools were used: 'ad hoc legislation, procurement, grants, fiscal privileges, bail outs, state guarantees [. . .] all administered with large discretion, and to changing ends' (Ciocca, 2007, pp. 116–17). Lack of transparency resulted in the exchange of favours between the private and the public sectors, cutting corners, and careerism, all captured by the novels of Maupassant in France[9] and De Roberto in Italy.[10]

Metal making saw double-digit growth in the 1880s (12 per cent per annum, up from 2.9 in 1861–80). Engineering, already the second largest manufacturing sector after food processing, grew annually by 5.3 per cent (up from 2.3). But the textile sector, not a target of government activism, also grew faster than the manufacturing sector on average. How much of the manufacturing growth acceleration can be attributed to the new activism by the left government? Probably not much of it, if other favourable factors are taken into account. Major institutional progress had been made in monetary and financial market unification (Toniolo, Conte, and Vecchi, 2003), and in the creation of business-friendly institutions (notably the Commercial Code of 1882). Foreign capital flowed in (Fenoaltea, 1988) as the result of a balanced state budget and the return to gold convertibility of the lira in 1883. A construction boom (4.5 per cent per annum, up from a negligible and volatile 0.36 per cent per annum during 1861–80) created considerable private demand for iron and steel, unrelated to government policy.

All in all, the government's chaotic panoply of support to manufacturing either slowed down growth, as maintained by economists at the time, or contributed little to it. Moreover, the brief cyclical expansion (1880–8) was followed by a slump in 1888–96, during which manufacturing grew by a meagre 0.84 per cent per annum while metallurgy, engineering, and textiles, as well as construction, all saw negative growth rates. If industrial policy is to be judged by its long-term impact, the left's activism does not pass the test.

As we have seen, during 1896–1925 Italy made a major quantitative and qualitative jump in modern industrialization, narrowing the gap with the core countries. Did industrial policy matter?

Giolitti, who directly or indirectly ruled the country from the end of the century to 1913, did not put an end to previous practices of the government paying excessively close attention to the needs of individual sectors and even of particular business groups. An active industrial policy, however, began to be conducted by the universal banks.

---

[8] In 1884 a steel-making company was created in Terni using electrically powered Bessemer converters and Martin–Siemens furnaces. A typical example of the industrial policy of the left, Terni was created by a group of private entrepreneurs, enjoying the state guarantee of substantial procurement, particularly for the navy. A government committee chose the location, taking into account, among other things, its distance from the border and from the sea (given the maximum reach of naval guns at the time). The largest banks provided most of the needed financial resources.

[9] See among others Guy De Maupassant's masterpiece, *Bel Ami* (1885).

[10] Long underrated, Federico De Roberto (1861–1927) is one of the great Italian novelists. His *I Vicerè* (1894) is a scathing critique of business corruption, as is his posthumous *L'Imperio* (1929), set at the same time.

It is impossible here to even review the vast literature on the contribution of German-type mixed banks to the manufacturing growth acceleration in Italy after the mid-1890s. The prevailing consensus (Confalonieri, 1994) is that, while Banca Commerciale and Credito Italiano introduced innovative banking practices and played an important role in the development of some sectors (notably hydropower), in underwriting equity and bond issues, and more generally in developing the financial market, they did not play the pivotal role as 'agents of industrialization' (i.e. as industrial policy-makers par excellence) assigned to them by Gerschenkron. The most important developmental role of the government during the Giolittian period was a time-consistent monetary and fiscal policy, which stabilized expectations by both domestic and foreign investors, lowered interest rates, crowded in private capital, and favoured a hefty inflow of emigrant remittances.

In every war economy, industrial policy is pushed to the extreme. Every tool available to the state—selective credit and taxation, price controls, licensing, tariffs, labour laws, and many others—is used to allocate resources to the production of war-related goods. Policy is enforced by special legislation, including the extension to civilians of the tough military penal code. For all its deficiencies and shortcomings, both military and industrial, Italy's wartime economic performance was quite satisfactory, given the relative backwardness of the economy, the inefficient public administration, and the social and political fractures that had emerged in the previous years. As far as industrialization is concerned, the First World War (unlike the Second) generated leaps forward in technical progress. There were two main drivers: economies of scale and import substitution. As for the former, the huge government demand for arms, ships, vehicles, and ammunition led to the creation or expansion of conglomerates, such as Ansaldo, for the vertically integrated production of steel, engineering products, warships, guns, trucks, and railway equipment. Another instance can be found in the wartime expansion of FIAT, the main producer of transport equipment. Import substitution was particularly relevant in fostering growth in the chemical industry, previously largely dependent on German imports. Montecatini developed the production of such products as superphosphates, nitrogen, synthetic colours, and sodium carbonate for the preparation of caustic soda. In several cases these products were inputs to other industrial processes, particularly explosives (Caracciolo, 1969; Galassi and Harrison, 2005). Some of the largest companies were downsized in the transition to the peace economy, and excess capacity emerged in some sectors (notably shipbuilding), but most of the qualitative changes to manufacturing induced by wartime 'industrial policy' were not lost in the transition. In particular, as engineers and skilled industrial workers had been largely exempted from serving in the trenches, the wartime manufacturing effort resulted in a permanent increase in the country's human capital through learning by doing and tacit knowledge.

The next relevant chapter in industrial policy was inaugurated by the protectionist U-turn of 1925, which favoured capital-intensive sectors (particularly steel making, engineering, chemicals, and sugar refining). Besides import duties, the usual allocative tools were employed: procurement, long-term credit at favourable conditions, grants and state guarantees. The revaluation of the lira, which started in the summer of 1926, was part of the new policy orientation. It helped in attracting foreign capital and, even more, in aiding large companies to repay foreign debts on favourable terms. Contrary to a widespread belief both at the time and among historians, the nominal revaluation had a relatively minor impact on the real exchange rate as it was accompanied by tight wage controls, and even by 'wage cuts' imposed by decree (Toniolo, 1980; Di Nino, Eichengreen, and Sbracia, 2013). The losers in this game were labour-intensive, export-oriented industries, which had led the post-war industrial boom, among them the rapidly expanding 'artificial silk' (rayon) sector in which Italy had a worldwide leading position as the second largest producer after the US.

The inward-looking nature of industrial policy was progressively reinforced in the 1930s. Administrative controls on capital movements and bilateral clearing agreements were added to the panoply as particularly effective allocative devices. An official autarky programme was eventually launched in 1935 as a reaction to the sanctions imposed by the League of Nations when Italy invaded Ethiopia.

The large number of state-owned enterprises (SOEs) is one of the most distinctive features of Italy's industrialization. SOEs originated in the inter-war years mostly as the unintended consequence of government bailouts. In the 1900s, the government nationalized the railway companies, merging them into a single state-owned company, as well as life insurance, but no SOEs existed in manufacturing before the First World War. Government intervention to ease the transition from a war- to peace-time economy in the socially explosive conditions of 1919–22 resulted in the state gaining indirect control of Ansaldo, a large metal-making and engineering conglomerate. In 1931 the government secretly bailed out the three largest universal banks of the country which, in the 1920s, had progressively turned themselves into holding companies: their combined equity portfolios held controlling stakes in about 50 per cent of the listed companies on the Italian stock exchange. As a condition for the supply of last resort liquidity, the government required a commitment by the banks to henceforth confine their business to short-term lending; holding of industrial stakes was explicitly forbidden. In 1933, the equity portfolio of the banks was 'provisionally' taken over by a state-controlled holding company, the Istituto per la Ricostruzione Industriale (IRI).[11] As far as 'industrial policy' was concerned, IRI coordinated and rationalized production within the group by directing financial resources where it deemed useful as well as by mergers and downsizing, the latter with little social cost as manpower could to a certain extent be reallocated within the group. From the very beginning, IRI also took responsibility for managerial training and selection for the entire group; a role efficiently performed, which particularly yielded fruit in the 1940s and 1950s.

During the post-war golden age of manufacturing growth, as tariffs rapidly lost importance, two main tools were used in industrial policy: credit allocation and public investment in manufacturing, largely but not exclusively channelled by SOEs. Active credit policies took place in the context of financial repression that

---

[11] On IRI see the six volumes edited by Pierluigi Ciocca (Ciocca, 2011–14).

characterized Italy and the rest of Europe from the 1930s through the 1970s and beyond. Under such conditions, Battilossi, Gigliobianco, and Marinelli (2013) argue that during 1948–70 Italian banks effectively promoted growth in the Italian economy. Co-integration analysis 'shows that the volume of credit to the industrial sectors tended to adjust to changes in the growth opportunities [of individual industries] as proxied by price/earning rates' (Battilossi, Gigliobianco, and Marinelli, 2013, p. 513). Credit allocation under financial repression was possibly not particularly detrimental to industrial growth. In the golden age, SOEs made a huge contribution to industrial investment, produced considerable R & D, and are credited with creating positive externalities for the private sector. 'IRI helped the development of the machinery industry by providing cheap intermediate inputs, compensating for the weakness of private firms in the field' (Crafts and Magnani, 2013, p. 80). It also created an extended network of superhighways (*autostrade*), which lowered transportation costs and favoured the rapid expansion of the car industry. ENI developed gas fields in the Po valley and freed the country's oil supply from the 'Seven Sisters' oligopoly.[12] Between 1958 and 1969 IRI's investments grew on average by 8.7 per cent per annum, and employment by 3.2 per cent (to 295,000), producing profits year after year (Ciocca, 2014, p. 147).

6.5 THE REGIONAL DIVIDE

An outstanding feature of Italy's modern economic growth is the stubborn persistence of regional inequalities in GDP per person. Whereas the country as a whole converged with the initially most advanced countries, a similar process did not take place within the country itself. Regional divides are observed in almost every country, but nowhere else is the phenomenon as deep and persistent as in Italy. Moreover, in contrast to other countries such as Spain, Italy is characterized by a persistent geographical pattern of inequality, with a 'continuing dominance of one area of the country' (see A'Hearn and Venables, 2013, p. 626).

An enormous literature exists on the 'Southern Question' (*Questione Meridionale*) dating back to the late nineteenth century.[13] In recent years, various estimates of regional GDP from 1861 to the present have produced some consensus about the evolution of the regional income gap. However, regional historical industrial statistics are still under-researched, with the exception of the painstaking analysis

[12] In 1963, at the peak of the 'economic miracle', a macroeconomic 'democratic planning' was designed 'to tackle the main structural problems of the economy [...] On the whole the program was heavily influenced by a dirigiste approach not uncommon in European economic culture of the time' (Crafts and Magnani, 2013, p. 81). Incomes policy proposals ran up against the weakness of the reform culture of the Communist Party (Magnani, 1997); the targets set by the *programmazione* were hardly compatible with the inefficiency of public administration; and the antitrust regulation and company-law reform proposals were defeated by the consolidated interests of large industrial groups (Barca, 1997; Ciocca, 2007).
[13] Among some of the most recent contributions are Iuzzolino, Pellegrini, and Viesti (2013), A'Hearn and Venables (2013), Felice (2013), and Daniele and Malanima (2007; 2014).

by Ciccarelli and Fenoaltea (2009, 2014), which unfortunately covers only 1861–1913.

In this chapter we begin to bridge the statistical gap. To do so, we rely for 1861–1913 on the series by Ciccarelli and Fenoaltea (2009).[14] For subsequent years we follow Fenoaltea's methodology by attributing to each region, at census benchmark years, a share of the national industrial and manufacturing production equal to the share of the regional labour force in the two sectors, using data produced by Vitali (1970).[15] This yields regional industrial and manufacturing value added at constant prices for sixteen Italian regions at benchmark years from 1871 to 1971.[16]

In Table 6.4 regional per capita industrial value added is shown in Geary–Khamis 1990 dollars to allow for comparisons with a selected number of countries. It shows that the Northwest, comparable in population size to Sweden, was as industrialized as the Scandinavian country by the 1930s, while the other Italian macro regions lagged behind most of Europe's countries.

The geographical pattern of Italy's industrialization can be summarized as follows: a large gap in per capita industrial value added between the Northwest and the rest of the country already existed in 1891; during 1891–1938 the South lagged behind in industrial growth per capita, while the Northeast and Centre progressed very similarly, losing some ground to the Northwest; the Second World War deepened the North–South divide while during 1951–71 all three other macro areas caught up with the Northwest.

A striking feature of Italy's industrialization is the concentration of manufacturing in the Northwest: in 1971, with about 27 per cent of Italy's population, the region produced more than half of the entire country's manufacturing value added. Note that the North–South divide in manufacturing is more pronounced than in industry as a whole. The Southern divergence began in 1911, when the area produced about one-third of the country's manufacturing value added, a share that dropped to one-eighth sixty years later. In 1891 manufacturing made up about 80 per cent of total industrial production in all four macro areas. A century later, the manufacturing/industry ratio was still 0.8 in the Northwest, but had fallen to around 0.7 in the Northeast and Centre, and had plummeted to 50 per cent in the South. One of the reasons for the weak Southern industrialization is its disproportionate reliance on construction and utilities rather than manufacturing.

A similar pattern is revealed when we consider the spatial distribution of the 'modern' manufacturing sector, defined, as above, by the chemical, engineering, and metal-making industries (Table 6.5). Up to the end of the nineteenth century,

[14] Data are at 1911 constant prices, which may affect the shares of manufacturing and construction presented below.

[15] This is the methodology Fenoaltea used in his 'first generation' estimates (see Ciccarelli and Fenoaltea, 2009). There are, obviously, two major flaws in this procedure: it does not take into account unknown but potentially large productivity differentials between regions, and it assumes the same ratio of labour force to employment across regions.

[16] For 1971 we rely on the Centre for North South Economic Research (CRENoS) dataset: www.crenos.it.

Table 6.4. Industrial value added per inhabitant: Italy, four Italian macro areas, and selected countries, 1891–1971 (Geary–Khamis 1990 dollars)

Year	ITA	NW*	NE*	CEN*	S*	FR	SP	JAP	BEL	FIN	SW	NL
1891	332	402	278	295	256	968	484	137	1,440	282	341	1,070
1911	497	761	472	380	391	1,231	555	287	1,637	491	719	1,337
1931	647	1,047	494	569	396	1,676	703	574	1,965	631	995	
1938	653	1,273	695	675	520	1,486		809	1,995	1,076	1,310	
1961	1980	4,102	2,065	1,884	1,009	2,484			2,942	2,532	3,022	
1971	3,515	5,869	3,596	3,023	1,919	3,991	2,581	3,423	4,395	3,777	3,840	4,607
Δ% 1891–1971	3.0	3.3	3.2	3.0	2.6							

* NW = Northwest; NE = Northeast; CEN = Centre; S = South.

Source: Regional GDP/per person in Italy, Felice and Vecchi (2013); Regional Industry/GDP, Table 6. Other countries: GDP per capita: Maddison (2010); Ind./GDP, Mitchell (2007); Ind./GDP France 1961 and 1971 INSEE; 1971 data for Spain, Japan, and the Netherland are from Groeningen Growth Centre (http://ggdc.net/).

Table 6.5. Distribution of value added by modern sectors across macro areas

	NW[a]	NE[a]	CEN[a]	S[a]	Total
1871	31.4	17.4	16.5	34.6	100
1881	35.8	16.6	15.4	32.2	100
1891	38.0	15.8	14.9	31.3	100
1901	40.7	14.9	14.4	30.0	100
1911	45.5	15.9	14.1	24.4	100
1921	49.5	14.4	13.4	22.7	100
1931	53.7	14.1	14.9	17.4	100
1936	52.8	15.0	14.5	17.7	100
1951	59.2	13.9	12.8	14.2	100

[a] NW = Northwest; NE = Northeast; CEN = Centre; S = South.

Sources: Our calculations; see text for data sources.

over one-third of 'modern' industries were located in the South, with the Northeast and Centre lagging behind. The Southern share had more than halved by 1951. By the 1970s, over 50 per cent of manufacturing produced in the Northwest was in the 'modern' sectors, which accounted for two-thirds of the total 'modern' production of the country.

The rapid concentration of the modern sectors in the Northwest began with the post-1896 industrial growth acceleration, and was favoured by the wartime demand for typically modern products and by post-1925 tariff and industrial policies. After the Second World War, large enterprises remained the engine of growth in the Northwest, while the Northeast and Central regions developed their own idiosyncratic industrialization pattern based on small and medium-size enterprises, often clustered in 'industrial districts', typically—if by no means exclusively—oriented to the production of medium- rather than high-tech goods. SOEs were largely responsible for the development of modern sectors in the South.

By focusing on just four macro areas, one misses at least one important feature of Italy's industrial (and general economic) growth, namely the large *within*-area dispersion of income levels. Fig. 6.2 shows modest convergence in industrial value added per person (upper graph) and divergence in income per capita (lower graph) for the sixteen original (1861) Italian regions. The scatter plots highlight the wide regional dispersion in both initial values and growth.

Regional divergence in per capita GDP (and in per capita manufacturing, as we shall see in the next section) is a well-known feature of Italy's modern economic growth. Little attention, however, has been paid so far to the difference between the industrial and GDP stories, which suggests that industrial growth was probably a necessary but not sufficient condition for regional GDP convergence. The quality of the industrial mix (e.g. manufacturing vs construction, modern vs traditional sectors) mattered.

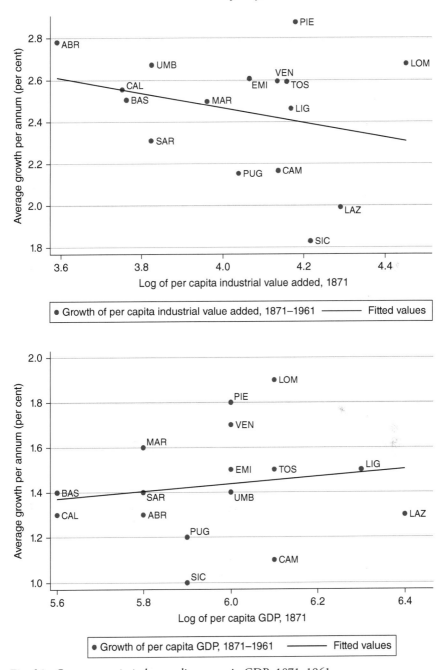

Fig. 6.2. Convergence in industry, divergence in GDP, 1871–1961

Note: Abbreviations refer to the sixteen Italian regions: ABR = Abruzzi; BAS = Basilicata; CAL = Calabria; CAM = Campania; EMI = Emilia; LAZ = Lazio; LIG = Liguria; LOM = Lombardia; MAR = Marche; PIE = Piemonte; PUG = Puglia; SAR = Sardegna; SIC = Sicilia; TOS = Toscana; UMB = Umbria; VEN = Veneto.

6.6 DRIVERS OF THE UNEVEN REGIONAL SPREAD
OF MANUFACTURING

As already mentioned, regional differences in per capita manufacturing output widened over the period under consideration (Fig. 6.3). In 1871, per capita value added by manufacturing in the South was about 70 per cent of the Northwest's; in 1961 the figure was just 30 per cent.

What drove this divergence? Deep history, government policies, institutions, geography, and human and social capital have all featured in the debate on the causes of the uneven spread of modern industry in Italy since the late nineteenth century.[17]

Galasso (2005) argued that Frederic II's centralization of state functions weakened the autonomy of the Southern cities, which could not match the industrial vitality of their Central and Northern counterparts: a weakness that was not redressed for the following six centuries. In the same vein, Putnam (1993) goes far back in history to find the roots of the North–South divide in the persistently low level of social capital (trust) that seems to characterize the *Mezzogiorno*.

A problem with attributing the relative weakness of Southern industrial growth to historical and geographical factors dating back several centuries is its inconsistency with the initially (1861) relatively small gap in GDP per person. Why did geographical, entrepreneurial, and social capital disadvantages not result in a wider income wedge long before unification? One (unfalsifiable) answer could be that those factors only became important in the context of modern economic growth.

The role of policies never ceased being debated ever since the famous polemical exchanges between Nitti and Fortunato at the turn of the twentieth century, with Nitti (1905) blaming the unified state's policies for the widening gap between North and South, and Fortunato stressing the original weakness of the Southern economy. The 'colonial conquest' of the *Mezzogiorno* by the Northern elites is where some authors lay the blame for the subsequent economic and social ills of the former kingdom of Naples (for a recent, sophisticated, revival of this approach, see De Oliveira and Guerriero, 2014). As already mentioned, tariff policies have taken centre stage in the debate, as have the various 'regional policies' aimed at promoting economic and industrial development in the South.

Some authors (see the reviews in Felice, 2013; Federico and Tena, 2014) explain the North–South divide in terms of a Southern lack of natural resources, and a lower level of human and social capital. A new economic geography approach stresses the importance of natural resources in combination with market access (A'Hearn and Venables, 2013; see also Missiaia, 2014).

All of these factors have probably contributed to the regional divide. To investigate their relative impact, we conducted several correlation exercises.[18] The general relationship we tested takes the following form:

---

[17] See Toniolo (2013) and the contributions therein.
[18] Correlations are obtained by regressing final-year levels (or the decadal growth) of per capita manufacturing on initial-year levels of each explanatory variable. These correlations are robust to a series of controls.

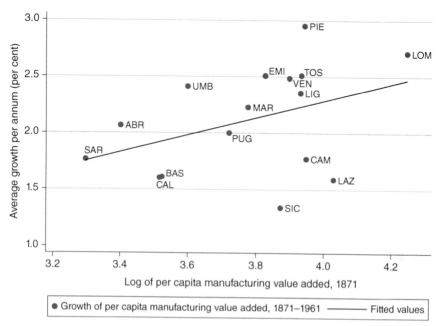

Fig. 6.3. Divergence in per capita manufacturing, 1871–1961

Note: Abbreviations as in Fig. 6.2.

$$Y_{it} = a + \beta X_{it-10} + \varLambda_i + \epsilon_{it}$$

where Y_{it}, our dependent variable, is per person value added in manufacturing in region i and year t, and $\varLambda_i$ are regional controls. The period of investigation runs from 1871 to 1961, and X_{it-10} are five possible explanatory variables lagged by ten years: the degree of *water availability*, which according to many authors (e.g. Fenoaltea, 2006; data from Ciccarelli and Fenoaltea, 2009) had a huge importance in allowing early industrial production (like silk) and in defining its location; the ease of access both to *domestic* and *foreign markets*, measured by a Harris (1954) index of *Market Potential*, which measures the distance-weighted potential demand faced by each region given its geographical location;[19] and endowments of *human and social capital*, two characteristics of the population often seen as major drivers of economic growth.[20]

All in all, these correlations suggest that geography-related variables are the most relevant in explaining regional divides. Over the entire period (1881–1961), almost two-thirds of the North–South gap in per capita manufacturing could potentially

[19] Proximity to foreign markets reduces transportation and information costs, and facilitates imitation and the transfer of technology.

[20] A more accurate description of the variables and details on the econometrics is in Gomellini and Toniolo (2015).

be explained[21] by differences in the ease of access to foreign markets. Proximity to domestic markets can explain, at most, a quarter of the final divide; *human and social capital* turn out to be less relevant in explaining the divergent paths in manufacturing.

6.7 CONCLUSIONS

In the late nineteenth century Italy was often regarded as the 'least of the great powers' (Bosworth, 1979). Sometimes it was demoted to the rank of 'first of the small powers'. The same ambiguity existed, at least until the 1960s, regarding Italy's relative economic position. As Federico and Vasta (2010, p. 229) noted, 'authors find it difficult to nail Italy down in a simple dichotomy between Core and Periphery: Blattman, Hwang and Williamson (2007) list it among the core countries, alongside the United Kingdom, while Williamson (2008) demotes Italy in the European periphery, with Russia and Spain'. In economic history the meanings of 'core' and 'periphery' vary according to research goals and time frame, as does the meaning of 'power' in political science: for much of the period covered in this chapter, Italy, or parts of it, would fall in the 'periphery' or 'core' according to the chosen variable of interest.

At the time of unification (1861–70), Italy's industrial sector was underdeveloped not only in absolute but also in relative terms: while Italy's GDP per person was about half that of the UK, industrial production per person was only 16 per cent of the UK level. Starting from this condition of typically peripheral industrial backwardness, in the following century Italy realized a pretty much 'normal' convergence with the 'core' in terms of both industrial output and GDP per person. Given its significant demographic size, Italy remained throughout one of the eight to ten largest world economies, and by the 1980s it had become the fifth or sixth largest world manufacturer.

After a slow start, Italy's industrialization process broadly followed the path taken by the main European countries: the pace of industrial output accelerated during 1896–1914, proved quite resilient to the shock of war, which brought about significant qualitative changes, increased significantly in the 1920s, and slowed in the 1930s while undergoing major structural changes. Italian industry participated fully in the second post-war golden age of the European economy. Throughout the century, Italian industry grew on average only marginally faster than industry in the world as a whole. The ebb and flow of protectionism also followed a general European pattern. Industrial policy was probably as invasive as, but less efficient than, those in France and Germany. State-owned enterprises and 'industrial districts' stand out as idiosyncratic Italian institutions fostering industrialization.

The lack of convergence in regional GDP per person is a well-known peculiarity of Italy's modern economic growth. While a number of studies exist on regional

---

[21] The *potential explanatory power* can be interpreted as the highest share of the North–South differential in the dependent variable that can be explained by a single variable. It is calculated as in Campante and Glaeser (2007).

GDP, we have produced for the first time consistent estimates of regional industrial and manufacturing output from 1861 to 1961. Industry progressively concentrated in the Northwestern regions, with the Northeast and Centre roughly maintaining their share of national industry. The South consistently lost ground from 1911 onward. A similar pattern holds for the geographical distribution of the 'modern' manufacturing sector (chemical, engineering, and metal-making industries). At the same time, Southern industrial output became increasingly dependent on construction, while manufacturing lost its initial relative weight. When we investigate the causes of the uneven geographical distribution of manufacturing, correlation analyses suggest that the degree of exposure to internal and foreign markets has a better chance of explaining differences in regional per capita manufacturing output than variables such as natural resources, and human and social capital, commonly associated with industrialization.

We have found evidence of a weak convergence among Italian regions in industrial (but not manufacturing) output per capita, which stands in contrast to the lack of convergence for GDP per capita.[22] The reasons for the different behaviour may not be the same in the case of peripheral countries, on the one hand, and peripheral regions within Italy, on the other. They form a large research agenda for economic historians, given the emphasis traditionally placed on industrialization as the main driver of modern economic growth. Our findings suggest that the composition of industrial output may impact on the growth of non-industrial sectors: Southern industry did converge on the North's, but its heavy reliance on construction and traditional labour-intensive industries may not have produced the same effects on agriculture and services as did the modern manufacturing located in the other areas.

To conclude, in 1861–71 Italy was definitely a peripheral industrial country, even if—given its population—it produced about 2.5 per cent of the world's industrial output. Its movement towards the 'core' did not start until the 1890s, but it then progressed 'as expected' by its initial backwardness. Japan is possibly the country most similar to Italy in the pattern of per capita industrial growth: its much larger population (about twice that of Italy throughout) made it possible to wage ten years of war against industrially weaker neighbours and four years of total war in the Pacific, starting from a relatively low but nonetheless substantial per capita industrial base. When did Italy (and Japan) join the 'core' of the industrial world? There are several possible answers to this question, depending on the yardstick employed. It can be argued that, by the eve of the Second World War, several qualitative features of Italian (and Japanese) industry, in particular the share of 'modern sectors' in manufacturing output, were similar to those of the core countries, even though the overall output level lagged behind. Alternatively, one may suggest that by the 1930s, the Northwest was a 'core' industrial country, the size of the Netherlands, while the South always remained on the edge between core and periphery.

---

[22] On the distinction between convergence in GDP per capita and manufacturing output per capita, see Rodrik (2013).

REFERENCES

A'Hearn, B. and Venables, A. J. (2013). Regional disparities: internal geography and external trade. In *The Oxford Handbook of the Italian Economy since Unification* (Ed., Toniolo, G.). New York: Oxford University Press, 599–630.

Baffigi, A. (2013). National accounts 1861–2011. In *The Oxford Handbook of the Italian Economy since Unification* (Ed., Toniolo, G.). New York: Oxford University Press, 157–86 (and appendix thereof, 631–713).

Bairoch, P. (1982). International industrialization levels from 1750 to 1980. *Journal of European Economic History* 11, 269–333.

Barca, F. (1997). Compromesso senza riforme. In *Storia del capitalismo italiano dal dopoguerra a oggi* (Ed., Barca, F.). Rome: Donzelli, 3–116.

Battilossi, S., Gigliobianco, A., and Marinelli, G. (2013). The allocative efficiency of the Italian banking system, 1936–2011. In *The Oxford Handbook of the Italian Economy since Unification* (Ed., Toniolo, G.). New York: Oxford University Press, 485–515.

Bénétrix, A., O'Rourke, K. H., and Williamson, J. G. (2015). The spread of manufacturing to the poor periphery 1870–2007. *Open Economies Review* 26, 1–37.

Blattman, C., Hwang, J., and Williamson, J. G. (2007). Winners and losers in the commodity lottery: the impact of terms of trade on growth and volatility in the periphery 1870–1939. *Journal of Development Economics* 82, 156–79.

Bonelli, F. (1978). Il capitalismo italiano. Linee generali di interpretazione. In *Storia d'Italia. Annali 1. Dal feudalesimo al capitalismo* (Eds, Ruggero, R. and Vivanti, C.). Turin: Einaudi, 1193–255.

Broadberry, S., Giordano, C., and Zollino, F. (2013). Productivity. In *The Oxford Handbook of the Italian Economy since Unification* (Ed., Toniolo, G.). New York: Oxford University Press, 187–226 (and appendix thereof, 631–713).

Cafagna, L. (1972). The industrial revolution in Italy 1830–1914. In *The Fontana Economic History of Europe*, Vol. 4 (Ed., Cipolla, C. M.). Glasgow: Collins/Fontana, 279–38.

Campante, F. and Glaeser, E. L. (2007). Yet another tale of two cities: Buenos Aires and Chicago. *National Bureau of Economic Research Working Paper* No. 15104.

Caracciolo, A. (1969). Crescita e trasformazione della grande industria durante la prima Guerra Mondiale. In *Lo sviluppo economico in Italia* (Ed., Fuà, G.). Milan: Franco Angeli, 187–240.

Carreras, A. and Felice, E. (2012). When did modernization begin? Italy's industrial growth reconsidered in light of new value-added series, 1911–1951. *Explorations in Economic History* 49, 443–60.

Castronovo, V. (1995). *Storia economica d'Italia. Dall'Ottocento ai giorni nostri*. Turin: Einaudi.

Ciccarelli, C. and Fenoaltea, S. (2009). *La Produzione industriale delle Regioni d'Italia, 1861–1913: una Ricostruzione Quantitativa*, Vol. I. Rome: Banca d'Italia.

Ciccarelli, C. and Fenoaltea, S. (2014). *La Produzione industriale delle Regioni d'Italia, 1861–1913: una Ricostruzione Quantitativa*, Vol. II. Rome: Banca d'Italia.

Ciocca, P. (2007). *Ricchi per sempre? Una storia economica d'Italia (1796–2005)*. Turin: Bollati Boringhieri.

Ciocca, P. (General Ed.) (2011–2014). *Storia dell'IRI*, Vols 1–6. Rome-Bari: Laterza.

Ciocca, P. (2014). *L'IRI nell'economia italiana*, Vol. 6. Rome-Bari: Laterza.

Confalonieri, A. (1994). *Banche miste e grande industria in Italia, 1914–1933*, Vol. I. Milan: Banca Commerciale Italiana.

Crafts, N. and Magnani, M. (2013). The golden age and the second globalization in Italy. In *The Oxford Handbook of the Italian Economy since Unification* (Ed., Toniolo, G.). New York: Oxford University Press, 69–107.

Daniele, V. and Malanima, P. (2007). Il prodotto delle Regioni e il divario Nord-Sud in Italia (1861–2004). In *Rivista di Politica Economica* 97(2), 267–316.

Daniele, V. and Malanima, P. (2014). Perché il Sud è rimasto indietro? Il Mezzogiorno fra storia e pubblicistica. In *Rivista di storia economica* 1, 3–36.

De Oliveira, G. and Guerriero, C. (2014). *Extractive States: The Case of Italian Unification.* Amsterdam: ACLE, University of Amsterdam.

Di Nino, V., Eichengreen, B., and Sbracia, M. (2013). Real exchange rates, trade and growth. In *The Oxford Handbook of the Italian Economy since Unification* (Ed., Toniolo, G.). New York: Oxford University Press, 351–77.

Federico, G. (1997). *An Economic History of the Silk Industry.* Cambridge: Cambridge University Press.

Federico, G. (2005). Seta, agricoltura e sviluppo economico in Italia. *Rivista di Storia Economica* 2, 123–54.

Federico, G. and Tena, A. (1998). Was Italy a protectionist country? *European Review of Economic History* 2, 73–99.

Federico, G. and Tena, A. (2014). The ripples of the industrial revolution: exports, economic growth, and regional integration in Italy in the early nineteenth century. *European Review of Economic History* 18, 349–69.

Federico, G. and Vasta, M. (2010). Was industrialization an escape from the commodity lottery? Evidence from Italy, 1861–1939. *Explorations in Economic History* 47, 228–43.

Federico, G. and Wolf, N. (2013). A long-run perspective on comparative advantage. In *The Oxford Handbook of the Italian Economy since Unification* (Ed., Toniolo, G.). New York: Oxford University Press, 327–50.

Felice, E. (2013). *Perché il Sud è rimasto indietro?* Bologna: Il Mulino.

Felice, E. and Vecchi, G. (2013). Italy's growth and decline, 1861–2011. *CEIS Research Paper* No. 293, University of Tor Vergata.

Fenoaltea, S. (1988). International resource flows and construction movements in the Atlantic economy: the Kuznets cycle in Italy, 1861–1913. *Journal of Economic History* 48(3), 605–38.

Fenoaltea, S. (2006). *L'Economia italiana dall'Unità alla Grande Guerra.* Rome-Bari: Laterza.

Fenoaltea, S. (2014). The fruits of disaggregation: the general engineering industry in Italy, 1861–1913. *Collegio Carlo Alberto Working Papers* No. 358, June.

Galassi, F. and Harrison, M. (2005). Italy at war 1915–1918. In *The Economics of World War I* (Eds, Broadberry, S. and Harrison, M.). Cambridge: Cambridge University Press, 276–309.

Galasso, G. (2005). *Il Mezzogiorno da 'questione' a 'problema aperto'.* Manduria: Piero Lacaita.

Gerschenkron, A. (1955). Notes on the rate of industrial growth in Italy, 1881–1913. *Journal of Economic History* 15, 360–75.

Gerschenkron, A. (1962). *Economic Backwardness in Historical Perspective: A Book of Essays.* Cambridge, MA: Belknap Press of Harvard University Press.

Giordano, C. and Giugliano, F. (2012). A tale of two fascisms: labour productivity growth and competition policy in Italy, 1911–1951. *Bank of Italy Economic History Working Papers* No. 28.

Giugliano, F. (2011). Crisis. Which crisis? New estimates of industrial value added in Italy during the Great Depression (mimeo).

Golinelli, R. and Monterastelli, M. (1990). Un metodo per la ricostruzione di serie storiche compatibili con la nuova contabilità nazionale (1951–89). Nota di lavoro n. 9001. Bologna: Prometeia.

Gomellini, M. (2004). Il commercio estero dell'Italia negli anni Sessanta: specializzazione internazionale e tecnologia. *Economic History Working Paper*, Banca d'Italia, Rome.

Gomellini, M. and Pianta, M. (2007). Commercio con l'estero e tecnologia negli anni Cinquanta e Sessanta. In *Innovazione tecnologica e sviluppo industriale nel secondo dopoguerra* (Eds, Antonelli, C., Barbiellini Amidei, F., Giannetti, R., Gomellini, M., Pastorelli, S., and Pianta, M.). Rome-Bari: Laterza, 358–594.

Gomellini, M. and Toniolo, G. (2015). The industrialization of Italy in the long-run (mimeo).

Iuzzolino, G., Pellegrini, G., and Viesti, G. (2013). Regional convergence. In *The Oxford Handbook of the Italian Economy since Unification* (Ed., Toniolo, G.). New York: Oxford University Press, 571–98.

James, H. and O'Rourke, K. H. (2013). Italy and the first age of globalization, 1861–1940. In *The Oxford Handbook of the Italian Economy since Unification* (Ed., Toniolo, G.). New York: Oxford University Press, 37–68.

Lafay, G. (1992). The measurement of revealed comparative advantage. In *International Trade Modeling* (Eds., Dagenais, M. G. and Muet, P. A.). London: Chapman & Hall, 209–34.

Maddison, A. (2010). *Statistics on World Population, GDP and Per Capita GDP, 1–2008 AD*, online database: http://www.ggdc.net/MADDISON/oriindex.htm

Magnani, M. (1997). Alla ricerca di regole nelle relazioni industriali: breve storia di due fallimenti. In *Storia del capitalismo italiano dal dopoguerra a oggi* (Ed., Barca, F.). Rome: Donzelli, 500–43.

Malanima, P. (2007). Wages, productivity and working time in Italy (1270–1913). *Journal of European Economic History* 36 (1), 127–71.

Missiaia, A. (2014). Market access and regional divergence in Italy (1871–1911) (mimeo).

Mitchell, B. R. (2007). *International Historical Statistics*. Basingstoke: Palgrave Macmillan.

Nitti, F. S. (1905). *La ricchezza dell'Italia.* Turin: Roux & Viarengo.

OECD (2013). *OECD Factbook 2013: Economic, Environmental and Social* Statistics. Paris: OECD Publishing.

Putnam, R. D. (1993). *Making Democracy Work: Civic Traditions in Modern Italy.* Princeton, NJ: Princeton University Press.

Rodrik, D. (2013). Unconditional convergence in manufacturing. *Quarterly Journal of Economics* 128, 165–204.

Romeo, R. (1959). *Risorgimento e capitalismo.* Rome-Bari: Laterza.

Romeo, R. (1988). *Breve storia della grande industria in Italia, 1861–1961.* Milan: Il Saggiatore.

Salsano, F. and Toniolo, G. (2010). *Da Quota 90 allo SME.* Rome-Bari: Laterza.

Toniolo, G. (1977). Effective protection and industrial growth: the case of Italian engineering. *Journal of European Economic History* 6, 659–73.

Toniolo, G. (1980). *L'Economia dell'Italia fascista.* Rome-Bari: Laterza.

Toniolo, G. (1990). *An Economic History of Liberal Italy.* London: Routledge.

Toniolo, G. (2013). An overview of Italy's economic growth. In *The Oxford Handbook of the Italian Economy since Unification* (Ed., Toniolo, G.). New York: Oxford University Press, 3–36.

Toniolo, G., Conte, L., and Vecchi, G. (2003). Monetary union, institutions and financial market integration: Italy, 1862–1905. *Explorations in Economic History* 40(4), 443–61.

Vitali, O. (1970). *Aspetti dello sviluppo economico italiano alla luce della ricostruzione della popolazione attiva*. Rome: Tipolitografia Failli.

Williamson, J. G. (2008). Globalization and the Great Divergence: terms of trade booms, volatility and the poor periphery. *European Review of Economic History* 12, 355–92.

Williamson, J. G. (2011). *Trade and Poverty: When the Third World Fell Behind*. Cambridge, MA: MIT Press.

Zamagni, V. (1993). *The Economic History of Italy, 1861–1990*. Oxford: Oxford University Press.

7

Industrialization in Egypt and Turkey, 1870–2010

Ulaş Karakoç, Şevket Pamuk, and Laura Panza

7.1 INTRODUCTION

This chapter examines the industrial performances of two large countries in the Middle East—Turkey and Egypt—during four historical periods: the period from 1870 to the First World War when industrialization remained very limited under open economy conditions; the inter-war era when industrialization began with the help of protectionism; the three decades after the Second World War when the import-substituting industrialization (ISI) model was adopted and rates of industrialization peaked in both countries; and trade liberalization and export orientation since 1980 when the performances of the two countries diverged significantly. In addition to providing brief accounts of Egypt and Turkey's performance, we will offer a comparative analysis of the outcomes in each period.

Egypt and Turkey have accounted for about half of the total population of the Middle East since 1870. Their combined populations have grown more than sevenfold from about 18 million in 1870 to more than 150 million in 2010 (Table 7.1). Egypt's borders have remained mostly unchanged since the nineteenth century. Turkey, on the other hand, was part of the Ottoman Empire until after the First World War and did not have borders of its own. For the sake of consistency, the narrative and all the quantitative series we present in this chapter will refer to the area inside the present-day borders of Turkey.

Per capita incomes in these two countries were roughly similar at the beginning of the period under study. Purchasing power parity (PPP) adjusted GDP per capita in 1990 international dollars was close to $800 in Egypt and Turkey in 1870. The two countries have diverged significantly since. While Egypt's GDP per capita rose more slowly, to $1,050 in 1950 and to about $4,000 in 2010, Turkey's GDP per capita almost doubled to $1,600 by 1950 and rose more than fivefold to 10,500 in 2010. As result, per capita incomes in 2010 were more than 150 per cent higher in Turkey than in Egypt (Table 7.1).

Egypt and Turkey embraced industrialization policies earlier than others in the region. They also achieved higher rates of manufacturing growth than most, if not all, other countries in the region from the 1930s. A comparative study can provide

Industrialization in Egypt and Turkey, 1870–2010   143

Table 7.1. Long-term trends in Egypt and Turkey, 1870–2010

| | Population | | GDP per capita | | | Manufacturing value added, annual growth rate (per cent) | | | |
| | Millions | | 1990 US$ (PPP) | | | Total | | Per capita | |
	Egypt	Turkey	Egypt	Turkey		Egypt	Turkey	Egypt	Turkey
1870	6.4	11.5	750	880					
1914	12.1	16.5	950	1,100	1870–1913	n.a.	1.2	n.a.	0.4
1950	21	21	1,050	1,600	1913–50	3.0	2.6	1.4	1.9
1980	45	44	2,100	4,750	1950–80	5.7	8.5	3.2	5.8
2010	79	73	4,000	10,500	1980–2010	4.1	5.2	2.2	3.3

Sources: GDP and population: Maddison (2007), Pamuk (2006); value added (Egypt), 1945–75: Ikram (1980, pp. 239–40); 1975–93: Radwan (2003); 1993–2010: World Bank indicators; value added (Turkey): Pamuk (2014) and Karakoç (2014).

insights into the impact of these policies. In contrast, in Iran, the other large country of the region, large oil revenues led to Dutch Disease effects which pulled resources away from industry, leading to lower manufacturing growth rates from the first half of the twentieth century.

This chapter will draw on official manufacturing series for the post-Second World War period and on recent value-added estimates for the inter-war era (Karakoç, 2014). For the pre-First World War years, we extrapolate backwards using the best available estimates of population, trade, and per capita income (Pamuk, 2006). The manufacturing value-added indices we present include factory production and traditional handicrafts, but not utilities, construction or mining. The inclusion of handicrafts is likely to lower measured manufacturing growth rates, since factory output grew much faster in the early stages of industrialization.

Egypt and Turkey adopted broadly similar trade and industrialization policies in each of the four historical periods we will identify below. Moreover, the trajectories of manufacturing in the two countries were similar to the pattern in many other developing countries. Neither country had tariff autonomy before 1914, since the Ottoman Empire, including Egypt, had committed to free trade treaties in 1838. It is likely that manufacturing output increased very slowly under these conditions (Table 7.1 and Fig. 7.1). During the second period, 1914–50, both countries adopted selective tariffs and moved towards protectionism, Turkey more strongly than Egypt. In both countries the beginning of industrialization can be dated to the 1930s, but manufacturing growth remained slow except in the 1930s. During the third period, 1950–80, both countries embarked on ISI policies. Average annual growth rates were close to 6 per cent in Egypt and 8 per cent in Turkey, and the share of manufacturing industry in GDP increased. Manufacturing exports remained limited, however, and most, if not all, of the output was directed towards the domestic market. After 1980 both countries liberalized their trade policies and attempted to promote manufacturing exports, with mixed results. Annual

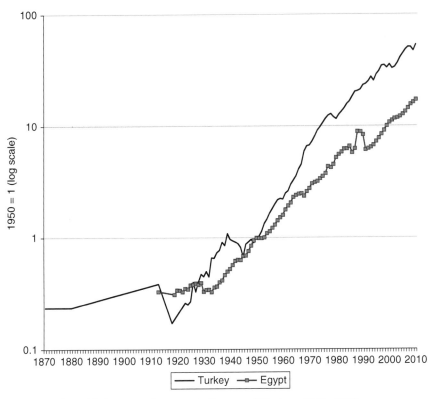

Fig. 7.1. Value added in manufacturing in Egypt and Turkey, 1870–2010

Sources: Egypt, 1919–45: Karakoç (2014); 1945–75: Ikram (1980); 1975–93: Radwan (2003); 1994–2010: World Bank indicators. Turkey: Pamuk (2014), Karakoç (2014).

manufacturing rates of growth slowed, while the differences in the industrial performance of the two countries became more pronounced. Per capita manufacturing output, the share of manufacturing in GDP, and the share of manufacturing in total exports were higher in Turkey in 2010 (Table 7.1 and Fig. 7.1).

We will identify a number of causal factors explaining these divergent trends. One was resource endowments. A significant difference between Turkey and Egypt was the availability of land. Egypt reached the limits of cultivable land before the First World War, but after that its population increased sixfold. In contrast, plenty of additional land was still available in Turkey in 1914. While population grew more than fourfold in Turkey during the twentieth century, this was matched by a threefold increase in cultivable land. This important difference in initial endowments helps explain part of the divergence between the two countries regarding not only agricultural but also industrial performance.

Another difference in initial conditions was social structure and the related political economy. Before 1945 private sector manufacturing was small scale and politically weak in both countries. As a result, agrarian interests were important in determining government policy. Egypt had a powerful class of large landowners favouring specialization in cotton, which helped delay the onset of industrialization. The British colonial administration in power from 1882 through the inter-war period also strongly favoured agriculture over industry. After the 1952 military coup, Egyptian governments started to eliminate the power of large landowners by distributing their land, and economic policy became strongly pro-industry. In Turkey, where small-scale family enterprises were more important in agriculture and landed interests were not as strong politically, government support for industrialization emerged earlier. While the Ottoman government did not and could not support industrialization, the new nation state strongly embraced protectionism and supported industrialization during the inter-war era, and again in the 1960s.

Government interventionism and the quality of the related institutions also mattered in explaining trends in the two countries. Government interventionism was important in creating high rates of manufacturing growth in both countries, especially during the ISI era. Yet, its content, goals, and implementation varied greatly over time. Perhaps most importantly, rather than being based on well-defined, impersonal rules, government support for manufacturing often involved support for individuals and firms close to the ruling party. As a result, the pursuit of favouritism or privileges from local and national governments remained a more popular activity for the private sector than productivity improvements or competition in international markets. There were also important differences between Egypt and Turkey in the impact of government interventionism on the private sector. The private sector was not promoted in Egypt, especially between the 1950s and early 1970s, at the height of Nasser's Arab socialism. In contrast, while the private manufacturing sector was initially quite weak in Turkey, it benefited from government support and steadily gained both economic and political strength from the end of the Second World War. However, here as well the private sector remained strongly dependent on government subsidies and tariff protection until the 1980s.

In terms of investment in human capital, both Turkey and Egypt lagged behind countries with similar levels of GDP per capita in Latin America and East Asia. This made it more difficult for manufacturing to move towards higher-technology, higher-value-added goods and sectors requiring higher skills. Low levels of human capital also help explain, at least in part, why the two countries did not have much success in increasing total factor productivity (TFP).

7.2 LIMITED INDUSTRIALIZATION UNDER OPEN ECONOMY CONDITIONS, 1870–1914

The sweeping changes transforming industrial production worldwide during the long nineteenth century also had a far-reaching impact on Middle Eastern manufacturing. The region, most of which belonged to the Ottoman Empire, became an exporter of primary commodities and an importer of manufactures, in common with most of the poor periphery. Increased integration with the world economy, in part due to steamships and railroads, accelerated the process of manufacturing decline (Issawi, 1982, p. 151), with the impact of the 1838 Anglo-Turkish Treaty being much discussed in the literature (Pamuk, 1987). A terms of trade shift in favour of primary commodity exports also explains much of the timing, extent, and spatial pattern of de-industrialisation (Pamuk and Williamson, 2012).

The collapse of Egyptian industry dates back to the 1840s, when Muhammad Ali's policy of state-led industrialization was replaced by one of laissez-faire (Panza and Williamson, 2015). The subsequent lack of any industrial strategy, coupled with very low external tariffs, persisted until 1914, discouraging manufacturing investment. From 1882, British rulers discouraged economic activities likely to compete directly with the homeland. Thus the Ottoman tariff rate increases in 1905 and 1908 did not apply to Egypt, and imported raw materials and machinery were taxed at the same rate as finished products. Excise duties were levied on a variety of locally produced goods, notably the 8 per cent duty on local cotton goods. This offset the 8 per cent import tariff, leaving the industry de facto completely unprotected (Panza, 2014, p. 161).

Egypt represented an extreme case of agricultural specialization. Cotton account-ed for more than 80 per cent of total exports in the 1880s, and over 90 per cent at the turn of the century (Panza, 2014, p. 158). The American Civil War increased the central importance of the raw fibre, and its share of government and private investment. Unsurprisingly, the second half of the nineteenth century saw only minimal industrial progress, despite considerable foreign investment and dramatic improvements in Egypt's transportation network (El-Gritly, 1947, p. 366): the share of industry (both mechanized and non-mechanized) did not exceed 2.3 per cent (Radwan, 1974). Agriculture, construction, finance, and trade attracted most foreign and domestic investment, being most profitable and relatively less risky.

Egyptian industry between 1870 and 1914 consisted of a small traditional manufacturing sector, co-existing with an even smaller mechanized sector, produc-ing for the low end of the income distribution. Employment was dominated by textiles and clothing (53 per cent of employment), both largely non-mechanized. Food processing, which ranked third (17 per cent), was also dominated by small, mostly unmechanized, family firms (Radwan, 1974, pp. 172–3).

Between 1899 and 1907, mechanization started in a few manufacturing sectors, mainly related to elementary raw material processing. Most important were sugar refining and cotton ginning/pressing, accounting for 65.6 per cent of capital invested in industry in 1899 (Radwan, 1974, p. 170; El-Gritli, 1947, pp. 367–9). Apart from these two sectors, there was very little modern indus-trial development.

Turkey's manufacturing production also declined during the nineteenth century, but less than in Egypt. Cotton textiles provide the most dramatic example, with the share of domestic producers falling from 97 to 25–35 per cent between the 1820s and the 1870s. More than half of the decline involved spinning and weaving by rural households. Most other branches of manufacturing shrank to a lesser extent or were not affected at all, either because the productivity increases in the European core were more limited, and/or because high transportation costs continued to protect Ottoman producers. Finally, exceptional cases such as carpet making and silk reeling saw increases in employment and production, due to growing demand in developed countries.

After 1870 Ottoman trade growth slowed, and the decline in textile manufacturing moderated and was even reversed in some areas, despite low tariffs. This slower manufacturing decline, which in some regions and sectors led to an incipient process of re-industrialization, was consistent with a reversal in the terms of trade. While these rose strongly in favour of primary commodities up to the mid- to late nineteenth century, they fell gradually thereafter, giving local industry some relief (Pamuk and Williamson, 2012). In some regions, small-scale urban workshops began using imported yarn to expand their output of cotton and mixed cotton cloths to meet local demand. Moreover, while hand spinning continued to decline, the volume of weaving rose, probably doubling between 1880 and the First World War. Significant amounts of textiles were shipped to long-distance markets elsewhere in Anatolia, Syria, and Egypt.

The decades before the First World War saw the establishment of a small number of factories in Turkey, mostly in the western part of the country, in Istanbul and Izmir but also in the Adana region in the south (Panza, 2014). Cotton, woollen and silk textiles, food processing, and construction materials such as cement and brick, were the most important branches. Nevertheless, the output of these mechanized factories remained limited when compared with domestic handicraft production. Total employment in large-scale manufacturing enterprises did not exceed several thousand during the 1910s (Quataert, 1993). While we can identify many obstacles to the rise of manufacturing in Turkey, such as limited availability of capital and a semi-skilled labour force, low tariffs and open economy conditions were the main determinants of the country's weak industrial performance before the First World War. Nor did the Ottoman (or Egyptian) currency provide any support for domestic manufacturing, being linked to gold.

Compared with the rest of the periphery, Egypt and Turkey were industrial laggards during this period (Bénétrix, O'Rourke, and Williamson, 2015). For example, while manufacturing production also declined in India, the latter started to re-industrialize earlier (Chapter 10). Unlike other major commodity suppliers, such as Argentina and Brazil (Chapter 13), Egypt and Turkey's specialization in primary commodity exports did not provide a platform for industrial development via Hirschman-type linkages. Low levels of industrialization in Egypt and Turkey before 1914 can thus be explained by the interaction of global and local dynamics. Low tariffs exposed domestic manufacturing to strong competition from abroad. Both countries remained vulnerable to international price shocks: improving terms of trade up to the 1870s contributed to manufacturing decline. The reversal of this trend from the 1870s onwards provided some relief to the import-competing sectors and can help explain the late nineteenth-century resistance of handicrafts in Turkey and to a smaller degree Egypt (Pamuk and Williamson, 2012).

Domestic tastes also afforded local handicrafts some staying power. Although British companies attempted to imitate local styles, often they could not do so satisfactorily, and thus there was still demand for domestic cloth, including cotton, woollen, and mixed varieties. Knowledge of local preferences helped domestic manufactures survive in the short run, while imported foreign techniques and foreign managers increased their efficiency and competitiveness in the longer run. Finally, Issawi argues that 'weavers were able to cut their costs greatly by using imported yarn; thus the Industrial Revolution, which had wiped out the spinners, gave the weavers a precarious reprieve' (Issawi, 1982, p. 152).

This was true particularly for Turkey, which experienced not only a stronger survival of domestic handicrafts, but also the beginnings of mechanized manufacturing production. Turkish geography offered more protection to domestic producers. Foreign goods were unable to penetrate regions distant from major trade routes or ports, especially before the railway boom late in the century. High transportation costs also provided considerable protection to domestic producers of bulky, nontextile goods, even in some coastal areas. On the other hand, Egyptian geography left the country more exposed to import penetration. The Nile valley in Lower Egypt, which included the vast majority of the population and cultivated land, represented a more compact and homogeneous area, and was thus easier and less costly to access. Large investments and improvements in transportation networks further facilitated import competition.

Finally, British colonialism was opposed to manufacturing development, implying no industrial policy and zero tariff protection in some sectors, like cotton textiles. Most government investments targeted agriculture and infrastructure. Moreover, the various Khedives who ruled the country were in no position to aid industry, not only because their power was subject to the colonial administration, but also because state revenues were tied to debt servicing. For all of these reasons, while manufacturing virtually collapsed in Egypt, Turkish handicrafts and industry, although badly hurt by foreign competition in the first half of the nineteenth century, resisted and adapted thereafter.

7.3 BEGINNINGS OF PROTECTIONISM AND INDUSTRIALIZATION, 1913–50

The period 1913–50 brought major changes to the structure of the world economy, together with deep political and social dislocations. The first wave of globalization resulted in a spectacular increase in the production and export of agricultural commodities and raw materials in the periphery. Two world wars, the instabilities of the 1920s, and the Great Depression largely disrupted this pattern. Although world production recovered by the end of the 1930s, world trade became fragmented within trade blocs and failed to recover (Feinstein et al., 2008). Political and economic rivalries and a lack of cooperation led many primary producers to adopt protectionism and more government intervention. Inter-war Egypt and Turkey were no exception.

Yet, there were crucial differences between Egypt and Turkey. Large-scale commercialization in agriculture, a lack of export diversification, land scarcity, and the existence of powerful landed and foreign interests continued to characterize the Egyptian economy until the 1940s. By 1914 the country had already reached the end of extensive growth based on the expansion of irrigation and cultivable land. Land became scarce and cotton yields fell from the turn of the century. Rapid population growth and persistent price declines from the mid-1920s put further pressure on per capita output, despite government-sponsored drainage projects and improved agricultural techniques.

Egypt gained nominal independence in 1922 but constraints on economic policy remained. First, the Egyptian pound remained tied to the British pound at a fixed rate until 1962. This may have been beneficial in the 1930s since Britain was still one of her main major trading partners, but whether the Egyptian pound was overvalued or not is far from clear (Hansen, 1991, pp. 79–83). Second, the tax system remained intact until the Capitulations were abolished in 1936, so the inefficient system based on land taxes, devised by the British before the turn of the century, remained a powerful constraint on the government's fiscal capacity. Finally, Egypt only regained tariff autonomy in 1930. The ensuing tariff reform introduced a three-tier scheme, based on mostly specific tariffs. The *ad valorem* equivalent for raw materials, fuel, and machinery was set at 4 per cent, while semi-manufactured goods were tariffed at 6–10 per cent and final goods at 15–30 per cent (Tignor, 1984, pp. 110–11). These rates were revised a number of times during the 1930s, and a depreciated currency surtax of 40 per cent was imposed in 1935 on imports of cotton and rayon piece goods from Japan, in order to stop a heavy inflow of cheap textiles from that country. The average nominal protection rate increased from 20–5 per cent in the 1920s to 40–50 per cent in the 1930s, rising five- or sixfold for cotton and woollen fabrics and even more for silk goods.

These measures reduced imports and boosted domestic manufacturing. Total imports declined by half in the first half of the 1930s and remained at these levels until the Second World War. The share of cotton textile imports in total domestic consumption declined steadily from 80 per cent in the 1920s to less than 40 per cent by 1939. Cotton textile imports were almost completely replaced by domestic production during the Second World War.

There were other developments that worked in favour of industrial growth as well (Hansen and Nashashibi, 1975, p. 4). Landowners looked for alternative investment outlets in the 1930s due to low and erratic cotton prices; relative prices moved in favour of manufactures; and wages remained low. Yet, tariff-induced industrial growth faced a serious constraint: limited domestic demand due to stagnating incomes. Direct national income estimates do not exist for this period, but estimates of consumption (e.g. of cereals, tobacco, passenger kilometres, and cotton textiles) and indirect income estimates (Yousef, 2002) confirm the largely accepted hypothesis that per capita national income remained stagnant between the eve of the First World War and the end of 1930s, due to the ongoing agricultural crisis (Hansen, 1979; Karakoç, 2014).

The Second World War brought significant dislocation. Foreign troops stationed in Egypt generated additional demand for manufactures. At the same time, imports were disrupted, particularly after Italy entered the war (Issawi, 1954, pp. 141–2; Tignor, 1984, pp. 176–9). Industrial output increased moderately during the 1920s (1.2 per cent per annum), accelerated slightly in the 1930s (2.8 per cent), and accelerated again during the war. Output growth during the 1930s and wartime was largely due to textiles whereas food-processing sectors stagnated. Furthermore, the share of modern factories in total output increased during the 1930s; more than half of cotton fabrics were produced by factories in the second half of the 1930s, though the trend was less pronounced in other sectors (Karakoç, 2014).

Turkey was different. Commercial agriculture was limited to the Aegean and Mediterranean coasts; the share of exports in national income was smaller; the export basket was more diverse and land was relatively abundant. Moreover, the political changes of the 1920s had a dramatic impact on state capacity as the military and civilian bureaucracy was able to pursue a nationalist and interventionist economic agenda throughout the inter-war period. Neither local wealthy elites nor foreign powers remained influential in policy making.

Industrialization was the primary objective of policy-makers from the very beginning, but the tools and results varied over time (Tezel, 1994, pp. 135–9). During the 1920s, the policy menu was rather small due to restrictions on import policies and limited state capacity. The 1923 Lausanne Treaty fixed tariff levels and prevented any revisions until 1929 for Turkey's main trade partners (Kurmuş, 1978). The average tariff rate thus remained around 16 per cent until 1929, implying negligible import protection. Policy-makers attempted to promote industry by trying to raise industrial loans and promulgating the 1927 Law for the Encouragement of Industry. This provided tax exemptions for domestic manufacturing enterprises (Tezel, 1994, pp. 263–6). A modest increase in output was achieved during the 1920s, mostly as a result of recovery from wartime disruptions (Karakoç, 2014).

In 1929 the government introduced a new tariff schedule. The average tariff rate increased from 15 to 35 per cent within a year. However, since the new duties were systematically biased in favour of final goods at the expense of raw materials and intermediates, effective rates increased more than nominal ones (Tezel, 1994, pp. 145–6). The tariff revision coincided with the advent of the Great Depression, which forced the government to take additional measures. Exchange controls and import quotas were immediately introduced in response to rapidly declining export revenues and deteriorating terms of trade. The main priority was to maintain the trade balance, avoid currency depreciation, and maintain a balanced budget. After 1933, clearing arrangements strengthened Germany's importance in Turkish trade.

From 1933, the government assumed a bigger industrial role, acting as entrepreneur and investor in industries such as textiles, leather working, mining, and sugar refining. State intervention reached such proportions that many scholars have classified the 1930s as an exclusively 'etatist' period (Boratav, 2011; Tekeli and Ilkin, 2009; Tezel, 1994). Large-scale state enterprises contributed to the rise of modern factory output at the expense of traditional handicrafts during this period, though it is hard to quantify the extent of this. However, the 'etatist' label is to a certain extent misleading, as the share of the state sector in total industrial employment did not exceed 10 per cent in 1938. Industrial growth was led overwhelmingly by the private sector, which benefited from backward and forward linkages with new large government enterprises (Pamuk, 2001).

Inward-looking policies had a significant impact on the domestic market, reducing imports, whose share in GDP fell from 12 to 8 per cent during the 1930s. The share of imports in the consumption of cotton fabrics fell from roughly 60 per cent in the 1920s to 20 per cent by the end of the 1930s. Furthermore, the composition of imports moved away from final goods towards raw materials and intermediate goods.

Textiles, food-related industrial output, and aggregate industrial output rose at 8.8, 7.9, and 7.9 per cent per annum, respectively, between 1925 and 1939 (Karakoç, 2014). However, since agricultural and services value added also rose, industry's share of GDP changed only slightly (Fig. 7.2). During the Second World War, manufacturing value added contracted by one-fourth, recovering to the 1939 level by the end of the 1940s. This wartime decline was the result of the large-scale mobilization of labour and draft animals, the collapse of world trade, and a downturn in domestic demand.

The industrial expansion of the 1930s was due to various factors. First, higher nominal and effective tariffs, exchange controls, and quotas allowed local producers to achieve boosted market share and prices in the domestic market. Second, the domestic terms of trade moved in favour of industrial goods in the 1930s, lowering the cost of raw materials in comparison with final goods prices. High tariffs reinforced this trend and further increased profits. Finally, the significant higher

Fig. 7.2. Share of manufacturing in GDP in Egypt and Turkey in current prices, 1870–2010 (per cent)

Sources: Egypt, 1913 and 1939–53: Hansen and Marzouk (1964), Hansen (1979); 1954–9: Issawi (1963); 1960–74: UN indicators; 1975–2010: World Bank indicators. Turkey: Pamuk (2014), Karakoç (2014).

agricultural output in the second half of the 1930s boosted farm income and manufacturing demand (Pamuk, 2001). On the supply side, firms enjoyed not only relatively lower raw material prices, but also wages. Real wages increased rapidly between 1929 and 1933 due to nominal wage rigidity and intense deflation, but lagged behind manufactured goods prices after 1933. The share of wages in total industrial output declined from 28 to 22 per cent during the 1930s (Boratav, 2011, p. 77).

Neither country used exchange rate policies to support manufacturing during the inter-war period. Egypt did not have exchange rate policy autonomy until the end of the Second World War. Turkish policy-makers avoided expansionary monetary or exchange rate policy, largely due to memories of high inflation during the First World War, and opted instead to adhere to an overvalued lira. Turkey's lack of exchange rate activism and strong protectionism is also consistent with Eichengreen and Irwin's (2010) argument that countries which avoided devaluation in the 1930s opted for more protectionism.

Summing up, the inter-war era saw an acceleration of industrial production in both countries but more so in Turkey. Both countries embarked on import repression policies after 1929–30 but policy support for industrialization was stronger, and protectionism more extreme, in Turkey, where tariff increases were complemented by various non-tariff barriers. Manufacturing was helped in both countries by low raw materials prices and real wages. An important difference was that Egyptian agriculture suffered from a secular constraint due to its closed land frontier, while an open land frontier made it possible for Turkey to increase agricultural production despite persistently low commodity prices. In both countries textiles led the growth acceleration, but food processing also contributed to overall growth in Turkey. Manufacturing output growth was around 2 per cent in Egypt and as high as 8 per cent in Turkey during the inter-war period, placing Turkey above and Egypt below the averages for Latin America and Asia during the inter-war years (Chapter 2). Because Turkey's population, economy, and manufacturing were hit much more powerfully during both world wars, however, overall growth between 1914 and 1950 was similar in the two countries.

7.4 THE ERA OF IMPORT-SUBSTITUTING INDUSTRIALIZATION, 1950–80

The three decades after the Second World War saw rapid industrialization and economic growth in most developing countries, where manufacturing growth was faster than in the industrial core (Chapter 2). Global political and economic developments, institutional arrangements such as the Bretton Woods system, and local political developments, all contributed to the acceleration of industrialization. In the Middle East, medium-sized and especially large countries such as Egypt and Turkey experienced the most rapid industrial growth (Fig. 7.1).

There were important common elements in the post-1945 industrialization experiences of Egypt and Turkey. In both countries governments pursued ISI strategies, promoting industrialization via strong protectionism, public sector enterprises, and tax exemptions and subsidies for industrial firms. Government policy and support focused on large-scale enterprises, although medium and even small-scale firms continued to contribute to manufacturing output. Textiles, food processing, and consumer durables accounted for a large share of manufacturing output. Large-scale public sector enterprises played a major role in the production of key intermediate goods such as steel, aluminium, and chemicals, while manufacturing technology was mostly imported. At the same time, however, the industrialization experiences of Egypt and Turkey were also marked by significant differences.

As the Second World War ended, Egypt remained overwhelmingly agrarian, with industry accounting for only 10 per cent of GDP (Fig. 7.2). Policy was still predominantly laissez-faire. The Free Officers' coup in July 1952, led by Gamal Abdel Nasser, ushered in a new regime that radically re-oriented Egypt's institutional settings towards Pan-Arabism and Arab socialism. The state's role in the economy increased sharply after the nationalization of the Suez Canal in 1956. Economic policy became more radical and ties with the Soviet bloc were strengthened. Ownership of the main sectors of the economy was transferred to the state, and foreign ownership was almost completely eliminated. The agrarian land reforms of 1952 and 1963 led to massive land confiscations, a considerable redistribution of wealth, and a drastic reduction in income inequality (El-Ghonemy, 2003, Chapter 4). The regime spent large sums on welfare, including health and education, and provided large numbers of public sector jobs (Owen and Pamuk, 1998, p. 132). Nevertheless, advances in literacy rates and overall educational attainment remained minimal (Hansen, 1991, pp. 228–9). In the 1970s average years of schooling were lower in Egypt than in many sub-Saharan African and Southeast Asian countries (Van Zanden et al., 2014).

Industrialization via import substitution represented another cornerstone of economic policy. Tariffs on competing manufacturing imports were raised, while those on raw materials and equipment were lowered. Rates of effective protection rose sharply, exceeding 100 per cent in cotton textiles and some foodstuffs (Mabro and Radwan, 1976, pp. 56–7; Hansen and Marzouk, 1964, pp. 191–8; Hansen and Nashashibi, 1975). Unlike in East Asia (Chapter 8), there was no deliberate industrial export promotion strategy, as the large domestic market was regarded as the main outlet for the country's industries (Hansen, 1991, p. 130). State control of manufacturing deepened and was formalized in five-year plans. Industrial output was dominated by basic consumer goods (textiles, shoes, food, beverages, and cigarettes) and essential intermediate goods (building materials, fertilizers, chemicals, paper, petroleum products, and some metals). In the late 1960s more than 30 per cent of the industrial labour force was employed in the textiles sector. Cotton yarn and fabrics represented 20 per cent of all merchandise export earnings, and accounted for two-thirds of manufactured exports (Mabro and Radwan, 1976).

Manufacturing investment and output increased by more than 9 per cent per annum until the early 1960s. Industry's share in GDP rose from 13.4 per cent in 1952 to 21.7 per cent in 1963 (Fig. 7.2). However, warfare, and particularly the

defeat in the Six Day War (1967), had far-reaching and negative implications for
the economy as a whole, including manufacturing (Owen and Pamuk, 1998,
p. 134). One strategy for industrial recovery was a limited relaxation of state
regulation and some encouragement for the private sector. This *siyasat al-infitah*
(open door) policy became the cornerstone of Anwar Sadat's agenda, laying the
foundations for liberalization and openness. While Egypt's industrial strategy
shifted towards the private sector, the state remained the central planner, major
employer, and resource allocator in industry, as government subsidies to manufacturing persisted (Djoufelkit-Cottenet, 2008).

After the *infitah*, Egypt's economy enjoyed a period of growth, with GDP
growing by more than 5 per cent per annum until 1980. Growth was predominantly
driven by the oil sector, which benefited from the return of the Sinai oil wells in
1979. Rising oil prices generated Dutch Disease dynamics, shifting resources from
agriculture and manufacturing, whose share in GDP declined steadily during the
1970s (Figs 7.1 and 7.2). Oil accounted for as much as 75 per cent of total exports,
while the share of manufactures fell from 35 per cent in 1972 to 11 per cent in
1980 (Fig. 7.3). The share of manufactured exports in GDP remained well below
5 per cent throughout this period.

Overall, while the post-Second World War years saw industrial growth in Egypt,
TFP did not improve significantly. It declined between 1964 and 1973 due to
difficulties in importing spare parts and raw materials, in turn related to foreign
currency shortages. In the following decade, increasing oil revenues and foreign
reserves eased these constraints. Another factor restraining productivity was slow

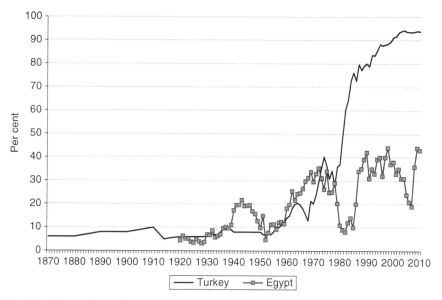

Fig. 7.3. Share of manufactures in total exports, 1870–2010 (per cent)

Sources: Egypt, 1919–54: Egypt, Annual Statement on Foreign Trade; 1954–73: Mabro and Radwan (1976);
1974–2010: World Bank indicators. Turkey: Pamuk (2014).

human capital accumulation, reflected in low literacy and enrolment rates, and reinforced by policies guaranteeing employment for graduates discharged from military service (Hansen, 1991, pp. 160–1, 229–30).

After 1945, domestic and international forces brought about major political and economic changes in Turkey as well. Domestically, many social groups had become dissatisfied with the single-party regime during the Second World War. The opposition demanded greater emphasis on private enterprise and the agricultural sector, and a more open economy. The emergence of the United States as the dominant world power after the war also shifted the balance towards a more open political and economic system. As the country was increasingly drawn into the American sphere of influence, the single-party regime abandoned its earlier emphasis on state-led industrialization.

Large increases in agricultural output were achieved after the Democrat Party came to power by winning the 1950 elections. However, the government tried to maintain high agricultural prices and incomes by printing money and buying wheat and other crops. The ensuing inflation and balance of payments crisis ended the experiment of agriculture as the leading sector. One criticism frequently directed at the Democrats was the absence of any coordination or long-term perspective in the management of the economy. As a result, one of the first initiatives of the military regime that toppled the Democrat Party in 1960 was to establish the State Planning Organization (SPO).

The economic policies of the 1960s and 1970s aimed to protect the domestic market and promote industrialization through import substitution, as in the 1930s. The five-year plans were binding for the public sector but only indicative for the private sector. In practice, however, the SPO played an important role in private sector decisions as well, since its approval was required for all investment projects that sought to benefit from subsidized credit, tax exemptions, or access to scarce foreign exchange. The agricultural sector was mostly left outside the planning process. Effective rates of protection remained very high in key sectors such as textiles, consumer durables, and some intermediate goods, and quotas were often set at low levels. Overvalued exchange rates served as another mechanism for subsidizing domestic industry (Hansen, 1991, pp. 352–3; Barkey, 1990, Chapter 4).

With the resumption of import substitution as the main strategy, family holding companies, large conglomerates which included manufacturing and distribution companies as well as banks and other services firms, emerged as the new leaders. State enterprises were directed to invest in large-scale intermediate goods industries, while private firms took advantage of the opportunities in the heavily protected and more profitable consumer goods sectors. From food processing and textiles in the 1950s, the emphasis shifted increasingly to radios, refrigerators, television sets, cars, and other consumer durables.

ISI policies were successful in accelerating the rate of economic growth, especially early on. GDP per capita increased by more than 4 per cent per annum on average during 1963–77. The rate of growth of manufacturing value added was considerably higher, averaging more than 10 per cent per annum. On the supply side, manufacturing growth depended overwhelmingly if not entirely on input growth. TFP growth remained well below 1 per cent per annum (Altuğ, Filiztekin, and Pamuk, 2008). Foreign direct investment in the ISI industries remained modest. Most new technology was obtained through patent and licensing agreements.

The large domestic market stimulated manufacturing output during this period. Despite the apparent inequalities in income, large segments of the population could buy consumer durables. Small and medium-sized agricultural producers were able to share in the expansion of the domestic market thanks to the growth in agricultural output and government price support programmes. In urban areas, real wages almost doubled during this period (Fig. 7.4), due to market forces as well as political and institutional changes. Most importantly, the rights obtained under the 1961 Constitution supported labour unions at the bargaining table (Keyder, 1987, Chapter 7; Barkey, 1990, Chapter 5; Hansen, 1991, pp. 360–78).

An important development with implications for Turkey's industrialization during this period was the emigration of several million, mostly male workers to Western Europe from 1961 until the 1973 recession. The remittances sent by these workers amounted to more than half of total earnings from commodity exports and kept the domestic market buoyant during the 1970s. They also began to create Dutch Disease effects during the mid-1970s, making it more difficult for ISI to proceed towards backward linkages. No study is available on the extent to which emigration may have raised Turkish wages during this period. After the 1970s, the

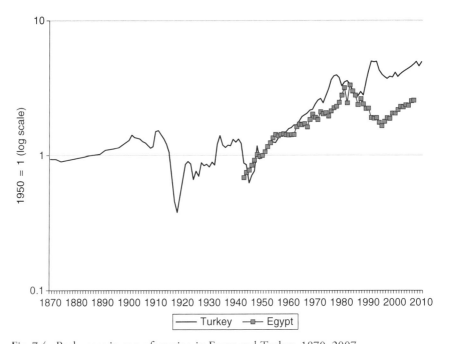

Fig. 7.4. Real wages in manufacturing in Egypt and Turkey, 1870–2007

Sources: Egypt, 1943–79 and 1987–2010: nominal wages (Mitchell, 1982) deflated by CPI (UN indicators); 1980–7: Radwan (2003). Turkey: Pamuk (2014).

absolute and relative importance of remittances declined, as the savings behaviour of workers began to change and Turkey's export earnings increased.

The years from 1963 to 1977 thus represented for Turkey what Albert Hirschman called the easy stage of ISI (Hirschman, 1966). By taking advantage of backward linkages, manufacturing value added increased in both final and intermediate goods, but not the technologically more difficult stage of capital goods. Both the relatively low education of the labour force and the related reluctance of the private sector to move into higher-technology sectors contributed to this outcome. The average years of schooling of the population above age 15 edged up from 1.5 in 1950 to only 4.2 in 1980. Literacy rates increased from 33 to 68 per cent during the same period. In both indicators, Turkey was well behind East Asia and Latin America as well as Eastern Europe, but above South Asia and Africa (Van Zanden et al., 2014). Moreover, manufacturing exports were also ignored until 1980, largely because of the sizable domestic market, and this proved to be the Achilles heel of Turkey's ISI. Even though the share of manufacturing in total exports reached 35 per cent in the 1970s, the low share of exports in GDP meant that the share of manufacturing exports in GDP remained less than 2 per cent. Boosting exports required a new government policy and institutional environment, but protection strengthened vested interests in favour of the old policies. Moreover, political conditions became increasingly unstable during the 1970s. As a result, no attempt was made to adjust even after the oil shock of 1973. Coalition governments chose to borrow abroad under unfavourable terms, and encouraged the private sector to do the same, leading to a major balance of payments crisis at the end of the decade (Keyder, 1987, Chapter 8; Barkey, 1990, pp. 109–67).

The three decades after the Second World War thus saw rapid industrialization, unprecedented economic growth, and rising living standards for broad segments of the population in both Egypt and Turkey. Governments played a key role in industrialization, through protectionism, public sector enterprises, and tax exemptions and subsidies for private industrial firms. Industrialization also produced problems similar to those experienced by many economies embracing ISI during this period. Like in Latin America (Chapters 12 and 13), Middle Eastern industrialization was mostly oriented towards the domestic market, not exports. The large domestic markets largely explain this, as does slow TFP growth. In short, exports were uncompetitive; as a result, foreign exchange shortages were chronic.

Manufacturing and GDP growth were higher in Turkey than Egypt during these three decades. Turkish growth was close to the Asian average, and above the Latin American average, during this period, while Egypt's manufacturing growth lay below Asian rates, close to those for Latin America (Table 7.1 and Chapter 2). A larger GDP, and thus domestic demand, led to a larger and more diverse manufacturing sector in Turkey. Agriculture played different roles in the two countries. While strong protectionism raised manufactured goods prices in both countries, the single-party government in Egypt supported industry and low food prices in the cities. In contrast, since agricultural producers made up more than half of Turkey's population and were an important voting bloc, agricultural prices were supported through large scale, multi-crop programmes. These policies boosted agricultural demand for manufactures but also helped delay the shift towards manufacturing exports.

Contrasting resource endowments in Egypt and Turkey also help explain differences in manufacturing performance. Rates of population growth were broadly similar in the two countries during most of the twentieth century (Table 7.1). However, Egyptian population–land ratios were much higher from the nineteenth century, and the limits to cultivated land had been reached by 1914. As a result, increases in agricultural production were much more difficult to achieve in Egypt, which lost its food self-sufficiency and had to spend large amounts of foreign exchange on imported cereals and other foodstuffs from the 1950s. On the other hand, Turkey remained under-populated, with a large proportion of empty if less productive land, whose limits were reached only in the 1960s. As a result, Turkish agricultural income could grow much more rapidly and contribute more strongly to domestic demand for manufactures. Turkey has remained self-sufficient in food since the 1930s. The other important difference in resource endowments between the two countries relates to oil. Large Egyptian oil revenues from the 1970s alleviated foreign exchange shortages but also generated Dutch Disease dynamics. In contrast, Turkish oil resources remained modest and only met a small fraction of the growing domestic demand for hydrocarbons from the 1960s.

7.5 TRADE LIBERALIZATION AND EXPORTS, 1980–2010

Egypt's policy shift towards a more open economy began with the rise of oil exports in the 1970s. The economy began to expand thanks not only to oil exports and high revenues from transit dues charged on Suez Canal traffic, but also to increasing remittances and Arab aid. However, the symptoms of Dutch Disease were unmistakable: an overvalued currency, rising wages, high inflation, and negative real interest rates. This promoted investments in housing, electricity, and transport, rather than in industry and agriculture (Owen and Pamuk, 1998, p. 136). With the drop in oil prices in the mid-1980s, the boom quickly came to an end, leading to a long recession characterized by high levels of inflation and declining real wages at the end of the decade (Fig. 7.4).

In response, the Mubarak regime agreed to launch a new round of economic liberalization and structural adjustment in 1991 under the direction of the World Bank, promoting privatization, deregulation, and greater market orientation. As a consequence, the private sector's contribution to the economy expanded considerably. By 2001 the private sector accounted for 67 per cent of total investment, compared to only 8 per cent in the 1980s and practically zero in the 1960s (El-Ghonemy, 2003, Chapter 4). The economic reforms also radically changed the structure of Egypt's manufacturing. With state ownership declining due to privatization, the private sector accounted for over 70 per cent of value added and over 60 per cent of manufacturing employment in 2003 (Djoufelkit-Cottenet, 2008, p. 8).

Trade liberalization boosted imports. Rates of protection dropped drastically; the overall rate of effective protection fell from 51 to 32 per cent between 1994 and 1998

(Cassing et al., 1998). In spinning and weaving, effective tariff rates dropped from 788 per cent in 1986 to 48 per cent in 1997 and 10 per cent in 2004 (Galal and El-Megharbel, 2005, pp. 19, 27). Non-tariff barriers were eliminated, as required for Egypt's admittance to the WTO. On the other hand, no effective policy was put in place to promote exports or achieve export-led growth. The share of manufacturing in the Egyptian economy remained much lower than in Middle Eastern countries where active industrialization policies were adopted, like Tunisia and Turkey.

The composition of manufacturing changed considerably during this period. The share of textiles in value added fell from 30 per cent in the early 1970s to 15 per cent in 1990, while the share of petrochemicals jumped from 2 to 30 per cent. This shift was mirrored by a similar change in the composition of manufacturing exports, with the agri-food sector's share falling from 12 per cent in 1973 to 4 per cent in 1990 and 2 per cent in 2005 (Djoufelkit-Cottenet, 2008, p. 8). Manufacturing exports remained well below 40 per cent of total exports, and were around 2 per cent of GDP in the 1990s and 2000s (Fig. 7.3). Two decades after the second round of liberalization, it is clear that manufacturing's importance has been shrinking and liberalization has not promoted its growth. Indeed, in 2010 manufacturing value added accounted for less than 15 per cent of GDP, compared with over 20 per cent in the 1960s (Fig. 7.1). In 2010 only 11 per cent of Egyptians were employed in manufacturing, a share only marginally higher than that at the beginning of the twentieth century. Manufacturing investment dropped significantly and TFP did not improve, in the absence of effective polices to foster investments in education or innovation.

In Turkey, the severe economic crisis at the end of the 1970s made it impossible to continue with inward-oriented industrialization policies. Against a background of falling imports and output, commodity shortages, and strained relationships with the IMF and international banks, the government announced a comprehensive and unexpectedly radical stabilization and liberalization package in January 1980. The military regime that came to power after a coup in September of the same year endorsed and continued the new programme. The aims of the new policies were threefold: to improve the balance of payments, to reduce the rate of inflation in the short term, and to create a market-based, export-oriented economy in the longer term. The package began with a major devaluation followed by liberalization of the trade and payments regimes, elimination of price controls, substantial price increases for the products of the state economic enterprises, elimination of many government subsidies, freeing of interest rates, and subsidies and other support measures for exports. Privatization of the state economic enterprises was delayed until the 1990s and even later, as this proved to be a very contentious issue politically. Reducing real wages and the incomes of agricultural producers was an important part of the new policies. The parliamentary government of Demirel had little success in dealing with labour unions due to strikes and other forms of labour resistance, but the military regime prohibited union activity and brought about sharp declines in labour incomes (Aricanli and Rodrik, 1990; Boratav, 2011).

Turkey's total exports rose sharply, from a mere $2.3 billion or 2.6 per cent of GNP in 1979 to $13 billion or 8.6 per cent of GNP in 1990, and to more than

$150 billion or more than 15 per cent of GDP in 2010. Equally dramatic was the rising share of manufactures in total exports, from about 35 per cent in 1979 to more than 95 per cent in 2010. Exports were encouraged by a more realistic and managed exchange rate and direct subsidies in the early 1980s, though the subsidies were soon abandoned. Another important factor in the long-term expansion of Turkey's manufacturing exports was the signing of the customs union agreement with the European Union in 1995, ensuring access to the large EU market. Turkey's most important exports included textiles, along with clothing in the early period, and iron and steel products and cars in later years (Yilmaz, 2011). The EU's share in Turkey's exports remained around 50 per cent from the 1960s until the crisis of 2008.

The expansion of exports was accompanied by the rise of new industrial centres across Anatolia. The industrial enterprises in these emerging centres were mostly small to medium-sized family firms with limited capital, employing few professional managers. They began production in low-technology and labour-intensive industries: textiles and clothing, food processing, metal industries, wood products, furniture, and chemicals. Labour productivity in manufacturing in these new districts remained below the level in more established industrial areas such as the Istanbul region; the rise of these centres was closely connected to their low wages (Filiztekin and Tunali, 1999; Yilmaz, 2011). Manufacturing wages in Turkey rose between 1980 and 2010, but by less than per capita incomes in the urban sector and the economy as a whole.

Beginning in the late 1990s, the growth of Turkish manufacturing based on market- and export-oriented policies began to stall. While exports continued rising and GDP per capita rose by more than 30 per cent, manufacturing's share of GDP declined from 24 per cent in 1998 to less than 16 per cent in 2010. The movement of relative prices against Turkish manufactures contributed to this trend. The decline in manufacturing's share of total employment must have been equally strong, although official statistics do not provide a sufficiently accurate picture. This appears to be an example of the premature de-industrialization observed in many developing countries in recent decades (Rodrik, 2015).

One problem for Turkish manufacturing is that it continues to produce mostly standard goods, attempting to take advantage of low wages and costs. The technological sophistication of Turkey's manufacturing output and exports remains low. As a result, firms have been increasingly forced to compete with Chinese and Southeast Asian manufacturers enjoying even lower wages. One cause of this problem is that manufacturing companies have been reluctant to invest in product development and innovation ever since the 1960s. This is at least partly related to the shortcomings of the education system, which has not delivered a labour force with the skills necessary for a more diversified and technologically more advanced industrial sector. Turkey still lags behind East Asia and Latin America, if not South Asia and Africa, in basic measures of education such as average years of schooling (Van Zanden et al., 2014). In addition, government policy for the support of manufacturing industry has been very weak, if not non-existent (Taymaz and Voyvoda, 2012).

Trade liberalization, privatization, greater reliance on markets, and exports of manufactures were the basic goals in both Egypt and Turkey during the Washington Consensus era. Manufacturing growth in the two countries was broadly similar during this period, close to that in Asia excluding Japan and above that of Latin America (Table 7.1 and Chapter 2). At the same time, however, the manufacturing and GDP per capita records of the two countries diverged considerably during these three decades. One striking example of the growing contrast is the ratio of manufactured exports to GDP, which averaged below 5 per cent in Egypt but was slightly above 15 per cent in Turkey during the first decade of the twenty-first century. Oil exports and Dutch Disease effects were not the only reason for the slower growth of manufacturing and manufacturing exports in Egypt. A weak private sector, a poor institutional environment, and low investment in schooling also played important roles. In Turkey, manufacturing industry was supported by a stronger private sector, a stronger manufacturing base from the ISI era, and easier access to EU markets after 1980.

7.6 CONCLUSION

This chapter has examined the industrialization experiences of two large countries in the Middle East from 1870 to 2010. Trade and industrialization policies in Egypt and Turkey were strongly influenced by global forces and were broadly similar in each of the four periods studied here. Since neither country had tariff autonomy during the nineteenth century, industrialization remained limited before the First World War. It was only after gaining tariff autonomy in 1929 (Turkey) and 1930 (Egypt) that they could adopt protectionist policies and increase manufacturing output. The degree of protectionism, and consequently of industrialization, was stronger in Turkey during the 1930s. Manufacturing output in both countries was further behind that of the early core industrializers in 1950 than it had been in 1870 or 1914.

Manufacturing in Turkey and to a lesser extent Egypt grew faster than in the core countries between 1950 and 1980, a period of unprecedented economic growth and rising living standards in both countries. Governments played a key role in industrialization, via protectionism, tax exemptions, and subsidies. Public sector enterprises played a major role in industrialization in Turkey from the 1930s and in Egypt after the Second World War. Government policy attempted to transfer resources from agriculture to support manufacturing in Egypt during this period, but less so in Turkey. Protectionism and various other government policies tended to shift the domestic terms of trade in favour of manufacturing. However, industrialization continued to be oriented mostly towards the domestic market in both countries and exports remained weak. Moreover, increases in output were achieved primarily by increasing inputs, with TFP growth being limited.

Manufacturing growth slowed in both countries after 1980, as they moved in the direction of trade liberalization, privatization, and manufactured exports. The divergence between the two countries' manufacturing performances also became more pronounced, although manufacturing growth has been similar in recent years. In Egypt, oil created Dutch Disease effects, diverting resources away from manufacturing. On the other hand, more export-oriented policies and freer access to EU markets helped Turkey expand its manufacturing exports after 1980. The two countries' growth rates also differed. Between 1950 and 2010 Turkey's GDP and GDP per capita increased at annual rates of above 5 and 3 per cent respectively, about 1 per cent per annum faster than in Egypt. Faster economic growth led to faster growth in domestic demand for manufactures; manufacturing industry both contributed to and was supported by more rapid economic growth in Turkey.

A number of factors can explain the industrial performance of these countries as well as the differences between them. Since economic policies in the two countries were broadly similar, they are not the key to understanding the differences. Initial differences in resource endowments, namely the relative scarcity of land in Egypt and the abundance of land in Turkey, contributed to the differences in industrialization outcomes from the end of the First World War until the 1980s, when the divergence between the two countries was strongest.

Turkey and Egypt lagged behind countries with similar levels of GDP per capita in Latin America and East Asia when it came to education and human capital, making it harder for manufacturing in both countries to transition towards higher-technology, higher-value-added goods and sectors requiring higher skills. Low investment in human capital also helps explain, at least in part, why the two countries have not had much success in improving TFP.

Finally, an important explanation for the long-term trajectory of industrialization as well as the low rates of TFP growth in both countries lies in the nature of government interventionism and the quality of related institutions. Interventionism spurred economic growth and development in many late industrializers, notably East Asia after the Second World War, by protecting infant industries and more generally by supporting the private sector. While government interventionism also played an important role in raising manufacturing growth in Egypt and Turkey during the ISI era, its content, goals, and implementation varied greatly over time. The military played an important role in the economy in both countries, especially Egypt, establishing close links with both the state apparatus and private enterprises. Perhaps most importantly, rather than being based on well-defined rules, government support for manufacturing industry or a specific sector often became support for individuals and firms close to the government. As a result, rent seeking, rather than productivity improvements or competing in international markets, often became the preferred strategy for the private sector. Individuals and firms preferred using their resources to stay close to and seek favours from the government, rather than invest in education, skills, and technology to improve competitiveness in domestic and international markets.

The impact of government interventionism on the private sector differed in the two countries. In Egypt, government policy reduced the size of the private sector via nationalizations and other means after the Second World War, so that the private sector was slow to become an important player in manufacturing, and more generally in the urban economy, after 1980. Private firms preferred investing in the oil or service sectors instead. In contrast, while the private sector was quite weak in Turkey at the end of the Second World War, its economic and political strength has risen steadily since then. A more solid manufacturing base inherited from the ISI era played a key role in Turkey's stronger export performance after 1980. Yet the private sector remains dependent on government favours in Turkey as well.

REFERENCES

Altuğ, S., Filiztekin, A., and Pamuk, Ş. (2008). Sources of long-term economic growth for Turkey, 1880–2005. *European Review of Economic History* 12, 393–430.

Aricanli, T. and Rodrik, D. (1990). An overview of Turkey's experience with economic liberalization and structural adjustment. *World Development* 18, 1343–50.

Barkey, H. J. (1990). *The State and the Industrialization Crisis in Turkey*. Boulder, CO: Westview Press.

Bénétrix, A. S., O'Rourke, K. H., and Williamson, J. G. (2015). The spread of manufacturing to the poor periphery 1870–2007. *Open Economies Review* 26, 1–37.

Boratav, K. (2011). *Türkiye İktisat Tarihi, 1908–2009*, 15th edition. Istanbul: Imge Kitabevi Yayınları.

Cassing, J., Fawzy, S., Gallagher, D., and Kheir-el-Din, H. (1998). *Enhancing Egypt's Exports*, Ministry for the Economy, DEPRA Report, Cairo.

Djoufelkit-Cottenet, H. (2008). Egyptian industry since the early 1970s: a history of thwarted development. *ADF Working Paper* No. 61, Paris.

Egypt, Ministry of Finance, Statistical Department (1910–46). Annual Statement on Foreign Trade.

Eichengreen, B., and Irwin, D. A. (2010). The Slide to Protectionism in the Great Depression: Who Succumbed and Why? *The Journal of Economic History* 70, 871–897.

El-Ghonemy, M. R. (ed.) (2003). *Egypt in the Twenty First Century: Challenges for Development*. London: Routledge, Curzon.

El-Gritli, A. A. I. (1947). The structure of modern industry in Egypt. *L'Egypte Contemporaine* 38, 363–79.

Feinstein, C., Toniolo, G., and Temin, P. (2008). *The World Economy between the World Wars*. Oxford: Oxford University Press.

Filiztekin, A. and Tunalı, İ. (1999). Anatolian tigers: are they for real? *New Perspectives on Turkey* 20, 77–106.

Galal, A. and El-Megharbel, N. (2005). Do governments pick winners or losers? An assessment of industrial policy in Egypt. *ECES Working Paper* No. 108, Cairo.

Hansen, B. (1979). Income and consumption in Egypt, 1886/1887 to 1937. *International Journal of Middle East Studies* 10, 27–47.

Hansen, B. (1991). *Egypt and Turkey: Political Economy of Poverty, Equity and Growth*. Washington, DC: World Bank.

Hansen, B. and Marzouk, G. A. (1964). *Development and Economic Policy in the UAR (Egypt)*. Amsterdam: North-Holland.

Hansen, B. and Nashashibi, K. A. (1975). *Egypt*. New York: National Bureau of Economic Research.

Hirschman, A. O. (1966). The political economy of import-substituting industrialization in Latin America. *Quarterly Journal of Economics* 82, 1–26.

Ikram, K. (1980). *Egypt, Economic Management in a Period of Transition: The Report of a Mission Sent to the Arab Republic of Egypt by the World Bank.* Baltimore, MD: World Bank/Johns Hopkins University Press.

Issawi, C. P. (1954). *Egypt at Mid-century: An Economic Survey.* London: Oxford University Press.

Issawi, C. P. (1982). *An Economic History of the Middle East and North Africa.* New York: Columbia University Press.

Karakoç, U. (2014). Sources of economic growth in interwar Egypt and Turkey: industrial growth, tariff protection and the role of agriculture. Unpublished Ph.D. dissertation, Department of Economic History, London School of Economics and Political Science.

Keyder, Ç. (1987). *State and Class in Turkey: A Study in Capitalist Development.* London: Verso.

Kurmuş, O. (1978). 1916 ve 1929 gümrük tarifeleri üzerine bazı gözlemler. Türkiye İktisat Tarihi Üzerine Araştırmalar.

Mabro, R. and Radwan, S. (1976). *The Industrialization of Egypt 1939–1973: Policy and Performance.* Oxford: Clarendon Press.

Maddison, A. (2007). *Historical Statistics for the World Economy, 1–2005.* Paris: OECD Development Studies Centre.

Mitchell, B. R. (1982). *International Historical Statistics: Africa and Asia.* New York: New York University Press.

Owen, E. J. R. and Pamuk, Ş. (1998). *A History of Middle East Economies in the Twentieth Century.* London: I.B. Tauris.

Pamuk, Ş. (2001). Intervention during the Great Depression: another look at Turkish experience. In *The Mediterranean Response to Globalization before 1950* (Eds, Pamuk, Ş. and Williamson, J.). London and New York: Routledge, 321–39.

Pamuk, Ş. (2006). Estimating economic growth in the Middle East since 1820. *Journal of Economic History* 66, 809–28.

Pamuk, Ş. (2014). Türkiye'nin 200 Yıllık İktisadi Tarihi, İş Bnkası Kültür Yayinlari. Istanbul.

Pamuk, Ş. and Williamson, J. G. (2012). Ottoman de-industrialization, 1800–1913: assessing the magnitude, impact, and response. *Economic History Review* 64, 159–84.

Panza, L. (2014). De-industrialization and re-industrialization in the Middle East: reflections on the cotton industry in Egypt and in the Izmir region. *Economic History Review* 67(1), 146–69.

Panza, L. and Williamson, J. G. (2015). Did Muhammad Ali foster industrialisation in 19th century Egypt? *Economic History Review* 68, 79–100.

Quataert, D. (1993). *Ottoman Manufacturing in the Age of the Industrial Revolution.* Cambridge: Cambridge University Press.

Radwan, S. (1974). *Capital Formation and Egyptian Industry and Agriculture 1882–1967.* London: Ithaca Press.

Radwan, S. (2003) Full employment: the challenge in the twenty-first century. In *Egypt in the Twenty First Century: Challenges for Development* (Ed., El-Ghonemy, M. R.). London: Routledge, Curzon.

Rodrik, D. (2015). Premature de-industrialization. *NBER Working Paper* No. 20935.

Taymaz, E. and Voyvoda, E. (2012). Marching to the beat of a late drummer: Turkey's experience of neoliberal industrialization since 1980. *New Perspectives on Turkey* 47, 83–111.

Tekeli, I. and İlkin, S. (2009). *Uygulamaya Geçerken Türkiye'de Devletçiliğin Oluşumu.* Ankara: Bilge Kültür Sanat.

Tezel, Y. (1994). *Cumhuriyet Döneminin Iktisadi Tarihi, 1923–1950*. Istanbul: Türkiye Ekonomik ve Toplumsal Tarih Vakfı.

Tignor, R. (1984). *State, Private Enterprise and Economic Change in Egypt, 1918–1952*. Princeton, NJ: Princeton University Press.

UN Indicators. Accessed at http://data.un.org.

Van Zanden, J. L., et al. (eds) (2014). *How Was Life? Global Well Being since 1820*. Paris: OECD Publishing.

World Bank Indicators. Accessed at http://data.worldbank.org/indicator.

Yilmaz, K. (2011). The EU–Turkey customs union fifteen years later: better, yet not the best alternative. *South European Society and Politics* 16, 235–49.

Yousef, T. (2002). Egypt's growth record under economic liberalism, 1885–1950: a reassessment using new GDP estimates. *Review of Income and Wealth* 48, 560–80.

PART II

ASIA

8

East Asian Industrial Pioneers
Japan, Korea, and Taiwan

Dwight H. Perkins and John P. Tang

8.1 INTRODUCTION

Many scholars have attempted to fit the East Asian industrialization experience into what is often called the 'flying geese pattern' of development. Japan in this view was the leader and innovator and the other economies of East Asia followed the leader. When this model was applied to all of East and Southeast Asia, however, it fitted poorly. Hong Kong and Singapore followed a much more laissez-faire approach, and while many Southeast Asian economies at times attempted an approach similar to that of Japan, the results were often failures. Korea and Taiwan, however, were colonies of Japan (from 1910 to 1945 and 1895 to 1945 respectively) and there is no doubt that their post-1960 industrial development policies and the nature of the associated supporting institutions were influenced by the Japanese experience, probably more so in Korea than Taiwan. Korea's post-independence leadership, for the most part, grew up under Japanese rule, while Taiwan's political leadership after 1945 came from the Chinese mainland.[1]

When Japan initiated its industrialization drive, however, it faced a different context from that facing Korea and Taiwan a half-century or more later. Japan was a true pioneer in that it was the first non-European/North American economy to achieve sustained industrialization and modern economic growth. In a broader sense, of course, Japan was a follower country that learned from the first pioneers of industrialization, notably England. The context Japan faced in the latter decades of the nineteenth century and the first decades of the twentieth, however, was very different from the context that faced England and the United States, although it had more in common with Germany.[2]

When Japan began to modernize its economy, it faced a world dominated by British free trade views and practices. Japan was forced to accept those views in the treaty that opened up the economy—mercantilist policies pushing exports and tightly restricting imports were impossible until much later. Japan's economy was

---

[1] These issues are the discussed at length in Perkins (2013).
[2] For a comparison of the German and Japanese development experiences, see Landes (1965).

influenced by the First World War, which cut off Asia from most trade with Europe. There followed a decade of comparative prosperity in much of the industrialized world, which then turned into the Great Depression of the 1930s and the Second World War. Facing a similar world situation after 1914, many economies in South America began an industrialization drive based heavily on import substitution behind high trade barriers. Japan followed a very different path, one that before 1914 took advantage of the world's open trading system, followed then by the trade protection provided by the First World War, but done without recourse to high tariffs and other trade restrictions. Japan changed course during the trade wars of the 1930s and this change was further reinforced by the country's decision to become a major colonial power in Asia with the help of the Japanese military.

The international context in which Korea and Taiwan began their industrial drive was different from that facing Japan earlier, in a number of ways. To begin with, a quarter-century had passed from the time when Japanese industrial development was governed by and then destroyed by war. During that time there had been steady industrial expansion and technological innovation, particularly in North America. The backlog of untapped technology available to newly industrialized nations was thus substantially larger than it was in the mid-1930s. Japan itself took advantage of this backlog and it is likely that it accounts for a significant part of the rapid growth spurt that Japan experienced between recovery from the Second World War, usually dated as 1953, and its slowdown to more normal high-income country growth rates in 1973. The backlog of technology available to Korea and Taiwan had accumulated not just for twenty-five years, but for more than half a century, and this was a major reason why industrialization in those two economies, once it started, proceeded at double-digit growth rates for three decades.

Korean and Taiwan's industrialization, unlike the earlier Japanese one, did not face a Great Depression and they could export into the wide-open economy of the United States during their first growth spurt. Also unlike Japan, they were not subject to a treaty prohibiting them from raising protective barriers for their domestic markets. Mercantilist policies promoting exports and limiting imports were possible in Korea and Taiwan in ways that they had not been in Japan before the Great Depression, because of Japan's treaty obligations on tariffs until 1899 and the implicit rules of the inter-war world economy thereafter. Nor did Korea and Taiwan face anything remotely comparable to the trade wars and build-up to all-out war in Europe and Asia that characterized the 1930s. South Korea and Taiwan, however, controlled territories that were determined by the outcomes of post-1945 civil wars, civil wars that to this day have not been formally ended. Industrialization policies in both economies were as a result heavily influenced by the possibility that economic failure could lead to their being swallowed up by the opposing sides in their civil wars.

In what follows we begin with a discussion of the Japanese industrialization experience before the Second World War. This is followed by an analysis of the industrialization of Korea and Taiwan after the Second World War.

8.2 JAPAN

Unique among emerging peripheral countries in the twentieth century, Japan began its industrial development in the late 1800s and successfully maintained the momentum over the following decades to become fully industrialized in the first half of the next century.[3] This transition is especially remarkable given the country's starting point: politically fragmented; agrarian; reliant on handicrafts and traditional techniques for manufacturing; and relatively isolated from international markets. By the early 1900s, however, the country had an integrated domestic market connected by railroads; was a leading exporter of textiles and light manufactures; and had burgeoning modern sectors in metal processing, machinery, and chemicals. Institutional and political change was also vigorous over this period, with the country adopting foreign practices like central banking, commercial and civil codes, the gold standard, and an overseas empire following wars with China and Russia.

While the contours of Japan's transition from a traditional to an industrial economy have been studied in great detail, identifying turning points in the process remains an active subject of scholarship.[4] Moreover, there is revived interest in the factors contributing to the country's successful industrial performance and their relative importance.[5] This chapter adds to the literature by providing an overview of Japan's pre-war economy, but focusing on the changes to its industrial structure and other features coinciding with the country's development.

8.2.1 Early Modern Period and Historical Background

The historical context of modern Japanese economic growth is well known. Following the opening of the country in the mid-1800s, the Tokugawa and Meiji governments rapidly adopted foreign technologies for national defence and to 'catch up' on leading industrial nations like the United Kingdom and United States.[6] Political centralization via institutional reform, infrastructure investment, and military conscription by the Tokyo-based Meiji government contrasted with the semi-autonomy exercised by domains in the Tokugawa period, facilitating the spread of literacy, legal institutions, and finance.[7] Universal primary education,

---

[3] Pre-conditions for modern industrial growth preceded the Meiji period, dating back to the Tokugawa era (1603–1868). These included a well-developed internal market for commodities and finance and significant human capital in terms of education and literacy; see Crawcour (1974; 1997a) and Lockwood (1954).

[4] E.g. Lockwood (1954), Ohkawa and Rosovsky (1973), and Ohkawa and Shinohara (1979). Historical data collections include the *Estimates of Long-Term Economic Statistics of Japan since 1868* and those produced by the Japanese Statistical Association (2007).

[5] Rousseau (1999), Morck and Nakamura (2007), Mitchener and Ohnuki (2009), and Tang (2011, 2013).

[6] The regime change from the Tokugawa (1603–1868) to Meiji periods and its underlying causes are discussed in Lockwood (1954), Gordon (2009), and Crawcour (1997a). Much of the following discussion is based on these sources.

[7] The current division of the country into 47 prefectures began from 1871, when nearly 300 hereditary domains were consolidated and assigned governors (initially, many of the former lords) chosen by the Meiji government, through 1888.

funded by local authorities, was announced in 1872 and made compulsory in 1890, and institutes were established to disseminate agricultural and technical best practices.[8] The 1873 tax and land reform, which also discontinued samurai stipends in lieu of government bonds, provided a more reliable public revenue stream to finance the modernization programme as well as model enterprises in engineering, arsenals, shipbuilding, and textile production.[9] However, only after the Matsukata deflation in the early 1880s did public finances stabilize, which followed a period of currency debasement and experimentation with a national banking system.[10] Major policies pursued by successive administrations included promulgating a constitution with limited suffrage; colonization of Taiwan and Korea; and renegotiating treaties with Western nations on extra-territoriality and tariff autonomy.

Straitened finances in the late 1870s resulting from trade deficits, modernization costs, and civil unrest suppression forced the government to privatize many of its model enterprises, providing a fillip to the private sector. Entrepreneurs like Shibusawa Eiichi and the zaibatsu conglomerates of Mitsui and Mitsubishi led the expansion of industry and technology, while many ex-samurai used their commutation bonds to invest in the nascent banking sector.[11] These banks and other intermediaries in turn provided local sources of financing for modern enterprises.[12] Private business also benefited from public investment in infrastructure and industries, with the government's share of capital investment averaging 30 to 40 per cent of the national total between the late 1890s and the First World War, at which point the country had emerged as an industrial economy.[13]

8.2.2 Timing of Japan's Industrialization

To date the onset of Japanese industrialization, scholars have used various metrics including growth rates for national output, industrial value added, and capital formation.[14] Based on these measures, Japan entered its 'modern economic growth' period in the early 1880s, the 1890s, or the early 1900s, respectively.[15] All these series have strengths and weaknesses, but share the objective of timing significant shifts in Japan's economic performance. National and per capita output by themselves abstract away from the composition of production, while industrial value

---

[8] Taira (1997), pp. 273–4, and Crawcour (1997b), p. 67. Pre-Meiji literacy rates were unusually high, approximately 40 and 10 per cent for males and females, respectively, and are implicated in the country's economic growth.

[9] Crawcour (1997a), pp. 43–4, and Onji and Tang (2015). Japan also accessed international capital markets, with its first bond offering of £1 million in 1870 used to finance the first railway and other public outlays.

[10] *Ibid.*, pp. 46–7.

[11] Morikawa (1992), Odagiri and Goto (1996), Tang (2011), Yamamura (1997).

[12] Tang (2013).   [13] Crawcour (1997b), p. 52.

[14] Ohkawa and Shinohara (1979), Bénétrix et al. (2015), and Ohkawa and Rosovsky (1973), respectively. These studies relate to the economic convergence literature, such as Barro (1997) and Rodrik (2013).

[15] Ohkawa and Shinohara (1979), p. 12; Bénétrix et al. (2015), Table 3; Ohkawa and Rosovsky (1973), p. 31.

added and capital formation growth rates are both relative measures that do not adjust for developing countries' varying initial stocks of industrial output and investment, especially when compared with leading economies that made their transition in an earlier, but more developmentally similar, period of time.

An alternative approach, useful for marking the country's full-fledged arrival to industrialized status as opposed to its take-off, would be to compare industry's share of output in Japan and in leading economies at a time when the latter would be recognized as being industrialized.[16] For example, using the United States as reference, its average share of manufacturing and construction output in total output between 1895 and 1914 was 11.8 per cent. Japan reached a similar stage of industrial performance in 1897. Similarly, Japan's share of machinery and transport equipment in total manufacturing exceeded 5 per cent in 1907, which was the average for the United States in the pre-First World War period (Fig. 8.1).[17]

This focus on the decade spanning 1897–1907 coincides with existing studies and highlights a familiar pattern of industrial development. Heavy industries like machinery manufacturing in Japan followed the same trajectory as the United States, with the two countries shifting toward more capital and resource intensive sectors over the sixty years leading up to the 1930s. In the case of the United States, the shift was from processed food products and textiles to lumber products and wood furniture, with a dramatic increase in the machinery output share in the early 1910s coinciding with the First World War. Similarly, Japanese food processing declined relative to higher-value products like silk and cotton textiles. At the same time, stone and mineral processing and chemical manufacturing grew steadily, with the former and machinery accelerating in trend starting in the early 1900s.[18]

While Japan remained far behind the United States in terms of the absolute and relative output of heavy sectors through the pre-Second World War period, its industrial structure increasingly resembled those of leading countries rather than those of peripheral ones. This is true not only in terms of the share of output among industrial sectors, but also in terms of the relative speed with which they grew to economic importance. In particular, technological diffusion in manufacturing was faster in Japan than the United States in the late nineteenth century, which is striking given the former's much lower initial per capita output.[19] To explain these

---

[16] Bénétrix et al. (2015) identify 1899 as the year when Japan joined the 'modern growth club', based on having ten years of average industrial growth exceeding 5 per cent.

[17] For Japan, manufacturing comprises ten sub-sectors: food products; textiles; lumber and wood products; chemicals; stone, clay, and glass products; iron and steel; non-ferrous metals; machinery; printing and publishing; and other manufacturing (Shinohara, 1972). For the United States, manufacturing and construction materials include 44 categories, which are then mapped into the broader industry classification equivalent for Japan (Wattenberg, 1976).

[18] See also Crawcour (1997b), pp. 51–2. The three sub-sectors of stone, clay, and glass products; iron and steel; and non-ferrous metals are grouped together in the Japanese data as they individually overlap with their more detailed American equivalents, which are also aggregated to the higher level of classification.

[19] Tang (2015).

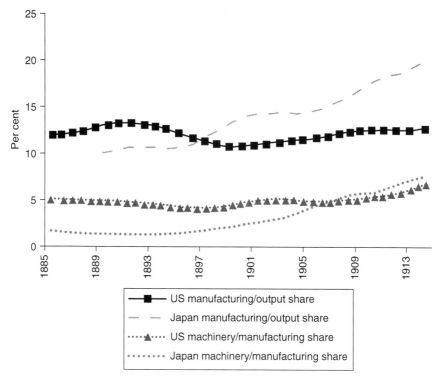

Fig. 8.1. United States and Japanese industry shares, 1885–1914

Sources: Wattenberg (1976), series F3 and P318-374 in constant 1913 dollars; Ohkawa, Takamatsu, and Yamamoto (1974), Table 25, and Shinohara (1972), Table 2, in constant 1934–6 yen. All series reported as five-year moving averages.

dynamics, the remainder of this section presents evidence regarding the contributions of trade, investment, and shocks to both the domestic and global economies.

8.2.3 The Impact of Trade

Although not colonized, Japan was subjected to numerous predations on its sovereignty, especially in its economic relations.[20] Besides extra-territorial privileges for foreigners residing in its eight treaty ports, Japan relinquished tariff autonomy, opening its domestic market to foreign manufactures and reducing potential revenues from its exports.[21] Import tariffs averaged 3.75 per cent between 1868 and 1898, but after regaining autonomy the following year they rose to an average

---

[20] Gordon (2009), p. 51.

[21] Tariffs were set at a maximum of 5 per cent *ad valorem* until 1899, when Japan began to successfully renegotiate its treaties; full autonomy was not negotiated until 1911, before which Japan could set a maximum of tariff of 15 per cent (*ibid.*, p. 117).

Table 8.1. Disaggregated trade shares by manufacturing sector, 1880–1930

Exports	1880	1890	1900	1910	1920	1930
Food products	39.0	27.5	14.3	12.8	10.9	9.1
Textiles	44.8	44.4	52.4	55.1	57.1	70.4
Chemicals	3.1	4.7	5.4	4.4	4.5	2.2
Stone and mineral products	6.4	14.0	15.0	12.7	10.7	5.3
Machinery	0.9	0.9	0.8	2.1	6.0	2.8
Printing and publishing	0.2	0.6	0.8	1.2	1.6	1.6
Other manufacturing	5.5	7.8	11.3	11.7	9.2	8.7

Imports	1880	1890	1900	1910	1920	1930
Food products	18.2	25.8	27.4	20.0	11.8	19.8
Textiles	57.1	44.3	40.2	39.0	40.6	36.4
Chemicals	4.8	5.0	5.1	7.2	7.2	7.6
Stone and mineral products	7.3	5.9	7.6	11.5	21.3	13.3
Machinery	5.6	12.7	12.9	10.7	6.9	8.4
Printing and publishing	1.1	1.2	1.4	2.3	1.4	1.5
Other manufacturing	5.8	5.1	5.3	9.3	10.8	13.1

Source: Japan Statistical Association (1987), Table 10-2-a in current yen. All series reported as five-year moving averages.

of 7.65 per cent up until the eve of the First World War.[22] Low barriers meant that trade grew rapidly over the Meiji period, averaging a quarter of national output in the early 1900s and increasing thereafter.

Given its undeveloped manufacturing sectors, Japan initially ran persistent trade deficits as foreign firms gained market share, especially in capital equipment.[23] This changed, however, as the economy shifted towards higher-value-added goods, which was reflected in the composition of Japanese trade. As shown in Table 8.1, starting from the Meiji period and up until the Second World War there was a marked decline in processed food products exports, while textiles grew to become the top foreign exchange earner for virtually the entire half-century. Machinery exports also increased, albeit more modestly. The pattern for imports is more ambiguous: textiles were steadily replaced by food products in the last two decades before the turn of the century, and then by stone and mineral products as well as miscellaneous commodities afterward.[24] This suggests that while domestic industries were producing more valuable goods for export at the inter-sectoral level, demand within the economy shifted from household consumption toward intermediate products used by firms. However, given the growth of Japanese

[22] Yamazawa and Yamamoto (1979), Table 22. Exchange rates did not play a significant role in the period between 1897 and 1914 as Japan was on the gold standard.
[23] Japan's low-tariff, high-growth experience in the pre-war era contrasts with that of most other countries; see Clemens and Williamson (2004).
[24] Note that the food products category for trade does not directly correspond with that for industry output, in that the former also includes unprocessed food items like grains and livestock.

machinery and its relatively constant import share over this period, the country was moderately successful in substituting away from foreign capital goods.

This movement into capital-intensive, higher-value-added production is illustrated by the two major sectors of textiles and metal processing. Since trade data are available at a more detailed level than those reported for industrial output, one can examine shifts in domestic demand and supply of traded goods to infer broader structural change among industries and the national economy. For instance, Table 8.2 shows trends for the three categories of textiles, which indicate that exports moved away from yarn and thread toward finished cloth between the 1870s and the Second World War. The change in shares was particularly rapid in the two decades prior to 1900, coinciding with the period when Japan's share of manufacturing in output matched that of the United States. After 1900, the third category of clothing and accessories began to grow, although the overall contribution remained in the single digits for most of the pre-war period.

For the heavier industries of metal goods and processing, the three categories of metal ores, metalworking, and machinery show a similar pattern of increasing value added over time. As Table 8.2 shows, the export share for machinery rose gradually in the 1880s before a rapid increase in the late 1910s, mirroring large decreases in ore exports in the same years. Import trends are less clear, with metal ores having high shares in the 1870s, then falling in the next two decades before rising thereafter. In contrast, machinery imports were highest in the 1880s and 1890s before declining until the 1920s. The First World War boosted domestic machinery exports, but this was a continuation of a rising trend during the previous decade. The war's impact on imported metal manufactures is also apparent, but much shorter lived.

Table 8.2. Disaggregated trade shares in textiles and metal goods, 1880–1930

Textiles		1880	1890	1900	1910	1920	1930
Yarn and thread	Exports	99.4	89.1	73.2	69.1	57.2	54.2
Fabric		0.4	10.3	25.3	26.3	34.4	39.7
Clothing		0.1	0.6	1.4	4.6	8.3	6.1
Yarn and thread	Imports	35.3	53.5	68.3	77.9	95.7	94.6
Fabric		63.2	43.4	30.6	21.0	4.1	5.0
Clothing		1.4	3.2	1.1	1.1	0.3	0.3
Metal goods		**1880**	**1890**	**1900**	**1910**	**1920**	**1930**
Ores	Exports	76.2	86.1	86.2	75.3	47.4	25.3
Metalwork		23.8	12.4	9.8	10.5	19.7	31.2
Machinery		0.0	1.5	4.0	14.3	32.9	43.6
Ores	Imports	52.4	28.4	34.6	47.3	72.9	54.7
Metalwork		8.4	27.9	19.1	14.8	7.2	5.7
Machinery		39.2	43.7	46.2	37.9	20.0	39.6

Source: Japan Statistical Association (1987), Table 10-2-a in current yen. All series reported as five-year moving averages.

Taken together, while capital- and energy-intensive sectors like machinery were important for Japan's sustained development into a mature industrial economy, the country relied on exports of its lighter manufactures to industrialize within the global economy. Furthermore, the decomposition of textiles and metal goods trade indicates that Japan moved away from import-substitution manufacturing to internationally competitive exports around the turn of the century. For textiles, the value of raw material imports exceeded that of finished cloth and clothing in the late 1890s, while for metal goods the change occurred in the 1910s. As discussed later in the chapter, both import and export shares by trade partner region also remained largely constant during this period, indicating the country's competitive success in these markets.

8.2.4 Domestic Factors

Shifts in industrial and trade composition are consistent with domestic trends in capital investment, firm size, and labour. Japanese firms grew in capitalization and workers, particularly in manufacturing. In terms of overall capital shares, there appear to be three distinct phases: before 1900, there was major investment in the transport and manufacturing sectors, led by railroads and textiles; high growth in commercial services like banking and trade in the early 1900s; and a resurgence of manufacturing after 1910, led by heavier industries like metal processing and machinery.[25] Average firm size also indicates the concentration of capital in the transport and mining sectors, while both manufacturing and commerce grew in firm numbers and capitalization.

The distribution of the labour force also changed during this period, with the share engaged in agriculture steadily decreasing between 1880 and 1920 in favour of manufacturing.[26] A comparison with the increase in manufacturing output indicates rising labour productivity in industrial sectors, maybe due to the greater availability of capital, which started from a low base and remained below levels in more advanced economies.[27] Lower Japanese industrial productivity, however, was mitigated by lower pay, with a large wage differential between male and female workers, and labour repression in the form of legislation curtailing unionization and strikes.[28]

8.2.5 Changing World Conditions

Shifts in Japanese industrial structure may have been partly due to conditions outside the control of domestic policy-makers. While Japan's involvement in the global economy and relatively free trade were externally imposed, exports (and to a lesser extent, capital inflows) helped finance its modernization programme and

---

[25] See Rousseau (1997) and Tang (2013; 2014). Data for capital investment and firms by major industry are from Japan Statistical Association (1987), Tables 10-5-a and 10-5-b.
[26] Data for industry labour shares from Umemura et al. (1988), Tables 5, 10, 12, 13, and 18.
[27] Gordon (2009), p. 97.   [28] *Ibid.*, p. 99.

Table 8.3. Export and import shares by region, 1880–1940

Export shares	1880	1890	1900	1910	1920	1930	1940
Korea		1.6	3.5	5.6	5.6	12.2	21.5
Taiwan			2.5	4.9	4.0	5.5	7.3
Northern China				3.3	5.1	4.4	19.4
Rest of Asia[a]	24.6	22.8	37.9	31.5	37.0	31.8	22.8
Europe, North America	74.5	73.1	54.0	51.9	42.8	41.0	19.8
Rest of the world	0.9	2.4	2.1	2.7	5.4	5.4	9.2
Import shares	**1880**	**1890**	**1900**	**1910**	**1920**	**1930**	**1940**
Korea		2.9	2.8	2.5	6.7	11.9	15.6
Taiwan			1.2	6.3	6.7	8.2	10.3
Northern China				2.1	6.0	5.6	8.6
Rest of Asia[a]	22.3	31.5	37.8	35.9	34.3	27.2	20.3
Europe, North America	77.6	65.3	57.6	51.8	39.5	40.6	35.5
Rest of the world	0.1	0.3	0.6	1.3	6.7	6.6	9.8

[a] Rest of Asia includes China, Hong Kong, Asiatic Russia, Southeast Asia, and other parts of Asia; Korea, Taiwan, and northern China (Kwantung and Manchuria) separately reported over time.
Source: Yamazawa and Yamamoto (1979), Tables 13 and 14 in current yen. All series reported in five-year moving averages.

build the capacity to produce more sophisticated goods.[29] The unexpected victories in the Sino- and Russo-Japanese wars boosted domestic investment in related sectors and increased access to nearby markets.[30] Reparations paid by China in the 1895 Treaty of Shimonoseki enabled Japan to finance its adoption of the gold standard, while the integration of Taiwan, Korea, and parts of northern China provided primary products to supply its heavy industries and feed the population.[31]

Similarly, the First World War was fortuitous for the Japanese economy in leaving the country physically unscarred while providing opportunities for its manufacturers and traders. European withdrawal from East Asian operations during the war meant Japan could readily substitute for shipping services and exports to the region, including India, Southeast Asia, and Oceania.[32] Shown in Table 8.3, Japanese exports to its colonies and the rest of Asia rose quickly in the 1910s, eclipsing those to industrial markets in Europe and North America shortly after. Japanese imports also shifted toward the Asia-Pacific as its economy took in

[29] Import tariffs comprised a minor share of government revenues: less than 2.3 per cent before Japan regained tariff autonomy in 1899, and less than 6 per cent from then until the war with China in 1937; see Yamazawa and Yamamoto (1979), Table 22.
[30] The 1872 Treaty of Kanghwa gave Japan access to three Korean treaty ports, which allowed for a significant expansion of bilateral trade (Gordon, 2009, p. 113). Korea was later annexed in 1910, while Taiwan was colonized in 1895 following the war with China.
[31] Matsukata (1899). Japan dominated Korean and Taiwanese trade, with about 90 per cent of Korean exports going to Japan in the 1870s and remaining high thereafter; Taiwanese exports grew from under 30 per cent in 1900 to 80 per cent in 1910, and exceeded 90 per cent for most of the 1930s (Gordon, 2009; Odaka et al., 2008, Table 9.1).
[32] Lockwood (1954), p. 38.

greater quantities of raw materials, continuing the trend from the turn of the century. As a share of total output, manufacturing nearly trebled over the 1910s, exceeding even American growth rates. The resumption of international peace tempered export growth, with its share of national output not returning to the pre-First World War high until after the Second World War. Higher machinery exports, however, continued and demand for imported metal ores resumed after a downturn in the 1920s.

Unlike industrialized economies in the inter-war period, Japan's experience of the 1920s and 1930s was neither roaring nor depressed. In March 1920, the Japanese stock market fell sharply due to investor uncertainty about post-First World War growth and was immediately followed in April by a series of bank runs.[33] The rest of the decade was punctuated by the 1923 Kanto earthquake, which killed an estimated 100,000 to 140,000 people in the greater Tokyo region and destroyed large numbers of industrial facilities and residences; and a financial panic in 1927 stemming from a reconstruction boom, bad loans, and bank failures. Compounding the problems was government interest in re-adopting the gold standard (abandoned in 1916), which led to fiscal austerity and tighter monetary policies.[34]

Recovery began in the early 1930s, in part due to the dramatic expansion of exports and industrial production in the first half of the decade. While Japan's military aggression in China was the most obvious feature of this period, the economy also experienced significant changes, starting with the depreciation of the yen in 1932 to 42 per cent of its value in the previous year.[35] This depreciation came months after the government reinstated an embargo on gold exports, promoting import substitution and industrial rationalization, and was followed by looser monetary policy and higher military and public works spending. While the value of trade doubled between 1932 and 1936, the volume of exports increased sixfold compared to imports, though the overall trade balance remained in slight deficit over these years. Exacerbating the deficit were the shift in textiles from silk to cotton goods, since the latter required raw materials imported from abroad; the need for metal ores and fuel for heavy industries; and the rise in protectionism against Japanese products.[36] Nevertheless, the patterns of economic restructuring and composition of trade persisted, in that textiles remained important but were steadily replaced by higher-value-added metal products and machinery. Hostilities with China and later the United States meant that capital-intensive sectors supporting the war effort received considerable investment at the expense of consumption, with significant government intervention to rationalize production.

8.3 KOREA AND TAIWAN

Japan surrendered its control of Korea in 1945 and the southern half of the Korean peninsula regained its independence in 1948 when the brief US occupation came to

---

[33] Shizume (2009).   [34] Nakamura (1987), pp. 59–61.
[35] *Ibid.*, pp. 62–4.   [36] *Ibid.*, pp. 68–9.

an end. War between the north and south broke out in June 1950 and continued for three years. During that time Seoul and Pyongyang and most other cities on the peninsula were reduced to rubble. Most of the physical infrastructure built by the Japanese colonial administration prior to 1945 was also destroyed. Most Japanese-built industries were in the north, as were what few mines existed on the peninsula. The south was cut off from these even before they were destroyed during the war. What South Korea inherited from the Japanese colonial period was mostly some human capital resulting from the Japanese colonial education system and some experience working in enterprises, many of which were owned and managed at the upper levels by Japanese. The Japanese colonial education system, for all of its inequities and its emphasis on the Japanese language, together with Korea's traditional high Confucian value placed on education, clearly gave the nation a stronger human capital base than that found in most low-income countries in the early 1950s. This base made it possible at the high end as early as the 1960s to send thousands of students to top universities abroad for advanced degrees in fields such as engineering and the natural sciences. At home it made possible the rapid expansion of an education system of steadily increasing quality at all levels.

There have been suggestions that import-substituting industrialization occurred during the period 1945–62, prior to the reforms that generated Korea's high-growth decades, and that this laid the foundation for what followed. Hyundai Corporation, for example, was founded in 1947 and did a great deal of construction work rebuilding what war had destroyed. Samsung began even earlier (in 1938) as a small export company in Taegu, selling dried fish and vegetables. Daewoo, however, was not founded until 1967. Thus much of the experience gained during the 1945–62 period was in business, but not particularly in starting and operating industrial enterprises. Nevertheless there were workers and even a few lower-level managers who had acquired experience in the few manufacturing establishments that did exist in the south before the Korean War, and others with experience in the north who migrated south at partition or during the war.

There were some modern food-processing and textile mills and a few other light industries, but the total value of manufacturing value added as late as 1961 was only 8 per cent of GDP. There were also traditional village handicrafts and food processing, but there is little data on these and no reason to think that their activities played a role in the development of modern manufacturing. There were virtually no exports of manufactures and very few exports of any kind, while imports were mostly financed with US aid. Thus there was some experience gained by running and working in industrial establishments but the total manufacturing workforce as late as 1963 was only 610,000 and that was mostly unskilled labour. The Korean chaebol and many other businesses would soon demonstrate that they could build and operate a much larger and more complex industrial economy, but the experience most of them brought from this earlier period was experience in how to do business, to buy and sell for a profit, and to mobilize construction crews.[37]

---

[37] The Korea data in this paragraph are mainly from Economic Planning Board (1980).

Taiwan did not suffer the same amount of destruction of its physical infrastructure, although destruction during the Second World War from Allied bombing was considerable. The years from 1949 until 1960 were mostly dominated by the retreat of the Kuomintang from the Chinese mainland, and then the settlement of 1.6 million mainlanders that accompanied that retreat. As in the case of Korea, most of the cost of imports was paid for by US foreign aid, and the NT$, like the Korean won, was seriously overvalued. Installed electric power capacity in 1960 was 260 megawatts, up from 61.5 megawatts in 1954. Manufacturing did grow rapidly after 1952, averaging 16 per cent per year, but from a tiny base, led by sugar, canned pineapples, alcoholic beverages, cement, cotton yarn, and cloth (Economic Planning Council, 1974). There were a few industrialists, notably those from the state-run China Petroleum Corporation plus a few private entrepreneurs who had joined the retreat of the Kuomintang government to Taiwan, but most of the business people were local Taiwanese, some of whom may have gained some relevant experience during the Japanese colonial period. All of these firms were very small in scale and that remained true for some time after the reform period began.

Taiwan's change in policies beginning in 1959–60, which led to the manufacturing and export boom of the 1960s and after, was driven by a number of considerations. Some of these were similar to what Korea would face two or three years later, but the Taiwanese change was more complex. There was no change in government in Taiwan; the Kuomintang and Chiang Kai-shek were in charge before, during and after the changes. The government economic officials who had come from the Chinese mainland were mostly from the state enterprise sector and many were imbued with a state-led planning model of growth that emphasized import substitution. The main changes in policy that ultimately had the most influence were those dealing with improving incentives for the private sector, unifying the multiple exchange rates then in force, reforming the banking system, and introducing measures to increase exports. The motivation for this last point was the desire to become less dependent on US aid. No one at the time, however, had any idea of how this last goal would come to dominate all of the others. And it was immediately apparent that exports mainly meant the export of manufactures. Taiwan had few minerals to speak of, and land reform along with other measures had reduced rice exports, a major export during the colonial period, to 3 per cent of total exports by 1960.

Thus a whole series of policies were introduced, and some of them, such as the devaluation of the exchange rate, began before 1960. In addition there were import tax rebates, low-interest loans for exporters, Export Processing Zones, and the 'Statute for Encouraging Investment'. This latter measure included everything from tax deductions for exporters to easing the then difficult process of obtaining land for manufacturing establishments. The export-processing law was not in place until 1965 but many of the other changes were implemented almost immediately.[38]

---

[38] For a more in-depth discussion of the process that led to the change in development policies, see Hsueh, Hsu, and Perkins (2001).

The changes in policy in Korea were if anything even more abrupt. US pressure did lead to a semblance of civilian democratic rule, but it also greatly reinforced the Korean government's desire to become less dependent on US aid. Even more clearly than in the case of Taiwan, increasing exports meant manufactured exports. Land reform in Korea had led the former rice surplus to be consumed domestically, Korea did not have a semi-tropical climate that could grow sugar and pineapples, and there were no minerals in the southern part of the Korean peninsula. That left only manufactures and Korea began to promote the export of manufactures with a series of measures that will be described in the next section. Korea also introduced banking and interest rate reform and a variety of other economic reform measures.

The governments of both Korea and Taiwan thus reached a decision to fundamentally change the direction of their economic development policies at roughly the same time (Taiwan a bit earlier) and for many of the same reasons. Both wanted to reduce their dependence on US aid. Both had few natural resources or agricultural products that could increase exports sufficiently to accomplish this goal of reduced dependence. It is also the case that both had experienced four to five decades of Japanese colonial rule. While Korea deeply resented this period and Taiwan did not, they both saw what Japan had accomplished decades earlier with a policy of industrialization that had manufactured exports as a major component. Finally, both understood that they had to create a more modern and efficient economy and society if their governments, and even their states, were to survive. It was therefore the political logic of the situation they found themselves in that led Korea and Taiwan to pick the development strategy that they then implemented. It was certainly not the dominant paradigm of development economists at the time.

8.3.1 Export-Led Industrialization: Korea, the First Phase

The changes in policy that led to the boom in manufactured exports and the accelerated growth of manufacturing were similar in both Korea and Taiwan, although there were differences in the specifics. The first key characteristic that the reforms had in common was the fact that both economies began their export push with a major devaluation. The second was that neither country pursued a broad liberalization of foreign trade. Their policies were geared to the promotion of exports through specific interventions that would overcome the many barriers to exporting that previously existed. Imports and the use of foreign exchange remained tightly restricted. Import substitution for a wide range of industrial sectors remained in place.

Devaluation of the won and the NT dollar came first. The changes in the exchange rate were dramatic. The NT$ lost half of its value relative to the US dollar, and the Korean won lost two-thirds of its value relative to the US dollar. Both maintained this level of devaluation through the 1960s and most of the 1970s. Neither the overvalued nor the undervalued exchange rate should be thought of as equilibrium rates. In addition to that, both systems remained riddled with state interventions in their international commerce on both the import and export side. The exchange rate that resulted from the devaluations of the late 1950s and early 1960s was in a sense undervalued and it remained that way through the 1960s and 1970s. Undervalued in this context, however, only means that both Korea and Taiwan probably could have promoted exports with a less pronounced devaluation. It was some time (the mid-1980s) before either economy could be said to be in a balance of payments equilibrium and at that point both economies experienced revaluation vis-à-vis the US dollar.

Given the numerous state interventions in international trade in both Taiwan and Korea, it is perhaps surprising that some analysts have argued that basically these two economies 'got their prices right': that is, they recreated what amounted to free market prices in a very un-free market environment. This argument was made in the book on Korea by Frank, Kim, and Westphal (1975) that was part of a set of studies on foreign trade regimes and economic development.[39] The alternative argument, made notably by Alice Amsden (1991), was that Korea deliberately 'got the prices wrong'—that is, Korea used trade barriers and other measures to ensure that infant industries, notably in the heavy industry sector, were protected from international competition and received prices well above world market prices for those products.

Frank, Kim, and Westphal's conclusion was based on a careful calculation of the effective rate of protection on a wide range of Korean products. Given the number of export subsidies and trade restrictions in Korea, this was a formidable undertaking. Their primary concern was to determine whether all of these restrictions and subsidies led to an efficient or inefficient allocation of resources for economic development. Since Korea's overall economic performance and its performance in industry in particular, during this period and the period that followed, involved very high growth rates, their conclusion that these restrictions and subsidies led to a relatively efficient outcome is no doubt correct. Their implicit argument that trade interventions produced a domestic price structure that was similar enough to the world price structure to produce a similar outcome is more questionable. There is not room to address their full analysis here, but other data developed for a different purpose were published around the same time.

As part of the early efforts to calculate the purchasing power parity GDP of various countries, the UN compared the prices in Korea with world (basically US) prices for 103 sectors (Fig. 8.2). As the figure makes clear, the domestic prices of roughly two-thirds of the tradable products listed had domestic prices below, and often far below, world prices. The commodities at that end of the spectrum included virtually all clothing items and all shoe categories, with PPP exchange rates often below 200 won/$1. At the other end of the spectrum were passenger automobiles (761 won/$1), ships and boats (519 won/$1), communications equipment (543 won/$1), construction machinery (387 won/$1), and refrigerators and freezers (980 won/$1). Alice Amsden's research focused particularly on the steel industry. Steel is not in the list because it is an intermediate product and

[39] The influential book by the World Bank (1993), Chapter 6, makes a similar argument that while a number of East Asian economies did promote import substitution, basically they distorted prices much less than in most other developing economies.

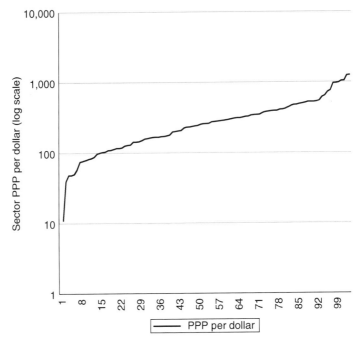

Fig. 8.2. Sector PPP per dollar for Korean tradable sectors, 1970

Note: The official won/US$ exchange rate in December 1970 was 316.65 won/US$1.00 and the rate in December 1969 was 304.45 won/US$1.00.

Source: Kravis, Heston, and Summers (1978), pp. 146–52.

purchasing power parity calculations use only final demand consumption and investment products, but steel was highly protected at this time. Many of these highly protected sectors became the focus of the Korean Heavy and Chemical Industry Drive of the 1970s and many of these highly protected sectors by the 1980s were a major component of Korean exports and no longer required protection.

This suggests that what Korea was pursuing was a classic infant industry strategy, where the government provided protection for industries in the learning phase but expected them to bring their costs down steadily and become exporters.

There was a major change in Korea's approach to industrial development in the 1970s. Government interventions in the 1960s were generally designed to help all exporters. The government did not target particular exporting firms or exporting industries. Most of the subsidies were available to anyone who met the criteria. This approach changed in a dramatic way with the Heavy and Chemical Industry Drive of the 1970s.[40] That drive was initiated by President Park, who empowered a government official, Oh Won Chol, to form a Blue House committee of government officials

[40] This discussion of the Heavy and Chemical Industry Drive is based mainly on Stern et al. (1995).

to draw up a plan for a drive by Korea to promote a range of major heavy industrial products, beginning with steel, shipbuilding, certain types of machinery, petrochemicals, and other chemicals. It was at that point that the government went to individual companies, typically the large chaebol such as Hyundai and Daewoo, and asked them to take on the task of developing one of these industries.

The incentives to do so were considerable. The government had already decided to provide much of the related infrastructure through the construction of a heavy industry industrial park, loans at below market rates were available, and in many cases the chaebol were given temporary monopolies over the domestic market for the particular item. Added to specific support measures was the general proposition that, given the active role played by government in directing and controlling the economy, companies wanted and needed to be seen as cooperative by that government. Thus government industrial policy decisions during the 1960s and 1970s were made mostly using technocratic criteria. That was to change as the country moved beyond the 1970s.

The performance of Korean manufacturing throughout the 1960s and 1970s was impressive by any standard. GDP grew at 9.2 per cent per year (1979/1961) while manufacturing grew at 17.9 per cent a year and the share of manufacturing in GDP rose from 13.5 per cent in 1961 to 27.7 per cent in 1979. Total exports from Korea in nominal US dollars grew at 42.7 per cent a year (1979/1964) and the share of manufactures in these exports rose from 55 per cent in 1964 to 89.9 per cent in 1979 (Table 8.4). The US market took 29 per cent of these exports in 1979, the Japanese market took 22.3 per cent, and the next largest economy, Germany, took only 5.6 per cent.

There were also rapid and large changes in the structure of industry and exports (Fig. 8.3). The producer goods industry surpassed the consumer goods industry by the late 1970s and exports of machinery and transport equipment surpassed those of the more labour-intensive consumer industries. The dominance of machinery and transport equipment exports increased further in the 1980s and beyond.

Table 8.4. Korean exports by sector

	Food, beverage, tobacco	Manufactured good classified by material	Machinery and transport equipment	Miscellaneous manufactures	Other
1967	14.0	31.7	4.4	30.4	19.5
1970	9.6	26.4	7.4	42.2	14.4
1975	13.2	29.4	15.0	35.8	6.6
1980	7.3	35.7	20.3	29.9	6.8
1985	4.1	23.3	37.6	27.6	7.3
1990	3.3	22.1	39.3	28.6	6.7

Sources: Economic Planning Board (1986), pp. 227–8; Economic Planning Board (1987), pp. 213–14; and National Statistical Office (1993), pp. 250–1.

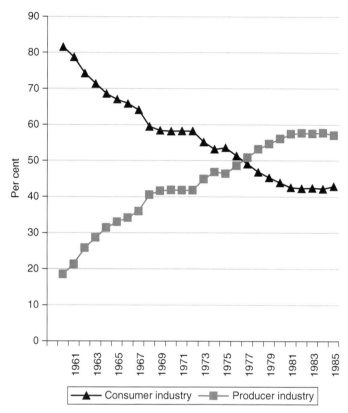

Fig. 8.3. Korea: the share of producer and consumer goods industries (per cent)

Note: The data up through 1979 are for light and heavy industry and only after that are derived from data on producer and consumer goods industries.

Sources: Economic Planning Board (1980), p. 281 and (1986), p. 104.

8.3.2 Industrial Development in Taiwan, 1960–79

Taiwan's manufacturing experience in the 1960s had many features in common with Korea, some of which, notably the devaluation of the currency and unification of the multiple exchange rates, have already been discussed.[41] Taiwan put up high tariff walls on products mainly produced for the domestic market and introduced a variety of subsidies and other incentives for exporters. The motive of the government was to earn foreign exchange. Any firm that could contribute to that end was given access to the various export support measures. Taiwan made somewhat greater use of Export Processing Zones, but in 1971 all of the zones together accounted for only 7.9 per cent of total exports; twenty years later that share had

---

[41] The discussion in this section is drawn mostly from Hsueh, Hsu, and Perkins (2001).

fallen to 5.2 per cent. The real value of such zones is to provide lessons in how to create a supporting environment for private exporting firms in the country at large, and they probably played that role in Taiwan.

Like in Korea, Taiwanese exporting industrial firms mainly produced labour-intensive products such as shoes, textiles, and garments. Most were very small in these early years. In 1974 there were 111 'big business groups' with an average of seven firms in each group but with an average employment of only a little over 300 per firm. These business groups were the larger economic organizations on the island. There were over 25,000 registered factories on Taiwan in the late 1960s, most of them quite small. However, many and perhaps most of these factories were not completely autonomous enterprises. Most were subcontractors to a central enterprise or to several enterprises that would assemble the various components into a product that could be exported.

Taiwan began to move beyond labour-intensive consumer manufactures at much the same time as Korea began its Heavy and Chemical Industry Drive. This heavy industry push in the 1970s was called the 'Ten Major Development Projects'. Petrochemicals were a priority, as was steel. Machinery and electronics remained mostly in the hands of small private enterprises. All of these government efforts in the heavy industry sector involved the establishment or expansion of state-owned enterprises. The China Petroleum Corporation, which had been founded on the mainland but had moved to Taiwan, was given a monopoly over upstream naphtha cracking plants and the corporation built two large plants in 1975 and 1978. The government also created two new state-owned enterprises, the China Petrochemical Development Corporation and Chung-Tai Chemicals, to produce mid-stream petrochemical products. There were also private firms in the sector, mainly involving mid-stream synthetic fibres, but 43 per cent of all investment in petrochemicals went to state-owned firms. Efforts to develop a shipbuilding indus-try were less effective. A state enterprise, the Taiwan Shipbuilding Corporation, already existed but could only build 100,000 ton cargo ships. The goal was to become a major producer of oil tankers of several hundred thousand tons and to that end the government provided 45 per cent of the investment in a new state enterprise, the China Shipbuilding Corporation, with the rest provided by foreign investors. Despite a variety of subsidies provided by the government, however, the China Shipbuilding Corporation never became internationally competitive. Korea's shipbuilding effort ran into similar head winds in the late 1970s, but the Korean government made a decision to provide what amounted to subsidies to companies that imported petroleum into Korea on Korean-made tankers. That saved Hyundai, the builder of the first supertankers, and Hyundai and Korea went on to become one of the largest shipbuilding countries in the world. A similar measure by Taiwan (to persuade ship owners flying the Chinese Nationalist Flag to buy Taiwanese-made ships) was not successful.

The Taiwanese government also made efforts to build an automobile industry to replace the small-scale producing units that already existed from the late 1960s, but which were only one step up from the assembly of imported parts that constituted the automobile sector in so many developing countries (there was a 60 per cent local content requirement in the Taiwanese case, beginning in 1965). Unlike Korea, Taiwan never became a producer of an internationally competitive product. These efforts in Taiwan did, however, produce an internationally competitive automobile parts sector. Automobile parts, in contrast with name brand complete automobiles, probably fitted the then small scale of most manufacturers on the island. In addition, the parts sector was largely private and producers either became efficient or went out of business.

The impact of these changes on the structure of Taiwan's industrial sector and its exports was rapid. By the late 1970s the share of machinery and transport equipment plus chemicals and petroleum far surpassed the share of textiles and apparel, which had begun to decline (Table 8.5). The shift in the structure of exports to the producer goods sector was not quite as rapid as in Korea, but by the mid-1980s these sectors combined had surpassed the share of the consumer goods sectors combined (Table 8.6).

Table 8.5. Taiwanese shares of industrial sectors in industry and mining (per cent)

	1961	1966	1971	1976	1981	1986
Food, beverages, and tobacco	21.4	14.0	9.2	9.7	6.5	6.1
Textiles and apparel	12.8	12.8	20.8	19.0	15.7	13.8
Lumber bamboo	3.0	2.4	3.3	2.5	2.5	3.1
Paper printing	5.6	3.8	3.3	2.1	2.8	3.2
Chemicals, petroleum rubber	17.1	22.2	22.2	20.6	21.1	24.8
Machinery, electrical machinery, transport equipment, metal products	6.9	10.8	17.3	22.5	26.1	25.0
Electricity, gas, water	8.8	9.8	8.8	6.6	8.2	7.7
Construction	1.0	3.1	3.7	5.0	5.0	2.4

Note: These shares are based on the weights used to construct Taiwan's industrial output index.
Source: Directorate General of Budget, Accounting and Statistics (1990), p. 288.

Table 8.6. Taiwanese sectoral export shares (per cent)

	Agriculture	Food, beverages, tobacco	Textiles, wood, paper	Electrical machinery	Metal products, machinery	Transport equipment	Other
1952	8.6	83.6	0.8	0	0	0	6.9
1955	5.7	84.6	2.4	0	0	0	7.3
1960	9.8	58.5	17.1	0.6	0.6	0	13.4
1965	14.9	39.1	26.2	2.7	2.4	0.4	14.2
1970	8.4	13.0	42.2	12.3	5.1	0.9	18.1
1975	5.1	11.2	37.6	14.7	6.1	2.1	23.1
1980	2.5	6.7	31.1	18.2	8.1	3.2	30.2
1985	1.7	4.5	27.6	21.0	9.8	4.1	31.3
1990	0.8	3.3	17.5	27.3	13.5	5.0	31.1

Source: Council for Economic Planning and Development (1994), pp. 192–3.

8.3.3 Changing Industrial Policies and the Increasing Role of Market Forces

Opposition to the highly interventionist approach to industrial policy peaked in the late 1970s in both Taiwan and Korea. The 1970s industrial policy that targeted specific industries and individual firms within those industries was the first to decline sharply, although it did not disappear altogether. The declining use of government policy to promote specific industries and firms began even before President Park's assassination in 1979 and continued under the Chun Doo-hwan government in the 1980s, a government more concerned with reining in inflation than in promoting heavy industries. In the case of Taiwan, its weakened international political situation together with the OPEC price increases of 1978 and 1979 led to concern by the government that Taiwan's heavy industry-oriented industrial policy in the 1970s was making the island overly dependent on petroleum imports that could be cut off or sharply reduced. By the mid-1980s opposition to petrochemical plants also became a source of major demonstrations against new plants, as Taiwan was making the transition to a more democratic and open political system.

A further consideration in the shifting approach to manufacturing was that wages in both economies and unit labour costs (Figs 8.4 and 8.5) were rising rapidly, making the labour-intensive industries of the 1960s and 1970s less and less competitive in international markets. In Taiwan there was a government-led shift in emphasis toward high technology. To educate the broader population in the importance of computers and information technology, the government took the lead by rapidly expanding the role and use of computers and information technology within the government itself. Universities were required to revamp their curricula to give greater emphasis to training relevant to high technology. The government directly sponsored research in a wide range of high-technology fields. Companies that started up firms in this area also received various direct incentives such as reduced taxes and easier access to credit, as had been the case with earlier export-oriented industries, but these incentives were secondary to the main effort. An important element in this effort was to encourage people who had left Taiwan to further their education abroad, mainly in the United States, to return home and set up firms in these high-technology sectors.

In Korea, the relative power of the chaebol had changed dramatically over the course of the 1960s and 1970s. By the mid-1980s they were less dependent on the government and the government was becoming more dependent on them as illegal sources of campaign funding among other things. This kind of corruption, however, does not appear to have had a major impact on industrial policy during the presidencies of either Chun Doo-hwan or Roh Tae-woo. A bigger issue facing the government was what to do about companies that had done what was asked of them during the Heavy and Chemical Industry Drive, but where the results of their efforts had produced large losses and threatened bankruptcy. There was an implicit assumption that if the company did what was asked of it, the government would help them out of any trouble that resulted. Much of the early 1980s was thus devoted to cleaning up various unsuccessful efforts of the 1970s campaign.

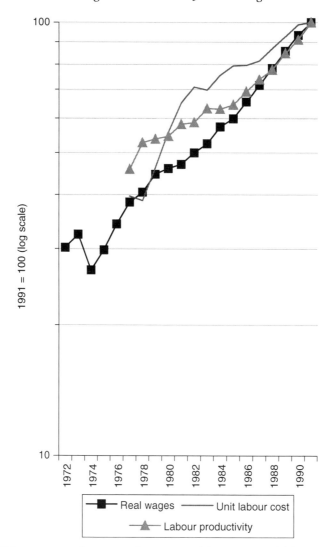

Fig. 8.4. Taiwanese manufacturing real wages, unit labour costs, and labour productivity
Source: Various issues of Council for Economic Planning and Development, *Taiwan Statistical Data Book*.

Unlike in Taiwan, there was never in Korea a clear decision to move away from heavy industry to an emphasis on information technology. On the contrary, heavy industries had become the mainstay of Korean exports by the 1980s and remained so into the next century. Machinery and transport equipment, for example, saw their share of Korean exports rise from 20.3 per cent in 1980 to 42.5 per cent in 1992, the last year of President Noh's term in office. Heavy industry products overall were 41.6 per cent of total exports in 1980 and 59.5 per cent in 1992 (and 72.3 per cent in 2000). Information technology products became an important

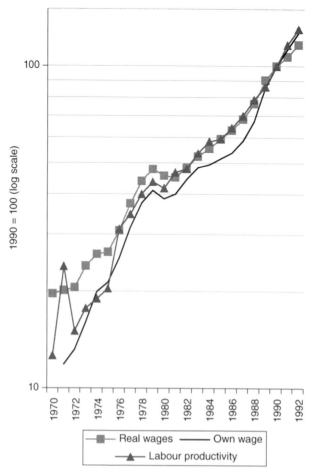

Fig. 8.5. Indices of Korean manufacturing real wages, own wages, and labour productivity

Source: Various issues of National Statistical Office, *Major Statistics of Korean Economy.*

part of heavy industry exports later, but they grew rapidly and accounted for 33.4 per cent of all heavy industry exports and 27 per cent of total exports in 2001.

Korea's government, like that of Taiwan, was concerned from the 1960s on with the fact that Koreans were increasingly being trained in high-technology areas mainly in the United States, but few were returning home to work in Korea. In an attempt to change this situation, the Korean government first created the Korea Institute of Science and Technology in 1966, a multi-disciplinary research institute mainly in the sciences and engineering. The Korean Advanced Institute of Science (KAIST) was established in 1971 as an educational and research institution, and rapidly rose to be among the highest-status universities in Korea (and in international university rankings). And the chaebol also had research institutes.

Overall research and development expenditures in Korea rose from 0.29 per cent of GDP in 1973 to 0.57 per cent in 1979 at the end of the Heavy and Chemical Industry program, before doubling to 1.02 per cent of GDP in 1982 and doubling again to 2.01 per cent in 1991.

Finally, by the 1980s and 1990s there was no longer a foreign exchange constraint in either Korea or Taiwan that could justify tight restrictions on imports, while the United States was becoming increasingly intolerant of trade restrictions as a means of infant industry protection, particularly given that most of the industries were no longer infants. Both economies thus greatly reduced the use of import restrictions as an instrument of industrial policy. Keeping the exchange rate undervalued was also no longer tolerated or justified and in both economies the currency was revalued to something closer to a market-driven exchange rate.

8.4 CONCLUSION

The Japanese, South Korean, and Taiwanese governments played leading roles in their respective industrialization drives, but the nature of those governments and their evolution from one kind of leadership to another differed. In Japan the Meiji restoration that began in 1868 kept much of the pre-modern elite in control, but fundamentally changed most of the institutions that had characterized the semi-feudal Tokugawa period. After that, however, that same elite ruled for six decades while experimenting with reforms that would facilitate Japan's catching-up with the world powers of Europe and North America. It was not until the Japanese military came to dominate the government that the nature of the ruling elite that governed economic policy changed fundamentally. The nature of the government and the manufacturing strategies pursued were also influenced by the external environment, notably the First World War that cut Europe off from active economic involvement with Asia, the Great Depression that was accompanied by rising protection and trade wars, and then the Second World War from which Japan did not recover until the early 1950s.

Korea and Taiwan were ruled by Japan until 1945. During that period Japan pursued economic development strategies that were driven by colonial interests and emphasized agriculture and mining exports. Independence in 1945 brought completely new governments to these countries, which were initially more interested in political and military goals than in industrialization or economic development. External pressures, due in part to their over-dependence on US aid, and the threat to their very existence, led to fundamental changes in policy in both economies in the early 1960s. What followed was similar, in that both governments led manufacturing development efforts that transformed their economies in a matter of decades.

Manufacturing development in Korea and Taiwan from the 1960s to the early 1990s was much faster than the growth of Japanese manufacturing in the pre-Second World War period, although Japan's own continued manufacturing growth after economic recovery from that war was equally rapid for two decades, and its pre-Second World War experience was more rapid than in most other industrial-ized economies at that time. A plausible hypothesis is that higher growth from the mid-1950s onward in all three countries was due in part to a large backlog of unused technologies, as well as of knowledge about what development strategies worked and which did not, allowing these economies, particularly Korea and Taiwan, to leapfrog ahead. Korea and Taiwan had the added advantage of being able to learn from Japan's experience starting from a similar economic foundation, whereas Japan had to figure out what would best fit. Korea and Taiwan's manu-facturing growth (and Japan's after the Second World War) also benefited from being able to pursue an export-oriented strategy in an increasingly open world market.

The faster pace of manufacturing growth in Korea and Taiwan also meant that the structure of industry and of industrial exports changed more rapidly than in Japan, although the nature of the structural changes was similar. All three countries began their industrial development drives with a focus on exports of labour-intensive products, but Korea and Taiwan experienced a more rapid shift from labour-intensive products to producer goods, notably machinery and transport equipment, with this occurring less than two decades after their rapid growth began. In Japan this shift began at the turn of the century, increased with the military build-up of the 1930s, and peaked in the post-Second World War era.

The industrial organization structure differed between the three economies, with the differences being between Korea and Japan, on the one hand, and Taiwan on the other. There were large business groups in both Korea and Japan—zaibatsu in Japan before the Second World War and keiretsu after the war, and chaebol in Korea. In Taiwan, most industrial firms during the first two decades of industrial development were small in scale, and business groups were looser combinations of these smaller firms, usually with a lead firm. Over time, this has changed as large groups have arisen, but these have not reached the level of dominance of the business groups of Korea and Japan.

Finally, rapid manufacturing growth is a transitional phase in all countries, and this was the case in Japan, Korea, and Taiwan. The starting point is an economy dominated by agriculture and handicrafts plus supporting commercial and financial services; there follows a period in which industrial growth dominates the economy. At purchasing power parity per capita incomes in the $14,000 to $17,000 range, however, industrial growth is increasingly replaced by services, including many modern services that did not exist in earlier periods.[42] In Korea and Taiwan, this transition into and then out of a focus on manufacturing took place over three decades. In Japan it took much longer, both because growth generally was much slower in the first half of the twentieth century than in the latter half, and because of the impact of the Second World War, which set Japan back for over a decade.

---

[42] The lower figure is the purchasing power parity per capita GDP (in 2011 prices) in Korea in the early 1990s and the higher figure is that for Japan in the early 1970s. This is when the share of manufacturing (in Korea) and of industry (in Japan) began to decline as a share of GDP (World Bank, 2014).

In Japan it took roughly seven decades from when industrialization started to when the share of industry in GDP began to fall.

REFERENCES

Amsden, A. (1991). *Asia's Next Giant: South Korea and Late Industrialization.* Oxford: Oxford University Press.

Barro, R. (1997). *Determinants of Economic Growth: A Cross-Country Empirical Study.* Cambridge: MIT Press.

Bénétrix, A., O'Rourke, K. H., and Williamson, J. G. (2015). The spread of manufacturing to the poor periphery, 1870–2007. *Open Economies Review* 26, 1–37.

Clemens, M. and Williamson, J. G. (2004). Why did the tariff-growth correlation change after 1950? *Journal of Economic Growth* 9, 5–46.

Council for Economic Planning and Development (1994). *Taiwan Statistical Data Book.* Taipei: Council for Economic Planning and Development.

Crawcour, S. (1974). The Tokugawa period and Japan's preparation for modern economic growth. *Journal of Japanese Studies* 1, 113–25.

Crawcour, S. (1997a). Economic change in the nineteenth century. In *The Economic Emergence of Modern Japan* (Ed., Yamamura, K.). Cambridge: Cambridge University Press.

Crawcour, S. (1997b). Industrialization and technological change, 1885–1920. In *The Economic Emergence of Modern Japan* (Ed., Yamamura, K.). Cambridge: Cambridge University Press.

Directorate General of Budget, Accounting, and Statistics (1990). *Statistical Yearbook of the Republic of China.* Taipei: Directorate General of Budget, Accounting, and Statistics.

Economic Planning Board (1980). *Handbook of Korean Economy.* Seoul: Economic Planning Board.

Economic Planning Board (1986). *Major Statistics of Korean Economy.* Seoul: Economic Planning Board.

Economic Planning Board (1987). *Major Statistics of Korean Economy.* Seoul: Economic Planning Board.

Economic Planning Council (1974). *Taiwan Statistical Data Book.* Taipei: Economic Planning Council.

Frank, C. R., Kim, K. S., and Westphal, L. (1975). *Foreign Trade Regimes and Economic Development: South Korea.* New York: National Bureau of Economic Research.

Gordon, A. (2009). *A Modern History of Japan: From Tokugawa Times to the Present.* Oxford: Oxford University Press.

Hsueh, L.-M., Hsu, C.-K., and Perkins, D. H. (2001). *Industrialization and the State: The Changing Role of the Taiwan Government in the Economy, 1945–1998.* Cambridge, MA: Harvard University Press.

Japan Statistical Association (1987). *Historical Statistics of Japan.* Tokyo: Japan Statistical Association.

Kravis, I., Heston, A., and Summers, R. (1978). *International Comparisons of Real Product and Purchasing Power.* Baltimore, MD: Johns Hopkins University Press.

Landes, D. (1965). Japan and Europe: contrasts in industrialization. In *The State and Economic Enterprise in Japan* (Ed., Lockwood, W.W.). Princeton, NJ: Princeton University Press, 93–182.

Lockwood, W. W. (1954). *The Economic Development of Japan*. Princeton, NJ: Princeton University Press.

Matsukata, M. (1899). *Report on the Adoption of the Gold Standard in Japan*. Tokyo: Government Press.

Mitchener, K. and Ohnuki, M. (2009). Institutions, competition and capital market integration in Japan. *Journal of Economic History* 69, 138–71.

Morck, R. and Nakamura, M. (2007). Business groups and the big push: Meiji Japan's mass privatization and subsequent growth. *Enterprise and Society* 8, 543–601.

Morikawa, H. (1992). *Zaibatsu: The Rise and Fall of Enterprise Groups in Japan*. Tokyo: University of Tokyo Press.

Nakamura, T. (1987). The Japanese economy in the interwar period: a brief summary. In *Japan and World Depression* (Eds., Dore, R. and Sinha, R.). New York: St Martin's Press.

Odagiri, H. and Goto, A. (1996). *Technology and Industrial Development in Japan*. Oxford: Clarendon Press.

Odaka, K., Saito, O., and Fukao, K. (2008). *Asian Historical Statistics: Taiwan*. Tokyo: Toyo Keizai Shinposha.

Ohkawa, K. and Rosovsky, H. (1973). *Japanese Economic Growth: Trend Acceleration in the Twentieth Century*. Stanford, CA: Stanford University Press.

Ohkawa, K. and Shinohara, M. (1979). *Patterns of Japanese Economic Development: A Quantitative Appraisal*. New Haven, CT: Yale University Press.

Ohkawa, K., Takamatsu, N., and Yamamoto, Y. (1974). National income. In *Estimates of Long-Term Economic Statistics of Japan since 1868* (Eds, Ohkawa, K., Shinohara, M., and Umemura, M.). Tokyo: Toyo Keizai Shinposha.

Onji, K. and Tang, J. P. (2015). A nation without a corporate income tax: evidence from nineteenth century Japan. *ANU Centre for Economic History Discussion Paper Series*, No. 2015–10.

Perkins, D. H. (2013). *East Asian Development: Foundations and Strategies*. Cambridge, MA: Harvard University Press.

Rodrik, D. (2013). Unconditional convergence in manufacturing. *Quarterly Journal of Economics* 128, 165–204.

Rousseau, P. (1999). Finance, investment, and growth in Meiji-era Japan. *Japan and the World Economy* 11, 185–98.

Shinohara, M. (1972). Mining and manufacturing. In *Estimates of Long-Term Economic Statistics of Japan since 1868* (Eds, Ohkawa, K., Shinohara, M., and Umemura, M.). Tokyo: Toyo Keizai Shinposha.

Shizume, M. (2009). The Japanese economy during the interwar period: instability in the financial system and the impact of the world depression. *Bank of Japan Review* 2009-E-2. Tokyo: Institute for Monetary and Economic Studies.

Stern, J. J., Kim, J.-H., Perkins, D. H., and Yoo, J.-H. (1995). *Industrialization and the State: The Korean Heavy and Chemical Industry Drive*. Cambridge, MA: Harvard University Press.

Taira, K. (1997). Factory labour and the industrial revolution in Japan. In *The Economic Emergence of Modern Japan* (Ed., Yamamura, K.). Cambridge: Cambridge University Press.

Tang, J. P. (2011). Technological leadership and late development: evidence from Meiji Japan, 1868–1912. *Economic History Review* 64(S1), 99–116.

Tang, J. P. (2013). Financial intermediation and late development in Meiji Japan, 1868 to 1912. *Financial History Review* 20, 111–35.

Tang, J. P. (2014). Railroad expansion and industrialization: evidence from Meiji Japan. *Journal of Economic History* 74, 863–86.

Tang, J. P. (2015). A tale of two SICs: industrial development in Japan and the United States in the late nineteenth century. Unpublished manuscript.

Umemura, M., Akasaka, K., Minami, R., Takamatsu, N., Arai, K., and Itoh, S. (1988). Manpower. In *Estimates of Long-Term Economic Statistics of Japan since 1868* (Eds, Ohkawa, K., Shinohara, M., and Umemura, M.). Tokyo: Toyo Keizai Shinposha.

Wattenberg, B. (1976). *The Statistical History of the United States from Colonial Times to the Present*. New York: Basic Books.

World Bank (1993). *The East Asian Miracle: Economic Growth and Public Policy*. Oxford: Oxford University Press.

World Bank (2014). *World Development Indicators (WDI) online*. http://databank.worldbank.org/data/views/variableSelection, accessed 5 August 2014.

Yamamura, K. (1997). Entrepreneurship, ownership, and management in Japan. In *The Economic Emergence of Modern Japan* (Ed., Yamamura, K.). Cambridge: Cambridge University Press.

Yamazawa, I. and Yamamoto, Y. (1979). Foreign trade and balance of payments. In *Estimates of Long-Term Economic Statistics of Japan Since 1868* (Eds, Ohkawa, K., Shinohara, M., and Umemura, M.). Tokyo: Toyo Keizai Shinposha.

9

Industrialization in China

Loren Brandt, Debin Ma, and Thomas G. Rawski

9.1 INTRODUCTION

China's recent economic boom, although widely viewed as a contemporary phenomenon, is the outcome of long-term processes with deep historical roots.[1] Here, we apply this perspective to analyse the trajectory that has transformed China from hesitant nineteenth-century experimentation into the world's largest manufacturer.

Table 9.1 summarizes our central quantitative results. The unusual speed of China's post-1978 industrial growth is well known. Much less appreciated is that rapid industrial growth extends back at least to 1912. Over a period spanning nearly a century, Chinese manufacturing has grown at an annual rate of more than 9 per cent. Table 9.2 provides further comparative perspective.

China's experience demonstrates, however, that industrialization is not simply the multiplication of commodity flows in and out of furnaces, mills, and machine shops. How growth occurs, the relative roles of the intensive and extensive margins, and more generally, the underlying microeconomic processes are key to maintaining long-run momentum, and to industrialization's economy-wide impact. Similar growth rates of manufacturing can conceal wide differences in the progress of industrialization, which we see as a fundamentally microeconomic process that enables firms and individuals to accumulate and deepen the technical, operational, managerial, and commercial skills that enable them to compete in ever more demanding markets, releasing multiple benefit streams that then reverberate throughout the economy. China's planned economy period, covering roughly 1952–78, recorded impressive rates of output growth, but did so under a policy and institutional environment that ultimately restricted the pace of change to a fraction of its potential, and carried high costs for the rest of the economy. Institutional and policy constraints similarly obstructed early industrialization efforts in the late nineteenth century.

[1] The authors have benefited from Guenther Lomas' dedicated research assistance, from data supplied by Bishnupriya Gupta, James Kung, Steven Nafzigar, and Li Nan, and from the comments and advice of Daniel Berkowitz, Kyoji Fukao, Hiro Good, Kevin O'Rourke, Dwight Perkins, Evelyn Rawski, Yingjun Su, Jeffrey Williamson, Haihui Zhang, Xiaodong Zhu, and Xiuying Zou. The usual disclaimer applies.

Table 9.1. Comparative growth of industrial output, 1912–2008

	China	Japan	India	USSR/Russia
1912–36	8.0	6.7	3.4	4.8
1912–49	4.1	2.5	3.9	3.9
1912–52	6.2	4.0	n.a.	4.8
1952–65	12.3	14.3	8.2	6.4
1965–78	10.2	8.2	4.3	3.8
1978–95	11.6	2.8	6.8	n.a.
1995–2008	13.8	0.7	7.8	3.1
1952–2008	11.9	6.1	6.8	n.a.
1912–2008	9.5	5.2	5.5	n.a.

Sources: China: calculated from authors' file 'Table 1 China Growth Rates 1912–2008_7.10.15', available on request. Index for 1912–49 from Minami and Makino (2014, Annex Table 4.D); link with 1952 from Liu and Yeh (1965, p. 66); index for 1952–2008 based on official data on industrial gross output; all output figures have been converted to 1980 prices. India: for 1911/12 to 1999/2000—data compiled by S. Sivasubramonian, courtesy of Bishnupriya Gupta for manufacturing (excluding small industry), in constant 1946–7 prices; for 2000/01 and thereafter, GDP originating in manufacturing (at 2005 factor cost) from India Data-Book (2014). Japan: linked index of production growth based on: for 1912–36: Ohkawa and Shinohara (1979, Tables A21–A22); for 1936–95: Statistics Japan (2012, Table 8-16); for 1995–2008: Statistics Japan (2011, Table 8-28). Russia: 1912–90 industrial output for the Russian Empire/USSR in constant 1913 roubles; 1991 and thereafter, industrial output for the Russian Federation, also in constant 1913 roubles. Data courtesy of Steven Nafziger.

Two factors have consistently served as important drivers of Chinese industry's global rise: openness to the international economy and domestic market liberalization.

Openness is important for the access it allows to new technology and know-how through foreign direct investment (FDI), imports of intermediates and capital equipment, and the movement of people and ideas. For a huge continental economy like China's in which the domestic market has typically absorbed upwards of 85 per cent of industrial output (Table 9.3), openness defined solely in terms of access to overseas markets cannot claim paramount importance. Domestic market liberalization is the crucial source of new opportunities and competitive pressure on incumbents and entrants to upgrade through product improvement and cost reductions, thus channelling resources to firms and sectors with high returns.

For latecomers like China, modern industry initially involves labour-intensive production requiring only modest capabilities. Over time, upgrading propels a shift into more skilled-labour and capital-intensive products and processes. Our review of a century and a half of Chinese industrialization shows that upgrading occurred most rapidly when the policy environment provided ample opportunity for the complementary interaction between openness and market liberalization, and helped roll back the institutional barriers that have often hindered the deepening of industrial capabilities.

While the past 150 years have seen wide variations in both international openness and domestic liberalization, we can identify several major dimensions of industrial development that have operated continuously throughout the period under review, albeit at different levels of intensity.

Table 9.2. Comparative industrialization: China, India, Japan, and Russia/USSR, 1912–2008

	1912	1933	1952	1965	1978	1995	2008
Cotton yarn production (m. lbs)							
China	221	990	1,445	2,860	5,240	11,928	38,214
India	647	1,268	1,452	2,068	2,006	3793	6,774
Japan	400	1,261	635	1,065	985	473	145
USSR/Russia		660			3,580	436	
Electricity production (bn kWh)							
China	0.1	2.8	7.3	67.6	256.6	1,007.0	3,496.0
India		2.1	6.1	31.4	110.1	396.0	841.7
Japan	1.1	19.5	52.0	179.6	564.0	990.0	1,146.0
USSR/Russia	2.0	16.4	119.1	506.7	1,293.9	860.0	983.0
Ingot steel production (m. tonnes)							
China	0.0	0.4	1.4	12.2	31.8	95.4	503.0
India	0.0	0.5	1.6	6.4	9.9	22.0	57.8
Japan	0.0	3.2	7.0	39.8	102.1	101.6	118.7
USSR/Russia	4.2	8.9	34.5	91.0	151.5	51.6	68.5
Cement production (m. tonnes)							
China	0.1	0.8	2.9	16.3	65.2	475.6	1,423.6
India	0.0	1.1	4.6	10.6	19.4	74.0	177.0
Japan	0.3	4.2	8.9	32.5	84.9	90.5	62.8
USSR/Russia	1.6	2.7	13.9	72.4	127.0	36.4	53.6
Industrial employment (m.)							
China[a]	0.7	1.1	5.3	16.6	53.3	147.4	126.3
India (formal only)	0.9	1.5	3.2	4.7	5.4		5.9
India[a] (formal + informal)						37.3	46.0
Japan	1.6	4.2	7.2	11.5	13.3	14.6	8.3
USSR/Russia	2.3	6.2–9.3	16.8	27.4	29.0		

[a] Employment data for manufacturing only.

Note: USSR/Russia data for 1995 and 2008 are for the Russian Republic.

Sources: List of sources available from the authors.

First, manufacturing activity and industrial capabilities have gradually spread across China's vast landscape. Factory production initially clustered along China's south-eastern coast, particularly in the Lower Yangzi region surrounding Shanghai, and subsequently in Manchuria. The war years (1937–49) brought a surprisingly large expansion of industry in China's interior (Table 9.4). The planned economy era (1949–78) modestly extended regional dispersion, most notably through the Third Front policies, as the state limited investment in previously dominant regions, which were seen as both militarily vulnerable and ideologically suspect, and developed industrial capacity inland. Although the post-1978 reform era allowed coastal regions once again to leverage their favourable location and

Table 9.3. Chinese exports of manufactures: scale and share of production and overall exports, 1933–2008

	Unit	1933	1952	1965	1978	1995	2008
Total exports	RMB bn	0.898[a]	2.71	6.31	16.76	1,245.18	10,039.49
of which: Manufactures	RMB bn	0.247[a]	0.41	2.84	9.22	1,065.24	9,492.50
Share of manufactures in exports	per cent	27.5	15.0	45.0	55.0	85.5	94.6
GVIO, current prices	RMB bn		34.9	140.2	423.7	9,189.4	60,737.92243
Manufacturing share in GVIO	per cent	83.4	88	88	88	88	88
GVIO manufacturing	RMB bn	2.645[a]	30.7	123.4	372.9	8,086.7	53,449.4
Share of manufacturing output exported	per cent	9.3	1.3	2.3	2.5	13.2	17.8
Trade ratio [X+M]/GDP	per cent	8.8	9.6	6.9	11.8	38.7	57.3

[a] 1933 data in billions of current pre-war yuan. GVIO: gross value of industrial output.

Sources: Exports: for 1952–2008, Compendium (2009, 60); for 1933, authors' calculations combining Republic of China exports with separate Manshūkoku data from Yamamoto (2003). Exports of manufactures: authors' file 'PRC Manufactured Exports', available on request. Manufacturing share in GVIO: authors' estimate based on file 'Share of Mining and Utilities in GVIO 1933–2008', available on request.

Table 9.4. Share of industrial output by region, 1933–2008

Region	1933	1952	1965	1978	1995	2008
NE	11.8	21.6	21.0	17.1	9.7	7.4
North	13.6	20.8	21.4	23.0	20.4	24.2
SE Coast	65.7	36.6	32.8	30.0	40.7	45.8
Central	7.9	11.0	12.3	15.0	16.0	12.9
NW	0.0	2.5	4.9	5.6	3.7	2.7
SW	0.9	7.5	7.6	9.3	9.6	7.0
Total	100.0	100.0	100.0	100.0	100.0	100.0
Herfindahl index	0.23	0.09	0.07	0.06	0.06	0.08

Regions:						
NE	Heilongjiang	Jilin	Liaoning			
North	Beijing	Tianjin	Inner Mongolia	Shanxi	Hebei	Shandong
SE Coast	Jiangsu	Shanghai	Zhejiang	Fujian	Guangdong	Hainan
Central	Henan	Anhui	Hubei	Hunan	Jiangxi	
NW	Shaanxi	Ningxia	Gansu	Qinghai	Xinjiang	
SW	Sichuan	Chongqing	Guangxi	Yunnan	Guizhou	Xizang

Sources: 1933: unpublished compilation by T. Kubo, Q. Guan, and F. Makino based on Liu (1937). We incorporate figures for Guangzhou, Qingdao, Chahaer, and Suiyuan into the provinces of Guangdong, Shandong, Hebei, and Inner Mongolia respectively. We add data for 1933 factory output in Manchuria compiled by Liu and Yeh (1965, p. 428), and partition the regional total among the three northeastern provinces in proportion to provincial electricity production in 1949 (Compendium, 2009, pp. 273, 307, 341). 1952–78: compiled from official PRC publications. 1995 and 2008: compiled from individual firms' 1995 (industrial) and 2008 (economic) census records.

superior resources of education, skill, and market experience to regain their share of national production, nationwide infrastructure expansion along with steeply rising land and labour costs in coastal cities encouraged growth in the central and western regions.

Second, the industrial product mix has expanded. Even without tariff protection, import substitution is visible from the late nineteenth century, particularly in cotton textiles. Import replacement on a more modest scale appeared elsewhere, particularly in segments of machine building, where the 1930s saw Chinese firms producing small quantities of textile machinery, machine tools, transportation equipment, and light armaments. Socialist planning grafted whole sectors, including trucks, petroleum refining, telecom equipment, nuclear fuel, and many others, onto the inherited industrial base. Although reform allowed market forces to exert growing influence over China's industrial product mix, government agencies continued to promote import replacement in computers, chemicals, machine tools, and other sectors that officials perceived as either essential building blocks for future development or militarily important.

Third, domestic upgrading has reduced the gap separating leading Chinese producers from global standards. Even without strong official support, progress in this direction became visible during the 1920s and 1930s, especially in cotton textiles. Chinese yarn producers moved beyond the coarsest grades of cotton yarn, improved labour and machine productivity, and absorbed management practices from British and Japanese rivals, while new academies offered training programmes in textile technology and civic organizations hired foreign technicians to facilitate the production and dissemination of Japanese-style equipment for handcraft weaving.

Beginning in the 1950s, the government of the People's Republic (PRC), tapping its new fiscal strength and the availability of technical support from its Soviet and East European allies, initiated what was then the largest technology transfer in human history. While the characteristic Soviet focus on production volume limited quality improvements and innovation, the accumulation of knowledge, resources, and experience under the planned economy created upgrading potential that could be captured once post-1978 reforms encouraged the revival of incentives and allowed greater flexibility in the allocation of resources.

Upgrading accelerated after 1978, spurred by the growing presence of foreign-invested firms, the unfamiliar demands of new export markets in rich countries, and the opportunities arising from growing access to international supply chains and cross-national information flows. The result was a growing dispersion of capabilities, as successful firms gradually moved toward global frontiers, leaving weaker units floundering in often overcrowded domestic markets for inferior goods.

Fourth, despite wrenching political discontinuity, successive advances built on prior developments. Early industrial efforts often involved individuals with modern education and/or overseas experience—both linked to international openness. Personnel from the pre-1949 National Resources Commission and from Japanese-controlled development efforts in Manchuria contributed disproportionately to early socialist planning. Even though the planned economy diverted investment away from Shanghai, China's pre-war industrial leader, the great metropolis figured centrally in the new system as a source of revenue from the profits of its consumer manufactures, and as a source of expert personnel—especially in textiles. Interior development was seeded with whole factory communities transported from Shanghai and other coastal locations. Reform-era development drew in similar fashion on the experience and skills accumulated within the plan-era state enterprise system, which became a source of expertise for both the township-village (TVE) firms and emerging private sector manufacturers (Li, Bathelt, and Wang, 2012; Dinh et al., 2013).

Finally, the Chinese diaspora has acted as a substantial source of financial and human capital in all periods except for the planned economy era. Its prominence reflects the unusual entrepreneurial propensity of ordinary Chinese, which survived several decades of intense anti-business propaganda under Mao and emerged as a key element in the astonishing reform-era expansion of private business (Table 9.5). Large numbers of micro-entrepreneurs in Wenzhou and other localities helped to propel Chinese exports to dominant positions in global market segments—an unusual, perhaps unique, phenomenon in global economic history.

Following a brief quantitative overview, we review development during three periods: the decades prior to the establishment of the PRC in 1949; China's era of socialist planning, which extends from the early 1950s to the late 1970s; and the succeeding period of economic reform, which begins shortly after the death of Mao Zedong (1976) and continues today.

Table 9.5. Breakdown of industrial output by ownership, 1933–2008 (per cent)

Sector	Foreign firm shares				Domestic firm shares				Per cent of domestic non-state		
	1933	1985	1995	2008	1933	1985	1995	2008	1985	1995	2008
Metallurgy	3.3	0.0	3.4	8.0	96.7	100.0	96.6	92.0	32.4	25.6	40.3
Power	100.0	0.0	5.1	4.6		100.0	94.9	95.4	8.0	13.8	6.5
Coal and coke	0.0	0.0	0.1	1.5	100.0	100.0	99.9	98.5	18.6	22.2	21.1
Petroleum	100.0	0.0	4.1	4.5		100.0	95.9	95.5	5.5	3.7	13.9
Chemicals	22.7	0.1	8.5	17.2	77.3	99.9	91.5	82.8	37.9	41.6	52.8
Machinery	20.6	0.6	15.7	35.0	79.4	99.4	84.3	65.0	28.4	43.9	55.7
Building materials	3.8	0.0	4.9	7.2	96.2	100.0	95.1	92.8	57.5	69.9	70.1
Timber	52.1	0.0	10.4	10.3	47.9	100.0	89.6	89.7	46.5	78.2	84.3
Food and drink	20.9	0.2	5.7	17.9	79.1	99.8	94.3	82.1	14.6	28.0	52.0
Textiles	25.6	0.1	13.7	10.8	74.4	99.9	86.3	89.2	33.6	76.1	74.3
Paper	13.0	0.1	5.8	15.3	87.0	99.9	94.2	84.7	62.7	47.0	70.5
Total	21.9	0.2	9.8	23.3	78.1	99.8	90.2	76.7	30.1	41.6	52.7

Sources: 1933: Liu and Yeh (1965), for China proper only (excluding Manchuria). Estimates for 1985 are from the industrial census summary volume, Industry (1989). Estimates for 1995 and 2008 are based on individual firms' records from the 1995 (industrial) and 2008 (economic) censuses.

9.2 QUANTITATIVE OVERVIEW

Table 9.1 provides a comparative perspective on China's long-term industrial growth ending with 2008, the most recent census year for which firm-level data are publicly available.[2] With the sole exception of Japan during its heyday of accelerated growth, the pace of Chinese industrial expansion exceeded that of India, Japan, and USSR/Russia during every sub-period for which meaningful comparison is feasible. Table 9.2 uses information on physical commodity output and industrial employment to provide crude comparisons of the scale of industrial activity in China, India, Japan, and USSR/Russia during the century beginning in 1912. These data portray early-twentieth-century China as an industrial pygmy, trailing India's production of cotton textiles and lagging far behind Japanese and Russian/Soviet production of electricity, steel, and cement.

Data for 1933 and 1952 suggest rough parity between Chinese and Indian industrial activity. An international comparison of industrial energy use during 1936/7 provides a clear ranking: industries in China (including Manchuria) and British India each absorb the equivalent of 19 billion kWh of electricity per year, one-third of the figure for Japan and one-sixth of the total for the USSR (US Department of State, 1949, pp. 96–7).

Manufacturing contributed 2.1 and 3.2 per cent of China's 1933 and 1952 GDP respectively (in 1933 prices); adding mining and utilities (but not handicrafts) raises the 1933 figure to 3.3 per cent (Liu and Yeh, 1965, p. 66). PRC compilations show a rapid increase in the GDP share of industry (including mining and utilities), which rises to 44.1, 41.0, and 48.6 per cent in 1978, 1995, and 2008 (Compendium, 2009, p. 10).

Beginning in the mid-1950s, Chinese industry rapidly outpaced India's. China's scale of industrial operations overtook Japan's shortly before the turn of the century, and surpassed the USSR's peak levels soon after 2000.

9.3 CHINA'S PRE-1949 INDUSTRIAL DEVELOPMENT

9.3.1 Overview

We observe three phases of pre-1949 industrialization: slow development during the late nineteenth century, including both officially inspired and private commercial efforts, followed by a more dynamic, market-driven expansion triggered by the Treaty of Shimonoseki (1895), which eroded barriers to private factory ventures.

---

[2] Unless otherwise noted, industrial growth rates are based on measures of gross output value (GVIO) rather than the value-added data used in conventional national income accounts. Following Soviet practice, GVIO has served as the standard metric for industrial output since 1949, whereas value added is a recent addition to the Chinese statistical repertoire. PRC materials use the term 'industry' to describe aggregates that include mining and utilities as well as manufacturing. We follow this convention: unless otherwise indicated, measures of GVIO and 'industrial' production or employment include mining and utilities as well as manufacturing.

Subsequently, Japanese military pressure culminating in the Sino-Japanese War (1937–45) and civil war (1945–9) prompted growing state intervention. Over this period, government became the chief driver of industrial development, leading to a rise in the share of military-linked activity and an enlarged output share for interior regions.

The Treaty of Nanking, which ended the Opium War (1839–42), obliged China to open five ports to unlimited trade, to limit tariffs to 5 per cent, and to exempt foreigners from Chinese law. Later agreements multiplied the number of 'treaty ports' and awarded similar privileges to citizens of multiple European nations as well as the United States and Japan. The resulting regime of obligatory free trade lasted until China regained tariff autonomy in 1929.

Falling international transport and communication costs complemented by rising trade volumes gradually aligned China's price structure, which displayed substantial domestic integration before the Opium War (Wang, 1992), with global values (Brandt, 1985). The resulting changes included price reductions (cotton yarn, ferrous metals) and increases (cotton, silk, tea), as well as the appearance of new products (machinery, kerosene, matches) that impacted prices of domestic substitutes and complements for traded goods.

9.3.2 Slow Development during the First Half-Century of Openness

Openness elicited a strong response in some segments of China's economy, such as Fujian's tea growers (Gardella, 1994, pp. 74ff). Development of manufacturing, however, was slow, both for semi-official initiatives directed by prominent regional leaders and for private ventures, some involving foreign entrepreneurs, that focused on processing of silk and other farm products. While the Jiangnan Arsenal impressed Japanese visitors, and China's Hanyeping complex initiated modern ferrous metallurgy ahead of Japan's Yahata works, the officially linked initiatives, most focused on defence-related production, delivered limited results and produced virtually no spillovers for the private sector.

An earlier literature mistakenly linked this slow growth to the supposed inability of modern factory goods to compete with the products of China's traditional sector (Murphey, 1977; Huang, 1985). In reality, modern technologies enabled factory products to outcompete many traditional products in price and quality. Given Japan's faster industrial advance under similar trade and treaty arrangements, attributing limited manufacturing growth to Western imperialism is equally unpersuasive (Esherick, 1972; Moulder, 1977).

Institutional and ideological constraints that drained potential profits from embryonic industrial ventures posed a key obstacle to modern industry. Shannon Brown (1978, 1979a, 1979 b) and others demonstrate how these difficulties undermined initiatives in soybean and silk processing. Entrenched local interest groups, possibly strengthened under the decentralization that accompanied the Taiping Rebellion (Brandt, Ma, and Rawski, 2014), thwarted potential competition by blocking newcomers' access to materials (soybeans, cocoons), storage facilities, and transport.

9.3.3 Accelerated Growth from 1896 to 1937

In addition to opening the growing roster of treaty ports to foreign-owned manufacturing activity, the stunning military defeat at the hands of Japan, a small and lightly regarded neighbour, prompted a sweeping reconsideration of traditional attitudes and structures. Rapid retreat of formal and, perhaps more important, informal restrictions and prejudices became the order of the day as even conservative leaders endorsed sweeping reform. A new company law introduced limited liability; the traditional examination system gave way to a new drive toward modern education; Confucian-educated gentry turned to constitutionalism, parliamentary democracy, and chambers of commerce as possible avenues to reverse China's decline.

This ferment facilitated a rapid acceleration of industrial enterprise formation. Table 9.6 shows the number of newly established modern Chinese private factories more than doubling between the 1880s and 1890s from 42 to 99, before increasing to 437 during the first decade of the twentieth century. This wave of entry, complemented by growing FDI (Remer, 1933; Hou, 1965) initiated several decades of rapid industrial growth that persisted through periods of disunity, war, and depression. Halting only with the outbreak of full-scale war with Japan in 1937, pre-war industrial growth outstripped that in Japan as well as India and Russia/USSR (Table 9.1). Work by Chinese scholars finds similarly high growth for Shanghai—the centre of pre-war manufacturing—between 1895 and 1912 (Ma, 2008).

Rapid growth from a minuscule base could not transform China into an industrial nation. At its pre-war 1936 peak, factory output accounted for only 3.1 per cent of GDP—far below the comparable Japanese figure of 25.1 per cent. Even with a substantial downward adjustment to the Liu-Yeh estimates of 1933 production,[3] handicrafts contributed nearly half of industry gross output (and value added) in 1933, comparable to Japanese circumstances during 1900–10 (Ohkawa and Shinohara, 1979, p. 37).

9.3.4 Key Features of Early-Twentieth-Century Industrialization

Labour-intensive production of consumer goods dominated China's early industrial landscape. Textiles, garments, and food processing accounted for two-thirds of 1933 industrial output with or without the inclusion of handicrafts (Table 9.7).

Industrial activity was regionally concentrated. Nearly two-thirds of 1933 industrial production was located in the southeast coastal provinces (Table 9.4), with half more narrowly clustered in Shanghai and the adjacent Jiangsu province.

---

[3] Liu and Yeh assign all non-factory production for food processing and textiles to the handicraft segment of China's 1933 industrial sector. Their estimate of 'industrial' output thus includes non-commercial household production for self-consumption. Our attempt to remove non-commercial handicrafts from the industrial total focuses on the largest segments, textiles and food processing. We assume that commercial handicraft textile production in 1933 amounted to 90 per cent of factory textile output and that commercial handicraft food processing activity amounted to 100 per cent of factory output in that sector, with output measured by gross value in both sectors.

Table 9.6. Number of domestic, privately owned modern factories established, by region and decade, 1841–1915

Region	1841–50	1851–60	1861–70	1871–80	1881–90	1891–1900	1901–10	1911–15	Pre-1911 total	Pre-1911 share
NE					1	6	47	47	54	9.1
North				1	3	11	77	90	92	15.6
SE Coast		4	3	3	37	69	203	209	320	54.1
Central				1		11	66	38	78	13.2
NW							1	5	1	0.2
SW	1					2	43	49	46	7.8
Total	1	4	3	5	42	99	437	438	591	100.0

Source: authors' tabulation of materials in Zhang [Chang] (1989).

Table 9.7. Breakdown of industrial output by sector

Year	Coverage	Metallurgy	Power	Coal and coke	Petroleum	Chemicals	Machinery	Building materials	Timber	Food and drink	Textiles	Paper
1933	Total	1.9	0.9	4.4	0.5	1.4	5.2	1.8	5.4	30.9	42.4	5.0
	Modern only	3.8	1.8	8.5	1.0	1.9	5.7	1.2	0.8	30.0	43.4	1.9
1952	Total	5.4	1.4	4.6	0.6	1.9	6.2	2.8	9.2	31.4	34.5	2.2
1965	Total	13.0	3.5	4.8	3.6	7.3	16.0	3.2	4.6	20.0	21.6	2.3
1978	Total	10.3	4.1	3.8	6.8	12.1	25.7	4.2	2.4	12.9	16.3	1.5
1995	Total	8.7	3.6	1.6	2.4	15.0	29.9	6.9	1.5	11.6	15.9	2.6
2008	Total	8.1	3.5	0.8	0.8	12.7	49.1	4.1	1.4	7.4	10.0	2.0

Notes: All data have been converted into 1980 prices. This classification reflects two-digit categories used in Chinese industrial data during the planned economy period. 'Machinery' includes metal products; 'Textiles' includes manufacture of garments and shoes. We omit a residual sector identified as 'other' (qita) in the sources.

Sources: For 1933, authors' rearrangement of gross output data compiled in Liu and Yeh (1965) into twelve-sector structure used for post-1949. We adjust their estimates of handicraft, food and textile output to exclude non-commercial production for household own consumption. For 1952–2008, Chinese yearbook and census data.

A further 10 per cent was located in China's northeast (Manchurian) region, largely tied to Japanese investments. Data on newly established private factories prior to 1911 (Table 9.6) show a similar pattern of regional clustering.

Extreme geographic concentration resulted in large variations in industry's GDP share. For Shanghai and the adjacent Lower Yangzi region, an area with a population of 60 million, the GDP share of modern industry during the early 1930s may have reached 15 per cent, three times the national total and comparable to the role of industry in Japan by the late 1920s.[4] Vast regions, especially in the west, experienced very limited development of modern industry prior to 1937.

Domestic entrepreneurs succeeded in rapidly overcoming their initial disadvantages—inferior technical knowledge, poorer financing, and treaty provisions exempting foreign firms from many Chinese taxes. Table 9.8, which decomposes 1933 factory activity in China proper,[5] puts the share of Chinese-owned firms in output and employment at 78 and 83 per cent respectively.[6]

Even though 90 per cent of 1933 factory production was sold domestically (Table 9.3), global market forces powerfully affected Chinese manufacturing throughout the pre-war period. New domestic producers usually faced the task of wresting market share from foreign manufactures, which attracted domestic buyers by offering alternatives for traditional products (manufactured yarn substituting for handicraft, cigarettes replacing pipe tobacco, kerosene being used for lighting rather than vegetable oil) and 'new' goods (matches, steam engines). As a result, China's pre-war factory output closely paralleled the economy's comparative advantage.

Cotton textiles, pre-war China's leading industry, illustrate this tight link between global markets and pre-war factory development. Imports of manufactured yarn and cloth established market niches that were subsequently captured by local producers. Imports of yarn declined steeply after peaking in 1903 and again in 1914, and China emerged as a net exporter of cotton yarn beginning in 1927. Fabric imports peaked in 1913; by 1932–6, their share in domestic consumption had dropped from over 25 per cent during 1901–10 to only 8 per cent (Hsiao, 1974, pp. 38–9, 86; Kraus, 1980, pp. 116, J-3; Feuerwerker, 1970; Brandt, 1989).

International influence permeated the development process. Chinese textile entrepreneurs hired foreign-trained technical staff, purchased imported equipment with advice from Shanghai-based foreign specialists, dispatched their sons to study abroad, and borrowed from foreign banks.

---

[4] Factories account for 15.8 per cent of Japan's 1929 GDP; calculated from Ohkawa and Shinohara (1979, p. 279), Ohkawa, Takamatsu, and Yamamoto (1974, p. 205) and Nakamura (1983, p. 80).

[5] Table 9.5 excludes Manchuria. Applying the 1931 share of Japanese-owned firms in Manchurian factory production (41.2 per cent—see Mantetsu keizai chōsakai, 1933, pp. 568–9) to Manchuria's 1933 factory output (Liu and Yeh, 1965, pp. 427–8) reduces the share of Chinese-owned firms in nationwide factory output for 1933 to 69.6 per cent.

[6] For earlier decades, scattered data suggest wide variation in the share of foreign firms. We do not have data for all of industry for earlier years, but for textiles, Feuerwerker (1970) suggests long-term stability in the proportion of foreign ownership. Data assembled by Yan Zhongping shows foreign dominance in pig iron, Chinese dominance in matches, and fluctuating shares in cigarettes and cement (Yan et al., 1955, pp. 127, 130).

Table 9.8. Gross output value and employment in manufacturing by type of firm, China proper, 1933

	Gross output value				Employment			
	Chinese firms	Foreign firms	Chinese firms	Foreign firms	Chinese firms	Foreign firms	Chinese firms	Foreign firms
	Million yuan		Share		Thousands		Share	
Metallurgy	83	2.8	96.7	3.3	20.1	0.9	95.7	4.3
Power								
Coal and coke	0.5		100.0	0.0	0.2		100.0	0.0
Petroleum								
Chemicals	86.7	25.5	77.3	22.7	42.3	8.9	82.6	17.4
Machinery	68.8	17.9	79.4	20.6	52.2	8.2	86.4	13.6
Building materials	45.8	1.8	96.2	3.8	36	1.1	97.0	3.0
Timber	5.6	6.1	47.9	52.1	1.7	1.7	50.0	50.0
Food and drink	597.8	158.1	79.1	20.9	72.8	28.3	72.0	28.0
Textiles	793.6	272.7	74.4	25.6	505.6	108.3	82.4	17.6
Paper	74.9	11.2	87.0	13.0	43.8	3.8	92.0	8.0
Other	13.8	1.5	90.2	9.8	7.9	1.4	84.9	15.1
Total	1,770.5	497.6	78.1	21.9	782.6	162.6	82.8	17.2

Note: This table excludes data for Manchuria, for which Liu and Yeh estimate 1933 output at 376.7 million yuan and 1933 factory employment at 129,500. In Manchuria, the share of foreign (i.e. Japanese) firms in 1931 gross output value for manufacturing was 41.2 per cent (Mantetsu keizai chōsakai, 1933, pp. 568–9). If 41.2 per cent of Manchuria's 1933 manufacturing output came from foreign-owned firms, the share of foreign firms in total manufacturing output for that year would be 30.4 per cent.

Source: Liu and Yeh (1965, pp. 426–8). Totals may not sum due to rounding.

Competition among imports and domestic goods from foreign- and Chinese-owned factories spawned market segmentation, with Chinese firms initially serving the lower price/quality segments of contested product markets (Sutton, 2012). Chinese textile entrepreneurs initially produced yarn rather than fabric, and concentrated on low-count varieties, leaving the finer grades to foreign rivals (Hou, 1965, p. 153).

Market evolution and competitive pressure pushed firms to upgrade. During the 1920s, access to Japanese machinery and shifts in local demand encouraged spinning firms to shift their focus from 'coarse low count yarn to . . . fine, high-quality, high-count' varieties (Köll, 2003, p. 265). Forcing out independent shop bosses and installing technically trained managers enabled some firms to secure steep productivity increases (Cochran, 2000, pp. 191ff; Zeitz, 2013). Chinese yarn producers matched the rising productivity of China-based Japanese firms and outperformed British-owned rivals during 1924–36; in factory weaving, incomplete data show Chinese firms raising output per loom from 59 to 84 per cent of the levels recorded by Japanese-owned industry leaders (Zeitz, 2013, p. 125; Chao, 1977, p. 313).

Matches present a similar picture, with imports giving way to domestic production first by foreign and then by Chinese-owned firms. Liu Hongsheng, China's 'match king', built his business in small cities ignored by foreign rivals, where customers put a premium on price over quality, and only later challenged the Japanese and Swedes in the Shanghai market, China's largest (Cochran, 1992, p. 61). Liu's strategy foreshadows the recent success of PRC start-ups in telecom equipment (Huawei) and construction machinery (Sany, Zoomlion, Liugong) that used capabilities accumulated through selling lower-quality goods to less demanding markets to break into high-end global markets that were initially dominated by prominent multinationals like Caterpillar and Ericsson (Brandt and Thun, 2010).

9.3.5 Impact on Handicrafts

Estimating the scale and growth of handicrafts is difficult, but several propositions are clear.

Enforced free trade and factory expansion disrupted some craft sectors while giving new life to others. The overall effect was probably beneficial: exports of selected handicrafts grew at an average rate of 2.6 per cent per annum during 1875–1928, while combined exports of sixty-seven handicrafts rose by an average of 1.1 per cent annually during 1912–31 (Hou, 1965, p. 171).

Cotton textiles illustrate this mixed outcome. Handicraft spinning, squeezed by the dual blows of falling prices for factory yarn and rising cotton prices, suffered a steep decline (Feuerwerker, 1970). But the same low prices of factory yarn strengthened handicraft weaving, which thrived by combining factory and homespun yarns (Reynolds, 1974). Grove (2006) describes the critical role of Japanese advice and Japanese intermediate technology (wooden handlooms with iron gears) in expanding small-scale cloth production in north China.

Despite rapid factory growth, handicrafts persisted as an important component of industrial output as late as 1955, when they accounted for nearly 20 per cent of overall industrial production (Chen, 1967, p. 210).

9.3.6 Wartime Developments

Japan's 1931 takeover of China's northeast region, followed by a brief but intense attack on Shanghai in early 1932, focused attention on the need to prepare for war with Japan. The response included the establishment of official planning bodies, efforts to develop a network of state enterprises in defence-related industries, and monetary and banking reforms aimed at strengthening official control over money and credit. With the Japanese-led breakaway state of Manshūkoku adopting its own planned economy regimen, the approach of war initiated a nationwide shift from private to public enterprise and from market to government allocation that presaged the socialist system of the 1950s.

Once full-scale combat began in 1937, the combined effects of physical destruction, disruption of commercial and transport networks, fiscal difficulties arising from the westward retreat of China's national government, and hyperinflation undermined private manufacturing and limited the implementation of industrialization plans, especially for Chiang Kai-shek's Nationalist government. Consumer manufacturing centred on Shanghai suffered catastrophic reductions in capacity utilization: operating rates in flour milling fell by nearly 90 per cent between 1936 and 1945; in textiles, the decline was even steeper (Minami and Makino, 2014, Annex Table 4.D).

Official industrialization efforts, however, moved forward despite the travails of war. Indeed, rapid manufacturing growth immediately following the cessation of civil war in 1949 reflects substantial wartime increases in manufacturing capacity— expansion that pushed 1952 output to double the 1933 level and 65 per cent above the 1936 figure. Wartime investments also altered China's industrial structure, raising the share of producer goods from 25 to 42 per cent of manufacturing output, increasing the share of central, southwest and northwestern regions from 8.8 to 21 per cent, and sharply reducing the Herfindahl index for provincial industrial output from 0.25 to 0.09 between 1933 and 1952 (Table 9.4).

9.3.7 Pre-1949 Outcomes

A century after British arms imposed a regimen of free trade, China in 1949 remained a primarily agricultural economy. Although industry grew rapidly during the early decades of the twentieth century, the share of manufacturing in overall output remained small. Even so, China recorded substantial progress along the path to industrialization. Following several decades of slow expansion, the shock of military defeat and the 1895 treaty provisions allowing foreign-owned factories in China's treaty ports unleashed a wave of reform. The ensuing acceleration of entry and growth provided China with a modest array of manufacturing industries, some of which—notably cotton textiles—achieved global visibility, that employed over 1 million workers in 1933 (Liu and Yeh, 1965, p. 428).

China's leading industrial regions, the Shanghai area and the northeast, reflected divergent sources of growth. In the Lower Yangzi region centred on Shanghai, private business was the main driver of pre-war industrial growth. Beginning around 1900, rapid expansion of consumer goods manufacturing powered an economy-wide transformation that paralleled Japan's earlier path. Expanding production of cotton goods, foodstuffs, matches, and other consumer goods promoted backward linkage into engineering and chemicals, stimulated the development of commodity and financial exchanges, and prompted banks to extend financing to manufacturing and even agriculture (Rawski, 1980, 1989; Ma, 2008). Prior to 1931, government involvement was mostly indirect; support of modern banks, 'the sector . . . that benefited most from its dealings with the government', was particularly significant (Kirby, 1984, p. 80). This changed after 1931 as the threat, and then the reality, of war with Japan pushed the Chinese state to assert growing control over industries and markets previously influenced mainly by private activity, and to inject itself directly into the allocation and operation of industrial resources.

In Manchuria, by contrast, government direction was evident throughout, with much factory investment coming from Japanese-controlled companies whose actions responded to Tokyo's economic priorities. Reflecting this circumstance, chemicals, machinery, and, from 1936, metals—the central components of detailed official plans that extended into the 1950s—stand out as the largest contributors to factory value added (Chao, 1982, p. 83).

These developments occurred in an open economy, with free trade (from 1842), substantial price integration with global markets (from the 1880s), minimal restriction of FDI (from 1895), rapid expansion of new forms of education and overseas study, and considerable return migration by overseas Chinese. Extensive openness magnified both the disruption (e.g. to handicraft spinning) and the opportunities resulting from the growth of international links.

Gradual emergence of growth-promoting institutions contributed to China's pre-war industrial growth. Private actors banded together to promote common interests. Köll (2003, p. 76) describes the spread of technical schools offering courses in textile engineering, the proliferation of technical journals and the emergence of an engineering profession, all foreshadowing developments that were vastly accelerated under state auspices after 1949. Local chambers of commerce facilitated the dissemination of know-how and provided 'voice' for newly emerging entrepreneurs (Chan, 1977).

State action, initially focused on sponsorship of semi-official enterprises during the late nineteenth century, subsequently emphasized indirect actions that smoothed the path of private ventures: passing a corporation law, identifying and disseminating commercially promising technologies, and pursuing tariff autonomy.

As a result, China's pre-war economy displayed many features of a market system. Prices were flexible and generally market-determined. There were few man-made obstacles to domestic or international mobility of goods, people, information, and ideas. Formal and informal entry barriers declined over time. Low revenue and, after 1911, weak central control restricted the state's ability to regulate and intervene.

This began to change soon after the Guomindang established the Nanjing government in 1927. Although restricted by weak finances and limited territorial control, the new administration set out to follow Japan and other rising powers by systematically deploying the levers of state power to build a modern industrial economy. Japan's assault on China's territorial integrity, which signalled a growing likelihood of all-out war, hastened the Guomindang's shift from supporting a largely private economy toward an emerging vision of a planned economy in which official direction of investment and state-owned enterprises (SOEs) would occupy leading roles.

The outbreak of war in 1937 led to 'an enormous expansion of Nationalist China's economic bureaucracy', nationalization of many existing industrial operations, and planned production and distribution of essential war materials (Kirby, 1990, pp. 127–8). By 1944, public sector firms accounted for more than half of total industrial output and an even higher share of heavy industry (Bian, 2002, p. 85).

While the defeat of Japan brought a renewal of China's long-smouldering civil strife, the Guomindang and Communists shared a common vision of an industrial sector oriented toward military strength, directed by government technocrats, and dominated by state-run firms. When Communist forces routed their Guomindang rivals, 'the large majority of Nationalist industrial planning personnel', including the 'entire senior leadership' of the National Resources Council, the KMT's lead agency for economic planning, 'remained on the mainland', imparting a strong element of continuity to the establishment of Soviet-aided socialist planning by the incoming PRC government (Kirby, 1990, p. 134).

9.4 CHINESE INDUSTRY UNDER SOCIALIST PLANNING, 1949–78

The Chinese economy recovered quickly with the end of hostilities and the establishment of the PRC in 1949. By the mid-1950s, China had succeeded in further institutionalizing and extending the system inherited from the preceding wartime era. In industry, two features were especially prominent: state ownership and the substitution of a planning system for markets.

Industry under socialism is as much a story of continuity as it is of change. State ownership had come to the fore during the 1940s. Nationalization of remaining private firms in the early 1950s and the concentration of new investment in the state sector simply reinforced this dominance. Between 1957 and 1978, the state sector consistently delivered over 80 per cent of gross value of industrial output (GVIO), with the remainder coming from a large number of small urban collective firms and, beginning in the late 1950s, from an even larger number of rural collective enterprises.

Through an enlarged and integrated version of separate planning bureaucracies inherited from the former Guomindang and Manshūkoku governments, China moved to fully replace markets with administrative resource allocation. Decisions about output, input use, and investment were now all in the hands of the planners.

Although China's plan system resembled its Soviet counterpart, there were important differences. The number of commodities for which planners constructed nationwide allocations was smaller than in the USSR. China's system was more decentralized, with substantial resources under the control of provincial and sub-provincial governments (Wong, 1985). This decentralization reflected a succession of initiatives that began during the mid-1950s and continued through the next two decades. Maskin, Qian, and Xu (2000) argue that this feature of the pre-1978 economy had important consequences for the system's reform-era trajectory.

A central objective of the new system was to mobilize resources that planners could direct toward strategic objectives. Control over prices was critical: by setting prices of final goods high relative to those for inputs, including wages, planners could concentrate profits in the hands of SOEs. Low profit retention rates—firms were required to remit more than 95 per cent of their profits—provided a revenue stream for the state that accounted for a large share of fiscal receipts.[7]

Security concerns and the desire to narrow the gap with the West put a high premium on investment and the expansion in China's producer goods sector, such as steel, machine tools, and chemicals. As in the USSR, and in sharp contrast to the

---

[7] Hsiao (1987, p. 12) gives annual fiscal 'receipts from enterprises' (including, but not limited to, industrial firms); this category accounted for over 50 per cent of budgetary revenue in fourteen of sixteen years between 1959 and 1974.

first three decades of the twentieth century, Chinese planning pursued industrial development without reference to comparative advantage. Moreover, with the notable exception of the sizable inflows of equipment, technology, and expertise from the Soviet bloc during the 1950s, Chinese leaders limited the country's ties to global markets. International isolation, which reflected a combination of ideological conviction and the impact of a US-led trade embargo, pushed China's trade ratio far below the levels attained during the 1930s (Table 9.3).

9.4.1 Achievements

These institutional arrangements delivered three decades of rapid industrial expansion, surpassing earlier rates of growth. After doubling between 1949 and 1952 with the revival of the economy, industrial output grew more than 11 per cent per annum between 1952 and 1978 (Table 9.1), while employment grew nearly tenfold, from 5.3 million in 1952 to 53.3 million in 1978 (Table 9.2).

In line with planners' objectives, quantitative expansion brought a pronounced shift in the structure of industry, which moved away from formerly dominant consumer manufactures toward intermediate and producer products. Entirely new industries appeared—for example, manufacture of trucks, tractors, radios, telecom, and power-generating equipment. The rise of machinery, from only 6.2 per cent of industrial output in 1952 to 25.7 per cent in 1978 (Table 9.7), highlights the direction and magnitude of structural change. By the 1970s, the sectoral composition of industry resembled that of a country with significantly higher GDP per capita, such as Japan in the late 1950s.

Declining spatial concentration, a trend already visible between 1933 and 1952, continued in the socialist plan environment (Table 9.7). China's first five-year plan (1953–7) concentrated investment in inland provinces, bypassing coastal regions that had dominated pre-war manufacturing. Planners also relocated personnel and factories from militarily vulnerable coastal cities to interior regions. Dispersion continued during the 1960s under the 'Third Front' programme, which situated industrial facilities in remote interior locations to guard against potential US or Soviet attacks (Naughton, 1988). With these shifts, the Herfindahl index for provincial industrial output continued the decline begun during the 1930s, falling from 0.09 in 1952 to 0.06 in 1978 (Table 9.4).

Beyond the cities, and largely outside the formal plan, development of rural industry represents an unusual feature of Chinese industrialization. Rural enterprises, most run by agricultural collectives, aimed to serve agriculture and to use local resources to satisfy local demand for cement, fertilizer, machinery, electricity, and coal. Promotion of rural industry began in the mid-1950s, experienced explosive but hugely wasteful growth during the Great Leap Forward (1958–60), and re-emerged in the late 1960s following major post-Leap retrenchment. By 1978, rural industry (including mining and construction as well as manufacturing) employed 19.7 million workers (Thirty Years, 2008, p. 248). Rural industry was particularly successful in the suburbs of major coastal cities that had also developed the largest non-agricultural sectors prior to 1949—that is, the regions disfavoured by both the early PRC investment plans and then by the Third Front policy.

By the 1970s, Chinese manufacturing, no longer limited to the production of low-end, labour-intensive consumer products, spanned virtually the entire range of industrial activity, including sophisticated operations involving petroleum refining, nuclear weapons, and earth satellites. Despite its brief duration, the flow of aid and trade from the USSR and its East European allies provided an unprecedented cross-national technology transfer that accelerated China's effort to broaden the span of domestic manufacturing.[8] Beyond the growth of output and extension of the product mix, socialist planning brought a vast expansion of industrial capabilities. The accumulation of production experience and the spread of mass education multiplied the stock of factory-level technical capabilities and human capital. In addition, the plan system underwrote a massive expansion of institutions, resources, and personnel for high-level technical training and research efforts. Ministries and major SOEs established networks of universities, technical schools, and R & D facilities. By the late 1970s, there were over 700 R & D institutes with over 500,000 scientists and engineers, nearly as many as in the United States (Gu, 1999, pp. 56–8; Nolting and Feshbach, 1981, p. 44).

9.4.2 Shortcomings

Despite important advances, the achievements of Chinese industry during the plan era fell far short of potential. The most obvious indicator is slow productivity growth (World Bank, 1985, p. 110; Kuan et al., 1988), despite a long list of favourable circumstances: unprecedented official promotion of industrial development, large inflows of Soviet technology and capital goods, huge increases in public expenditure on R & D, and rapid expansion of primary education and basic health care.

Rising capital per worker—the consequence of steep increases in investment spending, much of it directed toward industry[9]—coincided with surprisingly slow growth of industrial output per worker—with several sectors, including metallurgy, suffering declines in labour productivity between 1965 and 1978 (Field, 1982). Factoring in improvements in human capital suggests negative TFP growth (Zhu, 2012). This 'disappointing' outcome meant that 'rapid expansion of output came almost entirely from massive growth of labour and especially capital inputs' (Chen et al., 1988, pp. 585–7). The obvious implication is that the beneficial impact of multiple sources of productivity growth was

---

[8] During the 1950s, imports constituted nearly 20 per cent of newly added producer durables (Field, 1980, p. 233).

[9] The share of gross capital formation in aggregate expenditure, which Rawski (1989, pp. 260–1) places at 10.3 per cent during 1931–6 (excluding inventory accumulation), is estimated at 22.2, 25.4, 28.4, and 38.2 per cent for 1952, 1957, 1965, and 1978 respectively. Industry's share of basic construction, the largest component of investment spending, was 31.3 per cent in 1953, 43.9 per cent in 1956, and at least 50 per cent throughout 1957–78 with the exception of 1965, when the figure was 49.1 per cent (GDP, 2007, p. 19; Investment, 1987, p. 97).

overwhelmed by institutional blockages and policy failures.[10] With a rising share of GDP directed to investment to offset declining TFP, consumption languished.

Chinese observers were quick to highlight the institutional sources of poor outcomes. A 1982 editorial explained that 'the basic causes of low [industrial] labour productivity' included poor morale, bureaucratism and lax discipline 'in many factories' (Field, 1982, p. 656). Shigeru Ishikawa (1983, p. 275) highlighted shortcomings in the 'investment goods sub-sector', the core of the planned economy, which, despite receiving 'an extremely high proportion of investment funds... [and] scarce foreign currency', delivered weak results. 'The marginal output-capital ratio... decreased considerably over time and hence the expected rise in the growth rate of national income [and other important results were]... not realized.'

Rawski (1975) and others replicated previous work on Soviet industry which showed how material-balance planning and ambitious physical output targets led managers to pursue quantity at the expense of quality, variety, innovation, cost, and customer satisfaction; to systematically overstate input requirements and understate production capacity; and to hoard materials, labour and backup production facilities. Naughton (1995, pp. 49–50) found that the accumulation of inventories and unfinished construction in China was considerably worse than in the USSR.

Specific Chinese policies added further impediments. Of particular importance in this connection was enforced self-sufficiency at the national, regional, and even local level, which limited both international and domestic trade and moved investment priorities far away from comparative advantage. Suspicion of intellectuals and technical expertise, which periodically stripped firms, government offices, schools, and research institutions of scarce and valuable talent, also came with high costs.

9.5 CHINESE INDUSTRY DURING THE REFORM ERA, 1978–2008

Beginning in the late 1970s, a succession of reform initiatives gradually led to a hybrid that combines important elements of planning, state ownership, and official direction with a revival of the open, private, market-based system of the 1920s and 1930s. This novel arrangement has extended the rapid growth attained under the former plan system, but combined quantitative expansion with market liberalization, deep integration with global markets, and rapid upgrading that has enabled a growing array of Chinese manufacturers to approach global frontiers of technical sophistication and product quality.

We separate the reform era into two periods, with 1995 as the break point.

---

[10] Lardy (1983) makes a similar point regarding agriculture.

9.5.1 Early Reforms, 1978–95

China's initial reforms included selective opening to the global economy, most notably through the establishment of Special Economic Zones (SEZs) that welcomed foreign investment and allowed duty-free import of materials used to manufacture export goods, as well as incremental reform of state-owned enterprises. The critical element in early-stage reform, however, was market liberalization, which advanced along multiple axes.

Price and quantity determination, formerly the near-exclusive preserve of official plan bodies, moved toward market outcomes. Separate initiatives empowering firms to arrange the disposition of above-quota output and establishing 'dual pricing', i.e. market pricing of non-plan exchanges, injected scarcity-based marginal values into a formerly rigid pricing system (Naughton, 1995). By 1991, 'market forces' had surpassed 'state order' in determining prices of 'production materials'; in 1995, the share of market forces reached 77.9 per cent (Rawski, 2000, p. 320).

Introduction of partial profit retention (for firms) and bonuses (for workers) reversed the plan system's destruction of incentives and weakened the corrosive impact of soft budget constraints among state-owned firms.

Reforms began to dismantle plan-era restrictions that had limited the mobility of people, goods, technology, funds, and information across China's internal and international boundaries. These initiatives sparked what developed into vast flows of migrant labour to coastal industrial centres; they also undermined protectionist policies aimed at retaining local materials and blocking inflows of manufactures.

Finally, early reforms reduced impediments to entry and exit in a growing array of industries. Although SOE monopoly persisted in some sectors (Haggard and Huang, 2008), others opened up for entry by non-state actors—urban collectives, rural township and village enterprises (TVEs), private domestic ventures, and foreign-invested firms.

9.5.2 Outcomes to 1995

Notwithstanding the continuation of plan allocations and prices, the revival of incentives, domestic trade and market-determined prices allowed producers some scope to modify their product mix, choose among alternative suppliers or extend sales efforts into new markets without cumbersome bureaucratic approvals. New entrants, operating outside the plan system, could occupy market niches overlooked by the plan apparatus. Growing availability of materials and services outside the plan encouraged specialization, reversing the excessive vertical integration developed in the plan environment.

At the same time, growing openness steadily enlarged the global impact on China's formerly isolated and largely self-reliant industrial sector, which faced the prospect of accessing a backlog of overseas innovations dating back to the 1930s. Manufactured exports rose over 100-fold in US dollar terms between 1978 and 1995 (Table 9.3). Imports were heavily weighted with capital equipment, raw materials, and, reflecting

Table 9.9. Inward and outward FDI (US$ billion)

Year	1990	2000	2010
FDI inflow	3.48	40.71	105.70
FDI sources:			
Asia		25.48	
Hong Kong	1.91	15.50	60.60
Japan	0.50	2.92	0.71
Korea		1.49	2.70
Europe		4.76	
Germany	0.02	1.04	0.89
UK	0.01	1.16	0.71
North America		4.78	
US	0.46	4.38	3.02
Canada	0.41	0.28	0.71
FDI outflow	0.83	0.92	68.81

Source: Yearbook, 1991, 2001, 2011.

China's growing participation in global supply chains, industrial components, most delivered to the factory sector.

FDI increased dramatically (Tables 9.5 and 9.9). Firms with Hong Kong and Taiwan ties, run by entrepreneurs with long experience in producing and exporting consumer products, were especially prominent, constituting the majority of enterprises in the SEZs. Specializing in the assembly and export of textiles, apparel, footwear, and electronics, these firms became the leading source of China's exports. Nonetheless, the share of foreign-linked firms in industrial output (Table 9.5), the share of exports in sales of manufactured goods (Table 9.3), and the share of FDI in overall investment (Fixed Assets, 2002, p. 20) remained below 15 per cent throughout this period.

However, tariff and non-tariff barriers, remnants of the industrial plan system, ad hoc disruption of (especially private) business, and inadequate infrastructure (frequent power shortages, overcrowded railways, poor roads, primitive telecommunications) limited the economy's response to these opportunities, just as similar domestic constraints had restricted the responsiveness of private actors during the decades prior to 1937.

Industrial growth during the early reform years was somewhat higher than during 1965–78 (Table 9.1), with big increases in the growth of textiles and food processing (Table 9.10). Although the share of machinery, chemicals, and metallurgy changed little between 1978 and 1995 (Table 9.7), industry shifted toward the same coastal provinces that had led the development of private sector manufacturing prior to the Second World War (Table 9.4) and, reflecting the tripling of China's trade ratio from 11.8 to 38.7 per cent between 1978 and 1995 (Table 9.3), toward sectors and products in which China held a comparative advantage.

Growth occurred primarily outside the state sector, reducing the SOE output share from 80 to 49 per cent between 1978 and 1995 (Industry, 1985, pp. 31–2; Table 9.5). TVEs emerged as a key source of fresh momentum. Concentrated in

Table 9.10. Real annual growth rates for gross output value, 1952–2008 (per cent)

	1952–65	1965–78	1978–95	1995–2008
Sector				
Metallurgy	18.4	7.4	10.3	14.7
Power	18.8	10.7	10.5	15.0
Coal and coke	10.9	7.5	5.9	9.5
Petroleum	27.4	14.8	4.7	5.9
Chemicals	22.8	13.6	12.7	13.9
Machinery	19.0	13.4	12.3	19.8
Building materials	11.9	11.6	14.7	10.7
Timber	4.9	3.9	8.5	14.8
Food and drink	6.8	5.7	10.7	11.4
Textiles	6.7	7.0	11.2	11.3
Paper	10.8	5.8	15.2	13.1
Total	12.3	10.2	11.6	13.8

Sources: Table 9.1 and data underlying Table 9.7.

the once again dynamic coastal regions, these firms, largely owned and managed by township and village governments (although some were in reality private), absorbed labour released by the productivity growth that accompanied agricultural reform (Lin, 1992) and tapped expanding domestic trade networks to sell their products and obtain equipment, materials, and expertise. Powerful incentives, limited technical expertise, and hard budget constraints (Whiting, 2001) led TVEs to focus on labour-intensive consumer products. Flexible, ambitious, and aligned with China's comparative advantage, TVEs quickly entered international markets, accounting for 16.3 per cent of aggregate exports in 1990 and 28.9 per cent in 1995 (Thirty Years, 2008, p. 326; Yearbook, 2014, p. 329).

As waves of new entrants slashed returns in the consumer sector, China's leaders began to rethink the position of the state sector. Sectors like garments and beverages were designated as 'competitive industries'—meaning that market competition could determine the fate of SOEs in those product lines. Planning increasingly focused on a limited array of 'strategic' sectors seen as deserving special attention and support. Despite the reforms, state firms in the secondary sector (industry and construction) absorbed over half (and often much more) of aggregate investment outlays in every year between 1981 and 1995.[11] SOEs enjoyed priority access to bank lending. Licensing of advanced technology and joint ventures with overseas multinationals—for example, Beijing Jeep and Shanghai-Volkswagen—provided additional support for the expansion of SOE technical capabilities and competitiveness. Despite these advantages, SOEs lagged behind other firms in both financial returns (Holz, 2003, pp. 165–70) and productivity growth (Jefferson et al., 2000, pp. 797–804). This motivated efforts beginning in the mid-1990s to expand the reform effort.

[11] See authors' file 'Investment-by-sector-ownership', compiled from official statistical publications.

9.5.3 Reforms since 1995

On the domestic front, the government privatized (largely to insiders) or shut down large numbers of small, inessential or poorly performing SOEs: more than 75,000 SOE firms disappeared, and, with them, the jobs of 15–20 million workers. The state sector's share of industrial output fell from 48.6 to 24 per cent between 1995 and 2008 (Table 9.5). The remaining SOEs were larger and increasingly concentrated in sectors like steel, precision machinery, and chemicals that the state identified as strategic or 'pillar' industries.

A series of policy initiatives sought to make the SOEs more commercial and more innovative. A State-Owned Assets Supervision and Administration Commission (SASAC) was established to consolidate management of the state's ownership interests and take the lead in restructuring major SOEs to boost their competitiveness (Naughton, 2015). The government poured resources into the promotion of 'indigenous innovation' that would establish China as a producer (rather than, as in the past, a purchaser) of cutting-edge technology. The state also pushed Chinese firms, with SOEs again in the forefront, to 'go outward' by increasing overseas direct investment (Table 9.9) in order to deepen market experience and accelerate both the absorption and the development of advanced technologies.

Legal reforms that explicitly affirmed the legitimacy of private enterprise encouraged the rapid expansion of privately owned manufacturing, involving both new enterprise formation and privatization of TVEs and urban collectives. Restrictions on the movement of people and goods were further eroded.

On the external front, multiple initiatives—falling tariffs and non-tariff barriers, fresh measures to encourage FDI, allowing large numbers of firms to engage in international trade, and more generous currency retention rights for exporters—culminated in China's 2001 accession to the World Trade Organization (Lardy, 2002; Branstetter and Lardy, 2008). Reform leaders like Zhu Rongji saw a strong link between external and internal reforms. They viewed China's WTO agreements as a 'credible commitment' to the continued pursuit of market outcomes to which domestic players, especially major SOEs, would be compelled to adjust. From this perspective, the domestic impact of external reforms may have exceeded the direct benefits of WTO entry.

9.5.4 Outcomes since 1995

Industrial growth accelerated during this period (Table 9.1). The output share of textiles and food processing continued to decline, while machinery's share rose to almost half (Table 9.7).[12] The southeast coast continued to advance, raising its output share to 45.8 per cent by 2008 (Table 9.4).

While manufactured exports grew rapidly, China's rapidly expanding, highly competitive, and increasingly demanding domestic market absorbed over 80 per cent

---

[12] The extraordinarily high share of machinery in GVIO in 2008 may in part reflect inaccurately recorded relative price trends.

of incremental manufacturing output during both sub-periods of the reform era (Table 9.3). For most manufacturers, the opportunity to sell into this domestic market, the world's largest for products ranging from autos to mobile phones and nuclear power equipment, provided the biggest boost to growth. Although market opening has allowed foreign-linked firms to gain ground in a number of sectors, domestic enterprises have achieved strong competitive positions, in some cases—beer, home appliances, heavy construction equipment—recapturing market share initially ceded to foreign operators. As of 2008, domestic firms accounted for over three-fourths of industrial output (Table 9.5).[13]

The reforms increased the incentives for firms to invest in capability building, as well as their ability to upgrade. Incremental innovation and upgrading allowed firms to narrow the productivity gap vis-à-vis domestic and international leaders, similar to recent developments elsewhere in Asia as well as China's longer-term catch-up dating from the late nineteenth century. FDI, which accelerated following Deng Xiaoping's southern trip (1992) and continued at high levels thereafter, was a major contributor (Table 9.9). A significant portion of the FDI originated from relatively small firms based in Hong Kong and Taiwan. Large multinationals like Boeing, General Electric, Hitachi, and Volkswagen also established substantial Chinese operations.

Foreign firms initially focused on using Chinese land and labour to reduce production costs for components and final goods sold overseas. 'Processing' exports, an arrangement that allows duty-free importation of materials and components, propelled Chinese engagement with global production chains. As foreign firms gained familiarity with the rising capabilities of Chinese manufacturers, they turned to domestic suppliers to source an increasing range of components and help lower costs. This multiplied the dispersion of international standards and advanced business practices (inventory management, production scheduling, quality control, etc.) among domestic manufacturers, as the supply chain of a single assembly plant for vehicles or electrical equipment can involve thousands of component and material vendors. Finally, in anticipation of rapidly rising incomes and a growing middle class, FDI was increasingly directed toward serving the growing domestic market, a shift that intensified competition in many domestic product categories.

The experience of Chinese firms in telecoms and construction equipment illustrates the contribution of openness and liberalization to industrial upgrading. Huawei, initially dismissed as technically weak by both Chinese planners and their MNE partners, followed the path of China's pre-war 'match king' by building expertise in neglected markets—first in small cities in China's interior and then in Africa—to develop innovative products that subsequently penetrated high-end markets both within and outside China (Brandt and Thun, 2013). Reflecting

---

[13] PRC statistics classify the entire output of firms with any offshore (including Hong Kong, Taiwan, and Macao) ownership, no matter how small, as 'foreign'. The practice of 'round-tripping,' in which domestic funds are moved offshore and then repatriated to take advantage of regulatory provisions favouring foreign capital, leads official data to overstate output from foreign-linked firms by an undetermined, but probably declining, amount.

spillovers from China's growing R & D expenditures (Hu and Jefferson, 2008), research engineers designed inexpensive concrete pumps that allowed Sany, an obscure Hunan start-up, to develop into an internationally competitive manufacture of construction equipment (Brandt and Thun, 2015).

Growing market penetration and rising unit values confirm the growing sophistication and rapid upward migration of Chinese manufactured exports along international price/quality ladders (Schott, 2008; Mandel, 2013). The domestic (Chinese) content of exports has increased significantly, reflecting a deepening of local supply chains and capabilities (Kee and Tang, 2016). Manufacturing productivity growth, largely coming from the entry of new firms, now parallels the achievements of other successful economies during periods of similarly rapid industrial expansion (Brandt, Van Biesebroeck, and Zhang, 2012). The most dynamic outcomes are in sectors that are highly contested and readily accessible to foreign investors, and which obstruct neither entry nor exit by domestic firms (Brandt, Rawski, and Sutton, 2008; Brandt and Thun, 2015; Brandt et al., 2012, revised 2015).

At the same time, there is large-scale inefficiency within individual sectors: Hsieh and Klenow (2009) conclude that reducing efficiency gaps between firms within sectors to levels observed in US manufacturing could have raised productivity in China's factories by 30–50 per cent during 1998–2005. Preferential access to capital, energy and other key inputs is the likely culprit for these costs, which often show up in the form of excess capacity in firms and sectors. Table 9.11 reveals big differences in productivity dynamics between sectors with 1998 SOE output shares above or below 50 per cent. For sectors in which SOEs contributed the majority of 1998 output, outcomes are uniformly weak: continuing firms contribute negatively to productivity growth, as do new entrants, including new private firms—meaning that new firms enter with productivity levels below those of incumbents. For sectors with 1998 SOE shares below 50 per cent, the picture is

Table 9.11. Sectoral SOE shares and TFP growth, 1998–2007

Sectors	Total change in in TFP	Sources of change in TFP			
		Within	Between	Entry	Exit
SOE share > 0.50	−0.117	−0.048	0.007	−0.080	0.004
SOE share < 0.50	0.208	0.050	−0.024	0.175	0.007
All sectors	0.107	0.019	−0.014	0.096	0.006

Notes:
[1] Changes in TFP are based on estimates for a gross output function. TFP growth on a value-added basis can be obtained by multiplying these estimates by $1/V$, where V is value added as a percentage of gross output. A value-added ratio of 0.25 implies TFP growth on a value-added basis that is four times higher than on a gross output basis.
[2] Sector shares for SOEs are based on data for 1998.
[3] 'Within' represents the growth in productivity amongst firms operating in both 1998 and 2007; 'between' is the growth in TFP coming from the reallocation of resources to more productive firms; 'entry' is from new firms not in the sample in 1998 but present in 2007; and 'exit' is from firms operating in 1998, but no longer operating by 2007.
Source: Calculations based on firm-level data.

the opposite, with productivity rising, primarily because entering firms deliver above-average results, thus boosting sector-wide outcomes.

Our survey ends with a profound contradiction. As China navigates the fourth decade of a transition that produced results beyond anyone's wildest dreams, the strategy of placing state-owned firms at the core of the nation's development plans, a constant feature of economic policy making dating from the Chiang Kai-shek administration of the 1930s, emerges yet again as an obstacle to the achievement of ambitious economic goals. With the current administration seemingly committed to the traditional policy of populating the economy's commanding heights with state enterprises, we must ask whether the economy's forward momentum will be sufficient to carry the costs associated with state ownership.

9.6 CONCLUSION

Since its inception during the second half of the nineteenth century, modern industry in China has amassed an enviable record of rapid growth. Only the Second World War halted the long-term expansion of output, and even then on-going capacity growth pushed output to unprecedented levels once hostilities came to an end.

China's initial forays into manufacturing clustered around Shanghai and the southeastern coastal provinces, regions that subsequently maintained their leading position even as modern industry spread across China's cities and penetrated into the countryside. Nineteenth-century industrialization combined official ventures oriented toward defence-related sectors and private efforts focused on mechanized processing of farm products. Following several decades of mainly private initiatives oriented toward labour-intensive consumer manufactures, Japan's annexation of Manchuria in 1931 prompted a shift toward military-linked producer products and public ownership that continues to occupy a major plank of Chinese economic strategy.

Industrial expansion has involved qualitative change along with growing output volume. The initially narrow range of domestic manufactured goods has expanded dramatically. Chinese firms now populate every industrial segment. In a growing array of sectors, leading Chinese manufacturers can compete with leading multinationals. In sector after sector—yarn, machine tools, power generating equipment, computers—the transition of Chinese goods from laggards to formidable rivals follows a common path. Imports of novel products establish a market that domestic firms seek to penetrate. Their efforts, initially based on imitation, result in the production of cheap, low-quality domestic substitutes. Some of these producers of inferior goods mobilize sufficient capabilities to upgrade their products, thus beginning the ascent of that particular sector's price–quality ladder.

Crucial for growth, capability accumulation, and upgrading are openness to international flows of goods, capital, people, technology, and ideas; domestic market liberalization; and supportive institutions. We see these as mutually reinforcing, although Chinese reality defies simple analysis, and there may be substitutes for these essential ingredients (for example, personal networks extending into the ranks of government and Communist Party officials may partially offset the absence of secure property rights in today's PRC). The 1910s and 1920s saw substantial growth with minimal official support. Between 1949 and 1978, the PRC's planned economy delivered both rapid growth and considerable expansion of capabilities with limited openness and no domestic liberalization. And the current reform era has produced an astonishing burst of growth and upgrading in the face of massive institutional deficits and considerably less openness or liberalization than existed in the early twentieth century.

The objective of 'enriching the nation and strengthening the army' motivated official behaviour throughout our period, though the capacity of the state to underwrite militarily significant industrial efforts expanded hugely under the PRC. The shift from market dominance toward state control, conventionally attributed to the inception of Soviet-type planning during the 1950s, actually began much earlier. Chiang Kai-shek's Nanjing government began to embrace planning and state ownership from 1931; in the northeast, Japanese influence propelled a similar shift as early as the late 1910s. The question of the benefits and costs of state ownership, management, and control has thus permeated Chinese policy discussions during the past eighty years, and remains central today.

Looking ahead, we can anticipate continued deepening of industrial capabilities through multiple channels: domestic and overseas education, accumulation of production and marketing experience, increasing domestic R & D outlays, learning from large-scale inward and outbound FDI, and energetic, well-funded promotion of officially mandated nodes of 'indigenous innovation'. At the same time, immense industrial advance coexists with staggering inefficiency, an outcome that extends across multiple institutional settings—extensive planning with near-total public ownership prior to 1978, the initial reform period of the 1980s and early 1990s, and the more open and further liberalized system of the last two decades.

This chapter resonates with a larger body of work that highlights state-owned industry as the chief contributor to the vast inefficiencies that litter China's development path. It is not simply that SOEs, led by Communist Party appointees who must juggle (often conflicting) commercial and political objectives, have recorded consistently weak cost, profit, and productivity performance. We now have ample evidence that state ownership slows overall growth and impinges on financial stability and structural change.

China's leaders are well aware of these costs, and presumably understand that on-going efforts to attack corruption, encourage strong firms to absorb weak rivals, and exhort participants to follow official priorities cannot succeed where past reforms have failed. However, the value to Chinese elites of a large and growing state sector, which provides a treasure house of patronage and rents as well an army of powerful and responsive subordinates, banishes serious consideration of sweeping SOE privatization from the current policy agenda.

Will China's on-going momentum continue to override the current system's immense costs, maintaining something approaching the rapid progress of the past several decades? Might SOE giants slow the pace of innovation by blocking or absorbing potential rivals? Will SOE service oligopolies escalate system costs as the integration of telecoms and other services with manufacturing advances? Only time will tell.

REFERENCES

Bian, M. L. (2002). The Sino-Japanese War and the formation of the state enterprise system in China: a case study of the Dadukou iron and steel works, 1938–1945. *Enterprise and Society* 3, 80–123.

Brandt, L. (1985). Chinese agriculture and the international economy, 1870–1930: a reassessment. *Explorations in Economic History*, 22, 168–93.

Brandt, L. (1989). *Commercialization and Agricultural Development: Central and Eastern China, 1870–1937*. Cambridge and New York: Cambridge University Press.

Brandt, L. and Thun, E. (2010). The fight for the middle: competition and upgrading in Chinese Industry. *World Development* 38, 1555–74.

Brandt, L. and Thun, E. (2013). Going mobile in China: shifting value chains and upgrading in the mobile telecom sector. *International Journal of Technological Learning, Innovation and Development* 4, 148–80.

Brandt, L. and Thun, E. (2015). Constructing a ladder for growth: policy, markets and industrial upgrading in China. *World Development* 80, 78–95.

Brandt, L., Ma, D., and Rawski, T. (2014). From divergence to convergence: reexamining the history behind China's economic boom. *Journal of Economic Literature* 52, 45–123.

Brandt, L., Rawski, T., and Sutton, J. (2008). China's industrial development. In *China's Great Economic Transformation* (Eds, Brandt, L. and Rawski, T.). Cambridge and New York: Cambridge University Press, 569–632.

Brandt, L., Van Biesebroeck, J., and Zhang, Y. F. (2012). Creative accounting or creative destruction? Firm-level productivity growth in Chinese manufacturing. *Journal of Development Economics* 97, 339–51.

Brandt, L., Van Biesebroek, J. L., Wang, L. H., and Zhang, Y. F. (2012, revised 2016). WTO accession and performance of Chinese manufacturing firms. *CEPR Discussion Paper* No. 9166.

Branstetter, L. and Lardy, N. R. (2008). China's embrace of globalization. In *China's Great Economic Transformation* (Eds, Brandt, L. and Rawski, T.). Cambridge and New York: Cambridge University Press, 633–82.

Brown, S. R. (1978). The partially opened door: limitations on economic change in China in the 1860s. *Modern Asian Studies* 12, 177–92.

Brown, S. R. (1979a). The Ewo Filature: a study in the transfer of technology to China in the 19th century. *Technology and Culture* 20, 550–68.

Brown, S. R. (1979b). The transfer of technology to China in the nineteenth century: the role of direct foreign investment. *Journal of Economic History* 39, 181–97.

Chan, W. K. K. (1977). *Merchants, Mandarins, and Modern Enterprise in Late Ch'ing China*. Cambridge, MA: Harvard University East Asian Research Center, distributed by Harvard University Press.

Chao, K. (1977). *The Development of Cotton Textile Production in China*. Cambridge, MA: Harvard University East Asian Research Center, distributed by Harvard University Press.

Chao, K. (1982). *The Economic Development of Manchuria: The Rise of a Frontier Economy*. Ann Arbor, MI: Center for Chinese Studies, University of Michigan.

Chen, N. R. (1967). *Chinese Economic Statistics: A Handbook for Mainland China.* Chicago, IL: Aldine.

Cochran, S. G. (1992). Three roads into Shanghai's market: Japanese, Western, and Chinese companies in the match trade, 1895–1937. In *Shanghai Sojourners* (Eds, Wakeman, F. and Yeh, W. H.). Berkeley, CA: Institute of East Asian Studies, 35–75.

Cochran, S. G. (2000). *Encountering Chinese Networks.* Berkeley, CA: University of California Press.

Compendium (2009). *Xin Zhongguo liushiwunian tongji ziliao huibian* [China Compendium of Statistics 1949–2008]. Beijing: Zhongguo tongji chubanshe.

Dinh, H. T., Rawski, T. G., Zafar A., Wang, L., and Mavroeidi, E. (2013). *Tales from the Development Frontier: How China and Other Countries Resolve the Binding Constraints in Light Manufacturing to Create Jobs and Prosperity.* Washington, DC: World Bank.

Esherick, J. (1972). Harvard on China: the apologetics of imperialism. *Bulletin of Concerned Asian Scholars* 4, 9–16.

Feuerwerker, A. (1970). Handicraft and manufactured cotton textiles in China, 1871–1910. *Journal of Economic History* 30, 338–78.

Field, R. M. (1980). Real capital formation in the People's Republic of China, 1952–73. In *Quantitative Measures of China's Economic Output* (Ed., Eckstein, A.). Ann Arbor, MI: University of Michigan Press, 194–245.

Field, R. M. (1982). Slow growth of labour productivity in Chinese industry, 1952–81. *China Quarterly* 96, 641–64.

Fixed Assets (2002). *Zhongguo guding zichan touzi tongji shudian (1950–2000)* [Statistics on Investment in Fixed Assets of China, 1950–2000]. Beijing: Zhongguo tongji chubanshe.

Gardella, R. (1994). *Harvesting Mountains: Fujian and the China Tea Trade, 1757–1937.* Berkeley, CA: University of California Press.

GDP (2007). *Zhongguo guonei shengchan zongzhi hesuan lishi ziliao 1952–2004* [Data of Gross Domestic Product of China, 1952–2004]. Beijing: Zhongguo tongji chubanshe.

Grove, L. (2006). *A Chinese Economic Revolution: Rural Entrepreneurship in the Twentieth Century.* Lanham: Rowman & Littlefield.

Gu, S. L. (1999). *China's Industrial Technology: Market Reform and Organizational Change.* London: Routledge.

Haggard, S. and Huang, Y. S. (2008). The political economy of private sector development in China. In *China's Great Economic Transformation* (Eds, Brandt, L. and Rawski, T.). Cambridge, New York: Cambridge University Press, 337–74.

Holz, C. A. (2003). *China's Industrial State-Owned Enterprises: Between Profitability and Bankruptcy.* Hackensack, NJ: World Scientific.

Hou, C. M. (1965). *Foreign Investment and Economic Development in China, 1840–1937.* Cambridge, MA: Harvard University Press.

Hsiao, K. H. (1987). *The Government Budget and Fiscal Policy in Mainland China.* Taipei: Chung-Hua Institution for Economic Research.

Hsiao, L. L. (1974). *China's Foreign Trade Statistics, 1864–1949.* Cambridge, MA: East Asian Research Center, Harvard University, distributed by Harvard University Press.

Hsieh, C. T. and Klenow, P. (2009). Misallocation and manufacturing TFP in China and India. *Quarterly Journal of Economics* 124, 1403–48.

Hu, A. G. Z. and Jefferson, G. H. (2008). Science and technology in China. In *China's Great Economic Transformation* (Eds, Brandt, L. and Rawski, T.). Cambridge and New York: Cambridge University Press, 286–336.

Huang, P. C. C. (1985). *The Peasant Economy and Social Change in North China.* Stanford, CA: Stanford University Press.

India Data-Book (2014). *Data-Book Compiled for use of Planning Commission.* Posted at http://planningcommission.nic.in/data/datatable/data_2312/comp_data2312.pdf

Industry (1985). *Zhongguo gongye jingji tongji ziliao 1949–1984* [Statistical Materials on China's Industrial Economy, 1949–1984]. Beijing: Zhongguo tongji chubanshe.

Industry (1989). *Zhonghua renmin gongheguo 1985-nian gongye pucha ziliao jianyaoben* [Overview of Materials from the PRC 1985 Industrial Census]. Beijing: Zhongguo tongji chubanshe.

Investment (1987). *Zhongguo guding zichan touzi tongji ziliao 1950–1985* [Statistical Materials on China's Investment in Fixed Assets, 1950–1985]. Beijing: Zhongguo tongji chubanshe.

Ishikawa, S. (1983). China's economic growth since 1949—an assessment. *China Quarterly* 94, 242–81.

Jefferson, G. H., Rawski, T. G., Wang, L., and Zheng, Y. (2000). Ownership, productivity change, and financial performance in Chinese industry. *Journal of Comparative Economics* 28, 786–813.

Kee, H. L. and Tang, H. W. (2016). Domestic value added in exports: theory and firm evidence from China. *American Economic Review* 106, 1402–36.

Kirby, W. C. (1984). *Germany and Republican China.* Stanford, CA: Stanford University Press.

Kirby, W. C. (1990). Continuity and change in modern China: economic planning on the mainland and on Taiwan, 1943–1958. *Australian Journal of Chinese Affairs* 24, 121–41.

Köll, E. (2003). *From Cotton Mill to Business Empire: The Emergence of Regional Enterprises in Modern China.* Cambridge, MA: Harvard University Asia Center.

Kraus, R. A. (1980). *Cotton and Cotton Goods in China, 1918–1936.* New York and London: Garland Publishing.

Kuan, C., Hongchang, W., Yuxin, Z., Jefferson, G. H., and Rawski, T. G. (1988). Productivity change in Chinese industry: 1963–1985. *Journal of Comparative Economics* 12, 570–91.

Lardy, N. R. (1983). *Agriculture in China's Modern Economic Development.* Cambridge and New York: Cambridge University Press.

Lardy, N. R. (2002). *Integrating China into the Global Economy.* Washington, DC: Brookings Institution Press.

Li, P. F., Bathelt, H., and Wang, J. (2012). Network dynamics and cluster evolution: changing trajectories of the aluminium extrusion industry in Dali, China. *Journal of Economic Geography* 12, 127–55.

Lin, J. Y. (1992). Rural reforms and agricultural growth in China. *American Economic Review* 82, 34–51.

Liu, D. J. (1937). *Zhongguo gongye diaocha baogao* [Report of a Survey of China's Industries]. 3 vols. Shanghai: Jingji tongji yanjiusuo.

Liu, T. C. and Yeh, K. C. (1965). *The Economy of the Chinese Mainland: National Income and Economic Development, 1933–1959.* Princeton, NJ: Princeton University Press.

Ma, D. (2008). Economic growth in the Lower Yangzi region of China in 1911–1937: a quantitative and historical analysis. *Journal of Economic History* 68, 355–92.

Mandel, B. (2013). Chinese exports and US import prices. *Staff Reports, Federal Reserve Bank of New York*, No. 591.

Mantetsu keizai chōsakai (1933). *Manshū keizai nempō 1933* [Manchuria Economic Yearbook, 1933]. Tokyo: Kaizōsha.

Maskin, E., Qian, Y. Y., and Xu, C. G. (2000). Incentives, information, and organizational form. *Review of Economic Studies* 67, 359–78.

Minami, R. and Makino, F. (Eds) (2014). *Ajia keizai chōki tōkei 3: Chūgoku* [Long-Term Asian Historical Statistics 3: China]. Tokyo: Toyokeizai shinposha.

Moulder, F. V. (1977). *Japan, China and the Modern World Economy: Towards a Reinterpretation of East Asian Development ca. 1600–ca. 1918.* Cambridge: Cambridge University Press.

Murphey, R. (1977). *The Outsiders: The Western Experience in India and China.* Ann Arbor, MI: University of Michigan Press.

Nakamura, T. (1983). *Economic Growth in Prewar Japan* (Trans., Feldman, R. A.). New Haven, CT: Yale University Press.

Naughton, B. (1988). The third front: defence industrialization in Chinese interior. *China Quarterly* 115, 351–86.

Naughton, B. (1995). *Growing Out of the Plan: Chinese Economic Reform 1978–1993.* Cambridge: Cambridge University Press.

Naughton, B. (2015). The transformation of the state sector: SASAC, the market economy, and the new national champions. In *State Capitalism, Institutional Adaptation, and the Chinese Miracle* (Eds, Naughton, B. and Tsai, K.). Cambridge: Cambridge University Press, 46–71.

Nolting, L. E. and Feshbach, M. (1981). *Statistics on Research and Development Employment in the USSR.* Washington, DC: US Dept of Commerce, Bureau of the Census.

Ohkawa, K. and Shinohara, M. (1979). *Patterns of Japanese Economic Development: A Quantitative Appraisal.* New Haven, CT: Yale University Press.

Ohkawa, K., Takamatsu, N., and Yamamoto, Y. (1974). *Kokumin shotoku* [National Income]. Tokyo: Toyo keizai shinposha.

Rawski, T. G. (1975). China's industrial system. In *China: A Reassessment of the Economy* (United States Congress, Joint Economic Committee). Washington, DC: US Government Printing Office, 175–98.

Rawski, T. G. (1980). *China's Transition to Industrialism: Producer Goods and Economic Development in the Twentieth Century.* Ann Arbor, MI: University of Michigan Press.

Rawski, T. G. (1989). *Economic Growth in Prewar China.* Berkeley, CA: University of California Press.

Rawski, T. G. (2000). China's move to market: how far? what next? In *China's Future: Constructive Partner or Emerging Threat?* (Eds, Carpenter, T. G. and Dorn, J. A.). Washington, DC: Cato Institute, 317–39.

Remer, C. F. (1933). *Foreign Investments in China.* New York: Macmillan.

Reynolds, B. L. (1974). Weft: the technological sanctuary of Chinese handspun yarn. *Ch'ing-shih wen-t'i* 3, 1–19.

Schott, P. K. (2008). The relative sophistication of Chinese exports. *Economic Policy.* 53, 5–49.

Statistics Japan (2011). *Japan Statistical Yearbook 2011.* Accessed May 29, 2015 from http://www.stat.go.jp/english/data/nenkan/back61/index.htm

Statistics Japan (2012). *Historical Statistics of Japan.* Accessed May 29, 2015 from http://www.stat.go.jp/english/data/chouki/

Sutton, J. (2012). *Competing in Capabilities: The Globalization Process.* Oxford: Oxford University Press.

Thirty Years (2008). *Zhongguo xiangzhen qiye 30 nian* [30 Years of China's Township-Village Enterprises]. Beijing: Zhongguo nongye chubanshe.

US Department of State (1949). *Energy Resources of the World.* Washington, DC: US Government Printing Office.

Wang, Y. C. (1992). Secular trends of rice prices in the Yangzi Delta, 1638–1935. In *Chinese History in Economic Perspective* (Eds, Rawski, T. G. and Li, L. M.). Berkeley, CA: University of California Press, 35–68.

Whiting, S. H. (2001). *Power and Wealth in Rural China: The Political Economy of Institutional Change*. Cambridge and New York: Cambridge University Press.

Wong, C. (1985). Material allocation and decentralization: impact of the local sector on industrial reform. In *The Political Economy of Reform in Post-Mao China* (Eds, Perry, E. J. and Wong, C.). Cambridge, MA: Council on East Asian Studies/Harvard University, 253–78.

World Bank (1985). *China: Long-Term Development Issues and Options*. Baltimore, MD: Johns Hopkins University Press.

Yamamoto, Y. (2003). *Manshūkoku keizaishi kenkyū* [Research on Manshūkoku Economic History]. Nagoya: Nagoya daigaku shuppankai.

Yan, Z. P., et al. (1955). *Zhongguo jindai jingjishi tongji ziliao xuanji.* [Statistical Materials on the Economic History of Modern China]. Beijing: Kexue chubanshe.

Yearbook (Annual). *Zhongguo tongji nianjian* [China Statistics Yearbook]. Beijing: Zhongguo tongji chubanshe.

Zeitz, P. (2013). Do local institutions affect all foreign investors in the same way? *Journal of Economic History* 73, 117–41.

Zhang, Y. F. [Chang, Y. F.] (1989). 'Qingmo Minchu de minying gongye' [Private sector industry during late Qing and under the early Republic]. *Zhongyang yanjiuyuan jindaishi yanjiusuo jikan* [Quarterly Journal of the Modern History Institute of the Academia Sinica] 18, 315–561.

Zhu, X. D. (2012). Understanding China's growth: past, present, and future. *Journal of Economic Perspectives* 26, 103–24.

10

From Artisanal Production to Machine Tools
Industrialization in India over the Long Run

Bishnupriya Gupta and Tirthankar Roy

10.1 INTRODUCTION

This chapter documents India's transition from artisanal production to a modern industrial economy. India's comparative advantage as the dominant producer and exporter of cotton textiles in the world in the eighteenth century was based on cheap labour and skills acquired through family-based artisanal production over generations. This advantage disappeared with the advent of the capital-using technology of the Industrial Revolution. The increased output per worker achieved by substituting capital for labour dramatically reduced the cost of cotton yarn and cloth. Over the nineteenth century British producers displaced Indian handloom products, first in the world market and over time in the Indian domestic market, leading to the decline of Indian artisanal production. The share of local products in total consumption declined to 40 per cent by the last quarter of the nineteenth century. From this trough a recovery was led by a modern textile industry, organized in factories and using new technology imported from Britain. At the same time, other industries such as jute and tea also began to adopt new technology borrowed from the industrial countries. In the early twentieth century there were signs of revival and growth in artisan industries as well.

The fortunes of cotton textiles reflect the path of Indian industrialization: rise and fall of artisanal production followed by import substitution in simple consumer goods during the colonial period. A more mature phase saw a rise in the share of machinery and equipment including machine tools. The fortunes of this industry in the world market in part reflect the policy regimes of various governments: from merchant-ruler (the East India Company) and British colonial government to the more developmental state of independent India. This chapter focuses on the emergence of a modern industrial sector. It is both a narrative history of what happened and an attempt to explain the specific features of Indian industrialization.

10.2 1800–1947

Indian industrialization can be conveniently divided into two stages. The first was the colonial period (1858–1947) when the economy was open to trade, migration, and foreign investment, and state regulation was limited in scope. The second stage began with the post-colonial period, when import-substituting industrialization was implemented under state intervention (1947–c.1985).

The historiography of Indian industrialization in the colonial period tries to explain three long-term processes, each one directly or indirectly connected with the defining features of the time—openness and limited state intervention. These three processes are: de-industrialization or decline of the handicraft industries in the early nineteenth century, modest revival of the handicrafts in the twentieth century, and the rise and growth of factories from the 1860s. The latter process had a few peculiar features: (a) industrialization was concentrated in a few cities and towns, and until the First World War, almost entirely confined to Bombay, Calcutta, and Madras; (b) the composition of products manufactured was narrow, and there was little production of machines or intermediate goods; (c) none of the textbook preconditions for industrialization—cheap capital, high saving, agricultural revolution, or an activist state—were present in India in the 1850s, and (d) despite the growth in manufacturing, politicians and businesses after 1947 decided to change the paradigm completely from the one that had produced the industrialization.

10.2.1 De-industrialization

First, let us consider de-industrialization. Indian artisans had the largest share of the world cotton textile market in the seventeenth and eighteenth centuries. The onset of colonialism and the adoption of free trade as a tenet of British economic policy in India coincided with the Industrial Revolution, which shifted the balance of advantage in cotton textile production from Indian artisans to British factories (Broadberry and Gupta, 2009). A recent paper suggests that political and ecological crises in eighteenth-century India may have contributed to that shift (Clingingsmith and Williamson, 2008). Depending on the scale and availability of alternative employment, the resultant de-industrialization could have caused a consumption crisis and general economic decline, in addition to a decline in India's relative position in the world economy.

Reliable and direct measurement of the extent of the decline in handicraft employment cannot be found, because during the peak period of the decline (1820–80) few data were collected on employment and production. Indirect measures by Bagchi (1976) and Twomey (1983) suggest that the decline was large. There is some evidence also of a general economic depression between 1820 and 1840 in southern India, especially the Deccan uplands, which the fall in artisanal employment may have exacerbated. Reports on famines in 1876 and 1896, again in the Deccan plateau, mention textile artisans coming to relief camps in large numbers and enlisting for emigration to British colonies abroad. However, such facts and the available research do not add up to a detailed picture of what happened after Manchester textiles began to be imported into India in large quantities, c.1820.

We can do slightly better by working backwards from the state of the artisanal textile industry in 1900. It is possible to say that the impact of imports was significant on hand spinning of cotton yarn, and modest on handloom weaving of cloth. With the fall of spinning, an industrial activity that was once present in many regions and employed several million women disappeared. By implication, craft employment concentrated and became more male-biased. Possibly because so many of those displaced were part-time female workers, direct testimony of those made unemployed remains exceedingly rare. Outside cotton textiles, a de-industrializing process can be inferred in iron and steel, but again this cannot be measured precisely. As in textiles, the decline in iron seems to have been concentrated in the production of intermediate goods, namely pig iron, rather than in the iron products industry. The smelter was more likely than the black-smith to become unemployed due to imports.

10.2.2 Revival of Handicrafts

The revival of artisan industry dates from around 1900. Although employment in the crafts continued to fall between 1881 and 1931, the fall affected women household workers mainly, whereas male full-time workers were unaffected (Thorner, 1962). Despite the fall, 10 million artisans were reported to be working in 1901, and 90 per cent of industrial employment remained in handicrafts—that is, located in households or small workshops using hand tools—and fell outside the scope of factory acts. Output, income, and wages, too, did not fall in the first half of the twentieth century, and in some key instances they rose. Detailed national income statistics of acceptable quality start in 1900. Between 1900 and 1946 total net domestic product in small industry increased slowly (Fig. 10.3 below), but net product per worker increased by 40 per cent between 1900 and 1935. Between 1901 and 1939, the production of hand-woven cloth increased from 207 to 406 million square yards, implying a 127 per cent increase in output per loom and a 200 per cent increase in output per worker. Iron and steel data suggest a successful import substitution by domestic producers including artisans.

Evidence such as this has spurred scholarship suggesting that artisans should be seen as an example of industrialization rather than de-industrialization (Roy, 1999). Factory production grew much faster than handicrafts, but handicrafts remained stable rather than disappearing (Fig. 10.3). The new scholarship has shown that artisan textile producers survived because of consumer preference; they served customers who wanted handmade consumer goods for reasons of status, ritual, or display, or demanded a high degree of customization and product differentiation. These traditional preferences, however, were changing from the late nineteenth century along with migration, urbanization, and the emergence of a middle class. Artisans met these challenges with a variety of strategies, often by applying trad-itional decorative skills to modern utilitarian objects. They borrowed technologies and material from abroad, partly adopted the factory form of work, relocated towards major markets for their goods, and built close ties with cotton mills or the world market for the supply of cheap raw materials like yarn, dyes, metal thread, and synthetic fibre. The main sites of the re-organization process were small towns that received migrant artisans from depressed regions. These towns had easy access to big ports and consumer markets, yet avoided the high real estate prices and wages of the city. Somewhat similarly, artisanal industrialization is called 'small town capitalism' in a recent study of handloom weaving in western India (Haynes, 2012).

This scholarship usefully draws a connection between the colonial-period transformation of the crafts and the large number of small industrial firms present in post-colonial India. Handicrafts represented one root, but not the only root, of modern small-scale industry. Rural non-farm industry was another. Flourishing agricultural trade encouraged a variety of agro-processing industries involving rice, oilseeds, groundnut, or cotton. These tasks were done in small, usually seasonal, and partially mechanized factories, not of artisanal origin.

10.2.3 Growth of Factories

The third large process is the rise of factories. Officially, the definition of 'factory' in the factory acts was a unit that employed at least 100 workers and used power (1881 Factory Act). Not all large units were covered, however. The seasonal units just mentioned were not covered until 1911. On the other hand, cotton spinning and weaving mills, jute spinning and weaving mills, factories manufacturing cane sugar, paper, and wool textiles, and steel factories using the blast furnace were usually covered. In short, despite some flexibility in the definition, factories in colonial India meant units employing mechanical power, usually perennial, hiring on average several hundred workers, and subject to the application of the factory acts.

Between 1860 and 1940, employment in factories increased from less than 100,000 to 2 million (see Table 10.1 for available data on employment). Between 1900 and 1947, real national income originating in factories rose by 4.3 per cent per annum, and factory employment at 3.6 per cent (Sivasubramonian, 2000, pp. 201–3, 287–8, 293–4). In 1940, the port cities of Bombay and Calcutta and their immediate neighbourhoods were homes to about 200,000 factory workers each.

By some benchmarks, the growth of modern mechanized factories in India was an exceptional phenomenon in the tropical world. India had an earlier start than most late industrializing countries in the non-Western world. It led the contemporary developing world in two major industries of the Industrial Revolution, cotton textiles and iron and steel. In 1910, 55 per cent of the cotton spindles installed outside Europe, North America and Japan were installed in India.

Table 10.1. Employment in factories (thousands)

	Cotton and jute mills	British India, all factories	Princely states, all factories
1885	105	300	
1905	300	933	
1915	460	1,004	
1925	330	1,518	140
1935	295	1,611	270

Source: India, *Statistical Abstracts for British India.* Calcutta: Government Press, various years.

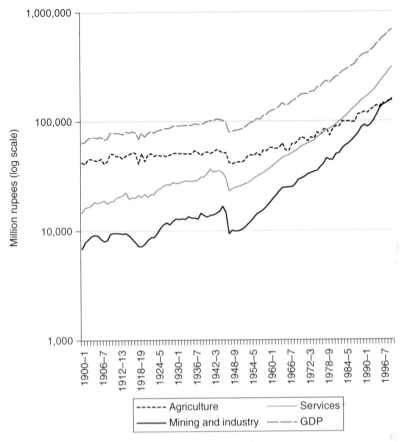

Fig. 10.1. Changes in GDP and its components in 1948–9 prices

Source: Sivasubramonian (2000, Appendices 7 and 8).

In 1935, 50 per cent of the steel produced outside Europe, North America, and Japan was produced in India (BKS, 1950). There were by then several concentrations of factory workers in the tropics, but possibly none with more factory workers than Bombay and Calcutta.

The impact of industrialization on the structure of the economy was limited, possibly more so in India than in the contemporary developing world. For example, countries in Latin America enjoyed higher inter-war industrial growth rates than India. As Figs 10.1 and 10.2 show, industry and services (trade, finance, transportation) experienced growth in the first half of the twentieth century, but the increase in their share of total GDP was modest. And yet, the extent of structural change in the fifty years before independence was not very different from that which occurred in the thirty years after independence (Fig. 10.2). It was only in the final decade of the twentieth century that the share of agriculture in GDP was exceeded by that of industry and services. The limited scale of structural change

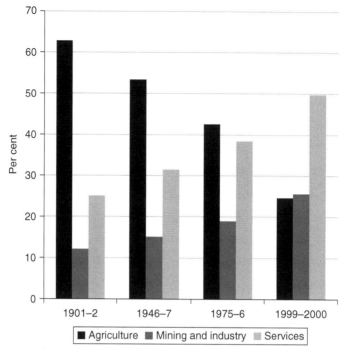

Fig. 10.2. GDP (1948–9 prices) by sector, 1901–2000 (per cent of total)
Source: Sivasubramonian (2000, Appendices 7 and 8).

reflected the fact that manufacturing enterprises remained concentrated in a few cities before 1947. The industrial sector was dominated by small-scale and cottage industry in 1900. In 1947 this still carried the same weight in industrial output as manufacturing, and it remained a significant part of the industrial sector even in 2000 (see Fig. 10.3). This, along with a slow-moving primary sector and rapid population growth, implied a disastrous early-twentieth-century economic record overall.

Nevertheless, the scale of factory expansion was sufficiently large to raise the question of why it happened at all.

10.2.4 Origin of Modern Industry

In chronological terms, India was a late industrializer. But as a type it was not, if, following accepted convention, we identify late industrialization with state intervention in exchange or production (Amsden, 1991). In the discourse on international development, the idea that an activist state could overcome the problems associated with arriving late lives on as 'big push', 'embedded autonomy', 'developmental state', and 'governed market'—some of these labels were coined to account for the recent industrialization of East Asia. The developmental state

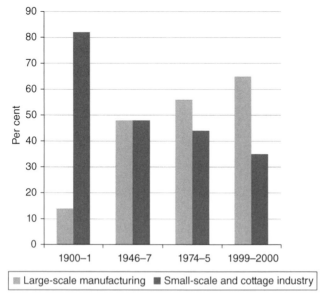

Fig. 10.3. Shares of industrial output (per cent)
Source: Sivasubramonian (2000, Appendices 7 and 8).

manipulates tariffs or regulates banks or manages the import of technology (Chang, 1999). The British colonial state in India was not an activist state in any of these senses. Not until late in the inter-war period did it set economic development as one of its goals. Until then a loosely defined notion of 'improvement' was sometimes cited by the regime as an aim, but improvement did not have a clear economic content, far less an industrializing one.

Nor were resource endowments and factor prices favourable for Indian industrialization. Received wisdom states that Britain industrialized under free market conditions thanks to favourable factor prices—that is, relatively low costs of capital and energy but high wages—and productive and energy-intensive agriculture which generated savings for investment and created path dependence in technological choices (Allen, 2009; Wrigley, 2006). Around 1850 in India, interest rates were two-to-three times higher than in the financial centres of Europe. The savings rate was around 5 per cent of GDP in 1920. Indian agriculture was characterized by some of the lowest yields even in the tropics. India's artisans may have been skilled but they had little access to the expensive capital market to start factories.

Why then did India industrialize at all? An answer can be offered using a business history approach. That is, instead of looking at the cost of resources, we can also consider transaction costs in factor markets, or the cost of accessing capital and labour. Port cities in the nineteenth century created the prospect of a unique encounter between European knowledge and skills on the one hand and India's advanced commercial tradition on the other, which reduced the transaction costs in accessing technology, skilled labour, and capital. Let us elaborate.

In the nineteenth century, the world was transformed by a revolution in transport and communication, and by industrialization in the British Isles. The resultant growth in world trade, along with migration of capital and labour, was directly or indirectly aided by the expansion of British political and military power. By 1858, the British ruled over much of India. The Indian port cities met these developments from a position of advantage. During the time that the East India Company conducted trade from these bases, the cities had grown in population, shipping, and scale of international and coastal trade. Between 1860 and 1940, the ports had been connected with the interior by railways and telegraph. They exported huge quantities of cotton, grain, seeds, indigo, and opium, and imported British textiles, machinery and metals, and chemicals from Germany and Belgium. Merchant firms engaged in these businesses were Indian, European, and Indo-European.

Although Europeans dominated the handicrafts export business, India's merchant capitalists dominated the export business in agricultural commodities. Further, because exports were dominated by agricultural goods, overseas trade, overland trade, and indigenous banking became ever more interdependent in the nineteenth century. Land trade and caravan trade in textiles, grain or cotton had been well developed before British rule, and bankers who financed long-distance trade could be found in the major towns located on rivers and caravan routes. As the Mughal Empire collapsed from the 1720s, a number of these merchants and bankers migrated, first to the capitals of rising states such as Hyderabad, Lucknow, and Pune, and later in the nineteenth century to the British Indian ports. Here, a string of British and European trading firms purchased agricultural commodities for export from merchants specializing in overland trade. The merchants themselves were financed not by the small number of corporate banks, but by indigenous bankers and money-lenders. By 1920, the biggest market for rediscounting of indigenous trade bills, the hundi, was located not in the interior, but in Bombay and Calcutta. These cities, thus, had an institutional edge over the interior.

The port cities also attracted skilled migrant workers from Britain more easily than did market towns in the interior of India. Capital and labour migration had been earlier constrained by the Company's monopoly charter, which restricted the establishment of new banks as well as free migration of European artisans, not to mention private merchants. In 1813, the charter ended in India, and an influx of European artisans and merchants began. Bombay's cotton exporters already had sufficient trading links with Liverpool, and went to England often enough to consider buying machinery and hiring foremen from there and setting up cotton mills in Bombay. The growth of modern enterprise, therefore, turned India into a net buyer of services from abroad. Excluding the government account, the net balance of payments met (out of a trade surplus) the salaries and pensions of engineers, foremen, artisans, teachers, doctors, managers, and scientists who migrated from abroad.

Pioneers in modern industry came from communities that had specialized in trading and banking activities, with some stake in the port cities. On the western coast, the Parsis, Khojas, Bhatias, bankers based in Ahmedabad, and the Bombay-based Baghdadi Jews, were the owners of mills. Some of these people had earlier traded in the Arabian Sea. Others, like the Parsis, joined trade after coming into contact with the Company and people connected with it. In Calcutta, Madras, and Kanpur, as well as the regions that formed their hinterland, Europeans dominated import–export trade, banking and insurance, and eventually jute, engineering, mines, plantations, railways, power, and dockyard. Commodity trade, however, was not in European hands, but in the hands of Indian traders, chiefly the Marwaris. By the end of the inter-war period, prominent Marwari firms in Calcutta had entered the jute industry, and on a smaller scale sugar, paper, cement, construction, and share broking.

An industrial entrepreneur in 1850 needed to solve two problems: raising large sums of money cheaply, and running unfamiliar machines. How well did they solve the problems?

10.2.5 Institutional Features

The financial and commercial origin of industrialists suggests that their key contribution lay in raising money for long-term investment. This was a difficult task in a world that offered a huge premium for seasonal agricultural loans. The mill-owners solved the problem of pooling large amounts of capital for investment, initially by using community networks, and later by adopting and making use of the joint-stock company organization. Corporate law followed these developments (Companies Act and amendments, 1850, 1857, 1860, 1866, 1882), and made raising money from the public easier. A particular institutional innovation, the managing agency contract, saved on scarce managerial resources and, by allowing a contracted remuneration to managers, reduced risks of financial loss to the managers.

There were, however, differences in corporate strategy along ethnic lines. Some authors suggest that Indians and Europeans specialized in different fields, consistent with their respective information and resource advantages (Morris, 1979; Gupta, 2014). Europeans raised money from London; the shares were purchased by other Europeans. Indians raised money from family and community resources. Europeans sold goods in export markets, through a transportation and communication network centred in London. Indians sold goods in India and China. The picture of specialization contrasts somewhat with an alternative picture of rivalry. Bagchi (1997), for example, suggests that in colonial Calcutta there were informal guilds that developed along ethnic lines that regarded each other with hostility. Direct evidence on racialist sentiments and how they worked remains scarce and anecdotal. Legally, race was not recognized in commercial law.

Besides, there were many examples of crossovers and collaborations cutting across ethnic divisions. In the inter-war period, a growing number of European capitalists set up small manufacturing firms. In relatively new areas of factory enterprise, such as sugar mills, Indian and European capital was present almost equally. The picture of antagonism between Indians and Europeans is largely an effect of the increasingly tense political situation of the 1930s that eventually destroyed the foundation of the British Empire in South Asia.

Although Indian industrialists successfully solved the problem of financing industrialization in a high-cost capital market, they had a rather poor record in attaining technical efficiency on the shop floor. Labour productivity and total factor productivity (TFP) were low in Indian factories, a syndrome variously attributed to the capitalists' preference for risk aversion (Tripathi, 1996), quality of labour (Wolcott, 1994), degree of unionization (Wolcott and Clark, 1999), and labour market institutions (Roy, 2008; Gupta, 2011a). Although both India and Japan were low-wage textile producers around 1920, Japanese cotton textiles succeeded in the Indian market in the inter-war period thanks in part to greater efficiency from the start, and in part to indigenization of textile machine production, which made a shift from mule to ring spinning more feasible in Japan (Kiyokawa, 1983). If the Japanese mill-owners took interest in technology, no such top-down interest in technology was in evidence in India. Persistence with British standards made for technological inertia. Such generalizations can seem overdrawn because Bombay's mills were extremely heterogeneous in respect of their openness to innovation. But there is no question that average Indian productivity, however measured, was low.

Too much attention to these Indian 'failures' can lead to an oversight of learning by doing at the work site. In the inter-war period, the percentage of Europeans among the supervisory staff in cotton mills fell sharply, from well over half to less than a quarter. Major fields of British-Indian engineering, such as railways, telegraphs, and canal construction, reveal numerous instances where British standards were modified to suit Indian conditions (Derbyshire, 1995). The diffusion of the stationary steam engine is another example of absorption and adaptation (Tann and Aitken, 1992). The progressive substitution of Indian foremen for foreign engineers proceeded apace in railway workshops, arsenal factories, field telegraphs, cadastral surveys, mineral prospecting, geological surveys, and meteorological services, along with cotton and jute factories. Civil engineering colleges started being established from the mid-nineteenth century (Ambirajan, 1995).

By the time independence came in 1947, the indigenous component in the technical and engineering workforce in the public services was prominent, and vocal as a lobby, pushing for more public investment in engineering education.

Why did the industrialization drive remain so concentrated in a few locations? A chronological account can answer that question to some extent.

10.2.6 Major Industries, Industrial Cities, and the World Wars, 1860–1947

Standard narratives of Indian industrialization are detailed regarding the early twentieth century, but relatively less clear on the eighteenth-century origins (Bagchi, 1972; Morris, 1983; Ray, 1979). A connected story drawing on existing scholarship and other sources is in order.

Calcutta became the capital of the newly acquired Company territories in India in 1772. By 1800, Calcutta had a sizeable settlement of Europeans and Indo-Europeans. The Company's military enterprise as well as the civilian population needed goods to be made locally, but that could not be procured easily from Indian artisans in the required number or quality. Cannons, small arms, hardware, glassware, cutlery, footwear and saddles, wines and spirits, and carriages, are some examples. Ships and boats were more easily repaired on the coasts by indigenous artisans who served the Indian seafaring groups. But the repair of ocean-going ships and gunships required skills that were not easily available.

Between 1772 and 1813, Henry Watson, a Company officer, James Kyd, an Indian-born artisan of mixed parents, and officers of the Company in Calcutta, established docks, shipyards, and ship-repairing stations on the Calcutta riverfront. They also started a cannon foundry and a distillery (these and other examples are discussed in Roy, 2013). Some of these enterprises were erected in abandoned premises that had existed from the early days of British settlement in Calcutta. Around 1780, a blast furnace was ordered, but not delivered. Some of the pioneering modern factory units were started soon after the charter ended in 1813: for example, the first steam-powered factory producing cotton yarn, which appeared in a river-front site called Fort Gloster in 1817 or 1818, and the famous charcoal-iron-smelting workshop in Porto Novo, a small port on the southeastern coast.

In Bombay, the origin of factories was somewhat different. Long before 1813, the Company's shipbuilding and ship-repairing tasks had been performed by the Parsi artisans of Surat and Bombay. Parsis worked in close partnership with the Europeans, and established a strong hold on ship-repair by keeping apprenticeship confined to the community. Young members of Parsi shipwright families were sponsored to be trained in England. These strategies led to an unusual degree of Parsi dominance in the dockyard in Bombay by 1840. When the charter ended in 1813, the Company sold its ships at a discount, which the Parsis purchased to conduct trade with Aden, Africa, and China. Profits made in these trades were redirected at first to real estate and financial speculation, and eventually to manufacturing industry.

Meanwhile, as warfare became more frequent in northern India, Indian capitalists left the moribund and declining cities in the interior and moved to the port cities under the Company's control. A number of unusual partnerships resulted from the joint influx of Europeans and Indians into the port cities. These were known as 'agency houses' in Calcutta. On a more limited scale these European and Indo-European partnerships appeared in Bombay and Madras as well. Few of these agency houses engaged in manufacturing or mining, but one or two exceptional ones did, such as Carr Tagore of Calcutta. In the mid-nineteenth century, more individuals with a stake in Indo-China trade became interested in factories. When the administration of India passed to the British Crown in 1857, a new set of people, who had been engaged in manufacturing or trade in the British industrial towns, came to India. Some of them had access to the London money market. They moved into industrial enterprise directly, especially in Calcutta.

The number of cotton textile mills increased from 1854 in Bombay. About the same time, a jute textile industry began to grow in Calcutta. A cotton mill industry also began in British-ruled Gujarat, especially Ahmedabad, from a slightly later date. Although Ahmedabad was not on the overseas trading map, as Bombay and

Calcutta were, there were specialized banking houses or *pedhis* in Ahmedabad. They performed money changing, issued and discounted bills of exchange, lent to governments, and occasionally took up revenue contracts. In 1880, there were 58 mills in India with an employment of 40,000. By 1914, the number of mills had risen to 271, and average daily employment to about 260,000.

The Calcutta jute mills were a European enterprise. Jute is a natural fibre grown mainly in southern West Bengal and Bangladesh. It was used as a raw material for sacking cloth. The demand for sacks increased in the nineteenth century in proportion with the volume of the international grain trade. Until the 1870s, Bengal raw jute was processed into sacking mainly in Dundee and Germany. But already by then, mechanized jute spinning and weaving had started near Calcutta, with considerable inflow of capital from Dundee. Between 1869 and 1913, the number of mills increased from 5 to 64, and employment from 5–10,000 to 215,000.

Between 1860 and 1914, the main market for Indian mill-spun cotton yarn was among the handloom weavers in China. A broad division of labour was maintained between Lancashire and Bombay in the Indian market for yarn, the former specializing in finer counts and middle-quality cloths, and the latter in coarser counts of yarn. A serious Indianization of the market began only around the turn of the century when Bombay lost the China market to Japan. Mills in Bombay started weaving their own yarn, and spinning and weaving finer counts of yarn. Both these moves brought the Indian mills into direct competition with Lancashire.

In metallurgy and engineering, factories were slow to develop, but emerged from around the First World War. The drive towards import substitution was always present in iron, which was one of the biggest import items. The drive had led to a number of state-sponsored charcoal-iron-smelting enterprises in the early nineteenth century being set up by British artisans and adventurers. Almost all of them failed, mainly because significant iron deposits occurred in regions that were relatively inaccessible before the railways. Private European-style blast furnaces, foundry shops, rolling mills, and mechanical forges only became successful around 1900, when sources of coal, manganese, limestone, and iron were linked to the railway system, and the expansion in demand from the railways for rolling stock, rails, sleepers, wires, bars, and rods reinforced the drive to promote local production. Coke smelting was becoming more common, and the development of mineral prospecting revealed important information about those inputs necessary in a blast furnace that were available within the easy reach of railways. An ordnance factory of Calcutta and a civil engineering school in Roorkee had metalworking shops, and by the First World War had produced hundreds of locally trained workers with experience in metallurgy.

Without these developments it would be hard to explain why Tata Steel, a project conceived in the 1880s, needed more than twenty years before it was considered ready for implementation. Almost from the start, the company owned an integrated steel factory, but also mines, transportation, and a coal washery. Judging by relative factor costs, India should not have gone into steel making. But it did, thanks to the confidence of Jamsetji Tata, and also to data available from geological surveys, an Indo-European advisory team, easy access to European know-how, and purchase contracts from the European-owned railways.

Large factories were few and far between outside these examples and outside the port cities. Ahmedabad has been mentioned; Madras developed a European textile industry. Among the other exceptional ventures of nineteenth-century origin, and located outside the ports, were two woollen textile mills at Dhariwal in Punjab and at Kanpur. Kanpur was an emerging factory centre, an important army base, and a source of army supplies since the Indian mutiny (1857), and both towns were situated on, or conveniently close to, trade routes in country wool. A few woollen mills were also set up in Bombay and Bangalore towards the end of the nineteenth century, after railway connection improved their access to wool originating in the interior tracts of Rajputana and Mysore.

In the inter-war period, by contrast, the majority of factory enterprises were small in scale and located away from the ports. Examples include a number of rice mills on the Madras coast, sugar mills in the Gangetic plains, and brick and tile works in southwestern India (Yanagisawa, 2010). At the same time, there was also a significant expansion of cotton mills and cotton gins and presses in the princely states.

The First World War was a landmark event. Indian jute bags, cotton canvas and tent cloth, and military clothing were in great demand. But disruption to supplies of machinery, raw materials, spares, and chemicals normally imported from Britain or Germany caused inflation. As the war progressed, industry overcame some of these supply constraints, and began to make large profits. The long-term impact of the war was a change in official policy. Until the war, the government followed a hands-off policy in respect of Indian industry, and a buy-British policy in respect of purchases for defence, railways or administration. Manchester textile interests had until then successfully countered moves to protect the Indian textile industry. After the war, the government began to look towards local sources and became more open to promoting such sources by means of protective tariffs. In cotton, protective tariffs became available, with the understanding that a new framework of preferential trade within the empire would minimize the losses to British industry.

The First World War had another effect. It enabled big business to expand, and made the leading entrepreneurs take an interest in national politics.

10.2.7 Business and Politics in the Inter-war Years

In the 1920s, the nationalist movement for political reform and independence under M. K. Gandhi's leadership began to attract funds from Indian merchants and industrialists. The dependence was mutual, for inter-war India confronted Indian industrialists with the ever more pressing need to seek political intermediation. One impetus was the increasingly militant trade unions in the cities; others included the government's currency policy, and crises in jute and cotton.

Indian business firms had a long-standing grievance against the empire. They resented the close control that London exercised on the Indian currency system, even though Indian rule functioned with a great degree of autonomy in many other domains (such as public goods and the fiscal system). Until 1920, London's control was justified on the ground that Britain's economic interests and Indian interests were compatible, and afterwards on the ground that the world's biggest money market was located in London. As the world economy came under strain and Britain stared at economic decline, that argument lost force and the control looked more cynical than ever. As the British economy weakened, some Indian businesses formed partnerships with the nationalists, and joined them in demanding autonomy.

The Great Depression made divisions within the capitalist class sharper than before. In jute, the world demand for sacking was growing less rapidly in the 1920s and 1930s than during the war. Facing depressed conditions, European economic interests in Calcutta formed an informal cartel (Gupta, 2005). By then, a small Indian-owned industry had begun, which refused to join the cartel. Europeans tried to use their proximity to the political elite and the government-backed Bank of Bengal to demand special privileges. Such attempts broke down because those who stayed out of the cartel grew faster than those who stayed in. The provincial government of Bengal temporarily played a partisan role, worsening political tensions between business communities. By 1940, Indian capitalists who funded the Congress had developed an uncompromising hostility towards foreign capital.

In the 1940s, when independence was imminent, a blueprint of development drawn up by Bombay's magnates and known as 'the Bombay Plan' delivered the message that the future of India should be a *closed* economy and a *state-dominated* economy. It is not quite clear where these two ideas came from. The majority of the individuals who signed the document had made money in the open economy. Why they turned their backs on that system must be understood with reference to politics as well as economics. The most likely explanation was that the plan represented a compromise between the capitalists and the pro-Soviet socialist lobby in the main political party, the Congress (Kudaisiya, 2014). Both groups keenly wanted a policy to industrialize India. The former wanted and were promised a protected home market. In return, the latter received support for an enlargement of the role of the federal state as investor and regulator. Thus emerged the foundation of one of the most aggressive forms of import-substituting industrialization the post-war world would see.

10.3 INDIA AFTER INDEPENDENCE

The newly independent state of India moved away from colonial economic policies. The first step was to set out an agenda for industrialization that represented a break with the global economy. Altering the global division of labour was critical to policy-makers at the time. Similar views were expressed in other parts of the underdeveloped world following the disruption in trading arrangements during the Great Depression and Second World War. The Economic Commission for Latin America raised similar concerns. The newly independent states of South Korea and Taiwan also adopted industrialization as a goal, which came to be guided by developmental states. Newly independent states in Africa moved in a similar direction a decade later, adopting policies of import substitution as the way forward.

While Alexander Hamilton and Friedrich List had evoked national prestige and the infant industry argument in motivating economy policy regarding industrialization, the rhetoric in post-colonial countries was to move away from an unequal exchange between rich industrial nations and economically backward colonies. Difference in policies between the newly industrializing countries concerned how to implement import substitution.

Hirschman's theoretical framework of import substitution saw this as a process that takes place in stages: first, substitution of imported consumer goods, where technology was simple, to be followed by substitution of more complex capital goods. Indian industrialization strategy attempted to jump straight into the production of capital goods, borrowing as a model that of Soviet industrialization. Planning for industrialization and modernization was the goal of the first government under Nehru, who saw 'dams as the temples of Modern India'. Nehru's vision differed entirely from the Gandhian vision of labour-intensive development that suited Indian factor endowments, opting instead for a top-down development strategy based on the experience of Soviet industrialization and relying on much greater use of capital.

In the Bombay Plan of the 1940s, the principle of public–private partnership was emphasized: the state was to play a guiding role not only through tariffs and advantages provided to the private sector, but via a more direct involvement of the state in building industrial capacity. Existing industrial interests were waiting to take advantage of policies of import substitution in coordination with the public sector. In post-independence India, the public sector became the main investor in the production of capital goods.

Who was to pay for industrialization? While the colonial economy had tried to deal with capital scarcity via capital flows from Britain, involving both portfolio investment and entrepreneurship by British investors, independent India chose to provide the required capital from internal sources. The gap between saving and investment was to be filled by foreign aid, and entrepreneurship was to be provided by the state. In 1950–1, gross domestic capital formation (GDCF) and gross domestic saving (GDS) were in balance. In the second plan GDCF increased to 17 per cent of GDP, while GDS fluctuated between 8 and 13 per cent. The gap was filled by foreign aid. During 1951–61, 12 per cent of incremental saving, 21 per cent of incremental investment, and 13 per cent of the increase in national income was aid-generated. In the second and third five-year plans, external assistance covered about a quarter of actual plan expenditure in the public and private sectors. Compared with colonial times, when 70–80 per cent of aggregate investment was in the private sector, after 1947 the public and private sectors shared investment about equally. Table 10.2 indicates that the share of machinery in gross fixed capital formation (GFCF) did not change much, but the share of GFCF in GDP increased significantly after independence. The data also point to an increasing role of the public sector in capital formation.

Table 10.2. Capital formation and the public sector

	Gross domestic capital formation as share of GDP	Share of the public sector	Share of machinery in gross fixed capital formation
1850–1	5.0[a]	2.24	3.3
1860–1	4.8[a]	2.61	9.2
1870–1	5.1[a]	14.96	24.5
1880–1	4.8[a]	25.21	18.5
1890–1	6.2[a]	17.48	36.8
1900–1	7.0[a]	21.59	47.5
1910–11	6.6[a]	25.20	49.5
1920–1	6.2[a]	32.68	49.5
1930–1	6.3[a]	31.95	47.3
1940–1	6.7[a]	19.81	46.4
1951–5	13.1 (11.6[a])	25.0	38.2
1956–60	17.3	38.9[b]	43.1
1961–5	17.7	43.2	44.0
1966–70	19.3	39.2	38.2
1971–5	19.7	40.2	41.5
1976–80	21.2	45.2	43.8
1981–5	20.8	51.4	54.1
1985–90	23.7	44.3	
1990–5	23.7	38.4	
1995–2000	24.8	29.2	

[a] Refers to the ratio to gross national income in 1980–1 prices.
[b] Refers to 1961–2.
Sources: Nagaraj (1990); Kohli (2004, 2006); Bina Roy (1996, Tables 46, 52, 55).

10.3.1 Planning for Industrialization

The Nehru–Mahalanobis model, as it is known after the statistician who designed the plan, put development of capital goods production at the heart of economic policy. It thus questioned the role of comparative advantage and suitability of factor endowments as the basis for economic growth. The Nehru–Mahalanobis framework held that economic growth depended on the share of investment in national income, and therefore on the output of investment goods. The economy consisted of two sectors—capital goods and consumer goods. The higher the share of the former, the higher would be the rate of growth. Agricultural stagnation was viewed as a consequence of a lack of capital goods invested in the sector.

A system of five-year plans was adopted, with specific targets set in each plan. The first plan set targets for infrastructure development. It was the second plan of 1956–61 that implemented the Mahalanobis model by developing capital goods production in the public sector. The plan regulated the involvement of the private sector by introducing industrial licensing, and many sectors remained outside the scope of private investment. This was a significant departure from the limited public investment in colonial India. The years that followed saw a rise in public sector investment. The state became a producer in several capital goods industries, including iron and steel, heavy machinery and machine tools, telecommunications and telecom equipment, minerals, oil, mining, aeronautics, railway equipment, and electricity generation and distribution. The emphasis was on reducing dependence on imports and self-sufficiency in industrial output, with unbalanced growth providing a 'big push' to industrialization. There was acceleration in industrial growth, and also in the growth of agriculture and services.

The Licence Raj, as it came to be known, presided over the regulation of trade, industry, and investment. A private entrepreneur could apply for a licence to set up a plant in a 'permitted' sector. Protection of domestic industry from external competition came via regulation rather than the exchange rate. Unlike in many other newly industrializing economies, such as Brazil and East Asia, multiple exchange rates were not used to protect some sectors and allow easy imports of others. The rupee remained overvalued and built an anti-export bias into the developing economy. Consequently, Indian traditional exports faced declining competitiveness in the world market, and the products of new industries could not gain an entry. Indian exports grew at just 2.3 per cent per annum between 1950 and 1973, at a time when world exports were growing at 7.9 per cent per annum. Exports accounted for 7.1 per cent of GDP in 1951, but only 3 per cent in 1965, and remained below 4 per cent in 1973.

The resulting foreign exchange shortage was dealt with through quantitative controls. India had one of the highest tariffs in the world, but the main instrument for trade regulation was non-tariff barriers (NTBs), making actual protection much higher. The highest protection rates were in consumer goods. The price mechanism played little role in guiding India's industrial development, and ad hoc criteria used to select the beneficiaries of industrial licences and import licences (Chibber, 2003) led to corrupt practices in the allocation of foreign exchange and industrial licences. Bhagwati's meticulous work on the effective protection of Indian industries showed high levels of protection, which over the long run led to inefficiency and rent seeking.

Independent India sought to build an industrial capacity that would make her self-reliant, and succeeded. The share of imported machinery in gross fixed capital formation in machinery was close to 40 per cent in 1960, but less than 15 per cent by 1970 (Rangarajan, 1982). The cost was inefficiency and an early slowdown in industrial growth, which contributed to low overall growth. The development literature sees India among the failures of import-substituting industrialization, in contrast to the successful industrializing economies of East Asia. South Korea and Taiwan adopted a standard model of import substitution that started with consumer goods and moved early to export promotion in consumer goods before moving to the next phase of import substitution in capital goods (Chapter 8). There is now a consensus that the East Asian miracle did not rely on the market to determine industrialization, but that a highly interventionist state effectively solved the 'coordination problem' of private investment (Rodrik, 1995). The Indian industrial sector faced a similar problem requiring state support, but the state may not have got the intervention right. Neither a lack of demand, nor supply-side inefficiencies, nor an inability to finance imports due to balance of payments constraints, slowed down industrial growth in East Asia, but they plagued the Indian economy from the mid-1960s.

Bishnupriya Gupta and Tirthankar Roy

Table 10.3. Industrial growth, 1951–98 (per cent, per annum)

	Basic goods	Capital goods	Intermediate goods	Consumer goods	Consumer durables	Total output
1950–65	9.4	14.4	7.1	4.6	9.5	7.5
1965–76	6.5	2.6	3.0	3.4	6.2	4.1
1981–91	8.0	5.3	11.2	8.9	12.0	6.5
1980–98	7.1	9.1	5.9	5.9	11.0	5.8
Share 1956	22.3	4.7	24.6	48.4		
Share 1980	39.4	16.4	20.5	23.6		

Note: Basic goods refer to basic materials used in production, which are therefore intermediate goods.
Sources: Sivasubramonian (2000, Tables 9.14 and 9.15); Nagaraj (2003).

As Table 10.3 shows, industrial growth was rapid between 1950 and 1965, driven by the growth in capital goods production. The decline in this sector led to a growth slowdown in the mid-1960s, a period which also experienced an agricultural crisis. Economic policy became more balanced, without much impact on industrial performance. The slowdown was also accompanied by a political crisis that eventually led to a leftward shift in economic policy. Banks were nationalized, and greater state control was introduced in the financial market. However, economic growth did not recover and the droughts of 1971–2 and the oil crisis of 1973 led to stagflation.

10.3.2 Dismantling Regulation

The economic crisis of the 1970s and the decline in the support of the ruling Congress Party ushered in a period of reforms from 1980, with reforms accelerating from 1991 onwards. Policy moved towards dismantling the Licence Raj, with an emphasis on economic growth rather than redistribution. Rather than announcing an IMF-style structural adjustment, the reforms proceeded by 'stealth' (Kohli, 2006). Rodrik and Subramaniam (2005) distinguish between 'pro-business' and 'pro-market' reforms. In the first phase, the reforms were 'pro-business' and removed many of the barriers faced by the private sector. Industrial policy saw the greatest change. The list of industries reserved solely for the public sector was shortened from eighteen to three. Defence aircrafts and warships, atomic energy generation, and railway transport remained under the public sector. Industrial licensing by the central government was abolished, except for a few environmentally sensitive industries. At the same time, the long-standing policy of reserving production of some labour-intensive products such as garments and shoes for the small-scale sector remained in place.

In the sphere of trade policy, reforms sought to phase out import licensing and reduce import duties. Table 10.4 shows changes in the protection of Indian industry using three indicators: effective rates of protection (ERP), non-tariff barrier (NTB) coverage ratios, and the share of imports in total consumption.

Table 10.4. Trade regulation by type of industry (per cent)

	Phase 1 1980–5	Phase 2 1986–90	Phase 3 1991–5	Phase 4 1996–2000
Consumer goods				
ERP	101.5	111.6	80.6	48.3
Import coverage ratio	98.3	98.3	41.8	27.6
Import share ratio	0.04	0.04	0.1	0.05
Intermediate goods				
ERP	62.8	78.5	54.2	33.3
Import coverage ratio	95.1	77.2	20.5	8.2
Import share ratio	0.13	0.15	0.18	0.14
Capital goods				
ERP	147.0	149.2	87.6	40.1
Import coverage ratio	98.7	87.6	45.7	33.4
Import share ratio	0.12	0.12	0.19	0.14
All industries				
ERP	101.5	125.9	80.8	48.3
Import coverage ratio	97.6	91.6	38.0	24.8
Import share ratio	0.11	0.12	0.16	0.12

Note: ERP measures the effective rate of protection; import coverage ratio shows the share of imports covered by NTBs; and import share ratio shows the share of imports in total consumption.
Source: Das (2003, Tables 3, 4, 5).

As the economy reduced the incidence of NTBs, the initial effect in the 1980s was a rise in average tariffs and ERP as many products moved from being protected by import quotas to being protected by tariffs (Gupta, 1993; Das, 2003). A second phase brought in 'pro-market' reforms that began with the devaluation of the Indian currency in 1991. Tariff rates began to decline across sectors and capital goods became freely importable (see Table 10.4).

10.3.3 Assessing Regulation and Reform

We can evaluate industrialization policies according to four criteria: growth; efficiency; structural change due to industrialization; and comparisons with similar economies.

Since the dismantling of the regulatory regime, economic growth has increased significantly, and its variance has declined (Basu and Maertens, 2007). While the surge in industrial growth from the 1950s was not sustained, growth increased significantly after 1980 and was followed by faster growth in the 1990s. Rodrik and Subramanian (2005) argue that the Indian economy was at some distance from the production possibilities frontier in the 1970s, and that the new environment incentivized the private sector and encouraged a move towards the frontier.

Table 10.5. Sectoral growth over the twentieth century (per cent, per annum)

	Primary	Secondary	Manufacturing	Small scale	Tertiary	GDP per capita	GDP per worker
1901–10	1.0	1.7	5.7	0.5	2.1	0.7	0.7
1911–20	−0.2	−3.5	1.6	−5.7	0.4	−0.5	−0.2
1921–30	0.7	5.6	4.8	6.2	3.4	1.1	−1.9
1931–40	0.0	0.9	7.1	−2.3	1.3	−0.8	−0.1
1940–7	−0.1	2.6	4.3	2.0	−1.4	−1.3	−1.3
1951–65	2.6	6.8	6.7	5.2	4.5	1.9	
1966–80	2.7	3.5	4.6	4.4	4.3	1.3	
1981–2000	3.2	5.7	7.2	5.9	6.7	3.5	
1991–2000	3.1	5.2	8.2	7.4	8.1	4.7	

Note: All estimates are in 1948–9 prices.

Source: Sivasubramonian (2000, Tables 7.3 and 9.4).

The 'pro-business' environment created favourable conditions for existing firms and led to a large productivity increase.

Taking a long-run view changes the assessment of the Licence Raj. GDP per capita growth during the period was well above the colonial-era growth rate. Tests for structural breaks in GDP and GDP per capita find the break points to be in the Nehruvian period, well before the economic reforms (Dongre and Hatekar, 2005; Gupta, 2011b). Alongside the high variability in secondary sector growth during first half of the twentieth century was sustained growth in modern manufacturing after 1920 (Table 10.5). The secondary sector comprises manufacturing in large-scale units (referred to as manufacturing) and industrial production in unregistered small-scale and cottage industries (referred as small-scale and cottage industry), and it is the small-scale sector that experienced high variance. Since this was the larger component of the secondary sector, its fluctuations had a bigger effect on growth. The share of large-scale manufacturing only overtook that of the small-scale units after 1950. Fig. 10.4 shows the relative growth of the two sectors over the twentieth century.

Most econometric tests looking for evidence of a structural break in *industrial* growth consider the period 1950 to 2000. Wallack's (2003) sectoral analysis does not find a structural break for industry and manufacturing, while Balakrishnan and Parameswaran (2007) find a structural break in industrial growth after 1980, coinciding with estimated break points in per capita GDP growth. Again, taking a long-run view brings new insights: India's industrial growth during the Licence Raj was better than the historical trend. Balakrishnan (2010, pp. 61–72) suggests that the institutional and policy environment of the colonial government did not foster industrial development; it was the Licence Raj that solved the coordination problems involved in building industrial capacity, and raised the rate of investment by increasing public sector involvement. This interpretation overlooks the steady growth in manufacturing after 1930 (Table 10.5). However, this growth involved a sector that was small in absolute size and mainly produced simple consumer goods.

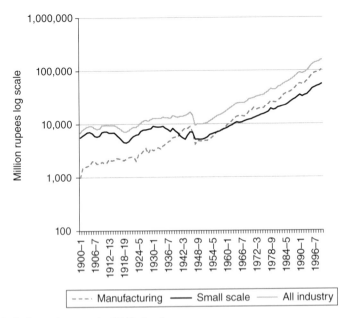

Fig. 10.4. Industrial output in 1948–9 prices

Source: Sivasubramonian (2000, Appendices 7 and 8).

The first phases of planning laid the foundation of a more diversified industrial sector, but did not ensure sustainable industrial growth. The economic reforms of the 1980s put the economy on a more sustainable growth path.

The capital goods sector had been the focus of the Mahalanobis plan. The sector did not decline as the focus shifted away from planned industrialization; rather, its composition shifted towards transport equipment. Machine tools, which were the key industry of the Mahalanobis plan, declined in importance with a growth rate of less than 2 per cent per annum in the 1990s (Nagaraj, 2003). Consumer durables became the most dynamic sector (Table 10.3).

Now we come to the efficiency effects. Bhagwati and Desai (1970) and Bhagwati and Srinivasan (1975) have highlighted the misallocation of resources and industrial inefficiency arising from protection. Estimates of total factor productivity show negative TFP growth in most industrial sectors during the period of import substitution, 1959 to 1979. The pro-business reforms of the 1980s led to an increase in industrial TFP growth. The pro-market reforms of the 1990s, on the other hand, slowed TFP growth in manufacturing from 1.9 per cent per annum to 0.7 per cent per annum as capital accumulation increased (Goldar and Kumari, 2003).

DeLong (2003) argued that the failure of economic policies in terms of promoting efficiency during the regulatory regime was largely offset by successes in mobilizing resources, to a great extent in the public sector. Total private savings rose from 6 per cent of GDP in the early 1950s to 15 per cent of GDP in the early

1960s, and 23 per cent by the 1980s. The reform years brought a significant increase in manufacturing and services TFP growth, relative to the period of regulation (Table 10.6). Notice that TFP growth in manufacturing in the 1980s was high, as suggested by Rodrik and Subramaniam (2005). However, TFP growth in Indian industry has in every period lagged behind that of the service sector.

This brings us to the third point, which is one of the most important aspects of Indian industrialization: India has not followed the standard pattern of structural change. In most economies the share of agriculture in employment and GDP declines with industrialization, and industry becomes the largest sector. In India, the declining share of agriculture in GDP was matched by a rising share of services rather than of industry. Industry has absorbed only a small proportion of labour re-allocating from agriculture. India's service sector-led growth is unique. Broadberry and Gupta (2010) point to an important difference in human capital between the industrial and service sectors. In 2000 the service sector had a concentration of workers with secondary and tertiary education, whereas industry still had a large number of workers with no basic education. This difference in human capital can be traced back to 1900 and may account for the differences in labour productivity between the two sectors.

Now we come to our last point. A comparison with other newly industrializing countries finds India lagging behind East Asia in capital formation and manufacturing value added per capita (Tables 10.7 and 10.8). The share of GFCF in manufacturing

Table 10.6. Sources of growth (per cent, per annum)

	Output per worker	Contribution of		
		Physical capital	Human capital	TFP
Agriculture				
1960–80	0.1	0.2	0.1	−0.1
1980–2004	1.7	0.4	0.3	1.1
Industry				
1960–80	1.6	1.8	0.3	−0.4
1980–2004	3.0	1.6	0.3	1.1
Manufacturing				
1960–80	2.0	1.5	0.3	0.2
1980–2004	4.0	2.1	0.4	1.5
1983–7	3.7	1.4	0.3	2.0
Services				
1960–80	2.0	1.1	0.5	0.4
1980–2004	3.8	0.7	0.4	2.7
India				
1960–80	1.3	0.8	0.2	0.0
1980–2004	3.7	1.4	0.4	2.0

Source: Bosworth, Collins, and Virmani (2007, Tables 4 and 5).

Table 10.7. Manufacturing value added per capita in US dollars, 1998

Argentina	1,253
Brazil	1,078
South Korea	2,142
Malaysia	946
Thailand	582
China	286
India	70

Source: Nagaraj (2003).

Table 10.8. Gross fixed capital formation in manufacturing and the share of machinery in industrial output

	Gross fixed capital formation			Share of machinery	
	1950	1970	1990	1975	1990
Brazil	13.0	19.7	13.5	23.4	24.9
South Korea	13.6	17.0	32.3	14.2	32.2
Malaysia	n.a.	26.8	23.9	16.9	28.1
Thailand	25.4	n.a.	48.8	9.6	11.8
India	11.6	27.5	10.4	23.3	23.7

Source: Amsden (2001, Tables 6.3 and 5.2).

was comparable to that in other newly industrializing economies in the 1960s, but was lower by the 1990s; the share of machinery in total manufacturing has been high in India, reflecting the country's application of the Mahalanobis model. India is one of the few late industrializers that developed the machinery sector early. The success stories of industrialization in the twentieth century, such as South Korea, had a small machinery sector in the early stages and successfully became exporters of manufactured consumer goods before moving into the production of capital goods. The Indian model of industrialization may have got some of the intervention 'wrong'.

Although the development of Indian manufacturing was impressive in the colonial period despite the lack of state support, India's performance does not compare well with that of the leading industrializing countries in more recent times. The role of the state in India recently has differed significantly from that of the developmental state of South Korea. Kohli (2004) points to colonial legacies regarding the role of the state in the two countries. The Japanese developmental state actively engaged in developing industrial capacity in South Korea towards the end of the colonial period, and also developed primary education and suitable infrastructure for industry. The British colonial state viewed India as an agricultural producer that met the needs of the imperial economy. Railways were built to meet the demands of trade, and there was little investment in developing human capital. The rise of industrial enterprise in India in the colonial period occurred despite the state. In independent India the role of the state in industrialization was interventionist rather than developmental.

Another comparison with the USSR is called for, since Indian policy-makers drew inspiration from the Soviet model of development. Despite putting the capital goods sector at the centre of industrialization strategy, the two economies differed significantly in many respects. The main difference lay in India's adoption of the 'mixed' economy, with a substantial role for private ownership of land, industry, and other businesses. This allowed the private sector to develop, despite its inefficiencies. Both countries enjoyed a spurt in industrial growth in the 1950s and 1960s, but Soviet per capita GDP growth was higher (Chapter 3). As economic growth slowed in both countries, their policies diverged. In India, economic reforms were able to incentivize the existing private sector, leading to faster growth. In the former USSR, in contrast, attempts to reform public enterprises caused disruption.

10.4 CONCLUSION

Indian industrialization took place against the backdrop of an economy that moved from a relatively open and unregulated market system in the 1800s, to a state-dominated and state-directed one in the mid-1900s. The first phase saw a decline of indigenous industry, a limited revival relying on imported inputs, a rise in British investment in India, and an increased ability and willingness of Indian merchants to invest commercial profits in manufacturing industry. The outcome was a growth of factories concentrated in a few port cities.

The post-independence closed economy phase built on the business and industrial infrastructure inherited from colonial times, adding a mainly state-owned capital goods sector and an import substitution policy. The autarkic-dirigiste regime gave rise to problems that are familiar to historians of post-war industrialization—foreign exchange crises, falling factor productivity, excess capacity, and poor-quality consumer goods. But the strategy did spread the industrialization impulse to a wider geographical area than before, strengthened the commitment of the state to industrialization, and gave political and economic power to big business of Indian origin.

The ongoing industrial transformation in India, which began with the reforms of the 1980s, led to efficiency gains and rising growth. However, the industrial sector in India has lagged behind a dynamic service sector, and the pattern of structural change in India has a correspondingly unique pattern.

REFERENCES

Allen, R. C. (2009). The industrial revolution in miniature: the spinning jenny in Britain, France, and India. *Journal of Economic History* 69, 901–27.

Ambirajan, S. (1995). Science and technology education in South India. In *Technology and the Raj: Western Technology and Technical Transfers to India, 1700–1947* (Eds, Macleod, R. and Kumar, D.). Delhi: Sage, 112–33.

Amsden, A. H. (1991). Diffusion of development: the late-industrializing model and greater East Asia. *American Economic Review* 81, 282–6.

Amsden, A. H. (2001). *The Rise of 'the Rest': Challenges to the West from Late-Industrializing Economies*. New York: Oxford University Press.

Bagchi, A. K. (1972). *Private Investment in India, 1900–1939*. Cambridge: Cambridge University Press.

Bagchi, A. K. (1975). *Private Investment in India, 1900–1939*. Cambridge: Cambridge University Press.

Bagchi, A. K. (1997). *The Evolution of the State Bank of India*, Vol. 2: *The Era of the Presidency Banks, 1876–1920*. London and New Delhi: Sage.

Balakrishnan, P. (2010). *Economic Growth in India*. Oxford: Oxford University Press.

Balakrishnan, P. and Parameswaran, M. (2007). Understanding economic growth in India: a prerequisite. *Economic and Political Weekly* 42, 2915–22.

Basu, K. and Maertens, A. (2007). The pattern and causes of economic growth in India. *Oxford Review of Economic Policy* 23, 143–67.

Bhagwati, J. N. and Desai, P. (1970). *India: Planning for Industrialization*. London and New York: Oxford University Press.

Bhagwati, J. N. and Srinivasan, T. N. (1975). *Foreign Trade Regimes and Economic Development: India*. New York: NBER and Columbia University Press.

BKS (1950). The European steel industry: production trends and the world market. *The World Today* 6, 265–74.

Bosworth, B., Collins, S. M., and Virmani, A. (2007). Sources of growth in the Indian economy. In *India Policy Forum 2006* Vol. 7 (Eds, Bery, S., Bosworth, B., and Panagariya, A.). Washington, DC: Brookings Institution and Sage, 1–69.

Broadberry, S. and Gupta, B. (2009). Lancashire, India and shifting competitive advantage in cotton textiles, 1700–1850: the neglected role of factor prices. *Economic History Review* 62, 279–305.

Broadberry, S. and Gupta, B. (2010). The historical roots of India's service-led development: a sectoral analysis of Anglo-Indian productivity differences, 1870–2000. *Explorations in Economic History* 47, 264–78.

Chang, Ha-Joon (1999). The economic theory of the developmental state. In *The Developmental State* (Ed., Woo-Cumings, M.). Ithaca, NY: Cornell University Press.

Chibber, V. (2003). *Locked in Place: State-Building and Late Industrialization in India*. Princeton, NJ: Princeton University Press.

Clingingsmith, D. and Williamson, J. G. (2008). Deindustrialization in 18th and 19th century India: Mughal decline, climate shocks and British industrial ascent. *Explorations in Economic History* 45, 209–34.

Das, D. K. (2003). Quantifying trade barriers: has protection declined substantially in Indian manufacturing? *Indian Council for Research on International Economic Relations Working Paper* No. 105.

DeLong, B. (2003). India since independence: an analytical growth narrative. In *In Search of Prosperity: Analytical Narratives on Economic Growth* (Ed., Rodrik, D.). Princeton, NJ: Princeton University Press, 184–204.

Derbyshire, I. (1995). The building of India's railways: the application of Western technology in the colonial periphery 1850–1920. In *Technology and the Raj* (Eds, Macleod, R. and Kumar, D.). New Delhi and London: Sage, 177–215.

Dongre, A. and Hatekar, N. (2005). Structural breaks in India's growth: revisiting the debate with a longer perspective. *Economic and Political Weekly* 40, 1432–5.

Goldar, B. and Kumari, A. (2003). Import liberalization and productivity growth in Indian manufacturing industries in the 1990s. *The Developing Economies* 41, 436–60.

Gupta, B. (1993). Trade liberalization and changes in the protection of Indian industry. In *Economic Liberalization in India and its Impact* (Ed., Gupta, S.P.). Delhi: Macmillan, 166–81.

Gupta, B. (2005). Why did collusion fail? The Indian jute industry in the interwar years. *Business History* 47, 532–52.

Gupta, B. (2011a). Wages, unions, and labour productivity: evidence from Indian cotton mills. *Economic History Review* 64, S1, 76–98.

Gupta, B. (2011b). India's growth in long run perspective. In *Handbook of South Asian Economics* (Ed., Jha, R.). London and New York: Routledge, 19–31.

Gupta, B. (2014). Discrimination or social networks: industrial investment in colonial India. *Journal of Economic History* 74, 141–68.

Haynes, D. E. (2012). *Small Town Capitalism in Western India: Artisans, Merchants and the Making of the Informal Economy, 1870–1960*. Cambridge: Cambridge University Press.

Kiyokawa, Y. (1983). Technical adaptations and managerial resources in India: a study of the experience of the cotton textile industry from a comparative viewpoint. *Developing Economies* 21, 97–133.

Kohli, A. (2004). *State Directed Development*. Cambridge: Cambridge University Press.

Kohli, A. (2006). Politics of economic growth in India, 1980–2005, part 1: 1980s. *Economic and Political Weekly* 41, 1251–9.

Kudaisiya, M. (2014). 'The promise of partnership': Indian business, the state, and the Bombay Plan of 1944. *Business History Review* 88, 97–131.

Morris, M. D. (1979). South Asian entrepreneurship and the Rashomon effect, 1800–1947. *Explorations in Economic History* 16, 341–61.

Morris, M. D. (1983). Growth of large-scale industry to 1947. In *The Cambridge Economic History of India*, Vol. 2: *c.1757–c.1970* (Eds, Kumar, D. and Desai, M.). Cambridge: Cambridge University Press, 553–676.

Nagaraj, R. (1990). Industrial growth: further evidence and towards an explanation and issues. *Economic and Political Weekly* 15, 2313–32.

Nagaraj, R. (2003). Industrial policy and performance since 1980: which way now? *Economic and Political Weekly* 38(35), 3707–15.

Rangarajan, C. (1982). Agricultural growth and industrial performance in India. *IFPRI Research Paper* No. 33. Washington, DC: International Food Policy Research Institute.

Ray, R. K. (1979). *Industrialization in India: Growth and Conflict in the Private Corporate Sector, 1914–1947*. Delhi: Oxford University Press.

Rodrik, D. (1995). Getting interventions right: how South Korea and Taiwan grew rich. *Economic Policy* 10, 55–107.

Rodrik, D. and Subramaniam, A. (2005). From Hindu growth to productivity surge: the mystery of the Indian growth transition. *IMF Staff Papers* 52, 193–228.

Roy, B. (1996). *An Analysis of Long Term Growth of National Income and Capital Formation in India (1850–51 to 1950–51)*. Calcutta: Firma KLM Private.

Roy, T. (1999). *Traditional Industry in the Economy of Colonial India*. Cambridge: Cambridge University Press.

Roy, T. (2008). Labour institutions, Japanese competition, and the crisis of cotton mills in interwar Mumbai. *Economic and Political Weekly* 43, 37–45.

Sivasubramonian, S. (2000). *National Income of India in the Twentieth Century*. New Delhi: Oxford University Press.

Tann, J. and Aitken, J. (1992). The diffusion of the stationary steam engine from Britain to India 1790–1830. *Indian Economic and Social History Review* 29, 199–214.

Thorner, D. (1962). 'Deindustrialization' in India, 1881–1931. In *Land and Labour in India* (Eds, Thorner, D. and Thorner, A.). New York: Asia.

Tripathi, D. (1996). Colonialism and technology choices in India: a historical overview. *The Developing Economies* 34, 80–97.

Wallack, J. (2003). Structural breaks in Indian macroeconomic data. *Economic and Political Weekly* 38, 4312–15.

Wolcott, S. (1994). The perils of lifetime employment systems: productivity advance in the Indian and Japanese textile industries, 1920–1938. *Journal of Economic History* 54, 307–24.

Wolcott, S. and Clark, G. (1999). Why nations fail: managerial decisions and performance in Indian cotton textiles, 1890–1938. *Journal of Economic History* 59, 397–423.

Wrigley, E. A. (2006). The transition to an advanced organic economy: half a millennium of English agriculture. *Economic History Review* 59, 435–80.

Yanagisawa, H. (2010). Growth of small-scale industries and changes in consumption patterns in South India, 1910s–50s. In *Towards a History of Consumption in South Asia* (Eds, Haynes, D., McGowan, A., Roy, T., and Yanagisawa, H.). Delhi: Oxford University Press, 51–75.

11

From Commodity Booms to
Economic Miracles
Why Southeast Asian Industry Lagged Behind

Jean-Pascal Bassino and Jeffrey Gale Williamson

11.1 INTRODUCTION

Three Southeast Asian nations—Indonesia, Malaysia, and Thailand—emerged unexpectedly in the 1960s and 1970s as fast-growing manufacturing countries.[1] While starting from very low manufacturing output per capita levels, they eventually became successful in promoting export-led, labour-intensive manufacturing. Their manufacturing growth rates closely matched those of Japan, South Korea, and Taiwan for more than two decades, and their performance attracted extensive foreign direct investment.[2] This sudden growth 'miracle' took place in the context of political instability and ethnic tensions, after more than two decades of modest success with post-independence import-substituting industrialization (ISI) strategies. During the 1950s, these countries experienced low per capita GDP growth due to the combination of rapid population growth and a slowdown in the expansion of agriculture and mining, two sectors which had until then been the main engines of growth. Led by manufacturing, growth accelerated from the 1960s onwards: the share of manufacturing[3] in GDP rose in Thailand and Malaysia from about 10 per cent in the late 1950s to more than 20 per cent in the late 1970s. In Indonesia, the upward trend started only in the 1970s but afterwards followed the same trajectory (Fig. 11.1).[4] These achievements were acknowledged by the World

---

[1] We are grateful for help with the data and comments to: Anne Booth, Ian Coxhead, Gregg Huff, Konosuke Odaka, Kevin O'Rourke, Dwight Perkins, Pierre van der Eng, and participants at the Oxford *Spread* Conference (2–4 October 2014).

[2] Singapore was the industrial pioneer in Southeast Asia in the 1950s and 1960s. But since it was essentially linked to British Malaya before independence, since it benefited from its position as a service hub for the entire region, since it was a city-state, and since it was of such small size, it is excluded from our analysis.

[3] Manufacturing is defined here as including UN Statistical Office ISIC divisions 15 to 37.

[4] The share of manufactures in total exports only increased significantly after the mid-1980s (Pangestu et al., 2015).

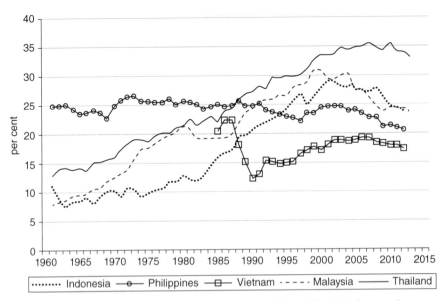

Fig. 11.1. Share of Southeast Asian manufacturing in GDP, 1960–2013 (per cent)

Note: Manufacturing refers to industries belonging to ISIC divisions 15–37. Value added is the net output of a sector after adding up all outputs and subtracting intermediate inputs. It is calculated without making deductions for depreciation of fabricated assets or depletion and degradation of natural resources. The origin of value added is determined by the International Standard Industrial Classification (ISIC), revision 3.

Source: World Bank (World Development Indicators website, accessed 9 May 2015).

Bank in its *East Asian Economic Miracle* report (World Bank, 1993) as almost matching South Korean and Taiwanese export-led industrial success a bit earlier.[5]

Neither the emergence of mainland China as an industrial power in the 1990s, and thus a competitor,[6] nor the Asian financial crisis of 1997, had an impact on the long-term trajectory of these emerging industrial Southeast Asian nations. By the early 2000s, the share of manufacturing in Thailand's GDP had reached around 35 per cent, well above South Korea, and it remained at that level for a decade, while it peaked above 30 per cent in Malaysia and Indonesia, before declining to 25 per cent. In contrast, Turkey's manufacturing share had followed a trajectory almost identical to that of Malaysia until the late 1990s, after which it declined steadily to below 20 per cent in the mid-2000s.[7]

The view that Southeast Asian countries shared common growth fundamentals gained more credibility when Cambodia and Vietnam joined the export-led manufacturing boom in the 1990s, and when even Myanmar joined the club in the 2000s. The only Southeast Asian nation to miss the 'miracle' was the Philippines. While it posted impressive manufacturing growth rates from the early twentieth

---

[5] See Chapter 8.   [6] See Chapter 9.   [7] See Chapter 7.

century to the 1960s, it stagnated thereafter. Still, the share of Philippine manufacturing in GDP reached about 25 per cent by the 1960s.

Before the 1960s,[8] Southeast Asian manufacturing had exhibited a dual structure: on the one hand, small cottage industry workshops using native labour-intensive technologies; on the other hand, a few medium or large-scale enterprises mostly involved in processing rice, sugar, tin, oil, and other commodities. These commodity-processing firms used imported capital-intensive technology and were owned and operated mostly by Chinese immigrants, Indian immigrants, or Westerners. Manufacturing accounted for a small share of employment, typically below 10 per cent (including the cottage industries).

Although it did not show signs of rapid industrial growth before the Second World War, Southeast Asia did experience impressive GDP per capita growth, close to 1 per cent per annum between 1870 and 1940. GDP grew at about the same rate between 1940 and 1970 as before 1940, but since population growth accelerated, GDP per capita stagnated or declined (Maddison, 2007). The share of manufacturing in GDP remained constant until the 1960s, from which it follows that manufacturing output growth barely exceeded population growth. Table 11.1 compares Southeast Asian annual real industrial output growth from 1870 to 2007 with three world leaders—Germany, the United Kingdom, and the United States, the two Asian giants—China and India—and three East Asian late-twentieth-century economic miracles—Japan, Korea (South Korea after 1945), and Taiwan. As in Chapter 2, the industrial history is broken up into two pre-First World War episodes (1870–96, 1896–1913), the First World War years (1913–20), the two inter-war decades (1920–38), the ISI years following the Second World War (1950–73), and the two periods up to the present (1973–1990, 1990–2007). During this long century, Japan, South Korea, and Taiwan recorded industrial growth rates faster than those of the Western leaders, and they were the fastest in the periphery. Between 1896 and 1990, the unweighted average of their growth rates exceeded that of the world leaders by: 2.7 per cent, 1896–1913; 7.1 per cent, 1913–20; and 4.2 per cent, 1920–38—all long before any post-war growth miracles. The figures were 7.1 per cent, 1950–73, and 7.3 per cent, 1973–90.

Except for the Philippines between 1896 and 1939, Southeast Asia was not part of this East Asian industrial catching-up until after the Second World War. Before the 1950s, most industrial sectors in Southeast Asia hardly grew at all. For example, only 7.1 per cent of the Malayan labour force was employed in manufacturing in 1921, declining to 6.9 per cent in 1931, and rising only modestly to 9.8 per cent in 1947 (Huff, 2002, p. 1082). Industry in Singapore and Thailand started growing faster than in the Western leaders only from the 1950s onwards, and Indonesia and Malaysia joined the club only after 1973. Even then, Southeast Asia did not record industrial catching-up growth rates on Japan or Taiwan until after 1973 and 1990, respectively, and never on South Korea. The only Southeast Asian country that

---

[8] The 1930s in Indonesia's case.

Table 11.1. Industrial output growth, 1870–2007: Southeast Asia and the rest (per cent, per annum)[9]

	1870–96	1896–1913	1913–20	1920–38	1950–73	1973–90	1990–2007
World leaders							
Germany	3.1	3.6	0.4	1.6	6.8	1.3	1.2
United Kingdom	1.9	1.5	−0.6	3.0	4.3	0.1	0.8
United States	4.6	4.9	4.5	1.2	4.4	1.9	4.2
Average	3.2	3.3	1.4	1.9	5.2	1.1	2.1
Asian Giants							
China	7.8	7.8	9.4	5.3	9.2	8.3	9.8
India	0.9	2.6	−4.3	3.4	6.9	5.1	6.5
Average	4.4	5.2	2.6	4.4	8.1	6.7	8.2
East Asian 3							
Japan	3.3	5.0	6.5	6.7	12.4	4.1	1.0
Korea		8.0	9.3	7.1	13.6	11.7	7.4
Taiwan		5.1	9.8	4.4	11.6	8.7	4.9
Average	3.3	6.0	8.5	6.1	12.5	8.2	4.4
Southeast Asia							
Cambodia							15.9
Indonesia	1.3	1.3	1.0	2.7	3.4	12.8	5.1
Lao PDR							8.5
Malaysia						8.5	7.1
Burma		0.1	3.5	2.6	3.2	3.0	12.0
Philippines		6.3	10.1	3.4	7.0	1.8	3.3
Singapore					16.2	6.9	6.1
Siam	0.9	2.3	1.6	2.3	11.2	8.1	5.9
Vietnam					7.6	1.9	10.7
Average	0.8	2.5	4.1	2.8	8.1	5.4	8.3

Source: Bénétrix, O'Rourke, and Williamson (2015, Table 7).

appeared to have joined the fast industrial growth club before the Second World War—the Philippines[10]—saw its industrial growth collapse after the ISI years (de Dios and Williamson, 2015).

What explains this dismal industrial performance in Southeast Asia before the 1960s? Why did Southeast Asia become a success story of rapid export-led manufacturing growth after the 1960s? To answer these two questions, we focus

[9] Between 1913 and 1934, industry's share in GDP rose in the Philippines from 16.1 to 23.8 per cent (Hooley, 2005, Table A.1), while it rose only marginally in Indonesia and Thailand (Booth and Deng, 2014, Table 3); manufacturing accounted for around 25 per cent of GDP in the Philippines in the early 1960s, while the share was around 8 per cent in Indonesia, Malaysia, and Myanmar, and 13 per cent in Thailand. See Fig. 11.1.

[10] The very high growth rate observed for China between 1870 and 1920 could mostly reflect the evolution of the modern sector, as it is likely that the underlying series do not entirely cover the large traditional cottage industry sector. The same remark may apply to Korea and Taiwan between 1896 and 1938. In the Philippines, the growth rate of the period 1896–1913 could be due to some extent to a change of coverage of the cottage industry in the transition from the Spanish to the US colonial administration. Still, such measurement problems existed for all periphery countries with which Southeast Asia could be compared.

on Indonesia (Netherlands East Indies until 1947), Malaysia (Malaya, Sabah, Sarawak, and Straits Settlements before 1957),[11] Myanmar (Burma until 1989), the Philippines, Thailand (Siam until 1939), and Vietnam (part of French Indochina before 1949). We distinguish four periods: de-industrialization and commodity export growth before 1913; a modest diversification into manufacturing during the First World War and the inter-war years; the development of consumer goods production under import substitution policies between the 1940s and the 1960s; and finally high-speed export-led industrialization up to the 1990s, helped greatly by foreign direct investment (FDI) but primarily driven by improvements in education and the demographic dividend that made young, literate labour abundant, particularly through the rapid rise of female labour force participation. To gauge the magnitude of the Southeast Asian industrial lag, we compare the region with Japan and Korea, the major success stories in Asia before China's emergence.[12]

11.2 SOUTHEAST ASIA IN THE FIRST GLOBAL CENTURY: DE-INDUSTRIALIZATION AND COMMODITY PROCESSING

The idea that the Third World suffered de-industrialization during the nineteenth century has a long pedigree.[13] However, quantitative evidence on the level of industrial activity in the nineteenth-century Third World is scant, and Southeast Asia is no exception. Most de-industrialization assessments rely on very sparse employment and output data. Manufacturing output is relatively easy to estimate for commodity processing, as these activities closely followed commodity exports. In Southeast Asia, they included rice milling in Bangkok, Rangoon, and Saigon, the three major hubs of the rice-exporting deltas of the Chao Phraya, Irrawaddy, and Mekong rivers, sugar milling in Java and the Philippines, and tin processing in Malaysia (joined by rubber processing in the early twentieth century). These manufacturing activities were undertaken mostly in enterprises owned by foreigners (Chinese immigrants, along with Indian immigrants in Burma, and Westerners) and they used imported capital goods such as milling and processing machinery powered by steam engines. This equipment was imported mostly from Britain, Germany, and France, and was operated by Western engineers, Chinese and Indian (in Burma) skilled workers, and local unskilled workers (including Chinese and Indian immigrants). Commodity export processing was a very large share of

---

[11] The Federation of Malaya was established in 1948 to unify British Malaya and the British colonies of Sabah (then North Borneo), Sarawak, and Straits Settlements (less Singapore), and became independent in 1957. Singapore joined Malaya in 1963, to form Malaysia, and then left in 1965.

[12] China is not included in the comparison, given the paucity of data available for the pre-Second World War period.

[13] Williamson (2011, Chapters 5 and 6).

manufacturing output. In 1917, sugar milling was almost 43 per cent of Indonesian manufacturing, and it was still more than 41 per cent in 1928.[14] In 1918, processing of all commodities accounted for more than 73 per cent of Philippine 'modern' manufacturing output, and hemp, copra, coconut oil, sugar, and tobacco accounted for 92 per cent of its exports (see below).

We do not have enough information to provide a quantitative assessment of the collapse of domestic textile production in the late nineteenth century as a consequence of the flood of cheap British and Indian cotton yarn, and cheap Japanese and Chinese silk yarn. But qualitative evidence offers little doubt that a collapse in domestic yarn production took place all across Southeast Asia. However, much of Southeast Asian imported (factory-made) yarn was processed into fabrics and dyed by local artisans.[15] Thus, the decline of the indigenous textile industries was partly offset by the specialization of cottage industry in products enjoying 'home preference'; in the Indonesian case the offset was more than partial, since if we include the processing of unbleached cloth, total output grew between 1870 and 1913 (van der Eng, 2007; 2013).

Price data are much more plentiful, and, as a consequence, the terms of trade can be used as a proxy for the de-industrialization forces facing Southeast Asia up to the early twentieth century: as manufactured import prices fell—driven by productivity growth in the industrial leaders—domestic production collapsed, and commodity export sectors expanded, driven by booming commodity prices pushed upwards by European demand. Such evidence suggests that while de-industrialization occurred everywhere in the poor periphery, it was probably much more dramatic in Southeast Asia than elsewhere (Williamson, 2011, Chapter 3). The long commodity price boom turned around after the First World War, something that should have favoured re-industrialization, except, as we shall see below, that skill scarcity, strong Japanese and Chinese competition, and adverse colonial fiscal, monetary, and commercial policies, all served to mute its impact. While these forces were shared everywhere in the poor periphery, they were more dramatic in Southeast Asia and sub-Saharan Africa (Frankema, Williamson, and Woltjer, 2015) than elsewhere. To make matters worse for local manufacturing, labour was relatively expensive in this resource-abundant frontier region.

Figure 11.2 plots the net barter terms of trade[16] (1900 = 100) from 1782 to 1913 for Indonesia, Malaya,[17] the Philippines, Siam, and Southeast Asia as a whole. While the Philippines and Siam underwent a spectacular price boom up to the 1860s, Indonesia's boom was more than twice as steep and much longer, peaking in 1896. Not only was it the biggest terms of trade boom in Southeast Asia, it was also the

---

[14] Based on personal correspondence from Pierre van der Eng (25 June 2015).

[15] This is well documented for Java (Boomgaard, 1991; van der Kraan, 1996), central and northern Vietnam (Gourou, 1955, pp. 460, 527; IGMI, 1943, p. 51), and the Philippines (Legarda, 1999).

[16] A country's net barter terms of trade is simply the ratio of its average export price to its average import price, where the averages are weighted by the relative importance of the traded goods in total exports or total imports.

[17] Malaya 1882–1913 is plotted in Fig. 11.2, but it starts much too late to be included in the analysis reported below.

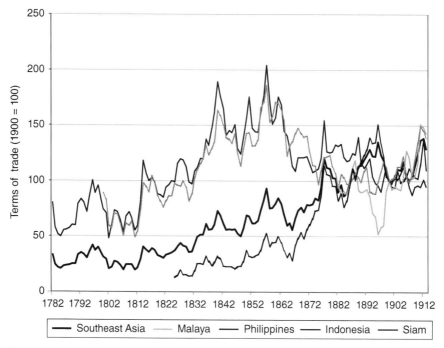

Fig. 11.2. Net terms of trade, 1782–1913

Source: Williamson (2011, Fig. 3.9).

biggest in the poor periphery. Since the Indonesian population was so large compared with the rest of the region, its trend dominates the Southeast Asian average.

Did the biggest terms of trade boom produce the biggest de-industrialization of import-competing manufacturing? The answer is definitely yes. The share of the home textile market supplied by Indonesian producers dropped from about 82 to 38 per cent from 1822 to 1870, before falling still further to about 11 per cent in 1913 (Williamson, 2011, Table 5.3). This evidence confirms dramatic de-industrialization in Indonesia up to the First World War.

Indonesia was not alone in suffering de-industrialization, since it happened everywhere in Southeast Asia. By the late 1890s, Burma's 'textile industry had suffered a serious decline and it was finally . . . destroyed by the 1920s' and 'weaving, . . . spinning, iron and metal making, pottery . . . and paper making' had declined in Siam (Resnick, 1970, pp. 57, 60). Like Indonesia, the Philippines started the nineteenth century with a well-developed textile industry. Indeed, by 1818 local cloth accounted for 8 per cent of Manila's exports:

> The province of Iloilo . . . developed valuable *piña*, dyed in bright and varied colours. This was woven chiefly with pineapple fibre, but might also contain cotton, silk and *abacá*. The industry sucked in migrants from far and wide . . . selling as far afield as Europe and the Americas. (Clarence-Smith, 2005, p. 8)

Table 11.2. Terms of trade volatility in Southeast Asia, 1865–1939

	1860s–1900s	Relatives	1910s–1930s	Relatives	1860s–1930s	Relatives
Southeast Asia	8.091	2.744	10.985	1.503	9.538	1.859
Burma	6.945	2.356	13.463	1.841	10.204	*1.989*
Indonesia	9.558	3.242	6.904	0.944	8.231	*1.604*
Philippines	7.823	2.654	10.004	1.368	8.914	*1.738*
Thailand	8.036	2.726	13.569	1.856	10.803	*2.106*
Three Colonizers	2.948	1.000	7.311	1.000	5.130	1.000
France	4.038	1.370	6.728	0.920	5.383	*1.049*
Germany	2.089	0.709	7.380	1.009	4.735	*0.923*
United Kingdom	2.716	0.921	7.825	1.070	5.271	*1.027*

Note: Volatility is measured by the Hodrick–Prescott filter with a smoothing parameter = 300. The regional averages are unweighted.

Source: Data underlying Blattman, Hwang, and Williamson (2007).

However, by 1847 almost 60 per cent of Philippine imports were textiles, and they increased ninefold over the half-century that followed (Legarda, 1999, pp. 149–50). By the 1880s, 'native textiles were in a sad state' (Legarda, 1999, p. 155). Spanish authorities did not use tariffs to fend off the flood of European manufactures. Indeed, the Philippine tariff system was thoroughly liberalized in the late 1860s (Legarda, 1999, pp. 198, 205), as it was in Indonesia (Booth, 1998, pp. 215–16). In short, it does indeed appear that Southeast Asia underwent the biggest terms of trade boom, the biggest Dutch Disease, and thus the biggest de-industrialization in the global periphery.

Although commodity export prices (and thus terms of trade) boomed up to the First World War, Southeast Asia was subjected to great terms of trade volatility and thus investment uncertainty in all sectors including manufacturing. Table 11.2 documents that terms of trade volatility between 1865 and 1913 was 2.7 times greater than that of the three industrial leaders, and 1.5 times greater even in the turbulent inter-war decades. The four Southeast Asian countries which had the most commodity price volatility included Burma and Thailand (both major rice exporters). Malaya did not have a long enough time series to be included in Table 11.2, but its two key exports, rubber and tin, had great price volatility and thus so did its economy.[18] The same applies to Vietnam, with rice accounting for about 70 per cent of total exports from the late nineteenth century to 1945.[19] The role of commodity price volatility in suppressing incentives in import-competing industries has been well established by economists (Hnatkovska and Loayza, 2005; Fatás and Mihov, 2006; Loayza et al., 2007; Poelhekke and van der Ploeg, 2009) and

[18] By the late 1920s, rubber and tin accounted for 68.6 per cent of total Malayan merchandise exports (Huff, 2002, p. 1077). New terms of trade data for Malaya confirm huge price volatility there from 1870 to 1913. Since doing the analysis, Professor Huff has shared with us new terms of trade data for Malaya 1872–1939 (6 May 2015). To give some sense of the immense volatility, peaks and troughs were: 1872, 100; 1878, 46.6; 1888, 111.6; 1896, 49; 1911, 141.7; 1925, 93.3; 1931, 33.5; and 1939, 69.3.

[19] Brenier (1914) and Annuaire Statistique de l'Indochine (various years).

Table 11.3. Population density in Southeast Asia, Japan, and Korea (inhabitants per square kilometre)

	1820	1870	1913	1950	1970	2000
Indonesia	9	17	27	43	61	107
Malaysia	1	2	9	20	33	66
Myanmar	5	6	18	29	40	65
Philippines	7	17	31	70	129	271
Thailand	9	11	17	39	72	120
Vietnam	20	32	59	77	129	240
Japan	82	91	137	222	276	335
Korea	63	65	71	138	211	311

Note: Population data for Myanmar unadjusted for changes in territory (lower Burma only up to 1890, including upper Burma thereafter).

Sources: World Bank for land area (http://data.worldbank.org/indicator/AG.LND.TOTL.K2); Maddison (2010) for population.

economic historians (Huff, 2002; Williamson, 2011, 2012), so there is no reason to doubt its role in Southeast Asia.

An additional factor explaining the decline of Southeast Asian manufacturing in the late nineteenth and early twentieth centuries is expensive labour relative to competitors such as Japan. Most of Southeast Asia was land abundant and labour scarce, as evidenced by the very low population density there compared with Northeast Asia (Table 11.3). The only exceptions were Java (in Indonesia), the Red River delta (in northern Vietnam), and the western part of Luzon (in the Philippines), but even these areas were close to extensive agricultural margins. In addition to high land/labour ratios, Southeast Asia enjoyed high labour productivity in agriculture by Asian standards (van der Eng, 2004). As urban and rural labour markets were well integrated throughout Southeast Asia, this resulted in relatively high wages in urban cottage industries and commodity processing manufacturing. The massive inflow of Chinese and Indian workers was not sufficient to induce a convergence of labour costs within the region and between it and the labour-abundant sources of its immigrants: the land frontier remained wide open until at least the 1920s in the midlands and highlands surrounding the high-density areas of Java, the Red River delta, or central Luzon, and until the 1960s in the rest of Southeast Asia. Nominal daily wages of unskilled workers, measured in grams of silver, were higher in Bangkok, Jakarta, Penang, Rangoon, Singapore, and Surabaya than in Tokyo in the 1890s (Bassino and van der Eng, 2013). Since the skill premium was much lower in Japan than in Southeast Asia, Japanese skilled labour remained cheaper than in most Southeast Asia cities until at least the 1910s. Under these circumstances, the most profitable manufacturing activities involved commodity processing, particularly milling and mining, but certainly not labour-intensive manufacturing. Southeast Asia simply had no comparative advantage in labour-intensive manufacturing prior to the inter-war years.[20]

---

[20] The same was true of Sub-Saharan Africa. See Chapter 14 by Austin, Frankema, and Jerven in this volume.

11.3 SLOW INDUSTRIAL GROWTH IN SOUTHEAST ASIA IN THE INTER-WAR YEARS

After the First World War, commodity prices collapsed, the terms of trade fell with them, and the relative price of import-competing manufactures rose in domestic Southeast Asian markets. Between 1913 and 1932, the terms of trade for Indonesia and the Philippines fell by 40.6 and 76 per cent, respectively, and they had not recovered by 1949 (still 22.9 and 34.7 per cent below 1913). The rice exporters Burma and Thailand suffered more modest declines from 1913 to 1932 (Burma down 12.6 per cent, and Thailand down 27 per cent), and both had surpassed 1913 levels by 1949 and the subsequent run-up to the Korean War peak. Malayan rubber prices fell by 86 per cent from 1910/19 to 1930/39, and its terms of trade fell by 51.1 per cent (see n. 18). But in spite of the rise in the relative price of import-competing manufactures, Southeast Asian manufacturing did not expand by much.

Industrial growth in inter-war Southeast Asia was mostly slow due to the combined effects of colonial exchange rate appreciation policy, skill scarcity, expensive unskilled labour, and Japanese and Chinese competition. Nevertheless, some diversification and deepening of modern manufacturing *did* occur during the inter-war decades.[21] And in some cases, modest pro-industrial colonial policy (for example, in 1930s Indonesia) did expand industrial output, and help pave the way for the post-war 'miracles'.

First, it is important to keep in mind the role of commodity price volatility when searching for causes of lagging industrial development. Pre-Second World War Southeast Asian economies were exposed to enormous world price shocks. The volatility of commodity prices already reported for the pre-1913 years was even greater between 1913 and 1940 (Table 11.4). For example, the international demand for rice from Burma, Indochina, and Siam, and sugar from Java,[22] declined sharply in the 1930s, and countries such as Indonesia found themselves excluded from key export markets. Their export bundles were dominated by just one or two

Table 11.4. Terms of trade bust, 1913–49 (1900 = 100)

	Burma	Indonesia	Philippines	Thailand
1913	100.0	100.0	100.0	100.0
1918	137.9	103.9	90.0	134.1
1929	113.2	72.5	54.7	105.1
1932	87.4	59.4	34.0	73.0
1939	99.5	70.9	39.8	89.4
1949	164.2	77.1	65.3	175.9

Source: Data underlying the series in Blattman, Hwang, and Williamson (2007).

---

[21] For instance, in the mid-1920s, Vietnamese production of cement, chemical products, explosives, glass, paint, paper, porcelain insulators, and matches in industrial plants employing a hundred or more workers expanded (Gouvernement Général de l'Indochine, 1928).

[22] Philippine sugar exporters had access to a protected US market.

Table 11.5. Export concentration in Asia around 1900

Country	Two major export commodities	Percentage of total exports
Burma	Rice, oil products	92
Indonesia	Sugar, coffee	60
Philippines	Hemp, sugar	89
Siam	Rice	100
Vietnam	Rice	68
Southeast Asia		**82**
Ceylon	Tea, coffee	100
India	Rice, jute	35
South Asia		**68**
China	Silk, tea	78
Japan	Silk, cotton goods	79
East Asia		**79**

Note: All regional averages are unweighted.
Source: All based on data underlying Blattman, Hwang, and Williamson (2007), except Vietnam proxied using share of rice in total export of French Indochina, based on data reported in Brenier (1914).

Table 11.6. Share of exports in GDP, 1901–38 (per cent)

	Indonesia	Thailand	Philippines	Vietnam	Burma
1901	12		28	19	30
1916	22	17	32	18	35
1926	26	22		25	36
1938	17	25	34	22	48

Note: Thailand 1916 = 1913, 1926 = 1929; Philippines 1901 = 1902, 1916 = 1918.
Source: Booth (2003, Table 2, p. 431).

commodities (Table 11.5), reflecting their specialization, so the price behaviour of one commodity was not offset by the behaviour of others. In addition, exports were a very large share of GDP. Between 1901 and 1938, that share (in per cent) was 30–48 in Burma, 28–34 in the Philippines, 18–25 in Vietnam, and 12–26 in Indonesia (Table 11.6). Since so much of rural household output was not marketed, the export share in marketed value added might have been double these figures.

Second, it is important to keep in mind that there were three kinds of manufacturing in the commodity-exporting economy—import competing, commodity processing, and local non-tradable. Commodity price booms suppressed import-competing industrial growth (the relative price of manufactures fell) but boosted commodity processing. Commodity price busts (the relative price of manufactures rose) improved the profitability of import-competitive manufacturing, but hurt commodity processing and local production of non-tradables—since local demand shrank during the bust. Total manufacturing in the inter-war years was dominated by the latter two, so manufacturing was hurt by commodity price busts. To give one example, the share of sugar milling in Indonesian industrial output fell from 41.2 per cent in 1928 to less than 12 per cent in 1935. In contrast with resource-poor China, Northeast Asia and much of the European periphery, where commodity processing was less important, any analysis of Southeast Asia (and Sub-Saharan Africa) must focus on the mix between those three manufacturing activities.

Third, the secular decline in Southeast Asia's net barter terms of trade between the world wars should, other things constant, have stimulated import-competing activities. But, as we shall see, other things were not constant.

Dutch Disease models are common in the development and growth literature, and they have been used to inform the 'resource curse' debate as to whether an abundant resource endowment implies poor growth prospects.[23] But that debate is not about manufacturing but rather about income per capita growth, and the latter was not slow in Southeast Asia over the first three quarters of the twentieth century. Indeed, three of the five regions where GDP can be documented—Malaya, the Philippines, and Singapore—had jumped over the Kuznets modern economic growth hurdle—namely, per capita income growth of 1 per cent or higher during a sustained period—for the quarter-century 1913–38. The GDP per capita growth rates were 2.4 per cent for Indonesia and 3.5 per cent for the Philippines 1902–13 (Maddison, 2010). For the six decades 1913–73, four Southeast Asian nations had jumped over the Kuznets hurdle. So, with the exception of Burma, the 'curse' certainly wasn't manifested by poor GDP per capita growth in pre-Second World War Southeast Asia. Rather, it was manifested by slow or even non-existent industrial growth (Table 11.1).

To account for this poor industrial performance, it is conventional to start with colonial policy. Britain was opposed to industrial development in its colonies on ideological free trade grounds. The French may have been a little less so, but neither wanted to lose their colonial markets for their exports. America forged free trade arrangements with the Philippines during the inter-war years. So, protection of domestic manufacturing was excluded there. Colonial tariffs were raised a bit in the 1930s to shore up collapsing colonial revenues, but this certainly didn't constitute an industrial development policy, except late in the decade.[24] Nor were subsidies used to help import-competing industries, no doubt partly because they would have been a drag on net colonial revenues. Colonial policy also muted any pro-manufacturing forces. To understand these forces, we find the Dutch Disease model which Gregg Huff applied to pre-Second World War Malaya most helpful (Huff, 2002). Although Huff draws extensively on the larger Dutch Disease literature—led by Max Corden and Peter Neary (1982) and Corden (1984)—he adds three colonial dimensions that make the de-industrialization forces powerful even during commodity price busts: credit scarcity, shrinking domestic markets, and the absence of currency depreciation, since colonial commitments to sterling exchange and gold standards made the latter impossible. On credit scarcity and

---

[23] It is somewhat of an irony that the term 'Dutch Disease' applies best to the Dutch East Indies.
[24] Indonesia provides one exception to this statement.

shrinking domestic markets, Huff has this to say about Malaya during commodity price busts:

> [A]lthough would-be industrialists benefited from a favorable [relative manufacture's price] and so a more attractive cost-price structure, a downward shock to credit supply and accompanying shrinkage in the size of the Malayan market effectively worked against any shift to manufacturing.   (Huff, 2002, p. 1093)

On the inability of colonial economies to depreciate their currencies during a commodity price bust, Anne Booth (1998, pp. 231–3) offers the best Southeast Asian example—namely, that Indonesia's real exchange rate *appreciated* during most of the pre-Second World War years.[25] French Indochina offers another example. Colonial authorities took into account the importance of China as the main market for Indochinese rice, and therefore kept the *piaster* on a silver standard but shifted their monetary policy to adopt a French franc peg in 1930. The decision was ill advised, since the *franc* became a gold exchange standard currency, and the Indochinese rice exporters underwent a loss of competitiveness due to the appreciated *piaster*. The story of fixed colonial exchange rates was pretty much the same elsewhere in Southeast Asia (Booth, 2003, pp. 439–56; Huff, 2003). One can only imagine how much these colonial policies suppressed industrial growth in Southeast Asia, given modern econometric studies of developing country performance since the 1950s (Rodrik, 2007; McMillan and Rodrik, 2011). Thus, one of the reasons that Southeast Asia had to wait so long to start its industrial catch-up on the leaders was that it first had to gain control of its exchange rate and trade policy.

Colonial attitudes towards local industry began to change during the 1930s, especially in Indonesia and Indochina. With the collapse of commodity prices, diversification into industry became the catchword (Shepherd, 1941). Indeed, in the face of the flood of Japanese manufactures into Southeast Asian markets (the Japanese share of Indonesian textile imports rose from 26 to 75 per cent between 1928 and 1933: van der Eng, 2013, p. 9), colonial authorities raised tariffs. They did so in part because of the decline in commodity export revenues, but they also set quotas. Both quotas and tariffs may have been used more to defend these markets for imperial manufactures (Booth, 2015, p. 46), but they also protected domestic industry. Indeed, the 'colonial government abandoned the principle that Indonesia's tariff served only fiscal purposes' also because the flood of Japanese textiles was destroying a new local weaving industry. These new policies 'gave the colonial government unprecedented powers to steer industrial development in Indonesia [up to] 1939' (van der Eng, 2013, pp. 10–11). With post-war independence, Indonesia and other parts of Southeast Asia were able to exploit this experience.

The cost of labour in Southeast Asia offers an additional explanation for the slow development of its import-competing industries. As we pointed out above, nominal unskilled wages were higher in Southeast Asia than in Japan up to the 1920s (Bassino and van der Eng, 2013), and they were much higher than in China and

---

[25] It should be noted, however, that the Indonesian colonial debt was denominated in gold-based currency, so the policy eased the debt service burden (van der Eng, 1998).

India throughout the inter-war years. In addition, due to skill shortages in Southeast Asian cities, their nominal skilled wages were greater than those of Tokyo throughout the inter-war years,[26] and far above those of Bombay and Shanghai. It is not surprising, therefore, that most foreign direct investment received by Southeast Asia in the 1920s and 1930s concentrated on plantations and mines (Lindblad, 1997), and that local manufactures had difficulty competing with Japanese imports, especially in the 1930s after the depreciation of the yen.

In spite of these difficulties, the inter-war period did witness a gradual transformation of Southeast Asian manufacturing, including the diffusion of modern technology to the traditional sector. The literature on industrial development and industrialization in emerging nations typically focuses on modern industry—that is, on large-scale, capital- and energy-intensive factories producing consumption importables, such as textiles, and capital goods importables, such as machinery—even though small labour-intensive operations that used little or no inanimate power remained dominant for a number of decades. The emerging and large-scale factories using modern technologies did not immediately destroy the small-scale workshop using traditional technologies: they co-existed during the transition so that dualism characterized early industrial development. Only at more advanced stages did large-scale, capital-intensive, and energy-intensive technology become ubiquitous. Understanding this transition is important to understanding industrial development more generally, and especially in Southeast Asia.

How the industrial output mix is measured matters in understanding the transition. In the inter-war and immediate post-Second World War years of anti-global policies and closed economies, distinguishing between capital and consumption goods production mattered in accumulation and growth debates (Domar, 1957; Bronfenbrenner, 1960). For the 1913–50 years, as we pointed out above, the distinction that matters for Southeast Asia and other commodity exporters is between commodity-processing, import-competing, and non-tradable domestic manufacturing. This tri-part distinction matters, since the three often or even typically offset each other, yielding little net industrial growth. Since Southeast Asia specialized in the export of commodities until the post-Second World War era, its industrial growth was based largely on commodity processing. To repeat the argument above, commodity price booms triggered commodity processing (and the production of the capital goods that did the processing), while the country suffered de-industrialization in the manufacture of importables like textiles. Unless they had some natural protection[27] or could build tariff barriers, import-competing manufactures collapsed. Some protective barriers did emerge in the 1930s, but most of Southeast Asia had to wait until post-war political independence to decide how high those barriers would be.[28]

---

[26] The skill premium was even higher in resource-abundant and land-scarce Sub-Saharan Africa during the same period (Frankema and van Waijenburg, 2012, Table 1).

[27] A large share of manufacturing activity in early stages of industrialization is that which is protected from foreign competition by distance, high weight-to-value ratios, consumer preferences, and perishability.

[28] Even earlier in the 1920s, there was a change in colonial policy that began to favor agricultural productivity growth, education, and health, led by the 'progressive' US policies in the Philippines and

Inter-war industry mix and industrial dualism in Southeast Asia is best documented for the region's fastest industrial grower, the Philippines. There were four key exports reported in the 1918 Philippine Census: coconut oil and copra accounted for 27 per cent of all exports, manila hemp for 43 per cent, sugar for 12 per cent, and tobacco products for 10 per cent.[29] While the Philippines was a net rice importer for most years, that commodity needed to be cleaned and then sent to the rice mills. These commodity export-processing industries grew three times as fast as the rest of manufacturing between 1903 and 1918, by which time they accounted for 73.4 per cent of 'modern' industrial output (industrial output excluding household or cottage industry).[30]

Philippine sugar mills were 51 per cent steam or water power driven by 1918, offering a good illustration of technology dualism in the transition to modern industrial growth. In another good illustration, cottage industry—or what the Philippine Manufacturing Census called 'household industry' or HH in what follows—accounted for 55.5 per cent of total manufacturing output in 1918. While this share may seem big, it was smaller than in China where in 1933 it accounted for three-quarters of total manufacturing value added.[31] Furthermore, the role of HH production varied considerably across industries. Many labour-intensive activities had been forced by foreign competition to retreat to isolated rural HHs: in 1918, 92 per cent of total textile output and 46 per cent of the hats were produced by HHs. Many industries had converted to factory organization (tobacco, corn milling, furniture, tanning, footwear, vegetable oils, rice mills, soap, sugar mills, brick and tile, abaca processing, pasta making, fish salting), and could report only trivial HH shares in total production. Some industries remained in dualism: HHs accounted for 55.9 per cent of copra drying, 53.9 per cent of textile dying, and 70.7 per cent of pottery production. All of these HH shares were much smaller in the 1939 Manufacturing Census.

Industrial dualism can also be observed in other Southeast Asian countries. For example, the share of power looms in total looms had risen in Indonesia from nothing to 18 per cent in 1940–1 (van der Eng, 2013, Table 1, p. 28), but it was still small. To take another example, shipbuilding had both traditional workshops and modern shipyards for repairing steamers in the main Southeast Asian ports of Jakarta, Surabaya, Haiphong, Saigon, Singapore, and others. Although they recorded lower manufacturing growth rates than did the Philippines, most Southeast Asian countries experienced some diversification of industrial activities. In the

---

the pro-growth attitudes of Japan towards its new colonies Korea and Taiwan. See Landes (1998, p. 437), Booth (2012, pp. 3–7) and Booth and Deng (2014).

[29] These four items needed processing before export: copra was dried and then pressed for the oil; sugar cane was processed at the mill; manila hemp was converted to rope, rugs, wall coverings, and other products in factories; and tobacco was dried, cut, and made into cigars and cigarettes. All of these were then packed for shipment.

[30] The import-competing growth estimates have an upward bias, since so many were under-reported or unreported in either 1903 or 1918. Qualitative evidence suggests that under-reported or unreported import-competing industries with high cottage industry shares were textiles, spinning, bags and sacks, iron agricultural implements, hats, and umbrellas.

[31] Chapter 9 in this volume.

export hub of Saigon, rice milling was a relatively capital-intensive industry in 1926–7 using steam-driven machines (GGI, 1928), but it was small scale and powered by hand or animals in rural areas. In northern Vietnam, manufacturing activities using capital-intensive and steam-driven technologies (powered by cheap local coal) included cement, glass, brewing, tobacco processing, printing, and paper mills, while others producing for the local market were cottage industries using hand-driven technologies.

Although it was more modest, the same industrial diversification and emerging dualism was apparent in Burma, at least as measured by the number of factories (Hlaing, 1965, Table 8, p. 32). Since it was factories and not cottage industry being reported by these official statistics, one can plausibly assume that fast factory growth rates meant a rising 'modern' share of industry: between 1899 and 1940, the number of factories grew by 5.2 per cent per annum. And the industry mix diversified as well, although modestly. The share of factories that processed export commodities (rice and saw mills, cotton ginning, petroleum refining, metal smelting) was huge in 1899, at 94.2 per cent. But that share fell to 86.7 per cent in 1940, domestic non-tradable producers (vegetable oil and flour mills, cement, printing) rising from 4.3 to 9.6 per cent, and import-competing manufacturers (spinning, weaving, knitwear, rubber goods) from 1.4 to 3.8 per cent.

In short, while there were some pro-industrial forces at work in Southeast Asia during the inter-war period, they were modest at best: the industrial share in GDP (including mining, manufacturing, construction, and utilities) only rose from 16.1 to 17.6 per cent in Indonesia, and from 17.1 to 17.3 per cent in Thailand (Booth and Deng, 2014, Table 3, p. 43).

11.4 TRANSITION: HUMAN CAPITAL ACCUMULATION AND ISI FROM THE LATE 1930s TO THE LATE 1960s

In the 1930s, Southeast Asia experienced a steady rise in public investment in education and some early attempts to promote ISI. Both were amplified during the Second World War and in the two post-war decades. Although these policies did not have a big immediate impact on industrial production, they paved the way for 'miracle' manufacturing growth after the 1960s.

Economists think that primary schooling is a critical ingredient of labour-intensive manufacturing in early stages of modern industrial growth, and that secondary schooling helps move countries up the industrial ladder to more skill-intensive activities. A large macro-econometric literature on modern East Asia supports that view (Jones, Ogawa, and Williamson, 1993; World Bank, 1993; Radelet, Sachs, and Lee, 2001; Lee and Hong, 2010).[32] Each of these studies finds that schooling is a central contributor to economy-wide per capita income and labour productivity growth after controlling for capital accumulation, good

---

[32] The literature is extensive, but see also Bils and Klenow (2000), Glewwe and Kremer (2006), and Manuelli and Seshadri (2014).

Table 11.7. Mean primary schooling enrolment rates in Southeast Asia, 1880–1960 (per cent)

	1880	1890	1900	1910	1920	1930	1935–40	1950/2	1960/1
Burma	9.4	8.5	11.5	11.8	10.3	13.4	13.3		
Indochina			0.5	1.0	2.8	6.9	10.8		
Indonesia	1.0	2.0	2.5	3.7	7.0	12.2	13.3		38.1
Japan	30.3	34.5	49.3	59.2	60.3	60.9	60.5	61.5	58.4
Korea				1.1	3.8	10.8	23.4		58.2
Malaysia				7.5	8.9	19.4	24.6		69.2
Philippines			19.3	28.4	35.8	32.4	44.8	70.6	53.8
Taiwan			2.0	3.1	19.5	26.1	52.8		83.0
Thailand		0.5		5.8	7.1	24.1	52.6	39.3	36.4
Japan = 100									
Burma	31.0	24.6	23.3	19.9	17.1	22.0	22.0		
Indochina			1.0	1.7	4.6	11.3	17.9		
Indonesia	3.3	5.8	5.1	6.3	11.6	20.0	22.0		65.2
Korea				1.9	6.3	17.7	38.7		99.6
Malaysia				12.7	14.8	31.9	40.7		118.5
Philippines				48.0	59.4	53.2	74.0	114.8	92.1
Taiwan				5.2	32.3	42.9	87.3		142.1
Thailand				9.8	11.8	39.6	86.9	63.9	62.4

Source: Benarot and Riddle (1988, Appendix, pp. 205–6) and Mitchell (1995: primary school enrolment (000s) from pp. 958–67, and children aged 5–14 (000s) from pp. 23–7).

government, openness, and other variables. A recent study of Southeast Asia covering the four decades between 1970 and 2010 finds, once again, that schooling has been an important determinant of GDP per worker growth (Phung, Coxhead, and Chang, 2015). Our strong prior is that it has been an even more important determinant of *manufacturing* output per worker growth, since the latter is certainly more schooling-intensive than agriculture and traditional services.[33]

This literature motivates the question: if schooling has mattered to Southeast Asian industrial growth since 1970, what was the source of that favourable schooling endowment? Available evidence suggests that much of Southeast Asia under foreign rule was severely disadvantaged by colonial policy before the 1940s (Sopheak and Clayton, 2007; Chaudhary, 2009). Table 11.7 reports that—with the exception of American colonial policy in the Philippines (Gomez and Pedro, 1992)[34]—primary enrolment rates in schools controlled by colonial administrations were very low in Southeast Asia in the 1920s. Again excluding the Philippines,

---

[33] Oddly enough, there is no study, to our knowledge, of the econometric determinants of manufacturing labour productivity growth in Southeast Asia.

[34] It should be noted, however, that enrolment rates were not insignificant in late-nineteenth-century Philippines. In 1866, the number of children attending primary school was 542 per 10,000 inhabitants, implying an enrolment rate of about 5 or 6, and the ratio of girl to boy students was a surprisingly high 0.72 (Census of the Philippine Islands, 1903, vol. 2, p. 591). The same source reports that 20.2 per cent of the population above 10 was able to read and write (*ibid*.: 81–2). The American pro-school colonial policy could to some extent be viewed as a continuation of Spanish colonial policy.

primary enrolment rates in Southeast Asia at that time were everywhere less than a sixth of Japan's (Table 11.7). This was especially true of French colonial primary school enrolment rates (Indochina 2.8),[35] but also Dutch colonial rates (Indonesia 7.0), and British colonial rates (Burma and Malaya 9.6). Enrolment rates were low even in Korea (6.3) and Taiwan (11.8). But they rose very steeply to 1935–40 as a result of Japanese colonial policy (38.7 in Korea and 87.3 in Taiwan).

Perhaps influenced by both American and Japanese pro-schooling colonial policies, primary school enrolment rates rose dramatically everywhere in colonial Southeast Asia up to the Second World War. Indeed, there was even impressive convergence on Asia's industrial leader, Japan (Table 11.7). Between 1910 and 1940, primary school enrolment rates rose from 1.7 to 17.9 per cent of Japan's in Indochina, from 6.3 to 22 per cent in Indonesia, from 12.7 to 40.7 per cent in Malaya, from 48 to 74 per cent in the Philippines, and from 9.8 to 86.9 per cent in Thailand. While it takes some time for the schooling rates of children to convert an adult industrial labour force from illiterate to literate, the process was certainly well under way in the inter-war years. What about the industrial growth leader in Southeast Asia? The primary school enrolment rate in the Philippines was 44.8 in 1935–40, at a time when Japan's was 60.5, so that the Philippines was already at 74 per cent of the Asian schooling leader. But the Philippines was not alone: late 1930s primary school enrolment rates were even higher in Thailand (Table 11.7: 52.6), having risen steeply from 1920.[36]

Enrolment rates could be misleading if official statistics do not record the number of children attending informal schools supported by private initiative (e.g. religious institutions) or by village authorities.[37] Similar to Meijii Japan, Buddhist temple schools in Thailand and Cambodia were reformed in the early twentieth century to offer a more comprehensive curriculum (Sopheak and Clayton, 2007). But it was only with the establishment of public schools that most Thai girls gained access to primary education. In all Southeast Asian cities, Chinese communities established privately funded primary schools for boys and girls. The fact that pro-school policies emerged in the inter-war period as part of the core political programme of the only Southeast Asian country that had remained independent, Thailand, says something about the lack of such policies in most of

---

[35] Share of school-aged children enrolled.

[36] Using age heaping as a numeracy index, Crayen and Baten (2010) find that late-nineteenth- and early-twentieth-century Southeast Asian levels were not too far below those of Northwest Europe, North America, and Northeast Asia, and well above those of South Asia. However, differences in numeracy across Southeast Asia do not correlate well with school enrolment in the early twentieth century.

[37] The return of an official survey on illiteracy undertaken in 1938 in two districts of central Vietnam, regarded by the authorities as representative, indicates that the percentages of boys between 10 and 20 able to read Romanized Vietnamese were 55 in one district and 22 in the other (22 and 18 per cent were able to read French); while the percentages of girls able to read Romanized Vietnamese were 60 and 28. The percentages were lower at higher ages, for both men and women, but around 30 per cent of men aged 51 to 60 were able to read Vietnamese in Chinese characters (Trinh, 1995, pp. 36–7).

Table 11.8. Average years of schooling aged 25–64, 1960–2010

	Years of schooling			Japan = 100		
	1960	1970	2010	1960	1970	2010
Korea	3.552	5.710	13.324	41.3	58.1	101.1
Japan	8.598	9.829	13.181	100.0	100.0	100.0
Burma	1.349	1.118	5.182	15.7	11.4	39.3
Indonesia	1.148	2.367	7.864	13.4	24.1	59.7
Malaysia	2.043	3.126	9.400	23.8	31.8	71.3
Philippines	3.744	4.727	10.030	43.5	48.1	76.1
Thailand	2.219	2.731	8.516	25.8	27.8	64.6

Source: Data underlying Cohen and Soto (2007, in electronic appendix cls-database).

colonial Southeast Asia until the 1930s. Primary schools played a major role in the nation-building agenda of all post-colonial Southeast Asian countries after 1945.[38]

With a lag of a couple of decades behind primary school enrolment rates, secondary school enrolment rates rose steeply in Southeast Asia after 1940. By 1970 and the start of modern 'miracle' growth, secondary school enrolment rates were 53 per cent of Japan in Malaysia and almost 48 per cent in the Philippines. By 1960, there is enough demographic and schooling data to say something about the average years of schooling achieved by adults aged 25–64 (a stock), not just the enrolment rates of children (a flow). That there was a revolutionary increase in Third World schooling after 1900 is well documented (Easterlin, 1981; Go and Lindert, 2010). That the revolution really took off in the periphery between 1960 and 1980 is also well documented (Schultz, 1987; Williamson 1993, pp. 147–52). Table 11.8 documents just how dramatic it was in Southeast Asia. Taking the Asian industrial leader, Japan, as our standard, between 1960 and 2010 average years of schooling of adults 25–64 rose from 15.7 to 39.3 per cent of Japan in Burma, from 13.4 to 59.7 in Indonesia, from 23.8 to 71.3 in Malaysia, from 43.5 to 76.1 in the Philippines, and from 25.8 to 64.6 in Thailand.

By the end of the 1960s, most of Southeast Asia was well endowed with educated labour ready for other forces to trigger an industrial 'miracle'. To the extent that schooling is a prime mover of modern industrial growth, Southeast Asia was under-equipped for it before the Second World War. But school enrolment rates were on the rise during the inter-war decades, and took off in the post-Second World War era up to 1970. The Southeast Asian schooling constraint was loosened in the 1920s and 1930s, and broken after 1950. However, the growth of schooling was not sufficient by itself to promote rapid manufacturing development.

ISI became explicit policy in Southeast Asia only in the 1950s, but it had two precedents. The first occurred in the inter-war period as Chinese entrepreneurs

[38] Thailand offers a post-war puzzle, since enrolment rates fell from 1935–40 to 1960–1, but they rose everywhere else in Southeast Asia. True, the rise in the Philippines was modest, but it was already at a relatively high level.

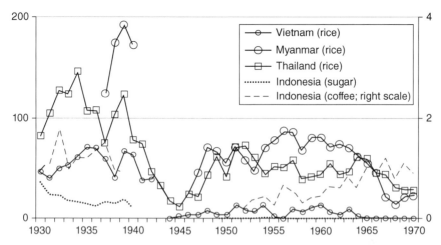

Fig. 11.3. Exports of main agricultural products (kg per capita) between 1930 and 1970
Sources: Mitchell (1995) for export volumes; Maddison (2010) for population, except Vietnam 1930–49 from Banens (2000).

established workshops in Southeast Asia using imported Chinese technology, Chinese skilled workers, and native unskilled labour for producing goods such as affordable chinaware or fireworks that were directly competing with imports from China. As we have seen, manufacturing received some stimulus by the switch to a less anti-industrial colonial policy in the 1930s. The second precedent occurred during the Second World War when, during Japanese occupation, Southeast Asia improvised a response to the disappearance of European and North American manufactured imports, and to the inability or unwillingness of Japan to fill the gap. Indeed, it was Japanese imperial policy to make Southeast Asia self-sufficient (Huff and Shinobu, 2013). Although these policies were introduced as an emergency response to exceptional conditions, they paved the way for the more formal post-independence policies introduced under post-war ISI.

ISI has been viewed as a response to the newly independent governments' desire to jump-start modern industrial growth.[39] But in Southeast Asia, it had another stimulant, the secular decline of commodity processing. Given the absence of adequate manufacturing data before the late 1950s, the decline cannot be measured directly, but it can be inferred by using export data. Fig. 11.3 shows the volume of some of the main commodities exported between 1930 and 1970 relative to total population (kg per capita). Rice exports from Myanmar, Thailand, and Vietnam, as well as coffee and sugar exports from Indonesia, peaked in the inter-war years. Since so much of Southeast Asian manufacturing was based on commodity processing, manufacturing faltered thereafter. Even with an expanding well-educated and

---

[39] Comprehensive discussions of ISI can be found in Chapter 10 on India and Chapter 13 on South America.

cheap workforce, Southeast Asian manufacturing found it impossible to compete with Japanese textiles and other consumer goods without protective barriers in the 1950s and 1960s.[40] ISI under tariff protection seemed to be the only option to enhance the profitability of domestic manufacturing in Southeast Asia. The ISI strategy had some success, at least in the short run: cotton yarn output per capita grew briskly between 1950 and 1970, as did electricity output per capita.

11.5 ECONOMIC MIRACLES: CHEAP SCHOOLED LABOUR, TECHNOLOGICAL TRANSFER, AND TRADE LIBERALIZATION

Southeast Asian per capita incomes diverged dramatically from the 1960s to the 1990s as a result of the successful industrial drive of Indonesia, Malaysia, Singapore, and Thailand (ASEAN 4) versus the disappointing performances of the Philippines and the stagnation of war-torn Cambodia, Laos, Myanmar, and Vietnam. The successes were celebrated as the Southeast Asian part of the Asian economic miracle when the World Bank (1993) compared the ASEAN 4 with South Korea and Taiwan, highlighting the importance of export-led industrial growth. However, the World Bank overlooked the divergence in per capita incomes across the region, illustrated best by Thailand (the biggest winner) and the Philippines (one of the biggest losers). In 1960, per capita GDP in Malaysia and the Philippines was 50 per cent higher than in Indonesia and Thailand (Maddison, 2010). By 1990, Thailand had a per capita GDP twice as high as the Philippines, and the income gap between Malaysia and Indonesia increased from 50 to 100 per cent.[41]

In confronting the causes of this uneven performance, we first consider shares of manufactured goods in total exports and then the stock of foreign direct investment (FDI) relative to GDP. Fig. 11.4 shows that Malaysia and Thailand followed the same upward trend in their shares of manufactured goods in total exports between the 1960s and the 1990s, both catching up with Singapore. Of course, these trends also imply a dramatic decline in commodity export dependence. And the relatively low percentages until the 1970s are consistent with the gradual transition from slow ISI to fast export-led industrialization reported in the previous section. Indonesia underwent a comparable trend but with a lag of almost 20 years, largely due to the Dutch Disease impact of its oil boom, and thus stagnation in its share of manufactured goods in total exports at very low levels until the late 1980s. Vietnam was later still, but its delayed trend was just as dramatic.

[40] The fact that the yen–US$ exchange rate was fixed at a yen-depreciated level helped Japanese producers maintain strong price competitiveness until the 1960s, in addition to non-price competitiveness resulting from the increasing sophistication of their production process.

[41] Within-country regional inequality also increased in Southeast Asia, as manufacturing was concentrated in urban areas where agglomeration economies could be exploited. See Chua et al. (2014, Table 2).

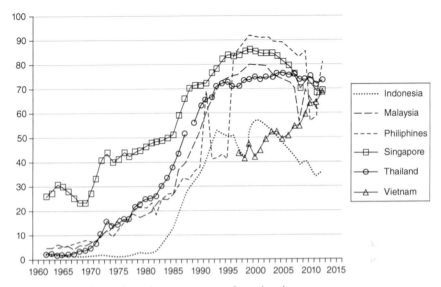

Fig. 11.4. Manufactured goods as percentage of merchandise exports

Note: Manufactures comprise commodities in SITC sections 5 (chemicals), 6 (basic manufactures), 7 (machinery and transport equipment), and 8 (miscellaneous manufactured goods), excluding division 68 (non-ferrous metals). *Source*: World Bank (World Development Indicators website, accessed 9 May 2015).

In order to exploit modern manufacturing technologies, market size is, of course, crucial. Southeast Asian domestic markets were very small in the inter-war years, and they could not compete with cheap Japanese consumer goods even in their own markets, let alone in world markets. Small domestic market size placed Southeast Asia at a disadvantage until the late ISI years. We use GDP as our proxy for domestic market size (Maddison, 2010). No doubt it might be a better proxy if GDP were interacted with urbanization—since most of the demand for local manufactures was generated by urban incomes—but it serves adequately enough to indicate the disadvantage. The proxy confirms that, with the exception of Indonesia, every Southeast Asian country had tiny domestic markets, much smaller than Japan, Brazil, Russia, and other countries which were catching up leaders in their regions before the Second World War. In 1929, domestic markets in Burma, Malaya, the Philippines, and Thailand ranged between about 6 to 14 per cent of Japan's domestic market. The market sizes of China, India, and Japan were eleven to twenty-four times larger than the average of the four Southeast Asian countries just listed, Russia was twenty times larger, and Brazil was more than three times larger. Indonesia was bigger and suffered a smaller scale disadvantage, but its domestic market was still only an eighth of the Russian domestic market. Given small domestic markets at the start, going open would have had a bigger impact on small Southeast Asian nations than on large emerging industrial nations, like Brazil or India.

Since every Southeast Asian country benefited from Japanese, US, and, to a lesser extent, European market access, the delayed expansion of manufacturing in Indonesia and the poor performance of the Philippines calls for alternative

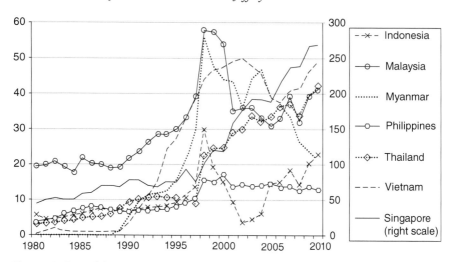

Fig. 11.5. Inward foreign investment stock as percentage of GDP
Source: UNCTAD (http://unctadstat.unctad.org/wds/TableViewer/tableView.aspx).

explanations. Indonesia presented unattractive features, in particular some of the most extreme forms of crony capitalism, and a chronic waste of financial resources due to over-investment in poorly managed state-owned enterprises during the oil booms (Robison, 1992). But the deregulation of investment barriers in the 1980s resulted in a rapid rise in the share of manufacturing in GDP.[42] Analysts have offered many explanations of the poor Philippine performance. One paper has described its experience as a 'perfect storm' of economic disasters, including: political instability, overlong protection, corruption, immigrant-remittance-in-duced Dutch Disease, and the rejection of all things Japanese, including their FDI (de Dios and Williamson, 2015). Indeed, all of these forces resulted in only a trickle of foreign capital into the Philippines.

These capital inflows were mostly FDI since international portfolio investment only became a significant source of financing for local investors in the 1990s (with the exception of Singapore). The stock of inward FDI accounted for a small and only slightly increasing percentage of GDP in Indonesia, the Philippines, and Thailand up to the late 1990s (Fig. 11.5). Singapore and Malaysia had the highest FDI stock to GDP ratios before the 1990s. Although there are no sector break-downs available, it seems likely that the high levels for Singapore were partly due to previous investments in finance and other services there. The high levels for Malaysia were mostly due to mining. We stress FDI since economists long ago reached the conclusion that this form of foreign investment is a carrier of technology, organizational efficiency, and managerial skills. This conclusion is confirmed by a recent econometric study of the region:

[42] This evolution can be compared with India's resulting from deregulation policy in the 1980s, discussed in Chapter 10 of this volume.

[T]he East Asian FDI boom continues to benefit [Southeast Asia] . . . These benefits originated from having export-oriented industries with improved labor skills and technological transfers, productivity growth and economic efficiency [following] the massive investment inflows from Northeast Asian economies. (Phung, Coxhead, and Chang, 2015, p. 80)

Needless to say, the larger the gap between best-practice technology in rich countries and traditional technology in poor countries, the better the chance that FDI will trigger a manufacturing miracle. Productivity growth in Southeast Asian manufacturing resulted from the combined effects of human capital investment and technology imported through FDI. Indeed, some time ago Alwyn Young argued that:

once one accounts for the dramatic rise in factor inputs, one arrives at estimated total factor productivity growth rates that are closely approximated by the historical performance of many of the OECD and Latin American economies. (Young, 1995, p. 644)

Another possible explanation for the heterogeneity of Southeast Asian industrial performance might be demography. Developing countries going through the middle stage of their demographic transitions have increasing shares of young working age populations (Bloom and Williamson, 1998). This so-called demographic dividend played a major role in the development of East Asia (Krugman, 1994; Bloom and Williamson, 1998), and we argued above that it also hastened the schooling revolution that helped carry the miracles. However, its contribution in Southeast Asia has been more limited (Williamson, 2013) and it cannot account for the region's uneven industrial performance.[43]

We are persuaded that one of the most powerful explanations of the uneven Southeast Asian industrial performance lies with differences in access to modern technology imported through FDI. Southeast Asia received only modest volumes of FDI until the 1980s.[44] However, these early inflows had an important impact on the development of manufacturing using labour-intensive technology compatible with Southeast Asian endowments—that is, cheap human capital. Japanese FDI played a much bigger role than did US and European FDI, since the Japanese manufacturing technology of the 1950s and 1960s was less capital intensive. It was also becoming obsolete in Japan just when it was appropriate for Southeast Asia. It was characterized by low capital requirements, and high primary and secondary schooling requirements, and was well suited for high female workforce participation.

---

[43] Between 1965 and 1990, working age population grew faster than total population in Southeast Asia, although the difference was much lower than in East Asia; this resulted in higher investment in human capital, saving, and female labour force participation than in South Asia and the rest of the developing world (Bloom and Williamson, 1998).

[44] Due to their concentration in manufacturing, Japanese FDI flows had a major effect on ASEAN manufactures exports (Urata, 1993). Manufacturing accounted for 45 per cent of total Japanese FDI to ASEAN in the period 1951–89, compared to 35 per cent of the total for South Korea, Taiwan, and Hong Kong, and only 27 per cent for the world as a whole (Urata, 1993, Table 10.1, p. 280).

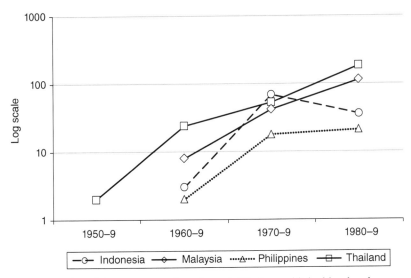

Fig. 11.6. Number of Japanese manufacturing subsidiaries established by decade
Source: compiled from individual data reported in Tōyō Keizai (2006), CD-ROM version.

Compared with South Korea, Southeast Asia was initially a second-best option for Japanese manufacturing firms,[45] but these countries became increasingly attractive as their comparatively cheaper workforce became almost as well equipped with primary schooling as in East Asia.

The flow of Japanese manufacturing FDI into Southeast Asia can be documented with company-level data reported in the annual Toyo Keizai survey. Fig. 11.6 indicates the total number of manufacturing subsidiaries established by decade. Thailand and Malaysia appear as the major recipients of Japanese manufacturing FDI, suggesting that these flows played an important role in contributing to their fast manufacturing growth. By contrast, the small number of Philippine subsidiaries indicates that it did not benefit much from Japanese technology transfer through FDI.

Available case studies illustrate a winning strategy based on the creation of joint ventures between local trading companies providing marketing know-how and foreign investors bringing modern (but labour-intensive) technology and organizational skills. In the case of Japanese FDI in Thailand, two of the most successful joint ventures of the early 1960s were the one linking Siam Motors with Nissan starting with an assembly plant in Bangkok in 1962, and the joint venture linking

---

[45] Perhaps mainly for political reasons, South Korea remained almost entirely closed to Japanese FDI up to the late 1990s, and the same remark applies to China until the 1980s. The economies of Taiwan, Hong Kong, and Singapore were too small to absorb the huge flows of outward Japanese FDI resulting from the rise in labour costs in Japan and the strategy of Japanese manufacturers to expand their activity overseas, particularly in lower-income countries. Southeast Asia benefited as a result.

the Sukree Group with Shikibo Spinning and Nomura Trading companies, starting with cotton spinning and weaving in 1963, and moving rapidly to synthetic yarns in 1968 (Suehiro, 1992, pp. 55–6). In addition to textile products, automobiles, and motorcycles, the list of production activities of these early Japanese subsidiaries also includes chemicals (cosmetics, plastics, rubber products, ink, and paint), and electric consumer durables (fans, radios, and TV sets). This suggests that the ISI experience with consumption goods production was an important precursor of subsequent export processing as it nurtured a generation of local entrepreneurs that gradually became accustomed to managing joint ventures with foreign partners, with a wide range of new manufacturing technologies. Furthermore, Southeast Asia had to leapfrog to comparatively capital-intensive export processing (chemicals, electric machinery, and transportation machinery) because Japanese manufacturers had previously located their most labour-intensive processing in Taiwan and Hong Kong, such as the assembly of toys, cheap watches, and low-quality garments. The first wave of FDI took advantage of local markets behind tariff and non-tariff barriers in Malaysia and Thailand. As these countries liberalized in the 1970s and 1980s, FDI rose substantially (Fig. 11.5). Indonesia was an important exception since it received comparatively little FDI, but nevertheless it experienced productivity gains and rising competitiveness in manufacturing (Amiti and Konings, 2007).

11.6 CONCLUSION: FACTOR ENDOWMENTS, SECOND-BEST INSTITUTIONS, FOREIGN MARKETS, AND GOOD LUCK

Resource-abundant and skill-scarce Southeast Asia has been a latecomer to modern manufacturing development. As long as nominal wages of skilled and unskilled workers were lower in resource-scarce and labour-abundant Japan or Korea, Southeast Asian manufacturing was limited to commodity export processing and some modest success with ISI-induced domestic manufacturing of consumer goods. The fundamental secular force at work seems to have been the evolution of this resource-abundant, labour-scarce, and skill-scarce region into a labour-abundant and skill-abundant region. But it also appears that Southeast Asia benefited from an extraordinary window of opportunity from the 1960s to early 1980s when China was entirely closed to foreign investment and unwilling to consider any kind of economic integration with the rest of Asia or the world. Indonesia, Malaysia, and Thailand were lucky that China was stubbornly engaged in an autarkic policy during these decades. Between the 1960s and the 1990s, rapid industrial growth occurred in much of Southeast Asia in spite of inadequate economic institutions. It is telling that when the World Bank 1993 *Economic Miracle* report assessed Japanese, Korean, and Taiwanese success, it highlighted the importance of sound institutional environments. Yet, abundant examples of corruption and crony capitalism could be found then even in the best Southeast Asian performers, like

282   *Jean-Pascal Bassino and Jeffrey G. Williamson*

Thailand and Malaysia (Suehiro, 1992, p. 50), let alone the Philippines (de Dios and Williamson, 2015). Southeast Asia did not undergo its industrialization drive because it had virtuous institutions but because public and private agents managed to play by some 'rules of the game' that can be described as second-best institutions (Rodrik, Subramanian, and Trebbi, 2004; Rodrik, 2008). An oil boom and some dysfunctional aspects of the Indonesian economy (Robison, 1992) were sufficient to delay the expansion of manufacturing there but not to prevent it, perhaps because other countries considered as potential targets for FDI had even worse institutions.

The fact that Vietnam joined the Southeast Asian manufacturing growth club in the 1990s, with Cambodia and Myanmar following in the 2000s, and all with labour costs lower than China and with comparable second-best institutions, suggests that the region retains a comparative advantage vis-à-vis Latin America, North Africa, the Middle East, Southern Asia, and Sub-Saharan Africa. These advantages were complemented by the gradual liberalization of trade policies, abundant and relatively cheap human capital, small gender gaps in education, high rates of labour force participation, and a willingness to participate in win–win regional cooperation. The impact of all of these factors was amplified by the ability to exploit FDI and the technology transfers it always carries.

REFERENCES

Amiti, M. and Konings, J. (2007). Trade liberalization, intermediate inputs and productivity: evidence from Indonesia. *American Economic Review* 97, 1611–38.

Bassino, J.-P. and van der Eng, P. (2013). The first East Asian economic miracle: wages, living standards, and foundations of modern economic growth (1880–1938). Unpublished paper.

Benarot, A. and Riddle, P. (1988). The expansion of primary education, 1870–1940: trends and issues. *Sociology of Education* 61, 191–210.

Bénétrix, A., O'Rourke, K. H. and Williamson, J. G. (2015). The spread of manufacturing to the poor periphery 1870–2007. *Open Economies Review* 26, 1–37.

Bils, M. and Klenow, P. J. (2000). Does schooling cause growth? *American Economic Review* 90, 1160–83.

Blattman, C., Hwang, J., and Williamson, J. G. (2007). The impact of the terms of trade on economic development in the periphery, 1870–1939: volatility and secular change. *Journal of Development Economics* 82, 156–79.

Bloom, D. and Williamson, J. G. (1998). Demographic transitions and economic miracles in emerging Asia. *World Bank Economic Review* 12, 419–55.

Boomgaard, P. (1991). The non-agricultural side of an agricultural economy: Java, 1500–1900. In *In the Shadow of Agriculture: Non-farm Activities in the Javanese Economy, Past and Present* (Eds, Alexande, P., Boomgaard, P., and White, B.). Amsterdam: Royal Tropical Institute, 14–40.

Booth, A. (1998). *The Indonesian Economy in the Nineteenth and Twentieth Century.* New York: St Martin's Press.

Booth, A. (2003). Four colonies and a kingdom: a comparison of fiscal, trade, and exchange rate policies in South East Asia in the 1930s. *Modern Asian Studies* 37, 429–60.

Booth, A. (2012). Measuring living standards in different colonial systems: some evidence from Southeast Asia, 1900–1942. *Modern Asian Studies* 46, 1–37.

Booth, A. (2015). A century of growth, crisis, war, and recovery, 1870–1970. In *Routledge Handbook of Southeast Asian Economics* (Ed., Coxhead, I.). London: Routledge, 43–59.

Booth, A. and Deng, K. (2014). Japanese colonialism in comparative perspective. Unpublished, SOAS.

Brenier, H. (1914). *Essai d'atlas statistique de l'Indochine.* Hanoi: IDEO.

Bronfenbrenner, M. (1960). A simplified Mahalanobis development model. *Economic Development and Cultural Change* 9, 45–51.

Chaudhary, L. (2009). Determinants of primary schooling in British India. *Journal of Economic History* 69, 269–302.

Chua, K. K., Limkin, L., Nye, J., and Williamson, J. G. (2014). Urban–rural income and wage gaps in the Philippines: measurement error, unequal endowments, and market failure. Unpublished paper, World Bank, Manila (May).

Clarence-Smith, W. G. (2005). Cotton textiles on the Indian Ocean periphery, c.1500–c.1850. Paper presented at the Global Economic History Network, Conference 8, Pune, India (18–20 December).

Cohen, D. and Soto, M. (2007). Growth and human capital: good data, good results. *Journal of Economic Growth* 12, 51–76.

Corden, W. M. (1984). Booming sector and Dutch Disease economics: survey and consolidation. *Oxford Economic Papers* 36, 359–80.

Corden, W. M. and Neary, J. P. (1982). Booming sector and de-industrialization in a small open economy. *Economic Journal* 92, 825–48.

Crayen, D. and Baten, J. (2010). Global trends in numeracy 1820–1949 and its implications. *Explorations in Economic History* 47, 82–99.

de Dios, E. and Williamson, J. G. (2015). Deviant behavior: a century of Philippine industrialization. In *Economics of Sustainable Development: Risk, Resources and Governance.* Honolulu: University of Hawaii Press, 372–99.

Domar, E. (1957). A Soviet model of growth. In *Essays in the Theory of Economic Growth.* New York: Oxford University Press, 223–61.

Easterlin, R. A. (1981). Why isn't the whole world developed? *Journal of Economic History* 41, 1–19.

Fatás, A. and Mihov, I. (2006). Policy volatility, institutions and economic growth. INSEAD, Singapore and Fontainebleau, France. Unpublished.

Frankema, E. and van Waijenburg, M. (2012). Structural impediments to African growth? New evidence from British African real wages, 1880–1965. *Journal of Economic History* 72, 895–926.

Frankema, E., Williamson, J. G., and Woltjer, P. (2015). An economic rationale for the African scramble: the commercial transition and the commodity price boom of 1845–1885. *National Bureau of Economic Research Working Paper* No. 212–13 (May).

Glewwe, P. and Kremer, M. (2006). Schools, teachers and education outcomes in developing countries. In *Handbook of the Economics of Education*, Vol. 2 (Eds, Hanushek, E. and Welch, F.). Amsterdam: Elsevier, 945–1017.

Go, S. and Lindert, P. H. (2010). The unequal lag in Latin American schooling since 1900: follow the money. *Revista de Historia Económica* 28, 375–405.

Gomez, F. and Pedro, A. (1992). The Philippines. In *Education and Culture in Industrializing Asia* (Eds, Wielemans, W. and Chan, P.). Leuven: Leuven University Press, 257–86.

Gourou, P. (1955). The peasants of the Tonkin Delta: a study of human geography. *Human Relations Area Files*, vol. 1, 111.

Gouvernement Général de l'Indochine. (1928). *Annuaire Economique de l'Indochine, 1926–1927*. Hanoi: Imprimerie d'Extrême Orient.

Hlaing, A. (1965). Trade and economic growth: a Burmese case. Ph.D. dissertation, University of London.

Hnatkovska, V. and Loayza, N. (2005). Volatility and growth. In *Managing Economic Volatility and Crises* (Eds, Aizenmann, J. and Pinto, B.). Cambridge: Cambridge University Press.

Hooley, R. (2005). American economic policy in the Philippines, 1902–1940: exploring a dark age in colonial statistics. *Journal of Asian Economics* 16, 464–88.

Huff, W. G. (2002). Boom-or-bust commodities and industrialization in pre-World War II Malaya. *Journal of Economic History* 62, 1074–115.

Huff, W. G. (2003). Monetization and financial development in Southeast Asia before the Second World War. *Economic History Review* 56, 300–45.

Huff, W. G. and Shinobu, M. (2013). Financing Japan's World War II occupation of Southeast Asia. *Journal of Economic History* 73, 937–77.

IGMI (Inspection Générale des Mines et de l'Industrie) (1943). Enquête sur l'artisanat indigène en 1938 (Hanoi: Gouvernement Général de L'Indochine, Bureau de l'artisanat). *Bulletin Economique de l'Indochine*, fasc.1, 46–63.

Jones, G., Ogawa, N., and Williamson, J. G. (Eds) (1993). *Human Resources and Development along the Asia Pacific Rim*. Oxford: Oxford University Press.

Krugman, P. (1994). The myth of Asia's miracle. *Foreign Affairs* 73, 62–78.

Landes, D. S. (1998). *The Wealth and Poverty of Nations: Why Some Are So Rich and Some So Poor*. New York: W. W. Norton.

Lee, J.-W. and Hong, K. (2010). Economic growth in Asia: determinants and prospects. *Asian Development Bank Working Paper Series* No. 220. Manila.

Legarda, B. J. (1999). *After the Galleons: Foreign Trade, Economic Change and Entrepreneurship in the Nineteenth-Century Philippines*. Madison, WI: University of Wisconsin Press.

Lindblad, J. T. (1997). Foreign investment in Southeast Asia in historical perspective. *Asian Economic Journal* 11, 61–80.

Loayza, N. V., Rancière, R., Servén, L., and Ventura, J. (2007). Macroeconomic volatility and welfare in developing countries: an introduction. *World Bank Economic Review* 21, 343–57.

McMillan, M. and Rodrik, D. (2011). Globalization, structural change, and productivity growth. *NBER Working Paper* No. 17143 (June).

Maddison, A. (2007). *World Population, GDP and Per Capita GDP, 1–2003* AD (August 2007 update), www.ggdc.net/Maddison.

Maddison, A. (2010). www.ggdc.net/maddison/Historical_Statistics/horizontal- file_02- 2010.xls.

Manuelli, R. E. and Seshadri, A. (2014). Human capital and the wealth of nations. *American Economic Review* 104, 2736–62.

Mitchell, B. R. (1995). *International Historical Statistics: Africa, Asia, and Oceania 1750–1988*. New York: Stockton.

Pangestu, M., Rahardja, S., and Ing, L. Y. (2015). Fifty years of trade policy in Indonesia: new world trade, old treatments. *Bulletin of Indonesian Economic Studies* 51, 239–61.

Phung, T., Coxhead, I., and Chang, L. (2015). Lucky countries? Internal and external sources of Southeast Asian growth since 1970. In *Handbook of Southeast Asian Development* (Ed., Coxhead, I.). Cheltenham, UK: Elgar, 60–86.

Poelhekke, S. and van der Ploeg, F. (2009). Volatility and the natural resource curse. *Oxford Economic Papers* 61, 727–60.

Radelet, S., Sachs, J. D., and Lee, J.-W. (2001). Determinants and prospects of economic growth in Asia. *International Economic Journal* 15, 1–29.

Resnick, S. A. (1970). The decline of rural industry under export expansion: a comparison among Burma, Philippines, and Thailand, 1870–1938. *Journal of Economic History* 30, 51–73.

Robison, R. (1992). Industrialization and the economic and political development of capital: the case of Indonesia. In *Southeast Asian Capitalists* (Ed., McVey, R.). Ithaca, NY: Cornell University Press), 65–88.

Rodrik, D. (2007). The real exchange rate and economic growth: theory and evidence. *Weatherhead Center for International Affairs Working Paper* No. 2008–0141, Harvard University.

Rodrik, D. (2008). Second-best institutions. *National Bureau of Economic Research Workng Paper* No. 14050. Cambridge, MA: http://www.nber.org/papers/w14050.

Rodrik, D., Subramanian, A., and Trebbi, F. (2004). Institutions rule: the primacy of institutions over geography and integration in economic development. *Journal of Economic Growth* 9, 1–165.

Schultz, T. P. (1987). School expenditures and enrollments, 1960–80: the effect of income prices, and population growth. In *Population Growth and Economic Development: Issues and Evidence* (Eds, Johnson, D. G. and Lee, R. D.). Madison, WI: University of Wisconsin Press), 413–76.

Shepherd, J. (1941). *Industry in South East Asia.* New York: Institute of Pacific Relations.

Sopheak, K. C. and Clayton, T. (2007). Schooling in Cambodia. In *Going to School in East Asia* (Ed., Postiglione, G. A.). Westport, CT: Greenwood Press, 41–60.

Suehiro, A. (1992). Capitalist development in postwar Thailand: commercial bankers, industrial elite, and agribusiness groups. In *Southeast Asian Capitalists* (Ed., McVey R.). Ithaca, NY: Cornell University Press, 35–63.

Tōyō Keizai (2006). Kaigai shushutsu kigyo soran 2005 [Operations of Japanese-controlled firms in overseas markets in 2005]. Tokyo: Tōyō Keizai Shinpōsha, CD-ROM edition.

Trinh, V.-T. (1995). *L'école française en Indochine.* Paris: Karthala.

Urata, S. (1993). Japanese foreign direct investment and its effect on foreign trade in Asia. In *Trade and Protectionism*, NBER-EASE, Vol. 2. Chicago, IL: University of Chicago Press, 273–304.

van der Eng, P. (1998). Exploring exploitation: the Netherlands and colonial Indonesia 1870 to 1940. *Revista de Historia Economica* 16, 291–321.

van der Eng, P. (2004). Productivity and comparative advantage in rice agriculture in Southeast Asia since 1870. *Asian Economic Journal* 18, 345–70.

van der Eng, P. (2007). De-industrialization and colonial rule: the cotton textile industry in Indonesia, 1820–1941. Unpublished, Australian National University, Canberra.

van der Eng, P. (2013). Why didn't colonial Indonesia have a competitive cotton textile industry? *Modern Asian Studies* 47, 1019–54.

Van der Kraan, A. (1996). Anglo-Dutch rivalry in the Java cotton trade, 1811–30. *Indonesia Circle* 68, 35–64.

Williamson, J. G. (1993). Human capital deepening, inequality, and demographic events along the Asia Pacific Rim. In *Human Resources and Development along the Asia Pacific*

Rim (Eds, Jones, G., Ogawa, N., and Williamson, J. G.). Oxford: Oxford University Press), 129–58.

Williamson, J. G. (2011). *Trade and Poverty: When the Third World Fell Behind.* Cambridge, MA: MIT Press.

Williamson, J. G. (2012). Commodity prices over two centuries: trends, volatility and impact. *Annual Review of Resource Economics* 4, 185–207.

Williamson, J. G. (2013). Demographic dividends revisited. *Asian Development Review* 30, 1–25.

World Bank (1993). *The East Asian Miracle: Economic Growth and Public Policy.* Washington, DC: Oxford University Press for the World Bank.

Young, A. (1995). The tyranny of numbers: confronting the statistical realities of the East Asian growth experience. *Quarterly Journal of Economics* 110, 641–80.

PART III

LATIN AMERICA

12

Industrialization and Growth in Peru and Mexico, 1870–2010

A Long-Term Assessment

Aurora Gómez-Galvarriato and Graciela Márquez Colín

12.1 INTRODUCTION

Mexico and Peru share a similar pre-colonial and colonial past, being the two largest pre-Hispanic civilizations in Latin America, and later the two wealthiest viceroyalties of Spain.[1] They both had a relatively substantial number of natives who survived contact with the European colonizers, similar extractive economic institutions, and great inequality. Both countries had a rich endowment of mineral resources, and their exploitation shaped early economic development. They also had a rugged geography that generated high transport costs, inhibited economic integration, and isolated a large part of the population that has historically been poorly integrated into the modern economy and has endured lower standards of living. Yet the economic connection between regions has been greater in Mexico as a result of less imposing geographical barriers, as well as the fact that the capital and largest metropolis lies in the centre of the country. In both countries, traditional and modern sectors co-existed, and despite significant efforts to diminish this duality, particularly in the twentieth century, it persists to the present.

Two significant differences between Peru and Mexico rest in the size of their markets. A territory five times bigger than Peru and a large border with the US poses different challenges and opportunities in shaping Mexico's manufacturing growth. Relative to Latin America as a whole, Mexico began to industrialize earlier, reaching higher levels of manufacturing GDP per capita and a greater share of manufacturing exports (see Figs 12.1 and 12.2). In contrast, Peru seems closer to the classic late-nineteenth-century commodity exporter and has followed the so-called primary-goods-exports model for a longer period. In this chapter we will assess the differences and similarities between the two countries with regard to their respective manufacturing development, and try to understand the reasons for these.

[1] We thank Jeff Williamson, Kevin O'Rourke, and the participants of the conference Industrialization in the Global Periphery 1870–2008 (Oxford University, 2–4 October 2014) for their comments. All remaining errors are ours.

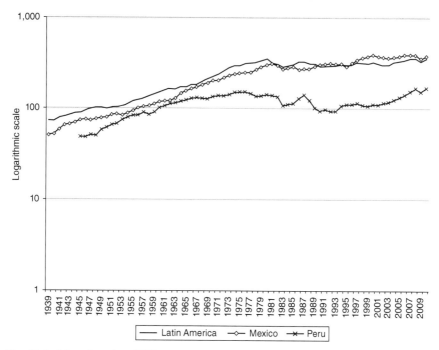

Fig. 12.1. Manufacturing GDP per capita
Source: See Appendix.

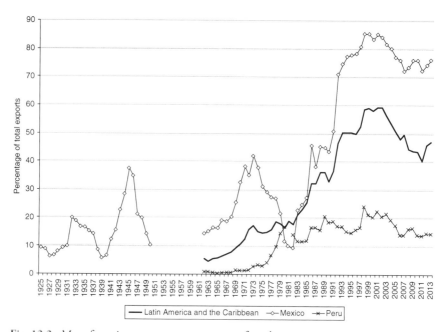

Fig. 12.2. Manufacturing exports as percentage of total exports
Source: See Appendix.

12.2 PERU AND MEXICO IN THE EXPORT-LED GROWTH ERA, 1880–1929

Mechanized manufacturing developed in Mexico exceptionally early relative to other countries in the periphery. Modern textile mills appeared in 1835, before any other country outside of Europe or British North America, except Egypt. Brazil, the other early industrializer in Latin America (see Chapter 13), established its first mills in the 1840s. Yet by 1853 it had only eight mills with 4,500 spindles, whereas ten years earlier, Mexico's textile manufacturing included fifty-nine mills with more than 100,000 spindles. Despite political turmoil and constant war during the nineteenth century, Mexico's textile manufacturing continued to grow and modernize. In 1879 domestic textile production claimed 60 per cent of the local market, which compares well with countries like India (35–45 per cent in 1887) and the Ottoman Empire (11–38 per cent in the 1870s), which had been important textile producers at the beginning of the nineteenth century. Mexico's cotton textile industry continued being the most important in Latin America until the 1920s when it was surpassed by Brazil (Gómez-Galvarriato, 2013, p. 15).

Manufacturing development emerged in other sectors as well. During the 1880s Mexico regained access to the international financial system after settling its foreign loans, in default since 1829. Political stability and institutional changes encouraged foreign investment that financed communications and transport infrastructure. All these factors promoted growth as well as an increasing integration of the national economy and of Mexico into world markets. Manufacturing grew at a faster rate, modernized, and diversified. Between 1892 and 1910 its production expanded at an average annual rate of 4.3 per cent, almost 50 per cent above total GDP growth (see Table 12.1).

The 1902 industrial census reported 6,234 manufacturing establishments with at least five workers each, spread throughout the country and predominantly powered by steam (Peñafiel, 1903, p. 99). Mexican manufacturing development between 1880 and 1930 went beyond export processing: by 1929 domestic manufacturing supplied almost two-thirds of consumer goods, more than one-third of intermediate goods, and more than one-fifth of capital goods (Cárdenas, 1987, p. 105).

Beginning in 1890, mineral processing increased as a result of the passing of the McKinley tariff in the United States, which imposed heavy duties on unrefined imports but exempted refined metals. In 1905 there were fifty-three metal foundries in Mexico, and in 1913 the country had forty-five of the 124 blast furnaces working in North America. The share of unprocessed raw minerals in total mining exports declined from 55 per cent in 1890 to 10 per cent in 1912, and to only 3 per cent in 1927. By this last year, 75 per cent of mineral exports were metallurgic products, such as bars, and 22 per cent were concentrated minerals. Apparently, the main reason why the metallurgic industry did not deepen further was the scarcity of coal, which was gradually surmounted at the beginning of the twentieth century (Kuntz, 2010, pp. 536–41). The founding of Mexico's first integrated iron and steel company in Monterrey in 1903, more than forty years before any other in

Table 12.1. Mexico: manufacturing indicators

Period	Total GDP	Manufacturing GDP	Manufacturing GDP/total GDP	Manufacturing exports/total exports
	Average yearly growth rate (per cent)		Average share (per cent)	
1870–90	–	1.3	–	–
1890–1913	2.9	4.3	10.7	–
1913–20	0.5	−1.9	–	–
1920–38	1.7	4.2	12.8	12.1
1920–9	1.7	4.5	11.3	7.9
1929–32	−6.8	−11.5	12.9	11.9
1932–8	6.3	12.6	14.4	15.7
1938–50	6.1	7.8	17.2	18.3
1938–45	6.0	9.2	17.3	17.2
1945–50	6.3	5.9	17.2	23.0
1950–73	6.4	7.8	20.2	21.7
1973–90	3.7	4.0	21.5	30.0
1973–81	6.7	6.7	22.6	26.4
1981–90	1.1	1.7	20.5	31.2
1990–2010	2.7	2.5	25.5	75.7
1990–2000	3.5	4.4	20.1	73.5
2000–2010	1.9	0.5	30.5	78.6

Source: See Appendix: calculations made according to the following availability of data. GDP: 1895–1910, 1921–2010; manufacturing GDP: 1877, 1892–2010; manufacturing exports: 1925–50, 1962–2010.

Latin America, cannot be explained without taking into account the spill-over effects of metal processing in northern Mexico (Gómez-Galvarriato, 1997, p. 202).

In Peru, the extraordinary export earnings induced by the guano boom (1840–77) generated a boom-and-bust export dependence. The currency became chronically overvalued and its detrimental effects on domestic manufacturing were further aggravated by the adoption of radical free trade policies (Gootenberg, 1991, pp. 132–4). The War of the Pacific (1879–83) triggered a severe crisis, since Peru lost nitrate deposits that could have compensated guano's decline. There was practically no development of mechanized manufacturing other than sugar and ore processing until the late nineteenth century. Most of the modern textiles factories dated from the 1880s and they only operated 1,015 looms in 1902 (Thorp and Bertram, 1978, p. 123). From 1890 until the outbreak of the First World War, manufacturing grew at a yearly rate of 4.8 per cent, relatively high because of its low initial levels. Expansion continued after 1914 at a similar rate (4.3 per cent) and accelerated to 5.5 per cent between 1920 and 1929 (see Table 12.2 and Chapter 2).

Concentrated around Lima, sugar mills, tanneries, and flour mills, as well as soap, pasta, and textile factories were the only mechanized establishments besides ore processing. In 1905, the number of factories was estimated at 291, a figure that rose to 505 in 1918 and 572 in 1923. A cotton textiles output spurt is apparent in the growing share of the domestic market supplied locally, from 5 per cent in

Table 12.2. Peru: manufacturing indicators

Period	Total GDP	Manufacturing GDP	Manufacturing GDP/total GDP	Manufacturing exports
	Average yearly growth rate (per cent)		Average share (per cent)	
1870–90	−3.0	−3.8	11.6	–
1890–1913	4.5	4.8	11.6	–
1913–20	3.8	4.3	11.1	–
1920–38	3.9	3.6	11.1	–
1920–9	6.0	5.5	11.1	–
1929–32	−7.8	−8.5	10.9	–
1932–8	6.9	7.1	11.2	–
1938–50	3.1	5.0	12.4	–
1938–45	1.9	3.0	11.9	–
1950–73	5.4	7.3	15.5	1.1
1950–60	5.5	5.8	14.0	–
1960–8	5.7	8.7	15.4	0.7
1968–73	4.6	8.2	18.5	1.5
1973–90	0.7	−0.6	18.3	11.6
1973–81	3.7	1.8	19.2	7.7
1981–90	−1.9	−2.6	17.4	15.2
1990–2010	4.9	5.4	17.2	17.8
1990–2000	4.2	4.8	16.5	18.1
2000–10	5.7	6.0	17.9	17.8

1891 to 20 per cent in 1898, 40 per cent in 1902, and more than 50 per cent in 1930. Likewise, the share of consumer goods in total imports (excluding foodstuffs) declined from 58 per cent in 1891 to 29 per cent in 1930 (Thorp and Bertram, 1978, pp. 34, 119–20).

Mexico and Peru exhibited labour scarcity throughout the nineteenth and the early twentieth centuries: thus, modern industry in both countries faced relatively high wages. Although real wages in Mexico fell from the mid-eighteenth to the early twentieth centuries relative to Western European nations, they were well above those in China and Japan (Challú and Gómez-Galvarriato, 2015).[2] In 1911, for instance, daily earnings per worker in a similar textile mill were US$0.46 in Mexico and US$0.18 in Japan (Gómez-Galvarriato, 2013, p. 62). There are no similar studies for Peru, but we know that daily wages in the sugar industry were US$0.67 by 1915, and US$0.58 in 1924 (Hunt, 2011, p. 210). Moreover, during this period there was substantial immigration of Chinese and Japanese workers to Peru and, though less so, also to Mexico (Ota, 1997, pp. 108–9; Yamawaki, 2002, pp. 52–3). In short, relatively high real wages made it difficult for these economies to produce labour-intensive manufactured goods for export, as Japan did during this period. Technical and skilled workers were even scarcer in both countries

---

[2] Real wages are deflated by consumer price indexes. In order to compare competitiveness levels it would be better to deflate them by the price of manufactures, but unfortunately these are not available.

because of low educational levels, implying that virtually all technical employees were foreign. However, illiteracy rates declined in Mexico from 82 per cent in 1895 to 61.5 per cent in 1930, and in Peru from 76 per cent in 1900 to 63 per cent in 1930.

The 50 per cent fall in silver prices during the 1880s and 1890s fostered the development of manufacturing in both Mexico and Peru. As Figs 12.3 and 12.4 show, terms of trade fell in both countries during these decades, but more in Mexico since this metal represented half of Mexico's exports, and only around one-fifth of Peru's. Since Peru and Mexico were on the silver standard, and silver depreciation was not coupled with an increase in domestic prices, they enjoyed several years of currency undervaluation that encouraged manufacturing growth.[3] At the same time, cost-reducing technological changes in silver mining increased output and thus compensated for declining silver prices (Beatty, 2000). However, by the turn of the century international price volatility was overshadowing the benefits of silver depreciation, leading both countries to adopt the gold standard, Peru in 1897 and Mexico in 1905.

A further compensating effect of falling terms of trade came from the diversification of the export basket, which incorporated non-precious metals and tropical crops and, after 1910, petroleum. Therefore, manufacturing production associated with export processing continued its expansion. Peru experienced an earlier recovery of its terms of trade than Mexico, together with overlapping export cycles (copper and lead, sugar, wool, rubber, cotton, and petroleum) that provided the basis for the continuation of export-led growth into the 1910s and 1920s, and contributed to the reduction of economy-wide volatility.

Tariff protection complemented the effect of a depreciating currency on local producers. As in other Latin American countries, between 1890 and 1913 Peruvian and Mexican tariff levels ranked among the highest in the world (above 30 per cent: Coatsworth and Williamson, 2004). Although the average nominal tariff declined in the late nineteenth century, Mexican policy-makers increased import duties selectively to promote manufacturing production by means of a cascading tariff structure (Márquez, 1998). In contrast, in the early 1900s booming cotton prices and a strong agricultural lobby led to a reduction in Peruvian tariffs. Between 1893 and 1903 the average tariff level declined from 39 per cent to 23 per cent (Bardella, 1989, pp. 149–51).

For Mexico, the impact of the First World War is difficult to separate from that of the Mexican Revolution (1910–20). Oil and sisal production grew significantly in response to increasing wartime demand, but manufacturing production dwindled as a result of the dislocation of the transport, monetary, and financial systems induced by the revolution. In spite of all these difficulties, Mexico was able to export some iron and steel products to the United States and even to Japan. Still, internal turmoil made it difficult for the manufacturing sector to take advantage of

[3] A similar phenomenon to that found for several developing countries between 1950 and 2004 (Rodrik, 2007).

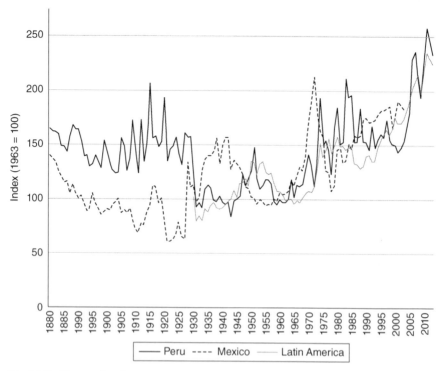

Fig. 12.3. Terms of trade
Source: See Appendix.

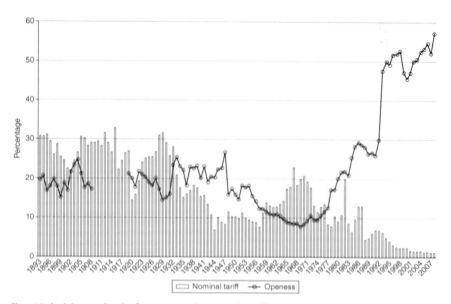

Fig. 12.4. Mexico: level of openess and nominal tariff rates
Source: See Appendix.

First World War demand. Instead, manufacturing production declined by 1.9 per cent yearly between 1913 and 1920.

The export booms during the First World War contributed to the strengthening of the Peruvian pound and it therefore appreciated substantially when the authorities set the gold parity before the end of the war (Pastor, 2012, p. 9). While export-processing products benefited from the export bonanza (in 1918 industrial exports represented almost one-third of total exports and half of total industrial production), the difficulties facing import-competing sectors reduced manufacturing growth to 4.3 per cent yearly between 1913 and 1920.

During the 1920s, Mexican manufacturing recovered the production levels of the 1900s, increasing at an annual rate of 5 per cent, well above GDP growth (see Table 12.1). However, it fell behind other Latin American nations, since foreign and domestic investment fell, and labour costs increased. Moreover, the cascading structure of protection faded away as workers, merchants, and industrialists lobbied in favour of their interests while the government was keen to fulfil their demands (Márquez, 2007, pp. 389–96). Nonetheless, the depreciation of the real exchange rate by 36 per cent between 1920 and 1929 fostered domestic manufacturing.

Peruvian manufacturing accelerated its rate of growth during the 1920s, growing annually at 5.5 per cent. The processing of exports together with an ambitious public works programme, financed through foreign lending, fed the demand for consumer and intermediate goods (Caravedo, 1976, pp. 38–44). Local and foreign investors established new ventures or expanded existing ones to supply this rising demand with locally produced manufactures that the tariff reform of 1923 sought to protect. At the onset of the world depression, manufacturing in Peru was closely linked to the export sector. Only in few instances, usually when exchange rate or tariff policies favoured it, did it spread to import-competing sectors.

12.3 1929–73: FROM EXPORT-LED GROWTH TO ISI

The Great Depression marked the end of the first era of globalization. Latin American countries were strongly hit by a collapse in the demand for their exports and suffered from the interruption of external capital flows and foreign direct investment (FDI). In order to seek a way out of the crisis, governments widened their participation in the economy. The falling trend in the terms of trade contributed to a yearly decline of GDP between 1929 and 1932 of 6.8 per cent in Mexico and of 7.8 per cent in Peru (see Fig. 12.3 and Tables 12.1 and 12.2). However, a diversified export basket and the stabilization of the terms of trade after 1932 guaranteed a swift recovery. Between 1932 and 1938 annual average GDP growth surpassed 5 per cent in both countries and that of manufacturing reached 7.1 per cent in Peru and 12.6 per cent in Mexico. The exchange rate policies adopted in the midst of the world depression (abandonment of the gold standard and large devaluations) not only alleviated the balance-of-payments crisis but also stimulated manufacturing growth (Díaz Alejandro and Seibert, 1979, p. 150).

The Mexican government followed moderately expansionist economic policies, mostly through investment projects in infrastructure, which complemented private investment and increased productivity. Between 1929 and 1939 more than half of the manufacturing growth can be explained by the rise of domestic demand, 37 per cent by the substitution of imports, and only 4 per cent by an increase in foreign demand (Cárdenas, 1987, pp. 112, 248). The share of consumer non-durables imported fell from 18 to less than 7 per cent, whereas the share of consumer durables and intermediate goods imported declined from 82 to 66 per cent and from 64 to 53 per cent, respectively. In contrast, the share of capital goods imported increased from 79 to 84 per cent, as a consequence of the demand of the growing manufacturing sector (Cárdenas, 1987, pp. 112, 116).

In Peru, the rapid recovery of export earnings increased aggregate demand by themselves, so the government did not need to carry out expansionist fiscal policies (Thorp and Bertram, 1978, pp. 184–5). The share of industrial goods in total imports declined from almost 50 per cent in 1933 to 36 per cent six years later, while most manufacturing growth focused on consumer goods. The market share of locally produced cotton textiles increased from 55 to 60 per cent, and that of cement went from 46 to 87 per cent, between 1930 and 1940 (Caravedo, 1976, p. 43; Thorp and Bertram, 1978, pp. 192–3).

The Second World War was another major external shock for Latin America, disrupting trade and financial flows. The shortage of manufactured goods fostered import substitution. Although Peru's terms of trade increased slightly between 1938 and 1945, its exports declined, and annual GDP growth slowed to 1.9 per cent. Manufacturing output growth reached an annual rate of 3 per cent, but was seriously limited by difficulties in importing capital and intermediate goods and the size of the market. Taking advantage of the high-quality cotton grown in the country, the domestic production of cotton textiles increased as a percentage of total consumption from 60 to 93 per cent (Thorp, 1979, p. 193).

Thanks to its proximity to the United States and the signing of a commercial treaty in 1942, the war offered Mexico the possibility of exporting manufactures. These increased their share in total exports from 8.6 per cent in 1938 to 38 per cent in 1945, despite the overvaluation of the peso (see Fig. 12.2), explaining more than three-quarters of manufacturing growth. Textiles drove most of this rise, representing around 60 per cent of manufactured exports and 15 per cent of total exports.

The good performance of the manufacturing sector was also facilitated by an increase in public investment, which grew at an annual rate of 15 per cent, financed by rising foreign trade revenues (Cárdenas, 2003, pp. 250–3). When the Second World War ended, the favourable conditions for Mexican manufacturing exports also ended, and the balance of payments worsened. In order to cope with the external deficit, in 1947 Mexico terminated the commercial treaty with the United States and raised trade barriers. As a consequence, the degree of openness (the sum of exports and imports relative to GDP) started a long decline, from a level of 27 to 8.4 per cent at its nadir in 1972 (see Fig. 12.4). These measures marked the entrance of Mexico into the protectionist 'inward-looking' import-substituting industrialization (ISI) club, in which it remained during the following three decades. The sharp increase in protectionism stimulated manufacturing growth, further reinforced by devaluations in 1949 and 1954.

Between 1950 and 1973, Mexico witnessed an annual growth of manufacturing output of 7.8 per cent, catching up with the fastest-growing countries in Latin America and increasing the manufacturing share of GDP from 17.9 to 23.2 per cent (see Fig. 12.1 and Table 12.1). Most of this expansion resulted from import substitution based on protectionist policies. In order to jump over the protectionist barrier, several multinationals established Mexican plants to produce appliances and cars. In addition, the government invested heavily in infrastructure, and widened the access to credit of manufacturing firms through development banks. In the early 1960s the government imposed a 49 per cent foreign ownership limit on new FDI in order to 'mexicanize' industry (Cárdenas, 2003, p. 255).

The fixed exchange rate policy followed by the Mexican authorities provoked a repetition of the devaluation–appreciation–devaluation cycle in 1948 and 1954 (and later in 1976). In each of these episodes the (temporary) stimulus to the manufacturing sector emerged only as a by-product of an exchange rate policy designed to correct trade deficits, but expansionary fiscal and monetary policies did not allow the undervaluation to persist. By 1960 the substitution of consumer goods was practically complete, so ISI policy focused on the substitution of intermediate and capital goods. Between 1950 and 1970 the share of intermediate products in total manufactures increased from 17.6 per cent to 29.2 per cent, and that of capital goods rose from 8.5 per cent to 17.6 per cent (see Table 12.3). These industries were generally less labour intensive, required a larger scale and thus a larger market, and demanded more imported inputs. The promotion of these types of industries often implied the establishment of state-owned enterprises as well as a less competitive economic structure that generated an increasing foreign trade deficit, and provided fewer jobs.

In order to cope with increasing trade deficits, in 1961 the Mexican government began a systematic export promotion policy, earlier than other Latin American nations. In 1962 it financed and promoted export-manufacturing through a financial trust (FOMEX) and specialized offices abroad (Bancomext, 1987, p. 235). Then in

Table 12.3. Mexico and Peru: manufacturing structure, 1929–2010

Mexico Sector	1929	1939	1940	1950	1960	1970	1980	1990	2000
Consumption goods	83%	79%	74%	61%	53%	53%	52%	39%	40%
Intermediate goods	15%	15%	18%	25%	29%	29%	30%	29%	29%
Capital goods	2%	6%	9%	14%	18%	18%	17%	32%	32%

Peru Sector				1995	1960	1970	1980	1998	2008
Consumption goods	–	–	–	59%	63%	60%	49%	53%	50%
Intermediate goods	–	–	–	39%	33%	33%	40%	38%	41%
Capital goods	–	–	–	3%	5%	7%	11%	8%	9%

Source: See Appendix.

1965 Mexico established the Border Industrialization Programme, meant to provide jobs to workers unemployed as a result of the end of the *bracero* programme (negotiated in 1942). In-bond assembly plants, known as *maquiladoras*, benefited from duty exemptions on inputs and machinery as long as they exported all output, while the US government granted privileged access to its market. Unlike other firms in Mexico, maquiladoras could be 100 per cent foreign owned. Initially, they were required to locate within 20 miles of an international border or coastline, but in 1972 the franchise extended to the rest of the country (Taylor Hansen, 2003, p. 1054). From 1965 to 1974 the number of maquiladoras soared from 12 to 455, and their employment went from 3,000 to 75,977 workers, most of them women (Martínez del Campo, 1985, pp. 273–6). Between 1970 and 1974, maquiladoras' value added increased yearly by 55 per cent, producing mostly electrical and electronic equipment, shoes, and apparel (ECLA, 1978, pp. 63–8).

The export promotion and maquiladora programmes proved fruitful as manufacturing performance in foreign markets improved considerably and expanded well above the rest of the economy. Between 1965 and 1974, non-maquiladora manufactured exports grew yearly by 18 per cent, with machinery, electrical, and transport equipment the fastest-growing industries, while maquiladora labour-intensive exports rose yearly by 36 per cent. By 1974, the share of manufactures (including those originated in maquiladoras) in total exports exceeded two-thirds. However, manufacturing exports did not alleviate trade imbalances, since other manufacturing sectors were intensive in imported inputs (ECLA, 1978, pp. 20–3).

In contrast to a firmly rooted ISI policy in Mexico, manufacturing development in Peru followed a different path characterized by the coexistence of export-led growth and milder industrial promotion policies up until the late 1950s. Thus, Peru remained an exceptionally open economy, as powerful export interests lobbied in favour of free trade (see Fig. 12.5). Another salient feature of the Peruvian economy was the implementation, from 1949, of a dual fluctuating exchange rate system, which avoided devaluation–appreciation–devaluation cycles. Remarkably, manufacturing in Peru achieved considerable progress, considering that the country never abandoned the export-led growth model and lagged behind the adoption of industrial promotion policies. An annual growth of 5.8 per cent between 1950 and 1960 increased the manufacturing share in GDP, reaching 14.2 per cent in 1961. One of the most successful endeavours was the development of the labour and resource intensive fishmeal industry, oriented primarily towards foreign markets and with strong linkages to the rest of local manufacturing (Bardella, 1989, pp. 436–42). Reinvestment of profits was the major financial source of domestic manufacturing, while the government-funded Banco Industrial granted loans primarily for the acquisition of machinery, equipment, and real estate. The welcoming attitude towards foreign investment was also crucial in the provision of funds supporting manufacturing growth.

Breaking with a long tradition of little intervention in the economy, in the late 1950s the Peruvian government implemented policies to foster manufacturing growth, which strengthened after the 1968 military coup (the so-called Peruvian Revolution) and extended up until 1975. Manufacturing growth rates between

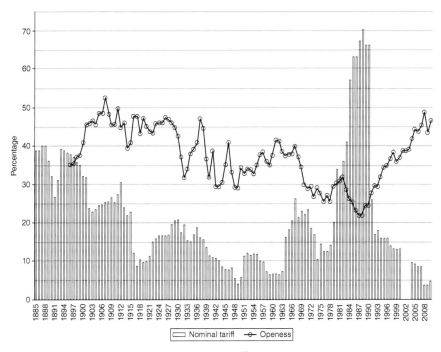

Fig. 12.5. Peru: level of openness and implicit tariff rates
Source: See Appendix.

1960 and 1968 reached 8.7 per cent, and between 1968 and 1973, 8.2 per cent annually (see Table 12.1). Manufacturing was stimulated by the devaluation of 1958, but this effect faded away with the adoption of a fixed exchange rate regime in 1960. The increasing appreciation of the currency ended with a large devaluation and the reintroduction of the dual exchange rate in 1968 (Pastor, 2012, p. 44).

The 1959 Industrial Act brought more lasting effects by implementing tax incentives, hikes in import duties on consumer goods, and reductions on inputs and capital goods. The 1970 Industrial Promotion Act reinforced the government's role in the economy by reserving exclusively to the state the production of cement, paper, basic chemicals, steel, fertilizers, and refined oil. Seeking to redistribute income and wealth in favour of wage earners and the rural poor, the government implemented land reform programmes and established cooperatives within private enterprises (Thorp, 1979, p. 114; Roca and Simabuko, 1999, p. 74).

The most dynamic sectors in Peru before 1970 were the inward-oriented assembly industries (cars and home appliances) as well as export-processing sectors, all of them with significant FDI presence. State-owned enterprises took the lead in the production of cement, steel, and fertilizers. Financing came primarily from the Banco Industrial, which supplied one-fourth of total credit to industry in 1960. The Inter-American Development Bank also played an important role financing medium and small enterprises, whereas American, Canadian, and German private banks funded the expansion of the fishmeal industry (ECLA, 1967, pp. 27–36).

Between 1968 and 1975 the military regime enhanced protectionism, controlled the main export commodities, imported industrial inputs and basic staples, and established more rigid labour regulations. Consumer goods accounted for more than 60 per cent of total output, and intermediate and capital goods together maintained their share below 40 per cent; chemicals, household durables, and vehicles were the more dynamic industries (Fitzgerald, 1979, pp. 262–3). In 1970, the share of semi-manufactured exports in total exports rose to 68.5 per cent, reflecting the boom in fishmeal exports, while the share of manufactured exports increased slightly to 1 per cent.

By the early 1970s the share of manufacturing in GDP had peaked in Mexico and Peru, at 23.2 per cent in 1973 and 21.1 per cent in 1974, respectively. However, serious constraints had been building up that would pose major challenges to manufacturing growth in the following decades. In both economies, the manufacturing sector reduced its capacity to absorb manpower, since the more dynamic industries (chemicals, non-durable goods) were capital intensive. Relatively high wages in Peru and Mexico reduced the competitiveness of manufactures in world markets. Wage increases were not driven by productivity growth but rather by increasingly powerful unions. Between 1958 and 1970, Mexican and Peruvian wages were on average around four times those in South Korea and Taiwan.[4] This wage gap also characterized Argentina, Brazil, Chile, Colombia, and Venezuela (Mahon, 1992, p. 254; Chapter 13 in this volume).

Educational levels did not keep up with those in Asian competitors either, nor did productivity. Literacy rates did improve steadily from the early twentieth century onwards, reaching 70.4 per cent in Peru and 76.3 per cent in Mexico in 1970, but the development of other technical skills proved less satisfactory. The average years of schooling in 1970, 3.7 in Peru and 2.9 in Mexico, were below the 3.9 average years in Latin America, let alone the 5.2 years in South Korea. Mexico retained a labour cost advantage relative to the United States, though: a study from the early 1960s indicates that the ratio of value added per worker to the wage in manufacturing was 4.08 in Mexico and 2.62 in the US. This study also shows that Mexico's manufacturing exports relied not only on cheaper labour but also on cheaper raw materials to compete internationally (Bancomext, 1965, p. 399).

Finally, growing fiscal and trade deficits were increasingly financed by external indebtedness, generating great macroeconomic vulnerability. During the 1960s Mexican foreign debt doubled relative to GDP, and by 1970 Mexico's foreign debt service represented 23.4 per cent of total exports (Cárdenas, 2003, p. 267). In Peru debt service payments soared from about 13 per cent of export receipts in 1968–72 to about 30 per cent by 1975–6 (Pastor, 2012, p. 53).

---

[4] For Mexico, the gap was largest in 1966, when its hourly wage was 0.5 dollars as compared with South Korea's 0.06 dollars and Taiwan's 0.11 dollars.

12.4 ECONOMIC CRISIS AND THE COLLAPSE OF ISI

The collapse of the Bretton Woods system together with the 1973 oil price shock caused uncertain financial conditions that gravely affected Latin America, because of higher energy costs, a recession in their export markets, volatile terms of trade, and excess liquidity abroad that greatly increased the availability of foreign lending.

In both countries, the combination of expansionary demand policies and rising energy costs accelerated inflation, appreciated the real exchange rate, and aggravated the trade deficit (see Tables 12.3 and 12.4). In Mexico, the discovery and exploitation of vast amounts of oil deposits fuelled economic growth for several years, but the government failed to implement appropriate demand management policies. Between 1973 and 1981 Mexico's terms of trade increased at an annual rate of 7.3 per cent and real GDP grew at 6.7 per cent, driven by oil exports (see Tables 12.1 and 12.3). Instead of sterilizing part of the oil bonanza, the government increased its expenditure from 13.4 per cent of GDP in 1972 to 31.6 per cent in 1982, mainly on non-tradables. More than half of public investment went to the oil sector, and very little was devoted to strengthening the production of agricultural or manufacturing tradable goods. Moreover, the growing overvaluation of the peso brought about a sharp rise in imports, mostly of capital and intermediate goods, which resulted in a huge current account deficit that reached 70 per cent of merchandise exports in 1982. Dutch Disease effects were exacerbated by a large increase in the external public debt that went from 10.2 per cent of GDP in 1973 to 32.7 per cent in 1982. Foreign borrowing brought about an even more severe stagnation of the non-oil tradable sector via an additional appreciation of the real exchange rate (Usui, 1997).

Manufacturing GDP grew at an annual rate of 6 per cent between 1973 and 1982, but the manufacturing share of GDP fell by 9 per cent. The Mexican economy did not 'petrolize', as happened in Venezuela, since oil production represented only between 10 per cent and 14 per cent of GDP in this period. However in 1981, oil represented two-thirds of total exports and 25 per cent of the government's revenue. In 1982, when oil prices declined and international interest rates increased, the situation became unsustainable and Mexico defaulted on its foreign debt, generating a financial crisis. GDP decreased by 0.5 per cent and manufacturing production by 2.9 per cent.

Peru faced severe economic difficulties even before the outbreak of the international debt crisis. After 1973, economic instability worsened the outlook for foreign investors, who were already alienated by the interventionist climate and expropriations. The rise of a new military government in 1975 shifted the economic strategy, with most extreme forms of government intervention in the economy being abandoned. The contraction of domestic demand resulting from the adjustment plans lowered manufacturing growth to 1.8 per cent between 1973 and 1981, but intermediate and capital goods slightly increased their share in total manufacturing production during this period (see Table 12.3).

The weaknesses of the Peruvian economy exacerbated as it entered into the 'lost decade' of Latin American development of the 1980s. A modest revival of FDI receded in the face of the nationalistic policies that reappeared in the second half of this decade. The country reached hyperinflation levels of 7,482 per cent in 1990 (see Table 12.2). Between 1981 and 1990 Peru's real GDP fell by 1.9 per cent per annum, while manufacturing GDP declined by 2.6 per cent annually.

Mounting economic and financial problems in the early 1980s masked significant increases of manufacturing exports throughout the 1970s and 1980s, taking advantage of regional integration efforts. In Peru, semi-manufactured exports' share in total exports declined from 68 to 40 per cent between 1970 and 1980, while that of manufactures increased from 1 to 15.6 per cent (ECLA, 1991, p. 119). In 1987, after several years of severe economic and financial troubles, semi-manufactures' and manufactures' contribution to total exports reached 61.4 per cent. The Andean Pact (later called Andean Community) allowed specialization and enlarged the market for mature Peruvian industries such as textiles.

Total factor productivity growth in Mexican manufacturing increased on average by 3.64 per cent per annum between 1963 and 1981. Its TFP growth during this period compares well with those of Japan, Korea, Turkey, and Yugoslavia (2.04, 3.71, 1.33, and 0.48 per cent per annum respectively: Samaniego, 1984, pp. 21–2). In the early 1970s, Mexican semi-manufactured and manufactured products amounted to 28.4 per cent and 27 per cent of total exports respectively. Together they comprised more than half of total exports (ECLA, 1991, p. 111). This experience in world markets is fundamental to better understanding the export boom that accompanied liberalization in Mexico and Peru during the last three decades.

12.5 LIBERALIZATION AND A NEW ERA OF EXPORT-LED GROWTH

Mexico and Peru liberalized their economies at a very fast rate, as part of the emergency economic policies meant to overcome their deep economic troubles. The main concern was to control inflation and to reduce their fiscal and trade deficits, and these objectives were placed above all others. Throughout the 1980s the manufacturing sector was severely hurt by skyrocketing interest rates, the abrupt opening up of the economy, and an overvalued exchange rate used to restrain inflation. Industrial policy was demonized, so few endeavours were carried out to strengthen domestic capabilities, and seek and develop areas of dynamic comparative advantage.

In Mexico, liberalization policies began in 1982 as a response to economic turmoil. Following a balance of payments crisis in 1982, the country eased restrictions on maquiladoras, which led to a large increase in export-processing trade with the United States. In 1985, Mexico broadened its opening to trade by joining the General Agreement on Trade and Tariffs (GATT), which entailed cutting tariffs across the board and eliminating non-tariff barriers. From 1983 to 1987 the percentage of goods that required import permits was reduced from

Table 12.4. Mexico: macroeconomic variables

Period	Terms of trade	Exports	Real exchange rate	Real wages	Prices	Openness	Tariff rate	Trade balance/GDP
	Average yearly growth rate (per cent)					Percentage		
1870–90	−4.4	8.5	−4.8	−1.7	3.0	–	–	–
1890–1913	−1.8	2.6	0.0	−0.3	2.6	19.4	28.1	2.7
1913–20	−4.0	16.5	−1.5	−1.0	0.0	0.0	25.4	0.0
1920–38	3.5	−4.9	4.0	14.5	−0.6	19.8	22.5	3.9
1920–9	3.9	−2.2	4.0	9.2	−2.9	20.0	24.0	2.9
1929–32	−16.0	−16.4	13.2	–	−4.4	16.8	28.7	3.1
1932–8	14.3	−2.6	−0.4	–	4.2	20.6	19.1	5.2
1938–50	0.9	0.6	0.6	−0.3	9.7	21.4	12.2	3.2
1938–45	0.5	0.2	−5.0	0.5	9.8	21.3	14.1	4.5
1945–50	1.3	−1.2	9.0	−1.2	9.8	21.4	10.0	1.3
1950–73	−1.4	4.1	−0.4	3.4	6.1	12.4	14.0	−2.2
1973–90	1.8	10.4	0.7	−1.7	47.7	18.5	10.3	0.6
1973–81	7.3	12.0	−6.5	−0.1	25.8	12.0	10.9	−2.4
1981–90	−2.9	9.0	7.6	−3.1	68.6	24.2	9.7	3.0
1990–2010	1.0	8.2	−0.6	1.4	11.3	45.2	3.2	−1.1
1990–2000	1.9	13.6	−2.5	1.2	17.6	40.0	4.4	−1.2
1990–2010	0.1	3.1	1.4	1.6	4.6	51.1	1.5	−1.0

Note: Calculations made according to the following availability of data. Terms of trade: 1870–2010; exports: 1880–2013; real exchange rate: 1886–1913, 1917–2010; tariff rate: 1893–2000, 2003–8; real wages: 1886–1913, 1917–29, 1939–2010; prices: 1886–1913, 1917–2010; openness, 1895–1910, 1921–2010; trade balance/GDP: 1895–1910, 1921–2010.

Sources: See Appendix.

100 per cent to 3.8 per cent, and the average nominal tariff declined from 27 to 10 per cent (see Table 12.1).

From 1984 the government gradually allowed the establishment of firms with majority or total foreign ownership, at first in some capital-intensive activities with a high export potential, and later in all productive activities (Moreno-Brid and Ros, 2010, pp. 775–6). The North American Free Trade Agreement (NAFTA), signed in 1994, consolidated and extended these reforms and tied them to reciprocal access to the US and Canadian markets. As Fig. 12.4 shows, the level of openness increased radically after the mid-1980s.

Between 1981 and 1987 manufacturing output declined at an annual rate of 0.4 per cent, ending a half-century of continuous expansion that had started in 1932. From 1982 to 1988 exports grew more than imports for the first time in several decades (see Table 12.4). In addition, the export mix changed dramatically with oil exports declining from 77.6 per cent of total exports in 1982 to 42.2 per cent in 1987, and the share of manufacturing exports increasing from 15.9 to 51 per cent. The growth in manufacturing exports was the result of the exploitation of underused installed capacity, the undervaluation of the exchange rate (that reached 37.7 per cent in 1987 relative to 1977), and a drop in real wages (see Table 12.5). While in 1982

Table 12.5. Peru: macroeconomic variables

Period	Terms of trade	Exports	Real exchange rate	Real wages	Prices	Openness	Tariff rate	Trade balance/GDP
	Yearly growth rate (per cent)					Percentage		
1870–90	−0.02	–	–	–	–	–	–	–
1890–1913	−0.86	7.7	−7.2	–	2.3	44.4	28.5	3.2
1913–20	5.40	1.8	10.3	–	11.4	44.7	14.9	9.8
1920–38	−3.77	5.3	11.4	–	−0.3	42.7	16.5	13.3
1920–29	−2.31	7.7	17.0	–	−0.4	45.6	15.8	0.1
1929–32	−14.90	−12.3	−22.7	–	−4.4	39.0	19.6	14.9
1932–8	0.04	11.8	24.1	0.2	1.3	39.4	16.7	17.3
1938–50	2.15	−1.3	−4.4	–	12.4	34.1	9.3	9.1
1938–45	0.39	−2.9	−21.0	–	8.0	34.6	11.2	12.1
1950–73	0.33	5.0	10.1	–	8.7	35.4	13.8	−2.5
1950–60	−2.25	7.5	11.7	–	8.2	35.2	9.5	−3.6
1960–8	1.66	6.5	−3.4	–	10.2	38.8	14.4	−2.2
1968–73	3.52	−2.1	31.9	–	9.0	31.1	20.9	0.002
1973–90	0.71	1.5	−3.3	−3.5	696.8	26.7	38.7	−0.9
1973–81	1.34	5.3	1.8	1.8	42.4	28.1	18.5	−3.0
1981–90	0.16	−1.8	−7.7	−11.2	1223.6	26.0	56.1	0.6
1990–2010	2.03	6.7	−1.2	−5.9	386.0	37.7	15.4	−0.2
1990–2000	−0.20	7.2	−0.3	−1.6	734.8	32.8	20.8	−3.3
2000–10	4.32	6.3	−2.1	−1.6	2.5	42.5	7.7	2.7

monthly wages in Mexico (US$327) were higher than in South Korea (US$277) and Singapore (US$306), by 1984 they had fallen to US$265, lower for the first time than in South Korea (US$304) and Singapore (US$306). By 1988 wages had declined further to less than US$100 (Villarreal, 2005, pp. 439, 471–4).

Maquiladora employment grew from 180,000, to 451,000 workers between 1984 and 1990, and to 1.3 million in 2000, over one-quarter of Mexico's total manufacturing labour force. Maquiladoras' real value added increased from $330 million pesos in 1990 to $1.5 billion in 2000. During the early 1990s maquiladoras generated more than half of manufacturing exports (Moreno-Brid and Ros, 2010, p. 780). These plants were concentrated along the Mexico–US border, which in 2002 accounted for 83 per cent of maquiladora employment (Hanson, 2002).

Before NAFTA, the US offshore assembly programme gave maquiladoras an advantage over integrated Mexican producers, since the importing firms were required to pay import duties only on the value added abroad. NAFTA apparently ended this special status for maquiladoras by giving all Mexican firms duty free access to the US market. However, new programmes were implemented to provide attractive fiscal and customs benefits to export manufacturing assembly firms.[5]

---

[5] After 2006 the programme was renamed Industria Maquiladora y Manufacturera de Exportación (IMMEX).

Since these programmes linked many of the benefits to the import of foreign inputs (such as exempting them from sales taxes), they generated a bias against the incorporation of domestic inputs.

After NAFTA, Mexico became increasingly linked to the United States: 76 per cent of Mexico's manufacturing exports went to the US in 1990 and 90 per cent in 2000 (Martínez, 2012, p. 24). Such concentration made Mexico very vulnerable to US economic cycles. During the 1990s low wages in Mexico were key to attracting multinational firms wishing to set up export assembly operations. Real wages fell during this decade, due in large part to a severe recession in 1995 (in which real GDP contracted by over 6 per cent in a single year). In 2000, wages in the United States were four or five times wages in Mexico (Hanson, 2002).

Perhaps one of the most salient impacts of liberalization was substantial FDI oriented towards export production. Manufacturing exports' share of total exports went from 44 to 83.5 per cent between 1990 and 2000 (see Fig. 12.2). Mexico's high-technology exports increased by 45 per cent during this decade, one of the highest growth rates in the world, and considerably faster than China's, which grew by 33 per cent (Lall, Albaldalejo, and Mesquita Moreira, 2004, p. 25). They surged in transport equipment and parts, and electrical and electronic equipment, precisely the same sectors that had grown faster in the 1970s (Martínez del Campo, 1985, pp. 262–3). Medium- and high-technology manufactured exports as a share of total manufacturing exports increased from 62 to 76 per cent between 1990 and 2000, whereas resource-based manufactures decreased from 24 per cent to only 7 per cent (Lall, Albaldalejo, and Mesquita Moreira, 2004, pp. 57–60). This contrasts with the rest of Latin America, for which medium- and high-technology manufactures represented only 36 per cent of manufactured exports in 2000. As a result, the share of capital goods in total manufacturing production increased from 17 per cent in 1990 to 32 per cent in 2000 (see Table 12.5). Although the Mexican export sector has been characterized as 'high technology', when it is analysed according to its locally generated value added it has specialized in relatively uncomplicated phases of assembly, distribution, and sales which are 'low technology' activities (Fujii and Cervantes, 2014, p. 10).

Total factor productivity and labour productivity in manufacturing practically stagnated between 1984 and 1987, increasing at the low annual rates of 0.8 per cent and 0.7 per cent respectively. Yet, between 1987 and 1990, as manufactures were increasingly destined for foreign markets, total factor productivity grew strongly, by 10.5 per cent annually (Brown and Domínguez, 1994, p. 284). However, it grew only by 1.2 per cent per annum between 1993 and 2000. Manufacturing industries varied widely as regards performance. Plant TFP fell by 4.3 per cent per annum in the apparel industry, but it rose in the machinery and equipment, computing equipment, and precision industries at annual rates of 5 per cent, 7.3 per cent, and 5.5 per cent respectively. Plant productivity in traded industries grew on average by 2 per cent per annum, while it stagnated in non-traded industries. Econometric analysis indicates that falling tariffs, an increase in the share of manufacturing industry participating in world markets, and increasing FDI flows to industry, explain productivity growth. However, the use of imported intermediate goods in the production process, which increased steadily from 28.5 per cent to 34.7 per cent of all non-wage costs of production during this period, had an adverse impact on productivity growth, particularly among foreign firms (López-Córdova, 2003, pp. 69, 80–5).

In Peru liberalization arrived later than in Mexico, but took place at an even faster rate. The disastrous economic experience of the 1980s paved the way to a radical opening-up of the economy and to market-oriented policies. Fujimori's government (1990–2000) implemented an extreme version of the so-called Washington Consensus. His government cancelled all previous industrial, labour, and income policy schemes, eliminated the main tax exemptions, reduced tariff protection, and lifted price controls, while financial, exchange, and trade regulations were liberalized. Job tenure was also eliminated and labour legislation was made more flexible, reducing union power. While real wages had been declining since 1974, between 1990 and 2000 they fell by 1.6 per cent annually (see Table 12.4). As in Mexico, Peruvian policy-makers advocated a radical government downsizing programme through privatization and lifted all restrictions on the inflow or outflow of foreign private capital (Roca and Simabuko, 1999, p. 74). In addition, the government reassured investors by bringing down inflation and carrying out policies to make foreign investment welcome once again. Consequently, investment and industrial production rose strongly.

Trade liberalization allowed manufactured imports to rise considerably through the first half of the 1990s, diminishing several lines of production such as automobiles, electrical equipment, and paper products. However, economic opening did not set back the industrial sector in an absolute sense. Rather, its output grew at annual rates of 5 per cent between 1990 and 2000 and 6 per cent between 2000 and 2010, the highest rates since 1950–73. Manufacturing growth was supported by relatively low real wages and higher investment rates. It took place mostly in resource-based sectors such as fishmeal, frozen seafood, sugar, jewellery, and zinc and copper metallurgy, but the apparel industry also saw important growth. Between 1990 and 2000 manufacturing value added increased at an annual rate of 3.6 per cent, and manufactured exports at 5.2 per cent yearly. The structure of manufactured exports remained unchanged during this period; around 70 per cent of Peruvian manufactured exports were resource based, while medium- and high-technology exports accounted for 5 per cent of manufactured exports (Lall, Albaldalejo, and Mesquita Moreira, 2004, pp. 57–8).

The spectacular rise of China's economic growth in the 2000s had a deep economic impact on the Mexican and Peruvian economies. China's growth generated a negative trade shock for manufacturing exporters and a positive shock for mining and agricultural exporters. According to Artuç, Lederman, and Rojas (2015), the net effect of China's foreign trade from 2001 to 2011 was to decrease Mexico's net manufacturing exports by 11 per cent, while it reduced those of Peru by only 2.5 per cent. At the same time, Chinese foreign trade expansion increased mining net exports by only 8 per cent in Mexico, but by 25 per cent in Peru, and agricultural net exports by 2 per cent in both countries. Argentina and Brazil, like Peru, also experienced a positive overall effect.

Mexico was one of the countries in Latin America hardest hit by Chinese economic growth, particularly after China's entrance to the WTO in 2001. More than in other Latin American countries, Mexico's export basket resembled that of China, particularly in those products where China was gaining market share. In contrast, Peru's economy was fostered by Chinese growth. During 2008–12 over a third of Peru's copper exports, 64 per cent of gold exports, and 22 per cent of other mineral commodities went to China. A correlation of 0.5 has been found between Peru's real GDP growth and China's investment growth during 1995–2012, transmitted mostly through its impact on Peru's terms of trade (IMF, 2014, pp. 53–6).

Mexico's manufacturing exports per capita grew by 15.3 per cent per annum between 1995 and 2000, slowing to 4.4 per cent from 2000 to 2010, which was still high by world standards. Yet, the growth of manufactured exports translated only modestly into overall economic growth. Mexico's GDP increased yearly by 3.5 per cent in the 1990s, and by only 1.9 per cent in the 2000s, making it one of the slowest-growing Latin American countries during this decade. While manufacturing production increased by 4.4 per cent during the 1990s, it almost stagnated in the 2000s, growing by only 0.5 per cent per annum during that decade (see Table 12.1). The slowdown was partly a result of the 2008 financial crisis that hit Mexico harder than other Latin American countries because of its high synchronization with the US economic cycle.

Mexico's slow growth can be partly explained by the low domestic value-added content in its manufacturing exports, and by the fact that most of the indirect domestic value added was concentrated in non-manufacturing sectors. The domestic value added in Mexico's manufacturing exports did not increase between 1995 and 2011. However, there is some hope that the domestic value-added content of Mexican exports might increase in the future, since the most dynamic export sectors, such as the automobile and aeronautic industries, also had a greater growth in terms of their domestic value added (Martínez, 2012, p. 49; Fujii and Cervantes, 2014, p. 6).

During the 2000s Peru became one of the fastest-growing economies in Latin America, reaching an annual GDP growth rate of 5.7 per cent. Once again, commodity exports were the driving force behind this economic performance. They increased at an annual rate of 7.2 per cent between 1990 and 2000, and at 6.3 per cent between 2000 and 2010 (see Tables 12.2 and 12.4). The terms of trade rose annually by 4.3 per cent in the latter period, driven by an increase in mining prices. In 2011 about 18 per cent of Peru's GDP came from the extraction and export of natural resources (IMF, 2014, p. 6). In contrast to Mexico, Peru's export markets were diversified: in 2013, 23.7 per cent of its exports went to the European Union, 17.6 per cent to the United States, 17.5 per cent to China, and 14.3 per cent to the Andean Community, Mercosur, and Chile (INEI, 2014). However, Peru's economic activity became increasingly vulnerable to a Chinese investment slowdown: in 2014 it was estimated that a one standard deviation decline in China's investment growth was likely to reduce Peru's real GDP growth by about 0.4 per cent (IMF, 2014, p. 62).

As in past export booms, manufactured exports were closely associated with primary products processing. By 2010, processed copper and fishmeal comprised 15 per cent of Peruvian total exports and labour-intensive knitted underwear exports 2.5 per cent. While the concentration in a handful of products was already a well-established pattern at least since the early 1960s, when fishmeal, sugar, and processed copper were the only manufactures listed amongst Peru's ten major exports, the rise of textile manufactures indicates a certain degree of diversification away from mineral- or agricultural-processing lines.

Real wages stagnated in both countries as a result of a reduction in the wage premium on education and working experience through this period. This took place because the more dynamic sectors in both countries demanded low-skilled workers, while the supply of more educated workers had increased. Although wages for low-skilled labour increased, the decrease in skilled-labour wages generated an overall stagnation of wages, while the labour income share in GDP decreased in both countries (Paz and Urrutia, 2014; Lustig, López-Calva, and Ortiz-Juárez, 2013).

In 2010, Mexico's manufacturing sector continued to be stronger than that of Peru, as it was one century earlier. In that year, the manufacturing value added per capita of Mexico (US$1,007.9) was more than twice that of Peru (US$448.6), and Mexico's manufactured exports per capita were 3.5 times higher (US $2,166.2). Moreover, the share of medium- and high-technology manufactured exports in total manufactured exports was more than 15 times higher in Mexico (78.7 per cent) than in Peru (5.2 per cent), but the share of their value added was only 2.6 times higher in Mexico (38.5 per cent) than in Peru (15 per cent). Mexico was ranked in 22nd place (above all Latin American countries) in UNIDO's competitive industrial performance index (UNIDO, 2013), and Peru in 63rd place. While Mexico's larger market size was an important factor explaining the different manufacturing performances of both nations until the 1980s, it was their geographical location and their natural resource endowments that shaped the different paths taken by each nation. However, at the beginning of the twenty-first century, industrial development was no longer closely linked to economic development.

12.7 CONCLUSIONS

The comparative study of manufacturing growth in Mexico and Peru over the long run tells us that Mexico's larger market and its proximity to the United States were crucial for its greater manufacturing development. Peru based its economic growth more on commodity exports, and manufacturing was slower to develop. Moreover, while Mexico concentrated most of its trade on the United States, Peru always had more diversified markets. Until the 1980s both countries had relatively high wage levels by international standards, inhibiting the development of labour-intensive manufacturing exports. At the same time their population lacked the educational and skill levels required to produce more sophisticated manufactures that could compete internationally in spite of their higher wage levels. Mexico and Peru had to rely on primary goods exports to generate the trade surpluses that could pay for the machinery and other intermediate goods that the manufacturing sector increasingly required. However, exports of semi-manufactures intensive in natural resources have been underestimated, since they are considered primary products in the statistical trade data.

This chapter shows that primary goods export-led growth was a driving force for manufacturing development rather than a hindrance when exports were diversified and the government conducted sound fiscal and monetary policies. Commodity export growth was only detrimental to manufacturing when commodity booms were concentrated in a single product, and were coupled with macroeconomic mismanagement that led to overvaluation, and excessive foreign indebtedness, as happened during Peru's guano boom of the mid-nineteenth century and Mexico's oil bonanza of 1978–81.

In both Mexico and Peru, ISI policies fostered manufacturing growth when they were coupled with macroeconomic stability, and policies that promoted domestic and foreign investment. However, ISI policies generated structural trade deficits that became more acute as import substitution progressed from consumer to intermediate and capital goods. Thus, when ISI policies were complemented with *other* policies that fostered, or at least did not hinder, the growth of exports, they were successful. In Mexico, this was the case during the late nineteenth and early twentieth centuries and from the 1930s until the mid-1960s, and in Peru during the 1890s and from 1950 until the early 1960s. During these periods, governments prevented overvaluation and invested in areas that increased the country's international competitiveness (such as transport infrastructure and education). The successful outcomes of ISI policies in countries such as Turkey and Southeast Asia show the feasibility of this strategy.

This chapter argues that macroeconomic stability is a necessary condition for achieving manufacturing development. In Peru and Mexico, real exchange rate appreciation, high interest and inflation rates, together with anti-private and anti-foreign business policies, which began in the late 1960s, undermined the development of manufacturing in the following decades. However, such economic disarray was not a consequence of ISI policies themselves, but rather the result of macroeconomic policies that sought to redress increasingly difficult political and social problems in countries with very high inequality. These policies were only feasible because the international bonanza of foreign lending in the 1970s nurtured them.

In contrast to the more successful East Asian countries, Mexico and Peru failed to use import substitution to build competitive capabilities, by underinvesting in education and infrastructure and by undermining the development of manufacturing exports through overvaluation and excessive tariff protection. Moreover, the severe economic mismanagement that produced periodic economic crises after 1973 destroyed some of the competitive capabilities that had been built during the previous years, as a result of hikes in interest rates, and collapses in demand, that forced many firms into bankruptcy.

After the 1980s crisis, Mexico and Peru liberalized much faster than East Asian countries. Mexico developed manufacturing exports through the maquiladora industry, and Peru went back to relying on commodity exports. Following the 'Washington Consensus', these two countries relied excessively on free markets to drive industrial growth and competitiveness. In contrast, in East Asia governments implemented policies to address market deficiencies, such as missing and incomplete capital markets; deficient or asymmetric information; unpredictable learning costs and externalities; and scale economies, imperfect competition, and information failures hampering investment in sectors of future comparative advantage (Lall, 1996; Stiglitz, 1996).

Mexico's slow rates of post-liberalization economic growth suggest that in order for export-led manufacturing growth to drive economic growth, it is necessary that exports have high domestic value added with strong production chains, and that the internal market be driven by income derived from exports—something that did not take place until 2010 (Fujii and Cervantes, 2014, p. 3). Moreover, Mexico's manufacturing export-led growth model does not seem to have reduced the country's vulnerability to external shocks relative to the old commodity export-led growth model, given its extreme reliance on only one foreign market. On the other hand, Peru appears to have returned to the old commodity-export-led growth model. Although it has provided high GDP growth in recent decades and a concomitant manufacturing growth, real wages have not risen, nor has external volatility been reduced.

APPENDIX

SOURCES

Total GDP

Peru: 1870–1949, Seminario (2014), pp. 817–20; 1950–2013, INEI, www.inei.gob.pe/estadisticas

Mexico: 1877–2003, linked series from INEGI, http://dgcnesyp.inegi.org.mx/; 2004–10, CEPALSTAT, http://estadisticas.cepal.org/cepalstat/WEB_CEPALSTAT/ESTADISTICASIndicadores.asp

Manufacturing GDP

Peru: 1870–2012, Seminario (2014), pp. 817–20.

Mexico: Linked series using: 1877–1910, El Colegio de México (1960), p. 106; 1911–25, own calculation built with data from Presidencia de la República (1963), pp. 81–92, and Gómez-Galvarriato (2013), pp. 18–19; 1926–50, Pérez López (1960), pp. 588–99; 1951–60, manufacturing GDP (pesos of 1960), INEGI, Estadísticas Históricas de México, 2014, Producto interno bruto total y por gran división de actividad económica, Table 8.3, http://dgcnesyp.inegi.org.mx/cgi-win/ehm2014.exe/CI080030010; 1961–70, manufacturing GDP (pesos of 1970), INEGI, Table 8.4, http://dgcnesyp.inegi.org.mx/cgi-win/ehm2014.exe/CI080030020; 1971–93, manufacturing GDP (pesos of 1980), INEGI,

Table 8.5, http://dgcnesyp.inegi.org.mx/cgi-win/ehm2014.exe/CI080030030; 1994–2003, manufacturing GDP (pesos of 1993), Table 8.6, INEGI, http://dgcnesyp.inegi.org.mx/cgi-win/ehm2014.exe/CI080030040; 2004–10: INEGI, Banco de Información Estadística, http://www.inegi.org.mx/sistemas/bie/default.aspx. Cuentas Nacionales. Producto Interno Bruto Trimestral. Valores a precios de 2008. Actividades Secundarias. Industria Manufacturera.

Manufacturing exports

Peru: 1962–2013, CEPALSTAT, http://moxlad-staging.herokuapp.com/home/es

Mexico: 1925–40, Cárdenas (1987), pp. 230–1; 1940–50, Ortíz Mena et al. (1953), p. 399; 1962–2013, CEPALSTAT.

Structure of manufacturing production

Peru: 1955 and 1960, Weeks (1985), pp. 103–10; 1970, 1980, and 1988, Portocarrero, Beltrán, and Romero (1992), pp. 27–8; 2008, INEI, www.inei.gob.pe/estadisticas/indice-tematico/economia/

Mexico: 1929–60, Villarreal (2005), pp. 254–5; 1960–2011, INEGI, Sistema de Cuentas Nacionales de México.

Real exchange rate

Peru: Banco Nacional de Reserva de Perú, Series Históricas, http://www.bcrp.gob.pe/estadisticas/cuadros-anuales-historicos.html

Mexico: Estimated using US price index, Lindert and Sutch (2006), Table Cc1–2, nominal exchange rate, INEGI (2010), Vol. II, pp. 1376–7; 1990–2012, Banco de México, Tipos de Cambio, http://www.banxico.org.mx/SieInternet

Prices

Peru: Banco Central de Reserva de Perú, Series Históricas, http://www.bcrp.gob.pe/estadisticas/cuadros-anuales-historicos.html

Mexico: 1885–1929, Gómez Galvarriato-Musacchio (2000), pp. 78–91; 1930–43, Bach y Reyna (1943) p. 51; 1943–62, Mexico, Presidencia de la República (1963), p. 109; 1963–8, Mexico, INEGI (2010), pp. 809–10; 1969–2014, Banco de Mexico, Indice de Precios al Consumidor.

Terms of trade

Peru: 1880–1928, Seminario (2014), pp. 648, 719 and 721; 1929–70 (1976); Moxlad, http://moxlad-staging.herokuapp.com/home/es

Mexico: 1880–1928, Kuntz (2010); 1929–70, ECLA (1976); 1970–2010, CEPALSTAT, http://moxlad.fcs.edu.uy/es/basededatos.html

Wages

Peru: 1969–2008, International Labor Organization, http://laborsta.ilo.org/STP/guest

Mexico: 1885–1900, Challú and Gómez-Galvarriato (2015); 1900–29, Challú and Gómez-Galvarriato (2015); 1939–75, Bortz (1988); 1975–80, International Labor Organization; 1980–2013, CEPALSTAT, http://moxlad.fcs.edu.uy/es/basededatos.html

Tariffs

Peru: 1885–1934, import customs revenue over total imports; 1934–79, Boloña (n.d.), pp. 287–8; 1980–97, Boloña and Illescas (1997), p. 40; 1998–2010, World Bank, World Economic Indicators, http://databank.worldbank.org/data/views/reports/tableview.aspx

Mexico: 1893–1910, estimated from Carmagnani (1994) and Mexico, SHCP, *Estadística Fiscal*, various years; 1911–29, estimated from Cosío Villegas (1932); 1930–40, estimated from Cárdenas (1987); 1941–2008, estimated from Mexico, INEGI (2010), pp. 1040, 1045–6, 1092, 1096–7.

Openness

We use as a measure of openness: (exports + imports)/GDP.

Peru: Seminario (2014), pp. 719–21; PWT 7.1, Alan Heston, Robert Summers, and Bettina Aten, Penn World Table Version 7.1.

Mexico: Own calculations with data from 1895–1929, Kuntz (2010); 1929–79, INEGI (2010), pp. 665–6; 1980–2010, CEPALSTAT, http://estadisticas.cepal.org/cepalstat

Manufactured exports as percentage of total exports

Mexico, Peru, and Latin America: 1962–2013, CEPALSTAT, http://moxlad.fcs.edu.uy/es/basededatos.html

Mexico: 1925–40, Cárdenas (1987), pp. 230–1; 1939–50, Ortíz Mena et al. (1953), p. 399.

Exports and imports

Peru: Seminario (2014), pp. 783–8.

Mexico: 1870–1929, Kuntz (2007), pp. 72–3; 1929–50, ECLA (1976), p. 51; 1950–80, ECLA (2009), Table 7.2.13; 1980–2008, ECLA (2009), Table 9.2.14; 2009–13, CEPALSTAT, http://moxlad.fcs.edu.uy/es/basededatos.html

REFERENCES

Artuç, E., Lederman, D., and Rojas, D. (2015). The rise of China and labor market adjustments in Latin America. *World Bank Policy Research Working Paper* No. 7155.

Bach, F. and Reyna, M. (1943). El nuevo índice de precios al mayoreo en la Ciudad de México. *El Trimestre Económico* 10, 1–63.

Banco Nacional de Comercio Exterior (Bancomext) (1965). *Manufacturas y semimanufacturas de exportación de los países en vías de desarrollo*. Mexico City, Mexico: Banco Nacional de Comercio Exterior.

Banco Nacional de Comercio Exterior (Bancomext) (1987). *Medio siglo de financiamiento y promoción del comercio exterior de México*, Vol. I. Mexico City, Mexico: Banco Nacional de Comercio Exterior and El Colegio de México.

Banco Nacional de Reserva de Perú, Series Históricas, http://www.bcrp.gob.pe/estadisticas/cuadros-anuales-historicos.html.

Bardella, G. (1989). *Un siglo de vida económica del Perú 1889–1989*. Lima, Peru: Banco de Crédito del Peru.

Beatty, E. (2000). The impact of foreign trade on the Mexican economy: terms of trade and the rise of industry, 1880–1923. *Journal of Latin American Studies* 32, 399–433.

Boloña, C. (n.d.). *Políticas arancelarias en el Perú, 1880–1980*. Lima, Peru: Instituto de Economía de Libre Mercado.

Boloña, C. and Illescas, J. (1997). *Políticas Arancelarias en el Perú, 1980–1997*. Lima, Peru: Instituto de Economía de Libre Mercado and Universidad San Ignacio de Loyola.

Bortz, J. (1988). *Los salarios industriales en la ciudad de México, 1939–1975*. Mexico City, Mexico: Fondo de Cultura Económica.

Brown, F. and Domínguez, L. (1994). The dynamics of productivity performance in Mexican manufacturing, 1984–90. *The Developing Economies* 32, 279–98.

Caravedo, B. (1976). *Burguesía e industria en el Perú, 1933–1945*. Lima, Peru: Instituto de Estudios Peruanos.

Cárdenas, E. (1987). *La industrialización mexicana durante la Gran Depresión*. Mexico City, Mexico: El Colegio de Mexico.

Cárdenas, E. (2003). El proceso de industrialización acelerada en México. In *Industrialización y Estado en América Latina. La leyenda negra de posguerra* (Eds, Cárdenas, E., Ocampo, J. A., and Thorp, R.). Mexico City, Mexico: Fondo de Cultura Económica, 240–76.

Challú, A. and Gómez-Galvarriato, A. (2015). Mexico's real wages in the age of the Great Divergence 1730–1930. *Revista de Historia Económica* 33, 83–122.

Coatsworth, J. and Williamson, J. (2004). Always protectionist? Latin American tariffs from independence to Great Depression. *Journal of Latin American Studies* 36, 205–32.

Cosío Villegas, D, (1932). *La Cuestión Arancelaria en México*. Mexico City, Mexico: Centro Mexicano de Estudios Económicos.

Díaz Alejandro, C. and Seibert, S. (1979). Algunas vicisitudes de las economías abiertas en América Latina. *Desarrollo Económico* 19, 147–59.

Economic Commission for Latin America (ECLA) (1976). América Latina: Relación de Precios del Intercambio. *Cuadernos Estadísticos de la CEPAL* 1(4).

Economic Commission for Latin America (ECLA) (1978). *Series Históricas del Crecimiento de América Latina*. Santiago de Chile, Chile: Cuadernos de la CEPAL.

Economic Commission for Latin America (ECLA), División de Estudios de Desarrollo Económico de la Cepal (1991). El comercio de manufacturas de América Latina. Evolución y estructura 1962–1989. Mimeo, LC/R 1056.A.

Economic Commission for Latin America (ECLA) (2009). *América Latina y el Caribe. Series históricas de estadísticas económicas 1950–2008*. Santiago de Chile, Chile: CEPAL.

El Colegio de México, Seminario de Historia Moderna de México (1960). *Estadísticas Económicas del Porfiriato*, 2 vols. México City, Mexico: El Colegio de México.

Fitzgerald, E. V. K. (1979). *The Political Economy of Peru, 1956–1978: Economic Development and the Restructuring of Capital*. New York: Cambridge University Press.

Fujii, G. and Cervantes, R. (2014). Changes in indirect domestic value added in Mexico's manufacturing exports by sectors and countries of origin and destination,

1995–2011. Mimeo, presented at the International Input Output Conference, 14–18 July, Lisbon, Portugal.

Gómez-Galvarriato, A. (1997). Definiendo los obstáculos a la industrialización en México: El desempeño de Fundidora Monterrey durante el Porfiriato. In *La Historia de las Grandes Empresas en México 1850–1913*. Mexico DF: Fondo de Cultura Económica and Universidad de Nuevo León, 201–43.

Gómez-Galvarriato, A. (2013). *Industry and Revolution: Social and Economic Change in the Orizaba Valley, Mexico*. Cambridge, MA: Harvard University Press.

Gómez-Galvarriato, A. and Musacchio, A. (2000). Un nuevo índice de precios para México, 1886–1929. *El Trimestre Económico* 62, 47–91.

Gootenberg, P. (1991). *Between Silver and Guano: Commercial Policy and the State in Postindependence Peru*. Princeton, NJ: Princeton University Press.

Hanson, G. H. (2002). The role of maquiladoras in Mexico's export boom. Paper presented at the conference, Prospects for Industrial Park in the Palestinian Territories, Rice University, https://migration.ucdavis.edu/rs/more.php?id=8.

Hunt, S. (2011). *La formación de la economía peruana: distribución y crecimiento en la historia económica del Perú y la América Latina*. Lima, Peru: Banco Central de Reserva de Peru and Instituto de Estudios Peruano.

INEI (2014). Encuesta Nacional de Hogares. Población en Situación de pobreza según ámbitos geográficos. http://www.inei.gob.pe/

International Monetary Fund (IMF) (2014). *Peru: Selected Issues Paper*. IMF Country Report No. 14/22ry.

Kuntz, S. (2007). *El comercio exterior en la era del capitalismo liberal, 1870–1829*. Mexico City, Mexico: El Colegio de México.

Kuntz, S. (2010). *Las exportaciones mexicanas durante la primera globalización, 1870–1929*. Mexico City, Mexico: El Colegio de México.

Lall, S. (1996). *Learning from the Asian Tigers*. London: Macmillan.

Lall, S., Albaladejo, M., and Mesquita Moreira, M. (2004). Latin American industrial competitiveness and the challenge of globalization. *Inter-American Development Bank, Occasional Papers* No. SITI-05.

Lindert, P. H. and Sutch, R. (2006). Consumer price indexes, for all items: 1774–2003. In *Historical Statistics of the United States, Earliest Times to the Present: Millennial Edition* (Eds, S. B. Carter, S. S. Gartner, M. R. Haines, A. L. Olmstead, R. Sutch, and G. Wright). New York: Cambridge University Press.

López-Córdova, E. (2003). NAFTA and manufacturing productivity in Mexico. *Economía*, Fall, 55–98.

Lustig, N., López-Calva, L. F., and Ortiz-Juárez, E. (2013). Declining inequality in Latin America in the 2000s: the cases of Argentina, Brazil, and Mexico. *World Development* 44, 129–41.

Mahon, J. E. (1992). Was Latin America too rich to prosper? Structural political obstacles to export-led industrial growth. *Journal of Development Studies* 28, 241–63.

Márquez, G. (1998). Tariff protection in Mexico, 1892–1910: ad valorem tariff rates and sources of variation. In *Latin America and the World Economy since 1800* (Eds, Coatsworth, J. and Taylor, A.). Cambridge, MA: Harvard University Press.

Márquez, G. (2007). Protección y cambio institucional en México (1910–1929). In *México y España ¿historias económicas paralelas?* (Eds, Dobado, R., Gómez-Galvarriato, A., and Márquez, G.). Mexico City, Mexico: Fondo de Cultura Económica.

Martínez del Campo, M. (1985). *Industrialización en México, hacia un análisis crítico*. Mexico City, Mexico: El Colegio de México.

Martínez Trigueros, L. (2012). La relevancia del comercio internacional en el desarrollo económico de México. In *La política del comercio exterior. Regulación e impacto* (Eds, Martínez Trigueros, L. and Hernández C.). Mexico City, Mexico: Secretaría de Economía and ITAM, 17–53.

Mexico, INEGI (2010). *Estadísticas Históricas de México*, 2 vols. http://dgcnesyp.inegi.org.mx/ehm/ehm.htm.

Mexico, Presidencia de la República (1963). *Cincuenta años de Revolución Mexicana en cifras*. México City, Mexico: Editorial Cultura.

Moreno-Brid J. C, and Ros, J. (2010). La Dimensión Internacional de la Economía Mexicana. In *Historia económica general de México* (Ed. Kuntz, S.). Mexico City, Mexico: El Colegio de México, 757–88.

Ortíz Mena, R., Urquidi, V. L., Waterson, A., and Haralz, J. H. (1953). *El desarrollo económico de México y su capacidad para absorber capital del exterior*. Mexico City, Mexico: Nacional Financiera.

Ota Mishima, M. E. (1997). *Destino México. Un estudio de las migraciones internacionales a México, siglos XIX y XX*. Mexico City, Mexico: El Colegio de México.

Pastor, G. (2012). Peru: monetary and exchange rate policies, 1930–1980. *IMF Working Paper* No. WP/12/166.

Paz, P. and Urrutia, C. (2014). Economic growth and wage stagnation in Peru: 1998–2012. http://ftp.itam.mx/pub/academico/inves/urrutia/14-04.pdf.

Peñafiel, A. (1903). *Estadística Industrial formada por la Dirección General de Estadística*. Mexico City, Mexico: Oficina Tipográfica de la Secretaría de Fomento.

Pérez, E. (1960). El producto nacional. In *Cincuenta años de Revolución*, Vol. 1. Mexico City, Mexico: Fondo de Cultura Económica, 571–94.

Portocarrero, F., Beltrán, A., and Romero, M. E. (1992). *Compendio estadístico de Perú: 1900–1900*. Lima, Peru: Universidad del Pacífico and Consorcio de Investigación Económica.

Roca, S. and Simabuko, L. (1999). Value and quality creation: natural resources, industrialization and standards of living in Peru 1950 to 1997. *Cuadernos de Difusión* 5, 69–123.

Rodrik, D. (2007). The real exchange rate and economic growth: theory and evidence. Mimeo, John F. Kennedy School of Government, Harvard University.

Samaniego Breach, Ricardo (1984). Evolution of total factor productivity in the manufacturing sector in Mexico, 1963–1981. *Serie de documentos de trabajo, Centro de Estudios Económicos, El Colegio de México* No. VIII.

Seminario, B. (2014). Las cuentas nacionales de Peru, 1700–2013. Mimeo.

Stiglitz, J. E. (1996). Some lessons from the East Asian miracle. *World Bank Research Observer* 11, 151–77.

Taylor Hansen, L. (2003). Los orígenes de la industria maquiladora en México. *Comercio Exterior* 53, 1045–56.

Thorp, R. (1979). The stabilization crisis in Peru 1975–78. In *Inflation and Stabilisation in Latin America*. Oxford: Macmillan and St Antony's College, Oxford, 110–43.

Thorp, R. and Bertram, G. (1978). *Peru 1890–1977: Growth and Policy in an Open Economy*. London: Macmillan.

United Nations Industrial Development Organization (UNIDO) (2013). *The Industrial Competitiveness of Nations: Looking Back, Forging Ahead*. Competitive Industrial Performance Report, 2012–13. Vienna.

Usui, N. (1997). Dutch Disease and policy adjustments to the oil boom: a comparative study of Indonesia and Mexico. *Resources Policy* 23, 151–62.

Villarreal, R. (2005). *Industrialización, competitividad y desequilibrio externo en México. Un enfoque macroindustrial y financiero (1929–2010)*. Mexico City, Mexico: Fondo de Cultura Económica.

Weeks, J. (1985). *Limits to Capitalist Development: The Industrialization of Peru, 1950–1980*. Boulder, CO: Westview.

Yamawaki, C. (2002). *Estrategias de vida de los inmigrantes asiáticos en el Perú*. Lima, Peru: Instituto de Estudios Peruanos.

13

Industrial Growth in South America
Argentina, Brazil, Chile, and Colombia, 1890–2010

Xavier Duran, Aldo Musacchio, and Gerardo della Paolera

13.1 INTRODUCTION

Between the late nineteenth century and the 1970s, the largest economies in South America had one of the most impressive rates of industrial catch-up in the world (Bénétrix, O'Rourke, and Williamson, 2015; Williamson, 2006).[1] Yet, despite the fact that these South American countries are all commodity exporters and share a similar culture, religion, and colonial origin, there is wide variation in their rates of industrial growth. They industrialized not only at different points in time, but also at different speeds.

In this chapter we take a long-term view and examine the patterns of industrialization in Argentina, Brazil, Chile, and Colombia. Rather than trying to provide a single explanation of how specific shocks or policies shaped the industrialization of the region, we show that there is too much heterogeneity for a single theory to work. Thus, we provide a range of alternative explanations, arguing that differences in initial conditions explain differences in pre-1930 industrial growth, while external shocks and macroeconomic and trade policy seem to explain the variation in rates of industrialization from the 1930s onwards.

The traditional history of the industrialization of Latin America has unfortunately been studied by periods, and the data used has often been estimated differently across the periods, thus leaving us with no readily available long-term series. Therefore, writing a South American industrial history required us to put together long-term series of manufacturing value added (i.e., industrial GDP), manufacturing labour productivity, and the manufacturing labour force from 1900 to 2010 (see the Data Appendix). Our manufacturing series cover industrial establishments of all sizes, different technologies (artisan vs mechanized), and a wide range of products. Most of our series reflect true manufacturing value added, after the first industrial census in the country concerned. However, Colombian data before 1953 are estimates of the quantum of manufacturing production, and for

---

[1] Maria de la Paz Ferro and Daniel Habermacher provided superb research assistance for this work.

Brazil the early industrial GDP indices are proxies using data on raw materials and statistics on textile production (Haddad and Contador, 1975). In addition to the data on manufacturing value added, we gathered information on population, openness to trade, exchange rates, terms of trade, and other series.

This new database allows us, for the first time, to uncover variation across countries and over time that the existing literature had either ignored or studied in piecemeal fashion at the country level. Our main insight is that industrial growth in South America has not been homogeneous. For instance, Argentina and Brazil, the largest economies in the region, enjoyed rapid catch-up before the 1930s, while only Brazil and Colombia saw very rapid and sustained catch up on the US, the global leader, in the 1930s. The post-Second World War golden age of growth was experienced in the four countries studied, but only Brazil and Colombia saw faster industrial growth than the industrial leaders in Europe and Japan. During the 1980s and early 1990s industrial growth slowed in most of the region, barring Colombia, but by the first decade of the twenty-first century most of the economies started to speed up again, but not sufficiently fast to catch up on the industrial leaders.

With our new time series in hand, we cannot find evidence to support most of the traditional hypotheses that have been used to explain the industrialization of South America. There are four basic explanations in the literature. First, there is the 'adverse shocks' hypothesis (Tavares, 1972; Nations/ECLA, 1951; Prebisch, 1950; Furtado, 1959), which argues that as a consequence of adverse international shocks, such as wars, downturns, or commodity price shocks, the relative price of exports decreased and/or import scarcity rose, financing channels were interrupted or there was a scarcity of foreign exchange, and the terms of trade declined. This hypothesis is related to Dutch Disease forces in the sense that it posits that Latin America de-industrialized when there were commodity booms because of Dutch Disease effects, while the region re-industrialized when the terms of trade declined and the local price of manufactures rose. The second hypothesis has been characterized as the 'endogenous industrialization view', seeing industrialization as a product of export-led growth (Diaz-Alejandro, 1976; Dean, 1969). This thesis argues, in sharp contrast to the previous one, that South America industrialized when commodity exports thrived, because the export boom attracted foreign investment and, via an income effect, stoked the growth of domestic industrial demand. Thus, commodity booms led to increases in manufacturing value added, but also to improvements in industrial productivity (Lederman, 2005; Haber, 2006; Williamson, 2011a).

A third hypothesis sees industrial growth as the product of import-substituting industrialization (ISI), or explicit policies that included tariff protection, exchange controls, special preferences for firms importing capital goods for new industries, preferential import exchange rates for industrial raw materials, and an ample set of industrial policy tools that ranged from subsidies, targeted credit, pressure on foreign companies to open plants in the region, or the direct establishment of state-owned enterprises (Hirschman, 1968; Baer, 1972). Most of these policies were not undertaken simultaneously until after the Second World War, yet a modified version of the ISI model was applied before the 1930s (Versiani, 1980; Coatsworth and Williamson, 2004). Finally, there is the 'stagnationist' hypothesis.

It argues that even if protection did lead to increases in manufacturing value added, it did not provide the incentives for firms to improve productivity over time: even when manufacturing value added increased, labour productivity stagnated. Thus, the 'stagnationist' hypothesis sees ISI as a policy that only succeeded in the short to medium term (Colistete, 2009; Macario, 1964; Diaz Alejandro, 1970; Krueger, 1978; Haber, 2006; Bulmer-Thomas, 2003).

Because our data show that none of these hypotheses explains all cases during the whole century, we argue that the industrialization of Latin America cannot be understood by appealing to a single theory. The drivers of industrial growth in each country are not the consequence of a common shock, or the adoption of a single set of policies. In fact, the evidence suggests that the most important external shocks, such as the First World War, the Great Depression, the Second World War, and the 1980s debt crisis, had heterogeneous effects on industry in Argentina, Brazil, Chile, and Colombia. While some countries were damaged by some of these shocks, others thrived.

Our argument is that the timing of the industrial take-off was powerfully influenced by initial conditions rather than by policies or external shocks, but that the subsequent variation in industrial growth and de-industrialization experiences was due to the response of policy to changes in external conditions. Market size, literacy, and infrastructure development at the end of the nineteenth century all favoured industrial growth in Argentina and Chile, but not in Brazil and Colombia, which were slower at developing infrastructure and integrating their markets. Later on, market size, the spread of infrastructure, trade policy, and macroeconomic policy explain why industrial growth sped up in Brazil and Colombia after the 1930s, while it slowed in Chile and Argentina. Finally, we argue that favourable terms of trade and economic liberalization explain relative de-industrialization in South America between 1990 and 2012.

The heterogeneous nature of industrial growth in Latin America can be seen in Tables 13.1 and 13.2. In Table 13.1 we compare manufacturing value added growth rates in South America with those in the industrial leader, the United States, and three other key early industrializers (the United Kingdom, Germany,

Table 13.1. Industrial GDP growth rates, South America vs global leaders (per cent, per annum, annual averages)

	Leaders (average)	GER	UK	USA	JAP	ARG	BRZ	CHL	COL
1900–19	3.2	2.7	1.0	5.8		4.8	9.8	2.4	
1920–30	2.6	1.0	2.9	3.9		6.5	2.6	1.5	3.1
1931–43	4.9	2.2	2.7	9.9	6.3	3.3	10.0	7.5	8.9
1944–72	5.6	4.7	4.3	3.1	10.2	5.3	8.7	5.4	6.9
1973–90	2.2	1.8	0.8	1.7	4.5	−0.6	4.0	1.8	3.9
1991–2009	0.8	0.03	−0.4	2.9	0.4	2.9	2.2	3.6	2.2

Notes: GER = Germany, JAP = Japan, ARG = Argentina, BRZ = Brazil, CHL = Chile, COL = Colombia.
Source: See Data Appendix. Developed country growth rates from Bénétrix, O'Rourke, and Williamson (2015).

Table 13.2. Convergence/divergence among South American nations and the developed country leaders

Leaders (average)	Growth in Latin America minus growth in leaders				Growth in Latin America minus US growth			
	ARG	BRZ	CHL	COL	ARG	BRZ	CHL	COL
1900–19	3.2	1.6	6.6	−0.8		−1.0	4.0	−3.4	
1920–30	2.6	3.9	0.0	−1.1	0.5	2.6	−1.3	−2.4	−0.8
1931–43	4.9	−1.6	5.1	2.6	4.0	−6.6	0.1	−2.4	−1.0
1944–72	5.6	−0.3	3.1	−0.2	1.3	2.2	5.6	2.3	3.8
1973–90	2.2	−2.8	1.8	−0.4	1.7	−2.3	2.3	0.1	2.2
1991–2007	0.8	2.2	1.5	2.9	1.5	0.0	−0.7	0.7	−0.7

Source and notes: As in Table 13.1.

and Japan). The wide dispersion in growth rates between our four Latin American countries, especially in the first three periods, can be seen immediately.

On the left-hand side of Table 13.2 we present these same South American growth rates, minus the average growth rate of the four leaders. Positive entries in the table imply industrial catching-up, while negative entries imply that the country in question's industry is falling further behind the leaders. The right-hand side of the table presents similar data, this time subtracting the industrial growth rate of the United States alone, rather than of all four industrial leaders.

13.2 PRE-1920 INDUSTRIAL GROWTH IN SOUTH AMERICA

The period before 1920 has always been considered the Belle Époque of GDP and industrial growth in Latin America. However, the phrase 'Belle Époque' refers to Latin America's performance in that epoch, relative to other periods, rather than to Latin America's growth performance compared with that of the developed world. When industrial growth in South America is compared with that of the industrial leaders, only Brazil and Argentina have an outstanding performance. When the South American performance before 1920 is compared with the United States (on the right-hand side of Table 13.2), only Brazil fares favourably. Thus, the Belle Époque was indeed an important period of initial industrial take-off for Argentina and Brazil, yet was a period of rapid catch-up only for Brazil.

Argentina was the industrial front-runner in the late nineteenth and early twentieth centuries, despite the fact that it experienced a sustained commodity export boom. Its industrial growth rate before the First World War was between 6 and 11 per cent (but the war years lowered the 1900–19 average to 4.8 per cent, as shown in Table 13.1). This early industrialization was an endogenous, private sector-led process driven by the dynamism of the export economy. The industrial boom was tightly linked to the development of agriculture, which produced forward and backward linkages, accelerating urbanization rates, and giving rise to a new consumer class that demanded manufactured goods. The initial industrial boom was dominated by the production of food, beverages, textiles, wool and leather, tobacco, and glass, with some important firms competing successfully with consumer goods imports. This was the beginning of what has been called an 'easy' import substitution process. During this first phase, the production of consumer goods represented 72 per cent of total manufacturing output. However, there were natural resource obstacles to the development of a competitive 'heavy' industry. These obstacles included the scarcity of coal, iron, and other minerals, which precluded the development of large-scale machinery and metallurgical firms. Firms thus relied heavily on imported intermediate and capital inputs (Rocchi, 2005; Diaz-Alejandro, 1970; Barbero and Rocchi, 2003).

Industrial growth in Brazil, Chile, and Colombia began later (much later in Colombia). In the 1910s Chile's industrial output was growing at a modest annual rate of 3 per cent, while Brazilian industry was growing at 14 per cent. The rapid Brazilian industrial take-off seems to have started at the beginning of the twentieth century. Textile and other industrial firms enjoyed buoyant internal demand associated with coffee booms (and coffee valorization programmes[2]), while they also had easy access to foreign and local equity and debt finance between 1905 and 1914, helping firms finance machinery imports. The result was a rapid spurt in industrialization during the fifteen years before the First World War (Haber, 1991; Suzigan, 1986; Musacchio, 2009). Cano (1977) highlights the importance of the almost forced import substitution during the First World War, when the disruption to shipping and capital inflows led to a shortage of foreign exchange and imported goods. Domestic producers took up the slack by increasing capacity utilization (Suzigan, 1986).

In Chile, Palma (2000) argues that in spite of a virtual world monopoly of sodium nitrate exports, the Chilean economy avoided Dutch Disease forces in the 1890s by implementing an active policy of manufacturing protection that propelled the local industry.

We do not have data for Colombian industrial GDP growth in this initial period, but we know that there were two coffee booms, following the valorization programmes in Brazil (in 1906 and after the late 1920s). The coffee booms, combined with increased protection for manufacturing, created a long-lasting non-durable consumer products industry for the first time, as well as a few shorter-lived coffee machinery producers. Moreover, it was during the second coffee boom that

---

[2] The coffee valorization programmes in Brazil, and later on in Colombia, were government programmes restricting the supply of coffee by stockpiling it to keep international prices stable. The first programme operated from 1906 to 1914, and subsequent programmes were tried in the 1920s, until Brazil began burning large amounts of coffee in 1931. By World War II Colombia and Brazil had organized a cartel under the Inter-American Coffee Agreement and by 1962 the cartel was global, with quotas for two dozen countries. These programmes stabilized the terms of trade and made coffee the most important source of foreign exchange for Brazil and Colombia throughout most of the twentieth century. For a detailed description of the programmes see Bates (1998).

Table 13.3. Average labour productivity growth rate: Argentina, Brazil, Chile, Colombia, and the United States

	Argentina	Brazil	Chile	Colombia	US
1900–19	1.4	4.8	3.9		1.0
1920–30	5.4	6.1	0.4	−2.5	4.4
1931–43	−1.4	5.6	4.3	5.5	3.5
1944–72	3.5	4.0	3.8	3.7	2.1
1973–90	1.6	3.7	−0.5	2.7	2.6
1990–2009	1.3	2.6	3.5	1.1	3.9

Source: See Data Appendix.

manufacturing was able to take advantage of the rise in market size due to investments in infrastructure (Echevarria, 1993).

In Argentina and Brazil, labour productivity growth was faster than that in the US during this period (Table 13.3). This supports the argument that Argentina and Brazil experienced endogenous industrialization with significant improvements in productivity (Haber, 2006).

13.2.1 Initial Conditions

What explains the early start of Argentina and the late start of Colombia? The heterogeneous timing of industrial take-off cannot be explained by any one of the industrialization hypotheses presented above. Instead, we argue that the explanation lies in the heterogeneity of their initial conditions, external conditions, policy, and outcomes. That is, heterogeneous initial conditions and the speed of technology adoption (related to absorptive capacity and market demand) explain the timing of industrial take-off better than any of the theories presented above. The rest of this section thus focuses on how initial conditions such as the stock of human capital, market size, and transportation structures determined the timing of industrial take-off in South America.

By 1900, Argentina, Brazil, Chile, and Colombia had all consolidated their status as independent countries. Colombia still waged a civil war, but it would soon be finished, and there followed a long period of relative peace. The inflow of migrants and capital from Europe was at its peak, contributing to expanding domestic markets and integration into the world economy (Obstfeld and Taylor, 2004; Stone, 1999; O'Rourke and Williamson, 1999; Williamson, 2011b).

A casual inspection of the demographic and educational data in Table 13.4 shows that initial conditions (at the beginning of the twentieth century) differed greatly between our four countries. Argentina and Chile were closer to European levels of literacy, while Brazil and Colombia lagged behind. As Sokoloff and Engerman (2000) remind us, low literacy rates retarded economic growth and might have been a crucial obstacle that postponed the take-off of the industrialization process. The adoption of new technologies and the capacity to innovate is

Table 13.4. Population, urbanization, and illiteracy rates (per cent), and transportation infrastructure: Argentina, Brazil, Chile, and Colombia, 1900–2000

Argentina

	Population (millions)	Urbanization rate	Illiteracy rate	Railway (km per million pop.)	Road (thousand km per million pop.)
1900	4.7	41	40	3,572.8	n.a.
1920	8.9	54	32	3,981.7	n.a.
1930	11.9	57	25	3,192.5	17.8
1940	14.2	60	18	2,913.6	28.7
1950	17.2	64	12	2,499.4	4.2
1960	20.3	72	9	2,164.8	3.8
1970	24.0	79	7	1,665.3	8.4
1980	28.4	83	5.6	1,201.2	n.a.
1990	33.0	87	4.3	1,082.2	n.a.
2000	37.3	89	3.2	957.6	5.8

Brazil

	Population (millions)	Urbanization rate	Illiteracy rate	Railway (km per million pop.)	Road (thousand km per million pop.)
1900	18.0	n.a.	65	851.6	n.a.
1920	27.4	n.a.	65	1,041.3	n.a.
1930	33.6	n.a.	61	967.5	3.6
1940	41.1	31	56	833.1	5.1
1950	53.4	36	51	686.4	n.a.
1960	69.6	45	40	550.3	7.1
1970	95.7	56	32	332.8	11.9
1980	123.0	66	25	241.1	n.a.
1990	151.2	75	19	200.6	n.a.
2000	176.3	81	15	172.4	11.2

Chile

	Population (millions)	Urbanization rate	Illiteracy rate	Railway (km per million pop.)	Road (thousand km per million pop.)
1900	3.0	43	47	1,471.4	n.a.
1920	3.7	47	37	2,205.5	n.a.
1930	4.3	49	25	2,094.9	8.4
1940	5.1	60	27	1,702.9	7.1
1950	6.1	61	21	1,396.0	n.a.
1960	7.4	68	16	1,137.2	7.4
1970	9.4	75	12	883.9	6.8
1980	11.1	81	8	568.1	n.a.
1990	13.1	83	6	521.9	n.a.
2000	15.2	85	4	324.8	5.3

Colombia

	Population (millions)	Urbanization rate	Illiteracy rate	Railway (km per million pop.)	Road (thousand km per million pop.)
1900	4.0	n.a.	61	142.1	n.a.
1920	6.2	n.a.	56	216.8	n.a.
1930	7.9	n.a.	48	329.7	3.0
1940	9.2	29	43	363.5	2.5
1950	11.6	43	38	304.2	n.a.
1960	15.4	48	30	204.6	n.a.
1970	21.4	57	22	160.3	2.3
1980	26.6	64	16	127.8	n.a.
1990	33.0	70	11	64.1	n.a.
2000	39.8	75	8	53.1	2.7

Source: MOxLAD (2014).

partly dependent upon a labour force (and management) that could learn new techniques.

Some have argued that the type of education imparted might also have been a deterrent to the adoption of sophisticated technologies. For example, Maloney (2002) shows that these countries failed to establish technical education during most of the nineteenth century. 'By 1926, Australia had twenty-seven times more graduates of technical schools per capita than Argentina, perhaps the most educated country in Latin America' (Maloney, 2002, p. 127). If this was the case, the genius to industrialize might have been embodied in European migrants who came with technical skills. In 1914, foreigners propelled industrial initiative in Argentina. More than 65 per cent of firms in Argentina were initiated and owned by first-generation immigrants (Diaz Alejandro, 1970).

Literacy and higher-order human capital may be good predictors of increases in per capita income levels, but they are insufficient to drive sustained manufacturing growth. Literacy and engineering rates alone would have led us to predict that Argentina and Chile, instead of Brazil, would be the industrial leaders by the mid-twentieth century (see Table 13.4 and Maloney, 2002).

Yet that did not happen. Brazil took the lead in terms of industrial sophistication and sheer size in the second half of the twentieth century. It started as a laggard: the initial industrialization of Brazil, between 1890 and 1930, did not have the kind of skill-biased technologies associated with the second industrial revolution (Goldin and Katz, 1996; Musacchio, Martínez Fritscher, and Viarengo, 2014). Brazil started rather with labour-intensive industry. Thus, the industrialization levels of Brazilian states in 1920 and 1940 are not correlated with educational levels. The Brazilian government did not introduce the kind of technical education necessary for the development of more sophisticated industries until the 1950s. The National Council for Research, a Brazilian version of the National Science Foundation, and the Technological Institute for Aeronautics (ITA) were launched in 1950, the National Institute of Applied Math (IMPA) in 1951, and the State University of Campinas—with a strong emphasis on engineering—was not founded until the early 1960s. The expansion of national laboratories and research centres continued in the 1970s and coincided with the dramatic changes in manufacturing revealed in Table 13.5 below, and with the rise of Brazil as a leader in innovation in areas such as agricultural research (e.g. with the creation of the Brazilian National Agricultural Research Company, known as Embrapa in 1973) and aeronautics.[3]

In any case, monocausal explanations of Latin American industrialization are always going to be insufficient to explain variation over time and across countries. Industrialization is a complex process that requires a multivariate explanation. For instance, one has to consider not just education, but urbanization levels, market potential, infrastructure, protectionist policies, and a variety of other important factors.

For instance, it is well known that urbanization is closely associated with increases in per capita income. Several studies even suggest that an increasingly

---

[3] To develop a native aeronautics industry, ITA worked closely with the Brazilian air force and the state-owned airplane manufacturer Embraer, which adopted key technologies from foreign firms.

urban economy promotes industrial growth (due to the benefits of agglomeration effects). However, the increases in rents experienced by an increasingly productive natural resource sector can generate two types of urban employment: tradables, like consumer goods; and non-tradables, such as services. South America's leading cities, Buenos Aires, Santiago, Sao Paulo, Medellín, and Rio de Janeiro were hybrids. Initially they relied more on the stimulus of internal demand based on exports, than on a supply-side push. Firms located in urban enclaves dealt first with processing and later with the substitution of imports. The Brazilian and Colombian urbanization processes came much later, but their industrial catch-up was extremely fast. After 1940, the acceleration of urbanization was probably caused by an industry-led boom attributable to the artificial change in relative prices favourable to manufacturing. This was certainly the case for Argentina and Chile, and in the Southeast of Brazil.

In Colombia urban concentration of the scale found in our other countries came much later. By 1912 there were two important urban centres, Bogotá and Medellín. The former was the political capital of Colombia, with 120,000 inhabitants, and focused on the production of foods. Medellín, with 70,000 inhabitants, had manufacturing focused on food, beverages, and textiles (Melo, 1987). Buenos Aires had 1.2 million inhabitants in 1910, Santiago 390,000 in 1900 and São Paulo 240,000 in 1900.

Moreover, the market potential for manufactured goods was not only determined by urbanization, but also by transportation costs (involved both in selling manufactured goods and in importing raw materials) (Krugman, 1993). Buenos Aires and Santiago, the key industrial hubs in Argentina and Chile, had the initial advantage of being close to the coast, and thus faced lower transportation costs for raw materials and enjoyed easier access to internal and external markets (by boat). In contrast, São Paulo, Bogota and Medellín had, initially, more difficult access to the coast. Until the early part of the twentieth century, the railway lines connecting the coast to the interior plateau of São Paulo were not fully developed. In Colombia, the location of the major urban centres of Bogotá and Medellín in the Andes probably made trade with the rest of the world, and within the country itself, harder than it was in any of the other three countries in our sample.

One way to gauge the transportation challenges of Colombia and Brazil is to look at their railway and road densities during the take-off period (Herranz-Loncán, 2014). Table 13.4 shows that Chile and Argentina had an initial advantage. Brazil, with its scattered population, was at a disadvantage and its transportation infrastructure did not compare well to those of Argentina and Chile, on a per capita basis, until after the Second World War. In Colombia, the poor rail and road infrastructure and the challenging topography complicated market integration until the second half of the twentieth century, when the large urban centres provided markets big enough for large-scale domestic industries to flourish. The road network in Colombia was small in relative terms even in the year 2000; comparable to the density of roads Brazil had had at the turn of the century.

Population size may be another factor determining the extent of specialization and diversification in manufacturing in these four countries. Murphy, Shleifer, and

Vishny (1989) described the benefits of size in models of 'take-off' or 'big push' industrialization, in which the take-off phase is characterized by a transition from a slow growth, constant returns to scale technology to endogenous growth and an increasing returns to scale technology. Size may also enhance industrial growth because it promotes product competition.

As we can see from Table 13.4, the Argentine economy had a size advantage when it came to its major urban centre (Buenos Aires). The country was more urbanized than any other country in the region and most of the population lived in the larger Buenos Aires area. That may explain Argentina's initial take-off and initial leadership as the early industrializer in South America. Brazil, despite its larger population, was a much more rural country and before 1900 most of the population centres were scattered around the country, with extremely poor communication and road networks.

Rapid population growth and urbanization in Brazil and Colombia after 1940 help to explain those countries' positive and sustained industrial performance and catch-up with Argentina in terms of manufacturing value added per capita. Population growth in Argentina and Chile did not keep pace with Brazil and Colombia.

13.3 INDUSTRIAL PERFORMANCE DURING THE INTER-WAR PERIOD

Industrial growth during the 1920s varied across South America. Argentina, Brazil, and Chile experienced growth spurts during the first half of the decade, but average growth rates then declined. For Argentina, the 1920s saw the most rapid industrial catch-up in the twentieth century. Industry grew at an average annual rate of 6.5 per cent, the result of export-led manufacturing demand and positive terms of trade. Incumbent firms in the 'traditional' sectors (food, beverages, tobacco, meatpacking houses, sugar mills, and tanning firms) experienced important capacity expansion and structural transformation, and new sectors developed, such as rubber products, chemicals, pharmaceuticals, machinery, and electrical equipment. The 'front-runner' was entering a second phase of industrialization. The share of the new sectors in manufacturing output increased from 13 to 21 per cent between 1920 and 1930. This process took place well before any implementation of an explicit state-led import-substitution strategy (Pineda, 2009). Argentina's performance during the 1920s supports the endogenous industrialization hypothesis.

The decline in the Chilean nitrate industry in the 1920s was due to the improvement in the production of synthetic nitrates in the core countries. The decade started with a 50 per cent nominal devaluation and increased protection that produced a transitory spurt in manufacturing. However, as the real exchange rate appreciated in the long run, the rate of manufacturing growth diminished and even became negative in some years (Palma, 2000; Muñoz, 1968). Thus, the 1920s proved to be the weakest for manufacturing growth in Chile.

Brazil enjoyed rapid industrial growth in the 1920s, driven to a large extent by the rapid advance of coffee exports and national income. The decade saw favourable terms of trade, a large importation of machinery for manufacturing, and a rapid expansion in coffee exports toward the end of the decade. According to Stein (1957) and Musacchio (2009), textiles continued to expand rapidly during this decade. At the end of the 1920s, the government instituted a coffee valorization programme to keep global prices high, while fixing the exchange rate to prevent its rapid appreciation. These measures not only provided an impetus for endogenous industrialization after the second half of the decade, but also allowed Brazil to maintain stable-to-favourable terms of trade during the Great Depression (Suzigan, 1986; Furtado, 1959).

The 1920s were years of unstable manufacturing expansion in Colombia. Industrial growth was fuelled by coffee booms, and large inflows of international capital after the Central Bank was set up in 1923. Incumbent firms expanded capacity and adopted modern management techniques. Foreign direct investment also helped to diversify the industrial sector by expanding oil manufactures. The development of the railroad network during the second half of the decade reduced the cost of transportation and its construction also increased the demand for manufactures. Qualitative evidence suggests that a mild process of endogenous industrialization was taking place in Colombia, aided by moderate protection.

Industrial output grew between 7.5 and 10 per cent per annum between 1931 and 1941 in Brazil, Chile, and Colombia, faster than in Europe and Japan, but not the US. In contrast, Argentina had industrial growth rates of only 3.3 per cent per annum, making it the only country of the four diverging from the industrial leaders.

Brazil and Colombia were not as hard hit by the depression thanks to the rapid recovery of their terms of trade, largely due to their coffee valorization programmes. In fact, Colombia experienced industrial growth of almost 9 per cent per annum during the 1930s and the Second World War, largely because of increasing coffee exports, a large depreciation in the exchange rate, protectionist policies, and an improved transportation infrastructure set up in the 1920s. This industrial growth spurt mostly involved consumer non-durable industries (Ocampo and Montenegro, 2007; Echevarría, 1993).

Chile probably suffered the most during the Great Depression: exports declined by 50 per cent between 1929 and 1932, imports by 83 per cent, and the terms of trade by more than 50 per cent. Chile needed to pursue another model and the policy reaction was immediate. The government engineered a devaluation of more than 300 per cent between 1932 and 1935, resulting in an increase of the real cost of imports of about 100 per cent. The result was an acceleration in average annual industrial output growth of 7.5 per cent (Muñoz, 1968). Manufacturing began an important structural transformation. In 1927 consumption goods still represented 83 per cent of manufacturing output, and Chile was unambiguously in its first phase of industrialization. However, the share of intermediate, heavy, and capital goods output in total manufacturing rose from 7.7 per cent in the early 1930s to 12.8 per cent by 1950, almost doubling. That is, the Great Depression accelerated the move towards import substitution of more sophisticated manufactures in Chile, and ISI policies played a big role in this. In 1938 the state development financial agency, CORFO (Corporacion de Fomento), was created to develop strategic plans for agriculture, industry, and mining, and to develop domestic technology research (Ffrench-Davis et al., 2001).

The adverse shocks hypothesis, which sees negative shocks as opportunities for industrialization, finds some support during this period. Not only did industrial output grow fast in Brazil, Chile, and Colombia, but labour productivity did as well. The only exception was Argentina, which suffered a terrible blow to its terms of trade and had, overall, negative labour productivity growth in the decade.

Why was the Great Depression an obstacle for Argentina while it acted as a boost for the remaining three countries? The front-runner was already attempting its second industrial revolution by the 1920s, and needed access to foreign markets and a continued inflow of foreign capital to finance the structural change. These were unavailable during the 1930s, while the post-depression years delivered a fatal blow to temperate climate crop prices, and international capital flows to developing countries were almost nil. Thus, Argentina followed a very different path than did Brazil or Colombia, due more to bad luck than to bad policy.

13.4 THE SECOND WORLD WAR AND IMPORT-SUBSTITUTING INDUSTRIALIZATION

The golden era of import substitution industrialization was 1944–73, when governments in the region implemented explicit protectionist policies to promote the substitution of consumer goods, and to some extent intermediate goods in Brazil (Leff, 1968). Rapid industrial growth during this period has also been attributed to rapid urbanization; manufacturing surpassed agriculture as the most important employer (although Argentina underwent this process earlier in the century) (Hirschman, 1968; Baer, 1972; Baer, 2008).

While Colombia, Chile, and Brazil continued deepening their industrialization in the 1930s, expanding their textile sectors and beginning to develop other industries (Stein, 1957; Lederman, 2005), Diaz Alejandro (1970) argues that Argentina missed an opportunity to implement a targeted industrial policy that would have enabled that country to follow a smooth transition to a more advanced industrial structure. According to Diaz Alejandro, since Argentina never experienced another export boom (its terms of trade in the post-1945 period was much lower than in 1900–30), the endogenous industrial growth phase was over. Instead a new phase began, during which the country faced recurrent current account deficits and external disequilibria. According to Diaz Alejandro, after the 1930s Argentina experienced a long period of drifting away from its South American front-runner status (Taylor, 1998). Although Argentina's terms of trade continued to decline, and it never experienced endogenous industrialization again, it did exhibit a relatively stable industrial growth rate after the Second World War, ranging between 4 and 6 per cent per annum. Brazil's industrial growth rate ranged between 7 and 11 per cent, Chile's was over 5 per cent, while Colombia maintained almost 7 per cent. The four countries were catching up on the world leader, the US, but only Brazil and Colombia managed to keep converging on the UK, Germany, and Japan.

13.4.1 Protectionism and Industrialization

Students of ISI in Latin America stress that such policies were intended to promote industrialization in stages. That is, governments would sequentially promote new industries with increasingly high value added and ever greater technological complexity. Consumer goods and basic building materials industries would be promoted first because of their simple technology and their low capital requirements. Then governments would support more complex consumer goods industries, which required more sophisticated technologies and higher capital requirements. Finally, governments were to target consumer durables, steel, engineering, chemicals, and other heavy industries (e.g. Brazil and Argentina ventured into aerospace) (Baer, 1972; Love, 2005). This sequencing could include as a final link the development of a domestic capital goods sector, or a complex sector of industrial raw materials. In practice, the sequence did not work like this. Instead, some industries lobbied governments to avoid developing intermediate goods that could lead to expensive inputs (Baer, 1972).

The golden ISI years in Argentina lasted from the 1950s to the early 1970s. The Peron administration (1946–55) opted—by default—for an inward-looking industrialization model that accelerated under the leadership of Arturo Frondizi (1958–62), an advocate of the so-called 'desarrollismo' ('developmentalist' approach). Already in 1960, state-owned enterprises controlled basic sectors of the economy such as iron, steel and petroleum, energy generation, telecommunications, and transport. Multinational corporations were engaged in the production of vehicles, pharmaceuticals, petrochemicals, tobacco, agricultural equipment, and food processing (Katz and Kosacoff, 2001). Structural change in industry was significant between 1950 and 1970: the share of heavy industry in total manufacturing increased from 20.5 to 32.4 per cent, while the share of capital goods manufacturing jumped from 9.7 to 22 per cent. In contrast, the share of consumer goods production dropped by a third. By the mid-1960s, a domestic ISI model was in place; the question by then was whether the battery of protectionist and fiscal policies supporting it were sustainable.

Table 13.5 depicts the change in industrial structure in Brazil during the post-1945 period. We separate manufacturing from the extractive industries, and subdivide it into groups that broadly represent the stages predicted by the import-substituting industrialization hypothesis. Brazil made the largest leap in industrial sophistication during the post-Second World War period. Manufactured consumer goods (associated with the first stage of import substitution) fell from 60 per cent of the total in 1939 to less than 30 per cent by the 1970s. In contrast, the share of heavier industries producing metals, chemicals, plastics, and pharmaceuticals (associated with the second stage of import substitution) almost doubled between 1939 and 1980, going from 17 to 30 per cent of total manufacturing. The rapid increase in these Stage II industries during the 1960s and 1970s is associated

Table 13.5. Industrial value added by type of industry, Brazil and Colombia, 1940–95 (per cent)

	c.1940	c.1955	c.1970	c.1980	c.1990	c. 1995
Brazil						
Transformation of natural resources:	14	15	13	11		
Consumer products (durables and non-durables)	59	41	34	28		
Heavy industry and industrial inputs	17	24	27	30		
Capital goods and high-technology products	5	15	20	24		
Others	1	2	2	4		
Colombia						
Consumer products (non-durables)	n.a.	66.3	30	32	31	33
Consumer products (durables)	n.a.	4.6	14	15	16	18
Intermediate goods	n.a.	16	39	34	36	34
Capital goods	n.a.	12	9	10	9	8
Transportation equipment	n.a.	n.a.	7	9	8	7

Sources: Brazil, compiled from IBGE (1990, p. 386). Colombia from ECLA (1957, p. 274); Garay (1998, p. 463).

with the explicit development plans of the military government (1964–85) promoting heavy industries. Finally, industries associated with Stage III, such as mechanical industries, electrical and telecommunications equipment, and transportation equipment (automobiles and airplanes), gained momentum after the 1950s and reached 24 per cent of total manufactures by 1980. This was the heyday of industrial policy in Brazil, when the government provided the subsidized financing, infrastructure, and raw materials needed to develop some of the most sophisticated industries in the country. State-owned enterprises were key to developing the airplane, petrochemicals, electricity, and telecommunications sectors (Musacchio and Lazzarini, 2014).

By 1949 the local capital goods industry provided over 60 per cent of the domestic demand for industrial equipment. This development is especially impressive given that the nascent capital goods industry developed despite competition from foreign imports until at least the 1960s, during which time machinery imports benefited from preferential exchange rate treatment and duty-free importation. In fact, the development of the Brazilian capital goods industry was so impressive that the 'domestic supply coefficient [for capital goods] was more than three times larger than in Argentina during the same years' (Leff, 1968, p. 8).

In Colombia, ISI policies also involved the development of industrial banks and creative exchange rate devaluation mechanisms to reduce the chance of recurrent foreign exchange crises. Manufacturing underwent a significant transformation between 1955 and 1970 (see Table 13.5). The production of durables and intermediate goods increased rapidly, rising from 4.6 and 16 per cent of manufacturing value added to 14 and 39 per cent, respectively. These shares would then remain constant for most of the twentieth century.

An additional important fact about the post-Second World War period is that our 'front-runner', Argentina, lagged behind, at least relative to Brazil, Colombia, and itself. Since there was no threat of external competition, Argentinian manufacturers focused on the domestic market and, according to Krugman (1993), experienced growth rates below their potential. But most importantly, ISI was an 'incomplete model' as the inadequate growth of industrial exports during this whole period was still an obstacle. Furthermore, attempts to develop large-scale, heavy industry required a continuous injection of public subsidies.

During the ISI golden age Chile was catching up on the US but lost the opportunity of catching up even faster, as did the UK, Germany, Japan, Brazil, and Colombia. Between 1950 and 1972, manufacturing grew at 5 per cent per annum in a context of very high monetary instability and stop–go macroeconomic policies. Chile did not implement a smooth ISI strategy, and the results were not stellar (Ffrench-Davis et al., 2001; Muñoz, 1968; Cortes Douglas, Butelmann, and Videla, 1981).

Having described the policy context and industrial performance in these four countries, we can now focus on the heated debates regarding the causes and limits of industrialization in Latin America during the ISI period. At least two important issues should be highlighted. First, the measurement of protection to domestic industrial producers is complex, and its correlation with industrial growth is debated. Second, there is still a debate as to what the right counterfactual is for Latin America in the post-Second World War period. Did Latin America industrialize rapidly because of ISI policies, or despite them? Could industrial growth rates have been higher if another set of policies had been implemented?

13.4.2 Overall Effect of ISI Policies

The contrasting performance of Brazil and Colombia on the one hand, and Argentina and Chile on the other, raises a puzzle. Was protection for domestic manufacturing behind the stellar performance of the former two countries? If it was, why did Chile and Argentina not achieve the same outcomes? In order to shed some light on this puzzle, Fig. 13.1 plots what we call real distorted import price indices for the four countries. These are the prices that local producers would have observed for competing imports. The index is the ratio of import prices (in domestic currency) to domestic prices. The prices of foreign goods in the domestic market are calculated by multiplying the import price index by the average tariff and the nominal exchange rate. Domestic prices are measured by the domestic price index for industrial goods (or the industrial GDP deflator). After a base year is selected, increases in the index above 100 imply that local producers faced greater protection from imports. The index is a useful but incomplete measure because it considers the effects of quantitative trade restrictions only via its effects on the domestic industrial price index.

Fig. 13.1 shows the log scale of the real distorted import price index (1939 = 100). We focus on trends rather than on levels and interpret the evolution of the index for each country. In Brazil macro and trade policies generated increasing protection for domestic producers up to 1980. Protection in Colombia was roughly increasing

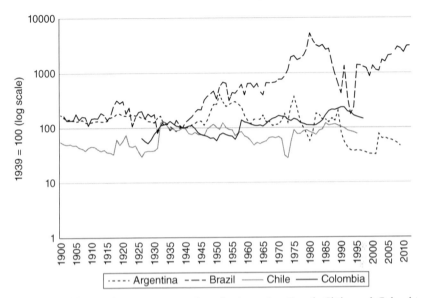

Fig. 13.1. Real distorted import price indices for Argentina, Brazil, Chile, and Colombia, 1900–2012 (1939 = 100)

Note: The real distorted import prices index = ((1+ avg. tariff) × nominal exchange rate × import price index)/ domestic industrial price index. We then index this series taking 1939 as the base year (1939 = 100).

Source: See Data Appendix.

between 1950 and 1990. In Argentina it increased up to 1950, and declined thereafter. In Chile, the index declined between 1948 and 1972 and increased thereafter. It is surprising that the Pinochet government seems to have implemented a set of policies that, although they included substantial trade liberalization, overall tended to protect domestic industrial producers.

To understand the overall effects of ISI policies it is important to derive synthetic indices such as the ones plotted in Fig. 13.1. The different macro and trade policies implemented during the ISI period generated complex effects on the economy, and it is even possible that their overall effect did not involve protection from import competition. The point seems even more important to take into consideration when one considers the complex political economy influencing ISI policies (the impact of trade unions, shifts from left to right, dictatorships, etc.). However, it seems that when a country aligned macro and trade policies so as to deliver truly effective industrial protection, it also experienced higher industrial growth. Thus, there seems to be suggestive evidence that increasing protection was indeed associated with increasing industrial growth. The period from the 1940s to the 1970s was characterized by a catch-up of industrial output and productivity on the leaders. Even though not all of our countries experienced faster industrial output growth than the US, they all experienced labour productivity growth that was almost twice as fast as in the US.

13.4.3 The Post-Second World War Period
as a Missed Opportunity

Did increasing protection lead to the highest possible industrial growth rates, or were there lost opportunities available that South American did not take, but that other regions at similar stages of development took? Fig. 13.1 suggests that more distortions were correlated with faster industrialization in Colombia and Brazil, but less so in Chile. Industrial catch-up on the US could be considered a clear indication of the success of ISI policies. But compared to other latecomers, how good were those ISI policies?

There are at least three reasons why the post-Second World War period could be considered a missed opportunity and/or a period of not so stellar industrial growth. First, using Asia as a counterfactual makes us question the importance of protectionist policies in promoting industrialization in Latin America. Second, the measures we have of industrial growth, the share of manufacturing in GDP, and labour productivity in manufacturing, are distorted by the fact that protectionism led to higher domestic prices for domestic producers. These rents were not necessarily a sign of progress for everyone in the economy. Third, protectionist policies also ended up hurting the capacity of South American countries to promote regional markets. Finally, the timing of the decline in manufacturing as a share of GDP (in the late 1970s) casts doubt on the hypothesis that ISI policies led to successful industrialization in the region.

In Northeast Asia the ISI policy mix included more incentives for domestic producers to export and compete in global markets, and more targeted tariff protection. For instance, in South Korea, even if tariff protection was spread around the same sectors as in Argentina or Colombia, tariffs were lower on average—for a shorter time—and were more targeted to promote specific industries or companies (Wade, 1990). The result of these policies was faster industrial growth than in the United States. In fact, manufacturing value added in South Korea grew at an average of 11.2 per cent in the post-1945 period, and continued at an accelerated pace in the 1980s (above 12 per cent per year) and in the post-1990 period (7.7 per cent per annum).

Comparisons with South Korea suggest that we need to improve our knowledge in at least two ways in order to better understand South America's ISI experience. First, what is the right counterfactual for Latin America? More precisely, is industrial catch-up on the US enough, or should we develop a measure of potential catch-up to judge our countries' performance during this period? Industrial catch-up on the world industrial leader may mask faster potential catch-up. After all, the industrial leaders were all on the brink of de-industrialization. Second, the East Asian 'gang of four' (South Korea, Taiwan, Hong Kong, and Singapore) were growing faster than Argentina and Chile. In addition, all four South American countries exhibited faster productivity growth in the 1930s than during the golden age of ISI (except for Argentina), which suggests that the potential for faster catch-up was there, but not achieved. If this conjecture is correct, our evidence may support the ISI stagnationist hypothesis.

Beyond this counterfactual using Asia, we know that the price distortions depicted in Fig. 13.1 were high for Brazil and Colombia, and that high protection is correlated with faster industrial growth. However, we also know that the shares of industrial value added in GDP were larger during this period, but in part because there were large rents in the protected industries. That is, value added and productivity figures may be inflated by the presence of such rents. With distortions such as tariff protection came high internal prices that made value added seem higher than if prices had been set in international markets.

Moreover, the distortions introduced by governments in South America also affected their capacity to promote a regional market for manufactures. In contrast with East Asia, where some manufactured products had to be competitive in international markets, the prices of Latin American manufactured goods were uncompetitive on world markets; furthermore, they could not be exported to neighbouring countries either, because they also wanted to develop their own industries using a similar policy mix. Thus, Latin America missed important opportunities to spur interregional trade: low productivity and high trade barriers became major obstacles, especially for intra-regional manufacturing trade (Badia-Miró, Carreras-Marín, and Meissner, 2014). Interregional integration and industrialization did not progress, despite efforts such as the 1940 Pinedo Plan, the 1944 John Hopkins report on 'Cooperación para la promoción del Intercambio in Argentina', which proposed the creation of a regional free trade area, or the Andean Pact between Bolivia, Chile, Colombia, Ecuador, Peru, and Venezuela.

All in all, maybe with the exception of Brazil, until the 1960s South American manufacturing production was mostly to satisfy domestic demand. The manufacturing sector in the region was a net importer, requiring foreign exchange continuously, which produced recurrent balance of payments crises. But the exclusively inward-looking characteristic of industry started to change by 1970: the share of manufacturing in total exports increased, governments lowered average tariffs, and some quantitative restrictions were removed. In addition, the creation of the free trade areas of ALADI (1980), which all four countries joined, and MERCOSUR (1990), which changed the export profiles of Argentina, Brazil, and to a lesser extent Chile, also allowed the region to expand manufactured exports.

Finally, the timing of de-industrialization also casts doubt on the hypothesis that ISI policies led to successful industrialization in the region. In the 1970s, all four countries experienced a deceleration of their industrial growth rates from 4 to 2 per cent. This implies that de-industrialization, measured as a declining share of manufacturing in total GDP, started for most countries *before* their governments dismissed ISI policies and *before* the crisis of the 1980s. That is, de-industrialization happened not as a consequence of the demise of ISI, but during the ISI period. De-industrialization started in Chile in 1971 (while Salvador Allende was still in power, and before any major change to ISI policies), and in Argentina and Colombia by 1975, also before any important departure from ISI programmes. In contrast, Brazil did not engage in any major liberalization until the late 1980s and early 1990s.

13.5 THE 1980s DEBT CRISIS AND ITS IMPACT
IN SOUTH AMERICA

The 1980s is again a period with mixed results. On the one hand, for Brazil and Argentina this is a decade of crisis. With the rapid rise in interest rates in the United States and the debt default of Mexico, capital markets were closed for these South American nations and their governments could not refinance their foreign debt. During this decade, industrial GDP growth rates decreased across the board, and despite rapid exchange rate depreciations, domestic industry suffered because of the contraction in domestic demand and the sudden stop in capital inflows (Frieden, 1991). Argentina and Brazil, in fact, ended up running hyperinflationary policies in the late 1980s, which forced their governments to open up and to establish fixed exchange rate regimes (in order to anchor prices). On the other hand, Chile and Colombia went through the crisis relatively unscathed, with moderate macroeconomic imbalances.

In all four countries, manufacturing output and productivity growth rates slowed substantially, and manufacturing as a share of GDP accelerated its decline. Simultaneously, the world leader, the US, and the close followers, the UK, Germany, and Japan, all experienced industrial output and productivity growth deceleration. Therefore, in relative terms Brazil and Colombia managed to catch-up, while Argentina and Chile increased its gap with these industrial leaders.

13.6 THE 1990s AND BEYOND

During the 1990s, a period of rapid structural change, we observe a rebound from the dismal 1980s, but with extremely modest rates of growth. The industrial complex in Argentina and Brazil maintained average growth rates close to 2 per cent, while Chile's industrial performance improved substantially, reaching average growth rates of 7 per cent. The success of Chile in the 1990s stems from the fact that its manufacturing sector gained international competitiveness, mostly in the so-called extractive industries, but also in some of the medium- and high-technology industries. According to our estimates, the Chilean manufacturing sector was the best performer of the 1990s and 2000s, with an average annual rate of growth of close to 4 per cent per year. This may be related to the fact that the Chilean terms of trade substantially improved after 1995, when the government ran a nominal exchange rate crawling peg to avoid sharp swings in the real exchange rate (Huelva and Núñez, 2010).

The 1990s were Colombia's worst decade of the twentieth century in terms of industrial growth, which stood at just over 2 per cent average growth per annum. While trade and capital market reform advanced and the terms of trade improved, there was a cycle of exchange rate appreciation–depreciation–appreciation that ended up hurting manufacturing growth (Tovar, 1998; Ocampo and Montenegro, 2007).

Finally, during the first decade of the twenty-first century, Brazil, Chile, and Colombia experienced modest average manufacturing growth while Argentina's output experienced a sharp decline, followed by a sharp rebound after 2005. During this period Chile's industrial growth rates were higher than in both the US and the other industrial leaders, while Argentina, Brazil, and Colombia did not lose too much ground on the US, and experienced industrial catch-up on the other industrial leaders (see Table 13.3).

13.7 CONCLUSION

This chapter has constructed new long-run series of industrial GDP growth and labour productivity growth, as well as a set of variables related to initial conditions, international trade, and macroeconomic policy. We have used these data to test four popular hypotheses: industrialization promoted endogenously by exports via an income effect in the domestic economy; industrialization occurred under adverse shocks that induced policies promoting industrialization; import-substituting-industrialization induced rapid manufacturing productivity growth; and import-substituting industrialization promoted uncompetitive domestic firms.

Industrial catch-up on the global leaders (the US, the UK, Germany, and Japan) did take place. But catch-up was not experienced during the whole period, and its pace was uneven over time and across countries.

The initial conditions facing these countries in 1900 were varied, and had an important impact on their subsequent industrial development. Argentina was characterized by higher human capital, and urbanization and transportation advantages, compared to the other three countries, and had begun its industrial development earlier. Brazil's size was not an advantage at this time: its large population was still poor, illiterate, sparsely located, and far from water transport. Strong industrial development only started at the turn of the twentieth century. Chile was relatively well endowed with human capital and low transport costs, but it had a small domestic market that was only moderately urbanized. It industrialized slowly. Like Brazil, Colombia's population was relatively illiterate, poor, sparsely located, and far from water transport. It was the industrial latecomer of this group.

There was an important heterogeneity across countries and periods in terms of the causes of industrialization and the policies adopted. Brazil's experience highlights the very different sources of industrial growth over time: strong endogenous industrialization (1900–30), an adverse shock and export boom (1930–44), ISI (1944–80), and weak endogenous industrialization (1991–2010). Chile's failure to catch-up on the US and the other industrial followers in the early stages of the twentieth century highlights the fact that industrialization via exporting was not automatic, even if many initial conditions had been already achieved. Argentina's failure to converge during the decade of fastest convergence in Latin America, the Great Depression, shows that even if most countries adopt similar policies, some are lucky and export and industrialize, while others do not. And Colombia's impressive Great Depression and ISI industrial performance highlights the importance of combining protectionist policies with interventions to reduce the disadvantages of initial conditions.

This chapter thus highlights the importance of considering the international context, internal policies, initial conditions, and the nature of the country's export products, in understanding industrialization. The point is particularly important in the context of the literature on Latin America's industrialization, as this has emphasized policies, while downplaying the importance of these other factors, as well as the heterogeneity of country experiences within the region.

Finally, the share of manufacturing in GDP followed an inverse U-shape in South America during this period. The relative importance of the industrial sector increased rapidly after the Great Depression, peaked in the 1970s, and then fell during a period of relative de-industrialization. We have seen that industrialization in most countries required protectionism. With a few exceptions, there was a large retrenchment from manufacturing once these economies started opening up to the world economy after the 1990s. We do not argue that the policies that promoted industrialization before 1980 should be tried again. On the contrary, our estimates show that the de-industrialization of South America started before the demise of ISI. Latin American policies before 1970 enjoyed only short-term success, and only in some industries did the region develop long-term comparative advantage.

DATA APPENDIX

Series on manufacturing value added for Argentina, Brazil, Chile, and Colombia have been produced by researchers and agencies at various times. The most frequently used sources include the World Bank's World Development Indicators (WB) and the Economic Commission for Latin America (ECLA). A project initially based at Oxford University and now at the Universidad de la República, Montevideo, collected and collated substantial ECLA data and has made it easily accessible for free via an internet website named MOxLAD (MOxLAD, 2014). The data on this website are slightly different from what we collected directly from ECLA reports (ECLA, 1966). After careful analysis, we decided to use manufacturing value added series put together by local experts in each country, rather than the MOxLAD or ECLA data. These series are usually longer, behave similarly to the ECLA series, and incorporate substantial local knowledge. That is, they purge distortions associated with political manipulation of the data from the series.

We have made additional adjustments to these manufacturing value added series. For Argentina we use manufacturing GDP in constant 1960 local currency units (LCU), constructed by Orlando Ferreres for 1875–2012 (Ferreres, 2005). For Brazil, we use IPEA's series of industrial value added in current LCU, deflated by the GDP deflator, for 1908–70. We then link this to the IPEA's real industrial value added series in LCU (deflated using the industrial GDP deflator) for 1971–2012 (IPEA, 2014). For Chile, we use the Díaz, Lüders, and Wagner (DLW) manufacturing value added series (in 1996 constant LCU) for the period 1900–2004, and extrapolate this to 2005–12 using real manufacturing GDP growth rates from Banco Central de Chile (Díaz, Schwarzenberg, and Wagner, 2007). Finally, for Colombia, we use the real manufacturing GDP for 1925–2012 from Banco de la República (1998). The four series are converted into indices with 1960 as the base year (1960 = 100).

We calculate growth rates of manufacturing value added and manufacturing labour productivity in LCU. Since we do not have PPP exchange rates for the whole period, we prefer to assume that policy-induced nominal exchange rate distortions are (eventually) translated into inflation, and are therefore accounted for in local currency series. Although this is not ideal, estimating century-long PPPs for the four countries is beyond the scope of this chapter. Furthermore, hyperinflation and exchange rate events in Argentina and Brazil suggest that this is probably the best way forward, as we know that the local expert series have taken hyperinflation, the adoption of new currencies, and exchange rate events into account. Thus, average long-term growth rates are comparable across countries and over time, although care was taken if important exchange rate or inflationary events took place precisely at the cut-off dates of our periodization.

REFERENCES

Badia-Miró, M., Carreras-Marín, A., and Meissner, C. M. (2014). Geography, policy, or productivity? Regional trade in five South American countries, 1910–1950. *National Bureau of Economic Research Working Paper* No. 20790.

Baer, W. (1972). Import substitution and industrialization in Latin America: experiences and interpretations. *Latin American Research Review* 7, 95–122.

Baer, W. (2008). *The Brazilian Economy: Growth and Development.* Boulder, CO: Lynne Rienner.

Barbero, M. and Rocchi, F. (2003). Industry. In *A New Economic History of Argentina* (Eds, Della Paolera, G. and Taylor, A. M.). Cambridge: Cambridge University Press, 261–94.

Bates, R. H. (1998). *Open-Economy Politics: The Political Economy of the World Coffee Trade.* Princeton, NJ: Princeton University Press.

Bénétrix, A. S., O'Rourke, K., and Williamson, J. G. (2015). The spread of manufacturing to the poor periphery 1870–2007. *Open Economies Review* 26, 1–37.

Bulmer-Thomas, V. (2003). *The Economic History of Latin America since Independence.* Cambridge: Cambridge University Press.

Cano, W. (1977). *Raízes da Concentração Industrial em São Paulo.* Rio de Janeiro: Difel.

Coatsworth, J. H. and Williamson, J. G. (2004). Always protectionist? Latin American tariffs from independence to Great Depression. *Journal of Latin American Studies* 36, 205–32.

Colistete, R. P. (2009). Revisiting import-substituting industrialization in Brazil: productivity growth and technological learning in the post-war years. Paper presented at conference on Latin America, Globalization, and Economic History, 24 and 25 April.

Cortes Douglas, H., Butelmann, A., and Videla, P. (1981). Proteccionismo en Chile: una vision retrospectiva. *Cuadernos de Economía* 18, 141–94.

Dean, W. (1969). *The Industrialization of São Paulo.* Austin, TX: University of Texas Press.

Diaz-Alejandro, C. F. (1970). *Essays on the Economic History of the Argentine Republic.* New Haven, CT: Yale University Press.

Diaz-Alejandro, C. F. (1976). *Foreign Trade Regimes and Economic Development: Colombia.* New York: National Bureau of Economic Research.

Díaz, J., Schwarzenberg, R. L., and Wagner, G. (2007). Economía Chilena 1810–2000: producto total y sectorial: una nueva mirada. *Pontificia Universidad Católica de Chile, Instituto de Economía, Documento de Trabajo* 315.

Echavarría, J. J. (1993). External shocks and industrialization: Colombia, 1920–1950. D.Phil. dissertation, University of Oxford, 1993.

ECLA, United Nations (1966). *The Process of Industrialization in Latin America.* Santiago: United Nations.

Ferreres, O. (2005). *Dos Siglos De Economía Argentina: Historia argentina en cifras*. Buenos Aires: El Ateneo: Fundación Norte y Sur.

Ffrench-Davis, R., Munoz, O., Benavente, J. M., and Crespi, G. (2001). The Industrialisation of Chile during Protectionism (1940–82). In *An Economic History of Twentieth-Century Latin America*, Vol. 3: *Industrialization and the State in Latin America: The Postwar Years* (Eds, Cardenas, E., Ocampo, J. A., and Thorp, R.). Houndmills, Basingstoke: Palgrave Macmillan, 114–53.

Frieden, J. A. (1991). *Debt, Development, and Democracy: Modern Political Economy and Latin America, 1965–1985*. Princeton, NJ: Princeton University Press.

Furtado, C. (1959). *Formação Econômica Do Brasil*. Rio de Janeiro: Ed. Fundo de Cultura Econômica.

Goldin, C. and Katz, L. F. (1996). Technology, skill, and the wage structure: insights from the past. *American Economic Review* 86, 252–7.

Haber, S. H. (1991). Industrial concentration and the capital markets: a comparative study of Brazil, Mexico, and the United States, 1830–1930. *Journal of Economic History* 51, 559–80.

Haber, S. H. (2006). The political economy of industrialization. In *The Cambridge Economic History of Latin America*, Vol. 2: *The Long Twentieth Century* (Eds, Bulmer-Thomas, V., Coatsworth, J., and Cortes-Conde, R.). Cambridge: Cambridge University Press, 537–84.

Haddad, C. L. and Contador, C. R. (1975). Produto, moeda e preços: Brasil 1861–1970. *Revista Brasileira de Estatística* 36, 407–70.

Herranz-Loncán, A. (2014). Transport technology and economic expansion: the growth contribution of railways in Latin America before 1914. *Revista de Historia Económica/Journal of Iberian and Latin American Economic History* 32, 13–45.

Hirschman, A. (1968). The political economy of import-substituting industrialization in Latin America. *Quarterly Journal of Economics* 81, 1–32.

Huelva, D. C. and Núñez, S. R. (2010). Cambio estructural de la industria manufacturera en Chile: 1979–2004. *Revista de Economía Mundial* 26, 27–51.

IBGE (1990). *Estatísticas Históricas Do Brasil. Séries Econômicas, Demográficas E Sociais De 1550 a 1988*. Rio de Janeiro: IBGE.

IPEA (2014). *Ipeadata*. Rio de Janeiro: IPEA. Available from www.ipeadata.gov.br/

Katz, J. and Kosacoff, B. (2001). Technological learning, institution building and the microeconomics of import substitution. In *An Economic History of Twentieth-Century Latin America*, Vol. 3: *Industrialization and the State in Latin America: The Postwar Years* (Eds, Cardenas, E., Ocampo, J. A., and Thorp, R.). Houndmills, Basingstoke: Palgrave Macmillan, 282–313.

Krueger, A. O. (1978). *Liberalization Attempts and Consequences*. Cambridge, MA: Ballinger and NBER.

Krugman, P. R. (1993). First nature, second nature, and metropolitan location. *Journal of Regional Science* 33, 129–44.

Lederman, D. (2005). *The Political Economy of Protection: Theory and the Chilean Experience*. Stanford, CA: Stanford University Press.

Leff, N. H. (1968). *The Brazilian Capital Goods Industry, 1929–1964*. Cambridge, MA: Harvard University Press.

Love, J. L. (2005). The rise and decline of economic structuralism in Latin America: new dimensions. *Latin American Research Review* 40, 100–25.

Macario, S. (1964). Protectionism and industrialization in Latin America. *Economic Bulletin for Latin America* 9, 61–101.

Maloney, W. F. (2002). Missed opportunities: innovation and resource-based growth in Latin America. *Economía* 3, 111–67.

Melo, J. O. (1987). Las vicisitudes del modelo liberal (1850–1899). In *Historia Económica De Colombia* (Ed, Ocampo, J. A.). Bogotá: Siglo XXI editores, 135–89.

MOxLAD (2014). *Montevideo–Oxford Latin American Economic History Database* (Eds, University of Montevideo and Oxford University). Montevideo. Available at http://www.lac.ox.ac.uk/moxlad-database.

Muñoz, O. (1968). *Crecimiento Industrial De Chile 1914–1965*. Santiago, Chile: Universidad de Chile, Instituto de Economía.

Musacchio, A. (2009). *Experiments in Financial Democracy: Corporate Governance and Financial Development in Brazil, 1882–1950*. New York: Cambridge University Press.

Musacchio, A. and Lazzarini, S. G. 2014. *Reinventing State Capitalism: Leviathan in Business, Brazil and Beyond*. Cambridge, MA: Harvard University Press.

Musacchio, A., Martínez Fritscher, A., and Viarengo, M. (2014). Colonial institutions, trade shocks, and the diffusion of elementary education in Brazil, 1889–1930. *Journal of Economic History* 74, 730–66.

O'Rourke, K. H. and Williamson, J. G. (1999). *Globalization and History: The Evolution of a Nineteenth-Century Atlantic Economy*. Cambridge, MA: MIT Press.

Obstfeld, M. and Taylor, A. M. 2004. *Global Capital Markets: Integration, Crisis, and Growth*. Cambridge: Cambridge University Press.

Ocampo, J. A. and Montenegro, S. 2007. *Crisis Mundial, Protección E Industrialización*. Bogotá: Editorial Norma.

Palma, G. (2000). From an export-led to an import-substituting economy: Chile 1914–39. In *An Economic History of Twentieth-Century Latin America*, Vol. 1: *The Export Age: The Latin American Economies in the Late Nineteenth and Early Twentieth Centuries* (Eds, Cardenas, E., Ocampo, J. A., and Thorp, R.). Houndmills, Basingstoke: Palgrave Macmillan, 217–64.

Pineda, Y. (2009). *Industrial Development in a Frontier Economy: The Industrialization of Argentina, 1890–1930*. Stanford, CA: University Press.

Prebisch, R. (1950). *The Economic Development of Latin America and Its Principal Problems*. Lake Success, NY: ECLA and UN Department of Economic Affairs.

Rocchi, F. (2005). *Chimneys in the Desert: Industrialization in Argentina during the Export Boom Years, 1870–1930*. Stanford, CA: University Press.

Sokoloff, K. L. and Engerman, S. L. (2000). History lessons: institutions, factors endowments, and paths of development in the New World. *Journal of Economic Perspectives* 14, 217–32.

Stein, S. J. (1957). *The Brazilian Cotton Manufacture: Textile Enterprise in an Underdeveloped Area, 1850–1950*. Cambridge, MA: Harvard University Press.

Stone, I. (1999). *The Global Export of Capital from Great Britain, 1865–1914: A Statistical Survey*. Houndmills, Basingstoke: Macmillan.

Suzigan, W. (1986). *Indústria Brasileira: Origem e Desenvolvimento*. São Paulo: Brasiliense.

Tavares, M. C. (1972). O processo de substituição de importações como modelo de desenvolvimento na América Latina. In *Da Substituição de Importações ao Capitalismo Financeiro* (Ed., Tavares, M. C.). Rio de Janeiro: Zahar, 47–150.

Taylor, A. M. (1998). On the costs of inward-looking development: price distortions, growth, and divergence in Latin America. *Journal of Economic History* 58, 1–28.

Tovar, J. (1998). La Industria Manufacturera, 1967–1995. In *Colombia: Estructura Industrial e Internacionalización 1967–1996* (Ed., Garay, L. J.). Bogotá: Ricardo Alonso, 453–530.

United Nations/ECLA (1951). *Economic Survey of Latin America, 1949*. New York: United Nations.

Versiani, F. R. (1980). Industrial investment in an export economy: the Brazilian experience before 1914. *Journal of Development Economics* 7, 307–29.

Wade, R. (1990). *Governing the Market: Economic Theory and the Role of Government in East Asian Industrialization*. Princeton, NJ: Princeton University Press.

Williamson, J. G. (2006). *Globalization and the Poor Periphery before 1950*. Cambridge, MA: MIT Press.

Williamson, J. G. (2011a). Industrial catching up in the poor periphery 1870–1975. *National Bureau of Economic Research Working Paper Series* No. 16809.

Williamson, J. G. (2011b). *Trade and Poverty: When the Third World Fell Behind*. Cambridge, MA: MIT Press.

PART IV
SUB-SAHARAN AFRICA

14

Patterns of Manufacturing Growth
in Sub-Saharan Africa
From Colonization to the Present

Gareth Austin, Ewout Frankema, and Morten Jerven

14.1 INTRODUCTION

Currently, Sub-Saharan Africa has the lowest manufacturing output per capita of any inhabited region on the planet. Most African economies, in contrast to the Asian NICs, have so far failed to supplement agricultural and extractive output by raising average productivity through the creation of a substantial number of jobs in higher-value-added manufacturing industries. From the perspective of mainstream growth theory, this appears to be an important *proximate* cause of comparative African poverty. This view has received new impetus from a recent study documenting unconditional convergence between leaders and followers in manufacturing labour productivity since the 1960s (Rodrik, 2013). The key message of the study is that failure to catch up in aggregate economic terms is not because manufacturing industries in the 'periphery' are underperforming, but rather because the proportion of industrial workers in the total labour force has remained too small to offer a substantial push to aggregate growth.

If industrialization of the global economic periphery is crucial to a sustained decline of global economic inequality in the twenty-first century, the case of Sub-Saharan Africa deserves special attention. Assessments of African economic development have become more optimistic recently due to encouraging rates of aggregate economic growth since *c.*1995 (IMF, 2012; Young, 2012; UNECA, 2013). While initial studies of the boom were largely silent on manufacturing growth, the matter has now begun to receive more attention (de Vries, Trimmer, and de Vries, 2013; McMillan and Harttgren, 2014; Rodrik, 2014; Diao and McMillan, 2015; Jerven 2015).

There are few signs yet that African countries are copying the Asian success-formula of moving up the value chain by promoting export of labour-intensive manufacturing produce (Sugihara, 2007; Austin and Sugihara, 2013). Nor do the growth rates of manufacturing output in the past decades offer encouragement. The more successful Asian and Latin American economies in the industrial convergence club have recorded annual average rates of manufacturing output growth surpassing 5 per cent for at least half a century and sometimes even over a full century (e.g. Japan, China, and Chile: see Bénétrix, O'Rourke, and Williamson (2015) and Chapter 2 in this volume). The only Sub-Saharan African country that achieved a more extended period of accelerated manufacturing output growth is South Africa (1924–78) during the heyday of its segregation and apartheid regimes. When other African countries caught the manufacturing train, it was for considerably shorter journeys. Moreover, among all the countries in the sample that have recorded a ten-year annual average growth rate of manufacturing output exceeding 5 per cent since 1980, not one has managed to sustain this acceleration to the present. Indeed, in Sub-Saharan Africa as a whole, the share of manufacturing in aggregate output actually declined between 1980 and 2010 (UNECA, 2013, pp. 7, 74).[1]

This chapter reviews the historical development of 'modern' manufacturing in Sub-Saharan Africa, including the transition from 'pre-modern' to 'modern' forms of manufacturing. We define 'modern' as production based on inanimate sources of energy, which began during colonial rule. Its promotion has been an object of government policy mainly since independence from overseas rule. It was adopted by South Africa and Southern Rhodesia (now Zimbabwe) under white minority regimes in 1924 and 1933 respectively, and in many of the other countries when they escaped from European rule around 1960. Modern manufacturing began later in sub-Saharan Africa than in some parts of Asia, Latin America, North Africa, and the Middle East, and its diffusion was certainly slower during the long twentieth century. Yet, for a deeper understanding of African manufacturing growth it is not sufficient to state that Africa is simply 'later' than the rest; the crucial question is whether there are signs that the *nature* of African industrial growth was or is different from experiences elsewhere. Only by exploring the deeper characteristics of the process, apart from rates of growth, may we hope to offer some cautious predictions for its future trajectory.

Bénétrix, O'Rourke, and Williamson (2015) have argued that Sub-Saharan Africa was no exception to their rule that, once 'peripheral' countries began to industrialize, their catching-up on the industrial leaders was 'unconditional' (see also Rodrik, 2013). However, arguably their historical sample is biased, in that for Sub-Saharan Africa it includes only the few countries in the sub-continent that achieved some notable scale of manufacturing before the 1950s (South Africa, Southern Rhodesia, and the Belgian Congo). We maintain, rather, that the story to date is more accurately summarized as *interrupted industrial growth* rather than catch-up growth; certainly for the Congo and Zimbabwe, but even, arguably, for South Africa. Moreover, taking account of the broader African experience, we argue

---

[1] The report of the UN Economic Commission for Africa gives two sets of figures on this, which agree on the fact of relative decline but differ on its magnitude, for reasons that seem unclear. The share of manufacturing value added in GDP is reported to have fallen from 16.6 per cent to 12.7 per cent in Sub-Saharan Africa, while rising in North Africa from 12.6 per cent to 13.6 per cent (2013, p. 74). Elsewhere in the document, the share of manufacturing in the aggregate output of the continent as a whole is given as slipping from over 12 per cent in 1980 to about 11 per cent in 2010 (p. 7).

that while 'unconditional convergence' in manufacturing output growth remains a dream, the conditions for achieving it are better at present than they were in the late nineteenth century, or even at the time when most African countries achieved independence from colonial rule (*c.*1960).

We explore the determinants of manufacturing growth in Sub-Saharan Africa by focusing on the interaction between changing factor endowments, global economic relationships, and government policies. Our argument is as follows. The sub-continent entered the colonial period with an emerging comparative advantage in land-extensive production, agricultural and mineral, which colonial governments and (in the 'peasant' colonies at least) African farmers and entrepreneurs proceeded to deepen. Colonial and post-colonial government policies contributed to the growth of population and human capital, which by the end of the twentieth century had greatly eroded the region's long-running characteristic of land abundance and labour scarcity. This historical transformation in the region's endowment structure facilitated the expansion (or in some areas, creation) of wage labour markets (Sender and Smith, 1986). Colonial governments and enterprises also enhanced capital formation and the development of consumer markets, including new financial institutions. Africa's known 'resource wealth' has been progressively augmented by a combination of the search for commercially valuable minerals and, more so, by technological innovations outside the continent which have created new markets for materials and fluids found in Africa, even as mining and pumping have reduced these reserves. In the setting of these changing endowment structures, the crucial issue for any prospective late-industrializing country is whether the ruling elite has had the *capacity* to adopt and the *dedication* to sustain policies that, in effect, defied—and, implicitly, sought to modify—the country's existing comparative advantage in primary production, by using its fiscal and regulatory powers to promote industrialization (Gerschenkron, 1962; Wade, 1990; Amsden, 1992).

We argue further that the changing dynamics of politics and international competition for resources and markets have played an important role in shaping the conditions for such commitments and policy agendas. The fact that white minority regimes were the first actively to encourage manufacturing development was because they had become independent (South Africa) or autonomous (Southern Rhodesia) first. The South African government started its programme in 1924, followed within a decade by Southern Rhodesia. The start of commercial copper mining in the 1920s in Katanga, in the southeast of the Belgian Congo, also spurred investments in complementary manufacturing industries. Following the independence of most of Africa around 1960, a larger number of tropical African countries adopted industrialization as a policy objective, despite relatively high costs for unskilled and especially for skilled labour. Import-substituting industrialization (ISI) polices were adopted by regimes with 'socialist' as well as 'capitalist' sympathies. But ISI policies were renounced when the same countries participated in economic liberalization programmes ('Structural Adjustment') in the 1980s and 1990s. Escalating government debts and conditional foreign aid reduced the opportunities for African governments to design independent economic policies.

Meanwhile, however, factor ratios within the sub-continent continued to move towards a relatively abundant and better educated labour force. This creates opportunities for labour-intensive industrialization (Austin and Sugihara, 2013), of which Mauritius has become the regional pioneer (Teal, 1999), with Ethiopia now looking to follow on a larger scale. Part of the reason why African economies have not (yet) been able to turn changing relative factor prices to their benefit is the tough competition they face from emerging economies in a neo-liberal global economic order.

Any long-term analysis of African economic development suffers data-availability constraints. There are relatively long manufacturing output series only for three countries, which happen to be the ones with significant early manufacturing growth: South Africa, Southern Rhodesia, and the Belgian Congo (Clarence-Smith, 1989; Mitchell, 2007). The scattered pre-war surveys of manufacturing published in the colonial blue books of British Africa are notoriously incomplete. For the post-colonial era there are many gaps in the data as well, and there is little or no quantitative data on the value of production in 'informal' manufacturing, which includes small-scale brewing and tool-making workshops. Thus, substitution effects between the informal and formal sectors remain invisible in the official data sources (Jerven, 2013). In an earlier study of colonial patterns of industrialization, Kilby noted that there was 'incomplete coverage of agricultural processing, cottage craft production, artisan industries and smaller establishments' (Kilby, 1975, p. 471), which not only limits comparisons across time, but makes it particularly hazardous to compare the industrial share of GDP from country to country, because 'definitions of industrial vary' (Austen, 1987, p. 247; see also Vandewalle, 1966, p. 39). Riddell, editing a volume on manufacturing growth in Africa, noted that 'little can be done . . . except to state at the outset that it throws considerable doubt about all the aggregate data used subsequently' (1990, p. 10). This is no less true for our study.

Within the framework of interactions between factor endowments, global economic relations and government policy, the following sections focus on the reasons for the abrupt discontinuity between pre-colonial handicraft production and the modern manufacturing introduced under colonial rule (section 14.2); the spatially and temporally uneven spread of modern manufacturing during the colonial period (section 14.3); a case study of interrupted manufacturing growth in the Belgian Congo (section 14.4); the widespread attempts to promote import-substituting industrialization in the 1960s and 1970s (section 14.5); and manufacturing performance during the subsequent era of economic liberalism, including recent trends (section 14.6). Section 14.7 concludes.

14.2 FROM PRE-COLONIAL HANDICRAFTS TO MODERN MANUFACTURING

On the eve of the European partition, *c.*1880, the two most important manufacturing activities were textiles plus iron smelting and smithing. While sizeable parts of Africa, such as Namibia and much of South Africa, including the Zulu kingdom, had predominantly pastoral economies, the arable and mixed-farming regions invariably had artisanal manufacturing of some sort. The biggest centre in absolute terms, and seemingly also as a share of output, was the central emirates of the Sokoto Caliphate, based in what is now northwest and north-central Nigeria. With some 6 million people around 1900, the Sokoto Caliphate was probably the most populous state in tropical Africa (Lovejoy, 2005, p. 8). From Kano, which became its commercial and manufacturing hub, cotton cloth was exported all over West Africa, and even to North Africa, as the German explorer Heinrich Barth reported from his visit in 1851 (1857, reprinted 1965, p. 511).

Rodney (1972, pp. 112–14) famously claimed that African handicraft industries such as textiles and iron smelting shrank even before colonial rule, because of growing competition from foreign imports. However, this view has been increasingly overtaken by new research. In West Africa the quality of African iron (Goucher, 1981), as well as of high-end weaving (such as Akan *kente* cloth from what is now Ghana), was such as to retain consumer loyalty even throughout the colonial period (for a fuller discussion, see Austin, 2008). In East-Central Africa, locally woven *machila* cloth produced in the lower Shire valley of Malawi continued to enjoy widespread popularity through the 1880s at least. More importantly, Frederick (2014) has estimated that the quantities imported (per capita yards of cotton cloth) before the twentieth century were too limited to have a significantly destructive impact. This changed at the outset of colonial rule, when per capita imports increased about fivefold between 1896 and 1913.[2]

The question arises why there was no direct transition from the handloom to the power loom, under the same entrepreneurs in the same workshops. Why—especially in contrast to Japan, the first non-Western industrializer—did the traditions of handicraft production apparently make little or no contribution to the origins of modern manufacturing, in the twentieth century, even in Nigeria?

At one level, it may have been because machines using inanimate energy were introduced by foreign firms that had already moved beyond human-powered tools. In other words, for African entrepreneurs the technology gap was simply too large to bridge. But this is an insufficient answer, when we note that African entrepreneurs were among the first importers and users of motor lorries in Ghana and Nigeria, and were therefore pioneers of the adoption of mechanization in transport (Heap, 1990; Drummond-Thompson, 1993). Why would they not copy or import power-looms as well?

A more fundamental answer emerges when we take a closer look at the endowment structure of African economies. Cultivable land was relatively abundant in most areas, but the natural environment imposed severe constraints on its productive uses. Just as opportunities to substitute capital for labour in agriculture and transport were constrained by *trypanosomiasis*, which prevented the use of large

---

[2] The de-industrialization thesis should be distinguished from the much more plausible argument that imported Indian and English cottons hindered proto-industrialization of the cotton industry, at least in West Africa, *c.*1650–*c.*1850 (Inikori, 2009).

animals in the tropical forests, and extensive if shifting bands of savannah, the rarity of coal and shortages of the kind of tree suitable for charcoal limited the production possibility frontier for iron. Despite the quality of local iron, and the existence of specialized iron-smelting communities engaged in iron trade, iron was scarce, and hence expensive, until the bottleneck was eased by imports.

Meanwhile, in West Africa especially, the narrow loom was preferred to the broad loom: at first glance a perverse choice because it reduced the quantity of output per hour. The explanation owes much to a combination of taste and environmentally conditioned constraints on the supply of yarn (Austin, 2008; 2013). Though cotton was very widely grown in the savannahs of tropical Africa, further expansion of output entailed a severe trade-off with food growing, as food crops and cotton had to be planted in the same short season (Tosh, 1980). In addition, the preference for the narrow loom was facilitated by the extreme seasonality of rainfall in much of tropical Africa, which meant that, despite the general scarcity of labour during the agricultural year, in the heart of the dry season the opportunity cost of labour was low (Austin, 2008; 2013; cf. Curtin, 1973).

The combination of inelastic supplies of raw cotton and high-quality weaving and dyeing explains the African practice of unpicking imported cloth to re-weave the threads with which it was made. As far as the finishing of cloth is concerned, it is notable that the initial exports of Manchester cloth to Kano, in the late nineteenth century, were of un-dyed cloth, which was then dyed in Kano for sale in local and regional markets (Johnson, 1976).

A demand-side explanation may be considered as well. African labour scarcity created incentives for the adoption of labour-saving production techniques, but the investments required for capital-embodied technologies (e.g. power looms) also correspond with higher minimum efficient scales, particularly if machines are suited for the production of lower-quality (bulk) cloth. Consumer markets in West Africa were not only considerably smaller than in Europe in terms of number and purchasing power of consumers, their development was also hampered by higher transportation costs. The transport constraint was partly eased by the construction of railways under colonial rule, but the same railways also cleared the way for expanded European textile imports. The rail networks, soon followed by motor roads, served as a key instrument of the characteristic colonial division of labour, under which Africa exported primary products in return for imported manufactures.

This division of labour has often been attributed to colonial policy (Rodney, 1972). However, while this division seemed natural as well as welcome to European politicians representing textile interests, it was not necessarily inevitable, if it had contradicted comparative advantage, especially in the 'free-trading' British empire of the early colonial years (in contrast to the more protectionist policies of Portugal and France). After all, the interests of Manchester mill-owners did not stop Indians from developing a modern cotton textile industry under British rule (Chapter 10). Moreover, as Kilby (1975, pp. 495–6) has shown for Nigeria, the market for manufactured goods in certain colonies was large enough to support local factories in several industries many years before such factories were established. On the other hand, Unilever established a soap factory in Nigeria in 1923, but it struggled in the face of competition from a British-based rival, as well as because of having to pay excessive prices for materials from a fellow Unilever subsidiary (Fieldhouse, 1978, pp. 345–79).

A fundamental obstacle to competitiveness for factories in Nigeria and other peasant colonies remained the high cost of labour. African comparative advantage was shaped by labour and capital scarcity and land abundance. The reservation wage of labour, hypothetical or actual, was relatively high, to the point that coercion (taking the form of slavery, pawning, and *corvée*) was a prerequisite for the existence of a labour market in parts of nineteenth-century West Africa (e.g. Austin, 2005, pp. 155–70, 495–8). As shown in Fig. 14.1, day wages of unskilled labour were considerably higher in British West Africa (Accra and Lagos) than in the major textile producing centres of British India (Bombay and Calcutta), especially before 1940. However, colonial responses to labour scarcity differed and it did not translate into high wages in major parts of East and Southern Africa, where labour coercion was more severe (Frankema and van Waijenburg, 2012).

In the mining regions of Southern Africa, labour coercion became particularly harsh. At the beginning of the South African gold mining industry, according to Harries, real earnings of black workers on the Rand and at Kimberley, who were often migrants from newly conquered areas or from the (at the time, lightly governed) Portuguese colony of Mozambique, 'compared favourably' to those of British agricultural workers (Harries, 1982, pp. 143, 161n). From the 1890s to the 1910s, however, black miners' wages were driven down by a combination of state policies designed to close the alternatives that Africans had enjoyed to supplying

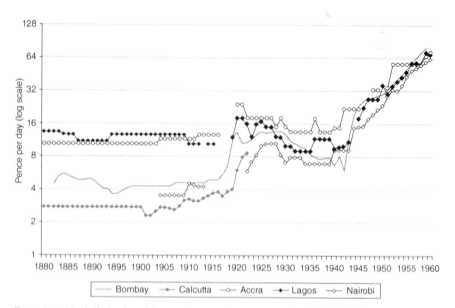

Fig. 14.1. Unskilled urban labourers' wages in pence per day, 1880–1960

Source: Wage and price data from Frankema and van Waijenburg (2012).

wage labour to white employers, and the creation of monopsonistic recruitment arrangements for mining companies (e.g. Lipton, 1986; Feinstein, 2005). Such reductions may already have occurred in the older British colonies of South Africa. According to de Zwart (2011, p. 65), nominal wages of black workers in Natal during the closing decades of the nineteenth century were lower than those paid in the capitals of at least some of the colonies that had been established further north, ranging between 5 and 9 pence per day, despite higher consumer price levels. In real terms, these wages were thus barely sufficient for subsistence. Wages paid in Nairobi were even lower and largely comparable with the rates observed in British India. By the 1950s the gap in nominal wages between British West Africa and India had largely been closed, owing much to the increasing political clout of the Indian independence movement.

Austin has argued that, in a context of labour and capital scarcity, the logical next step in expanding African economies was specialization in land-extensive production in agriculture and mining. Indeed, African entrepreneurs in coastal West Africa had already revealed a comparative advantage in these areas (Austin, 2013; 2015), and it was further spurred by a favourable shift in the net barter terms of trade of African export commodities that followed the British Industrial Revolution (Hopkins, 1973; Law, 1995; Williamson, 2011; Frankema, Williamson, and Woltjer, 2015). As the Atlantic slave market shrank, from 1807, the demand for industrial inputs such as palm oil, gum, and oilseeds such as groundnuts rose. African producers responded to rising prices by increasing supplies. A similar transition to 'legitimate commerce' began in Angola and other areas when the external slave trade was eventually suppressed there as well. In the so-called 'peasant' colonies, African entrepreneurs were relatively free to mobilize and invest sufficient capital, and they themselves deepened the comparative advantage in agricultural exports, notably by the adoption of the exotic crop cocoa in Nigeria and Ghana, and by pioneering the adoption of the motor lorry there.

The result was not a wholesale handicraft de-industrialization. In southeast Nigeria, during the age of 'legitimate commerce' female weavers in the town of Akwete, just outside the palm oil-exporting zone, developed a new, more expensive style of cloth for the expanding market provided by the growth of exports (Kriger, 2006, pp. 45–7). During the early colonial decades, female dyers in Abeokuta, southwest Nigeria, sold their dyed cloth to the cocoa farmers of Nigeria and Ghana (Byfield, 2002). However, there was a widespread transfer of labour from low-productivity dry-season manufacturing, especially cotton spinning but also weaving, to what was now the more rewarding activity of export agriculture. Even so, in French Soudan (Mali), handicraft weavers (most of them seasonal) fought off the competition of factory-made cloth throughout the colonial period, outbidding French merchants for the most of the colony's cotton crop as late as 1948–9 (Roberts, 1996). In East African cotton growing regions such as Uganda and Nyasaland, local cloth production fared worse, as Indian and British firms bought up nearly all the cotton. Meanwhile, foreign imports of metal and metalware were largely unchecked by artisanal production; but this was not because African iron lacked quality, but rather because African producers increasingly ran out of the charcoal they needed for smelting (Goucher, 1981).

14.3 THE UNEVEN SPREAD OF MODERN MANUFACTURING

Modern manufacturing emerged widely during the colonial period, but in most cases the process was slow, and it remained largely confined to the production of lighter consumer goods for domestic markets. As Table 14.1 shows, by the end of the colonial era, excluding South Africa, the largest manufacturer in Sub-Saharan Africa was Nigeria, reflecting the fact that it had much the largest GDP, which in turn was based on a combination of by far the largest population and considerable agricultural (and some mineral) exports. As of 1960, for the sample of the larger countries shown in Table 14.1, the shares of manufacturing in GDP varied from 3 per cent in Tanganyika to c.9–10 per cent in Kenya and Senegal, 14 per cent in the Belgian Congo, and 16 per cent in Southern Rhodesia. In South Africa, manufacturing was about 20 per cent of a much larger GDP (Lipton, 1986, p. 402).[3] The majority of the African countries absent from Table 14.1 must have had shares below 5 per cent, if only because of small market size, given that locational advantage could be important. According to the same source as that

Table 14.1. Manufacturing output in context for selected African countries, 1960 (US 1964 dollars)

	Manufacturing/ GDP (%)	Population (millions)	GDP (m. $)	Per capita income (S)	Manufacturing output (m. $)
Southern Rhodesia (Zimbabwe)	16.0	3.6	751	206	120.2
Belgian Congo	14.0	14.1	910	58	127.4
Senegal	9.5	3.1	678	218	64.4
Kenya	9.5	8.1	641	79	60.9
Uganda	6.5	6.7	583	87	37.9
Ghana	6.3	6.8	1,503	222	94.7
Cameroun	6.0	4.7	511	109	30.6
Ethiopia	6.0	20.7	1,021	49	61.3
Northern Rhodesia (Zambia)	5.5	3.2	511	155	28.1
Côte d'Ivoire	5.3	3.2	584	181	31.0
Sudan	4.8	11.8	909	77	43.6
Nigeria	4.5	40.0	3,500	88	157.5
Angola	4.3	4.8	726	151	31.2
Tanganyika	3.0	9.6	671	67	20.1

Source: Kilby (1975, p. 472, Table 112—Population, income and manufacturing output in selected African countries, 1960).

[3] Note that this figure comes from a different series from that used in Table 14.1.

underlying Table 14.1, as late as 1965 Dahomey, with a population of 2.4 million, had a 2.6 per cent share of manufacturing in GDP (though Gabon with 400,000 people had 6.1 per cent) (Kilby, 1975, p. 472).

Most of tropical Africa's progress in manufacturing occurred after the Second World War. Elsewhere, for example in Southeast Asia, the world wars and the Great Depression, along with the associated slowdowns in world trade, gave some impetus to local industry in various colonies (see Chapter 11). In particular, the French response to the Depression—of pursuing autarky on an imperial scale—provided protection for manufacturing investments, as was seen with textile mills in Indochina. In Senegal a groundnut-refining industry promptly emerged (producing shelled nuts and groundnut oil). However, its growth was soon curtailed by the French government, which limited exports to France to 5,900 tonnes a year, and effectively prohibited new entries to the industry (Boone, 1992, pp. 47–9).

By the end of the Second World War, the British Colonial Office was seeking to include the promotion of manufacturing in state-supported development programmes, but this was rejected by a more powerful ministry, the Treasury, partly because they saw African development as a means of assisting the recovery of the British economy, rather than increasing overseas competition for British firms, and partly because they thought that any infant industries in Africa were unlikely to grow up (Butler, 1997). On the last point, a partly similar attitude was shown by the Watson Commission, which investigated the causes of riots in the Gold Coast in 1948. While recommending an accelerated timetable for political independence, it observed: 'At every turn we were pressed with the cry of industrialisation. We doubt very much if the authors of this cry really understood more than their vague desire for something that promised wealth and higher standards of life.' While accepting that 'there is clearly room for many secondary industries which would enrich the country', they were 'unable to foresee, in any circumstances, the Gold Coast emerging as a unit of heavy industries in the world markets' (Great Britain, 1948, p. 54).

Still, from a very low base, the 1950s saw a spurt in the growth of manufacturing across British and French Africa. In part, this responded to the growth of consumer markets, underpinned by expanded earnings from export agriculture, and in some cases also from mining wages, facilitated by the Korean War boom. In part, too, European firms were responding to the accelerated process of decolonization. British trading companies sought to establish themselves in manufacturing before they were excluded from retailing by nationalist governments. French manufacturers, though still not expecting early independence, decided on direct investment to pre-empt competition from cheaper foreign producers. In both Senegal and Nigeria, the 1950s spurt in manufacturing mainly comprised French and British companies seeking to protect existing markets (Hopkins, 1973; Kilby, 1975; Boone, 1992).

The consumer industries that spread most widely across colonial Africa were food and beverages, cigarettes, cotton textiles, footwear, furniture, soap, and perfume. Export processing of cash crops (including cotton ginning and oil-seed crushing), ore smelting, sawmilling, and cement production could also be found.

Viewing industrial development in a wider sense, there was also considerable investment and works associated with the construction of railways. However, outside South Africa, and to a lesser extent Southern Rhodesia, there were only very limited developments in the iron and steel, engineering, machinery, transport equipment, and chemical sectors. Hence, most of the growth in manufacturing was based on the processing of food, cash crops, and raw materials; there was little production of intermediate products and virtually none of capital equipment (Kilby, 1975).

To understand the temporal and geographic disparities in the spread of manufacturing growth, it is useful to consider the differences between settler, concession, and peasant colonies. In the peasant colonies, land remained overwhelmingly under African ownership and control, allowing space for African entrepreneurship, albeit with European oligopolies or monopolies in some sectors. In settler and concession economies, a large or even overwhelming proportion of land was alienated, respectively, for the use of European settlers or, mainly, for European companies. The presence of relatively large European populations broadened and deepened the market for manufactured consumer goods. In Senegal, for instance, it stimulated the growth of small factories producing carbonated drinks, biscuits, and bricks as early as the 1920s (Boone, 1992, p. 48). Substantial European populations also enhanced supplies of relevant manufacturing skills (Kilby, 1975). The latter applied obviously to settler economies, but also to the part-concession, part-settler economy of the Belgian Congo and to the capital of French West Africa, Dakar. The growth of modern manufacturing in the colonial era owed much to locational cost advantages. These evolved from proximity to raw materials or from natural protection for products with high transportation costs per unit value, such as beer and cement. Until oil became readily and cheaply available, access to coal to generate electricity was a major locational advantage as well, in South Africa, Southern Rhodesia, and Nigeria.

But differences in government systems in settler and non-settler colonies made a decisive difference to the extent of political and financial investment in manufacturing, and made significant differences to the outcomes. The largest manufacturing industries were created in areas where a locally resident population, albeit a white minority, controlled the government: South Africa became effectively independent within the British Empire in 1910, while Southern Rhodesia became autonomous in 1923 under a parliament largely elected by settlers. In contrast, following Salazar's establishment of a dictatorship in Portugal in 1926, the large Portuguese populations in the colonies were formally excluded from government, restricting—though not extinguishing—their ability to lobby for manufacturing or anything else (Clarence-Smith, 1989, pp. 177–8). This does much to explain why, in 1960, manufacturing constituted only 4.3 per cent of Angola's GDP. Again, Ghana, which had been a 'peasant colony', or more appropriately, an 'indigenous rural capitalist' colony, had the highest per capita income in tropical Africa as of 1960, but the share of manufacturing in GDP was only 6.3 per cent (Table 14.1).

Along with Kenya, which was basically a settler colony until the 1950s but one in which the administration remained under metropolitan control, South Africa and

Southern Rhodesia had seen a determined effort by the government to make unskilled labour artificially cheap. By a series of measures mostly unavailable to pre-colonial states (even had they wanted to adopt them), the above-mentioned alliance of governments and mining companies had driven down the cost of labour to well below the reservation wage of un-coerced labour. The most important measures were the reservation of land for European use, the imposition of native direct taxes, and bans or restrictions on African tenancy: obliging Africans to offer their labour for sale (Arrighi, 1973b; Mosley, 1983; Frankema and van Waijenburg, 2012).

In South Africa, systematic labour coercion meant that the real wages of black gold miners were not only lower in 1911 than they had been in the late nineteenth century, but higher than they would be again until the early 1970s (Lipton, 1986, p. 410). Feinstein (2005, pp. 109–12) has provided a quantitative illustration of the importance of this policy. Without it, the mining industry in South Africa would have been a fraction of its actual (historical) size, at least until the 1930s. For governments, mining revenues provided the war chest necessary for subsidizing electricity production, and if necessary other industries, in pursuit of the interests of white settlers and workers. The latter, expressing themselves through the Labour Party in South Africa, wanted the guarantee of more, and more skilful, jobs. The former were willing to pay higher prices for consumer goods if it meant a more diversified economy, less dependent on the metropole. Once the Pact government in South Africa (Nationalist and Labour), elected in 1924, had implemented protectionist measures as part of its comprehensive programme of promoting manufacturing, the South Rhodesia parliament felt obliged to respond with a similar programme of import-substituting industrialization, launched in 1933 (Phimister, 2000). The South African case, in particular, fits the paradigm of a 'developmental state' with regard to manufacturing, though certainly not in terms of the welfare of most of the population. Afrikaner nationalism and white labour made for a highly motivated industrial lobby. Both in South Africa and, from 1944, in Southern Rhodesia, the state subsidized the creation of iron and steel plants (cf. Fine and Rustomjee, 1996).

Manufacturing growth in the Belgian Congo was also partly driven by the consumption demands of a sizable white minority (about 90,000 people in 1960), but primarily by the needs of the mining industry (Buelens and Cassimon, 2013). Without the 'discovery' of vast copper reserves in the Katanga province and the acute demand for it during the First World War, sending world market copper prices through the roof, the area would have been one of the least attractive places to invest in manufacturing. Katanga was underpopulated, it had no wage labour markets or consumer markets of any significance, and the area was tucked away in the vast Congolese interior, a thousand miles from the Atlantic coast. But with the development of the mines, the locational disadvantage turned into a high degree of natural protection for manufacturing industries that were needed to cater to the mines and the mine-workers. That said, labour and land policies were the key in Congo as well to turning copper mining into a commercially feasible proposition. The powerful mining companies, especially the Union

Minière du Haute-Katanga (UMHK), financed the colonial state and could exert great influence on labour-recruitment practices, as it did with labour stabilization (paying higher wages to enable migrant male workers to become, with their families, permanent urban dwellers). We will return to the Congo case below to illustrate how interrupted industrial growth has worked in practice.

While the settler regimes were effective in combating the problem of a physical scarcity of labour that in itself pointed to high labour costs, cheap migrant labour was not necessarily efficient for manufacturing. Hence factories, preceded by some of the mining companies, sought to 'stabilize' their African workforces by offering 'family' wages rather than 'bachelor' wages. Pioneered by the South African Chamber of Mines, the implementation of this policy in South Africa—which, to be profitable, required opening semi-skilled and even some skilled jobs to blacks—was long delayed by the resistance of organized white labour. Though the white union's violent protests (the Rand Revolt) were defeated in 1923, the white Labour Party got revenge in the elections of the following year, which put it into power in coalition with the National Party, forming the government that adopted ISI as policy. After that, black workers' real wages in manufacturing did creep up somewhat, despite the rigorous repression of miners' wages (Lipton, 1986), suggesting that some stabilized labour emerged even in South Africa. Meanwhile, from the late 1920s, in Katanga the Belgian mining companies, and soon Belgian manufacturers, implemented labour stabilization, in the interests of labour productivity. This example was followed in Southern Rhodesia, especially in the 1950s (Arrighi, 1973b, pp. 216–17). Meanwhile, as independence approached in most countries, African economies remained largely dependent on imports of manufactured goods financed by exports of unprocessed primary products.

14.4 INTERRUPTED GROWTH: THE CASE OF THE CONGO

The development of modern manufacturing in the Belgian Congo (later known as Zaïre and Democratic Republic of Congo) presents a particularly dramatic case of interrupted industrial growth in Sub-Saharan Africa, but the mechanisms steering growth, stagnation, and, eventually, a full collapse were important aspects of a wider African pattern. Especially important were low investment in African human capital, the strong connections between the mining and manufacturing sectors, and the great vulnerability of African manufacturing to world market shocks.

Compared to the disruptive kleptocratic style of economic governance that emerged under Leopold II (until he was deposed in 1908), industrial and infra-structural investments after the First World War (by which time the Congo had become a Belgian colony instead of a private royal fiefdom) contained the promise of a more sustainable road towards economic growth. GDP per capita in the Congo was distinctly higher in 1960 than in neighbouring countries (Maddison, 2010), while the Congolese population had recovered from a serious collapse and enjoyed notably higher living standards than around 1900. Part of this long-term process of welfare growth (and recovery) resulted from structural economic change.

The growth of modern manufacturing in the Congo may be loosely divided into two periods (Lacroix, 1967). During the first phase from *c.*1920 to *c.*1940, copper mining gained momentum, railway infrastructure expanded, and commercial centres emerged. Foreign firms (mostly Belgian and British) invested in plantation cultivation of tropical cash crops such as cotton, palm oil, coffee, cacao, and tobacco. To feed, clothe, and house a rapidly expanding but now stabilized male wage labour force and their families, the mines and plantations needed processed foods from grain mills and slaughter houses, beer, soap, cotton fabrics, cement, electricity, and specific chemicals to be used in mining operations (Buelens and Cassimon, 2013, p. 234). In addition, raw copper ore also had to undergo several stages of refinement to lower transport costs per unit value.

Manufacturing growth benefited from the phenomenal profit margins generated by the copper industry. Buelens and Marysse (2010) have estimated that the equity shares of colonial companies yielded an average annual rate of return of 7.2 per cent between 1920 and 1955, which was about 2.5 times the return on Belgian stocks (2.8 per cent). The lure of big profit also spurred investments in large-scale infrastructural projects. The Congolese railway network covered over 5,000 kilometres by the end of the colonial era, twice as much as in Nigeria (Mitchell, 2007, pp. 721–2). The inauguration of the '*voie national*' by King Albert I in 1928, connecting the mines in Katanga to the Congo river in Ilebo (Port Francqui) over a distance of about a thousand miles through the tropical forest, symbolized the intertwined forces of colonial extraction and investment.

The second phase, from 1940 to 1960, differed from the first as it entailed a move towards ISI policies (motivated by the experiences of the Depression and the Second World War), increasing investments in energy infrastructure (hydro-electricity in particular) and a modest shift in manufacturing production from consumer goods to intermediate and capital goods (iron and steel, machinery). After a severe setback during the Great Depression, when copper prices collapsed, industrial growth picked up again during the war. The Congo was an important supplier of strategic raw materials (copper, uranium) to the Allied war effort, while on the other hand the drastically reduced availability of manufacturing supplies from Europe enhanced investment in a wide range of local industries. The index of manufacturing production in the Belgian Congo given in Table 14.2 shows the

Table 14.2. Volume index of manufacturing production in the Belgian Congo, 1939–57 (1947–9 = 100)

Year	Food	Textiles	Chemicals	Construction	Others	Total
1939	41	21	35	19	10	29
1948	100	102	76	105	95	99
1957	296	618	473	492	387	377

Source: Centrale Bank van Belgisch-Congo en Ruanda Urundi (1959, p. 4).

Table 14.3. Industrial production in Belgium and the Belgian Congo, 1957

Commodity	Units	Belgium	Belgian Congo	Congo as per cent share of Belgium
Electricity	Million kWh	12,611	2,320	18.4
Sugar	Tons	369,335	19,332	5.2
Beer	Thousand hl	10,185	1,382	13.6
Water and lemonade	Thousand hl	2,966	320	10.8
Margarine	Tons	95,253	669	0.7
Cigarettes	Millions	10,546	4,045	38.4
Cement	Tons	4,705,000	463,952	9.9
Lime	Tons	29,249,000	100,460	0.3
Bricks	Thousands	2,242,933	293,876	13.1
Ceramics	Thousand m²	1,625	137	8.4
Shoes	Thousand pairs	12,117	2,851	23.5
Tissues	Thousand m²	702,105	52,982	7.5
Blankets	Thousand pieces	11,768	1,976	16.8

Source: Buelens and Cassimon (2013, Table 11.2). Data obtained from Centrale Bank van Belgisch-Congo en Ruanda-Urundi (1959).

impact of the war boom and the continued acceleration of manufacturing growth during the 1950s. From the 1940s to the early 1970s international copper prices were high, especially compared to the 1930s, and the Congo was well on its way to becoming an African economic 'powerhouse'. The number of officially registered industrial enterprises rose to about 12,000 in the early 1950s (Buelens and Cassimon, 2013, p. 237). Table 14.3 shows that, in comparison to the metropole (with a comparable population size of *c*.10 million), the volume of industrial production in the Belgian Congo was indeed substantial.

We lack the space to give a detailed reconstruction of the collapse of Congolese manufacturing, and offer a brief summary instead. Political instability occurred almost immediately after the official transfer of power. The Katanga secession war led to turmoil in the newly independent country, and put a halt to investment. Only after Mobutu had fought his way to power in 1965 did the dust start to settle, for a period of about eight years. In his early years in office, Mobutu pursued the grand development schemes which had come to the drawing table in the final years of Belgian rule (1958–60). He introduced an open door policy to foreign investors by granting tax exemptions. Foreign investors (e.g. General Motors, Good Year, Fiat) came in and industrial output grew by about 50 per cent during 1966–72 (Chomé and Komitee, 1977, p. 120). But Mobutu's investments in various mega-projects lacked economic common sense. The Inga Falls project, a gigantic hydro-power dam in the lower Congo, turned into an outright failure and became a serious drain on the government budget. The economy hit reverse gear when international copper prices went into free fall in the wake of the 1973 oil crisis.

Copper prices did not recover to pre-1973 levels until the end of the twentieth century (Abbeloos, 2013, p. 264). The shock laid bare one of the fundamental weaknesses of the Belgian colonial state: the budget relied predominantly on direct and indirect receipts from copper exports. Mobutu's response may perhaps best be summarized as denial. He overloaded the state with foreign debt, increasingly allowed his personal clientele to strip state assets, and plunged the country into an extended period of hyperinflation from 1988 to 1996, eroding the macro-economic conditions required for a recovery. During the 1990s and early 2000s the country was caught up in endemic warfare, creating the conditions for millions of excess deaths as a result of disease and undernourishment (Prunier, 2009). Primary school enrolment rates, which had approximated 100 per cent in 1970, plummeted to under 40 per cent in 2000 (Frankema, 2013, p. 161).

To be sure, even in the context of widespread post-colonial conflict across the continent, the Congolese economic and political collapse represented a worst case. But this does not mask one of the fundamental problems of industrial growth in Africa's former concession and settler colonies: the detrimental impact of racial discrimination on the socio-economic mobility and human capital accumulation of native Africans. Forced labour programmes were focused on supplying the mines and plantations with manual labour power, while higher-skilled jobs and management positions were exclusively reserved for whites. The colour bar was also strictly applied in education. Primary education was almost entirely left to Catholic and Protestant missionary schools. The few public schools in the larger urban centres would offer lower-grade secondary education to Congolese children, but nothing more (Depaepe and van Rompaey, 1995; Dunkerley, 2009; Frankema, 2013).

The colonial government started to reform the education system in the late 1940s, by allowing tiny numbers of Congolese children to attend European secondary schools and reducing the education monopoly of the Christian missions. Yet, ironically, when the first university opened its doors in 1954 near Leopoldville (Kinshasa), the first cohorts of Congolese students had yet to complete secondary school. By 1960 only a few hundred Congolese were in university, of whom thirteen were enrolled in natural sciences and eighteen in engineering (Mantels, 2007). Frankema (2013) has argued that this legacy of racial discrimination in education had a detrimental effect on the quality of post-colonial governance. After dropping out of secondary school, Mobutu received a two-year training in accounting and secretarial work in the army. He was among the best educated of his generation. Technical and engineering skills were thus barely available after the Belgians had retreated, and the few highly educated Congolese usually preferred salaried careers in the public sector.

14.5 FROM IMPORT SUBSTITUTION TO 'STRUCTURAL ADJUSTMENT'

On the eve of independence, many African politicians anticipated that industrialization would go hand in hand with the development of new independent nation states (Mytelka, 1989). As in other developing regions in the 1950s to 1970s, the early post-colonial African states adopted ISI policies in an attempt to kick-start industrial development (see Chapters 8, 10–13). The policies usually consisted of a combination of infant industry protection, increased investments in key infrastructures (transport, energy), and more or less ambitious output targets to secure a rapid replacement of manufacturing imports by domestically produced manufactures (Killick, 1978). Indeed, the key objective of ISI was to achieve self-sufficiency in the production of domestic consumer goods, rather than obtaining stakes in export markets by developing internationally competitive industries. This development agenda was not only embraced by 'socialist' governments, notably Ghana under Nkrumah (1951–66) and Tanzania under Nyerere (1961–85): it was also subscribed to by 'capitalist' governments, such as Côte d'Ivoire under Houphouët-Boigny (1960–93). Indeed, another staunchly capitalist regime, Kenyatta's in Kenya (1964–78), adopted five-year plans to promote industrialization and adopted protectionist policies to curb import competition.

Yet there were important differences in the degree of state intervention across early post-colonial African economies. Most of the former French colonies, including Côte d'Ivoire and Cameroon, remained within the franc zone. Most of the former British colonies, together with Sekou Touré's Guinea and Congo-Zaïre, opted for monetary independence. In many cases (including Ghana, Guinea, Tanzania, Congo-Zaire, and Zambia), the latter route became associated with increasingly overvalued, largely non-convertible currencies and a battery of quantity and price controls, not only on imports but also on internal markets. Structural macro-economic disequilibria resulted in hyperinflation by the 1980s. Kenya steered a middle path, with an independent currency but periodic devaluations, which largely prevented major price distortions.

In theory, currency overvaluation provided an indirect subsidy to domestic manufacturing enterprises, as it permitted them to acquire imported raw materials, intermediate goods, and capital goods below world prices. This happened to some extent in Kenya, but in the likes of Ghana extreme currency overvaluation functioned as a punitive tax on exports, which not only reduced the incentive to re-invest in export agriculture, but also eroded foreign reserves and produced structural current account imbalances. This eventually resulted in acute shortages of strategic import products. Ironically, the government which made the strongest rhetorical commitment to industrialization, Ghana under Kwame Nkrumah and some of his successors, ultimately delivered less of it than those such as Côte d'Ivoire under Felix Houphouët-Boigny, whose policies merely aimed at the gradual growth of light consumer goods industries around a continued growth of export agriculture (Table 14.5).

In the former peasant colonies, state intervention in the promotion of manufacturing represented a break with colonial economic policies. This policy reform may be called a partial success (in its defence, see Sender and Smith, 1986, pp. 67–109). Certainly it created economic rents, facilitating the politicization of employment in public enterprises and allowing foreign as well as state enterprises to enjoy domestic markets without striving to improve their efficiency (e.g. Boone, 1992). But it also enhanced the availability of capital to local manufacturing industries and offered the latter protected access to growing (especially urban) consumer markets. To illustrate the substitution effects of ISI policies and the associated process of capital

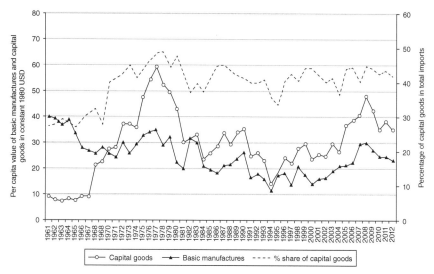

Fig. 14.2. Composition of imports in Senegal, 1961–2012

Notes: Left-hand vertical axis: per capita value of basic manufactures and capital goods in constant 1980 USD. Right-hand vertical axis: Percentage of capital goods in total imports. Capital goods imports corresponds to SITC 2 category 7: machinery and transport equipment. Basic manufactures corresponds to SITC 2 category 6, comprising a large range of intermediate and finished consumer manufactures such as textiles, leather, wood, cork, paper, metals, and rubber products. Total manufacturing imports comprises SITC categories 5 to 8, including chemicals (5) and miscellaneous manufactures (8).

Source: United Nations, *Yearbook of International Trade Statistics* (several issues 1964–2013). Population data from UN, *World Population Database*, accessed 1 October 2014.

accumulation, Fig. 14.2 presents both the per capita value of capital goods imports and their share in total manufacturing imports in Senegal since 1961. It serves to illustrate a common pattern among ISI adherents in Africa: after a rapid rise in capital goods imports, both in (nominal) per capita terms and as a share of manufactured imports, the economic downturn of the late 1970s to early 1990s interrupted this process of capital formation. Although the share of capital goods imports in total manufacturing imports remained higher than in the early 1960s, the declining per capita values were not replaced by increasing domestic output of capital goods.

Table 14.4 indicates that aggregate rates of annual manufacturing growth in post-independence Sub-Saharan Africa stayed above population growth (2–3 per cent) until the start of the 1980s. Although we lack data for the colonial era, it is probably safe to say that the 1960s and 1970s saw the highest rates of growth of manufacturing during the twentieth century. At the same time it should be noted that African manufacturing industries failed to capture even a modest share of the international market for manufacturing merchandise. Exports remained largely confined to some cross-border trading among neighbours.

Even South Africa, where the manufacturing share in GDP had surpassed agriculture and mining by 1946, and where the capital goods industry made a sizeable contribution, failed to transform itself from being a modest regional

Table 14.4. Aggregate annual average growth rates of industry and manufacturing in Sub-Saharan Africa, 1961–2000

Sub-Saharan Africa	Industry (annual per cent growth)	Manufacturing (annual per cent growth)
1961–70	7.7	8.8
1971–80	4.0	5.1
1981–90	1.3	1.9
1991–2000	1.3	1.1
2001–10	4.3	3.4

Source: World Bank, *World Development Indicators* (2003). 2001–10 calculated with data from *World Development Indicators* (2013). Jerven's calculations based on ten-year averages.

exporter of manufactures (mainly supplying its neighbours) into a global manufacturing exporter. For South African manufacturers the advantage of low-waged unskilled labour was increasingly outweighed by the disadvantages of a domestic market restricted by the low purchasing power of the vast majority of the population, and artificially expensive skilled labour. The supply of the latter was restricted by lack of investment in black education, as well the colour bar which curtailed its use (Lipton, 1986; Feinstein, 2005).

South Africa was not the only country where idiosyncratic factors mattered. It is important to take account of such country-specific features, and to emphasize the large inter-country differences in manufacturing growth. Table 14.5 presents the growth rates of manufacturing output during 1965–88 in the most populous twelve countries in Sub-Saharan Africa (all those with populations of 10 million or more by 1988) besides South Africa. The first sub-period, 1965–73, covers ISI policies before the first oil crisis, showing modest convergence in manufacturing on the world leaders in the majority of countries. The second sub-period, 1973–80, brought the exogenous shock of higher oil prices, offset a few years later in some countries by a boom in beverage crop prices. Higher oil prices enabled governments of oil-exporting countries such as Nigeria to increase direct and indirect subsidies to manufacturing. But in the oil-importing majority of African countries, the net effects on manufacturing were negative, reducing the capacity to import inputs, and depressing the domestic market.

The third sub-period, 1980–8, saw the transition to structural adjustment programmes (SAPs): schemes of economic liberalization promoted by the World Bank and International Monetary Fund that were voluntarily and involuntarily adopted by African governments for a range of reasons. The dates at which individual countries began 'adjustment' varied. Ghana made the move in 1983, Nigeria and Tanzania in 1986; Zambia vacillated.

The former settler economies did not escape the trend towards economic stagnation or decline that took hold in many countries at some stage in the 1970s and 1980s, albeit for different reasons. Rhodesian industry was initially stimulated by the reduced competition it faced during the period of international sanctions imposed during the settler regime's unilateral declaration of independence from Britain in 1965, but stopped growing in the 1970s. Above all, South

Table 14.5. Average annual growth rate of manufacturing output (per cent)

	1965–73	1973–80	1980–8
Sudan	n.a.	6.7	5.0
Ethiopia	8.8	2.6	3.7
Kenya	12.4	6.9	4.6
Tanzania	8.7	2.6	−2.5
Uganda	4.0	−12.4	2.3
Nigeria	15.0	17.2	−2.9
Senegal	4.0	1.5	3.4
Ghana	6.5	−2.8	3.1
Côte d'Ivoire	10.9	8.3	8.2
Cameroon	7.4	9.0	6.2
Zaire (Congo DRC)	n.a.	−5.7	1.7
Rhodesia/Zimbabwe	n.a.	0.4	2.1

Sources: 1965–80 from World Bank (1989, Table 2); 1980–8 from World Bank (1990, Table 2).

African manufacturing, after decades of expansion facilitated by repression of black labour (low wages, reinforced by the ban on black trade unions) and tariff protection, entered a productivity crisis primarily resulting from the artificially high cost of skilled labour mentioned above. The marginal efficiency of investment shrank steadily during the last twenty years of apartheid (Lewis, 1990). The ingrained contradiction of the apartheid economy between the promotion of capital accumulation through artificially cheap unskilled labour, and the political incapacity to invest in the skills required to move manufacturing on to a path of rising total factor productivity, underlay the stagnation of the economy during the last fifteen years before the end of the apartheid regime in 1994 (Feinstein, 2005). This economic morass was reinforced, rather than caused, by international sanctions when they began to bite in the 1980s.

The first decade of economic liberalization was one of stagnation or net decline at the level of Sub-Saharan Africa as a whole, despite dramatic recoveries in the two most successful adjusters, Ghana and Uganda. In the majority of African countries, macro-economic conditions continued to worsen, especially as a result of unmanageable debt accumulation. It took most countries until the late 1990s to reschedule their debts and implement all the liberalization and privatization programmes prescribed by the Washington Consensus. While aggregate regional GDP per capita growth picked up from the mid-1990s, the overall policy model remains the economic liberalism established in the 1980s. Under this model, the region as a whole experienced at least a 'lost decade', in terms of growth of both manufacturing and GDP, to *c.*1995, followed by—to date—twenty years in which GDP has outpaced population, by about 2 per cent a year. The most plausible explanation for this contrast in performance under the same policy regime is that, as before, African economic growth rates primarily respond to external demand for African commodities (Jerven, 2011; 2014).

While the current wave of economic expansion in Africa is more widespread and, in aggregate, apparently faster than any previous one, with the possible exception of

1890–1914, it would be unimaginable without the (this time Chinese-led) boom in the prices of primary commodities that started in the mid-1990s, after nearly two decades of price weakness (Jerven, 2010). It should be added that further technical advances in mining and oil drilling reinforced Africa's comparative advantage in extractive industries, for example by allowing re-filtering of iron ore slag in Sierra Leone and elsewhere, and permitting deep-water oil drilling off West Africa. The South African economy has also resumed growth since the advent of majority rule in 1994, but at a very modest rate, despite South African companies taking advantage of the opportunity to enter markets in the rest of Africa on a much larger scale than before. Manufacturing, overall, has expanded in absolute terms but declined in relative terms (UNECA, 2013). This is not very surprising, given that the problem of a lack of international competitiveness in manufacturing has not been resolved: how would these industries thrive without a shield?

14.6 WILL MANUFACTURING SUSTAIN AFRICA'S GROWTH REVIVAL?

Despite Africa's long history of labour scarcity, factor endowments have been moving, and continue to move, in a direction that facilitates labour-intensive industrialization. Population rose six times over the twentieth century, and population growth rates accelerated especially after 1945. Moreover, increasing investment in education and public health counts as one of the biggest achievements of post-independence governments (Sender, 1999): poor though the African record still looks in cross-sectional terms, it was much better in 1980 than in 1960, and, despite retrogression in some countries during economic liberalization in the 1980s, on the whole there has been further progress since the mid-1990s. Yet, to date, Africa's growth revival has been led not by labour-intensive manufacturing, but rather, as with earlier growth episodes, by commodity exports (Jerven, 2010).

   Though there is fragmentary evidence that labour costs in Africa have fallen relative to other parts of the world, Teal's comparison of Ghana and Mauritius at the end of the last century (Teal, 1999) illustrates a generalization that still largely applies today: without significant advances in labour productivity, continental African real wages remain too high to be internationally competitive in manufacturing. Teal estimated that the wages paid in Mauritius, a sugar plantation economy that successfully transformed itself to become a manufacturing exporter (mainly of textiles) after 1970, were about six times higher than in Ghana; but that this gap was still insufficient to offset a labour productivity gap of over 600 per cent (1999, p. 991). It is not encouraging to note that even the Mauritian textile industry has struggled since, in the face of intensified competition (Joomun, 2006). The industry's share of Mauritian exports declined from 55 per cent in 1995 to 16 per cent in 2010; a fall in the overall contribution of manufacturing to exports that was only partly compensated by a rise in 'miscellaneous manufactured goods' from 0 to 20 per cent of exports during the same years (Sannassee, Seetanah, and Lamport, 2014).

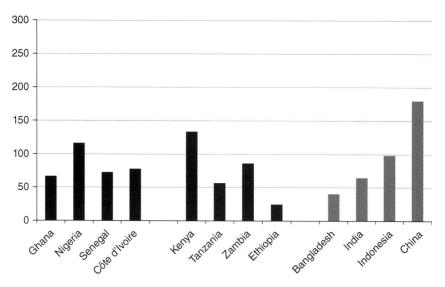

Fig. 14.3. Minimum wages in a selection of African and Asian countries, 2010–11 (US dollars per month)

Source: Official minimum nominal monthly wages taken from ILOSTAT, converted into US dollars using exchange rates from *World Development Indicators* (2014).

Fig. 14.3 shows the official minimum monthly wages in 2010–11 for a selection of African and Asian countries, expressed in US dollars using official exchange rates. While the enforcement of minimum wage legislation probably varies across the sample, the figure shows that there is no apparent clear-cut labour cost advantage in African economies compared to emerging Asian economies such as India or Vietnam. In some cases (notably Kenya and Nigeria), the minimum wages are distinctively higher. Chinese wages have only recently surpassed the upper bound of Sub-Saharan wages. The reasons for this are unclear. Exchange rate overvaluation may explain part of this phenomenon, but it can hardly be the result of trade union power, which is generally weak in the neo-liberal era, and if 'efficiency wages' are being paid (wage premiums to encourage worker commitment in the absence of cheap and effective supervision), as has been suggested (Austin, 2013, p. 219), they have yet to have a discernible effect at the macro level.

It remains extremely hard to pin down to what extent sources other than commodity exports are driving African growth. Having examined survey data on real material consumption per household for 1990–2006—thus including several years before the start of the boom indicated by the GDP figures—Young (2012) found that such consumption was growing fast enough (3.4–3.7 per cent per year) for him to proclaim an 'African growth miracle'. But other studies take a more cautious approach. McMillan and Harttgen (2014) report that part of recent African growth stems from structural change, but also note that structural change in Africa does not follow the 'classic' historical pattern. The share of the labour force employed in agriculture in African countries declined on average by 10 per cent between 2000 and 2010, but only a fifth of this decline was absorbed by manufacturing. The rest went into services, formal and informal. As people move out of the lowest productivity sector, agriculture, structural change contributes to growth (see also Diao and McMillan, 2015). Yet, to what extent consumption growth and structural change operate independently from the commodity export boom remains difficult to assess.

Surely, the rising concentration of Africans in urban centres opens up new opportunities for scale economies and specialization, including a 'von Thunen' type of agricultural transformation in the vicinity of growing consumer markets, which may be further supported by the recent 'communication revolution' which releases spatial constraints that were innate to the historically dispersed settlement patterns in the region (Frankema, 2014, pp. 22–3). Rodrik's view is largely in line with the historical account we have provided:

> the African pattern of structural change is very different from the classic pattern that has produced high growth in Asia, and before that, the European industrializers. Labor is moving out of agriculture and rural areas. But formal manufacturing industries are not the main beneficiary. Urban migrants are being absorbed largely into services that are not particularly productive and into informal activities. The pace of industrialization is much too slow for the convergence dynamics to play out in full force. (Rodrik, 2014, p. 9)

If African real wages continue to fall relative to those in the current 'workshop of the world', China, there remains the question of whether entrepreneurs will convert this into manufacturing growth. Foreign direct investment (FDI) has been rising recently, some of it in the traditional form of Western-owned breweries for domestic markets, but also export-oriented shoe and cotton yarn factories in Ethiopia, owned by Chinese and Indian participants. The explanation for the apparent rise of Ethiopia as the first African country to attract considerable inflows of (Asian) FDI in modern labour-intensive manufacturing industries may be historical: Ethiopia represents the oldest peasant society south of the Sahara, has by far the longest record of state centralization, and was one of the two countries that remained independent from European colonial rule. Moreover, its relatively high population densities currently convert into relatively low minimum wages (Fig. 14.3). It is not inconceivable that the exceptional historical path of Ethiopian 'development' has given rise to a favourable combination of labour costs, discipline, and diligence that is hard to find elsewhere in the continent (Frankema and van Waijenburg, 2015).

FDI in extractive industries in Africa has also increased, especially in oil. In the past, transnational corporations investing in Africa had a capital-intensive bias, reflecting not local labour-market conditions so much as their own habit of using the same techniques of production wherever they operated (Arrighi, 1973a, p. 113). This habit may be a liability in the context of falling costs of labour, including skilled labour. As comparative experience shows, it is difficult to maximize productivity without congruence between the technologies employed and the resources and culture of the economies and societies in which the investment takes place (Abramovitz, 1986). African enterprise has the advantage of offering potentially greater linkages with the rest of the economy than foreign investment (even including investment by foreign minorities, such as Indians and Levantines in East and West Africa respectively, and now Chinese almost all over the sub-continent). But it is perhaps only in Nigeria that there is a history going back even thirty years of private (not privatized) factories employing several hundred people under African ownership (Forrest, 1994). African capitalists are mostly small scale, whether in trade, agriculture or manufacturing.

Regarding the latter, an important feature of the last century was the emergence of new forms of small-scale manufacturing, such as motor repairs and motor parts. Such industrial growth in Nigeria and Ghana has not yet emerged clearly in the national income accounts (Dawson, 1991; Forrest, 1994). The Ghanaian population census of 2000 recorded just over 1 million people working in manufacturing, with just over half of them women. Whatever their actual contribution to national output, small firms in Africa today, as in the colonial era, operate almost invariably in markets characterized by low entry costs and 'excess competition', making it hard to accumulate profits (Austin, 2013). African firms may occasionally be created big, but they rarely start small and grow big; and, again with the partial exception of Nigeria, they rarely outlive their founders (Iliffe, 1983).

To judge from both African and East Asian history, if there is one thing that could assist both foreign and indigenous manufacturing enterprises in Africa, it would be the presence of states with the capacity and dedication to promote structural change in the cause of long-term growth. Mkandawire (2001) has argued plausibly that the absence of the 'developmental state' in Africa has been exaggerated. Several of the current governments in the sub-continent may be viewed as 'developmental'. However, in the most populous country, Nigeria, the state is still a long way from delivering certain basic public goods, such as security and, even for urban areas, reliable electricity. Clearly, there is much neglected business for many African governments to undertake if they want to facilitate the growth of manufacturing.

14.7 CONCLUSION

We have reviewed the progress of manufacturing in the colonial and post-colonial economies of Sub-Saharan Africa in the framework of the interactions between the region's specific endowment structures, global economic relationships, and government policies. In a diverse sub-continent, it is possible to make the following nine generalizations about 'the' African case within the global spread of modern manufacturing. First, as of *c.*1900 resource endowments—both in terms of aggregate factor ratios (land abundance, labour scarcity), and on a disaggregated view (powerful environmental obstacles to the full utilization of the land and labour)—favoured neither a Western-style capital-intensive route of development, nor an East Asian-style labour-intensive one. This helps explain the second feature, a striking discontinuity between handicraft and machine-based production: artisanal manufacturing had been based primarily on a seasonal abundance of labour, which was reduced or eliminated by the growth of primary-product exports, while factories were implanted from outside—where they were introduced at all. Handloom weaving, in particular, survived in some areas, but thrived mostly where its difference from factory-made cloth could be maximized, by artisans specializing in luxury handmade products. Third, in the decades before the European Scramble for Africa, African producers—especially but not exclusively in West Africa—were already responding to the export opportunities created by industrialization in the West in ways that revealed a deepening comparative advantage in land-extensive agriculture and mining. Fourth, colonial governments reinforced that specialization, notably through their infrastructural investments and regulations.

It is thus unsurprising that, fifth, only independent or self-governing regimes invested heavily in promoting manufacturing, whether calculating that it was possible to shift the comparative advantage of the country concerned to industry, or simply in the hope that defying the existing pattern of comparative advantage would not be costly. The first such regimes were the white-minority governments of South Africa and Southern Rhodesia, which adopted import-substituting industrialization having already taken drastically coercive measures to reduce the cost of African unskilled labour. They achieved considerable manufacturing growth, especially South Africa. But labour repression contained its own limitations: the early growth was replaced by stagnation in the 1980s, by which time productivity growth was stymied by the high cost of artificially scarce skilled labour. Elsewhere in Africa, many of the majority-rule governments that followed the colonial regimes that departed around 1960 also embarked on import-substituting industrialization, in defiance of relatively high labour costs, and generally without the resources or commitment to carry it through.

Our sixth generalization is that the main achievement of these governments was better provision of education and health services, which greatly improved upon the modest achievements of colonial governments in increasing the supply, and improving the preparation, of future workers. Seventh, colonial companies and governments, sooner or later, undertook policies of labour stabilization. This move in itself made sense from the perspective of both capital- and labour-intensive paths of development. The former path required skilled or semi-skilled workers, whom an itinerant, shifting workforce could not supply. The labour-intensive path entails cheap labour as a starting point, but goes on to require investments in labour quality (Austin and Sugihara, 2013). Eighth, so far large foreign companies in Africa have tended to use the capital-intensive technologies they apply elsewhere, without worrying about congruence with local conditions. It remains to be seen whether, helped by a relatively cheaper and better-educated workforce, this approach will contribute to more sustained industrial growth in future. Finally, while private African manufacturing enterprises are mostly small, occasionally (in Nigeria) medium sized, they tend to be labour intensive, benefiting from greater labour abundance. But they need government intervention, especially the provision of public goods, making it easier for them to accumulate profits, if they are to become a leading force in a twenty-first-century industrialization of Africa.

REFERENCES

Abbeloos, J.-F. (2013). Mobutu, Suharto, and the challenges of nation-building and economic development, 1965–97. In *Colonial Exploitation and Economic Development: The Belgian Congo and the Netherlands Indies Compared* (Eds, Frankema, E. and Buelens, F.). London: Routledge, 251–73.

Abramovitz, M. (1986). Catching up, forging ahead, and falling behind. *Journal of Economic History* 46, 385–406.

Amsden, A. H. (1992). A theory of government intervention in late industrialization. In *State and Market in Development: Synergy or Rivalry?* (Eds, Putterman, L. and Rueschemeyer, D.). Boulder, CO: Lynne Reiner, 53–84.

Arrighi, G. (1973a). International corporations, labor aristocracies, and economic development in Tropical Africa. First published 1970, reprinted in *Essays on the Political Economy of Africa* (Eds, Arrighi, G. and Saul, J. S.). New York: Monthly Review Press, 105–51.

Arrighi, G. (1973b). Labor supplies in historical perspective: a study of the proletarianization of the African peasantry in Rhodesia. First published in Italian 1969, English 1970, reprinted in *Essays on the Political Economy of Africa* (Eds, Arrighi, G. and Saul, J. S.). New York: Monthly Review Press, 180–234.

Austen, R. A. (1987). *African Economic History: Internal Development and External Dependency.* London: James Currey; Portsmouth, NH: Heinemann.

Austin, G. (2005). *Labour, Land and Capital in Ghana: From Slavery to Free Labour in Asante, 1807–1956.* New York: University of Rochester Press.

Austin, G. (2008). Resources, techniques, and strategies south of the Sahara: revising the factor endowments perspective on African economic development, 1500–2000. *Economic History Review* 61, 587–624.

Austin, G. (2013). Labour-intensity and manufacturing in West Africa, 1450–2010. In *Labour-Intensive Industrialization in Global History* (Eds. Austin, G. and Sugihara, K.). London: Routledge, 201–30.

Austin, G. (2015). The economics of colonialism. In *Oxford Handbook of Africa and Economics* (Eds, Monga, C. and Lin, J.). Oxford: Oxford University Press, 522–35.

Austin, G. and Sugihara, K. (Eds) (2013). *Labour-Intensive Industrialization in Global History.* London: Routledge.

Barth, H. (1965, originally 1857). *Travels and Discoveries in North and Central Africa,* Vol. I. London: reprint by Frank Cass.

Bénétrix, A. S., O'Rourke, K. H., and Williamson, J. G. (2015). The spread of manufacturing to the poor periphery 1870–2007. *Open Economies Review* 26, 1–37.

Boone, C. (1992). *Merchant Capital and the Roots of State Power in Senegal, 1930–1985.* Cambridge: Cambridge University Press.

Buelens, F. and Cassimon, D. (2013). The industrialization of the Belgian Congo. In *Colonial Exploitation and Economic Development: The Belgian Congo and the Netherlands Indies Compared* (Eds, Frankema, E. and Buelens, F.). London: Routledge, 229–50.

Butler, L. J. (1997). *Industrialisation and the British Colonial State: West Africa, 1939–1951.* London: Frank Cass.

Byfield, J. (2002). *The Bluest Hands: A Social and Economic History of Women Dyers in Abeokuta (Nigeria), 1890–1940.* Portsmouth, NH: Heinemann.

Chomé, J. and Komitee, Z. (1977). *Zaïre. Ketens van Koper.* Louvain: Kritak.

Clarence-Smith, G. (1989). The effects of the Great Depression on industrialisation in Equatorial and Central Africa. In *The Economies of Africa and Asia in the Inter-war Depression* (Ed., Brown, I.). London: Routledge, 170–202.

Curtin, P. D. (1973). The lure of Bambuk gold. *Journal of African History* 14, 623–31.

Dawson, J. (1991). Development of small-scale industry in Ghana: a case study of Kumasi. In *Small-Scale Production: Strategies for Industrial Restructuring* (Eds, Thomas, H., Uribe-Echevarría, F., and Romijn, H.). London: Intermediate Technology Publications, 173–207.

Depaepe, M. and van Rompaey, L. (1995). *In het teken van de bevoogding. De educatieve actie in Belgisch-Kongo, 1908–1960.* Leuven: Garant.

Diao, X. and McMillan, M. S. (2015). Toward an understanding of economic growth in Africa: a re-interpretation of the Lewis model. *National Bureau of Economic Research Working Paper Series* No. 21018.

Drummond-Thompson, P. (1993). The rise of entrepreneurs in Nigerian motor transport: a study in indigenous enterprise. *Journal of Transport History* 14, 46–63.

Dunkerley, M. E. (2009). Education policies and the development of the colonial state in the Belgian Congo, 1916–1939. Ph.D. thesis, University of Exeter.

Feinstein, C. H. (2005). *Conquest, Discrimination and Development: An Economic History of South Africa.* Cambridge: Cambridge University Press.

Fieldhouse, D. K. (1978). *Unilever Overseas: Anatomy of a Multinational 1895–1965.* London: Croom Helm.

Fine, B. and Rustomjee, Z. (1996). *The Political Economy of South Africa: From Minerals-Energy Complex to Industrialisation.* Boulder, CO: Westview.

Forrest, T. (1994). *The Advance of African Capital: The Growth of Nigerian Private Enterprise.* Edinburgh: Edinburgh University Press.

Frankema, E. (2013). Colonial education and post-colonial governance in the Congo and Indonesia. In *Colonial Exploitation and Economic Development: The Belgian Congo and the Netherlands Indies Compared* (Eds, Frankema, E. and Buelens, F.). London: Routledge, 153–77.

Frankema, E. (2014). Africa and the Green Revolution: a global historical perspective. *NJAS—Wageningen Journal of Life Sciences,* 70–1, 17–24.

Frankema, E. and van Waijenburg, M. (2012). Structural impediments to African growth? New evidence from real wages in British Africa, 1880–1965. *Journal of Economic History* 72, 895–926.

Frankema, E. and van Waijenburg, M. (2015). The African poverty debate: why historians' contributions matter. Mimeo.

Frankema, E., Williamson, J. G., and Woltjer, P. J. (2015). An economic rationale for the African Scramble? The commercial transition and the commodity price boom of 1845–1885. Paper presented at the RIDGE Workshop on Comparative Studies of the Southern Hemisphere in Global Economic History and Development, Montevideo, 26–7 March.

Frederick, K. (2014). External trade and internal production dynamics in Southern East Africa: the case of Nyasaland's lower Shire valley. Paper presented at the Fourth European Congress on World and Global History, Paris, 4–7 September.

Gerschenkron, A. (1962). *Economic Backwardness in Historical Perspective.* Cambridge, MA: Harvard University Press.

Goucher, C. L. (1981). Iron is iron 'til it rust: trade and ecology in the decline of West African iron-smelting. *Journal of African History* 22, 179–89.

Great Britain (1948). *Report of the Commission of Enquiry into Disturbances in the Gold Coast 1948,* Colonial No. 238. London: HMSO.

Harries, P. (1982). Kinship, ideology and the nature of pre-colonial labour migration: labour migration from the Delagoa Bay hinterland to South Africa, up to 1895. In *Industrialisation and Social Change in South Africa: African Culture, Class Formation and Consciousness, 1870–1914* (Eds, Marks, S. and Rathbone, R.). Harlow: Longman, 142–66.

Heap, Simon (1990). The development of motor transport in the Gold Coast, 1900–1939. *Journal of Transport History* 11, 19–37.

Hopkins, A.-G. (1973). *An Economic History of West Africa*. London: Longman.

Iliffe, J. (1983). *The Emergence of African Capitalism*. London: Macmillan.

IMF (2012). *Regional Economic Outlook. Sub-Saharan Africa: Sustaining Growth amidst Global Uncertainty*. Washington, DC: International Monetary Fund.

Inikori, Joseph E. (2009). English versus Indian cotton textiles: the impact of imports on cotton textile production in West Africa. In *How India Clothed the World: The World of South Asian Textiles, 1500–1850* (Eds, Riello, G. and Roy, T.). Leiden: Brill, 85–114.

Jerven, M. (2010). African growth recurring: an economic history perspective on African growth episodes, 1690–2010. *Economic History of Developing Regions* 25, 127–54.

Jerven, M. (2011). The quest for the African dummy: explaining African post-colonial economic performance revisited. *Journal of International Development*, 23, 288–307.

Jerven, M. (2013). *Poor Numbers: How We Are Misled by African Development Statistics and What to Do about It*. Ithaca, NY: Cornell University Press.

Jerven, M. (2014). On the accuracy of trade and GDP statistics in Africa: errors of commission and omission. *Journal of African Trade* 1, 45–52.

Jerven, M. (2015). *Africa: Why Economists Got it Wrong*. London; New York: Zed Books.

Johnson, M. (1976). Calico caravans: the Tripoli–Kano trade after 1880. *Journal of African History* 17, 95–117.

Joomun, G. (2006). The textile and clothing industry in Mauritius. In *The Future of the Textile and Clothing Industry in Sub-Saharan Africa* (Eds, Jauch, H. and Traub-Merz, R.). Bonn: Friedrich-Ebert-Stiftung.

Kilby, P. (1975). Manufacturing in colonial Africa. In *Colonialism in Africa, 1870–1960* (Eds, Duignan, P. and Gann, L. H.). Cambridge: Cambridge University Press, 475–520.

Killick, T. (1978). *Development Economics in Action: A Study of Economic Policies in Ghana*. New York: St Martin's Press.

Kriger, C. (2006). *Cloth in West African History*. Lanham, MD: AltaMira Press.

Lacroix, J.-L. (1967). *Industrialisation au Congo: la transformation des structures économiques*. Paris: Mouton.

Law, R. (ed.) (1995). *From Slave Trade to Legitimate Commerce: The Commercial Transition in Nineteenth-Century West Africa*. Cambridge: Cambridge University Press.

Lewis, S. R., Jr (1990). *The Economics of Apartheid*. New York: Council on Foreign Relations Press.

Lipton, M. (1986). *Capitalism and Apartheid: South Africa, 1910–84*. Aldershot: Gower.

Lovejoy, P. E. (2005). *Slavery, Commerce and Production in the Sokoto Caliphate of West Africa*. Trenton: Africa World Press.

Maddison, A. (2010). *Historical Statistics on World Population, GDP and Per Capita GDP, 1–2008 AD*. Available at: http://www.ggdc.net/maddison/.

Mantels, R. (2007). *Geleerd in de tropen Leuven, Congo & de wetenschap, 1885–1960*. Leuven: Universitaire Pers Leuven.

McMillan, M. S. and Harttgen, K. (2014). What is driving the 'Africa growth miracle'? *National Bureau of Economic Research Working Paper Series* No. 20077.

Mitchell, B. R. (2007). *International Historical Statistics, Africa, Asia and Oceania, 1750–2005*. 5th ed. Basingstoke: Palgrave Macmillan.

Mkandawire, T. (2001). Thinking about developmental states in Africa. *Cambridge Journal of Economics* 25, 289–313.

Mosley, P. (1984). *The Settler Economies: Kenya and Rhodesia 1900–1963* (Cambridge: Cambridge University Press).

Mytelka, L. K. (1989). The unfulfilled promise of African industrialization. *African Studies Review* 32, 77–137.

Phimister, I. (2000). The origins and development of manufacturing in Southern Rhodesia, 1880–1939. In *Zimbabwe: A History of Manufacturing 1890–1995* (Eds, Mlambo, A. S., Pangeti, E. S., and Phimister, I.). Harare: University of Zimbabwe Publications.

Prunier, G. (2009). *From Genocide to Continental War: The 'Congolese' Conflict and the Crisis of Contemporary Africa*. London: Hurst & Co.

Roberts, R. L. (1996). *Two Worlds of Cotton: Colonialism and the Regional Economy in the French Soudan, 1800–1946*. Stanford, CA: Stanford University Press.

Rodney, W. (1972). *How Europe Underdeveloped Africa*. London: Touissant l'Ouverture Press.

Rodrik, D. (2013). Unconditional convergence in manufacturing. *Quarterly Journal of Economics* 128, 165–204.

Rodrik, D. (2014). An African growth miracle? *National Bureau of Economic Research Working Paper Series* No. 20188.

Sannassee, R. V., Seetanah, B., and Lamport, M. J. (2014). Export diversification and economic growth: the case of Mauritius. In *Connecting to Global Markets: Challenges and Opportunities* (Eds, Jansen, M., Jallab, M. S., and Smeets, M). Geneva: World Trade Organization, 11–23.

Sender, J. (1999). Africa's economic performance: limitations of the current consensus. *Journal of Economic Perspectives* 13, 89–114.

Sender, J. and Smith, S. (1986). Trade, industrialization and the state in the post-colonial period. In their *The Development of Capitalism in Africa*. London: Methuen, 67–109.

Sugihara, K. (2007). The Second Noel Butlin Lecture: labour-intensive industrialisation in global history. *Australian Economic History Review* 47, 121–54.

Teal, F. (1999). Why can Mauritius export manufactures and Ghana not? *The World Economy* 22, 981–93.

Tosh, J. (1980). The cash-crop revolution in tropical Africa: an agricultural reappraisal. *African Affairs* 79, 79–94.

United Nations Economic Commission for Africa (2013). *Making the Most of Africa's Commodities: Industrializing for Growth, Jobs and Economic Transformation: Economic Report on Africa 2013*. Addis Ababa: Economic Commission for Africa.

Vandewalle, G. (1966). *De conjuncturele evolutie in Kongo en Ruanda-Urundi, van 1920 tot 1939 en van 1949 tot 1958*. Antwerpen: SWU.

Vries, G. de, Timmer, M. P., and de Vries, K. (2013). Structural transformation in Africa: static gains, dynamic losses. *GGDC Research Memorandum* No. 136.

Wade, R. (1990). *Governing the Market: Economic Theory and the Role of Government in Industrialization*. Princeton, NJ: Princeton University Press.

Williamson, J. G. (2011). *Trade and Poverty: When the Third World Fell Behind*. Cambridge, MA: MIT Press.

World Bank (1989). *Sub-Saharan Africa: From Crisis to Sustainable Growth*. Washington, DC: World Bank.

World Bank (1990). *World Development Report 1990*. Washington, DC: World Bank.

Young, A. (2012). The African growth miracle. *Journal of Political Economy* 120, 696–739.

General Index

Printed and bound by CPI Group (UK) Ltd, Croydon, CR0 4YY